DEATH AND THE ROYAL SUCCESSION IN SCOTLAND, c.1214–c.1543

St Andrews Studies in Scottish History

Series Editor
Professor Emeritus Roger Mason (Institute of Scottish Historical Research, University of St Andrews)

Editorial Board
Professor Dauvit Broun (University of Glasgow)
Professor Michael Brown (Institute of Scottish Historical Research, University of St Andrews)
Dr David Ditchburn (Trinity College, Dublin)
Professor Emerita Elizabeth Ewan (University of Guelph)
Professor Clare Jackson (Trinity Hall Cambridge)
Dr Catriona MacDonald (University of Glasgow)
Dr Malcolm Petrie (Institute of Scottish Historical Research, University of St Andrews)

Sponsored by the Institute of Scottish Historical Research at the University of St Andrews, St Andrews Studies in Scottish History provides an important forum for the publication of research on any aspect of Scottish history, from the early middle ages to the present day, focusing on the historical experience of Scots at home and abroad, and Scotland's place in wider British, European and global contexts. Both monographs and essay collections are welcomed.

Proposal forms can be obtained from the Institute of Scottish Historical Research website: www.st-andrews.ac.uk/ishr/studies.htm. They should be sent in the first instance to the chair of the editorial board at the address below.

Professor Emeritus Roger Mason
Institute of Scottish Historical Research
St Andrews University
St Andrews
Fife KY16 9AL
UK
email: ram@st-andrews.ac.uk

Previous volumes in the series are listed at the back of this book.

DEATH AND THE ROYAL SUCCESSION IN SCOTLAND, c.1214–c.1543

Ritual, Ceremony and Power

Lucinda H.S. Dean

THE BOYDELL PRESS

© Lucinda H.S. Dean 2024

All Rights Reserved. Except as permitted under current legislation no part of this work may be photocopied, stored in a retrieval system, published, performed in public, adapted, broadcast, transmitted, recorded or reproduced in any form or by any means, without the prior permission of the copyright owner

The right of Lucinda H.S. Dean to be identified as the author of this work has been asserted in accordance with sections 77 and 78 of the Copyright, Designs and Patents Act 1988

First published 2024
The Boydell Press, Woodbridge

ISBN 978 1 83765 172 6

The Boydell Press is an imprint of Boydell & Brewer Ltd
PO Box 9, Woodbridge, Suffolk IP12 3DF, UK
and of Boydell & Brewer Inc.
668 Mt Hope Avenue, Rochester, NY 14620–2731, USA
website: www.boydellandbrewer.com

A catalogue record for this book is available
from the British Library

The publisher has no responsibility for the continued existence or accuracy of URLs for external or third-party internet websites referred to in this book, and does not guarantee that any content on such websites is, or will remain, accurate or appropriate

This book is dedicated to my husband, Richard Dean, and my parents, Joanna Clarke and Mark Stewart-Clarke. Thank you for everything you have done to support me with this book.

Publication of this volume was made possible by a grant from the Scouloudi Foundation in association with the Institute of Historical Research.

Contents

List of Illustrations	viii
Acknowledgements	xi
List of Abbreviations	xiv
Note on Money	xviii

	Introduction	1
1	The Last Canmore Kings	21
2	Contested and Compromised: Ceremonies and Succession under the Balliol and Bruce Kings	65
3	Stating Their Place: Ceremonial Legitimisation of the Stewart Dynasty, c.1371–c.1424	113
4	Foreign Queens, the Home-Grown Elite and Minor Kings, 1430s to 1470s	146
5	The Pinnacle of Stewart Power? James IV and James V	184
	Conclusion	224

Timeline of Key Events	240
Appendix I: Transcription from John Scrymgeour of Myres, NLS, Adv. MS 31.5.2, fols 15r–16r	253
Appendix II: Attendees and Officiators at Scottish Inaugurations and Coronations	256
Appendix III: James IV and Margaret's Wedding Costs, 1503	267
Appendix IV: Select Expenses from James V's French Journey, 1536–37	269
Bibliography	271
Index	302

Illustrations

Plates

1 Alexander II Great Seal [mounted and enthroned], c.1235. Crown Copyright, National Records of Scotland, Laing Seal Impressions, RH17/1/11–12 — 41

2 Scone Abbey Seal appended to Letter of Renunciation by Patrick Bishop of Murray and commendator of the abbey of Scone in favour of Patrick Kynnard of Kynnard, 7 February 1568. Perth and Kinross Archives, MS169/1/2/189 — 47

3 Inauguration of Alexander III from Bower in *Scotichronicon*. Parker Library, Corpus Christi College, Cambridge, CCC MS 171, fol. 206r — 48

4 Alexander III Great Seal [mounted and enthroned]. Crown Copyright, National Records of Scotland, Laing Seal Impressions, RH17/1/13–14 — 57

5 'The Base Slabs of St Margaret's Tomb/Feretory', Dunfermline Abbey, photographed by the author, October 2011 — 69

6 'The Funeral of Alexander III' in *Scotichronicon*, Parker Library, Corpus Christi College, Cambridge, CCC MS 171, fol. 225v — 73

7 Seal of the Guardians [St Andrew and Lion Rampant], c.1292. Crown Copyright, National Records of Scotland, Laing Seal Impressions, RH17/1/17–18 — 74

8 John Balliol Great Seal [mounted and enthroned], c.1292. Crown Copyright, National Records of Scotland, Laing Seal Impressions, RH17/1/19–20 — 82

9 David II Great Seal [mounted and enthroned], c.1359. Crown Copyright, National Records of Scotland, Laing Seal Impressions, RH17/1/27–RH17/1/28 — 100

ILLUSTRATIONS

10 Edward Balliol Great Seal [mounted and enthroned], 1350. Crown Copyright, National Records of Scotland, Laing Seal Impressions, RH17/1/30–1 — 101

11 David II Privy Seal, c.1359, and Edward Balliol Privy Seal, c.1350. Crown Copyright, National Records of Scotland, Laing Seal Impressions, RH17/1/29, RH17/1/32 — 104

12 Tomb of Alexander Stewart, 'the Wolf of Badenoch', c.1410x1420, Dunkeld Cathedral, photographed by the author, 2016 — 118

13 Robert II Privy Seal, n.d. Crown Copyright, National Records of Scotland, Laing Seal Impressions, RH17/1/35 — 126

14 Seal of Euphemia queen of Scotland, 10 October 1375. Crown Copyright, National Records of Scotland, Laing Seal Impressions, RH17/1/36 — 127

15 James I Great Seal [enthroned], c.1436. Crown Copyright, National Records of Scotland, Laing Seal Impressions, RH17/1/42 — 142

16 Coin (obverse), unicorn, from reign of James III (1484–1488 issue). The Hunterian, Lord Stewartby Collection, S/4779 — 178

17 Coin (obverse), groat, from reign of James III (c.1471–1483 issue). The Hunterian, Lord Stewartby Collection, S/2372 — 179

18 'Dirge of the King of Scots' from Das Gebetbuch Jakobs IV. von Schottland (Book of Hours of James IV of Scotland). Österreichische Nationalbibliothek, Cod.1897, fol. 141v — 192

19 'King James IV at Prayer' from Das Gebetbuch Jakobs IV. von Schottland (Book of Hours of James IV of Scotland). Österreichische Nationalbibliothek, Cod.1897, fol. 24v — 196

20 The Royal Honours of Scotland (crown, bonnet, scabbard, sceptre and sword). Historic Environment Scotland, SCRAN 008-001-008-645-C — 221

Maps

1 Potential route of funeral procession of William I, 1214. Contains Ordnance Survey data © Crown Copyright and database right (2023) — 33

2 Southern Scotland and Northern England, thirteenth and fourteenth centuries. Contains Ordnance Survey data © Crown Copyright and database right (2023) — 37

ILLUSTRATIONS

3	Sites associated with death and burial of Alexander II, and inauguration of his son, 1249. Contains Ordnance Survey data © Crown Copyright and database right (2023)	44
4	Potential route of funeral procession of Alexander III, 1286. Contains Ordnance Survey data © Crown Copyright and database right (2023)	72
5	Potential route of funeral procession of Bruce, 1329. Contains Ordnance Survey data © Crown Copyright and database right (2023)	94
6	Potential route of funeral processions of Robert II and Robert III, 1371 and 1390	129
7	Potential route of funeral procession of James II, 1460. Contains Ordnance Survey data © Crown Copyright and database right (2023)	172

Note: These maps were created by Crane Begg for this publication (2023) and are used here with his kind permission

Genealogical Tables

1	Scottish Kings from Mael Coluim III to Margaret Maid of Norway	20
2	The Balliol and Bruce Dynasties	64
3	The Stewart Dynasty	112

The author and publisher are grateful to all the institutions and individuals listed for permission to reproduce the materials in which they hold copyright. Every effort has been made to trace the copyright holders; apologies are offered for any omission, and the publisher will be pleased to add any necessary acknowledgement in subsequent editions.

Acknowledgements

This book has been a long time in the making. Consequently, there are many people to whom I am grateful for the help they have given, either directly or indirectly. Without the scholarship that came before, and that which has emerged during the study's long gestation, this work would not have been possible. I am also greatly indebted to all who have supported, encouraged and challenged me on my academic journey over the last two decades – from colleagues and mentors to family and friends, please accept my heartfelt gratitude.

Several organisations and institutions have supported the research that underpins this monograph and its production: with important thanks due to the Arts and Humanities Research Council, the Strathmartine Trust, the Royal Historical Society, Society of Renaissance Studies, European Science Foundation (Humanities), Scottish Historical Review Trust, the UHI Mini Sabbatical Fund and the Scouloudi Publication Grant. I also owe a huge debt to the archives and libraries, and the wonderful staff working at these institutions, who have helped me *in situ* or via email communications with everything from hunting out obscure references and helping with palaeography conundrums to more practical image reproductions and permissions: National Records of Scotland, the National Library of Scotland, the National Archives at Kew, the British Library, the Aberdeen City Archives, Edinburgh City Archives, Österreichische Nationalbibliothek, Historic Environment Scotland, the Hunterian (Glasgow), Perth and Kinross Archive, Corpus Christi College Library (Cambridge), Statens Archiver Copenhagen, Bibliothèque nationale de France, the College of Arms, and the university librarians at Stirling, UHI and Edinburgh. Equally, huge thanks to Caroline Palmer and the team at Boydell & Brewer and the series editor, Professor Roger Mason, for assistance in producing this fine volume.

I would not have embarked upon the research journey that has led to this monograph without the encouragement of my undergraduate and MRes supervisor, Professor Marisa Linton, so I will always be indebted to her for encouraging me to push myself further. I am hugely grateful to the staff and student community at the University of Stirling, particularly Dr Michael Penman and Dr Alastair Mann for their supervision and support, and the late Dr Alasdair Ross for letting me use the desk in his 'bookstore

ACKNOWLEDGEMENTS

cupboard' when there was no other space for a postdoc tutor to camp out between classes. There are several friends and colleagues made at Stirling whose support and advice, spare room or sofa-surfing provision, comments on drafts or help with map design have been invaluable right through to the present. Dr Kate Buchanan (and her husband, Mike), Dr Anne Dance, Dr Amy Hayes (and her husband, Stephen), Dr Vicki Hodgson, Dr Katy Jack, Dr Allan Kennedy, Rachel Meyer, Dr Emma Macleod, Dr Nicola Martin, Dr Kat Neumann, Professor Richard Oram (and his wife, Emma), Dr Emily St Denny and Michelle Joyce Tuxworth (and her partner, Craig): to you all, I am forever grateful for your friendship, encouragement and support.

The work that has arrived on the pages here has also been influenced, encouraged, debated and discussed with many other scholars and colleagues. I fear listing names and forgetting someone, so this is by no means a comprehensive list but there are some who require particular mention: Dr Elena Woodacre and all the members of the Royal Studies Network and attendees of the Kings and Queens Conference series who have become like an extended academic family; the late Professor Ronnie Mulryne, Dr Margaret Shewring and all the members of the European Society for Festivals Research, who were instrumental in my early forays into conferences and publications; and many other fellow scholars for sharing in the highs and lows of early career research and its aftermath with unfaltering kindness and enthusiasm, including Dr Allan Kennedy, Dr Amy Blakeway, Dr Rachel Delman, Dr Simon Egan, Dr Morvern French, Dr Claire Hawes, Dr William Hepburn, Dr Lynn Kilgallon, Dr Catriona Murray, Dr Helen Newsome, Dr Jamie Reid-Baxter, Dr Lizzie Swarbrick and Dr Tom Turpie. I also extend a huge appreciation to all those who have kindly offered their time to read drafts and offer comments on my work, who have not been named previously, including the anonymous reviewers, Professor Elizabeth Ewan, Dr Norman Reid, Professor Alice Taylor and Vikki Lewis (who selflessly proofread the whole darn thing), and all my wonderful colleagues at the Centre for History, UHI, who have been steadfast in their support (despite the many ups and downs) and contributed greatly to this volume through reading of drafts, fruitful conversations and general moral support. As well as those who have mentored and supported me, I am also hugely thankful to all the students I have taught and supervised, particularly at UHI, for their conversations and inspiring strength. Research is not a singular pursuit and many dialogues feed into the resulting publications – thanks to all for the parts that you have played in this one.

My deepest thanks and eternal gratitude also extend to my family and friends who are too numerous to name in full – Amy, Phil, Haydan, Leah, Janet and Dickie, Steve and Carol, and all the Clarke, Dean and Wetherald clans, who undoubtedly think I'm slightly barking but also love me unwaveringly, and to Laura, Vikki, Simon, Sarah and your lovely partners and families, and to the new friends I have made in the Highlands since 2017, who have helped me leave my desk for fresh air and good company, particularly Jamie, Rachel and Lois. While they care not a jot for history, I'm also hugely grateful to the pets and horses who have often been essential to my health and wellbeing at the toughest of times: Buster, Angel, Jura, Freya, Makka, Zara, James and, most recently, Poker.

Lastly, there are no words that can really express the thanks I owe to my mum and dad, Joanna Clarke and Mark Stewart-Clarke, and my husband, Richard Dean, whose support – financial, practical, moral and emotional – and love have underpinned everything I have achieved in the writing of this book and my life more generally. I could not have done any of this without you.

Abbreviations

ACA	Aberdeen City Archives
ADCP	*Acts of the Lords of Council in Public Affairs 1501–1554: Selections from the Acta Dominorum Concilii*, ed. Robert K. Hannay (Edinburgh, 1932)
Annals of Howden	Roger de Howden, *The Annals of Roger de Hoveden comprising the History of England and other countries of Europe from AD 732 to AD 1201*, trans. and ed. Henry T. Riley, 2 vols (London, 1853)
APS	*The Acts of Parliament of Scotland*, ed. Thomas Thomson and Cosmo Innes, 12 vols (Edinburgh, 1814–75)
Barbour, *Bruce*	John Barbour, *The Bruce*, ed. Archibald A.M. Duncan (Edinburgh, 1997)
BL	British Library
Bellenden's Boece, *Chronicle*	Boece, Hector, *The Chronicles of Scotland Compiled by Hector Boece. Translated into Scots by John Bellenden, 1531*, ed. Edith Batho and H. Winifred Husbands, 2 vols (Edinburgh and London, 1941)
Boece, *Historia*	Boece, Hector, *Scotorum historiae a prima gentis origine cum aliarum & rerum & gentium illustration non vulgari: præmissa epistola nu[n]cupatoria, tabellisq[ue] amplissimis, & non pœnitenda Isagoge quæ ab huius tergo explicanbuntur diffusius* (Paris, 1526)
Buchanan, *History*	Buchanan, George, *The History of Scotland translated from the Latin of George Buchanan; with Notes and Continuation to the Reign of Queen Anne*, ed. James Aikman, 4 vols (Glasgow, 1827)
CDS	*Calendar of Documents relating to Scotland preserved in her Majesty's Public Record Office London*, ed. Joseph Bain et al., 5 vols (Edinburgh, 1881–1986)

ABBREVIATIONS

Chron. Auchinleck	'The Auchinleck Chronicle', from the Asloan MS (NLS MS. Acc. 4233), 'Appendix 2', in Christine McGladdery, *James II* (Edinburgh, 2015), 261–76
Chron. Bower	Bower, Walter, *Scotichronicon*, ed. Donald E.R. Watt et al., 9 vols (Aberdeen and Edinburgh, 1987–98)
Chron. Buriensis	*Chronica Buriensis: The Chronicle of Bury St Edmunds, 1212–1301*, ed. Antonia Edmunds (Edinburgh and London, 1964)
Chron. D'Escouchy	*Chronique de Mathieu D'Escouchy, Nouvelle Édition revue sur les Manuscrits et publiée avec notes et éclaircissements*, ed Gaston du Fresne de Beaucourt (Paris, 1863)
Chron. Fordun	Fordun, John, *Chronicle of The Scottish Nation*, trans. and ed. William F. Skene (Edinburgh, 1872)
Chron. Guisborough	*The Chronicle of Walter of Guisborough: previously edited as the Chronicle of Walter of Hemingford or Hemingburgh*, ed. Harry Rothwell (London, 1957)
Chron. Hardyng	*The Chronicle of Jhon Hardyng, from the firste begynnynge of Englande, vnto the reigne of kyng Edward the fourth And from that tyme is added a continuacion [by Richard Grafton]*, facsimile edition (Amsterdam, 1976)
Chron. Lanercost	*The Chronicle of Lanercost, 1272–1346*, trans. and ed. Herbert Maxwell (Cribyn, reprint 2001)
Chron. Melrose	*Medieval Chronicles of Scotland: The Chronicle of Melrose (from 1136 to 1264) and The Chronicle of Holyrood (to 1163)*, trans. and ed. Joseph Stephenson, reprint (Dyfed, 1988)
Chron. Melsa	*Chronica monasterii de Melsa*, ed. Edward A. Bond, 3 vols (London, 1867)
Chron. Wyntoun	Wyntoun, Andrew of, *The Original Chronicles of Andrew of Wyntoun*, ed. F.J Amours, 6 vols (Edinburgh and London, 1903–14)
CPL	*Calendar of Entries in the Papal Registers relating to Great Britain and Ireland: Papal Letters*, ed. W.H. Bliss et al., 16 vols (London, 1893)
Diurnal	*An Diurnal of Remarkable Occurrents that have passed within the country of Scotland since the Death of King James Fourth til the Year MDLXXV* (Edinburgh, 1833)

ABBREVIATIONS

ER	*The Exchequer Rolls of Scotland: Rotuli Scaccarii Regum Scotorum*, ed. John Stuart, George Burnett et al., 23 vols (Edinburgh, 1878–1908)
Extracts Aberdeen	*Extracts from the Council Register of the Burgh of Aberdeen, 1398–1625*, ed. John Stuart, 2 vols (Aberdeen, 1844–48)
Extracts Edinburgh	*Extracts of the Records of the Burgh of Edinburgh, 1403–1589*, ed. James D. Marwick, 5 vols (Edinburgh, 1869–92)
Foedera	*Foedera, Conventiones, Literæ, et cujuscunque generis Acta Publica inter Reges Angliæ. Et alios quosvis Imperatores, Reges, Pontifices, Principes, vel Communitates etc.*, ed. Thomas Rhymer et al., third edition, 10 vols (Hague, 1739–45)
Fyancells MS	College of Arms, [John Young] The Marr. of Margarete da: to Hen: VII to the King of Scots, MS 1st M.13 bis., fols 75–115v
Fyancells Coll.	John Young, 'The Fyancells of Margaret, eldeſt Daughter of King of the King Henry VIIth to James King of Scotland', in *Johannis Lelandi antiquarii De rebus Brittannicis Collectanea*, ed. Thomas Hearne, 6 vols (London, 1774), IV, 258–300
HR	*Historical Review*
IR	*Innes Review*
Leslie, History	Leslie, John, *The History of Scotland from the death of King James I in the year MCCCXXXVI to the year MDLXI* (Edinburgh, 1830)
Leslie, Historie	Leslie, John, *The Historie of Scotland wrytten first in latin by the most reuerrend and worthy Jhone Leslie, Bishop of Ross*, trans. James Dalrymple (1596), ed. E.G. Cody and William Murrison, 2 vols (Edinburgh and London, 1888–95)
LPHVIII	*Letters and Papers, Foreign and Domestic, of the Reign of Henry VIII*, ed. John S. Brewer, James Gardiner and R.H. Brodie, 21 vols (London, 1862–1932)
Maior, History	Maior, John, *A History of Greater Britain as well England as Scotland, Compiled from the Ancient Authorities by John Major, by Name indeed a Scot, but by Profession a Theologian 1521*, trans. and ed. Archibald Constable and Æneas J. G. Mackay (Edinburgh, 1892)

ABBREVIATIONS

NRS	National Records of Scotland
NLS	National Library of Scotland
NMS	National Museum of Scotland
ODNB	*Oxford Dictionary of National Biography* (Online resource)
Pitscottie, *Historie*	Lindesay of Pitscottie, Robert, *The Historie and Cronicles of Scotland: From the Slauchter of King James the First To the Ane thousande five hundrieth thrie scoir fyftein zeir*, ed. Æneas J. G. Mackay, 2 vols (Edinburgh and London, 1899)
Pluscarden	*The Book of Pluscarden*, ed. Felix J.H. Skene, 2 vols (The Historians of Scotland Series, Vol. 10, Edinburgh, 1880)
PSAS	*Proceedings of the Society of Antiquaries of Scotland*
RMS	*Registrum Magni Sigilli Regum Scotorum (Register of the Great Seal)*, ed. John M. Thomson et al., 11 vols (Edinburgh, 1882–1914)
Rot. Scot.	Rotuli Scotiae in Turri Londonensi et in Domo Capitulari Westmonasteriensi Asservati [Scottish Rolls Preserved in the Tower of London and the Chapter House of Westminster Abbey], ed. David Macpherson et al., 2 vols (London, 1814–19)
RPS	*Records of the Parliament of Scotland*, ed. Gillian H. MacIntosh, Alastair J. Mann, Roland J. Tanner et al. (St Andrews, 2007–13), accessed online at www.rps.ac.uk
RRS	*Regesta Regum Scottorum – Handlists of Acts and Acts of Mael Coluim IV to David II*, ed. James Maclean Scouler, Grant G. Simpson et al., 7 vols (Edinburgh, 1960–)
SHR	*Scottish Historical Review*
STS	*Scottish Text Society*
TA	*Accounts of the Lord High Treasurer of Scotland*, ed. Thomas Dickson and James Balfour Paul, 12 vols (Edinburgh, 1877–1916)
TNA	The National Archives, Kew

Note on Money

All values are in £ Scots unless otherwise stated. It was not until the 1390s that Scotland formally broke away from the English sterling, although there had been Scottish coins minted substantially earlier and they were increasingly common in the thirteenth century under Alexander II and Alexander III. In the late fourteenth century the English enforced an exchange rate of 2:1 (£ Scots: £ sterling). Elizabeth Gemmill and Nicholas Mayhew suggest that this vastly undervalued the Scottish coinage, which was closer to two thirds of the value of its English counterpart at this time.[1] Across the subsequent centuries under consideration the value of the Scottish coinage fluctuated substantially.

Some Useful Exchange Rate Information[2]

Until around 1360 the Scottish coinage held value against the English sterling:
  1390–1430s: £1 (sterling): £1⅓ to £2 Scots
  1430–1480s: £1 (sterling): £2 to £3½ Scots
  1483: £1 (sterling): £5 Scots
  Late 1480s to 1530: £1 (sterling): £3 to £4 Scots
There are sharper rises and falls in value in the 1530s and then steady devaluing across the sixteenth century that saw £6 Scots to a sterling in 1560s, £7 Scots to a sterling in 1580s and £10 Scots to a sterling by the 1590s.

French currency in the fourteenth century was roughly 1:6 (with the Scots this time stable at 1). It fluctuated between 1:3 and 1:1½ through the fifteenth century, before plateauing at 1:2 through the first half of the sixteenth century.

A merk was worth 13s. 4d.

There was a huge variety of coinage in use in each country (with a variety of values), but this note can act as a rough guide in most cases and where a direct exchange rate can be drawn from the financial material used, this will be noted in the footnotes.

---

[1] Elizabeth Gemmill and Nicholas Mayhew, *Changing Values in Medieval Scotland: A Study of Prices, Money, and Weights and Measures* (Cambridge, 1995), 111–42.
[2] The exchange rate information comes from tables compiled by John M. Gilbert, 'The Usual Money of Scotland and Exchange Rates Against Foreign Coin', in David M. Metcalf (ed.), *Coinage in Medieval Scotland (1100–1600): The Second Oxford Symposium on Coinage and Monetary History* (Oxford, 1977), 131–53.

Introduction

In January 1543, a sombre procession set out from Falkland Palace in Fife towards Edinburgh. The king of Scotland, James V, had died in late December aged thirty only days after the birth of his daughter and heir, Mary.[1] Between his death and early January, the king's body was prepared for his final journey: prayers were said for his soul, his body embalmed, vigils held in the palace chapel, and dule wear (funeral garb) prepared for attendees. The body and accompanying procession moved slowly, likely pausing for overnight vigils at Dunfermline amongst James's ancient and saintly ancestors before being conveyed by boat from Fife across the Forth and making its way towards Edinburgh. The number of people in attendance grew on approach to the burgh, including the queen and her ladies in a chariot draped in rich black cloth drawn by horses fitted out with black harnesses. The procession carried the coffined king and his effigy through the streets towards Holyrood Abbey in the Canongate. The effigy, in regalia made for the occasion, acted as a replacement for the body and may have been intended to represent a visual embodiment of the body politic or the royal dignity that lived on despite the mortality of human monarchs.[2] The deceased king was accompanied not only by his queen but also by heralds, macebearers, the burgh elite and members of the court, including James Hamilton, earl of Arran, duke of Châtellerault and governor of the realm, in a 'dule cape of stait'. All were led by black-clad paupers bearing torches to the sounds of 'lamentable trumpetis' and 'qwisselis of dule'. The interior of Holyrood Abbey was draped in black. Before the altar stood a *chapelle ardent* or hearse – a chapel-like structure decorated with 648 great and small arms, clubs, swords and other tools of war, all in gold and bright colours amidst a sea of black. Beneath the structure, the king's effigy lay resplendent in the flickering light of a plethora of candles and torches.[3]

---

[1] The king's death is dated variously: 14 December (Leslie, *Historie of Scotland*, 259–60; *Diurnal*, 25); 16 December (NRS, Exchequer Records: Accounts of the Treasurer, Nov 1542–Mar 1542/3, E21/40, fol. 1; *TA*, VIII, 141); and 20 December (Pitscottie, *Historie*, I, 407–8).
[2] Ralph Giesey, *The Royal Funeral Ceremony in Renaissance France* (Geneva, 1960); Ernst Kantorowicz, *The King's Two Bodies: A Study in Medieval Political Theology*, reprint (Princeton, 1997).
[3] Financial materials and the account of John Leslie largely provide the details of James V's funeral: NRS, E21/40, fols 4r–14v (note: the manuscript has recently been re-foliated and the folio numbers used herein utilise these amendments); *TA*, VIII,

The realm mourned the loss of the monarch and prepared to crown their first queen regnant. 'The king is dead, long live the queen': the ritual cycle of death and the royal succession marked both an end and a new beginning.

The phrase – 'Le roi est mort, vive le roi' – stands at the heart of this study. It emphasises the unambiguous connection between death and succession. That death begins the ritual cycle of succession may be an obvious observation, but it is often overlooked and not just in the Scottish context. There is a substantial body of research on royal funerals, inaugurations and coronations, particularly for England and France.[4] However, despite the directly or indirectly integrated nature of these events, very few studies consider these rituals as a ceremonial whole.[5] This book explores the cycle of rituals and ceremonies associated with succession in Scotland: incorporating funerals, accession ceremonies, marriages and the ceremonial promotion of heirs. By considering the interwoven ceremonies that facilitated or marked the transferral, negotiation and renegotiation of royal power within the cycle of dynastic succession, it addresses continuity and change in the ongoing dialogue between the monarch and the kingdom.

The importance of ceremony and ritual has been increasingly recognised in Scottish historiography, particularly following the cultural turn of the 1980s to 2000s.[6] Nonetheless, its treatment is still rather haphazard, with

141–67; NRS, Exchequer Records: Libri Emptorum, James V and Regent Arran, 14 Aug. 1542–7 Aug. 1543, E32/8, fol. 127v; Leslie, *Historie of Scotland*, 259–60. See also NLS, John Scrymgeour's Heraldic Collection: The maner hou herrauldis and purſevants ſould know of obſesquis, Adv. MS. 31.5.2, fols 15r–16v (Appendix I for transcription); David Lindsay, 'The Testament of Squyre Meldrum', in *Sir David Lyndsay: Selected Poems*, ed. Janet Hadley Williams (Glasgow, 2000), 174–82; Caroline Edington, *Court and Culture in Renaissance Scotland, David Lindsay of the Mount* (Amherst, 1994), 112–14; Andrea Thomas, *Princelie Majestie: The Court of James V of Scotland, 1528–1542* (Edinburgh, 2005), 210–17.

[4] Numerous works on funeral and coronation rituals are referred to herein and listed in the bibliography, including work by Jonas Bak, Joel Burden, Johanna Dale, Anna Duch, Ralph Giesey, Ralph A. Griffiths, Elizabeth M. Hallam, Richard A. Jackson and Roy Strong.

[5] Giesey has a short chapter considering the funeral as part of the inaugural ritual in France, Griffiths discusses the importance of funerals in legitimising succession and Joel Burden looks at both coronations and funerals but deals with them separately: Ralph Giesey, 'Inaugural Aspects of French Royal Ceremonials', in Janos Bak (ed.), *Coronations: Medieval and Early Modern Monarchic Ritual* (Berkeley, 1990), 35–45; Ralph A. Griffiths, 'Succession and the Royal Dead in Later Medieval England', in Frédérique Lachaud and Michael Penman (eds), *Making and Breaking the Rules: Succession in Medieval Europe, c.1000–1600* (Turnhout, 2008), 97–109; Joel F. Burden, 'Rituals of Royalty: Prescription, Politics and Practice in English Coronation and Royal Funeral Rituals c.1327 to c.1485' (PhD thesis, University of York, 1999). The seminal work of Ernst Kantorowicz, originally published in 1957, analyses the political theology that informed ceremonial choices, particularly relating to death, rather than the practicalities of ritual and ceremony: Ernst Kantorowicz, *The King's Two Bodies*.

[6] Many of the works from this cultural turn are referred to herein and listed in the bibliography. For a summary of Scottish historiography and key works on various aspects of the cultural turn, see Lucinda H.S. Dean, 'Crowns, Wedding Rings, and Processions:

most studies considering one ceremony, or a small group of ceremonies, in isolation. There has also been a polarisation of research around two chronological periods and specific ceremonies within these. The first of these focuses on early inaugurations, with notable interest in that of Alexander III in 1249 as this boasts one of the fullest surviving source bases – narrative, material and illustrative – in comparison to other Scottish inaugural occasions prior to the later sixteenth century.[7] Positioned in the midst of the thirteenth century (often considered a 'golden' period) and prior to the Great Cause (1290–92) and the Wars of Independence (1296–1328, 1332–57), this inauguration has been discussed as a pivotal moment for understanding Scottish medieval kingship.[8] Despite such considered attention, these discussions of inauguration practice rarely situate the ceremony in conversation with funerary rituals.[9] The second prominent area of research focuses on spectacle and diplomacy – weddings, tournaments and baptisms – predominantly in the sixteenth century.[10] Gordon Kipling has lamented the propensity to focus

Continuity and Change in the Representations of Scottish Royal Authority in State Ceremony, c.1214–c.1603' (PhD thesis, University of Stirling, 2013), 1–3, fns 2–11.

[7] In addition to detailed accounts in *Gesta Annalia* and Bower's *Scotichronicon*, plus shorter entries in other chronicles, this ceremony has the only contemporary depictions of a medieval Scottish inauguration in the Scone seal (Plate 2, see 47) and a fifteenth-century manuscript illumination from Bower (Plate 3, see 48). *Chron. Fordun*, 289–90; *Chron. Bower*, V, 290–3. The seal was in use by the 1280s but depicts a youthful king without a beard: Archibald A.M. Duncan, *The Kingship of the Scots 842–1242: Succession and Independence* (Edinburgh, 2002), 136; Dauvit Broun, *Scottish Independence and the Idea of Britain From the Picts to Alexander III* (Edinburgh, 2007), 172–4. For work on 1249, see M.D. Legge, 'Inauguration of Alexander III', *PSAS* 80 (1945–46), 73–82; John Bannerman, 'The King's Poet and the Inauguration of Alexander III', *SHR* 68 (1989), 120–49; Nick Aitchison, *Scotland's Stone of Destiny: Myth, History and Nationhood* (Stroud, 2000); Duncan, *Kingship of the Scots*, 127–50; Archibald A.M. Duncan, 'Before Coronation: Making a King at Scone in the Thirteenth Century', and Dauvit Broun, 'The Origin of the Stone of Scone as a National Icon', in Richard Welander, David Breeze and Thomas O. Clancy (eds), *The Stone of Destiny: Artefact and Icon* (Edinburgh, 2003), 139–67, 183–97; Broun, *Scottish Independence and the Idea of Britain*, 161–88.

[8] For further on the myth of the 'golden age', see the work of Norman H. Reid: 'Alexander III: The Historiography of a Myth', in Norman H. Reid (ed.), *Scotland in the Reign of Alexander III, 1249–1286* (Edinburgh, 1990), 181–213; *Alexander III, 1249–1286: First Among Equals* (Edinburgh, 2019), 1, 313–42.

[9] Where ceremonies are the primary focus of the research, inauguration is considered independently to other rituals, see fn. 7 and J. Cooper, 'Four Scottish Coronations Since the Reformation', *Transactions of the Aberdeen Ecclesiological Society and Transactions of the Glasgow Ecclesiological Society*, Special Issue (Aberdeen, 1902), 8–10. The previous king's funeral is considered in conjunction with the inauguration in some recent monographs of reigns e.g.: Reid, *Alexander III*, 6–19.

[10] A range of work on the sixteenth-century spectacle and diplomacy is referred to herein and listed in the bibliography, including the work of Michael Lynch, Louise O. Fradenburg, Alastair A. MacDonald, Douglas Gray, Sarah Carpenter, Andrea Thomas, David Stevenson, Maureen Meikle and Katie Stevenson. There has also been some work on the sixteenth-century coronations of James V (1513) and James VI (1567): Andrea Thomas, 'Crown Imperial: Coronation Ritual and Regalia in the Reign of James V', in Julian Goodare and Alastair A. MacDonald (eds), *Sixteenth-Century Scotland: Essays*

on renaissance triumph without full recourse to the medieval foundations, and focusing on singular events has led to some Scottish scholars making statements about the advanced or unique nature of events without reference to what had preceded it.[11] Analysing ceremonial examples across a long chronology has been identified by Gerd Althoff, and others since, as a valuable approach for identifying when and why change occurred, as well as what was usual and unusual in ritual activities.[12] Consequently, a *longue durée* approach has been embraced here to address a lacuna in Scottish scholarship through a tried and tested methodology.

The study begins with the funeral of William I in 1214 and ends with the death of James V in 1542. It thus covers four reigning dynasties: Canmore (until 1290), Balliol (1292–96, 1332–57), Bruce (1306–71) and Stewart (1371–1603/1714). A study over a long chronology cannot realistically incorporate all rituals and ceremonies associated with kingship. Yet, by analysing those taking place at critical junctures in the cycle of succession, the study provides a more comprehensive understanding of the shifting motivations and political contexts that underpin ritual decision making. The cycle of death and succession pertaining to the ruling monarchs is the primary focus here, so ceremonies and rituals associated with queens and royal children are only incorporated when directly integral to this cycle. The chapters take the reader through a narrative cycle of rituals set against their respective contexts, and primarily in chronological order, for two core reasons. First, context and interpretation are essential to understanding and analysing these events. Ceremonies, rituals and the records that relay them, are products of their environment and, as other scholars have illustrated in the wider European context, hold a wealth of understanding about the social, political and cultural milieu that produced them.[13] Sydney Anglo even suggests that it

---

in Honour of Michael Lynch (Leiden, 2008), 42–67; Michael Lynch, 'Scotland's First Protestant Coronation: Revolutionaries, Sovereignty and the Culture of Nostalgia', in Luuk A.J.R. Houwen (ed.), *Literature and Religion in Late Medieval and Early Modern Scotland* (Leuven, 2012), 177–207.

[11] Gordon Kipling, *Enter the King: Theatre, Liturgy, and Ritual in the Medieval Civic Triumph* (Oxford, 1998), 8. For an example of a problematic claim from a study of one sixteenth-century ceremony, see the comment about the baptismal celebrations in 1566 being 'the first truly Renaissance festival which Great Britain had ever witnessed': Michael Lynch, 'Queen Mary's Triumph: the Baptismal Celebrations at Stirling in December 1566', *SHR*, 69 (1990), 1–21, at 21.

[12] Gerd Althoff, 'The Variability of Rituals in the Middle Ages', in Gerd Althoff, Johannes Fried and Patrick J. Geary (eds), *Medieval Concepts of the Past: Ritual, Memory and Historiography* (Cambridge, 2002), 71–89, at 75.

[13] For example, although certainly not limited to these alone: Sydney Anglo, *Spectacle, Pageantry and Early Tudor Policy* (Oxford, 1969); Lawrence M. Bryant, 'The Medieval Entry Ceremony at Paris', in Bak (ed.), *Coronations*, 88–90; Lawrence M. Bryant, *Ritual, Ceremony and the Changing Monarchy in France, 1350–1789* (Farnham, 2010); Sergio Bertelli, *The King's Body: Sacred Rituals of Power in Medieval and Early Modern Europe*, trans. R. Burr Litchfield (University Park, PA, 2001), 67; Kevin Sharpe, *Selling the Tudor Monarchy: Authority and Image in Sixteenth-Century England* (New Haven,

INTRODUCTION

is possible to read the 'fluctuations of English policy' in the ceremonial decisions of Tudor monarchs.[14] The second reason, taking inspiration from Kevin Sharpe, is to provide a logical narrative for the reader – particularly those unfamiliar with this period of Scottish history – with distinct subsections provided to identify specific ritual or ceremonial types easily.[15]

Michael Penman states: '[t]he history of succession to the Crown of medieval Scotland is dominated by the crisis of inheritance of 1286 to 1292...'[16] This crisis is a crucial context for understanding the later medieval Scottish political landscape in which the cycle of death and succession took place. However, Chapter 1 begins with the death of William I in 1214 and covers the reigns of the last Canmore kings, Alexander II (r.1214–49) and Alexander III (r.1249–86). This period of relative stability offers a prime starting point as it marks the culmination of the developments of the previous centuries, thus providing the foundations, prior to the succession crisis and wars that followed, from which to explore subsequent developments. Chapter 2 begins with the funeral of Alexander III in 1286 and covers the period most marked by war and civil strife, during which time two dynasties were raised to the kingship and Scotland experienced brief periods largely under English control.[17] The cycle of succession was unsurprisingly disrupted by competing dynastic claims and external incursions, but the final three chapters on the Stewart dynasty aptly illustrate that threats could also come from within. The shift from Bruce to Stewart was relatively peaceful, but transferral and negotiations of power from 1371 to 1543 were often no less fraught with complexities. Chapter 3 addresses the period of consolidation of the Stewart dynasty, following the death of the childless David II, when members of the extended royal family emerged as the prominent threat to the personal authority of Robert II, Robert III and even James I.[18] Dynastic

---

2009), particularly at 8; Andrew Brown, *Civic Ceremony and Religion in Medieval Bruges, c.1300–1520* (Cambridge, 2011), 39–72; Giesey, *The Royal Funeral Ceremony*, 53–78; Richard A. Jackson, *Vive Le Roi! A History of the French Coronation From Charles V to Charles X* (Chapel Hill and London, 1984), particularly 155–67; Peter Arnade, *Realms of Ritual: Burgundian Ceremony and Civic Life in Late Medieval Ghent* (Ithaca and London, 1996); Alastair Mann, 'The Scottish Parliaments: the Role of Ritual and Procession in the Pre-1707 Parliament and the New Parliament of 1999', in Emma Crewe and Marion G. Müller (eds), *Rituals in Parliaments, Political, Anthropological and Historical Perspectives on Europe and the United States* (Frankfurt, 2006), 135–58.

[14] Anglo, *Spectacle, Pageantry*, particularly at 3–4.
[15] Sharpe, *Selling the Tudor Monarchy*, xxix.
[16] Michael Penman, '*Diffinicione successionis ad regnum Scottorum*: Royal Succession in Scotland in the Later Middle Ages', in Lachaud and Penman (eds), *Making and Breaking the Rules of Succession in Medieval Europe*, 43–59, at 43.
[17] For an introduction to the period, see Michael Brown, *Wars of Scotland 1214–1371*, reprint (Edinburgh, 2010).
[18] Robert II was side-lined by his adult sons, 1384–90; the duke of Albany (Robert III's brother) was confirmed as lieutenant before Robert III was crowned in 1390 and Robert III only really held power from 1393 to 1399, despite reigning until 1406. The duke of Albany was involved in the murder of Robert III's eldest son (1402) and was governor

rivalry within the extended Stewart family also played a role in the murder of James I in 1437, which provides the dramatic beginning to Chapter 4, and the rebellions of the 1480s that led to the death of James III, whose enigmatic funerary arrangements open Chapter 5.[19] The period covered in the final two chapters also includes two further violent deaths related to war (James II in 1460 and James IV in 1513) so this period witnessed the accession of four minor kings, three of whom were less than ten years old. The study ends with the death of James V, the last Scottish monarch to be buried on native soil.

The description of the funeral of James V in 1543, at first glance, could be mistaken for a fifteenth- or sixteenth-century royal or elite heraldic funeral in any number of European kingdoms or principalities, incorporating many frequently used symbols and practices. Indeed, that the ceremony was recognisable to foreign audiences was important to an outward-looking Renaissance monarch like James V of Scotland. However, this ceremony was not identical to any other: it was at once identifiable, uniquely malleable, universally understood but locally defined. Societies do not remain static. Consequently, as Sergio Bertelli has argued, neither can the ceremonies, rituals and symbols that societies adopt, develop or invent.[20] The idea that ritual and ceremony were constantly evolving could appear contradictory as ritual is commonly associated with actions undertaken repetitively in a prescribed and easily recognisable way by actors in a public forum. However, this is too simplistic a definition, as illustrated by even a brief foray into the voluminous work seeking to define ritual. Ritual is defined by scholars as simultaneously emotive or empty, enacting or representative, prescriptive and fixed or fluid and performative, as something that facilitates communal identity and cohesion or has the potential for contention and dispute, and as a mirror reflecting reality or an aspirational idealised model.[21] Due to the fact that '[r]ituals are inherently ambiguous in their function and meaning', Edward Muir encourages engaging with the various meanings and definitions in conjunction with

---

through most of James I's absence (as a prisoner in England, 1406–24). See Stephen I. Boardman, *The Early Stewart Kings: Robert II and Robert III, 1371–1406* (East Linton, 1996); Karen Hunt, 'Governorship of Robert Duke of Albany (1406–1420)', in Michael Brown and Roland Tanner (eds), *Scottish Kingship 1306–1542: Essays in Honour of Norman Macdougall* (Edinburgh, 2008), 126–54.

[19] On the murder of James I and role of his uncle: Michael Brown, '"That Old Serpent and Ancient of Evil Days": Walter, Earl of Atholl and the Death of James I', SHR 71 (1992), 23–45; Michael Brown, *James I* (Edinburgh, 1994), 172–93. James III was directly challenged by his brother in 1482 and, subsequently, by elites using his fifteen-year-old son as a figurehead: Norman Macdougall, *James III*, revised edition (Edinburgh, 2009), 318–58; Norman Macdougall, *James IV*, reprint (Edinburgh, 2006), 1–48.

[20] Bertelli, *The King's Body*, 2.

[21] For example: Peter Burke, 'Performing History: The Importance of Occasions', *Rethinking History* 9 (2005), 35–52; Althoff, 'The Variability of Rituals', 71–89; Burden, 'Rituals of Royalty', 10–28; Frances Andrews, 'Ritual and Space: Definitions and Ways Forward', in Frances Andrews (ed.), *Ritual and Space in the Middle Ages: Proceedings of the 2009 Harlaxton Symposium* (Donington, 2011), 1–29, at 4–14; Edward Muir, *Ritual in Early Modern Europe* (Cambridge, 1999), *passim*, particularly at 1–9.

one another for fruitful analysis.[22] Taking Muir's advice, as many have done before, this study will not seek to provide a narrow definition but embrace the inherent multiplicity of this term. There are, nonetheless, a few points about ritual that require further consideration.

The first is the relationship between ritual, ceremony and symbolism. Ritual and ceremony are used interchangeably across a wide range of interdisciplinary scholarship, and the lines between them are inherently blurred.[23] Althoff even suggests that trying to 'delimit ritual vis-à-vis related phenomena such as rite, custom, ceremony, or habit' is far less important than acknowledging the fluid boundaries between them.[24] However, Olaf Mörke notes that ceremony incorporated ritual 'action' to create 'drama', which 'visually accentuated ritual', and this idea informs the use of ceremony in this study, where it will primarily refer to an overarching event in which ritual elements or actions were combined in a performance or dramatic event.[25] As rituals can be seen as the building blocks of a ceremony, so symbolism is often referred to as 'the raw material of ritual'. However, like ritual and ceremony, there is no one simple definition or use of this term as rituals were themselves also 'manifestations of symbolism'.[26] Taking onboard both of these definitions, this study will engage with the flourishing dialogue around the expansion and cultivation of the symbols of power adopted by the Scottish monarchs – such as the imperial crown, the unicorn and the thistle – and the vibrant cultural forces that underpinned these developments, while speaking to how ritual and ceremony were harnessed as an integral symbolic form of communication between the ruler and ruled.[27]

Another key point identified in most scholarship of ritual is that rituals required participants and an audience. However, the impact of engagement with ritual and the reaction – emotional or otherwise – of participants and audiences, and how far these can and should be assessed, is an issue of

---

[22] Muir, *Ritual in Early Modern Europe*, 3–6.
[23] Examples influential discussions of ritual that use ritual and ceremony interchangeably: Arnade, *Realms of Ritual*; Muir, *Ritual in Early Modern Europe*; Andrews, 'Ritual and Space', 1–29; David Ditchburn, 'Rituals, Space and the Marriage of James II', in Andrews (ed.), *Ritual and Space in the Middle Ages*, 179–96.
[24] Althoff, 'The Variability of Rituals', 72.
[25] Olaf Mörke, 'The Symbolism of Rulership', in Martin Gosman, Alasdair MacDonald and Arjo Vanderjagt (eds), *Princes and Princely Culture 1450–1650, Vol I* (Leiden, 2003), 31–49, at 37.
[26] Marcello Fantoni, 'Symbols and Rituals: Definition of a Field of Study', in Samual Cohn Jr, Marcello Fantoni, Franco Franceschi and Fabrizio Ricciardelli (eds), *Late Medieval and Early Modern Rituals: Studies in Italian Urban Culture* (Turnhout, 2013), 15–40, at 16–17.
[27] See the works of Katie Stevenson and Roger Mason referred to herein and listed in the bibliography, for example: Roger Mason, *Kingship and the Commonweal: Political Thought in Renaissance and Reformation Scotland* (East Linton, 1998), 104–38; Katie Stevenson, 'Chivalry, British Sovereignty and Dynastic Politics: Undercurrents of Antagonism in Tudor-Stewart Relations, c.1490–c.1513', *HR* 86 (2013), 601–18; Katie Stevenson, *Power and Propaganda, 1306–1488* (Edinburgh, 2014), 182–214.

debate.[28] Frances Andrews identifies a pertinent practical issue associated with exploring participation and audience interactions: the authors recording medieval rituals rarely offer specifics about those taking part, which she suggests indicates an 'innate ambivalence' in contemporary narratives towards engagement with and response to ritual that, in turn, can hinder a full analysis.[29] This is certainly true for records of Scottish ritual that are often lacking details about participants and can be void of information about audiences. Consequently, while this study considers the size, profile and roles of participants and audiences where possible, how they responded or what they understood is often impossible to comment on with the evidence that survives.[30] Fantoni's discussion of the inclusivity of ritual, as a medium that included people from across society in the establishing, re-establishing or emphasising hierarchical order through shared beliefs and understanding, is important when considering participants and audience in Scotland.[31] Indeed, William Hepburn's recent study of the court and household of James IV speaks to the importance of performance within and by the court, likening it to immersive theatre in which identities and status could be shaped and restated.[32] Ritual and ceremony provide a means of exploring the dynamics between the ruler, political community (parliament, court and urban), foreign observers (friend or foe) and the wider population.[33] Althoff argues that 'medieval public communication was ritual and demonstrative' and thus the politics of this era was performative and imbued with ritual actions.[34] This speaks to a strand of recent scholarship that has contributed to our understanding of how power was negotiated between crown, magnates and parliament in fifteenth-century Scotland through analysing the relationship between political language and public performance.[35] The analysis that follows can further build on this by exploring the ways that rituals functioned in the political landscape and what this reveals about the dynamics of power within the Scottish polity.

Records of ritual are inherently problematic, and not only due to an ambivalence toward, or absence of commentaries on, participants and audience. For understanding the rituals and ceremonies of succession and power transfer, the extant Scottish sources present some specific as well as common chal-

---

[28] For some examples, see Muir, *Ritual in Early Modern Europe*, 2–3, 9, 259; Burden, 'Rituals of Royalty', 25–8; Andrews, 'Ritual and Space', 5; Lauren Ristvet, *Ritual, Performance, and Politics in the Ancient Near East* (Cambridge, 2015), 30.
[29] Andrews, 'Ritual and Space', 5.
[30] Burden, 'Rituals of Royalty', 25–6.
[31] Fantoni, 'Symbols and Rituals', 32–3.
[32] William Hepburn, *The Household and Court of James IV of Scotland, 1488–1513* (Woodbridge, 2023), 102–22.
[33] Arnade, *Realms of Ritual*, 5.
[34] Althoff, 'The Variability of Rituals in the Middle Ages', 73.
[35] Claire Hawes, 'Community and Public Authority in Later Fifteenth-Century Scotland' (PhD thesis, University of St Andrews, 2015); Lynn Kilgallon, 'Communal Authority, Counsel and Resistance in the Reign of James I: A Conceptual Approach', *SHR* 100 (2021), 1–24.

lenges. There are no extant medieval *ordines* (singular *ordo*) – liturgical orders of ceremony – for inaugurations, coronations or royal funerals for Scotland. Evidence exists for an order of ceremony being penned for the first official coronation with anointing following the papal bull granting unction in 1329, but the document itself has not survived.[36] Johanna Dale structured her comparative study of twelfth-century liturgical kingship in England, France and the Empire around her source types and her first two chapters utilise *ordines*.[37] Such documents vary in the level of detail – some are little more than lists of prayers – and most scholars who use them openly admit their inherent flaws as prescriptive documents composed by ecclesiastics.[38] Nonetheless, they do still form a significant body of source material for the study of inaugural ritual that Dale states is 'absolutely fundamental to understanding the liturgical resonances inherent in the images of medieval kingship' and they also survive for royal funerals in some instances.[39] The only extant orders of ceremony for later medieval Scotland are secular in origin, recorded in either records of the parliament or in copies of medieval texts collated by Scottish heralds in the seventeenth century.[40] These secular records are no less problematic than those with ecclesiastical origins, particularly for understanding the extent to which a ceremony was liturgically driven, and they must be treated with the same caution, especially where they were collated or written after the Scottish Reformation.

Bryant notes, however, that it is important to remember that the political and liturgical rules of ritual emerged and evolved before *ordines* existed, so overreliance on these should be avoided.[41] In Scotland, the absence of liturgical texts and the challenges presented by surviving secular records are at once problematic and liberating in preventing an over reliance upon

---

[36] *ER*, I, 381; Duncan, 'Before Coronation: Making a King at Scone', 153.
[37] Johanna Dale, *Inauguration and Liturgical Kingship in the Long Twelfth Century* (York, 2019), 22–3, 28–105.
[38] For example: Janet L. Nelson, *Politics and Ritual in Early Medieval Europe* (London, 1999), 283–307, 329–39; Jacques Le Goff, 'A Coronation Program for the Age of St Louis. The Ordo of 1250', in Bak (ed.), *Coronations*, 46–57; Burden, 'Rituals of Royalty', particularly 30–72.
[39] Dale, *Inauguration and Liturgical Kingship*, 36. Burden provides a useful overview of funeral ordines in the English context: 'Rituals of Royalty', 50–72.
[40] For example: *RPS*, 1371/1–2 (memorandum regarding coronation of Robert II in 1371); Jerome Lindsay, 'Forme of the coronatioun of the Kings of Scotland', *Register of the Privy Council of Scotland*, ed. John H. Burton et al., 36 vols (Edinburgh, 1877–1933), Second Series, II, 393–5; NLS, Sir James Balfour of Denmilne's Manuscript Collection, Coronations: Descriptions of coronations and other ceremonies in the hand of Sir James Balfour, seventeenth century, Adv. MS. 33.7.10, fols 6–14r, and Adv. MS. 33.2.26, fols 30–1. For discussions of origins, see Roderick Lyall, 'The Medieval Coronation Service: Some Seventeenth Century Evidence', *IR* 28 (1977), 3–21; Lucinda H.S. Dean, 'Crowning the Child: Representing Authority in the Inaugurations and Coronations of Minors in Scotland, c. 1214 to 1567', in Elena Woodacre and Sean McGlyn (eds), *The Image and Perception of Monarchy in Medieval and Early Modern Europe* (Nottingham, 2014), 254–80.
[41] Bryant, *Ritual, Ceremony and the Changing Monarchy in France*, 5, 21.

prescriptive texts. Malcolm Vale's study of the princely courts and culture in medieval Europe encompasses 'both the material and non-material' – material, artistic, literary and musical sources alongside more traditional document sources – within a single framework.[42] This model is central to the methodology followed here. The paucity of various types of material and non-material records in Scotland across such a long chronology in the late medieval to early modern period is notable, so it requires casting the net wide to counteract these challenges. This study relies primarily on three types of evidence, all of which are discussed in more detail where appropriate in the text, which require a brief introduction here: narrative and descriptive sources, financial accounts and material culture.[43]

Late medieval Scotland has a rich collection of surviving chronicles. Three well-known narrative sources form the core of this chronicle tradition – *Gesta Annalia* (previously attributed to John of Fordun), Andrew of Wytoun's *Original Chronicle* and Walter Bower's *Scotichronicon*. All three have attracted substantial scholarly attention, particularly focused on the common sources utilised by them that are no longer extant.[44] *Gesta Annalia* is a work of two parts, largely untouched by Fordun himself: *Gesta Annalia I*, which Dauvit Broun convincingly argues was written or compiled at St Andrews in the thirteenth century, and *Gesta Annalia II*, which was a fourteenth-century addition covering 1285 to 1363.[45] Comparisons between *Gesta Annalia*, historians Wyntoun and Bower have illustrated that shared sources were used, but subtle differences between the texts illustrate that each chronicler also had unique sources of information and that a distinct purpose or patronage shaped their narratives.[46] The malleability of narrative is a key point of consideration for all the Scottish, English and continental chronicles drawn into this analysis of ritual. There is a direct correlation to Gabrielle M. Spiegel's medieval French exemplars in the sharing of common source materials and the emergence of narrative spaces for airing 'competing

---

[42] Malcolm Vale, *The Princely Court: Medieval Courts and Culture in North-West Europe, 1270–1380* (Oxford, 2001), particularly 1–11.
[43] For a fuller breakdown of all the sources and challenges with them, see Dean, 'Crowns, Wedding Rings and Processions', 13–22.
[44] For biographical material on these chroniclers, see Donald E.R. Watt, 'Fordun, John (d. in or after 1363)', *ODNB* (2004), https://doi.org/10.1093/ref:odnb/9875. Date accessed: 27 February 2021; Caroline Edington, 'Wyntoun, Andrew (c.1350–c.1422), Prior of St Serf, Lochleven, and Historian', *ODNB*, (2004), https://doi.org/10.1093/ref:odnb/30164. Date accessed: 27 February 2021; *Chron. Bower*, IX, particularly 204–9, 315–64.
[45] Dauvit Broun, 'A New Look at *Gesta Annalia* Attributed to John of Fordun', in Barbara E. Crawford (ed.), *Church, Chronicle and Learning in Medieval and Early Renaissance Scotland: Essays Presented to Donald Watt on the Occasion of the Completion of Bower's Scotichronicon* (Edinburgh, 1999), 9–30; Broun, *Scottish Independence and the Idea of Britain*, 215–34.
[46] Stephen Boardman, 'Chronicle Propaganda in Fourteenth-Century Scotland: Robert the Steward, John Fordun, and the "Anonymous Chronicle"', *SHR* 76 (1997), 23–43; Broun, 'A New Look at *Gesta Annalia*', 13–17.

INTRODUCTION

interests'.[47] In the context of English medieval chronicles, Chris Given-Wilson states that 'truth' was a flexible term with more than one meaning which affected choices made about language, inclusion and exclusion by medieval and early modern authors.[48] The post-modernist literary turn pushed academics to question the interpretive nature and construction of the narrative sources upon which they rely. When dealing with records of ritual specifically, Philippe Buc warned that from the moment ritual is conceived or performed it is open to interpretation, so such narratives are inherently flawed and a record outlining a perfectly orderly ceremonial occasion should raise immediate questions.[49] Yet, the authors of such sources did have to use commonly understood customs and rules as their building blocks in shaping their narratives of ritual to present believable accounts for contemporaries. For this reason, Althoff argues that such sources can and should be used for 'investigations of practice' and the 'forms and functions of public communication'.[50] Consequently, this study draws on such chronicle texts with a considered appreciation of authorship, composition, motivation and purpose. This is particularly the case where discrepancies occur within the chronicle accounts, as these indicate narrative choices and are used to achieve a deeper understanding of underpinning ideas that circulated about ritual elements and their association with royal power and succession.

Later fifteenth- and early sixteenth-century Scotland suffers from a distinct shortage of contemporary narrative sources.[51] This necessitates some reliance here as elsewhere on sixteenth-century histories, largely produced after the Reformation and the expulsion of Mary Queen of Scots, which adds denominational and ideological layering to their interpretation.[52] The later period also witnesses an increased survival of ambassadorial accounts

---

[47] Gabrielle M. Spiegel, *The Past as Text: The Theory and Practice of Medieval Historiography* (Baltimore and London, 1999), 195–212.

[48] Chris Given-Wilson, *Chronicles: The Writing of History in Medieval England* (London, 2004), 2–6, 57–65; Matthew Kempshall, *Rhetoric and the Writing of History* (Manchester, 2011), 89–90.

[49] Philippe Buc, 'Ritual and Interpretation: The Early Medieval Case', *Early Medieval Europe* 9 (2000), 183–210, at 186, 200–1. See also Muir, *Ritual in Early Modern Europe*, 1–9. For Buc's challenges of 'ritual' as a concept, see *The Dangers of Ritual: Between Early Medieval Texts and Social Scientific Theory* (Princeton, 2001).

[50] Althoff, 'The Variability of Rituals', 87.

[51] For comprehensive summaries about the challenges of mid-late fifteenth-century sources, see Christine McGladdery, *James II* (Edinburgh, 2015), 203–34; Macdougall, *James III*, xiii–xvii.

[52] Key sixteenth-century chronicles or histories include Hector Boece (c.1465–1536) *Scotorum historia* (1527), Robert Lindsay of Pitscottie (c.1532–c.1586) *The Historie and Cronicles of Scotland* (completed 1576x1586, published 1728), John Leslie bishop of Ross (1527–96) *The Historie of Scotland* (presented in the vernacular to Mary in 1570s, published in Latin 1578, many translations), George Buchanan (1506–82) *Rerum Scoticarum historia* (1582) and also anonymous commentators, such as *An Diurnal of Remarkable Occurrents* (c.1575).

recording Scottish ceremonies.[53] Ambassadors and other foreign visitors were usually outside observers but, like chroniclers and history writers, they often held inherent loyalties that colour their reports and the level of detail they record varies greatly. The account of John Young, Somerset herald, who accompanied Margaret Tudor to Scotland to marry James IV in 1503, offers unparalleled descriptions of clothing, accessories and performative actions through the eyes of a spectator and participant. Young, rather unusually, shows little interest in the politics of the union; rather his concerns centre on how noble virtues were performed through sartorial splendour.[54] Young was not alone in his appreciation of material display and its role: Gilbert Hay's fifteenth-century *Buke of the Gouvernance of Princis* underscores contemporary expectations that a king must elevate himself above his subjects in the manner he adorned his body.[55] As Catherine Richardson argues, literary sources offer another way to broaden modern appreciation of the meaning that medieval and early modern people located in the material culture around them.[56] Narrative and diplomatic sources, however, rarely offer the level of detail and insight that Young provides. Often the records of ambassadors are brief and perfunctory, while chronicles and histories frequently provide only basic information – when, where and, occasionally, who attended or took part. Dale turns these limitations of narrative into a positive, proposing that, where minimal details survive, they reflect that which is most significant.[57] This is an approach taken here as limited information can often speak at great volume, whether about what is noteworthy or what is unusual. It is also important to recognise that a lack of detail on the actions and objects of ceremony in the accounts of a chronicler or ambassador does not necessarily mean a lack of investment in performance and display.

Financial materials can offer hard evidence of such investments, which can then be employed in reconstructing rituals and ceremonies, such as undertaken in the opening vignette of James V's funeral where financial accounts were used to supplement a brief contemporary description. The analysis of these records, and ceremonial details reconstructed from them, fundamen-

---

[53] Two prime examples record weddings, first that of James II (*Chron. D'Escouchy*, 175–83) and second of James IV (*Fyancells MS*, fols 75–115; *Fyancells Coll.*, 258–300). There are also published calendars that provide an invaluable resource for material and investigating original materials: *CDS*, I–V, *passim*.

[54] *Fyancells Coll.*, 265; *Fyancells MS*, fol. 76r; Sarah Carpenter, '"To Thexaltacyon of Noblesse": A Herald's Account of the Marriage of Margaret Tudor and James IV', *Medieval English Theatre* 29 (2007), 104–20, at 105–7.

[55] *Gilbert Haye's Prose Manuscript (d. 1456) Vol. II: The Buke of the Knychtehede and the Buke of the Gouvernance of Princis*, ed. J.H. Stevenson (Edinburgh and London, 1914), 92. For more on the importance of dress and textile display, see Lucinda H.S. Dean, '"richesse in fassone and in fairenesse": Marriage, Manhood and Sartorial Splendour in Sixteenth-Century Scottish Kings', *SHR* 100 (2021), 378–96.

[56] Catherine Richardson, 'Written Texts and the Performance of Materiality', in Anne Gerristen and Giorgio Riello (eds), *Writing Material Culture History* (London, 2015), 43–58, at 53–6.

[57] Dale, *Inauguration and Liturgical Kingship*, 106–8.

tally underpins this research from the fourteenth century onwards, when the *Exchequer Rolls* of Scotland survive more consistently.[58] An overhaul of the financial administration in Scotland by James I in the 1420s saw the introduction of the Comptroller, the Treasurer and the *Treasurer's Accounts* and led to a period of change in accounting practices, the understanding of which is hampered by the fact that the first decades of the *Treasurer's Accounts* have not survived.[59] The first extant *Treasurer's Accounts* cover August 1473 to December 1474 and more consistent records survive from 1488 onwards, although significant gaps still exist.[60] The first volume of the printed editions offers a verbatim transcription of the original manuscripts, but later volumes provide only abridged content.[61] This is not the place for a reappraisal of the published editions of the *Treasurer's Accounts*, which are still highly valuable, but the omissions often consist of the details of repeat entries or minor items. These can include Yule or Easter gifts – where similar items were given to numerous people – and lower cost items, such as those related to the manufacture of clothing including lining cloth, sewing silks and maker's fees.[62] Omissions of minor incremental costs are not always problematic. However, where finer details of individual items or the total spent on a specific event are sought, such as in the provisioning for the weddings of James IV in 1503 and James V in 1537, the manuscripts are referenced so that these additional minor costs are drawn into the calculations (see Chapter 5 and Appendixes III and IV). Supplementary accounts including household books are also used, but these survive inconsistently during the sixteenth century only and are predominantly in manuscript form.[63] Without this body of financial material and the careful in-depth interpretation of it within this study, the scale and detail of many of the Scottish ceremonies analysed here would be lost to posterity.

Financial records and narrative texts provide much of the evidence for material culture in this analysis due to a scarcity of surviving objects and sig-

---

[58] *ER*, I–XXIII, *passim*. Fragments of the Exchequer Rolls survive for the 1260s, copied in a seventeenth-century hand: John Stuart and George Burnett, 'Preface', *ER*, I, xxxv–xxxvii. For detailed information on the records, officers, practices and procedures of the Exchequer, see Atholl L. Murray, 'The Exchequer and Crown Revenue, 1437–1542' (PhD thesis, University of Edinburgh, 1961). Manuscript spot checks were undertaken and referenced where appropriate, but largely the published editions are used.

[59] *TA*, I, xiii–xxv. On the development of the office of the Treasurer, see Murray, 'The Exchequer and Crown Revenue', 272–319.

[60] *TA*, I–XII, *passim*.

[61] *TA*, I, xxxv–xxxvi.

[62] Recent scholarship by Melanie Schuessler Bond also speaks to the challenges with these printed records for the study of clothing in the Scottish court: *Dressing the Scottish Court, 1543–1553: Clothing in the Accounts of the Lord High Treasurer of Scotland* (Woodbridge, 2019).

[63] *Accounts of the Masters of Works for Building and Repairing Royal Palaces and Castles*, ed. H.M. Paton et al., 2 vols (Edinburgh, 1957–82) is one of the few published resources. Supplementary accounts used include *Liber emptorum* and *Liber domicilii*. For more on supplementary accounts, see Murray, 'The Exchequer and Crown Revenue', 207–25.

nificant losses and remodelling of critical built fabric. Catherine Richardson emphasises how historians fruitfully approach material culture 'in the absence of objects' through textual sources, and the combination of quantitative and qualitative methodologies that she advocates reflect the approach taken here.[64] This study joins Morvern French in emphasising the importance of considering materiality in the Scottish context and where objects survive, such as the royal honours and seal impressions, this study will draw these into the analysis.[65] Historians have often considered seals problematic due to the formulaic nature of their designs and a lack of realism, but there is increasing recognition of the potential seals have to offer historical enquiry if an appreciation of their form and function is embraced.[66] By using observation of design changes in this form of material culture, which, alongside coinage, was 'amongst the most public means of image projection' for monarchs in pre-modern Europe, this study adds to the dialogue about the potent messages that seals can contain about kingship.[67] Moreover, in a Scottish context, the royal gold or silver seal matrix may have been carried with other regalia in the coronation from the fifteenth century or earlier, and it was physically broken at the point of power transfer to be replaced by the seal of the new monarch.[68] This use of the seal indicates that objects incorporated into royal rituals were not inert props, but were firmly embedded as active agents with the ability to enact change, reflect interpersonal communications and shape

---

[64] Richardson, 'Written Texts and the Performance of Materiality', 43–4.

[65] Morvern French, 'Magnificence and Materiality: The Commerce and Culture of Flemish Luxuries in Late Medieval Scotland' (PhD thesis, University of St Andrews, 2016). For the royal honours: Historic Environment Scotland (HES), Crown, EDIN052; HES, Sword, EDIN053a; HES, Sceptre, EDIN054. See Plate 20, see 221. See also Lucinda H.S. Dean, *The Scottish Royal Honours: Objects, Ceremony, Use* (Edinburgh, forthcoming).

[66] Pertinent examples include: Grant G. Simpson, 'Kingship in Miniature: A Seal of Minority of Alexander III, 1249–1257', in Alexander Grant and Keith Stringer (eds), *Medieval Scotland: Crown, Lordship and Community: Essays Presented to G.W.S Barrow* (Edinburgh, 1993), 131–9; John Cherry, 'Medieval and Post-Medieval Seals', in Dominique Collon (ed.), *7000 Years of Seals* (London, 1997), 124–42; Nicholas Vincent, 'The Seals of King Henry II and his Court', and Adrian Ailes, 'Governmental Seals of Richard I', in Phillipp Schofield (ed.), *Seals and Their Context in the Middle Ages* (Oxford, 2015), 7–34, 101–10; Cynthia J. Neville, 'Making a Manly Impression: The Image of Kingship on Scottish Royal Seals of the High Middle Ages', in Lynn Abrams and Elizabeth L. Ewan (eds), *Nine Centuries of Man: Manhood and Masculinity in Scottish History* (Edinburgh, 2017), 101–21; Dale, *Inauguration and Liturgical Kingship*, 191–214; Rachel M. Davis, 'Material Evidence? Re-approaching Elite Women's Seals and Charters in Late Medieval Scotland', *PSAS* 150 (2021), 301–26.

[67] Vincent, 'The Seals of King Henry II', 7.

[68] On the carrying of the seal in Scotland: Lyall, 'The Medieval Coronation Service', 3–21; Dean, 'Crowning the Child', 271–7. Numerous examples of the breaking of the Great Seal survive in Scotland, including during the minority of James V when the seal was broken and remade at least three times: *RPS*, 1524/8/2; *RPS*, 1525/2/9; *RPS*, 1525/2/11; *RPS*, 1526/2/16; *RPS*, 1526/6/5; *ADCP*, 1 August 1524, 204–5; *Diurnal*, 9; William K. Emond, 'The Minority of King James V, 1513–1528' (PhD thesis, University of St Andrews, 1988), 41.

interactions.[69] Similarly, as Fantoni stresses, the physical spaces of ritual action were not a mere decorative backdrop but had a physical impact on the ceremonies that were performed.[70] While the material culture and physical locations employed in Scottish ceremonies have rarely survived unchanged, or often at all, the materiality of ritual is an essential component to be analysed. Consequently, where it is possible to do so, the material record (in all its forms) will be analysed here to provide fuller understanding of the performance of royal power.

Through its consideration of the material and non-material records of the ritual cycle of death and succession, this book adds to existing debates about Scottish kingship and the polity within which it functioned from the thirteenth to the sixteenth century. For over one third of the period under consideration, Scotland lacked a fully empowered adult monarch at the helm.[71] This was a hazard of hereditary monarchy across Europe, but Scotland suffered particularly badly. Dougal Shaw has proposed that the frequency of absent adult royal power meant that 'the country's coronation remained correspondingly immature'.[72] This statement requires serious challenge. First, the common presumption that kingdoms where the ceremonies were not overtly Christianised or maintained strong secular elements were in some way 'lesser' is highly contestable. Second, the suggestion that the lack of an adult monarch impedes the development of ritual and the polity from which it emerges does not sit comfortably with recent scholarship on the Scottish parliament, guardianship, the office of the regent and the practical exercise of power. These two challenges to Shaw's conclusion provide apposite hooks from which to hang the remaining debates and contexts that are threaded through this study.

On the first point, it is in comparison to the highly elaborate liturgical English coronation that Shaw made his judgments of the equivalent Scottish ceremony.[73] Traditional studies of ritual tend to associate ceremonial 'success' with developments such as the introduction of anointing, found first in kingdoms like France and England.[74] However, there is a growing body

---

[69] For more on debates about objects as active agents: Leora Auslander, 'Beyond Words', *American Historical Review* 110 (2005), 1015–44, at 1016–18, 1034–44; Anne Gerristen and Giorgio Riello, 'Introduction: Writing Material Culture History', in Gerristen and Riello (eds), *Writing Material Culture History*, 1–14.

[70] Fantoni, 'Symbols and Rituals', 31–2.

[71] Alexander II, Alexander III, David II, James I and all the subsequent Stewart kings herein came to the throne as minors. Periods of absentee kingship, foreign intervention, etc., prior to 1371: 1286–92 (guardianship, Great Cause), 1296–1306 (guardianship, brief English rule), 1334–42 (guardianship, David II absent in France for protection), 1346–57 (guardianship, David II prisoner in England) and 1384–93 and 1399–1406 (lieutenancies, during old age or ill health of Robert II and Robert III).

[72] Dougal Shaw, 'Scotland's Place in Britain's Coronation Tradition', *Court Historian* 9 (2004), 41–60, at 47.

[73] Ibid., 47.

[74] Muir, *Ritual in Early Modern Europe*, 248–9.

of work considering kingdoms in Europe that actively rejected unction or developed with different dominant influences offering challenges to this Anglo-French paradigm around what should be considered ceremonial norms and, indeed, rulership 'norms' more generally.[75] As a kingdom often considered on the periphery rather than a central powerhouse of Europe, which intermittently fought for its independence, Scotland offers a prime example of how ritual functioned, changed and developed over time, and what this reveals about the complexities of a polity beyond the central core of western Europe. Some Scottish medievalists, including Archibald A.M. Duncan, have also assumed that the secular nature of the Scottish inauguration was a 'weakness', particularly in comparison to England.[76] This book actively extends the ongoing discussion, most recently contributed to by Alice Taylor and Norman Reid, that challenges the traditional views surrounding the impact of Anglo-Norman influences and the associated Anglicisation of the Scottish kingdom.[77] During the period under consideration, Scotland was influenced by many cultures beyond its bounds. This was complicated at times by English encroachments on Scottish royal power, particularly in the thirteenth and fourteenth centuries, but even when the English were directly involved in managing Scottish rituals neither party sought to mirror those of England. This should not be presumed to equate with inferiority, rather it stresses that which Bertelli argues in more general terms: Scotland's rituals and ceremonies were indicative of its unique origins and reflected the kingdom's particular political, cultural and social landscape.[78]

Scotland had a long Christian heritage. The kings invested heavily in demonstrations of piety, the church and crown shared a struggle for independence from England and there was ongoing interaction with the papacy.[79] The idea of the Christianisation or 'liturgification' – a term coined

---

[75] For example: Teófilo F. Ruiz, 'Unsacred Monarchy: The Kings of Castile in the Late Middle Ages', in Sean Wilentz (ed.), *Rites of Power: Symbolism, Ritual and Politics Since the Middle Ages* (Philadelphia, 1999), 109–44; Christian Raffensperger, 'The Kingdom of Rus: Towards A New Theoretical Model of Rulership in Medieval Europe', Grischa Vercamer and Dušan Zupka (eds), *Rulership in Medieval East Central Europe: Power, Ritual and Legitimacy in Bohemia, Hungary and Poland* (Leiden, 2021), 325–39, and other chapters in this volume.

[76] Duncan, *Kingship of the Scots*, 80–1.

[77] Alice Taylor, *The Shape of the State in Medieval Scotland, 1124–1290* (Oxford, 2016), passim, at 17–19 (fns 83 and 84 summarise key scholarship in this area); Reid, *Alexander III*, passim.

[78] Bertelli, *The King's Body*, 2.

[79] For example: Paul C. Ferguson, *Medieval Papal Representatives in Scotland: Legates, Nuncios, and Judge-Delegate, 1125–1286* (Edinburgh, 1997); Geoffrey W.S. Barrow, *The Kingdom of the Scots: Government, Church and Society from the Eleventh to the Fourteenth Century*, second edition (Edinburgh, 2003), 151–68, 203–30; Donald E.R. Watt, *Medieval Church Councils* (Edinburgh, 2000); Dauvit Broun, 'The Church and the Origins of Scottish Independence in the Twelfth Century', *Records of the Scottish Church History Society* 31 (2002), 1–35; Michael Penman, 'Royal Piety in Thirteenth-Century Scotland: The Religion and Religiosity of Alexander II (1214–49) and Alexander II (1249–86)', in

by Duncan – still has some validity for describing one of the ways in which the royal rituals of succession developed.[80] Scottish kings and the church intermittently sought many of the overt symbols of Christian kingship. Nonetheless, Reid is right to question the extent to which Scottish kings saw themselves as divine or sacral, particularly with reference to the thirteenth century.[81] There were ongoing tensions between the liturgical and the secular in Scotland; these are revealed here as central to the ceremonial developments. The Scottish inauguration ritual of the thirteenth century was distinct from the 'Christianised core' that features in Dale's study of twelfth-century inaugurations, in part because Scotland only received the right to anoint its monarchs from the papacy in 1329.[82] In her study, Dale promotes the use of the term 'inauguration' in an effort to extricate the complex liturgical underpinning to the making of kings from the act of crowning and refocus rather on the act of anointing.[83] In a Scottish context, however, there needs to be a distinction between the ceremonies before and after these ritual elements were introduced. For this reason, this study will use 'inauguration' before the introduction of unction and 'unction and coronation' or 'coronation' after this point. This is not to suggest that there was a wholesale 'liturgification' of the Scottish ritual cycle following the introduction of these elements; indeed, there is substantial evidence that indicates this was not the case.[84] Other secular aspects of Scottish king making, such as a secular enthronement, acclamation and the recitation of the genealogy of kings, maintained a prominent place beyond 1329. This study will argue that the hybrid blending of secular and liturgical ritual elements in the Scottish ceremonial cycle of death and succession made it different, rather than inferior to southern and continental exemplars.

The second aspect of Shaw's statement is the implication that the absence of adult authority, particularly in minorities, caused fundamental issues in terms of the maturity of the Scottish coronation. This too is ripe for challenge. Recent scholarship on the Scottish parliament and political assembly during periods of minority and absentee kingship in the late thirteenth and fourteenth centuries argues that this period witnessed the continued growth of ideas of the 'community of the realm', the fuller formation of parliament as an entity and increased 'political consultation and participation'.[85] The

---

Janet Burton, Phillipp Schofield and Björn Weiler (eds), *Thirteenth Century England XII: Proceedings of the Gregynog Conference, 2007* (Woodbridge, 2009), 13–30.
[80] Duncan, *Kingship of the Scots*, 127–50, at 145.
[81] Reid, *Alexander III*, 31–5, quote at 33.
[82] Dale, *Inauguration and Liturgical Kingship*, passim.
[83] Ibid., 94.
[84] See also Lucinda Dean, 'Where to Make the King (or Queen): Space, Place and Location in Scottish Inaugurations and Coronations from 1214 to 1651', in Oliver O'Grady and Richard D. Oram (eds), *Royal and Lordly Inauguration and Assembly Places in North-West Europe* (Donington, 2023), 48–73.
[85] Keith M. Brown and Roland J. Tanner, 'Introduction', and Alison A.B. McQueen, 'Parliament, the Guardians and John Balliol, 1284–1296', in Keith M. Brown and

political elite demonstrated investment in a concept of royal power or dignity that was separate from the monarch and took a shared responsibility in the promotion of royal power. This existed in the twelfth and thirteenth centuries – as identified most recently in the work of Taylor and Reid – and can be traced throughout the minority-riddled fifteenth and sixteenth centuries – as shown in the work of Claire Hawes and Amy Blakeway.[86] Work on English royal minorities by Charles Beem, David Carpenter and Joel Burden illustrates the effective use and development of public ritual events, such as funerals and coronations, to express stability, continuity and reconciliation during minorities.[87] This was not only an English phenomenon. That the guardians and political community of thirteenth-century Scotland, particularly the secular elite, saw it as their right to invest royal dignity on their chosen king is central to Reid's argument in his study of Alexander III's reign; their roles in the ceremonies of king making emphasised such rights.[88] Such interest and understanding of the centrality of ritual has also been illustrated in Blakeway's work on the sixteenth century where it was harnessed by Scottish regents.[89] This book expands upon this dialogue by analysing the extent to which the Scottish political elite and widowed queens invested in the ceremonial cycle to emphasise the stability and continuity of royal power in the absence of an adult king. It will also argue that personal goals and desires must not be underestimated. In a realm where many monarchs came to the throne as children, royal weddings and the crowning of consorts were critical junctures in the cycle of succession and projection of royal authority, particularly where they marked the end of a minority. Such ceremonies often appear underpinned by a desire to reclaim or renegotiate the level of royal authority vested in the king personally, but this held the potential for con-

---

Roland J. Tanner (eds), *The History of the Scottish Parliament 1: Parliament and Politics in Scotland, 1235–1560* (Edinburgh, 2004), 1–49; Archibald A.M. Duncan, 'The Early Parliaments of Scotland', *SHR* 45 (1966), 36–58; Norman Reid and Michael Penman, 'Guardian – Lieutenant – Governor: Absentee Monarchy and Proxy Power in Scotland's Long Fourteenth Century', in Frédérique Lachaud and Michael Penman (eds), *Absentee Authority Across Medieval Europe* (Woodbridge, 2017), 191–218; Michael Penman, '"The King Wishes and Commands"? Reassessing Political Assembly in Scotland, c.1286–1329', in Mario Damen, Jelle Haemers and Alastair J. Mann (eds), *Political Representation: Communities, Ideas and Institutions in Europe, c.1200–c.1690* (Leiden, 2018), 125–41, quote at 141.

[86] Taylor, *Shape of the State*, passim, at 4 (aims outlined), 445–7 (concluded); Norman Reid, 'The Kingless Kingdom: The Scottish Guardianship of 1286–1306', *SHR* 61 (1982), 105–29; Reid, *Alexander III*, passim; Hawes, 'Community and Public Authority', passim, particularly 73–121; Amy Blakeway, *Regency in Sixteenth-Century Scotland* (Woodbridge, 2015), passim.

[87] See chapters by Charles Beem, Christian Hillen and Frank Wiswall, James S. Bothwell, Gwilym Dodd and Ralph A. Griffiths, in Charles Beem (ed.), *The Royal Minorities of Medieval and Early Modern England* (New York, 2008); David A. Carpenter, *The Minority of Henry III* (London, 1990); Burden, 'Rituals of Royalty', 1–112, 164–94.

[88] Reid, *Alexander III*, 37–9.

[89] Blakeway, *Regency in Sixteenth-Century Scotland*, 55–67.

frontation. By considering how rituals of death and succession were managed during the reigns of adult kings, minorities and in the face of dynastic crisis, this work offers new insights into the Scottish kingdom and the figures who dominated and maintained its royal dignity across the late medieval and early modern periods.

Genealogical Table 1   Scottish Kings from Mael Coluim III to Margaret Maid of Norway.

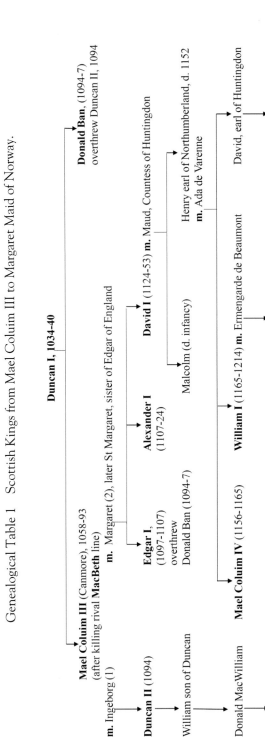

1

The Last Canmore Kings

William I, or the Lion, of Scotland died in Stirling on 4 December 1214. The following day, after an overnight vigil for the king, prominent nobles and the bishop of St Andrews took his son, Alexander II, to Scone for his enthronement. Celebrations and feasting lasted for three days before the new king joined his father's body on a procession from Perth to Arbroath. The late king was buried at the abbey of Arbroath, his own Tironensian foundation dedicated to St Thomas Becket, on 10 December 1214.[1] The swift organisation of events indicates that William's old age and ill health had encouraged advance preparations, and the immediacy of the inaugural rite points to its integral role in the legitimate transfer of power for contemporaries. However, this ordering differed from William's accession in 1165, when the inauguration took place some fifteen days after the funeral of his brother and predecessor, Mael Coluim IV, but this followed the 'unanimous' choice of an adult by the nobles and prelates.[2] Alexander II was not an adult; he was only sixteen years old when his father died, and succession in Scotland was not straightforward.[3]

Male primogeniture – the accession of the eldest son of the primary hereditary line – increasingly dictated Scottish royal succession during the centuries prior to 1214.[4] However, primogeniture posed a potential threat to the perceived right of powerful nobles to be involved in the process of 'selecting' a king so was not immediately embraced. In Scotland, as in Norway and Ireland, an adult male brother or cousin had been preferable to a child or even a youth in preceding centuries due to an adult king's capability to fight to protect his kingdom.[5] Mael Coluim III's efforts to assign the succession

---

[1] Scott convincingly demonstrates that *Gesta Annalia* drew from well-informed contemporary sources for this period and Bower records the same order of events: *Chron. Fordun*, 275–6; *Chron. Bower*, V, 3; W.W. Scott, 'Fordun's Description of the Inauguration of Alexander II', *SHR* 50 (1971), 198–200.
[2] *Chron. Melrose*, 14; *Chron. Fordun*, 254–5; *Chron. Bower*, IV, 281.
[3] Indeed, Gordon Donaldson suggests that succession was rarely straightforward in any kingdom: 'Reflections on the Royal Succession', in James Kirk (ed.), *Scotland's History: Approaches and Reflections* (Edinburgh, 1995), 103–17, at 105–6.
[4] Penman, '*Diffinicione successionis*', 43–59, at 43.
[5] J.H. Stephenson, 'The Law of the Throne: Tanistry and the Introduction of the Law of Primogeniture: A Note on Succession from Kenneth MacAlpin to Robert the Bruce', *SHR* 25 (1927), 1–12, at 1–6; Alasdair Ross, *Kings of Alba* (Edinburgh, 2011), 3–4, 80–144 (see *Gesta Annalia* quoted at length on this subject, 144); Duncan, *Kingship of the Scots*, 16–17, 27. Similar succession practices existed for twelfth-century elites in Scotland: Taylor, *Shape of the State*, 42–5. Such trends also existed in Scandinavia, for example, in

by primogeniture to his sons faced challenges from his brother, Domnall mac Donnchad III (r.1094–97). These challenges received support from the nobles, despite both Mael Coluim III's sons being adults. Howden's *Annals* recorded that 'the Scots chose their king' and then expelled English members of the royal court.[6] This emphasises that the leading subjects believed it their right to challenge direct hereditary lineage where there was reason – in this case, the overtly English nature of the incoming king's court. Duncan has identified that Henry (c.1115–52), son of David I (c.1084–1153), was named as '*rex designatus*' in charters of the priory of St Andrews and that there was support for the accession of Henry's twelve-year-old son, Mael Coluim IV (r.1153–65), following the death of David I in 1153.[7] This appears to signal further embedding of primogeniture in Scotland, but Richard Oram and Alex Woolf have demonstrated direct challenges to Mael Coluim IV by the illegitimate children of Alexander I (d.1124), supported by Somerled of Argyll.[8] Even by the 1190s William and Mael Coluim IV's younger brother, David earl of Huntingdon, was preferred by nobles to William's proposal of his daughter and her foreign husband, Otto of Brunswick, prior to the birth of a male heir.[9] Direct hereditary kingship by primogeniture still had its limits and it was certainly not a given that the king's designation of an heir was above question. The retention of elements of 'election' and acceptance in the ritual cycle of succession indicates that tradition and established power structures were not subsumed by incoming influences; rather, new concepts and symbols were adapted and woven into the Scottish ceremonial fabric.

The twelfth and thirteenth centuries were defining years for Scottish kingship. This makes the juncture between these two centuries – the transfer of royal power between William and Alexander II in 1214 – a logical place to start exploring the rituals that mourned, made and celebrated kingship. Recognisable geographic boundaries of the kingdom of Scotland were largely secured in this period, systems and structures of governance were advanced locally and centrally, and there was an influx of reforming orders

---

early medieval Norway the king was the 'best man' so, while lineage and descent were of important, he also needed to be a successful warrior: Sverre Bagge, *From Viking Stronghold to Christian Kingdom: State Formation in Norway, c.900–1350* (Copenhagen, 2010), 147–8. In Ireland, where multiple smaller kingdoms existed for much longer, seniority and *febas* (worth or excellence) remained dominant over primogeniture until the sixteenth century: Bart Jaski, *Early Irish Kingship and Succession* (Dublin, 2000), 24–30.

[6] *Annals of Howden*, I, 179. Translator notes in fn. 99 that the term *elegerunt* – to choose – emphasises the principally elective nature of Scottish succession.

[7] Archibald A.M. Duncan, *Scotland: The Making of the Kingdom*, reprint (Edinburgh, 1996), 12–26, 172–3 (Mael Coluim as *rex designatus*). See also Stephenson, 'The Law of the Throne', 6–11; Duncan, *Kingship of the Scots*, 53–81; Ross, *Kings of Alba*, 159–218; Dauvit Broun, 'Contemporary Perspectives on Alexander II's Succession: The Evidence of King-Lists', in Richard D. Oram (ed.), *The Reign of Alexander II* (Leiden, 2005), 79–98.

[8] Richard D. Oram, *Domination and Lordship: Scotland 1070–1230* (Edinburgh, 2011), 111–14; Alex Woolf, 'The Song of the Death of Somerled and the Destruction of Glasgow in 1153', *Journal of the Sydney Society for Scottish History* 14 (2013), 1–11.

[9] Duncan, *Making of the Kingdom*, 239–40, 611; Duncan, *Kingship of the Scots*, 105–7.

and reorganisation of the church sponsored partly by the crown.[10] These centuries also saw an increased assertion of a distinctive Scottish identity and independent dynastic kingship in the face of English claims of supremacy over king, kingdom and church.[11] Scottish kings legitimised their kingship through ceremonies that spoke to European 'norms' but, notably, without the Anglo-French Christianised elements of crowning and unction that are often considered the standard.[12]

Through its analysis of rituals, this chapter will complement and extend recent historiographical debates around the extent of Anglo-Norman influence by arguing that the secular nature of Scottish kingship rituals was different, not inferior.[13] However, it also interrogates Reid's suggestion that Scottish kings in the thirteenth century demonstrated a rather lacklustre desire for 'the overt symbolism of Christian kingship'.[14] Scottish ceremony certainly retained a core of self-consciously traditional and secular aspects, but there were also distinct efforts during the thirteenth century to incorporate recognisable English and continental influences to bolster Scottish kingship on an international stage.

Rituals and ceremonies offered physical and representative manifestations of the inner workings of kingship and power structures, as well as the wider society in which they functioned. This chapter works through the pivotal ceremonial in the cycle of succession in the thirteenth century: the inauguration of Alexander II, the funeral of William I, the weddings of Alexander II, the inauguration of Alexander III, the funeral of Alexander II and the weddings of Alexander III and his children. Taking careful heed of Buc's reminder that all rituals have function, and that the narratives of ritual seek to harness function as power, it works to draw in evidence from official and material sources in addition to the narratives of ritual.[15] However, it is important to note that due to source survival, particularly a dearth of Scottish financial records, this chapter is quite heavily reliant upon interpretations of narrative chronicles. There are challenges with this approach, particularly as many of the narratives were collated or written either in later centuries or by English authors and compilers, and often the entries recording rituals and ceremonies

---

[10] For examples of studies of the development of the Scottish kingdom during this period: Duncan, *Making of the Kingdom*; ibid., *Kingship of the Scots, 842–1292*; Geoffrey W.S. Barrow, *Kingship and Unity: Scotland 1000–1306*, revised edition (Edinburgh, 2003); Barrow, *The Kingdom of the Scots*; Oram, *Domination and Lordship*; Taylor, *Shape of the State*.

[11] Archibald A.M. Duncan, 'John King of England and the King of Scots', in Stephen D. Church (ed.), *King John: New Interpretations* (Woodbridge, 1999), 247–71, particularly at 268–9; Duncan, *Kingship of the Scots*, 99–105; Broun, 'The Church and the Origins of Scottish Independence', 1–35; Broun, *Scottish Independence and the Idea of Britain*, 189–212; Rees R. Davies, *The First English Empire* (Oxford, 2000), 4–30.

[12] Dale, *Inauguration and Liturgical Kingship*, 4–9, passim.

[13] Taylor, *Shape of the State*, passim, particularly 1–40; Reid, *Alexander II*, passim, particularly 5–41.

[14] Ibid., 30–41, quote at 33.

[15] Buc, 'Ritual and Interpretation', 183–210.

are brief in nature. The evidence available does impact how far this chapter is able to address prominent issues about the actors, actions and audience of ritual, and leads to a degree of speculation in some of its conclusions. Yet, it is essential to provide this analysis to lay the foundations for exploring subsequent centuries and to better understand where inspirations and developments in those periods emerge.

Raising the Red Fox Cub as King and Burying the Lion

Rather than challenging the idea of primogeniture, the contenders for the Scottish throne in 1214 sought to use it. The MacWilliams (or FitzDuncans) were disinherited by David I in the previous century but were heirs of Donnchad II, eldest son of Mael Coluim III and his first wife, Ingibjörg, which made them the senior line.[16] This meant that the MacWilliam claimant, Domnall Bán, was an adult whose claim was rooted in the concept of primogeniture. Consequently, the threat to the existing hereditary line was a potent reality and explains the speed with which the teenaged Alexander II – nicknamed the 'red fox cub' by his adversary John of England (r.1199–1216) – was placed upon the throne before his father was buried. This was not a uniquely Scottish problem. In thirteenth-century Norway, a kingdom similarly on the northern periphery of Europe and where election was a central element of the succession, Håkon IV sought to embed primogeniture through a combination of old and new rituals for his son and heir, Magnus, within the king's own lifetime: the traditional election and acclamation in the *thing* (1257) and then through the recently acquired rite of coronation and unction (1261).[17] Similarly, despite the relative stability of succession and the ordering of coronation after burial by the thirteenth century, pre-mortuary inaugural rituals had also been a feature in both England and France during the previous century due to the instability of primogeniture and challenges to the succession.[18] There is no evidence of pre-mortuary inauguration for

---

[16] *Chron. Fordun*, 276; Stephenson, 'The Law of the Throne', 10–11; Richard D. Oram, *Alexander II: King of Scots, 1214–1249* (Edinburgh, 2012), 18–21, 25, 29–30; R. Andrew MacDonald, *Outlaws of Medieval Scotland: Challenges to the Canmore Kings, 1058–1266* (East Linton, 2003), *passim*, particularly at 62–75; Penman, '*Diffinicione successionis*', 43–59, at 45–6.

[17] David Brégiant, *Vox Regis: Royal Communication in High Medieval Norway* (Leiden, 2016), 276–80. The *thing* or *þing* was a political assembly made up of representatives of the political community.

[18] The twelfth-century Capetian dynasty crowned the heir to the throne prior to the death of his predecessor during efforts to secure the transition from elective to hereditary monarchy: Alain Erlande-Brandenburg, *Le Roi est mort: étude sur les funérailles les sépultures et les tombeaux des rois de France jusqu'à la fin du XIIIe siècle* (Paris and Geneva, 1975), 18–19; Jackson, *Vive le roi*, 6; Giesey, 'Inaugural Aspects of French Royal Ceremonials', 37. Henry II of England (r.1154–89) campaigned for the coronation of his eldest son from

Alexander II, but William I sought public recognition of his heir from an early stage.

Contemporary and near contemporary chronicles record that, in October 1201, William gathered his nobles at Musselburgh to swear fealty to the infant Alexander, possibly in the presence of a papal legate, Giovanni di Salerno or John of Salerno.[19] The legate's presence coincided with the gifting of a papal sword in a 'golden sheath, enriched with precious stones' and a papal hat to William as a mark of papal favour.[20] Charles Burns demonstrates that this was one of the earliest examples of this particular gift from a pope to a temporal ruler.[21] Material signs of papal gratitude and personal recognition were valuable in challenging internal secular claims to the throne, as well as acting to consolidate papal support for the Scottish church's independence – first voiced in the bulls *Super anxietatibus* (30 July 1176) and *Cum universi* (1189x1192) – in response to the pretentions of the English archbishops of Canterbury and York.[22] If the oath-giving ritual was united with the receipt of significant papal gifts in the presence of a papal legate, William arguably created a pseudo-inaugural event for his son witnessed by the leading nobility of the realm that tied Alexander's right to succeed to both oaths of those secular lords and symbolic objects granted by the papacy.

Alexander's training for kingship led to his inclusion in diplomacy from a young age, including a journey to London in 1212 where the English king knighted him and other Scottish nobles. English and Scottish chronicles record that Alexander and his entourage arrived in London with 'the greatest pomp and state', suggesting efforts to raise his profile on the diplomatic stage and position him as a leader among his peers.[23] However, the fact that this took place in London – at the heart of the English kingdom – raised questions around a superior/inferior relationship between the kingdoms and their monarchs. Jenny Benham demonstrates that physical place was used as

---

1161 to 1170, which Matthew Strickland argues was a response to the instability of the civil war (1139–53) between Empress Matilda and Stephen of Blois that marred his own youth: *Henry the Young King, 1155–1183* (New Haven, 2016), 40–4; Duncan, *Making of the Kingdom*, 228.

[19] *Chron. Melrose*, 31 [fourth ides October or 12 October]; *Chron. Fordun*, 271 [Feast of St Simon and St Jude or 28 October]; *Chron. Wyntoun*, V, 47; Gaetano Moroni, *Dizionario di erudizione storico-ecclesiastica*, 103 vols (Venice, 1840–61), LXX, 44. Ferguson places Salerno at York after August and Perth by December, so the legate could easily have been in Musselburgh in October: Ferguson, *Medieval Papal Representatives in Scotland*, 65–71. See also Oram, *Alexander II*, 14–24.

[20] Charles Burns, 'Papal Gifts to Scottish Monarchs: The Golden Rose and the Blessed Sword', *IR* 20 (1969), 150–95, at 161–2.

[21] The Italian text is recorded in Moroni, *Dizionario di erudizione storico-ecclesiastica*, LXX, 44: 'd'una spada con Guiana d'oro, arricchita di pietre preziose'. See also Bellenden's Boece, *Chronicle*, 327; Burns, 'Papal Gifts', 161–2.

[22] Broun, 'The Church and the Origins of Scottish', 1–35, particularly at 28–9.

[23] *Chron. Fordun*, 273–4; 'Annales S. Edmundi, ed. Lieberman, 150' and 'Roger Wendover, Vol. I, 60', in *Annals of the Reigns of Malcolm and William*, 381. King John's expenses for Prince Alexander at Clerkenwell: *CDS*, I, no. 518.

a tool to underscore the relative power and status of rulers in negotiations in the Middle Ages: rulers of equal status negotiated or concluded peace in border regions, while inferior rulers travelled into the heart of a superior ruler's kingdom.[24] David Carpenter has argued that the Treaty of Norham in 1209 demanded homage from Alexander to John of England when the former succeeded the throne.[25] This was tantamount to reinstating the Treaty of Falaise of 1174 – oaths by William I to Henry II recognising the English king as overlord of Scotland – which was subsequently declared void with the Quitclaim of Canterbury in 1189.[26] When Alexander travelled to England in 1212, John already held both of William's daughters hostage and the visit witnessed confirmation of the English king's rights to arrange Alexander's marriage 'as his liege man'.[27] The English king was thus in an unquestionably powerful position. However, the act of sending Alexander to London – where he was publicly identified by others as the heir to the Scottish throne and knighted as the 'first among equals' of his Scottish peers – was a means by which William could promote his son's dynastic right to both the English king and his own leading subjects when he was facing serious internal threats to stability as he got older and increasingly unwell.

Historians doubt whether William I sought coronation and unction or promoted Scottish sovereignty, and these doubts are well founded.[28] While there is little evidence of foreign observers, the combination of Alexander's inauguration with William's funeral appears to have been designed to project a veneer of dynastic stability to a native audience, particularly to those who sought to challenge the succession. The inauguration at Scone – the traditional site for making Scottish kings and a predominant site for gatherings of the political community – was recorded as one with more 'pomp and ceremony' or 'grandeur and glory' than any before it.[29] Direct evidence of how

---

[24] Jenny Benham, *Peacemaking in the Middle Ages: Principles and Practice* (Manchester, 2010), 19–68, and on place in Anglo-Scot relations specifically, 51–7. See also Rees Davies, *The First English Empire*, 72; Barrow, *Kingship and Unity*, 48.

[25] *Magna Carta, with A New Commentary*, trans. and ed. David A. Carpenter (London, 2015), 238–41, 318, 352–3, 473–5.

[26] For more information, see Duncan, *Kingship of the Scots*, 230–8.

[27] Alice Taylor, 'The Scottish Clause in the Magna Carta in Context: Homage, Overlordship and the Consequence of Peace in the Early Thirteenth Century', in Sophie Ambler and Nicholas Vincent (eds), *Magna Carta: New Interpretations* (forthcoming). My thanks to Alice Taylor for sharing her thoughts and work prior to publication. On Margaret and Isabella's hostageship, see Katherine Weikert, 'The Princesses Who Might Have Been Hostages: The Custody and Marriages of Margaret and Isabella of Scotland, 1209–1220s', in Matthew Bennett and Katherine Weikert (eds), *Medieval Hostageship, c.700–c.1500: Hostage, Captive, Prisoner of War, Guarantee, Peacemaker* (Abingdon, 2017), 122–39.

[28] Duncan, *Kingship of the Scots*, 114–16; Broun, *Scottish Independence and the Idea of Britain*, 189–212.

[29] Quotes from: *Chron. Fordun*, 275–6; *Chron. Bower*, V, 3. See also *Chron. Melrose*, 38. On Scone as a traditional meeting/inauguration site: David Caldwell, 'Finlaggan, Islay – Stones and Inauguration Ceremonies', and Simon T. Driscoll, 'Govan: An Early Medieval

it was more glorious than William's own in 1165 is lacking.[30] Nonetheless, William's material gains and personal experiences of ceremonial occasions provide some insights into how and why this may have been so. For example, William received a golden rose as a papal gift during his reign.[31] Contemporary and later chroniclers record that the golden rose was 'marvellously-fashioned', 'set upon a wand, also of gold' and filled with sweet smelling balsam, which – according to Burns – was poured into the object during its papal blessing.[32] An inventory, created at the removal of the regalia by Edward I of England in 1296, records a rose of gold among the confiscated items, suggesting it was kept or used alongside the rest of the regalia – potentially as a sceptre or part of a sceptre – until its removal.[33] A sword and sceptre, or rod, were linked to Scottish inaugurations in the eleventh-century Northumbrian pontifical, associated with Iona, which indicates that early kings of Scots were invested with these items.[34] A sword and an orb had appeared on royal seals of Scotland prior to 1214, as well as in the illuminated letter depicting David I and Mael Coluim IV enthroned in a Kelso charter of 1159.[35] In the latter, the heir-in-waiting holds a long rod topped with a cross. It was only during the thirteenth century that a floriated sceptre made an appearance on seal images, perhaps visually representing the papal rose's incorporation into the regalia.[36]

Evidence for the specific use of regalia items in 1214 is absent from the records, but the power of ritual objects was appreciated by contemporaries. William had practical experience of an English coronation-like ceremony utilising a host of material symbols of majesty. In 1194 he carried one of three coronation swords, alongside two English earls, for the second coronation of Richard I (r.1189–99) at Winchester celebrating his return from a year-long

---

Royal Centre on the Clyde', in Welander, Breeze and Clancy (eds), *The Stone of Destiny*, 61–75, 77–83; Oliver J.T. O'Grady, 'The Setting and Practice of Open-Air Judicial Assemblies in Medieval Scotland: A Multidisciplinary Study' (PhD thesis, University of Glasgow, 2008), *passim*, particularly at 9–17.

[30] *Chron. Fordun*, 254–5. See Duncan, *Kingship of the Scots*, 98–9.

[31] It is widely thought that Pope Lucius III made the gift. *Gesta Annalia*, Bower and *Pluscarden* erroneously link this to William's death in 1214, whereas the *Chronicle of Melrose* dates the event to 1182: *Chron. Fordun*, 275; *Chron. Bower*, IV, 475; *Pluscarden*, 38; *Chron. Melrose*, 22. Charles Burns notes that as Pope Lucius was dead by 1214 he could not have made the gift then, and the papal interdict was lifted in 1182: Burns, 'Papal Gifts', 155–6, sketch of a papal rose opp. 156. See also Duncan, *Making of the Kingdom*, 272–3; ibid., *Kingship of Scots*, 137–8.

[32] *Chron. Fordun*, 275; *Pluscarden*, 38. See also Burns, 'Papal Gifts', 157.

[33] *Documents Illustrative of the History of Scotland from the Death of King Alexander the Third to the Accession of Robert Bruce MCCLXXXVI–MCCCVI*, ed. Joseph Stevenson, 2 vols (Edinburgh, 1870), II, 142–4.

[34] John Stuart, *Scottish Coronations* (Paisley, 1902), 13–18; Cooper, 'Four Scottish Coronations', 5–7.

[35] For an image of the illumination: G.W.S. Barrow, 'David I (c.1085–1153)', *ODNB* (2004), https://doi-org.uhi.idm.oclc.org/10.1093/ref:odnb/7208. Date accessed: 29 July 2022.

[36] Dean, *The Scottish Royal Honours*, Chapter 2 (and associated plates).

imprisonment by the Emperor, Henry VI (r.1191–97).[37] Nigel Saul suggests that Richard saw the rite as a means of symbolically reinstating his diminished authority, which illustrates the strength of contemporary perceptions around the power of rituals and their symbolic objects.[38] Richard was recorded as resplendent in the trappings of sacral Angevin kingship as found in the 1189 order of coronation: royal robes or mantle, a gold crown, a sceptre, a golden wand or rod topped with a dove, a ring, swords, *armils* (bracelets) and spurs.[39] Three to four supporting officiant bishops assisted the archbishop of Canterbury, clergy processed 'with cross, torch bearers, censers and holy water going before them' and a silken canopy was carried above the king on lances accompanied by processions of nobles.[40] The haste with which Alexander II's inauguration occurred in 1214 suggests that preparations occurred during William's life time, and the aging king may have drawn on these experiences in such preparations.[41] Like those recording the glorious return of Richard I, however, the chroniclers recording 1214 had every reason to underscore the splendour of the inauguration in order to create a more robust image of the dynastic succession at a moment riddled with internal and external threats.

Rituals of kingship were not static entities, but they needed to be recognisable and honour tradition. Thus, even if William sought to emulate aspects of the ceremony he had witnessed, it was not feasible to imagine any wholesale transferral of English ceremonial norms into a Scottish context, despite near fifty years passing since the last inauguration. There was no anointing or crowning and the dominant ecclesiastical presence in English coronations was not replicated in 1214. William Malveisin, bishop of St Andrews, accompanied Alexander II to Scone, where the abbot and monks of the abbey would have been present. Yet, the roles of these individuals may have been limited to officiating in an inauguration Mass and blessing the regalia of the monarch. Moreover, other important bishops were conspicuous in their absence: the bishop of Glasgow and bishop-elect of Ross, remained with the queen and dead king rather than attending the inauguration.[42] Duncan and Broun have identified the increasing involvement, or at least desire for such, of churchmen in the process of royal inauguration throughout the thirteenth century, and this

---

[37] *Annals of Howden*, II, 321–2; *The Historical Works of Gervase of Canterbury*, Rolls Series, 73, ed. William Stubbs, 2 vols (London, 1879–80), I, 524–7. Briefer entry in 'Historia Rerum Anglicarum of William Newburgh', in *Chronicles of the Reigns of Stephen, Henry II and Richard I*, Rolls Series 82, ed. Richard Howlett, 4 vols (London, 1881–9), I, 408.
[38] Nigel Saul, *The Three Richards: Richard I, II and III* (London, 2006), quote at 45; Ralph V. Turner and Richard R. Heiser, *The Reign of Richard the Lionheart: The Ruler of the Angevin Empire, 1189–1199* (Harlow, 2000), 230.
[39] *Annals of Howden*, II, 321–2; *Works of Gervase*, I, 526; 'Twelfth Century Coronation Order' and 'Coronation of Richard I', in *English Coronation Records*, ed. Leopold G.W. Legge (Westminster, 1901), 30–42, 46–53.
[40] Ibid., 51; *Annals of Howden*, II, 321; *Works of Gervase*, I, 526–7.
[41] Duncan also suggests that preparations were made in advance: *Kingship of the Scots*, 116. The Saturday after the inauguration was the feast day of St Nicholas, when feasting would have occurred as a matter of course.
[42] *Chron. Fordun*, 27–6; *Chron. Bower*, V, 3.

had much earlier roots.[43] Indeed, the earliest reference to a Scottish inaugural event identified ecclesiastical involvement: Adomnán's seventh-century life of St Columba recalls the role of Columba in the making of King Áedán, in c.574.[44] The eleventh-century Northumbrian pontifical, associated with Iona, also includes a Mass as the final element of proceedings prior to feasting.[45] More contemporary are references to the bishop of St Andrews either blessing William or officiating over part of the ritual for his inauguration in 1165.[46] Chronicles with clerical authorship may have retrospectively emphasised ecclesiastical roles, but the process of secular enthronement is also strikingly evident in their record. This reflects definite limits to church involvement. In the case of Ireland, Fitzpatrick has proposed that 'at its most potent, ecclesiastical resolve was capable of translating an inauguration ceremony from a traditional royal assembly to a church site'.[47] While there was a consecrated abbey at Scone from the reign of Alexander I (r.1107–24) onwards, the enthronement of Scottish kings continued to take place outside the church, suggesting that the church faced similar challenges in influencing this secular rite in Scotland. This does not, however, automatically undermine the legitimacy of the ritual for those undertaking and recording it.

The other named attendees at the inauguration of 1214 were all secular earls (see Appendix II, 'Alexander II'). *The Chronicle of Melrose* states that there was a great number of the nobility, while *Gesta Annalia I* names seven earls: Fife, Strathearn, Atholl, Angus, Menteith, Buchan and Lothian or Dunbar.[48] The identification of seven earls aligns with the territorial division of Scotland in *De Situ Albanie* (c.1202x1214) and later claims made in the Appeal of the Seven Earls sent to Edward I during the Great Cause in the 1290s.[49] Bower only lists five earls, missing out Fife and Lothian or Dunbar,

---

[43] Duncan, *Kingship of the Scots*, 150; Broun, 'The Church and the Origins of Scottish Independence', 1–35.

[44] *Life of Saint Columba (Colum-kille) AD 521–597 founder of the Monastery of Iona and first Christian missionary to the Pagan Tribes of North Britain*, trans. and ed. Wentworth Huyshe (London, 1900), Book III, Ch. V, 193–4. See also Cooper, 'Four Scottish Coronations', 4; M.G.J. Kinloch, 'Scottish Coronations, AD 574–1651 (Part One)', *Dublin Review* 130 (London, 1902), 263–77, at 267–7; Stuart, *Scottish Coronations*, 1–13.

[45] Ibid., 13–8; Cooper, 'Four Scottish Coronations', 5–7.

[46] *Chron. Fordun*, 254–5 [blessed, translated as conscrated]; *Chron. Bower*, IV, 281 [officiating with other bishops].

[47] Elizabeth Fitzpatrick, *Royal Inauguration in Gaelic Ireland, c.1100–1600: A Cultural Landscape Study* (Woodbridge, 2004), 177.

[48] *Chron. Melrose*, 38; *Chron. Fordun*, 275–6. Fordun lists the earl of Lothian, but this title was not commonly used from mid-twelfth century onwards when Patrick, fifth earl (d. 1232), began using the title Dunbar: *The Scots Peerage founded on Woods edition of Sir Robert Douglas's Peerage of Scotland containing an Historical and Genealogical Account of the Nobility of the Kingdom*, ed. James P. Balfour Paul, 9 vols (Edinburgh, 1904–1914), III, 239–79, at 252.

[49] Thanks to Alice Taylor for flagging up this importance of the *De Situ Albanie* in this context. See Taylor, 'The Scottish Clause in the Magna Carta'; Taylor, *Shape of the State*, 33–7; Dauvit Broun, 'The Seven Kingdoms in *De Situ Albanie*: A Record of Pictish Political Geography or Imaginary Map of Alba?', in Edward J. Cowan and R. Andrew

but indicates that others accompanied the young king from across the 'three estates'.[50] The use of this term reflects the political language of Bower's own era. However, this language choice and the use of the seven earls of *Gesta Annalia I* indicate that both chroniclers sought to depict Alexander's succession as one supported by the whole kingdom at a time when such support was hardly demonstrable. These clerical authors also underscore the critical role of these secular individuals as those who 'raised him to the throne'.[51] Ecclesiastical figures played a part, but the secular earls dominated the ritual roles (as far as they are described) in the making of Alexander II. This marked a clear distinction with the ecclesiastically dominated ceremonies of England and France, and perhaps suggests more common ground with those realms that still honoured a form of customary election such as Castile, Norway or the Empire.[52]

Ecclesiastical figures were prominent in the funerary ritual for William I: Walter, bishop of Glasgow, Robert, bishop-elect of Ross, and the chancellor, William del Bois, who may have been archdeacon of Lothian by this point, remained with the queen in Stirling.[53] Bower recorded that these men were to provide support for William's grieving widow, Queen Ermengarde, in making the required preparations for the burial.[54] Anna Duch has demonstrated that the preparation of a high status body after death required the skill and knowledge of specially trained individuals. For royalty in England, this task was also increasingly undertaken – in part at least – by high status bishops or members of the royal household.[55] Consequently, the involvement of these

---

MacDonald (eds), *Alba: Celtic Scotland in the Medieval Era* (Edinburgh, 2012), 24–42. See also 'Appeal of the Seven Earls', 'Appeal of the Seven Earls', in *Anglo-Scottish Relations, 1174–1320: Some Selected Documents*, ed. Edward L.G. Stone (Oxford, 1965), no. 14.

[50] *Chron. Bower*, V, 3.

[51] *Chron. Fordun*, 275–6. Bower records that Alexander II was 'crowned' (*Chron. Bower*, V, 3), but the act of crowning (and accompanying unction) had to be sanctioned by the pope and William I had demonstrated no efforts to seek this rite.

[52] Reid makes a comparison with Castile due the centrality of election and shunning of anointing: *Alexander III*, 34–5. For more detail, see Ruiz, 'Unsacred Monarchy', 116–26. Election was central to laws of succession in Norway, even after increased acceptance of hereditary succession, and the Golden Bull (1356) of Charles IV enshrined the election of the emperor by seven princes, even though one dynasty ultimately gained power in the fifteenth century and maintained it for over 350 years: Bagge, *From Viking Stronghold to Christian Kingdom*, 166–9; Daniel Waley and Peter Denley, *Later Medieval Europe, 1250–1520*, third edition (Abingdon, 2013), 67–76, particularly at 73; Matthias Schnettger, 'Dynastic Succession in an Elective Monarchy: The Habsburgs and the Holy Roman Empire', in Elena Woodacre, Lucinda H.S. Dean, Chris Jones et al. (eds), *The Routledge History of Monarchy* (London, 2019), 112–29.

[53] *Chron. Fordun*, 275–6; *Chron. Bower*, V, 3. William del Bois (d.1232), or Boscho, chancellor from 1211 to 1224 and archdeacon of Lothian (possibly from 1214, but only titled as such 1227–32): *People of Medieval Scotland Database*, no. 42, https://www.poms.ac.uk/record/person/42/ Date accessed: 28 February 2021.

[54] *Chron. Fordun*, 275–6; *Chron. Bower*, V, 3.

[55] Anna Duch, 'The Royal Funerary and Burial Ceremonies of Medieval English Kings, 1216–1509' (PhD thesis, University of York, 2016), 79–82.

bishops and members of the royal household may have been far more 'hands on' than previously appreciated. During the days of the inauguration and subsequent feasting, William's body was prepared and transported to Perth, where the inaugural and funeral parties converged to travel to Arbroath. This journey took around a week in total, so washing, embalming and evisceration were likely undertaken for the comfort of those travelling with the corpse; this may have involved removal of heart.[56] The burial of entrails at the site of evisceration and a separate heart burial at a chosen site were increasingly common across Europe.[57] Such practices are recorded for later Scottish kings, most notably Robert Bruce, but unfortunately there is no evidence to confirm whether it occurred on this occasion.[58] *Gesta Annalia I* comments that those remaining at Stirling did so to 'abode with the king' – this indicates the potential for vigils over his body in which ecclesiastics would have been vital.[59] Vigils over the dead had strong roots in Christian liturgy, particularly in the rites over the Easter period, acting as protection for the soul and a point for further intercessory prayers.[60] It was likely that vigils were held at various stopping points between Stirling, Perth and Arbroath as public displays of royal bodies were common as proof of a good death, and also allowed wider audiences the opportunity to take part in mourning.[61]

William's selection of his Tironensian foundation at Arbroath for burial meant abandoning Dunfermline, which housed the tombs of his predecessors back to Mael Coluim III and Margaret.[62] The creation of a dynastic mausoleum in Scotland was comparable to the developments of Saint-Denis in

---

[56] For an account of preparation and display of the body of Håkon IV of Norway at Kirkwall, Orkney, in 1263: Brégiant, *Vox Regis*, 285–6. This does not refer to evisceration, but Duch's detailed analysis of prescriptive and medical texts on this process demonstrates it was increasingly common: Duch, 'Royal Funerary and Burial Ceremonies', 73–85.
[57] For further discussions on the separation of body and organs, see Elizabeth A.R. Brown, *The Monarchy of Capetian France and Royal Ceremony* (Aldershot, 1991), see chapter 'Death and the Human Body in the Later Middle Ages: The Legislation of Boniface VIII on the division of the Corpse', 221–70; Elizabeth Hallam, 'Royal Burial and the Cult of Kingship in France and England, 1060–1330', *Journal of Medieval History* 8 (1982), 359–80, at 363–4; Danielle Westerhof, *Death and the Noble Body in Medieval England* (Woodbridge, 2008), 75–95; Anna Duch, 'My Crown Is in My Heart, Not on My Head: Heart Burial in England, France and the Holy Roman Empire from Medieval Times to the Present' (Masters thesis, University of North Texas, 2013), 36–108.
[58] For separation of heart in case of Robert I, see Chapter 2, 89, 97–8.
[59] *Chron. Fordun*, 275–6.
[60] On the liturgy of Easter, see Eamon Duffy, *The Stripping of the Altars: Traditional Religion in England 1400–1580* (New Haven, 1993), 23–35; John Harper, *The Forms and Orders of Western Liturgy from the Tenth to the Eighteenth Century: A Historical Introduction for Students and Musicians*, reprint (Oxford, 2001), 139–52.
[61] Hallam, 'Royal Burial', 366; 'Succession and the Royal Dead', 101–3; Brégiant, *Vox Regis*, 285–6.
[62] *Chron. Bower*, V, 3; *Chron. Fordun*, 275–6; Steve Boardman, 'Dunfermline as a Royal Mausoleum', in Richard Fawcett (ed.), *Royal Dunfermline* (Edinburgh, 2005), 139–54, at 140–2.

Paris,[63] and occurred significantly earlier than the later thirteenth-century focus on Westminster as a mausoleum by the English monarchy.[64] However, some peripatetic monarchies did not settle on one site until much later and there were also numerous foreign counterparts who sought burial at monastic houses that they had founded personally, particularly following the surge of new religious orders fuelled by eleventh-century religious reforms.[65] Arbroath was also, according to Keith Stringer, one of the richest monastic houses in Scotland and represented 'the most outstanding single act of devotion to Becket in … the late twelfth century'.[66] Here the commonly held desire for personal salvation appears to have been married with efforts to make a potent declaration about Scottish kingship. At a basic level, William demonstrated the wealth to fund an elaborate new mortuary space for himself. As was often the case with veneration of cross-border saints, dedicating his foundation to St Thomas Becket of Canterbury held multi-layered meaning.[67] This included choosing a saint martyred on the orders of the king who had subjected William and Scotland to the Treaty of Falaise, which could be read as a statement of Scottish defiance toward the promises made in 1209 and 1212.[68] Moreover, the selection of Arbroath did not have to mean the total abandonment of Dunfermline: there was potential for it to be incorporated as a stopping point on the journey to William's final resting place.

Specific evidence for the exact route of the funeral procession and the stopping points at which vigils could be held – beyond the three key points

---

[63] Erlande-Brandenburg, *Le Roi est mort*, particularly 68–96; Brown, *The Monarchy of Capetian France*, see 'Burying and Unburying the Kings of France', 242–3; Hallam, 'Royal Burial', 361.

[64] Under Henry III (r.1216–72) the focus was on the tomb of Edward the Confessor, while the focus on Westminster as mausoleum occurred under Edward I (r.1272–1307) following the death of his queen in 1290. See Hallam, 'Royal Burial', 359–80; John Steane, *Archaeology of the Medieval English Monarchy* (London, 1999), 41–70; Mark Duffy, *Royal Tombs in England* (Stroud, 2003); David M. Palliser, 'Royal Mausolea in the Long Fourteenth Century (1272–1422)', in W. Mark Ormrod (ed.), *Fourteenth Century England III* (Woodbridge, 2004), 1–16; Griffiths, 'Succession and the Royal Dead', 97–109; Paul Binski, *Westminster Abbey and the Plantagenets: Kingship and the Representation of Power* (New Haven and London, 1995), 1–9, 90–120.

[65] Hallam, 'Royal Burial', 367–9; Ruiz, 'Unsacred Monarchy', 126.

[66] Keith Stringer, 'Arbroath Abbey in Context, 1178–1320', in Geoffrey W.S. Barrow (ed.), *The Declaration of Arbroath: History, Significance, Setting* (Edinburgh, 2003), 117–41, quote at 119.

[67] Tom Turpie, 'A Monk from Melrose? St Cuthbert and the Scots in the Later Middle Ages, c.1371–1560', *IR* 62 (2011), 47–69; ibid., 'Scottish or British? The Scottish Authorities, Richard III and the Cult of St Ninian in Late Medieval Scotland and Northern England', in Katherine Buchanan and Lucinda H.S. Dean with Michael Penman (eds), *Medieval and Early Modern Representations of Authority in Scotland and the British Isles* (Abingdon, 2016), 124–40.

[68] Stringer, 'Arbroath Abbey', 119–20. On Scottish royal veneration Becket, see Michael Penman, 'The Bruces, Becket and Scottish Pilgrimage to Canterbury, c.1174–c.1406', *Journal of Medieval History* 32 (2006), 346–70, particularly at 348–53; Penman, 'Royal Piety', 18–19.

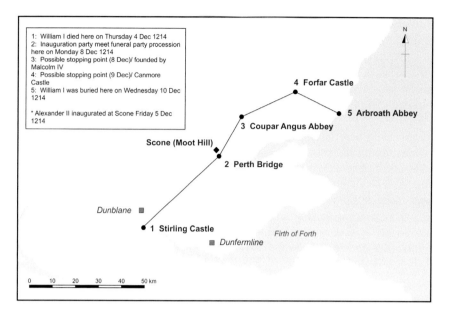

Map 1   Potential route of funeral procession of William I, 1214. Contains Ordnance Survey data © Crown Copyright and database right (2023).

of Stirling, Perth and Arbroath – is sadly lacking. Barrow notes the surprising speed with which medieval road travel could occur (upward of thirty miles per day), but also the slower progress of heavy siege machinery (ten to twelve miles per day).[69] Consequently, a funerary procession travelling in December could be estimated to have been travelling at a pace between these two (perhaps fifteen to twenty miles per day). The cortege had to travel between seventy and eighty-five miles, dependent on route, between 5 December and 10 December, so overnight stopping points must have been selected at suitable prominent places along the route (Map 1). Travelling from Stirling north-east towards Perth might have meant stopping at the prominent cathedral at Dunblane; it would have been possible to travel to Perth via the dynastic mausoleum of Dunfermline, but this would have added significantly more miles. The journey from Perth to Arbroath, if taken by land rather than water, may have passed Mael Coluim IV's Cistercian foundation at Coupar Angus en route to the favoured Canmore residence at Forfar.[70] These stopping points for vigils are necessarily speculative, but making use of sites with dynastic connections through physical locations and spatial associations – as

---

[69] Geoffrey W.S. Barrow, *Scotland and its Neighbours in the Middle Ages* (London, 1992), 204.
[70] Forfar was a prominent castle of the later Canmores and Oram notes that Alexander II returned there for Christmas 1214: *Alexander II, 1214–1249*, 27. It may have been possible for the body to have been transported by boat from the harbour at Perth to Arbroath, but there is no indication that this was the case.

well as ones that were regularly travelled to and from – made both practical and symbolic sense.

The physical location on the route about which there is the most evidence for specific activity is Perth: according to the chronicle accounts, efforts were made to visually confirm dynastic connections and Alexander's right to succeed. The funeral party met the inauguration party at Perth Bridge on 8 December.[71] The choice of a crossing point in a liminal space outwith the burgh could potentially symbolise a transitional moment in the transfer of power from father to son as the latter was enthroned but the former had still to be laid to rest. The convergence of these two groups would naturally lead to the funeral procession swelling in size. *Gesta Annalia I* also states that a cross was raised at the site, suggesting efforts to physically memorialise this point in the journey when the newly installed heir and deceased king moved forward together towards the latter's final resting place.[72] Across Europe during the thirteenth century royal funeral ceremonies were becoming increasingly elaborate and processional routes were attracting commemorative structures in France and England by the second half of the century.[73] This evidence from Scotland suggests an earlier use of procession commemoration or indicates that later chroniclers were projecting current ideas into the past; although, there are no discernible examples of processional route monuments being raised in later medieval Scotland.

By this point, William's ageing brother David, earl of Huntingdon (1152–1219), had also joined the inaugural party and at Perth his actions were recorded as follows:

> [...] getting off his horse, he [Earl David] took upon his shoulder one handle of the bier, and, with the rest of the earls who were there, devoutly carried the body as far as the boundary, where a cross was ordered to be set up [...][74]

The speed of the funeral procession's progress indicates the use of horse-drawn vehicles, but the body appears to have been carried ceremonially over short distances on the shoulders of mourners. David's older age would have limited his ability to carry the bier with his fellow peers, but the extract indicates a symbolic moment inserted into the funeral procession (at a point where the audience was largest) where his positioning close to the body of his brother could be illustrative of bonds being remade following earlier hints at discord between them.[75] Placing the young king and the late king's brother –

---

[71] *Chron. Fordun*, 276.
[72] *Chron. Fordun*, 276.
[73] Hallam, 'Royal Burial', 366–7; Griffiths, 'Succession and the Royal Dead', 107; Brégiant, *Vox Regis*, 284–7.
[74] *Chron. Fordun*, 276.
[75] Taylor notes that when the nobles swore fealty to Alexander in 1201, David did not offer his fealty until 1205: 'The Scottish Clause in the Magna Carta'.

the previous heir apparent – together acted to emphasise the stability (real or imagined) of the hereditary succession. The presence of the successor at the funeral remained important in the Middle Ages where succession by primogeniture was still being established. For example, in thirteenth-century Norway, Magnus VI was recorded leading the procession for the second funeral of his father, Håkon IV, following the return of his body to Norway.[76] The presence of the late king's brother as coffin bearer, even if only for a short period, rather than as a competitor for Alexander's kingship, publicly reinforced the acceptance of primogeniture and the rightful succession of William's son and, as such, could easily have warranted the monumental commemoration *Gesta Annalia I* recorded. It was also a particularly potent display of unity in the light of competing MacWilliam claims and the baronial dispute on the verge of erupting south of the border.

Messages about Alexander II's dynastic rights as the heir to William's throne – whether beholden to the king of England or not – reverberated throughout the ceremonies of the young king's life to 1214. In the face of challenges to the integrity of an independent Scottish kingship and dramatic shifts in the balance of the power between England and Scotland, this period witnessed the active accumulation and ritual use of material signs of the majesty and religiosity of the Scottish royal house. There were also ongoing negotiations between Scottish nobles and clerics about the rituals of Scottish kingship, with a notable dominance of secular lords and emphasis on consensus with the choice of monarch. The details of William's funeral procession highlight the importance of reconciliation and the provision of a representative entourage to accompany the king on his final journey – a necessarily impressive public projection of royal authority. The processional journey's endpoint with the burial of William's body at Arbroath marked a key moment in the transferral of power to Alexander that had begun with the king's death. Nevertheless, succession was a cyclical process and the rituals that helped to secure it did not end at the graveside, nor did the influences and context shaping the ceremonies of kingship fade as the cycle continued.

Marriage, Succession and the Attempts to Level the Playing Field

Marriage marked a prominent step in the ceremonial cycle of succession as an event that promised an heir to continue the dynasty. In the case of Alexander II, Oram argues that no earlier king of Scots had secured such 'an

---

[76] Brégiant, *Vox Regis*, 286–7. Other examples include Emperor Henry II carrying the coffin of Emperor Otto III in 1002 and Louis VIII's role at the funeral of Philip Augustus in 1223: John W. Bernhardt, 'King Henry II of Germany: Royal Self-Representation and Historical Memory', in Althoff, Fried and Geary (eds), *Medieval Concepts of the Past*, 39–69; Erlande-Brandenburg, *Le Roi est mort*, 18–19.

exalted bride'.[77] This was a highly prestigious match, but Alexander's marriage to Joanna, daughter of John of England, in June 1221 also necessitated careful navigation of the continuing legacy of English superiority in political relations with Scotland. Alexander travelled to York in 1220 to complete his marriage arrangements in the shadow of his first independent interactions with England. Despite coming to the throne as a minor aged sixteen, he had risen with the northern nobles of England between 1215 and 1217. He received the fealty of several rebellious northern English nobles and 'the men of Yorkshire', besieged Carlisle successfully and rode to Dover to swear allegiance to Louis, son of the French king, who was invited to replace John by his rebellious subjects.[78] These gains rapidly trickled away after John's death; with the enemy gone, the pope placed Scotland under interdict for its role in the rebellion. After raising the interdict in 1218, Pope Honorius III renewed the special daughter status of Scotland, which had first been granted by the bull *Cum universi* in 1192, but still denied Scotland an independent archbishop. Moreover, Alexander failed to get papal support in overturning the terms of the treaty of 1209.[79]

Alexander married Joanna in York in mid-June 1221. The issue of the inferior status of a monarch who travelled outwith his lands to treat for peace re-emerged with the marriage occurring on English soil, amidst peace negotiations that made null many of Alexander's initial triumphs as king and with his sisters still in English hands and unmarried.[80] Even if the bull of 1218 neutralised York's metropolitan claims over Scotland, a marriage in the archbishop's cathedral with the papal legate, Pandulf, watching over the proceedings complicated matters.[81] Despite initial appearances, however, York was

[77] Oram, *Alexander II*, 69. From 1070, when Mael Coluim III married Margaret, daughter of the exiled heir to the Anglo-Saxon throne of England, numerous matches were made with England and on the continent, but these matches were for daughters. For example, Edith (Matilda), eldest daughter of Mael Coluim III and Margaret, married Henry I of England (c.1100) and William's discussions with Philip Augustus, king of France, about marrying his daughter to the French king played into the breakdown of Anglo-Scottish relations in 1209. See Oram, *Domination and Lordship*, 16, 51–7, 96–7, 118, 123–4, 146–7; Duncan, 'John King of England and the King of Scots', 259–61.
[78] Oaths of the English to Alexander: *Chron. Melrose*, 43–4. For further on the Anglo-Scottish political context, see Duncan, *Making of the Kingdom*, 520–7; Duncan, 'John King of England and the Kings of Scots', 247–71; Richard D. Oram, 'An Overview of the Reign of Alexander II', and Keith Stringer, 'Kingship, Conflict and State-Making in the Reign of Alexander II: The War of 1215–17 and Its Context', in Oram (ed.), *The Reign of Alexander II*, 1–49, 99–156 (Table 1, 153); Brown, *Wars of Scotland*, 50–4; Oram, *Alexander II*, 26–69.
[79] Ibid., 53–8; *Early Sources of Scottish History A.D. 500 to 1286*, ed. Alan Orr Anderson, 2 vols (Edinburgh, 1922), 425–6, 435–6, fn. 5; *Chron. Bower*, V, 92–101; Brown, *Wars of Scotland*, 124–5; Ferguson, *Medieval Papal Representatives*, 73–85.
[80] Benham, *Peacemaking in the Middle Ages*, 44–68.
[81] CDS, I, nos 761–2; *Chron. Fordun*, 283–4; Mary Anne Everett Green, *Lives of the Princesses of England from the Norman Conquest*, 6 vols (London, 1849), I, 381–8; Duncan, *Making of the Kingdom*, 256–80; Ferguson, *Medieval Papal Representatives*, 81–5; Oram,

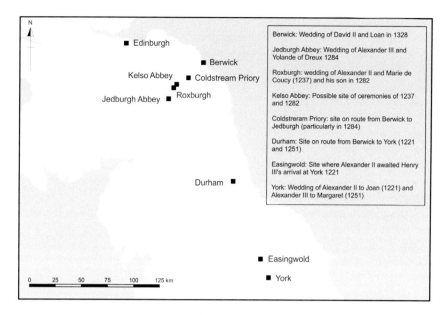

Map 2 Southern Scotland and Northern England, thirteenth and fourteenth centuries. Contains Ordnance Survey data
© Crown Copyright and database right (2023).

not a wholly uneven playing field. First, it was not a usual site for the English king to hold court, so Henry III (r.1216–72) also had to make a specific and intentional journey to attend. Second, the men of Yorkshire had sworn fealty to Alexander at Melrose in 1216, only five years previously, and there were Scottish links with the city, particularly its churches and hospitals, going back generations.[82] Finally, Alexander was a twenty-three-year-old young man, while Henry was barely more than a boy at fourteen. Consequently, the relative status of the two leading attendees fell into a greyer area than would have been the case if Alexander had travelled to an English royal centre, such as Northampton, London or Winchester, to meet an adult king.[83] This made the articulation of identity and position in the social hierarchy, via the medium of the entry ceremonial, all the more important for Alexander and the Scots.

On his journey south (Map 2), Alexander was met at various stages by English crown men, including Walter de Gray, archbishop of York, William de Warenne, earl of Surrey, Robert de Vieuxpont, Geoffrey de Neville, plus

---

Domination and Lordship, particularly 334–46.
[82] *Chron. Melrose*, 44. For references to Scottish royal patronage in York from David I to William I, particularly of the hospital of St Peter's in York, see *RRS*, I, nos 17, 76, 141, 318; *RRS*, II, nos 103, 225.
[83] Benham, *Peacemaking in the Middle Ages*, 60–1.

the sheriffs, nobles and barons of Northumberland, the Tees and York.[84] The English records of 1221 illustrate that Alexander identified an escort 'as his own and his predecessors' right' and thus demanded such from Henry, with the archbishop of York and leading northern nobles named specifically, including some who had previously sworn fealty to him.[85] Additionally, as highlighted by Oram, when Alexander heard that Henry III was delayed, the Scottish king insisted on waiting at Easingwold so that they could make their 'adventus' together and on equal terms, despite being in English territory.[86] While Benham's analysis of the twelfth century shows that escorts, often led by the bishop of Durham, were common for leading a Scottish king into English territory, Alexander's demands indicate his awareness of past precedents and clear expectations regarding his treatment.[87] Moreover, in a manner similar to Giovanna Guidicini's statement about the dynamic quality of civic spaces in royal entries to Edinburgh, this performance 'gave a three-dimensional, experiential quality to the political dialogue' that was occurring between the two kings and their political communities in which members of the English audience for Alexander's demonstration also functioned as actors in the performance.[88]

A further attempt to bring about ritual parity between the two kings occurred around this time: Alexander II sought the right to coronation. In the hiatus between Alexander's meeting in York in 1220 and the marriage in 1221, he requested that the papal legate to Scotland, Master James, perform a crowning ceremony for him and suggested postponing the wedding while the legate sought permission from the pope.[89] Broun has argued that the use of the terms crowning or coronation in this case, rather than any specific mention of anointing, suggests that Alexander acknowledged the difference in status between the two kings.[90] That said, the request recognised the potential of a Christianised papally-sanctioned ritual to rebalance the scales, so Pope Honorius's refusal, imbued with his conviction in English overlordship, would have been particularly hard felt. When these efforts are combined with Alexander's demands about his arrival and the royal entry,

---

[84] TNA, Close Rolls, 5 Hen. III, part 1 [1220–1221], C54/24, m. 10, m. 11 dorso; *CDS*, I, no. 803; Oram, *Alexander II*, 68.

[85] TNA, C54/24, m. 10, m. 11 dorso; *CDS*, I, no. 803.

[86] TNA, Letters from Richard March, bishop of Durham and Chancellor to Hubert de Burgh, justiciar, SC1/1/134–9; *CDS*, I, nos 805–6; Oram, *Alexander II*, 68.

[87] Benham, *Peacemaking in the Middle Ages*, 44–56, 83–4.

[88] Giovanna Guidicini, *Triumphal Entries and Festivals in Early Modern Scotland: Performing Spaces* (Turnhout, 2020), 21. See also for discussions about immersive theatre analogy: Hepburn, *The Household and Court of James IV*, 102–22.

[89] Postponement of the date of the wedding with Joanna: TNA, Special Collections: Ancient Correspondence: Alexander II, king of Scots, to Henry III, SC1/5/9. Supplication to the papacy: *CPL*, I, 83; Ferguson, *Medieval Papal Representatives*, 88; Duncan, *Kingship of the Scots*, 118–9; Oram, *Alexander II*, 60–9; Broun, *Scottish Independence and the Idea of Britain*, 203–4.

[90] Ibid. Arguably, in this issue of semantics and definition, a coronation includes anointing: Dean, *The Scottish Royal Honours*, Chapter 7.

they illustrate definite posturing from the Scottish king as he prepared to meet the boy king of England.

Many English and Scottish chronicles record the marriage of Alexander II and Joanna, but specific details are sparse on the respective royal displays, or indeed the responses to them.[91] Joanna's dower – worth a total of £1,000[92] – was sealed at York on the 18 June and the wedding appears to have occurred on the following day 'with the exceeding splendour that was fitting such an occasion'.[93] Expenses for this splendour are elusive and the lack of extant material, particularly for Scotland, make nineteenth-century conclusions that the English crown shouldered the entirety of the expense impossible to assess.[94] Surviving English financial records (recorded in sterling) indicate that Alexander was granted £15 expenses during his visit; the city and the mayor of York were reimbursed £50 and a further £14 went to the city farm between the 20 and 22 June.[95] The money granted to Alexander was a figure deemed sufficient by Lars Kjær for a yearly payment to an English knight in the 1260s, providing an understanding of the level of expense incurred by the Scottish king for a short visit that hints at elaborate levels of display.[96] The surviving reimbursements to York indicate that the city and mayor, and probably the archbishop, may have also footed more of the bill than the records can illuminate.[97] Such expectation of hospitality was the norm for the period. It is seen across ceremonies where sufficient accounts survive, and Taylor identifies similar reimbursements claimed by Scottish sheriffs for occasions when Alexander III was in residence in their localities later in the century.[98]

No Scottish financial accounts are extant to offer any further illustration of how Alexander II used his attire, entourage, horses or gifts. However, as

---

[91] BL, Annales Angliæ ab anno 1195 ad anno 1316, Add. MS 5444, f. 26r; BL, Thomas Rymer Collections, Add. MS 4575, fol. 216v; BL, Miscellaneous Treatises, Gloucester Chronicle AM 1–AD 1303, Cotton Vespasian A II, fol. 54r; 'Annales de Theokesberia [Teweksbury]', 'Annales prioratus de Dunstaplia', 'Annales de Wigornia [Worcester]' in *Annales Monastici*, ed. Henry Richard Luard, 5 vols (London, 1864–69), I, 65, III, 68–9, IV, 413; *Chron. Melrose*, 56; *Chron. Fordun*, 283–4; *Chron. Wyntoun*, V, 81.

[92] At this point Scots and sterling currency of equal value, see Note on Money, xviii.

[93] TNA, Patent 5 Hen. III, part 1, C66/24, m. 6 dorso; *Foedera*, I, part i, 85; *CDS*, I, no. 808; *Chron. Melrose*, 56; Everett Green, *Lives of the Princesses of England*, I, 386–7; Oram, *Alexander II*, 68–9. Oram highlights that it was probably in the days of business prior to the actual ceremony that the marriage of Alexander's eldest sister Margaret to Hubert de Burgh was discussed and perhaps finalised.

[94] Everett Green, *Lives of the Princesses of England*, I, 386–8.

[95] Ibid., 387; TNA, C54/24, m. 7; *CDS*, I, nos 809–10.

[96] Lars Kjær, 'Food, Drink and Ritualised Communication in the Household of Eleanor de Montfort, February to August 1265', *Journal of Medieval History* 37 (2011), 75–89, at 78.

[97] The extant registers and rolls of the Archbishops of York start with the Register of Walter de Gray, archbishop in 1221, but the first ten years of his episcopate are no longer extant/missing (1215–25).

[98] For similar use of the surrounding area in provisioning court of Alexander III, see 55, 59–60; Kay Staniland, 'The Nuptials of Alexander III of Scotland and Margaret Plantagenet', *Nottingham Medieval Studies* 30 (1986), 20–45; Taylor, *The Shape of the State*, 385–6.

Bryant has argued, ritual and spectacle were opportunities for the powerful to articulate identity.[99] Visual symbols and material objects would have been essential tools for Alexander in such articulations. The lion rampant of Scottish heraldry, thought to have originated with William the Lion, was first used on the reverse of Alexander II's Great Seal (see Plate 1).[100] Heraldry and heraldic devices developed in twelfth-century Europe from a simple method of identification to a system governed by rules and, by the thirteenth century, some chroniclers recorded great men just by referring to their devices, suggesting the prominence of such within society.[101] The use of the lion on his Great Seal indicates that Alexander was aware of the power of symbols, even at this early point in his reign. Consequently, it is not a great leap to suggest that the lion rampant adorned the king's horse, as well as the banners and tabards of his retinue. The use of regalia by either party is difficult to determine, and particularly so in the case of the Scottish king due to the inconsistencies around descriptions and depictions of a crown. Alexander's inauguration did not include a crowning, but Edward I removed a crown with other regalia from Scotland in 1296. Alexander is not depicted wearing a crown on his Great Seal (see Plate 1), although some of his coins depict him so adorned and earlier Scottish kings had been depicted with crowns, most famously David I and Mael Coluim IV.[102] The efforts to secure a ceremonial crowning, if not a full coronation, indicate not only Alexander's awareness of the symbolic significance of this object but also that – if it did not already exist – he may have commissioned one in preparation.[103] It seems unlikely that the Scottish king would have appeared before the English king without a crown when he sought to accentuate a level of symbolic parity between them. Similarly, the parading of regalia items in processions was relatively common, as illustrated by William I's role in carrying one of the English regalia swords in the ceremony following Richard I's return from imprisonment.[104] If the papal sword and rose sceptre were paraded in 1221, these could have provided tangible material evidence of Scotland's special relationship with the papacy. These objects potentially also signified papal control, particularly with

---

[99] Bryant, *Ritual, Ceremony and the Changing Monarchy in France*, 69.
[100] Bruce A. McAndrew, *Scotland's Historic Heraldry* (Woodbridge, 2006), 23–4; Walter de Gray Birch, *History of Scottish Seals from the Eleventh to the Seventeenth century*, 2 vols (Stirling, 1905), I, 26–7 (and accompanying plates).
[101] For discussions of early development of heraldry, see Maurice Keen, *Chivalry*, reprint (New Haven and London, 2005), 125–34; Adrian Ailes, 'Heraldry in Medieval England: Symbols of Politics and Propaganda', in Peter Coss and Maurice Keen (eds), *Heraldry, Pageantry and Social Display in Medieval England* (Woodbridge, 2008), 83–104, at 83–5.
[102] Ian H. Stewart, *The Scottish Coinage* (London, 1955), 134. For image of the illumination, see Barrow, 'David I (c.1085–1153)', *ODNB* (2004), https://doi-org.uhi.idm.oclc.org/10.1093/ref:odnb/7208. Date accessed: 29 July 2022. For further on the removal of the regalia, see Chapter 2, 80–1, 99.
[103] On Alexander II potentially introducing crown wearing as an adult, see Duncan, 'Before Coronation', 151–2.
[104] See 27–8.

Plate 1 Alexander II Great Seal [mounted and enthroned], c.1235. Crown Copyright, National Records of Scotland, Laing Seal Impressions, RH17/1/11–12.

Pandulf watching over the rituals, as the special relationship positioned the pope as nominal head of the archbishop-less Scottish church.[105] Nonetheless, the symbolism of these objects in a city whose archbishop had previously claimed supremacy over the Scottish church would have been potent.

Unfortunately, the marriage did not provide an heir to offer security for the cycle of succession by 1238, when the queen died in England.[106] Alexander did have at least one illegitimate son, but the necessity for a forty-year-old man to produce a legitimate male heir was reflected in his remarriage within eighteen months. His second marital choice, Marie de Coucy, was daughter of Enquerraud (or Ingram) de Coucy, an extremely wealthy and important French lord of royal Capetian blood.[107] The Scottish ambassadors, William de Bondington, bishop of Glasgow and the chancellor, and Sir Walter fitz Alan, justiciar, accompanied Marie from France, and the couple married at Roxburgh on Whitsunday [15 May] 1239.[108] The choice of Roxburgh, near the border with England, for this second marriage could have been purposefully antagonistic. Yet, it was equally likely to be linked to the wealth of the area for providing necessary supplies, proximity to merchant communities, and the ease of attendance for foreign guests from both northern England and

[105] A.D.M. Barrell, *Medieval Scotland* (Cambridge, 2000), 47–8.
[106] Joanna was buried in England, notably at the expense of Henry III: Oram, *Alexander II*, 134, 146–8.
[107] *Early Sources of Scottish History*, II, 417 (fn. 6), 514 (fn. 4). Oram notes that Marie's father was listed as a prominent figure in the dauphin Louis' campaigns in England from 1216–17, where he may have met Alexander II at Dover: *Alexander II*, 156–7. Louis IX of France and his wife Margaret of Provence did not have their first child until 1240, so there would not have been an eligible 'daughter of France' for the Scottish king had such an ambitious attempt crossed Alexander's mind.
[108] *Chron. Wyntoun*, V, 94–7; *Chron. Fordun*, 287; *Matthew of Paris's English History from the Year 1235 to 1273*, trans. and ed. J.A. Giles, 3 vols (London, 1852–54), I, 165.

Europe via well used trade routes between the prominent monastic houses and burghs of the borders and the port of Berwick (Map 2, see p. 37).[109] Little is known of the marriage rite and celebrations beyond this, due to the Scottish chronicles primarily focusing on the birth of a male child on 4 September 1241 rather than the wedding.[110] Following seventeen years of childless marriage, the focus on Marie's child-bearing capabilities is unsurprising when the continuation of royal power through a legitimate successor was so vital.

Ritual Rites and Dynastic Stability: Continuing Alexander II's Mission Beyond the Grave

Alexander II died in the summer of 1249 on the island of Kerrera, less than eight years after the birth of his long-awaited son and heir. Oram and Reid suggest that Alexander's health had been poor for some time prior to his death and that he had already chosen Melrose as his burial place.[111] Even though the final MacWilliam claims to the throne were brutally dispatched in 1230, the king's actions throughout the 1240s – following the birth of his son – demonstrate a renewed vigour in efforts to promote dynastic stability. By 1244 a betrothal was secured between his infant son and the infant daughter of Henry III to counter renewed tensions that had emerged between the two monarchs in the previous years.[112] This potential union refocused Alexander's attention upon how the status and sovereignty of Scottish kings should be represented. John Malden argues that it was during the period of negotiations that the double tressure flory counter-flory (the double band with lily symbols) was added as a border for the lion rampant of Scottish royal arms to act as a visual heraldic statement of Scotland's independent royal status.[113] In 1245, moreover, Alexander and the abbot of Dunfermline, Robert de Leldeleth or of Kenleith, later chancellor of Scotland, first sought the offi-

---

[109] Roxburgh was a leading thirteenth-century royal burgh with a castle commanding the crossing of the Tweed and the Teviot rivers, and it was one of the first Scottish towns to have a royal mint along with Berwick, see E. Patricia Dennison, *The Evolution of Scotland's Towns: Creation, Growth and Fragmentation* (Edinburgh, 2018), 14–16, 53. Barrow also includes the road route between Roxburgh and Berwick as one of Scotland's substantial medieval main roads: *Scotland and Its Neighbours*, 206.
[110] *Chron. Melrose*, 67–8.
[111] Oram, *Alexander II*, 190; Reid, *Alexander III*, 5.
[112] APS, I, 108; CDS, I, no. 1654; *Foedera*, I, part i, 150–1; *Matthew of Paris's English History*, I, 406; Donald E.R. Watt, 'The Minority of Alexander III in Scotland', *Transactions of the Royal Historical Society*, Fifth Series 21 (1971), 4–6; Duncan, *Making of the Kingdom*, 536; Oram, *Alexander II*, 96, 157–75.
[113] John Malden, 'Alexander II and the Double Tressure', in Oram (ed.), *Reign of Alexander II*, 211–20, at 213–16. Duncan argues that this could have been in 1250 following the canonisation of Margaret, but there is convincing evidence to support Malden's claim: Duncan, *Kingship of the Scots*, 151.

cial canonisation of the founder of the Canmore line, Margaret.[114] Both Taylor and Robert Bartlett posit that this was, in part, driven by the priorities of Dunfermline Abbey, but the timing suggests that the king and Abbot Robert had complementary designs.[115] The dynasty's importance was also promoted in the thirteenth-century production of king-lists that accentuated descent from the Canmore line of Margaret and Mael Coluim III, rather than from Cinead mac Alpin and still earlier Irish origins.[116] The 1240s, then, was a period of increased symbolic posturing and realigning Scottish kingship with a narrative of the Canmore dynasty, alongside active consolidation of royal power within and on the edges of the realm, to provide robust foundations for Alexander III's succession.[117]

Whereas Alexander III's inauguration has been the subject of much previous analysis, the evidence for Alexander II's death and burial is sparse and it has rarely been considered as an integral part of the ceremonies of succession of 1249. The inauguration of the seven-year-old Alexander III took place on Tuesday 13 July 1249 at Scone, while the contemporary *Melrose Chronicle* and a charter confirmation by Alexander II, presumably undertaken on his death bed, place the king's death on Kerrara on or after 8 July.[118] The journey from Kerrara to Melrose was a long one, whichever route was selected, and would have taken a minimum of a week and possibly significantly longer (see Map 3).[119] Consequently, the practicalities related to the distances involved suggest that the inauguration occurred first, with limited attendance, allowing time for a larger host to gather at or on the way to Melrose to bury the king in the wake of the inauguration. There were no dynastic rivals for the throne in 1249, but Alexander's death on the island of Kerrera – where the king was extending royal power in the west – created logistical difficulties due to the distance between the late king and important ritual sites. In conjunction with the heir's young age, this was potentially destabilising at a critical moment in the transfer of power. The contemporary response was to have

---

[114] *Registrum de Dunfermlyn*, ed. Cosmo Innes (Edinburgh, 1842), no. 281; *The Heads of Religious Houses in Scotland form the Twelfth to the Sixteenth Centuries*, ed. D.E.R. Watt and N.F. Shead (Edinburgh, 2001), 68; Penman, 'Royal Piety', 19–20.

[115] *The Miracles of Saint Æbbe of Coldingham and Saint Margaret of Scotland*, trans. and ed. Robert Bartlett (Oxford, 2003), xxxvi–xxxvii; Alice Taylor, 'Historical Writing in Twelfth- and Thirteenth-Century Scotland: The Dunfermline Compilation', HR 83 (2010), 228–52.

[116] Dauvit Broun, *The Irish Identity of the Kingdom of the Scots in the Twelfth and Thirteenth Centuries* (Woodbridge, 1999), 165–200, particularly 195–8. Also summarised in Oram, *Alexander II*, 226–30.

[117] For the most recent and comprehensive discussion of Alexander's consolidation in Scotland, see Oram, *Alexander II*, particularly 76–107, 149–91.

[118] RMS, II, no. 3136; *Chron. Melrose*, 87; *Chron. Fordun*, 288; *Chron. Bower*, V, 290–1; Oram, *Alexander II*, 190–1.

[119] Map 3 principally functions to indicate the disparate nature of the sites involved. It offers some possible suggestions of routes, but evidence does not give any specifics about the journeys taken; we only have the start and end points.

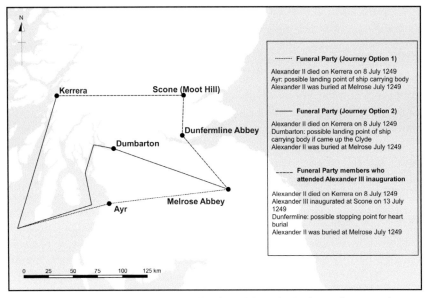

Map 3 Sites associated with death and burial of Alexander II, and inauguration of his son, 1249. Contains Ordnance Survey data © Crown Copyright and database right (2023).

the new king recognised by representatives of the political community in an inaugural ritual to provide a tangible confirmation and recognition of the king's accession as quickly as possible. The funeral was less urgent, but it offered – as in 1214 – a culmination to the ceremonial events that could be attended by a fuller representative group and utilise processional movement through the country to counter potential instabilities. Ritual had to be adaptable, but it is also inherently associated with repetition and the inclusion of recognisable features. In 1249, the dating and geographical evidence suggests that, at least for the ordering of events, those organising the ceremonies looked back to 1214 for inspiration or even a model. This warrants some cautious speculation – at least in the case of the funerary rites where hard evidence is sparser – around other ritual actions or components that may have borrowed from previous experience. In the case of the inauguration, paradoxically, it is the volume of surviving material and the inconsistencies in the way narratives record ritual that offer the most interesting points of analysis. By drawing these two approaches together, this analysis speaks to the ways that rituals of death and succession were or may have been used in conjunction in 1249.

A distinct division of the royal party, as recorded in 1214, does not feature as obviously in the narrative accounts of 1249, but Duncan notes that a relatively small number of major earls – Fife, Strathearn and Menteith

– were named in attendance at the inauguration.[120] It is unlikely that the queen was present at the deathbed as found in 1214. Evidence for Marie de Coucy's exact location is lacking, but Reid suggests her political role in the minority has been underestimated and has proposed that she was residing with her son and involved in the inauguration, rather than travelling with Alexander II on a military campaign.[121] The king's final charter identifies some of those present with him on Kerrara: Clement, bishop of Dunblane, Alan Durward, justiciar of Scotia, David of Lindsay, justiciar of Lothian, Alexander the Steward, Walter of Moray or Murray, William of Brechin, Walter Bissett and Robert of Meynors.[122] Of these signatories, only Alan Durward was recorded at Scone for the inauguration.[123] Although others may have travelled with Durward to take part in the inauguration, it is likely that the bishop of Dunblane – who was not one of the bishops recorded at Scone – and officials, such as the Steward, remained with the deceased king to prepare and transport the body to Melrose. All three brief chronicle entries about Alexander's death comment similarly on the king taking the final sacrament, confirming the presence of at least one ecclesiastic to perform this.[124] Clement, bishop of Dunblane, was university educated and a leading member of the Scottish clergy closely associated with the king, whose abilities to stabilise his own diocese saw him entrusted with the reforming of the vacant diocese of Argyll.[125] Duch's emphasis on the status of those who took care of the preparation of royal bodies for display and burial is also relevant here: the bishop was a potential candidate not only for performing the sacraments but also for the vital, if less savoury, role of preparing the corpse, with the assistance of other members of the household and possibly local islanders.[126] The evisceration of the body for transportation would have provided other body parts for separate burial, and entrails were quite often buried at the place of death.[127] Considering Alexander's challenges with lingering loyalties of those in the west to Norse kings, burying part of his body on the west coast could have been a potent symbolic act laying claim to the region. Unfortunately, despite the need to dispose of any removed viscera, there is no evidence that such a ceremonial statement was made.

---

[120] Duncan, *Kingship of the Scots*, 139. All three earls are named by *Chron. Fordun*, 289.
[121] Reid, *Alexander III*, 76–7.
[122] *RMS*, II, no. 3136; Oram, *Alexander II*, 190.
[123] *Chron. Fordun*, 289–90; *Chron. Bower*, V, 290–3.
[124] Ibid., 290–1; *Chron. Melrose*, 87; *Chron. Fordun*, 288.
[125] John Dowden, *The Bishops of Scotland* (Glasgow, 1912), 196–8; Oram, *Alexander II*, 182, 212–13.
[126] Duch, 'Royal Funerary and Burial Ceremonies', 73–85.
[127] Examples include Henry I, d.1135 (viscera buried at Rouen), Eleanor of Castille, d. at Lincoln 1290 (viscera buried at Lincoln) and Henry V, d.1422 in France (viscera buried at Saint Maur des Fosses): Duffy, *Royal Tombs*, 22–3; Duch, 'Royal Funerary and Burial Ceremonies', 73–85, 96–7, 203, 223; Brown, *The Monarchy of Capetian France*, see 'Death and the Human Body', 227–8; Hallam, 'Royal Burial', 364.

Gesta Annalia I and Bower both record rising tensions among the Scottish nobles in the wake of Alexander II's death when key secular figures – Alan Durward and Walter Comyn – challenged each other over whether to knight the young king before his inauguration.[128] Reid has questioned the traditional historiographical stance that Alexander III's minority was inherently factional. In this particular affair, he suggests Durward's motive for proposing that the king should be knighted was not for personal gain, as usually argued, but rather as a continuation of Alexander II's drive to bring parity of status between kings as knighting was common for kings of France and England prior to coronation.[129] Taylor states that Alexander III's minority also witnessed growth in the minting of new Scottish coins, which offers evidence of continued use of material displays to represent Scotland as an equal player after the king's death.[130] The minority leaders may have had their quarrels, but there was a common goal in supporting and promoting the crown. The occurrence of a debate over ceremonial procedure offers an insight into wider contemporary investment in such rituals, as well as tensions that could occur around influential practices from elsewhere impinging on native practices.

The contemporary *Melrose Chronicle* offers a brief statement that underscores the continuing importance of the nobility within the 'election' and the enthroning of the king with an apparent absence of any ecclesiastical involvement:

> ...according to the custom of the kingdom, [Alexander III] was appointed king, and placed upon his father's throne by the nobility in the third of the ides of July [13 July], and was honoured by all as lawful heir.[131]

Secular lords were also prominent in both *Gesta Annalia I* and Bower's *Scotichronicon*: in the debate about knighting and subsequent acclamation, in the outdoor enthronement and homage and, finally, in the recitation of the genealogy by the Gaelic poet.[132] Key secular figures – the earls of Fife and Strathearn and the Gaelic poet – also feature in the thirteenth-century Scone seal imagery and the fifteenth-century illustration from Bower's chronicle (see Plates 2 and 3). Though notably absent in the *Melrose Chronicle*, members of the clerical estate appear in the illustrative representations and later narrative accounts. In the latter, David de Bernham, bishop of St Andrews, was recorded as the officiant, while the presence of Geoffrey or Galfrid, bishop of Dunkeld, and the abbot of Scone was noted, though neither was assigned a role.[133] The similarities between the later narratives indicate that Bower

---

[128] *Chron. Bower*, V, 290–3; *Chron. Fordun*, 289–90. Alexander III was not knighted until December 1251 at the same time as his wedding to Henry III's daughter, Margaret. See 55; Duncan, 'Before Coronation: Making a King at Scone', 140–2.
[129] Reid, *Alexander III*, 84–143.
[130] Taylor, *Shape of the State*, 53–5.
[131] *Chron. Melrose*, 87.
[132] *Chron. Fordun*, 289–90; *Chron. Bower*, V, 290–3.
[133] Duncan states that the abbot is not mentioned until 1306, except for on the Scone

Plate 2 Scone Abbey Seal appended to Letter of Renunciation by Patrick Bishop of Murray and commendator of the abbey of Scone in favour of Patrick Kynnard of Kynnard, 7 February 1568. Perth and Kinross Archives, MS169/1/2/189.

largely relied on *Gesta Annalia I*, or both used the same original.[134] However, the divergences of word choices and selected details offer an opportunity to explore the ongoing developments in ritual roles and spaces, both at the time and later, as well as revealing the careful path that needs to be taken when analysing narratives of ritual.

Broun and Duncan have explored how the author of *Gesta Annalia I* inserted both the detail of the stone of destiny and an extended genealogy recited by the poet (c.1285), whereas Bower included a Latin genealogy and pays little heed to the stone.[135] The stone had, of course, been languishing in Westminster for over a century by the time the *Scotichronicon* was composed so may have faded in significance.[136] On the specifics of the officiant's actions and where these took place, Bower and *Gesta Annalia I*'s accounts also diverge. Bower states that the bishop of St Andrews was chosen to knight the young king. Duncan suggests that, in doing so, Bower provides a distinctly ecclesiastic understanding of inaugural actions by filling 'the office of king', as Lanfranc, archbishop of Canterbury, had done in the case of William II in England.[137] Such understanding of the proceedings betray Bower's fifteenth-century experience of a Scottish coronation, which is out of place when considering

---

seal, but he appears named as present in *Gesta Annalia I*: *Chron. Fordun*, 289; Duncan, *Kingship of the Scots*, 136–7, 144.

[134] *Chron. Bower*, V, 290–5; *Chron. Fordun*, 289–90.

[135] Note that Broun comments that some intrusions into *Gesta Annalia I* may have been written later than 1285 but, if this was an insertion, it must have occurred before the stone's removal in 1296: Broun, *Scottish Independence and the Idea of Britain*, 174–9, 216–19.

[136] Ibid., 161–88, 215–34; Duncan, 'Before Coronation: Making a King at Scone', 167, 183–97.

[137] *Chron. Bower*, V, 292–3; Duncan, *Kingship of the Scots*, 133. On the impact of Bower's ecclesiastical background: Legge, 'The Inauguration of Alexander III', 78–9.

Plate 3   Inauguration of Alexander III from Bower in *Scotichronicon*. Parker Library, Corpus Christi College, Cambridge, CCC MS 171, fol. 206r.

1249. Bower also attributed to the bishop the act of blessing and ordaining the king, and offering and receiving the king's oath, all of which occurred in a different physical space, presumably within the abbey church, before the secular enthronement outside.[138] *Gesta Annalia I*, on the other hand, states that once seated on the royal throne outside: 'the bishop of St Andrews, assisted by the rest, consecrated him as king'.[139] Bower's separation of the ecclesiastical and secular parts of the inaugural ceremony across distinctive indoor and outdoor spaces appears to draw on developments observable in the Scottish coronation of the following century.[140] *Gesta Annalia I*, however, describes the use of a transitional space – a cross in a graveyard – a Christianised space but still outside the church indicating an incremental blurring of traditions and roles. This speaks to Taylor's argument for a gradual process of change in the development of the Scottish 'state' more broadly over the twelfth and thirteenth centuries.[141] It also echoes clerical interventions occurring in other ceremonies and rituals – such as marriage – which were witnessed more widely across Europe during the thirteenth century, particularly following the Fourth Lateran Council of 1215.[142] The use of an outdoor Christianised space for the ecclesiastical and secular elements in *Gesta Annalia I* presents an overlooked transitional stage in ritual development between the secular ceremony outlined by the Melrose chronicler and the version in Bower, which draws, in part, from his contemporaneous fifteenth-century knowledge and understanding. These developments were shaped by both the specific Scottish context and the wider European environment in which the church sought to maintain and extend control.

Duncan's work on the thirteenth-century inauguration draws frequent attention to the continuing 'liturgification'.[143] There is good reason and evidence for this: Alexander II sought the rites of unction and coronation and pursued papal canonisation of a dynastic saint; William I made material gains of papal origin for the Scottish regalia, and ecclesiastics were taking increasingly prominent roles in the promotion of Scottish kingship and sovereignty.[144] Nonetheless, the extent of 'liturgification' can be overstated

[138] *Chron. Bower*, V, 292–3.
[139] *Chron. Fordun*, 289–90.
[140] See Chapter 3; Lucinda H.S. Dean, 'Making the Most of What They Had: Adapting Indoor and Outdoor Spaces for Royal Ceremony in Scotland, c. 1214 to c. 1603', in Krista De Jonge and Ronnie Mulryne with Richard Morris (eds), *Architectures of Festival in Early Modern Europe* (Abingdon, 2017), 99–117, at 102–6; Dean, 'Where to Make the King (or Queen)', 58–65.
[141] Taylor, *Shape of the State*, passim.
[142] 'Canons 50–52, Lateran IV 1215, Twelfth Ecumenical Council', in *Disciplinary Decrees of the General Councils: Text, Translation and Commentary*, ed. Henry J. Schroeder (St. Louis, 1937), 279–82; Jennifer Ward, *Women in Medieval Europe, 1200–1500* (Harlow and London, 2002), 26–44, particularly 30–2.
[143] Duncan, *Kingship of the Scots*, 127–50; Duncan, 'Before Coronation: Making a King at Scone', 139–67; Reid, *Alexander III*, passim.
[144] Robert Kenleith, abbot of Dunfermline, could be compared to Abbot Suger of Saint-Denis, who combined efforts to enhance the position of his abbey through associations

when secular elements remained pronounced, even through the lens of later ecclesiastical chronicle writers. The centrality of the nobility and the outdoor enthronement are significant, but so too is the arrival of the Gaelic poet or historian.[145] The act of reciting the genealogy of the kings becomes enshrined in the Scottish ceremony as it develops, albeit with different secular figures voicing the recitation over time. Its distinctive prominence is particularly interesting in light of Reid's argument about its role as a confirmation of the king's relationship with the nobility: a declaration through lineage that he was 'one of them' and thus, with their acknowledgement, was confirmed as king.[146] Bannerman and Duncan trace the function of the Gaelic individual back to early founders of Alba and their Irish origins, indicating the sense of a long tradition, but the poet – or *fili* – by this time was likely a royal court figure resident in Fife.[147] Earlier chroniclers and accounts of previous inaugurations, such as 1214, do not mention the Gaelic recitation of the genealogy, so the reasons for its centrality in the later accounts of 1249 raise questions about the emphasis of the chroniclers.[148] The *Chronicle of Melrose* offers far less detail: the king was raised to his throne 'according to the custom of the kingdom' by the nobility, emphasising his appointment and the support for his 'lawful' succession.[149] This may have been due to the recitation being part of 'the custom' and, as such, needed no explanation, as was the case with other excluded details in this brief account. However, the retrospective emphasis on the Gaelic and secular traditions, from the pens of later chroniclers or compilers, could intimate that these authors felt it necessary to offer a reminder of the importance of such traditions in the post-war period when Scottish kings had been granted unction. Either way, the consistency of focus on secular elements across the various chroniclers further problematises the historically presumed adoption of Anglo-Norman norms in Scotland.[150] The thirteenth century was a period of change, but thirteenth-century ceremony also had deep roots in a complex pre-Anglo-Norman past that shaped developments in distinctively Scottish ways.[151]

---

and enhancement of the twelfth-century French monarchy, or the role of Archbishop Eystein Erlendsson of Nidaros for his involvement in the introduction of crowning and the *Laws of Succession* in Norway (1163), as well as the promotion of the cult of St Olaf, including the ritual use and rehousing of relics: Hallam, 'Royal Burial', 361; Brégiant, *Vox Regis*, 33–53.

[145] For detailed discussion of the Gaelic poet, see Bannerman, 'The King's Poet', 120–49.
[146] Reid, *Alexander III*, 37.
[147] Bannerman, 'The King's Poet', 120–49, on the poet in Fife, 135–48; Duncan, *Kingship of the Scots*, 147–8.
[148] Broun, *Scottish Independence and the Idea of Britain*, 177–8.
[149] *Chron. Melrose*, 87.
[150] The extent of the Anglo-Norman influence has most recently been challenged by Taylor, *Shape of the State*, 17–18, *passim*, and Reid, *Alexander III*, 37–8, *passim*. Both include extensive lists of reading on both sides of debate.
[151] For the most recent and comprehensive summary of earlier influences on Scotland, see Reid, *Alexander III*, 19–31.

One increasingly pan-European ritual that could have offered symbolic opportunity for those in charge of the minority government was a separate heart burial. This discussion is necessarily speculative as a separate heart burial for Alexander II is not specifically recorded, but the details of Scottish royal funerals and burials are almost universally sparse in narrative sources. The excavations at the high altar at Dunfermline (1818–19) to exhume Robert I's tomb also located a separately encased heart, which was not Bruce's own as his heart was buried at Melrose, and the owner of this heart is still unknown.[152] Alexander's choice of the Cistercian abbey of Melrose for burial could indicate a lack of interest in the growth of the cult around Margaret and, by association, Dunfermline. Yet, this would not tally with Alexander's involvement – along with the abbot of Dunfermline, Robert of Kenleith – in securing her canonisation, and scholars have demonstrated that the king's pious devotions were complex and varied.[153] Favouring Melrose could be associated with Alexander's desire to compensate the abbey for destruction during earlier warfare, but it could also illustrate renewed interest in Northumberland and Margaret's Anglo-Saxon heritage, as found in the Dunfermline tradition particularly. Melrose also housed the relics of another saintly ancestor, Waltheof, to provide an additional emphasis on the sanctity of his dynasty.[154] A separate interment of Alexander's heart at Dunfermline would have spoken to these complex devotions and accentuated the dynastic continuity, particularly if the young king carried the heart to Dunfermline for burial either en route to or from Melrose: a journey that could have easily passed through Dunfermline (see Map 3, p. 44).

Evidence for a separate heart burial at Dunfermline is sadly lacking, but the central role of the abbot of Dunfermline during this period of transition is undeniable. In 1249, only two months after the inauguration of Alexander III, the papacy granted Margaret's canonisation to the abbot along with the right to forty days of indulgences for those visiting the saint.[155] The young king, his mother, prelates and nobles all attended the translation of St Margaret in June 1250.[156] Compared to Henry III's preparations for the new

[152] Henry Jardine, 'Extracts from the Report made by Henry Jardine […] relative to the Tomb of King Robert Bruce and the Church of Dunfermline', *Archaeologia Scotica: The Transactions of the Society of Antiquaries of Scotland* 2 (1822), 435–54, at 446.
[153] Penman, 'Royal Piety', 17–22, 25 (reference to separate heart burial in fn. 74); Oram, *Alexander II*, 213–23. On role of Kenleith: Taylor, 'Historical Writing', 251–2.
[154] Taylor, 'Historical Writing', 228–52; Penman, 'Royal Piety', 19–22; Oram, *Alexander II*, particularly 221–2; Grant G. Simpson, 'The Heart of King Robert I: Pious Crusade or Marketing Gambit?', in Crawford (ed.), *Church, Chronicle and Learning*, 173–86, at 180; Derek Baker, 'Waldef [Waltheof] c.1095–1159, abbot of Melrose', *ODNB* (2004), https://doi.org/10.1093/ref:odnb/28647. Date accessed: 28 February 2021.
[155] *Registrum de Dunfermlyn*, nos 290–1; *The Miracles of … Saint Margaret of Scotland*, xxxvi–xxxvii. Indulgences were remissions of temporal punishment for sins and often given more liberally on significant Marian feast days, at Christmas and Easter or at shrines, see Duffy, *The Stripping of the Altars*, 193, 288–91.
[156] *Chron. Fordun*, 291; *Chron. Bower*, V, 296–9.

shrine and translation of Edward the Confessor, announced in 1245 and not completed until 1269, the Scottish efforts have been viewed as 'rushed and low key'.[157] That the first request for canonisation of Margaret occurred in 1245 was unlikely to have been coincidental. Having secured an agreement for the marriage for his son to Henry's daughter (1244), Alexander II appears to have grasped an opportunity to demonstrate his own saintly ancestry on hearing of Henry's translation plans. Ultimately, Alexander did not live long enough to see the marriage or canonisation, but both originated in his reign. The situation that presented itself in 1249 to 1250 is clear in *Gesta Annalia I*, whose account of the translation runs directly and without pause from this ceremony to the decision (encouraged by churchmen) to send an embassy to Henry III to conclude Alexander III's marriage to Margaret.[158] Receiving the canonisation with a royal wedding on the horizon, the Scots saw the necessity to continue their former monarch's efforts and place the young Scottish king at the centre of the translation of the relics of his saintly great-great-great grandmother – a far closer saintly relative than Henry III could claim – ahead of any meeting between the two kings.

This same period also witnessed further efforts to seek parity for Scottish kingship, as the minority council took up Alexander II's pursuit of the rite of unction and coronation for Alexander III. This request was refused in 1251 but the tone of the response points to a papacy increasingly opposed to the interference of Henry III on the issue of the Scottish coronation, now deemed an issue between the papacy and the Scots alone.[159] Duncan offers material evidence of the designs of the clerical estate to forward the mission to secure the rite of unction in the small seal of Alexander III. In use from approximately 1250, the seal carries a legend linking Alexander to St Columba and the first 'ordained' Scottish king, Áedán, to underscore the right of the Scottish kings to unction.[160] Taylor has convincingly demonstrated that the Dunfermline manuscript, containing a *Vita* of St Margaret and two shorter chronicle sections, was composed in the 1250s with the express purpose of providing further evidence of Alexander's right to be anointed through ancestral associations to Alfred – the first Anglo-Saxon monarch to be anointed – via St Margaret.[161] This analysis places the abbot and his community at the heart of this ongoing campaign. Abbot Robert and other clerics joined leading nobles, including Durward, in their concerns for the projection of parity for the kingship of the realm.[162] The marriage between the Scottish child-king and the daughter of Henry III had the potential to

---

[157] Penman, 'Royal Piety', 20; Binski, *Westminster Abbey*, 4.
[158] *Chron. Fordun*, 291.
[159] TNA, Special Collections: Papal Bulls, Intimation to the king of England that the pope cannot grant his requests that the king of Scotland should not be anointed or crowned without his assent, SC7/20/11; *CDS*, I, no. 1798.
[160] Duncan, *Kingship of the Scots*, 152–3.
[161] Taylor, 'Historical Writing', 228–52, at 246–50.
[162] Reid, *Alexander III*, 88, 91, 94–5.

destabilise the efforts to create a level playing field during Alexander II's lifetime, but equally provided the motivation to continue in his footsteps. Whether the late king's heart was laid to rest at Dunfermline or not, the political community surrounding the infant king reflected a commonly held determination to create visible and tangible demonstrations of a stable cycle of succession, while continuing to pursue ritual means – amongst others – to shore up the kingship and country against possible incursions.

The Marriages of Alexander III and his Children

In comparison to the marriage of Alexander II in 1221, there is a relative abundance of evidence for the union of Alexander III and Margaret Plantagenet on Christmas Day in 1251. However, there is a problematic imbalance in the source survival: there are no extant Scottish financial accounts, whereas such records are plentiful for England, and the fullest description is found in *Chronica Majora*, written by an English monk of St Albans, Matthew of Paris.[163] Paris's record is, at least, not a straightforward Anglo-centric view of proceedings. Paris was well informed, but Kjær suggests that he used the events at York to provide a well-crafted criticism of Henry III's kingship, and the country writ large, for a monastic audience.[164] Consequently, Paris's critique focuses on the vain luxuries of all attendees – who were recorded as 'glorying in their silks and variegate ornaments' – and the discord in the streets marring a sacred religious festival as the two parties jostled for superiority and grandeur.[165] However, in so doing, Paris inadvertently supplies tangible evidence of Scottish efforts to compete for status with the English in this contested space. Additionally, while the young king's Scottish entourage was described as significantly smaller than that of the English king, he was also accompanied by the queen mother, Marie de Coucy, who returned from France with a large host of Frenchmen described as both 'numerous and pompous' by Paris.[166]

---

[163] Financial accounts: TNA, Close Rolls 35–6 Hen III, C54/64–5; TNA, Liberate Rolls, 36 Hen. III, C62/28; TNA, Patent Rolls, 36 Hen III, C66/63; TNA, Pipe Rolls, 35 Hen III, E372/95; CDS, I, nos 1815–72. Examples of descriptive accounts include BL, Chronicle of English History to 1274, Cotton MS Nero A IV, fol. 109v; *Chron. Fordun*, 291; *Chron. Bower*, V, 301; *Chron. Wyntoun*, V, 115; *Pluscarden*, 57–8; *Matthew of Paris's English History*, II, 466–71.

[164] Lars Kjær, 'Matthew Paris and the Royal Christmas: Ritualised Communication in Text and Practice', in Janet Burton, Phillipp Schofield and Björn Weiler (eds), *Thirteenth Century England XIV: Proceedings of the Aberstwyth and Lampeter Conference, 2011* (Woodbridge, 2013), 141–52, particularly at 144–8. See also Staniland, 'The Nuptials of Alexander III', 20–45.

[165] *Matthew of Paris's English History*, II, 466–71, quote at 469.

[166] *Matthew of Paris's English History*, II, 468. Marie de Coucy returned to France in 1250, after the translation of the relics of St Margaret, but returned in 1251: CDS, I, nos 1785–6, 1791, 1795; Watt, 'The Minority of Alexander III', 8; Reid, *Alexander III*, 99.

The sacred nature of kingship was central to the symbolism and display of Henry III; thus, it makes sense that the leading figures in the Scottish minority government would have sought to imbue Alexander III's kingship with divinity and authority to help level the playing field, particularly where age and power sat in the hands of the English.[167] Two key ritual actions recorded for the young king – his refusal to make homage for Scotland and his challenge to traditional demands made by the English earl Marshal for his palfrey following the ceremonies – offer examples of ritualised posturing designed to demonstrate the sovereign status of the young king.[168] Even if these episodes were fabricated or scripted, as Reid suggests, the Scottish king was still presented in these interpretations as a confident monarch aware of his position despite his youth.[169] The use of regalia as tangible material symbols to complement and enhance such ritual actions seems likely, even though evidence for the wearing of regalia by either the English or Scottish king is limited. Paris does not comment on the clothing and adornment of specific individuals, but his general comments about the use of 'variegate ornaments' does imply the employment of material adornments in the symbolic articulation of identity and status by those present.[170] One near contemporary manuscript recording the marriage includes a rudimentary stylised sketch of a pair of bishops blessing the young couple. The illustrator saw fit to depict Alexander with a crown, despite probable English authorship, and Alexander was depicted in various seals wearing a crown, which suggest this symbolic object may have been used to assist with indicating a level of parity in royal status.[171] It was also possible – as speculated for 1221 – that the papal sword and sceptre topped with the golden rose could have been conspicuously carried in an entry procession. The inclusion of such regalia, emphasising royal status and papal support for Scottish sovereignty, would also have mirrored the minority council's efforts to seek unction and imbue the young king with sacred connections through in the reinterring of Margaret after her canonisation.

Despite Scottish efforts, the wedding offered Henry III both ritual and political advantages.[172] Material culture was certainly employed to express

---

[167] For example, see David A. Carpenter, *The Reign of Henry III* (London, 1996), 427–61; Nicholas Vincent, *The Holy Blood: King Henry III and the Westminster Blood Relic* (Cambridge, 2001), 7–19, 35–7, 154–85.
[168] *Matthew of Paris's English History*, II, 469–70.
[169] Reid, *Alexander III*, 101–2.
[170] *Matthew of Paris's English History*, II, 469.
[171] BL, Cotton MS Nero A IV, fol. 109v. This text and accompanying Geoffrey de Monmouth's *Propheti Merlini* (fols 63r–75v) date to the early fourteenth century.
[172] On political relations: Duncan, *Making of the Kingdom*, 559–70; Watt, 'The Minority of Alexander III', 9–23; Brown, *Wars of Scotland*, 46–56. One political advantage was an infiltration of Scotland's court with the entourage he sent with Margaret, including Robert of Norwich, Stephen Bauzan and Matilda Cantelupe, widow of William de Cantilupe, two unnamed maids, 'Ridellus de Briggelak' and two of his knights, 'Geoffrey de langele, justiciar of the forest' and the king's marshals (all supplied with clothing): TNA, 36 Hen III, C54/65, m.29; *CDS*, I, no. 1841; *Matthew of Paris's English History*, II, 471–3.

English wealth and generosity illustrated in surviving financial records, which covered everything from the provision of beasts and wildfowl collected from the northern counties to the 'exquisites' presented throughout the ceremonial proceedings to Margaret, Alexander and others.[173] Complementary clothing and adornments made for the king and his twelve-year-old son – similarly fashioned with the gold leopards of the English royal arms – symbolically emphasised the relative stability of the Plantagenet dynasty's line of succession.[174] This would have provided a marked contrast with the relatively precarious nature of the Scottish succession personified in the boy king. The material excesses may have been criticised by Paris, but potent messages could and were made through such sartorial choices.[175] Henry also exploited ritual objects and actions to position himself as the magnanimous bestower of honours, particularly upon his younger counterpart. This included knighting Alexander and presenting him with an ornately decorated sword, with a scabbard of silk and a silver pommel, along with a belt and a pair of decorative silver gilt spurs.[176] Equally, amongst the numerous gifts that Alexander and Margaret received from Henry was Margaret's first seal matrix as queen of Scotland.[177] As an object that created the physical mark of royal power in wax, this gift reflected how Henry might figuratively, and literally, impress his royal authority upon the young couple in subsequent years.

Following the union, Henry also granted a pardon – to Alan, son of the earl of Atholl, for crimes, including murder, committed in Ireland – at the behest of his daughter, Margaret.[178] Henry had similarly pardoned a criminal, following the 'staged' intercession of his wife, Eleanor of Provence, in her coronation in 1236. Carmi Parsons argues that the latter was a carefully scripted performance designed to emphasise that any power of the queen emanated from the king, and thus this became a common feature in subsequent coronations of English queens.[179] There is no evidence of a crowning or symbolic ritual marking Margaret's transition from English princess to Scottish queen,

---

[173] TNA, 35 Hen III, C54/64; TNA, C62/28; TNA, C66/63; TNA, E372/95; *CDS*, I, nos 1815–72. See also Staniland, 'The Nuptials of Alexander III', 20–45.

[174] TNA, C54/64, m. 30–1 dorso; *CDS*, I, nos 1825, 1829, 1838; For further examples see Staniland, 'Nuptials of Alexander III', 29–30, 32–3, 36–7. For discussions on the development of the leopard badge of English kings: Caroline Shenton, 'Edward III and the Symbol of the Leopard', and Adrian Ailes, 'Heraldry in Medieval England', in Coss and Keen (eds), *Heraldry, Pageantry and Social Display*, 69–104.

[175] *Matthew of Paris's English History*, II, 471.

[176] *Chron. Wyntoun*, V, 115; *Chron. Fordun*, 292; *Chron. Bower*, V, 301; *Pluscarden*, 57–8; *Matthew of Paris's English History*, II, 467–8; TNA, C54/65, m. 30–1; *CDS*, I, nos 1824, 1828, 1831.

[177] *CDS*, I, nos 1903, 1928. For other gifts to Margaret: TNA, C54/65, m. 29–30; TNA, E372/95, m. 7 dorso; TNA, C62/28, m. 14–18; *CDS*, Vol. I, nos 1816, 1819, 1825–7, 1841, 1854. Alexander also received a set of 'precious' bed-hangings decorated with gold and coloured fabrics as a Christmas gift: TNA, C54/65, m. 30; *CDS*, I, no. 1826.

[178] TNA, C66/63, m. 16; *CDS*, I, no. 1865.

[179] John Carmi Parsons, 'Ritual and Symbol in the English Medieval Queenship to 1500', in Louise O. Fradenburg (ed.), *Women and Sovereignty* (Edinburgh, 1992), 60–77, at 64–5.

other than the wedding, but if this intercession was also staged it may have been associated with her transformation. More unusually, and apparently largely overlooked, is evidence of intercession by Alexander on behalf of sixteen English men, outlawed for murder and other crimes from around the country, resulting in a pardon granted by Henry on 31 December, just a week after the young couple's wedding.[180] Paris describes a theatrical episode in which Alexander seeks a pardon for the transgressions of Philip Lovel (not one of the criminals but rather an out-of-favour courtier) on bended knee, where the young king first declared his orphan status and then asked for Henry's protection as a pseudo-father before requesting the pardon.[181] The speeches and actions described by Paris appear to be narrative tools utilised to emphasise Henry's dominant position. However, the survival of official records of numerous pardons given at Alexander's behest within a week of the wedding, and the fact that the other ritual actions recorded by Paris present a young king of Scots proactively repelling English attempts to demonstrate superior power, do offer some credence to a ritualised intercession to seek the pardon for prisoners. Such a ritual would have spoken volumes about the subservient position of the Scottish king, particularly in the eyes of the English court who had witnessed the ritual intercession of Eleanor at her coronation.

The English king had reason to employ material and ritual means to bolster his new son-in-law's status, but the same tools were equally employed to demonstrate his dominance in this relationship. Initially, this reflected reality as Henry did exert significant influence during the minority of Alexander III.[182] Journeys made to England by Alexander and Margaret, such as the royal couple's visit to Woodstock and London in 1256, were opportunities for Henry to reemphasise the balance of power through bringing the Scottish king into the heart of England.[183] However, the king and queen of Scots were treated as guests of honour. In 1256 – following celebrations for the feast of the Assumption of the Virgin at Woodstock and pious offerings made at St Albans – the couple entered London, which 'was decorated with banners, chaplets, and manifold ornaments' to honour 'the arrival of great personages', alongside Henry, Queen Eleanor and Prince Edward.[184] Such occasions provided first-hand experience of the full force of Henry III's ceremonial excesses, lavish feasting, rich decorative displays, well-known largesse and gift giving, all imbued with a distinct religiosity and divine connotations.[185] Such shows

---

[180] TNA, C66/63, m. 14; CDS, I, no. 1852. Some of the names include 'of x' in the rolls, and where places are identifiable these range across several counties from Yorkshire and Northumberland to Norfolk and Oxfordshire.

[181] *Matthew of Paris's English History*, II, 471–2.

[182] For the most recent assessment of Henry's influence in the minority, see Reid, *Alexander III*, 75–118.

[183] Benham, *Peacemaking in the Middle Ages*, 19–68.

[184] *Matthew of Paris's English History*, III, 184–91; CDS, I, nos 2053–6. On the proposed influence of the journeys to England on piety, see Penman, 'Royal Piety', 17–18.

[185] Staniland, 'The Nuptials of Alexander III', 20–45; Carpenter, *Reign of Henry III*, 427–61; Benjamin Wild, 'Secrecy, Splendour and Statecraft: The Jewel Accounts of Henry III',

Plate 4   Alexander III Great Seal [mounted and enthroned].
Crown Copyright, National Records of Scotland, Laing Seal Impressions,
RH17/1/13–14.

would likely have left an impression on the Scottish king as he grew up and, by the time Alexander attended the coronation of Edward I in 1274, reports suggest he had taken a leaf from Henry's book as he 'exceeded all others in lavish hospitality and gifts'.[186] Yet, Henry was only one of the influences on the Scottish king. Alexander worked with Scotland's leading men, who had shaped the rituals of his early reign following the path laid down by his father, and with his French mother, Marie de Coucy, whose influence has potentially been underestimated according to a recent reassessment by Reid.[187] Later seals of Alexander's reign bear the hallmark of all these influences. A multitude of lions rampant decorate the caparison of the horse and the shield in the elaborate heraldic design on the mounted image, while the background is covered in fleur-de-lys (Plate 4). These design elements projected his Scottish and French heritage. The counterseal enthroned image depicts a crowned king holding a sceptre and clutching his robe with the other hand. These two objects – the sceptre and the robe – were prominent items of the Scottish regalia, but the throne is in a marked gothic style that suggests lingering influences of Henry's material display.[188]

The birth of Alexander III's heirs, and particularly the weddings he orchestrated for them, provided him with the opportunities to fully emerge from England's shadow through alliances designed to ensure the stability of the Scottish succession. This included the marriage of his daughter, Princess Margaret, who left Scotland in early August 1281, to Eric II, king of Norway.[189]

HR 83 (2010), 409–30; Kjær, 'Matthew Paris and the Royal Christmas', 141–52.
[186] Chron. Lanercost, I, 8–9.
[187] Reid, Alexander III, particularly 119–43.
[188] Birch, History of Scottish Seals, 27–30; McAndrew, Scotland's Historical Heraldry, 24.
[189] APS, I, 421–4; Chron. Fordun, 302; Chron. Bower, V, 409–11; Chron. Wyntoun, V, 128–9; RRS, IV, part i, no. 132.

The terms of this marriage agreement speak to concerns around succession, particularly confirming the rights of Margaret and her children to the succession should the male hereditary line fail.[190] With such concerns for the maintenance and stability of the dynasty, it is unsurprising that Alexander's most potent use of ritual to underscore the succession were vested in his eldest son and heir. As Cynthia Neville has recently demonstrated, Alexander and his advisors exerted considerable effort in the preparation of his son, also named Alexander, for his role as future king, including the creation of a separate household, the appointment of tutor-advisors and an education that provided him with skills in diplomacy.[191] With the creation of an appanage, or territorial endowment, for the young prince, including the lordship of Man in 1275, Alexander III marked his son out as his heir presumptive in a way that was familiar in Scotland, England and France.[192] Such public identification of the heir designate by Alexander reproduced and amplified the public oaths and ceremonies that William I used to mark out Alexander II as heir.

The marriage of young Alexander to Marguerite or Margaret of Flanders, daughter of Guy, count of Flanders, was a rite of passage that offered stability for the succession. While not as prestigious as a marriage to the daughter of a ruling monarch, this match strengthened Scotland's foreign connections and trade links with Flanders – one of the primary importers of Scottish wool – and allowed further extrication from English influences.[193] It also provided Alexander and his heir with an opportunity to host a royal marriage that promised the continuation of the dynastic succession. The date chosen to have the union 'solemnized in great state' was the Sunday after Martinmas – 15 November 1282 – or the eve of the feast day of St Margaret, the blessed ancestor of the dynasty.[194] With a major religious feast such as this, the celebrations usually began the evening before and often continued for a week after the feast day, meaning that the wedding and its wider celebration would likely have been imbued with liturgical associations to St Margaret.[195] The use of Masses and prayers across this extended period would thus have offered

---

[190] Ibid., no. 132, at 158, 162.

[191] Cynthia J. Neville, 'Preparing for Kingship: Prince Alexander of Scotland, 1264–1284', in Elizabeth Ewan and Janay Nugent (eds), *Childhood and Youth in Pre-Modern Scotland* (Woodbridge, 2015), 155–72.

[192] Ibid., 160.

[193] *RRS*, IV, part i, nos 133–5; *Inventaire chronologique des documents relatifs à l'histoire d'Écosse conservés aux Archives du royaume à Paris. Suivi d'une indication sommaire des manuscrits de la bibliotheque royale*, ed. Jean B.A.T. Teulet (Edinburgh, 1839), 3; Neville, 'Preparing for Kingship', 166–71. Duncan notes possible involvement of Edward I, as Guy of Flanders was allied with the English king against France; however, the terms of the agreements reflect exclusively Scottish concerns: *Making of the Kingdom*, 591–2. For a synthesis of research on Scottish trade and diplomatic links with Flanders, see David Ditchburn, 'Scotland and Europe', in Bob Harrison and Alan R. MacDonald (eds), *Scotland: The Making and Unmaking of the Nation, 1100–1707, Vol. I* (Dundee, 2006), 103–20, at 113–15.

[194] *Chron. Bower*, V, 409–11; *Chron. Fordun*, 302; *Chron. Wyntoun*, V, 135.

[195] Harper, *The Forms and Orders of Western Liturgy*, 53–7.

pertinent reminders of the sanctity of the dynasty and any offspring that the union might produce. Female saints provided important role models to medieval wives and queens. Turgot's *Life of St Margaret* was written in the twelfth century for her daughter, as she embarked on her role as queen, so the liturgy and sermons likely proffered advice for the bride to look to her saintly namesake as a guiding figure.[196]

The wedding was celebrated 'amid unbounded joy and compliments' of 'many Flemish knights and ladies' and Scottish prelates, nobles and knights at the royal burgh of Roxburgh. As for Alexander II and Marie de Coucy's wedding in 1239, the choice of location took advantage of a burgh situated on a primary trading route connecting the rich border abbeys with the port of Berwick, where the bride's entourage would have arrived (Map 2, see p. 37).[197] The specific space used for the marriage ritual is not clear, but the burgh and its environs provided a choice of elaborate high capacity venues, including Kelso Abbey and St John's church in Roxburgh.[198] Following the nuptials, the celebrations were said to continue with fifteen days of feasting.[199] While no financial accounts remain extant for 1282, *Exchequer Roll* fragments from 1264 to 1266, surviving in later copies, offer insight into the provisioning of the royal household at the royal hunting lodge of Forfar. In addition to large quantities of malt and flour for beer and bread, the accounts document that sheep, chicken, wildfowl and sixty stone of cheese were brought from a variety of nearby locations, beef and wild boar was collected from the adjacent – presumably royal – forests, and over eight hundred eels were brought from Loch Cluny in nearby Perthshire.[200] The account clearly indicates how foodstuffs were collected from the surrounding area, as seen at York in 1221 and 1251.[201] The surviving accounts also refer to the purchase of furs and cloth, imported and collected by Augustin the tailor from the fair at Dundee, and illustrates that Alexander's household was one that sought material comfort and sartorial display even in quiet times.[202] Indeed, Taylor's work on the thirteenth-century financial materials reveals that over this accounting period around two thirds of the expenditure went on hospitality and conspicuous consumption.[203] As such, with the addition of a handsome

---

[196] On St Margaret as a model for Scottish queens, see Amy V. Hayes, 'The Late Medieval Scottish Queen, c.1371–c.1513' (PhD thesis, Aberdeen, 2015), 23–4, 28–9, 42–5, 65–6.
[197] *Chron. Bower*, V, 409–11; *Chron. Fordun*, 302; *Chron. Wyntoun*, V, 135.
[198] The abbot of Kelso has long claimed equal status to bishop, providing the abbey with elevated status, and discoveries of substantial sarcophagi and carved masonry at St John's speak to the high status decorations and wealth of the burgh: Christine Henderson, *Kelso Abbey: A Brief History* (Kelso, 2012), 10–12; *Old Roxburgh, Floors Castle Estates, Kelso: An Archaeological Evaluation and an Assessment of their Results*, Document Reference: 52568.06 (Salisbury, 2004), 16–17, figs 1 and 6.
[199] *Chron. Fordun*, 302; *Chron. Bower*, V, 409–11.
[200] *ER*, I, li–lii, 7–9.
[201] See 39, 41–2, 55, 59–60, and Staniland, 'Nuptials of Alexander III', 20–45.
[202] *ER*, I, li–lii, 7–9.
[203] Taylor, *Shape of the State*, 385–7.

tocher for Marguerite partly paid, it is likely that the marriage witnessed much indulgence, excess and exuberant demonstrations of royal majesty.

A pronounced shift in young Alexander's own understanding of his royal status in the year prior to his marriage can be demonstrated in his manner of presenting himself in letters and seals. Neville evidences a shift from referring to himself as simply the son of the king of Scots to identifying as the 'firstborn son of the illustrious king of Scots' both in his letter texts and in the legend on his seal.[204] Such self-promotion, along with Alexander III's clear designation of his heir through means comparable to both his predecessors and European contemporaries, emphasise the fact that primogeniture was being normalised by the crown as the rule rather than the exception in Scotland. With the succession sealed in two marriage treaties and a male heir provided with the training for leadership, Prince Alexander's wedding must be considered a triumphant moment in Alexander III's ritual demonstrations. It could be considered curious then that such an occasion did not lead to a renewed pursuit of the rite of unction and coronation. At the relative peak of his political power, Håkon IV used the wedding of his son, Magnus, in 1261 as an opportune moment, witnessed by foreign – including a Scottish diplomatic envoy sent to bargain for control of the Hebridean islands – and native audiences, to have his son crowned in a full coronation having secured the papal approval to do so in 1247.[205] Reid proposes that Scottish kings only sought unction when politically expedient.[206] Perhaps as Alexander's bride was the daughter of a count, the necessity for the Scots to compete for parity – as found where marriages brought the Scottish king into the orbit of an anointed king – was not so pressing. Yet, in the previous year, Alexander III's daughter was married to the anointed king of Norway and the early 1280s was a period of relative confidence in which contemporary kings of comparable realms took advantage of embedding their position through papal rites that sanctified their kingship.

The relative influence of leading secular and religious lords in Norway and Scotland is something to pause and consider here. Bérgiant's work argues that there was a decline in the power of the nobility in comparison to the rapid acceleration in the role and power of the church in Norway, particularly in relation to kingship, following the creation of an archdiocese at Nidaros. Influential archbishops, such as Eystein Erlendsson, who sought to position the church as the most powerful player in king-making, can also be seen as a driving force in ritual development.[207] There was no comparative decline in the power of the nobility in Scotland, rather the evidence of rituals of kingship in thirteenth-century Scotland indicate that the nobility remained central to king-making. Bérgiant concludes that unction marked the king out as sacred, no longer *primus inter pares*, but invested with divine grace which

[204] Neville, 'Preparing for Kingship', 167–8.
[205] Brégiant, Vox Regis, 276–83.
[206] Reid, Alexander III, 5–41, particularly 41.
[207] Brégiant, Vox Regis, passim.

nobody in the nobility could pretend to', so arguably the Scottish nobility likely saw little benefit in the introduction of such a rite.[208] The most vigorous advocates of the Scottish efforts to gain sacral kingship through unction and coronation in the thirteenth century were Alexander II and his advisors, specifically Robert Kenleith, abbot of Dunfermline, a churchman with much to gain for his own abbey. However, there does not appear to have been a similarly motivated secular or regular cleric in the later reign of Alexander III encouraging the king to take advantage of this, despite many of the episcopal appointments of this period being men favoured by the king, including those who served as royal officials.[209]

Due to the lack of effort to secure unction by the adult Alexander III, Reid suggests limited interest in 'the overt symbolism of Christian kingship' and associates this with the fact that Scottish kings viewed themselves as 'first among equals'.[210] This chapter has demonstrated that there was a dominant secular core to the inaugural rituals of Scotland's thirteenth-century monarchs, but also emphasises the long term impact of religious men on the ceremonies that determined the ritual cycle of Scottish kingship. In comparison to Norway, a relatively recently Christianised kingdom, king-making rituals in Scotland had been permeated by Christianity and influenced by ecclesiastical men for centuries. Consequently, the ceremonies that emerged in thirteenth-century Scotland reveal the ways that secular and religious rites intertwined over time. There were occasions when unction and coronation were actively sought to create parity with other European kings, particularly – it would appear – when Scottish kingship was perceived vulnerable or when a Scottish king was in direct competition with an anointed king, particularly if he was English. Ecclesiastics were often proactive in such efforts, as found in comparable kingdoms from Norway to France. Though church and king sought independence from overbearing southern neighbours, the lack of an independent archbishop to head the Scottish church may also have affected the church's ability to dominate kingship ritual in the way that Bérgiant argues was the case in twelfth and thirteenth-century Norway, where even the secular election was increasingly permeated by church influence.[211] Despite this, the inauguration of Alexander III – particularly in the use of space for the enthronement – illustrates how the lines between secular traditions and ecclesiastical rites could easily become blurred over time. There were notable aspects of the inauguration that remained largely the domain of secular

---

[208] Ibid., 267–8.
[209] Reid discusses the high number of episcopal appointments required between 1274 and 1286, due to the general course of nature, which may have played into this situation: Reid, *Alexander III*, 239–42.
[210] Ibid., 32–7, quotes at 33 and 37.
[211] Brégiant, *Vox Regis*, particularly at 45–59.

actors, including acclamation, outdoor enthronement on a stone or throne, the recitation of the genealogy and the role of earls in raising the king to the throne, but Gesta Annalia I suggests that the bishop of St Andrews was involved in blessing the king once ensconced on his outdoor throne.[212] Many of the inaugural 'traditions' appear in the written record in detail for the first time in 1249, so their origins are obscure in some cases. Yet, the fact that ecclesiastical chroniclers of later centuries record the dominance of the secular elements underscores the limitations for the church, and their active endorsement of such traditions, in thirteenth-century king making.

The analysis of the cycle of death and succession in this chapter has identified the individuals, actions, influences and ideas that defined the rituals and ceremonies of kingship in thirteenth-century Scotland. Death and remembrance of the previous king were woven into the king-making process, and here – where limited evidence exists – ecclesiastical figures were notably prominent for obvious reasons: the last rite was a sacrament over which clerics had a monopoly. In a realm where succession by primogeniture was still a relatively new concept, a speedy inauguration was essential – even where the heir faced little real competition – which points to the importance of the ritualised actions in the process of king making. The haste could lead to a physical division of the royal court, but the funeral could be used to draw the court and country together, particularly with the heir positioned alongside the deceased king to emphasise the path of dynastic progression. Consequently, the funeral – and particularly the processional aspect – was an integral ritual element of succession. It functioned, as Griffith has suggested for medieval England, 'to sustain the institution of monarchy beyond the earthly life of an individual king' and appears to have been witnessed by a significantly larger audience than the inauguration.[213] The details of the treatment of the royal body in death are elusive as neither orders of ceremony for funerals nor financial accounts survive for this period. Exploring timelines, geographies and the identities of those who remained with a body can, however, allow for extrapolations about the role of clerics in preparing bodies for the funeral and the potential for separate heart and viscera burials. The use of processional elements that integrated funerals and inaugurations at times of potential instability feature conspicuously in surviving records. Public dynastic statements also underpinned the rituals that promoted the designation of young heirs by William I, Alexander II and Alexander III. The very creation of an heir designate was also a central phase in the cycle of succession, and marriage similarly presented opportunities for Scottish kings. However, with two of the marriages occurring in English territory and one for a minor, these weddings could also pose challenges to the projection of Scottish sovereignty, which was an ongoing concern throughout this century.

---

[212] Chron. Fordun, 289–90.
[213] Griffiths, 'Succession and the Royal Dead', 98.

There has been a tendency, undoubtedly created in the chaos that followed these reigns, to see the thirteenth century as a 'golden age'; one marked by increased royal authority, centralisation of power, expansion into the extremities of the realm and, arguably, one that witnessed royal power being firmly asserted. Yet, it was also a period of transition and development in a more piecemeal and gradual manner than one witnessing any rapid wholesale change. The rituals that defined Scottish kingship through the cycle of death to succession were similarly malleable: neither fixed nor complete. Prior to the 1280s, Scotland's kings were still in a process of negotiating their status within the realm and beyond. This was particularly notable in terms of the sacral nature of Scottish kingship and their status in relation to their southern neighbours. The necessity for rituals to respect and endorse the long-established process by which the Scottish nobility 'made' their kings as one from within their ranks was pronounced. Likewise, there were periods of confidence when efforts to secure unction and sacralise the kingship waned, but moments of political expediency when those aspects of ritual parity and full Christian majesty were sought more keenly. The subsequent crisis, however, was one in which Scottish fears about parity of kingship subsided in the face of threats to its very existence as a separate entity.

Genealogical Table 2   The Balliol and Bruce Dynasties.

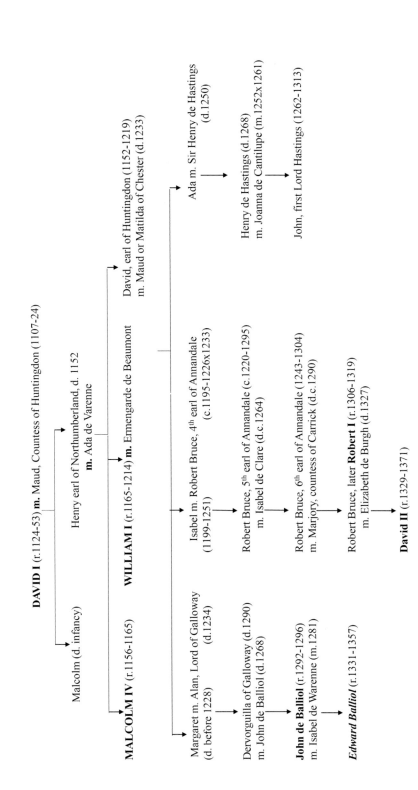

2

Contested and Compromised: Ceremonies and Succession under the Balliol and Bruce Kings

After the death of Alexander III in 1286 the subsequent decade saw the end of the established Canmore line, which was followed by a prolonged contest between claimants for the throne. The volatile political environment in which the Balliol and Bruce dynasties emerged and re-emerged as rulers required increased effort to secure legitimacy and created further obstacles in the negotiation of ritual status, both within the realm and beyond. In these circumstances, arguably, the most important audience for demonstrations of authority were those in Scotland, as the two dynasties vied for support. Yet, continued English – and to a lesser extent French – interventions meant that rituals of the Scottish ceremonial cycle of succession were, in some instances, recorded with more interest and detail by fourteenth-century English chroniclers than witnessed previously (with the notable exception of marriages between Scottish kings and English princesses). Complex circumstances tied to the succession litter this period: the Canmore succession crisis and rule of the Guardians (1286–92), the Great Cause (1290–92), the installation and removal of John Balliol (r.1292–96), Robert Bruce's usurpation (1306), the subsequent late birth of a Bruce heir (1324), the accession of a minor with a delayed coronation (1329–31), Scotland having two inaugurated kings from 1332 and the lack of a direct heir for the second Bruce king, David II.[1] Bannerman suggests that the succession crisis of the late thirteenth century resulted in 'abnormal circumstances' and this can be extended across all these events.[2] The impact of such abnormalities upon either individual rituals or the ceremonial cycle itself, the primary sources that they generated – particularly partisan chroniclers and English bureaucratic attention – and what an analysis of these reveals about kingship in the wider cultural and political landscape are the primary concerns of this chapter.

Periods of contested kingship, interregnum, English pretensions to overlordship, civil conflict and war with England dominated the late thirteenth and early fourteenth centuries in Scotland. This affected the secular and ecclesiastical individuals who made up the 'community of the realm' as much

---

[1] There is extensive literature on this period, but some good introductions include: Reid, 'The Kingless Kingdom', 105–29; Archibald A.M. Duncan, 'The Wars of the Scots, 1306–23', *Transactions of the Royal Historical Society* 2 (1992), 125–51; Brown, *Wars of Scotland, 1214–1371*, 157–254; Penman, '*Diffinicione successionis*', 43–59.
[2] Bannerman, 'The King's Poet', 137.

as it did those who claimed the right to rule. Historians have increasingly argued that this period reshaped the political community's expectations of the monarch and their own role in governance.[3] The accession of each new monarch often involved renegotiation. This chapter analyses the way in which Scotland's monarchs, and leaders of the Scottish political community, navigated kingship and the reassertion of royal authority through contested and even compromised rituals. It argues that the management, or indeed mismanagement, of the images and messages projected through the ceremonies of this period augment an understanding of this ongoing process of negotiation. Recent research has begun to explore how these dynasties attempted to forge their place in history through means of patronage, piety, liturgy and ceremony in a period dominated by war and conflict, but Robert Bruce monopolises these discussions just as the chronicles, epic poetry and histories promoting his narrative intended.[4] To widen the focus, this chapter builds on recent scholarship that has sought to unpick the subsequent undermining, blackening or even erasure of Balliol kingship during periods of Bruce and Stewart ascendancy.[5]

This chapter primarily considers the interlinking ceremonies at moments of dynastic crisis and contested succession, in the years between 1286 and 1306 and 1328 and 1332. A comparative approach has been adopted, particularly in discussions of the inaugurations of John Balliol and Robert Bruce and then those of David Bruce and Edward Balliol, to address issues of continuity and change. Weddings and the rituals involving Scottish queens do not feature as prominently, as all four kings were married prior to their

---

[3] See chapters by McQueen, Tanner, Penman and Boardman, in Brown and Tanner (eds), *Parliament and Politics in Scotland, 1235–1560*, 29–122; Roger Mason, 'Beyond the Declaration of Arbroath: Kingship, Counsel and Consent in Late Medieval and Early Modern Scotland', in Steve Boardman and Julian Goodare (eds), *Kings, Lords and Men in Scotland and Britain, 1300–1625: Essays in Honour of Jenny Wormald* (Edinburgh, 2014), 265–82; Penman, 'The King Wishes and Commands?', 125–41; Reid and Penman, 'Guardian – Lieutenant – Governor', 191–218.

[4] Michael Penman, 'Christian Days and Knights: The Religious Devotions and Court of David II of Scotland, 1329–71', *HR* 75 (2002), 249–72; Michael Penman, '"Sacred Food for the Soul": In Search of the Personal Piety and Devotions to Saints of Robert Bruce, King of Scotland, 1306–1329', *Speculum* 88 (2013), 1035–62; Lucinda H.S. Dean, 'Projecting Dynastic Majesty: State Ceremony in the Reign of Robert the Bruce', *International Review of Scottish Studies* 40 (2015), 34–60; Michael Penman, 'Who is this King of Glory? Robert I and the Consecration of St Andrews Cathedral, 5 July 1318', in Buchanan and Dean with Penman (eds), *Medieval and Early Modern Representations of Authority*, 85–104. Work on the guardianships prior to 1306, most recently by Norman Reid, considers material legacy through seals and charter titles: Reid and Penman, 'Guardian – Lieutenant – Governor', 200–5.

[5] Alan Young, *Robert the Bruce's Rivals: The Comyns, 1212–1314* (East Linton, 2001); Amanda G. Beam, *The Balliol Dynasty 1210–1364* (Edinburgh, 2008); Alan Young and George Cumming, *The Real Patriots of Early Scottish Independence* (Edinburgh, 2014). Edward Balliol is also the subject of forthcoming work by Andy King, 'Edward, by the Grace of God, King of Scotland: Perceptions of the Kingship of Edward Balliol, 1332–1356' (working paper). Thanks are due to Andy King for sharing this working paper with me.

accession. The exception is David II: his union to Joan Plantagenet, or of the Tower, occurred when David was a child, as part of his father's wider programme of ceremonial display. Consequently, this is analysed alongside Robert I's funeral to assess his use of ceremony in the consolidation of his dynasty. David's second marriage, as an adult, and other efforts to secure a line of succession are considered briefly in closing to address issues arising from his inability to father a son and the animosity toward his heir designate, Robert the Steward.

For a period in which death and violence were commonplace, it is curious that the place of death in the ritual cycle is less certain as circumstances detach it from the succession. Yet, as death *should* mark the start of a new revolution of the cycle of succession, so this chapter begins with a reassessment of the death and burial of Alexander III.

The Ritual Cycle Resumes: The Funeral of Alexander III

> I cannot recall having read of such a famous feast ever before in Scotland. But alas! an unusual feast of this kind a short time later brought forth for the Scots a fast, or that herald of sickness an insatiable hunger. ...Laughter is [always] mixed with grief, and mourning takes over from extremes of joy: after such splendour the kingdom lamented ingloriously, when a short time afterwards it lost itself and as a consequence its king.[6]

Ominous foreboding oozes from Walter Bower's fifteenth-century record of the wedding of Alexander III and his second wife, the French noblewoman Yolande of Dreux, in 1285. However, this is only possible with the hindsight gained by writing after the fact. Bower was not alone in amalgamating the marriage of Alexander III with his death and Scotland's subsequent descent towards crisis. Indeed, the more contemporary Franciscan *Chronicle of Lanercost* links the two events in more direct terms:

> At the feast of All Saints in this year, Alexander, King of Scotland, took a second wife, Yoleta by name, daughter of the Comte de Dreux, to his own sorrow, and to the almost perpetual injury of his kingdom...[7]

In *Gesta Annalia II* the two events are just chronologically concurrent with no sense of menacing portent. Rather, here, the chronicler eulogises Alexander's kingship and the peaceful times of his reign – a standard response to a monarch's death – before bemoaning Scotland's unhappiness at the loss of

---

[6] *Chron. Bower*, V, 419.
[7] *Chron. Lanercost*, I, 37–8. Little argues that the chronicle was composed by two individuals, based on stylistic shift, and that the first section (covering 1201 to c.1297) was composed between 1280 and 1297 by a Franciscan who travelled widely in northern England and southern Scotland: A.G. Little, 'Authorship of the Lanercost Chronicle', *English Historical Review*, 31/2 (1916), 269–79, at 272–6.

a leader who 'left no lawful heir'.[8] The latter statement was inaccurate in 1286 as Alexander had a living granddaughter, so *Gesta Annalia II* too was influenced by hindsight.[9] All three chronicles, collated during or after the turmoil that followed Alexander's death, tend to fixate on the subsequent crisis, rather than any mourning that may have taken place, and historians have largely – understandably, considering the impact of the crisis on the subsequent decades – followed in these footsteps. The aim here is to pause to consider Alexander III's funeral as the ceremonial starting point for a new rotation in the ritual cycle of kingship and succession, driven by the king it memorialised, even if the succession was rather more uncertain than it had been for some time.

The funeral of Alexander III, like many a Scottish royal funeral before and after, leaves little in the way of a paper trail. Scholars such as Steve Boardman and Penman have emphasised that a renewal of royal interest in Dunfermline as a royal mausoleum occurred under Alexander III, which makes this a sensible place to start.[10] Alexander III's first wife, Margaret (d.1275), and both of his sons, David (d.1281) and Alexander (d.1284), were all buried at Dunfermline and the king planned his burial in the same sacred space.[11] The mid-late thirteenth century saw royal mausoleums flourishing beyond Scotland. During the 1260s Louis IX (later canonised as St Louis) undertook a programme of rebuilding and reinterment at Saint-Denis near Paris. He installed matching tombs for his Capetian and Carolingian forebears to affirm the abbey's status as '*cimetière aus Rois*' to make powerful statements about dynastic and personal power.[12] In England, Westminster increased its royal ceremonial status: first, through the reinterment of Edward the Confessor and Henry III's elaborate tomb and, later, under Edward I, it took on a multi-functional role as both coronation church and royal mausoleum.[13] Hallam argues that competition between Louis IX and Henry III fuelled the elaboration of death rituals and mausoleum design.[14] Alexander III's involvement in the reinterment of his saintly ancestor Margaret as a minor, under the direction of Abbot Robert of Dunfermline, likely had a marked impact. However, SangDong Lee suggests that Alexander's interest in Dunfermline occurred most notably as an adult in the 1270s after the death of his wife.[15] A similar competitive desire may have underpinned

[8] *Chron. Fordun*, 304–5.
[9] Dating of *Gesta Annalia II*, see Broun, *Scottish Independence and the Idea of Britain*, 216–19.
[10] Boardman, 'Dunfermline as a Royal Mausoleum', 139–54; Penman, 'Royal Piety in Thirteenth-Century Scotland', 22–6.
[11] *Chron. Fordun*, 302; *Chron. Bower*, V, 403, 409–11; *Pluscarden*, 78–9.
[12] Erlande-Brandenburg, *Le Roi est mort*, 68–96, particularly 81–3, figs 131–51 (for images of tombs); Hallam, 'Royal Burial', 371–4.
[13] See Chapter 1, 32 n.64.
[14] Hallam, 'Royal Burial', 371–2, 375, 377.
[15] SangDong Lee, 'The Development of Dunfermline Abbey as a Royal Cult Centre, c.1070– c.1420' (PhD thesis, University of Stirling, 2014), 140–51.

Plate 5 'The Base Slabs of St Margaret's Tomb/ Feretory', Dunfermline Abbey, photographed by the author, October 2011

Alexander's choices, as this followed the completion date of Louis IX's project at Saint-Denis and coincided with increased tension with England after the accession of Edward I. There may be no extant record of Alexander III seeking unction and coronation, but this was not the only means of raising the status of his kingship and elaborating the cycle of succession in competition with his fellow monarchs.

The lack of extant tomb monuments at Dunfermline is problematic, but the base of St Margaret's tomb shrine survives and was crafted from highly polished black Frosterley marble (Plate 5). If Alexander III sought closer association with his dynastic and saintly heritage, using the same marble offered visual and physical links between his new scheme of burials and the tomb of St Margaret. The space that Alexander III's tomb inhabited has recently been the subject of some lively debate but, if proposals by Penman, Erica Carrick Utsi and Lee are accepted, the location of the tomb on the south aisle on the pilgrimage route towards St Margaret's feretory, at the far east end of the church, offered a further means of physically associating Alexander III with his saintly ancestor for the pilgrims making their way around the stations of the church.[16] Robert I's use of the same black Frosterley marble in his tomb design at Dunfermline in the fourteenth century further increases the likelihood that such material association existed across multiple generations.[17] Design influences for Alexander III may also have emanated from the arrival of Yolande of Dreux. Familial statuettes upon tomb chests, used as part of dynastic pious displays and popular in the Low Countries and northern France, were increasingly witnessed in Scotland by the fourteenth century.[18] In an environment of mounting concerns about the succession, such design features could be manipulated to emphasise his dynasty's lineage.

An extant Scottish poem (c.1290x1306) implies that Alexander's tomb remained unfinished.[19] Penman speculates that this – along with its actual positioning by the chapel of St John the Baptist in the south aisle – may speak to the wariness of the Dunfermline monks toward Alexander III's 'uncertain soul', as he died alone without final confession and thus could not be buried alongside shriven kings like David I and Mael Coluim IV.[20] While this proposition is convincingly argued, it suggests that the decision about where Alexander's tomb was positioned came after his death and that the monks, rather than the monarch, dictated this. With the sudden death of a king in his prime, Alexander's involvement in positioning his tomb may have been less, but having already buried his wife, prominently alongside David I, and his two sons at Dunfermline, it seems unlikely that this had not been decided. Choosing a position on the ambulatory route to St Margaret's shrine, as to sit in the direct path of visiting pilgrims and closer to St Margaret, seems to

---

[16] Lee, 'The Development of Dunfermline Abbey', 253–5, and plans of tomb arrangements, figs 4 and 4(2), 274–5; Michael Penman and Erica Carrick Utsi, *In Search of the Scottish Royal Mausoleum at the Benedictine Abbey of Dunfermline, Fife: Medieval Liturgy, Antiquarianism, and a Ground-Penetrating Radar Pilot Survey, 2016–19* (Stirling and Ely, 2020), 118–19. Martin MacGregor and Caroline Wilkinson posit that Alexander III was buried in front of the altar after the altar was moved eastward following the twelfth-century burials of David I and Mael Coluim IV, but the ground penetrating radar undertaken by Utsi does not seem to support this conclusion: 'In Search of Robert Bruce, part III: Medieval Royal Burial at Dunfermline and the Tomb Investigations of 1818–19', *IR* 70/2 (2019), 171–201, at 177–83. See also *Chron. Lanercost*, I, 42; Ian Fraser, 'The Tomb of the Hero King: The Death and Burial of Robert I and Discoveries of 1818–19', in Fawcett (ed.), *Royal Dunfermline*, 139–76, at 159–61.

[17] Michael Penman, 'A Programme for Royal Tombs in Scotland? A Review of the Evidence, c.1093–c.1542', in Michael Penman (ed.), *Monuments and Monumentality in Later Medieval and Early Modern Europe* (Donington, 2013), 239–53. 243–4. See 93–4 n.39.

[18] Anne M. Morganstern, *Gothic Tombs of Kinship in France, the Low Countries and England* (University Park, PA, 2000), 10–31. Yolande of Dreux's father's lands were primarily in the regions of Normandy and Ile de France with strong links to the Low Countries.

[19] '*Liber Extravagans*', ed. Dauvit Broun with A.B. Scott, in *Chron. Bower*, IX, 54–127, at 57, 77.

[20] Penman and Utsi, *In Search of the Scottish Royal Mausoleum*, 118.

speak to Penman's broader argument about placing tombs within an abbey church that functioned as a pilgrimage site and royal mausoleum.[21] While Dunfermline monks may have had concerns about the king's soul, it was also not unusual for royal tombs to be completed by the successor, as was the case for Henry III.[22] Moreover, in the turbulent years after 1290, it is perhaps unsurprising that finishing the tomb was not a high priority. Yet, in 1286 the full impact of the succession crisis had yet to be felt. The infant queen, Alexander's granddaughter Margaret Maid of Norway, to whom many of the leading nobles and clergy had sworn oaths in 1284, still lived.[23] But with Margaret in Norway and unable to be physically raised to the stone at Scone, it was imperative for the Scots to offer ceremonial continuity and dynastic stability in marking the king's death.

Gesta Annalia II records that the king was buried in state at Dunfermline, after meeting his end in an accident near Kinghorn on 19 March 1286, but it gives no date for the funeral nor details of the journey between these places.[24] Michael Brown posits that Alexander III was buried on 29 March, some ten days later; although the source of this information is unclear, it implies that time was taken to honour the king's death.[25] The distance from Kinghorn to Dunfermline is roughly thirteen to fifteen miles depending on the route: manageable in a day on horseback or a couple of days by foot, this journey was significantly shorter than distances covered by funeral processions discussed in Chapter 1. However, Alexander III's death was unexpected. He was not old or ill, as in William I's case when preparations were clearly made in advance to facilitate the speed of the subsequent ceremonies. The route taken is unknown. The southern coast of Fife had notable parish churches at Kinghorn-Wester (Burntisland), Aberdour and Inverkeithing that could have broken the journey into blocks of a few miles if travelling by land (Map 4).[26] From Kinghorn, the body could have been transported by ship to Inverkeithing or North Queensferry – a port at the crossing point from Fife to Edinburgh, south of Inverkeithing – due to the prominence of sea travel and ferry ports along the Fife coast.[27] However, a land journey would have extended the opportunities for vigils and public processions through the royal heartlands of Fife, and provided time for members of the elite to gather at Dunfermline for the funeral. An illustration of the funeral exists in the 'working copy' of Walter Bower's *Scotichronicon* (Plate 6) depicting four nobles carrying the coffin, covered by a rich cloth decorated with a large

---

[21] Penman and Utsi, *In Search of the Scottish Royal Mausoleum*, particularly 120–32.
[22] Duff, *Royal Tombs*, 72–81.
[23] Beam, *The Balliol Dynasty*, 90–1 (includes list of key individuals who swore the oath in 1284).
[24] *Chron. Fordun*, 304–5.
[25] Brown, *Wars of Scotland*, 157.
[26] 'Burntisland/ Kinghorn-Wester', 'Aberdour Parish Church', 'Inverkeithing Parish Church', *Corpus of Scottish Medieval Parish Churches*, https://arts.st-andrews.ac.uk/corpusofscottishchurches/sites.php. Date accessed: 28 February 2021.
[27] Barrow, *Scotland and Its Neighbours*, 207–8.

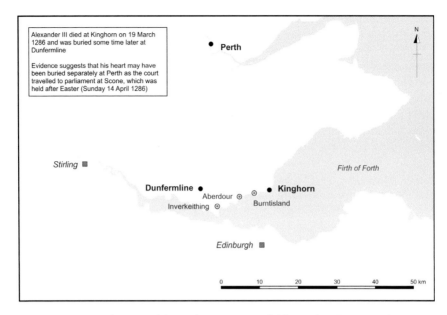

Map 4   Potential route of funeral procession of Alexander III, 1286. Contains Ordnance Survey data © Crown Copyright and database right (2023).

cross, followed by monks singing the offices of the dead. James I's funeral in 1437 was more contemporaneous with Bower's chronicle compilation in the 1440s and the clothing reveals fifteenth-century influences upon the illustrator.[28] Yet, William I's funeral in 1214 offered precedent for carrying the coffin in this manner, at least for part of the journey, and this would have been feasible whether the journey predominantly took place by land or sea.

Whereas the discussion of a separate heart burial in the case of Alexander II in Chapter 1 was necessarily speculative, a verse recalled by Bower notes that Alexander III's heart 'rests in peace in Perth' offering a more tangible indication that a separate heart burial occurred in 1286.[29] This would have required the evisceration and embalming of the king's corpse prior to leaving Kinghorn.[30] As the first parliament of Margaret's minority took place at Scone, not as Brown suggests at Dunfermline, Perth was situated between the site of burial and the meeting place of the inaugural parliament.[31] This

---

[28] On fifteenth-century clothing in 'working copy' of Bower, see *Chron. Bower*, IX, 169–76.
[29] *Chron. Bower*, V, 420–1.
[30] Kinghorn's parish church had received endowments from Scottish monarchs since the twelfth century making a suitable holy site for the preparation of and first vigils over the king's body: 'Kinghorn-Easter/Magna Kinghorn Parish Church', *Corpus of Scottish Medieval Parish Churches* (St Andrews and Stirling, 2008), https://arts.st-andrews.ac.uk/corpusofscottishchurches/sites.php. Date accessed: 28 February 2021.
[31] *Chron. Bower*, VI, 8–9; Brown, *Wars of Scotland*, 159.

Plate 6 'The Funeral of Alexander III' in *Scotichronicon*, Parker Library, Corpus Christi College, Cambridge, CCC MS 171, fol. 225v.

Plate 7   Seal of the Guardians [St Andrew and Lion Rampant], c.1292. Crown Copyright, National Records of Scotland, Laing Seal Impressions, RH17/1/17–18.

parliament – starting in late April, some fourteen to fifteen days after Easter (Sunday 14 April 1286) – selected six guardians to act in the monarch's absence at the site of royal inauguration, and these guardians likely undertook an oath in a ritual.[32] The choice of Perth for the burial of Alexander III's heart is thus of great importance to understanding how the ceremonial of death was drawn into these 'abnormal' circumstances. A separate heart burial at Perth amidst the liturgical feast of Easter, just two miles from the inauguration site where parliament would be held, extended the rituals of mourning and linked the king's death with the temporary succession of the guardians. Connecting all these elements together using processions and recognisable liturgy was a tangible means of placing the royal dignity, usually transferred to the new monarch in their inauguration, symbolically into the hands of the guardians for safekeeping.

Regnal years, Reid and others have argued, appear to start at the death of the previous monarch; however, in 1286 the inauguration and acceptance by God, as well as acclamation by nobles and clergy, were still critical for the transfer of royal dignity.[33] This is particularly potent in extant material culture evidence, as the guardians elected not to use a seal design with a direct reference to Margaret or her regnal years, but rather the lion rampant – symbol of Scottish royalty – and St Andrew on the cross – the patron saint of the realm and its political community (Plate 7).[34] Reid argues that the fact that the community could hold the royal dignity in this manner

---

[32] Reid and Penman have also recently posited that a ritual was likely: 'Guardian – Lieutenant – Governor', 204–5.
[33] Ibid., 202. See also, the Treaty of Birgham and the statement about seal and the importance of *'Deu, e a la église, e a la comunaté du reaume'* in making the monarch: *Documents Illustrative of the History of Scotland*, I, 162–73, at 169.
[34] Birch, *History of Scottish Seals*, 32–3.

implies that kingship was reliant on both hereditary right and election, which is a dichotomy recognisable in aspects of the Scottish inauguration.[35] This echoes broader European trends of political thought circulating in the later thirteenth century on the sovereignty of kings and the extent to which their power emanated from the people of the kingdom they ruled.[36] It also demonstrates an understanding of a concept of royal dignity as something that transcended the mortality of individual kings, as found in the idea of the king's two bodies.[37] While Alexander III's funeral came before the official selection of the guardians, the ceremonies employed leading up to the parliament reflected the ritual means by which the succession was managed throughout the thirteenth century and was thus an adaptation of tradition to circumstance. While immediate challenges made to Margaret's position in the subsequent parliament demonstrated the problems faced by those who actively sought to uphold her right to the throne, ceremonial statements underscore attempts made by the guardians to maintain the integrity of the realm and the royal dignity in the absence of the monarch.

From a 'Fixed' Election to Murder and Usurpation, c.1290–1306

With the death of Margaret in 1290, a contest for the Scottish throne began. The judicial process managed by Edward I to select a monarch from among the claimants to the throne, known as the Great Cause, marked a sizeable departure from the norm and placed the ritual accession of the victor in uncharted territory for Scotland, and indeed in a broader European context. However, it was still rooted in ideas of dynastic legitimacy and election by a political community.[38] Through the thirteenth century, inauguration was the primary means of attaining legitimacy, as it was a critical point at which the royal dignity was invested and was usually bound to death and funerary practices. Yet, in the two episodes of king-making analysed here, there was no body to bury or mourn. The child-queen Margaret died on her journey; she did not reach Scotland in 1290, or fulfil the marriage to Edward I's heir arranged in the Treaty of Birgham; rather her body was returned to Norway to be identified by her father and buried at Christ Church in Bergen.[39] The

---

[35] Reid, 'The Kingless Kingdom', 124–7.
[36] John Watts, *The Making of Polities: Europe, 1300–1500* (Cambridge, 2009), 43–157, particularly 73–98.
[37] Kanotorowicz, *The King's Two Bodies*.
[38] Described in a range of contemporary and near-contemporary chronicles, for example: *Chron. Melsa*, II, 252–6; *Chron. Buriensis*, 98–103; Thomas Gray, *Scalacronica, 1272–1363*, trans. and ed. Andy King (Woodbridge, 2005), 30–5; *Chron. Lanercost*, I, 84–5; *Chron. Hardyng*, fols clxii v–clxiii r; *Chron. Bower*, VI, 4–39; *Chron. Fordun*, 306–14. For further information on the Great Cause, see *Edward I and the Throne of Scotland, 1290–1296: An Edition of the Record Sources for the Great Cause*, ed. Grant Simpson and E.L.G. Stone, 2 vols (Oxford, 1977–78), *passim*, particularly, see I, 1–24; Brown, *Wars of Scotland*, 165–8; Beam, *The Balliol Dynasty*, 102–18.
[39] Knut Helle, 'Norwegian Foreign Policy and the Maid of Norway', *SHR* 69 (1990),

death that accelerated Robert Bruce's journey to the throne in 1306 was the murder of an enemy, while his predecessor still lived as an exile in Picardy.[40] As a result, a rupture occurred in the way that kingship traditionally transitioned and the funeral was temporarily dislodged from the ritual cycle. This section offers a comparative discussion of the inaugurations of 1292 and 1306 to analyse the way 'royal dignity' was invested when the natural hereditary cycle of succession was broken and what this can indicate about kingship. Five main areas emerge to address in this comparison: what facilitated the rise to kingship, attendees and officiators, regalia and the throne, the location of the ritual and, finally, the use of a crown and liturgical developments.

A small blessing in this complex period is a spike in the creation and survival of records, particularly due to the thirteenth-century English penchant for bureaucracy. Such evidence largely sits in the annals of partisan chroniclers and official records manufactured in times of conflict, which necessitates careful treatment of the narratives and records of these ceremonies.[41] The sources that record the accessions of John Balliol and Robert Bruce are many, but the detail they offer on specific ritual elements is often minimal: the events that facilitated accession attract far more attention in both cases. Nonetheless, the chronicles largely agree on the following basics. After being selected as king and receiving oaths from key Scottish lords and offering loyalty to Edward I, John's inauguration took place at the abbey of Scone on 30 November 1292. It was conducted in the manner deemed traditional for the realm – although there is minimal explanation of this – before John travelled to give homage to Edward I for the kingdom of Scotland at Newcastle.[42] Robert Bruce's inaugural ceremony also occurred at Scone between 25 and 27 March 1306 – the first being the Annunciation of the Virgin and the second Palm Sunday – during the crisis incited by the murder of his rival, John Comyn, on 10 February at Greyfriars in Dumfries.[43] Isabella, countess of Buchan and the adult representative of the earldom of Fife, enthroned

---

142–56, at 155–6. See also Geoffrey W.S. Barrow, 'A Kingdom in Crisis: Scotland and the Maid of Norway', *SHR* 69 (1990), 120–41; Michael Prestwich, 'Edward I and the Maid of Norway', *SHR* 69 (1990), 157–74; Brown, *Wars of Scotland*, 157–65.

[40] Note on naming: in this section Robert Bruce refers to Robert I (r.1306–29), and Bruce the Competitor (c.1215–95) refers to his grandfather and competitor to the throne in the Great Cause.

[41] A comparable set of records exist for the deposition of Richard II: *Chronicles of the Revolution, 1397–1400*, trans. and ed. Chris Given-Wilson (Manchester, 1993).

[42] *Chron. Melsa*, II, 256; *Chron. Buriensis*, 115; *Scalacronica*, 32–5; *Chron. Lanercost*, I, 86; *Chron. Hardyng*, fols clxii v–clxiii r; *Chron. Bower*, VI, 38–9; *Chron. Fordun*, 315; *Pluscarden*, 104; *Chron. Guisborough*, 238–9.

[43] Ibid., 367; *Chron. Fordun*, 333; *Chron. Bower*, VI, 317; *Pluscarden*, 176; *Scalacronica*, 50–3; *Chron. Lanercost*, 176. On the murder at Greyfriars, see Barbour, *The Bruce*, 78–81, bk. 2, lines 25–48. For secondary discussion see Ranald Nicholson, *Scotland: The Later Middle Ages* (Edinburgh, 1978), 71; Geoffrey W.S. Barrow, *Robert Bruce and the Community of the Realm*, third edition (Edinburgh, 2001), 145–8; Brown, *Wars of Scotland*, 199–200; Alexander Grant, 'The Death of John Comyn: What Was Going On?', *SHR* 86 (2007), 176–224.

and possibly crowned Robert, and the collected 'baronage' (usually largely unspecified) gave oaths of fealty to the new king.[44] There is less certainty here in the chroniclers' accounts, however, as to whether this was in 'the traditional manner' or not. Despite the brevity of detail on the two inaugural ceremonies, comparing how aspects of the rituals were treated in different texts can prove a fruitful exercise.

John Balliol's inauguration in 1292 is bookended by episodes of English intervention in his kingship: the judicial process of his election preceded it and his homage to Edward in Newcastle in December concluded it.[45] For most chroniclers, John's departure to make oaths of homage, which placed John and Scotland into vassal status, followed immediately after the inauguration. This potentially undermined the ceremony's role in legitimising John's kingship. Chronologically, one event did follow the other. Yet, for some chroniclers writing after the fact, particularly those promoting the victorious Bruce-Stewart line as rightful Scottish monarchs, the temptation to exaggerate this connection to prophesy John's downfall was too strong to resist. Bower and *Gesta Annalia II* record that John took his oaths of homage to Edward with only the support of a small number of key figures (all unnamed) and 'against the will… of the kingdom'.[46] By the later fifteenth century this had morphed into John 'shamelessly and most foolishly' undertaking homage to 'King Edward the tyrant' without consulting any of the barons, prelates or the community.[47] These chroniclers actively sought to reduce Scottish complicity in the Anglo-sponsored election and inauguration, and the subsequent oaths, by shifting the blame onto an individual pariah. Contemporary evidence, particularly documents produced by the English chancery that include witness lists recorded for surety of the process on Edward's part, contradict such sentiments. Indeed, they indicate a healthy Scottish attendance at the ritual process of selection and inauguration (see Appendix II, 'John Balliol').[48]

The inauguration of John in 1292 occurred on the feast day of St Andrew – 30 November – the same saint chosen by the guardians to represent the community on their interregnum seal.[49] Beam suggests that the choice of 20 November for John's pre-inauguration oaths provided a symbolic connection

---

[44] Isabel Comyn, Countess of Buchan, née MacDuff of Fife, recorded as *filia*/daughter of the earl of Fife (*Chron. Guisborough*, 367), acted as representative of her nephew, the under-aged ninth earl: Andrew MacDonald, 'Macduff family (per. c.1095–1371)', *ODNB* (2004), https://doi-org.uhi.idm.oclc.org/10.1093/ref:odnb/50328. Date accessed: 8 September 2022.
[45] *Chron. Melsa*, II, 256; *Chron. Buriensis*, 115; *Scalacronica*, 32–5; *Chron. Lanercost*, I, 86; *Chron. Hardyng*, fols clxiiv–clxiii r; *Chron. Bower*, VI, 38–9; *Chron. Fordun*, 315; *Pluscarden*, 104; *Chron. Guisborough*, 238–9.
[46] *Chron. Bower*, VI, 38–9; *Chron. Fordun*, 315.
[47] *Pluscarden*, 104.
[48] Appendix II, 'John Balliol'. For examples, see *Foedera*, I, pt. iii, 112–16; *Edward I and the Throne of Scotland*, II, 22–3, 44–5, 72, 80–5 [table of auditors], 101–5, 116–27, 252–3, 263.
[49] See Plate 7; see 74.

between Edward I and John as Edward's regnal year began on this date.[50] Yet, it is important to remember the largely Scottish audience of the events of November 1292. For this community, surely the symbolism of the inaugural date was more potent for imbuing John with legitimacy rooted in the guardianship, St Andrew and sovereign identity. As caretakers of the 'royal dignity' after Alexander III's funeral, the guardians sought Edward I's help to settle the dispute over who would be king and then passed the royal dignity to that individual, accompanied by the symbolic breaking of the guardians' seal (19 November 1292).[51] English incursions in 1292 were bound to create anomalies, not to mention challenging previous Scottish efforts to generate parity through the rituals of kingship. It is unwise, however, to underestimate the Scottish community's involvement in key ceremonial choices, or their complicity in the political process, which ultimately honoured ideals of choice and election.

The opposite was arguably the case in the inauguration of Robert Bruce in 1306, when a small number of individuals dictated the decisions made and actions taken with little in the way of choice or process. Even the pro-Bruce Scottish chroniclers relay a sense of urgency after the murder of John Comyn at Dumfries in 1306, when Robert Bruce took 'with him as many men as he could get, [and] hastened to Scone': a statement almost universally copied over the centuries.[52] Even Bruce's most fervent advocate, John Barbour, compiling his epic poem in the 1370s, admits that it was only after the inauguration that Robert was able to gather a fuller following and hints that, even then, it was gathered using more than loyalty.[53] The 'hastening to Scone' was likely a literary means of amplifying the drama of Bruce's journey to victory from the lowest depths, as over forty days lay between the murder and the inauguration – a period that later became the standard for allowing parliament to gather.[54] There is no definitive list of attendees in 1306 but Guisborough suggests that four bishops and five earls attended the ceremony, which was similar to that listed for John in 1292.[55] Records of Edward I's punishments of Bruce's supporters reveals the identities of some of the bishops and earls who were present, as well as pointing to other lesser barons, knights and squires, female members of Bruce's inaugural party and other Bruce family members who

---

[50] Beam, *The Balliol Dynasty*, 113–14.
[51] *Edward I and the Throne of Scotland*, 252–3.
[52] *Chron. Fordun*, 333; *Chron. Bower*, VI, 317; *Pluscarden*, 176.
[53] Barbour, *Bruce*, 88–9, bk. 2, lines 185–9. In the Old Scots verse, Barbour uses the word 'purchesand' in relation to gaining support, which is indicative of financial exchange: 'Owtane that he off the barnage/ That thidder come tok homage/ And syne went our all the land/ Frendis and frenschip purchesand/ To maynteym that he had begunnyn'.
[54] Surviving letter by an unknown individual writing from Berwick, who seems to be a Balliol/Comyn supporter, records how Robert sought to gather men to him in the southwest before leaving for Scone: 'News of the Earl of Carrick [1306]', in *Anglo-Scottish Relations*, no. 34, 130–4.
[55] *Chron. Guisborough*, 367. See also Appendix II, 'John Balliol'.

were involved (see Appendix II, 'John Balliol' and 'Robert I'). The number of named individuals in 1292 and 1306 could arguably indicate that, despite the supposed rush in 1306, the number of leading men in attendance may have been similar. Notable figures appeared on both lists, including the bishops of St Andrews and Glasgow, the earl of Menteith and James the Steward. In both cases attendance was relatively robust, but neither could boast a full complement of bishops and earls, and there were conspicuous absences from both ceremonies. This reflects the contested nature of the succession, which forced leading figures to choose sides, retreat to their own lands or ride the tide of favour between the options as best they could.

The earl of Fife – a key figure in the secular enthronement of the thirteenth century – was notably absent from both inaugural occasions due to Duncan, ninth earl of Fife, being both a minor (born c.1289x90) and held in English wardship.[56] The handling of this anomaly offers insight into the ceremonies and the messages that they projected. Guisborough's chronicle, and indeed Edward I, recognised the hereditary role of the earl to enthrone the king in a memorandum instructing *nostrum* (our) John de St John to take the role of earl of Fife because of the earl's minority.[57] In this choice, the secular nature of the Scottish enthronement remained intact and this neutral figure avoided any potential disquiet among the Scottish nobility that could have arisen by selecting one from their number. However, in not seeking a Scottish replacement, an English knight – not even a high-ranking earl – took one of the pre-eminent roles in making this Scottish king. Using a lower status English actor, who lacked traditional hereditary right, infers a decision made with little direct Scottish input; although, interestingly, there is no suggestion in the surviving records that there was any challenge or response to this incursion from the Scots, as one may have expected. By contrast, in 1306, a representative of the house of the earls of Fife was chosen to take the role. Isabel countess of Buchan, sister of the late earl of Fife and aunt to his heir, rejected her husband's loyalties to Balliol and the Comyns to support Robert Bruce.[58] Drawing Isabel into this role acted on tradition to underscore the Scottish nature of Bruce's inauguration in comparison to Balliol. Nonetheless, this choice arguably suggests that Bruce required the legitimacy offered by the closest hereditary figure to the earl of Fife, in a way that Balliol – chosen by a majority of his peers, then inaugurated on the stone of Scone and invested with the ancient Scottish regalia – did not.

---

[56] McDonald, 'Macduff Family'.
[57] *Chron. Guisborough*, 238–9; *Foedera*, I, pt. iii, 115–16. For more on the career of John de St John, see Malcolm Vale, 'St John, John de (d.1302)', *ODNB* (2004), https://doi.org/10.1093/ref:odnb/24499. Date accessed: 28 February 2021.
[58] *Chron. Guisborough*, 367. On Isabella's hereditary right, see footnote no. 44; Fiona Watson, 'Buchan (née MacDuff), Isabel, countess of Buchan (born c.1270, d. after 1313)', *ODNB* (2004), https://doi.org/10.1093/ref:odnb/54144. Date accessed: 28 February 2021.

John Balliol's reign did not end with his death – he was living in exile in France in 1306 – but his removal from the throne by Edward I in 1296 had a material impact on Robert Bruce's inauguration.[59] Following John's surrender to Edward, the chroniclers describe the ritual humiliation of John who was presented with a white baton (symbolising his surrender), stripped of his royal ornaments and taken to England along with 'the stone on which the king was enthroned'.[60] The English records illustrate what Penman has argued was essentially the beginning of 'a systematic removal' of objects emblematic of Scottish kingship, followed by the records that documented and empowered a sense of Scotland's history and identity.[61] Edward had used similar tactics of removing the tangible manifestation of royal power elsewhere, including Wales.[62] Some regalia items did not appear in Edward's collection, including the papal sword, and Bishop Robert Wishart, to whom Robert Bruce fled for absolution after the murder of Comyn, provided him with a robe (possibly made from purple episcopal vestments) and a royal banner.[63] Even so, it was not possible for Robert to be invested with the full regalia of his ancestors in 1306, nor was he enthroned on the stone at Scone. Materially this inauguration was lacking key legitimising objects used in the previous century. Yet, the chronicles are largely void of any reaction to the loss of these items or what impact this had upon Bruce's inaugural ceremony or Scottish kingship. Even in the extensive communications with the papacy rebutting Edward's claims to Scotland, known as Baldred Bissett's pleading (c.1301) and relayed in the *Scotichronicon*, the only material object mentioned for its forced removal is the royal seal – not the regalia or the stone.[64] Rather than suggesting that anything 'changed' due to the removal of such objects, the Scottish accounts of 1306 refer in standard terms to customary and traditional rites, with Bower and *Gesta Annalia II* even referring to 'the royal seat or throne' despite the removal of the stone.[65] References to rituals and ceremonies occurring in a traditional manner were not unusual in a Scottish or wider European context but, as so many traditional ritual objects

---

[59] For the fullest discussion of Balliol's downfall, see Beam, *The Balliol Dynasty*, 143–64.
[60] Quote from *Scalacronica*, 17–18. See also *Chron. Fordun*, 321; *Chron. Bower*, VI, 76–7; *Chron. Wyntoun*, V, 292–5; Grant G. Simpson, 'Why Was John Balliol Called Toom Tabard?', *SHR* 47 (1968), 196–9; Beam, *The Balliol Dynasty*, 159–61.
[61] *Documents Illustrative of the History of Scotland*, II, 142–6, at 144; Michael Penman, *Robert the Bruce, King of Scotland* (New Haven and London, 2014), 46–7.
[62] Marc Morris, *A Great and Terrible King: Edward I and the Forging of Britain* (London, 2008), 163–4, 192, 194–5, 200.
[63] 'News of the Earl of Carrick', 133; BL, 'Articuli proponendi contra Epi[sca]pum Glasguensis super consilio assensu et adhorentia per ip[su]m factis Roberto de Brus in principio rebellionis contra Angliæ', in BL Add. MS 4575, fols 247r–52v, at fol. 250v; *Scotland. Documents and Records Illustrating the History of Scotland, and the Transactions between the Crowns of Scotland and England, Preserved in her Majesty's Exchequer*, ed. Frances Palgrave (London, 1837), I, 366–7.
[64] *Chron. Bower*, VI, 168–89, at 186–9.
[65] Ibid., 316–17; *Chron. Fordun*, 333.

were absent in 1306, these specific references to tradition suggest efforts to smooth over glaring abnormalities.

The stone of Scone was in place for the inauguration of 1292, but the question of what John Balliol was enthroned upon offers an interesting case study to address the manipulation of the material objects of the inauguration for a chronicler's own purposes. For many of the chroniclers, and Edward I in a memorandum to his officials, John was simply raised upon a 'royal or kingly seat or throne' but three chronicles – including the relatively contemporary Walter of Guisborough – refer to a 'regal stone' as the throne itself or as a component of it.[66] Of those who do not mention the stone, *Gesta Annalia II* is of particular interest. A detailed insertion about the stone was made by the author of *Gesta Annalia I* into an earlier account of the inauguration of Alexander III, and this was unique. Yet, the stone was seemingly unimportant to the author of *Gesta Annalia II* in the mid to late fourteenth century. The ritual significance of this object is still debated, and the difference in focus may be indicative of the chronicle's complex makeup. Nonetheless, excluding an object previously promoted as 'reverently kept… for the consecration of the king…' from the description of John's inauguration implies efforts to undermine its legitimacy in comparison to Alexander III, or indeed to create less of a contrast between John and Robert Bruce.[67] When combined with the brevity of the content of this chronicle for John's reign – three entries, including the inauguration and the ritual dethroning, over a four-year period – *Gesta Annalia II*, or Fordun in his collation, actively attempted to diminish the worth of Balliol's kingship and the ritual actions that confirmed it.[68]

For Walter of Guisborough, writing c.1290 to 1305, the stone was of central importance in John's inauguration: it is one of the main features in his short account, alongside the oath made by John to his kingdom in accepting his kingship and the traditional role of the earl of Fife to enthrone the king.[69] Described as large, fashioned into or contained within a throne,

---

[66] *Chron. Melsa*, II, 256; *Chron. Buriensis*, 115; *Scalacronica*, 32–5; *Chron. Lanercost*, I, 86; *Chron. Hardyng*, fols clxiiv–clxiiir; *Chron. Bower*, VI, 38–9; *Chron. Fordun*, 315; *Pluscarden*, 104; *Chron. Guisborough*, 238–9; *Foedera*, I, pt. iii, 115–16.

[67] *Chron. Fordun*, 289–90, 315. These two episodes occur in different halves of the chronicle, as identified by Broun, but there are still aspects of the earlier chronicle (*Gesta Annalia I* to c.1285) that show signs of having been amended and adapted later, and the insertion about the stone is a prime example, see Broun, 'A New Look at *Gesta Annalia*', 13–17.

[68] Ibid., 315–16.

[69] *Chron. Guisborough*, 238–9; John Taylor, 'Guisborough [Hemingford, Hemingburgh], Walter of (fl.1290–1305)', *ODNB* (2014), https://doi.org/10.1093/ref:odnb/12892. Date accessed: 28 February 2021. Other chronicles recording the stone are from the fifteenth century, Pluscarden and Hardyng, and the latter may have used Guisborough as a source: *Chron. Hardyng*, fols clxiiv–clxiii r; *Pluscarden*, 104; Duncan, 'Before Coronation: Making a King at Scone', 167; Duncan, *Kingship of the Scots*, 141–2; Skene, 'Introduction', *Pluscarden*, xxv; Henry Summerson, 'Hardyng, John (born 1377x8, d. in or after 1464)', *ODNB* (2004), https://doi.org/10.1093/ref:odnb/12296. Date accessed: 28 February 2021.

Plate 8   John Balliol Great Seal [mounted and enthroned], c.1292. Crown Copyright, National Records of Scotland, Laing Seal Impressions, RH17/1/19–20.

the stone sat beside the high or great altar in the abbey church.[70] Both of these descriptions are fairly unique to Guisborough and might, at first glance, be presumed to refer to how the stone was encased in a throne and kept at Westminster Abbey by Edward I.[71] However, *Gesta Annalia I* previously makes reference to the stone being 'reverently kept' in the monastery at Scone, if not specifically in the church.[72] Duncan observed that, if the stone measuring 26.5 cm in height was not contained within some kind of seat or throne, sitting upon it 'would have entailed an undignified royal squat', and both Alexander III and John's Great Seals depict a far more elaborate throne than previous kings, perhaps capable of housing the stone (Plate 4, see p. 57, and Plate 8).[73] As such, Guisborough's account seems rooted in some logic and knowledge of the stone at Scone.

Vague comments that the inauguration occurred in the 'fashion or manner of the country' could imply an outdoor enthronement. However, Guisborough's account situates the stone within the church in 1292 and there is no comment about moving the stone outside for any part of the ceremony, so this casts some doubt on whether John was enthroned in the manner of his predecessor.[74] Practical considerations such as the weather, particularly in late November in Scotland, could have resulted in a change of plan even if an outside enthronement had been intended. Such circumstances could have accelerated the gradual 'liturgification' of the Scottish ceremony: that is, the

[70] 'Apud monasterium de Sconis positus erat lapis pergrandis in ecclesia dei iuxta maius altare concauus quidem et ad modum rotunde cathedre confectus': *Chron. Guisborough*, 238–9.
[71] Binski, *Westminster Abbey and the Plantagenets*, 135–8.
[72] *Chron. Fordun*, 289–90.
[73] Duncan, *Kingship of the Scots*, 140.
[74] *Chron. Guisborough*, 238–9. Others record the stone as a relic kept within the abbey, but the impression is that it is brought outside for enthronement: *Chron. Fordun*, 289–90.

long-term process that saw parts of the rite, such as the Mass, move inside the church prior to 1292.[75] Edward I had little to gain from making connections with the divine for the Scottish monarchs, but by holding the entire event within the church, organisers could control access to the space at a time when there were prominent members of the Scottish political community who did not support John's accession. However, if John was not raised to the throne in a truly public space, this could detrimentally affect the legitimacy that the inauguration sought to secure for a Scottish audience, particularly as subsequent inaugural and coronation rituals would suggest the outdoor enthronement retained or regained importance.

Both English and Scottish ecclesiastics and nobles were present for oath-giving ceremonies at Norham (20 November) and Newcastle (25 and 26 December) in 1292, so it is likely that many attended the inauguration. The lists include the pre-eminent bishops of Scotland, William Fraser, bishop of St Andrews, and Robert Wishart, bishop of Glasgow, in addition to John Sanford, archbishop of Dublin, Anthony Bek, bishop of Durham, William de Luda, bishop of Ely, and John de Halton, bishop of Carlisle.[76] Extant sources do not record the roles undertaken by these ecclesiastics, but the Scottish prelates were unlikely to relinquish their hard-earned ritual gains in the inauguration Mass. Beam has pointed to the likely central roles of the bishop of St Andrews and the bishop of Durham, due to their involvement in securing the kingship for John.[77] The lack of overt ecclesiastical involvement in John's inauguration may be symptomatic of Edward I's desire to restrict divine connotations attached to Scottish kingship, but it also reflected the secular nature of the Scottish ceremonies.

Edward I's letter to the French jurors during the Great Cause, recorded by Bower, stated that Scottish kings were 'not crowned or anointed, but only set on a certain royal seat by the earls, magnates and prelates of the kingdom in place of coronation'.[78] Henry III had continually sought to intercept Scottish efforts to seek parity through unction in preceding reigns and Edward was keenly aware how ritual could reinforce his superiority as a king. Indeed, he received evidence direct from the Scots about the right of secular earls to elect, enthrone and confer the honours of the realm upon the king through the 'Appeal of the Seven Earls', one of a number of appeals by Bruce the Competitor between September 1290 and May 1291.[79] References to seven earls or ancient kingdoms had a long heritage so, while the appeal is dubious in its authenticity, there were precedents for its claim and, in stressing the rights of the nobility in making Scottish kings, it offered evidence of a dispar-

---

[75] Duncan, *Kingship of the Scots*, 150.
[76] *Foedera*, I, pt. iii, 112–13. See Appendix II, 'John Balliol'.
[77] Beam, *The Balliol Dynasty*, 112–13.
[78] *Chron. Bower*, VI, 10–11.
[79] 'Appeal of the Seven Earls' and for discussion of date, see 44, fn. 2; Penman, '*Diffinicione successionis*', 46–8; Duncan, *Kingship of the Scots*, 137.

ity that emphasised the pre-eminence of English kingship in Edward's eyes.[80] Thus, the desire of members of the Scottish community to retain a place in the inaugural process gave Edward the fuel he needed to retain a sense of distance between the extravagant liturgical coronation he received and the largely secular inauguration of his counterpart. That this was accepted by the Scots, however, suggests the ceremony was one in which the attending Scots felt their major expectations had been fulfilled.

Both contemporary and later accounts illustrate confusion as to whether John was crowned by the hand of another in 1292.[81] This was hardly a new conundrum for chroniclers. Scottish kings certainly had a crown as one was removed with the other regalia in 1296. Yet, as Duncan has posited, the Scottish inauguration likely saw the king wearing a crown that he placed on his own head rather than being invested with it by another, as expected, in a full coronation.[82] Edward sought to maintain the secular, and to him inferior, nature of the Scottish inauguration to his own advantage. Consequently, it is unlikely that he sanctioned the crowning of John Balliol by another's hand when this would have raised the status of the Scottish king. There were no such constraints on the ritual actions for Robert Bruce in 1306. Despite the removal of ceremonial objects by Edward in 1296, various accounts refer to the crowning of the king including Guisborough, the fifteenth-century *Book of Pluscarden* and a communication recording that an Englishman, Geoffrey de Coigners, had concealed 'a certain coronet of gold with which Robert de Brus lately caused himself to be crowned'.[83] The latter statement could indicate that Robert placed the crown on his own head. Equally, it may accuse Robert of something more heinous: inducing others to undertake the action in a manner above the station of the Scottish king, as the English saw it, and tradition maintained so far.

There is good reason to suggest that Bruce – guided by Robert Wishart, bishop of Glasgow – took a more obvious liturgical and ritual leap into the unknown in 1306. John Watt has proposed, when discussing Philip IV of France, that where authority was openly threatened, or a king felt 'wounded', it often created some of the most absolute statements of royal prerogative.[84] Bruce could have made no clearer statement to his own attending subjects and Edward I than to have himself anointed and crowned as king, taking the right that his Canmore ancestors had sought and not received. While Scotland did not receive the papal bull permitting unction and coronation until 1329, it is possible that the bull provided retrospective permission as found in other medieval kingdoms, such as Norway. Here unction – unsanctioned by the papacy for almost a century – was introduced by leading ecclesiastics to bolster

---

[80] See 27.
[81] *Chron. Hardyng*, fols clxii v–clxiii r; *Chron. Lanercost*, 86; *Chron. Fordun*, 315; *Foedera*, I, pt. iii, 115–16; Buchanan, *History*, 395–6.
[82] Duncan, *Kingship of the Scots*, 138–9.
[83] CDS, II, no. 1914; *Chron. Guisborough*, 238–9; *Pluscarden*, 104.
[84] Watt, *Making of Polities*, 90.

kingship in times of civil war and crisis, while also empowering the church within the political community at the expense of the nobility.[85] Robert Bruce had committed a heinous crime in February 1306 when he murdered John Comyn in church, and he turned to Bishop Wishart for absolution.[86] Wishart may have pushed for anointing for his own peace of mind, to absolve Robert and cleanse (or re-baptise) him in readiness for receiving the crown, as much as for the aggrandizement of Bruce.[87] However, considering the suggestion in a contemporary letter about Robert's actions in 1306 that he promised to 'abide under the direction of the clergy' in return for his absolution, Wishart may also have taken a tactical opportunity to embed a liturgical church-controlled rite at the heart of Scottish king-making.[88] Such an action would have run counter to papal restrictions on both Scottish royal and ecclesiastical power, but it was not without wider European precedent. The crowning and possible anointing likely took place on the prominent religious Feast of the Annunciation of the Virgin (25 March).[89] Penman argues that the idea of baptism and renewal continued in the subsequent Palm Sunday Mass over which William Lamberton, bishop of St Andrews presided.[90] Such a ceremony, echoing Christ's entry into Jerusalem, would have been heavily laden with rich religious symbolism appreciated by all in attendance.[91] The challenges to Scottish kingship that emerged in this period – particularly through the stripping of royal power from John Balliol in 1296 and the crisis arising from the murder at Greyfriars – created the perfect storm for driving forward liturgical demonstrations of the divine nature of Scottish kingship.

Wishart and Lamberton denied their presence at Scone, initially, for their own personal preservation, but both were present in 1306 and these individuals were specified as the churchmen who 'traditionally' invested the monarch in the bull of 1329.[92] Moreover, Edward I's reaction to the ceremony

---

[85] Bagge, *From Viking Stronghold to Christian Kingdom*, 59–60, 159–69; Brégiant, *Vox Regis*, *passim*, particularly 33–59.
[86] 'News of the Earl of Carrick', 133.
[87] Penman, *Robert the Bruce*, 96–7. See also T.A. Boogaart II, 'Our Saviour's Blood: Procession and Community in Late Medieval Bruges', in Kathleen Ashley and Wim Hüsken (eds), *Moving Subjects: Processional Performance in the Middle Ages and the Renaissance* (Amsterdam, 2001), 69–116, at 70–2; Dale, *Inauguration and Liturgical Kingship*, 77–8.
[88] 'News of the Earl of Carrick', 133.
[89] On the prominence of Marian worship in Scotland, see Audrey-Beth Fitch, *The Search for Salvation: Lay Faith in Scotland 1480–1560*, ed. Elizabeth Ewan (Edinburgh, 2009), 113–50.
[90] Penman, *Robert the Bruce*, 97; Penman, 'Who is this King of Glory?', 85–104.
[91] The same religious festival used for the ceremonial for James I's entry to Edinburgh in 1424, see Chapter 3, 137–40. For more on the Palm Sunday liturgy see Harper, *The Forms and Orders of Western Liturgy*, 51–3, 137–52.
[92] For denial: BL, Add. MS 4575, fols 247r–52v; *Scotland. Documents and Records*, I, 366–7. For involvement of the bishops in 1306, see *Chron. Guisborough*, 367; *Pluscarden*, 176; 'Notice of a Manuscript of the Latter part of the Fourteenth Century, entitled *Passio Scotorum Perjutatorum*', trans. and ed. James Stuart, PSAS 19 (1884–5), 166–92, at 167–84; 'News of the Earl of Carrick', 133. For bull of unction, see 'XXX. Bull of John

was extreme and all involved felt his wrath, with vicious attacks on Bruce's family and adherents.[93] Scone Abbey was under scrutiny until at least 1307, with searches carried out for relics and other valuable items; Henry Mann, abbot of Scone, along with Bishop Lamberton, Bishop Wishart and Isabella, countess of Buchan, were all imprisoned and the last was infamously placed in a wooden cage at Berwick.[94] On hearing of the capture of Wishart, Edward I proclaimed he was 'almost as much pleased as if it had been the earl of Carrick [Robert]'.[95] Sonja Cameron and Alasdair Ross highlight the relatively quick release of Lamberton in comparison to Wishart, whose exile continued until 1315 along with Bruce's queen and other female relatives.[96] The length of incarceration and severity of punishment were equally harsh for Isabella, countess of Buchan, implying that these individuals were seen as on a par with Bruce's queen in value and treachery.[97] This suggests that they had gone beyond merely assisting Bruce in raising himself to the throne in the manner of his predecessors; rather, they were involved in creating an occasion designed to make the Scottish king an equal to his English rival and remove any lingering undertones of subservience.

John Balliol and Robert Bruce both required an inauguration that provided and enforced the legitimacy of their rule without the usual integration with the funeral of a predecessor. Balliol had won the legitimate contest for the throne with the support of a large proportion of the Scottish political elite and, although his kingship was rapidly undermined, it is essential to remember this. Later Scottish chroniclers have coloured the narratives of each king to respectively undermine the legitimacy of John and distance Robert from a tainted legacy. Even with these interventions, extant details highlight that abnormalities within the 1292 rituals did not destabilise John's kingship, at least initially, whereas every ritual effort was vital for the legitimacy of Bruce's kingship. Yet, John's inauguration did little to continue efforts to secure ritual parity for the Scottish kingdom. The questionable nature of Robert's claim and instability it generated, on the other hand, potentially saw a major cere-

---

XXII Concerning the Coronation of the Kings of Scotland', in *Facsimile of the National Manuscripts of Scotland*, 3 vols (Edinburgh, 1867–72), II, 24–5.
[93] For a range of entries that touch on collaborators and punishments, see CDS, II, nos 1771–1963.
[94] CDS, II, nos 1777, 1780, 1785–86, 1812–16, 1818, 1824–25, 1827–28, 1903 (refers to a letter of February 1307 from Clement V to Edward I regarding the 'translation' of important documents – including charters dating back to David I – from Scone to the abbey at Reading), 1906; CDS, III, no. 24.
[95] Ibid., II, no. 1786.
[96] Sonja Cameron and Alasdair Ross, 'The Bad Bishop: Robert Wishart and the Scottish Wars of Independence' (working paper); Penman, *Robert the Bruce*, 158. Many thanks to Alasdair Ross for sharing this unpublished collaborative work on Robert Wishart with me.
[97] The last mention of Isabella, countess of Buchan, is at Berwick in 1313 but she is not listed amongst those released in 1315 suggesting she died in captivity: CDS, II, no. 313; Penman, *Robert the Bruce*, 158.

monial shift propelling the Scottish inauguration toward ritual parity, despite, or even due to, the violent English efforts to retain superiority.

The Rise of the Bruce: Ambitious Displays and Dynastic Challenges

And from that day many of the Scots went back, and clave no longer his company; so that his kingdom was divided, and confusion came upon them, for a nation rose against his own nation, together with the English army…[98]

This extract from a fourteenth-century English parody poem is unsurprisingly hypercritical of Robert I's rise to kingship, but it identifies a crucial reality about his early reign. Despite the efforts to legitimise Robert's kingship in his inauguration, he was not viewed as the rightful king of Scots by many Scottish peers and subjects, nor by various foreign contemporaries. Indeed, for the former, he had usurped the throne from its rightful heir and killed the man who protected the legitimate succession; for the latter, he was a sacrilegious murderer rapidly excommunicated. Even once Robert had successfully laid waste to his enemies and won support through military successes, such as Bannockburn (1314) and the siege of Berwick (1318), his hold on power was one that needed continued authentication in the eyes of others. He employed ceremony as one of many means of affirming and validating his kingship.[99] For example, following the successful siege of Berwick in 1318, Penman has demonstrated how Robert manipulated the liturgical calendar and its associated rituals. Robert's entry to the town of Berwick was fused to Palm Sunday celebrations, as was the case in 1306, and in the wake of excommunication he managed to create an 'impressive royal, church and state occasion' around the consecration of St Andrews Cathedral on 5 July 1318.[100] This event marked an increasing confidence in his kingship, but it was also reactionary and fuelled by necessity. His kingship and the stability of the realm were open to internal threats, such as the Soules Conspiracy (1318–20), and outside censure, including reinforced excommunication from 1318 to 1329

---

[98] 'Passio Scotorum Perjuratorum: Omelia Ejusdem', 173.
[99] On patronage and piety, see Penman, *Robert the Bruce*; Penman, 'Sacred Food for the Soul', 1035–62. The Declaration of Arbroath is a prime example of Brucian propaganda; see Alice Taylor et al., 'The Declaration of Arbroath: A New Dynamic Digital Edition', *The Community of the Realm. 1249–1424: History, Law and Charters in a Recreated Kingdom* (COTR project, 2019), https://cotr.ac.uk/guidelines/dynamic-declaration-arbroath/. Date accessed: 28 February 2021; Grant G. Simpson, 'Declaration of Arbroath Revitalised', *SHR* 56 (1977), 11–33; Roland Tanner, 'Cowing the Community? Coercion and Falsification in Robert Bruce's Parliaments', in Brown and Tanner (eds), *Parliament and Politic in Scotland, 1235–1560*, 50–73, at 55–61; Barrow (ed.), *The Declaration of Arbroath*, *passim*. On ceremony, see Dean, 'Projecting Dynastic Majesty', 34–60; Penman, 'Who is this King of Glory?', 85–104.
[100] Ibid., 91–100.

and the consistent refusal of recognition by the English king.[101]

Similarly problematic was the issue of succession. For much of his reign, Robert had no legitimate sons and had lost all his brothers in the fight for the kingdom by 1318.[102] While the birth of twin sons, John and David, in 1324 was a significant success that led to an increased flurry of patronage and provided an important ritual focal point, Robert was already fifty years old and had suffered bouts of debilitating illness since at least 1308.[103] Death and the royal succession were at the centre of the king's concerns in the closing years of his life. In 1328, following the deposition of Edward II of England in 1327, Robert was finally able to secure a peace with England that included a recognition of his kingship and a betrothal for his surviving son, David.[104] The wedding of his son allowed Robert one of his most obvious opportunities to level the playing field with England. However, preparations for the king's death punctuate the same financial records that facilitate an analysis of the wedding. This reveals the unambiguously intertwined nature of these two ceremonies and is the reason why these events are analysed side-by-side rather than one after the other in this chapter. The first substantive run of *Exchequer Rolls* includes the final two years of Robert's reign and provides invaluable insight, particularly as neither event receives much coverage in the narrative accounts.[105] The volume of evidence for these ceremonies in the financial accounts confirms that a minimal entry, or even the absence of information, in the narrative chronicles does not automatically reflect a lack of investment in that event by the Scottish crown.

The main costs associated with the wedding of David and Joan of the Tower were £2,300, excluding smaller entries and additional supplies in livestock and other goods, despite financial challenges faced toward the end of the reign.[106] Supplies came from the locality and abroad. Basics such as grain,

---

[101] Michael Penman, '"A fell coniuracioun agayn Robert the douchty king": The Soules Conspiracy of 1318–1320', *IR* 50 (1999), 25–57; Barrow, *Robert Bruce*, 233–311; Penman, *Robert the Bruce*, 149–295.

[102] Ibid., 101–5, 177–93; Colm McNamee, *The Wars of the Bruces: Scotland, England, Ireland, 1306–1328* (East Linton, 1997), 31–3, 37–8.

[103] Barrow, *Robert Bruce*, 418–19; Penman, *Robert the Bruce*, 302–4; Matthew H. Kaufman and William J. MacLennan, 'King Robert the Bruce and Leprosy', *Proceedings of the College of Physicians* 30 (2000), 75–80.

[104] Sonja Cameron and Alasdair Ross, 'The Treaty of Edinburgh and the Disinherited (1328–1332)', *History* 84 (1999), 237–56; Penman, *Robert the Bruce*, 282–91.

[105] *ER*, I, 59–260. Examples of narrative sources: *Chron. Fordun*, 345; *Chron. Bower*, VII, 42–5, epitaphs for Robert, 47–57, and record of heart on crusade, 64–7; *Chron. Lanercost*, 260–1, 264; BL, Old Chronicle, Harley MS 4690, fol. 75r; BL, Monachus de Bridlington, Harley MS 688, fols 316v–317r. Barbour has a longer section for marriage and the death of Bruce, which includes a crowning of David and Joan and a deathbed scene for Bruce, but the wedding and funeral receive only generic descriptions: Barbour, *Bruce*, 746–7, 754–7, bk. 20, lines 85–111, 294–308.

[106] Penman suggested £1,000 for this ceremony, but the three 'bulk' costs from the accounts total £2,308, 11s. 4 d. and there are several smaller individual entries and incoming livestock and goods recorded: *ER*, I, 118–19, 149, 185; Michael Penman, *David II*

flour, malt, barley, oats, beef, mutton and fifty-six casks of wine arrived at Berwick brought from around the Scottish realm.[107] Two foreign merchants – *Petrus machinarum*[108] and Thomas de Carnato – purchased exotic goods on commission, ranging from foodstuffs – such as pepper, cinnamon, olive oil, galangal, cumin, a bale of ginger (1,060 lbs), 40 lbs of saffron and sugar of varying quality – to silks and precious metals.[109] These means of procuring goods may seem normal, but the wedding of 1328 marks the first occasion when the Scottish financial sources yield sufficient material to assess the scale of ceremony and feasting found at an extraordinary event. Even the smallest details offer more of the picture: payments to repair a wall around the cemetery of the Trinity church in Berwick that imply a sizeable crowd collected and damaged the structure.[110] The makeup of this crowd is unknown, but their desire to view the spectacle left physical traces.

The accounts are similarly revealing for the funeral of Robert I, as narrative records predominantly focus on the king's deathbed speech and the posthumous crusade of Bruce's heart, under the keeping of Sir James Douglas, rather than the funeral.[111] The epic poem *The Bruce* (c.1375) records the most detail: it explicitly refers to the disembowelment and embalming necessary for the removal of Bruce's heart and suggests an extended period of grieving and vigils.[112] Even so, beyond the statement that 'they took him to Dunfermline with great ceremony and solemnity', there are no details of the funeral procession from Cardross, where Bruce died, to his chosen burial site of Dunfermline, nor the rituals that occurred in the abbey.[113] The financial accounts add rich detail to these bare bones. For example, the use of torches and candles in funerary liturgy had a long tradition across Europe, and the volume of wax, weight and type of candles and torches used in a funeral was increasingly important during the fourteenth century as an indication of status and intended to harness the apotropaic power of candles for the deceased.[114] The weight and type of individual candles used in 1329 are not discernible, but the overall volume of wax purchased for torches and candles weighed near 9,000 lbs.[115] This was directly comparable with French kings

---

(Edinburgh, 2005), 18–19. On the financial issues, see Penman, *Robert the Bruce*, 290–4.
[107] *ER*, I, cxvi–cxvii, 185–92.
[108] Translated in the preface to the exchequer rolls as 'Peter the machinist': *ER*, I, cxiii–cxv.
[109] NRS, Exchequer Records: Exchequer Rolls, June 1328, E38/7; *ER*, I, cxiii–cxv, 118–19, 149–50. Thomas de Carnato produced a full list of goods purchased that remains extant.
[110] Ibid., I, 217–8.
[111] *Chron. Fordun*, 345; *Chron. Bower*, VII, 44–5, 64–5; *Chron. Lanercost*, 264; Barbour, *Bruce*, 748–57, bk. 20, lines 153–308.
[112] Ibid., 757, bk. 20, lines 277–98.
[113] Ibid., 756, bk. 20, lines 299–301. Old Scots: 'Has ressavyt in gret daynté,/ With gret fayr and solemnyté,/ Thai haiff had hym to Dunferlyne'.
[114] James Monti, *A Sense of the Sacred: Roman Catholic Worship in the Middle Ages* (San Francisco, 2012), 597–8, 600–1, 615–26; Duffy, *Royal Tombs*, 23–4, 107–8.
[115] NRS, Exchequer Records: Exchequer Rolls, July 1329–December 1329, E38/9–10;

of the early fourteenth century – a third of the costs of the funeral of Louis X (d.1316) went on 7,000 lbs of wax and the illuminations attracted commentary from contemporaries, while Philip V's funeral included 13,000 lbs of wax for the illuminations in 1322.[116] Robert may have witnessed Alexander III's funeral in 1286, which likely drew on the Catholic traditional use of candles and torches, and the elaborate funeral and subsequent anniversaries for Edward I's queen, Eleanor of Castile, while present at the English court in the 1290s.[117] Moreover, Robert likely took a final opportunity to directly position himself as superior to Edward II (d. 1327), whose solemn exequies appear to have been void of candles despite conforming to many other standard traditions.[118]

One of the main uses of candles in comparable funerals was to decorate the 'hearse' or wooden chapel erected over the body of the deceased, and the financial records illustrate that such a structure was raised for Robert I at Dunfermline. This is the first known reference to this kind of structure in a Scottish ceremony. The sixteenth-century funerals of James V and his wife Madeleine also featured such structures, richly decorated with hundreds of heraldic escutcheons and, in James's case, depictions of weapons of war.[119] The chapel structure at Dunfermline was painted and richly decorated with black material, candles and 2 lbs of gold leaf.[120] Though undescribed, the painted decoration likely depicted heraldic or dynastic symbols, which the Scottish crown had increasingly incorporated in other material representations, such as the use of the lion rampant on coins and seals since the thirteenth century.[121] Heraldic designs likely also featured in the wedding ceremony the previous year. Food was increasingly used in royal displays in ways that moved beyond the sheer quantity provided and exotic ingredients involved, and heraldry commonly featured in such designs.[122] In 1328 purchases of large quantities of almonds, loaves of sugar and 'colours for food' could point to ingredients used to form marzipan or sugar paste to create

---

ER, I, 150–1, 193, 232. The funeral liturgy would have extended beyond the immediate ceremony with wax used across this elongated liturgical performance.

[116] Brown, *The Monarchy of Capetian France*, see 'The Ceremonial of Royal Succession in Capetian France, the Funeral of Philip V', 251, and 'The Ceremonial of Royal Succession in Capetian France: The Double Funeral of Louis X', 231.

[117] Penman, *Robert the Bruce*, 20–1, 31–2; Duch, 'Royal Funerary and Burial Ceremonies', 219–22.

[118] Ibid., 150–1, particularly fn. 197.

[119] For examples: NRS, E21/32, fols 11v, 26; E21/40, fols 4r–v, 6v; NRS, E31/7, fols 98v, 102v; TA, VI, 334, 352, VIII, 141–2; Thomas, *Princelie Majestie*, 210–17; Dean, 'Crown, Wedding Rings and Processions', 80–91.

[120] NRS, E38/9; ER, I, 150, 197, 215.

[121] Birch, *History of Scottish Seals*, I, 43–5; Stewart, *Scottish Coinage*, 25–31; McAndrew, *Scotland's Historic Heraldry*, 24–32.

[122] The best evidence survives for the fifteenth century when the designs were complex, for example, see the *soltetes* coronation feast of Katherine de Valois in 1421: Burden, 'Rituals of Royalty', 197–220. For the wedding of James II and Mary of Guelders in 1449, see Chapter 4, 165.

decorative displays used alongside two thousand 'confections' purchased for the feast.[123] However, the finer details of these displays must remain speculative as the surviving financial accounts only record the raw ingredients rather than detailed descriptions of the finished products. Expenses of around £265 were lavished on coloured and striped cloth for knights, attendants and men-at-arms, suggesting that they were highly visible in processions and knightly contests that took place; although the colours of the cloth are not specified, it is likely that the red and yellow associated with the lion rampant featured.[124] The knights accompanying the horse-drawn litter that carried the body of the king in 1329 were similarly singled out and provided with the fine quality dule wear (hooded black funerary garment).[125] Large numbers of pieces of silk and leaves of gold backed with papyrus paper were also purchased, potentially to be used as offerings by the nobility, with the Steward – heir apparent after the infant David Bruce – singled out specifically.[126] Such offerings to the dead appear in both the English fifteenth-century *Liber Regie Capelle* and the sixteenth-century Scottish heraldic manuscript from John Scrymgeour's collection, in which the cloth offered is described respectively as gold and black.[127] The evidence of Robert's funeral, and indeed for David's wedding, demonstrate that the roots of the heraldic spectacles of the fifteenth and sixteenth centuries were firmly taking hold by the first half of the fourteenth century.

As Stevenson has argued, heraldic display was a central facet of Brucian propaganda and it reflected the wider European context of the Edwardian era of war, when Europe witnessed a proliferation of heraldic symbolism and chivalric culture.[128] This chivalric culture was at the centre of Barbour's retelling of Bruce's history and, as Foran posits, chivalric discourse created

---

[123] NRS, E38/7; *ER*, I, cxiii–cxv, 118–19. The loaves of sugar likely contained a better quality product for a different or specific use in comparison to a further 70 lbs of cheaper, and thus presumably lower quality, sugar bought in a barrel for kitchen provisions.

[124] Chroniclers speak of great festivities rather than jousting specifically, but Mary Anne Everett Green refers to over 360 lances or spears provided by Isabella for a mock spear fighting: *Lives of the Princesses of England*, III, 105.

[125] NRS, E38/10; *ER*, I, 176, 213, 255–6.

[126] Ibid., 221; NRS, E38/10.

[127] *Liber Regie Capelle* was composed by the Dean of the Chapel Royal, William Say, c.1448. It is an extended version of 'Rubrica de Regis Exequiis' from the *Liber Regalis seu Ordo Consecrandi Regem Solum, Ordo Reginam cum Rege, Ordo Consecrandi Reginam Solam, Rubrica de Regis Exequiis*, which is thought to date from the reign of Richard II, c.1380–90. Version referenced herein: *Liber Regie Capelle: A Manuscript in the Biblioteca Pública, Évora*, ed. Walter Ullmann (Woodbridge, 2008), 112–13. For John Scrymgeour's manuscript: NLS, Adv. MS. 31.5.2, fols 15r–16v. For transcription, see Appendix I.

[128] Stevenson, *Power and Propaganda*, 184. The Edwardian era was defined by Peter Coss as the period beginning with the Welsh Wars of Edward I and ending in the early victorious stages of the Hundred Years War in the reign of Edward III: 'Knighthood, Heraldry and Social Exclusion in Edwardian England', in Coss and Keen (eds), *Heraldry Pageantry and Social Display*, 39–68. For general discussion of the expansion of heraldry across Europe, see Keen, *Chivalry*, 125–34.

solidarity between king and community by promoting him as the 'captain of his knights'.[129] With this ideal in mind, it is hardly surprising that chivalry and heraldry featured in rituals and ceremonies that marked the gradual transfer of power and an attempted consolidation of support around the infant son of a warrior king. With the knights physically close to their king and captain, the solidarity in the display in the funeral of 1329 was tangible, but Robert I's absence from Berwick in 1328 was problematic. Barbour records that Robert's ill health was the cause of his absence, although he did manage other journeys in his final year of life.[130] The decision not to accompany his son to Berwick may also have been about resituating the solidarity of the community of knights – led by Thomas Randolph, earl of Moray, and Sir James Douglas – around the young heir in a public forum that celebrated the Scottish achievements and concluded peace with England. This realignment of the nobility around the heir and his young wife gives some credence to the suggestion by Barbour that:

> For he [Robert] thoct he wald in his lyff
> Croun his young son and his wyff
> And at that parliament sua he did.[131]

A crowning ceremony, in a gathering of the members of the estates of parliament, would certainly fit with the acknowledgment of rituals as significant tools for creating stability and legitimacy. There were, of course, precedents for such actions prior to the death of the ruling king in contemporary realms, such as Håkon IV crowning and anointing his son and heir, Magnus, in 1261 following the Norwegian civil wars (1130–1240).[132] However, Penman suggests that Barbour may have fused together disparate events linked to succession in his poem: the marriage of 1328 and the parliament of 1326 at Cambuskenneth Abbey, where the succession was confirmed and guardians were identified, in a year that also marked the creation of a separate household for the earl of Carrick [David].[133] It is not clear where or when the crowning or crown wearing took place, but combining either with oath-taking rituals for the Steward and others at Cambuskenneth – where Robert drew the line in the sand for those who had not come into his peace in 1314 – would have bound the parliament attendees to the son of the king in a particularly

---

[129] Susan Foran, 'A Nation of Knights? Chivalry and the Community of the Realm in Barbour's *Bruce*', in Steve Boardman and Susan Foran (eds), *Barbour's Bruce and its Cultural Contexts: Politics, Chivalry and Literature in Late Medieval Scotland* (Cambridge, 2015), 137–48, at 142.

[130] Barbour, *Bruce*, 744–7, bk. 20, lines 73–84; Penman, *Robert the Bruce*, 296–9.

[131] Barbour, *Bruce*, 748–9, bk. 20, lines 123–5.

[132] Brégiant, *Vox Regis*, 276–80. See also, Henry II crowning young Henry in twelfth-century England following the turmoil of the civil war between Matilda and Stephen: Strickland, *Henry the Young King*, 40–5.

[133] Penman, *Robert the Bruce*, 269–70. For settlement of the succession in 1326, see *RPS*, 1326/2.

poignant physical space. However, David would only have been two years old in 1326. The choice of Berwick for the wedding in 1328 emphasised the achievements of the previous two decades that culminated with this union, so a crowning of, or crown wearing by, the child king and his new queen may have been powerfully utilised here. It is also possible that either a crowning or crown-wearing ceremony occurred on both occasions.[134] Wherever the crowning took place, it represented an extension of the type of oath-giving ritual that had been used by the later Canmores for their heirs.

The town of Berwick had been central to Bruce's attempts to reclaim Scotland's former boundaries: it was the last town retaken from the English and the site from which he had laid down terms in 1327 (Map 2, see p. 37). Moreover, the ability to choose the venue made a distinct departure from the Anglo-Scottish marital unions of his predecessors, when the English king had determined the site in English territory.[135] While it was still in the border region and a highly contested place, with reference to Benham's discussion of peace making, this location clearly indicates a degree of equality between rulers.[136] Holding the wedding in Berwick overtly emphasised the victories Robert had achieved for his dynasty, and this prosperous border burgh – one of the largest in the realm – was able to support ceremonies designed to reflect an image of plenitude and opulence that would rival those of his contemporaries in scale and design.[137] Place was also significant in the decisions around Robert I's funeral. From as early as 1314, Robert had decided on burial at Dunfermline – near the tombs of his kingly predecessors – to bolster his fledgling dynasty through connection with his Canmore ancestors, including St Margaret and Alexander III.[138] The materiality of this tomb physically accentuated kinship links by employing Frosterley black marble from Durham, which was used for both the base of St Margaret's shrine at Dunfermline (see Plate 5, p. 69) and Bruce's reinterment of William I at Arbroath.[139] A further significance to the

---

[134] Dale suggests the use of non-inaugural crown-wearing ceremonies are an underestimated part of political life in the medieval period: *Inauguration and Liturgical Kingship*, 135–8.

[135] See the discussions in Chapter I, 37–41, 53–7.

[136] Benham, *Peacemaking in the Middle Ages*, 19–68.

[137] David Ditchburn and Alastair J. Macdonald, 'Medieval Scotland, 1100–1560', in Robert A. Houston and William W.J. Knox (eds), *The New Penguin History of Scotland: From the Earliest Times to the Present Day* (London, 2001), 96–181, at 97.

[138] *RRS*, V, no. 44. In this letter to William Lamberton, bishop of St Andrews, it is recorded that Robert wished to be buried: '*propter honorem sepulture regum predessorum nostrum*'. See also Boardman, 'Dunfermline as a Royal Mausoleum', 144–5; Penman, 'A Programme for Royal Tombs in Scotland', 244–7. On the king's devotional practices, see Penman, 'Sacred Food for the Soul', 1035–62. For recent debates about the position of Robert I's tomb, see MacGregor and Wilkinson, 'In Search of Robert Bruce, part III', 171–201; Penman and Utsi, *In Search of the Scottish Royal Mausoleum*, 102–13.

[139] George D.S. Henderson, 'Royal Effigy at Arbroath', in W. Mark Ormrod (ed.), *England in the Fourteenth Century: Proceedings from the 1985 Harlaxton Symposium* (Woodbridge, 1986), 88–98; G.S. Gimson, 'Lion Hunt: A Royal Tomb-Effigy at Arbroath Abbey', *PSAS* 125 (1995), 901–16; Penman, 'A Programme for Royal Tombs', 243–4. The effigy

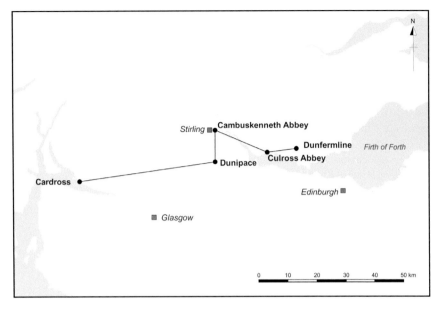

Map 5   Potential route of funeral procession of Bruce, 1329. Contains Ordnance Survey data © Crown Copyright and database right (2023).

selection of Dunfermline occurs when considering the journey required from Cardross, near Dumbarton, where Robert died on 7 June 1329, to his final resting place in Fife.[140] Two stopping points on the sixty- to seventy-mile route are identifiable due to expenses accrued at Dunipace and Cambuskenneth for vigils, and this illustrates that the funeral procession passed the site of the victory at Bannockburn, near Stirling, on 24 June 1314 (see Map 5).[141] It is possible to extrapolate other potential stopping points. For example, Culross in Fife was situated between Cambuskenneth and Dunfermline, and

---

itself was white Italian marble carved in Paris and shipped via Bruges and England to Dunfermline: NRS, E38/10; ER, I, 213–14, 288. It likely adopted a French style with weepers or kinship figures around the tomb as now visualised in the digital recreation and model housed at Dunfermline: 'Lost Tomb of Robert the Bruce Finds Its Final Resting Place', Historic Environment Scotland: About Us – News (HES, 26 April 2019), https://www.historicenvironment.scot/about-us/news/lost-tomb-of-robert-the-bruce-finds-its-final-resting-place/. Date accessed: 28 February 2021. See also Fraser, 'The Tomb of the Hero King', 169–76; Penman, 'A Programme for Royal Tombs', 243–4; Brian and Moira Gittos, 'Motivation and Choice: The Selection of Medieval Secular Effigies', in Coss and Keen (eds), Heraldry, Pageantry and Social Display, 143–67, at 151. On familial statuettes on tomb chests in the thirteenth and fourteenth centuries, and origins in France and Low Countries, see Morganstern, Gothic Tombs of Kinship, 10–91.

[140] This was where the king was eviscerated and embalmed, and where his entrails were buried, with oblations undertaken by the rector of Cardross: NRS, E38/10, NRS; ER, I, 215.

[141] Ibid., 297.

was also central to the cult of St Serf mirroring the dedication of the church at Cardross where the procession began.[142] Surviving documents do not offer a date for Robert I's burial at Dunfermline. However, the use of significant dates – both liturgical and secular – to exaggerate the potency of events was common in his reign, from the choice of date for the inauguration through to the way that this was reflected in the dates and liturgy surrounding the settling of the Treaty of Edinburgh-Northampton in 1328.[143] Either passing the site at Bannockburn or arranging the burial on 24 June, some two weeks after his death, were eminently feasible. By combining the funeral ceremony with the memorialisation of this victory against England, Robert's kingship was inextricably fused to the cause of Scottish independence.

Thomas de Carnato records the acquisition of a seal matrix for David. As the description records the silver seal matrix on a chain was ordered 'for the lord king now reigning', suggesting he had not been reigning when the order was initially made, it was probably ordered prior to his father's death.[144] This object symbolises the preparation undertaken to provide the material means of continuation of royal rule through the cycle of death and succession. The role of David in his father's funeral is unclear. Robert the Steward, now fifteen years old, was named as one who received cloth to make an offering at Dunfermline, but the financial accounts do not indicate that the young king was similarly provisioned to take part in this ceremony. Yet, David's instrumental role in the peace through his betrothal and marriage, the emphasis on the succession through rituals in parliament and the importance laid on demonstrating the dynastic links all suggest that he was present. Robert I's ill health and the challenges it caused were entwined with the ceremonial displays of 1328 to 1329, but this demonstrated the ritual cycle of succession in motion, and the extent of the efforts made to provide legitimacy in the transition are palpable in the records.

The Paradox of a Kingdom with Two Crowned Kings, 1329–32

Following the death and funeral of Robert I, a curious pause in the ceremonial transfer of power or 'royal dignity' occurred. Despite a direct living heir and the receipt of a papal bull granting the rite of unction in June 1329, David II's coronation did not take place until November 1331. The papal bull provided external recognition of Scottish kingship with liturgical parity to contemporaries – something Scottish monarchs had sought intermittently for over

---

[142] David Hugh Farmer, *The Oxford Dictionary of Saints* (Oxford, 1978), 354.

[143] On dates and liturgy connected to the treaty, see Penman, 'Who is this King of Glory?', 100.

[144] *ER*, I, 150. The entry is in an account returned on 5 August 1329, and reads: '*Et pro vno sigillo aureo ad opus regis, cum cathena argentea deaurata, et vno sigillo argenteo, cum cathena argetea, pro domino rege nunc regnante, cviij s.*'

a century.[145] Nonetheless, arriving the month Robert I died, it was a bittersweet victory. David was only five years old, so his accession was a test of the highest order for the Bruce dynasty and for Scotland more broadly as a kingdom still nursing the fresh scars of war.[146] This did not, however, precipitate a rush to raise the young king to the throne as witnessed in the thirteenth century. The prolonged hesitation combined with Edward Balliol, heir to John Balliol, being placed on the throne less than a year after David was crowned and anointed raises questions as to the perception and understanding of unction in the Scottish context in this transitional stage. Whether Edward Balliol was anointed or raised to the throne in a manner far more akin to his father in 1292, any inauguration of another without death, deposition or abdication appears to be a further abnormal situation bred of the contested nature of Scottish kingship in the fourteenth century. A similar situation arose in the context of civil war in twelfth-century Norway: King Sverre was elected as king in 1177, and this was seven years before Magnus Erlingsson, who was anointed and crowned in 1163, was killed in 1184. However, Sverre was denied unction until 1194 and the system of election in Norway, prior to the introduction of unction and crowning, had allowed for a means of sharing the kingship between legitimate claimants in a manner uncommon for kings of Scots.[147] The unusual circumstances arising around the Scottish succession in 1331 and 1332 support a close comparison of the respective ceremonies and the rituals within them. This section will analyse the partisan and patchy sources of this era to better understand the role of ritual in these abnormal times by considering the events that facilitated accession, crowning and regalia, the issue of anointing, attendees and officiators and, finally, feasting. There are a multitude of reasons posited for the delay to David II's coronation, but none is entirely satisfactory. The pre-emptive crowning in parliament that potentially occurred in 1326 or 1328 may have alleviated the pressure to raise David to the throne with the haste that occurred in the previous century. However, the pre-inaugural oath-taking ceremonies orchestrated for Alexander II and Alexander III had not provided the necessary stability and legitimacy to postpone inauguration. Consequently, for this explanation to suffice, the pre-mortuary recognition for David must have been significantly more binding. Other ceremonial reasons could account for a delay, including the unfulfilled return of the stone of Scone promised in the treaty of 1328, awaiting holy oil for unction from Rome or a standoff between Dunfermline and Scone for the right to anoint, as one held the blessed St Margaret and the other the right to house the honours or regalia of Scotland.[148] Penman

---

[145] 'Bull of John XXII Concerning the Coronation', 24–5. See 26, 38–9, 49, 52, 60–1.
[146] On the first wars of independence, see Brown, *Wars of the Scots*, 179–231.
[147] Brégiant, *Vox Regis*, particularly 33–5, 123–8.
[148] On the return of the stone: 'Letter of Edward III to the Abbot and Convent of Westminster Ordering Delivery to the Scots of the Stone of Destiny', in *English*

also points to both David's youth and potential political disquiet causing delay, but both these issues would have engendered haste in orchestrating the inauguration in the previous century.[149] Discussions of Sir James Douglas's departure on his mission to take Robert I's heart on crusade also offer a counterbalance to this being a period of political instability. There is a consensus that this journey implied a level of confidence in the Bruce succession and the peace with England; after all, it meant the departure of the second named guardian and one of Scotland's finest warriors from the country.[150] Considering the turmoil occurring in England following the accession of Edward III and the unpopularity of his mother's regime in the late 1320s, such convictions were logical and rational.[151]

One consideration overlooked thus far, which arises from a specific focus on the interconnectivity of death and succession ceremonies, is whether there was a direct link between the journey of Robert I's heart – more specifically its return and burial – and the delay in the coronation. The journey of Bruce's heart on crusade around the neck of Sir James Douglas in 'a case of fine silver' was a ritualised statement about the status, piety and wealth of the dynasty.[152] As Sonja Cameron has argued, despite the Douglas dominance of the display, it was sanctioned and paid for by Robert, prior to death, and the guardian Randolph, with Douglas holding court in his king's name while in Sluys and presumably beyond.[153] This was then the closing act – a continuation of the elaborate funeral – in which Bruce had always intended that his heart would be buried at Melrose Abbey.[154] Few questions have

---

Coronation Records, 77–8. Robert I's favour of Scone and Dunfermline fluctuates. The abbot of Scone, Thomas de Balmerino, is listed first of the abbots in the Cambuskenneth parliament, 6 November 1314, but legislation about entailing the crown lists the abbot of Dunfermline first (*RPS*, 1314/1, 1315/1, 1318/30). Moreover, in 1323 petitions settle lands in Dunfermline's favour (*RPS*, 1323/7/1–2) and Robert installed a perpetual light to St Margaret in the abbey in the early 1320s (see *RRS*, V, no. 88, dated c. Aug 1320 x July 1321). Scone was favoured for parliament, particularly where succession was discussed, and had the right to house the Scottish royal honours confirmed in 1325 (see *RPS*, 1315/1, 1318/30; *RRS*, V, no. 285. Thanks to Richard Millar for the latter reference). On the delay, see Penman, *David II*, 44–5; Dean, 'Crowns, Rings and Processions', 121–3.
[149] Penman, *David II*, 44–5.
[150] Ibid., 41–2; Simpson, 'The Heart of King Robert I', 173–86; Sonja Cameron, 'Sir James Douglas, Spain and the Holy Land', in Terry Brotherstone and David Ditchburn (eds), *Freedom and Authority, Scotland c.1050–c.1650: Historical and Historiographical Essays presented to Grant G. Simpson* (East Linton, 2000), 108–17.
[151] W. Mark Ormrod, *Edward III* (New Haven, 2013), 55–89.
[152] Barbour, *Bruce*, 752–67, bk. 20, lines 186–500, quote 758–9, bk. 20, lines 314–15; *Chron. Bower*, VII, 65; John Froissart, *Chronicles of England, France, Spain and the Adjoining Countries from the Latter Part of the Reign of Edward II to the Coronation of Henry IV*, trans. Thomas Johnes, 12 vols, third edition (London, 1803–10), I, 71–4; *The True Chronicles of Jean le Bel, 1290–1360*, trans. Nigel Bryant (Woodbridge, 2015), 52–4.
[153] Cameron, 'Sir James Douglas, Spain and the Holy Land', 114.
[154] *RRS*, V, nos 379–80. There has been some confusion around whether the intended burial place was the Holy Sepulchre in Jerusalem, but Robert's grants to Melrose specifically mention his intentions that his heart should be buried there. See also Cameron, 'Sir

been asked about the heart burial itself and this interment surely offered a further opportunity for dynastic display. The exact date for the return of the heart is unknown, but it may not have been until 1331. Douglas died on 25 August 1330, with his bones returned at an unknown later date along with the heart of the king.[155] The chronicle narratives focus more on the death of Douglas in Spain than on the return of the heart, but Bower's chronicle situates David's coronation directly after Douglas's death and epitaph making a textual link between Douglas's mission and the accession ritual.[156] The papal bull *Desterande feritatis* in 1299, with which Pope Boniface VIII banned separation of the body, necessitated papal permission for the separation of Bruce's body.[157] This retrospective permission was received in August 1331, while summons for the coronation parliament followed in September.[158] This may be a coincidence, but it also identifies another highly plausible reason for delaying the coronation as, with the papal sanction in hand, Bruce's heart could be buried as the final part of an extended memorialisation. If the young king, now seven, attended this event before travelling to Scone for the coronation and parliament, thus reconnecting the cycle of death and succession, it would have acted as a potent continuation of the work done by Bruce to mitigate the potential fragility of the legacy left to his son.

For Edward Balliol, it was Edward III's seizure of power in England in 1330 followed by the death of the Scottish guardian, Thomas Randolph, earl of Moray, in 1332 that began the cycle toward his accession to the throne on 24 September 1332. Andrew of Wyntoun's fifteenth-century chronicle poignantly foregrounds his rule with the high number of deaths at Dupplin Moor:

[Th]e bodies [th]at slayn war at Duplyne,/ Nowmeryt ful and sowmyt syne,/ In reknynge passit thre thowsande,/ Left on [th]at feylde [th]ar ded lyande.[159]

Nonetheless, the young Bruce king still lived. He was not dead, nor was he deposed, nor did he abdicate in a carefully managed process, such as that orchestrated following the removal of Edward II in England in 1327.[160] The reason for this was simple: Edward Balliol's claim to kingship was based on his father's claim to throne and the illegitimacy of the Bruce dynasty. This is emphasised in parliamentary records from 1334 relating to Edward's accession to the throne, which refer to the heirs of Sir Robert Bruce – meaning the Com-

---

James Douglas, Spain and the Holy Land', 116–17.
[155] Barbour, *Bruce*, 770–3, bk. 20, lines 579–611; Froissart, *Chronicles*, I, 76–7; *Chron. Bower*, VII, 67–73.
[156] Ibid.
[157] Brown, *The Monarchy of Capetian France*, see 'Death and the Human Body in the Later Middle Ages', 221–70.
[158] Papal permission: CPL, II, 345; Simpson, 'The Heart of King Robert I', 177. Parliament records are limited but a summons to the sheriff of Berwick survives: RPS, A1331/1.
[159] *Chron. Wyntoun*, V, 420–3, at 421 [Cotton MS version].
[160] Seymour Phillips, *Edward II* (New Haven, 2011), 508–55; Ormrod, *Edward III*, 40–54.

petitor, Robert I's grandfather – as 'having no right thereto'.[161] John Balliol had died in late 1314 at his ancestral castle at Hélicourt, but his was not a royal death and his funeral is an unknown entity.[162] Thus, Edward's kingship emerged out of the ritual removal of John Balliol in 1296. The parliamentary records also reflect that John's removal, the rights of the English king to hold Scotland and dispossession by the heirs of Bruce were the foundations of Edward's kingship.[163] Sir Galfrid Scrope, Edward III's justiciar in Scotland, goes so far as to state – in a document sealed by Edward Balliol and members of the Scottish clergy and nobility – that 'through the help of God and the said lord, the lord king of England, you have your position in the kingdom of Scotland'.[164] The contractual nature of Edward's kingship was explicit, rooted as it was in support of the English king, but also with 'the assent of the prelates, earls, barons, knights and all others assembled at our present parliament'.[165] A continued heavy emphasis on the need for the consensual support of the estates of the realm was thus as critical for Edward as it has been for his father.

For both David and then Edward the explicit inclusion of crowning at their accession marked a development in the process of king-making.[166] Surviving evidence for the regalia in the 1330s is scant, but tentative suggestions can be made. Alexander Brook has argued that the cut of the diamonds found in the crown that remains extant today were of Indian origin, the style of which can be dated back to the fourteenth century.[167] Robert I was not in the position to purchase diamonds in 1306, but longer-term investment in magnificent regalia sits comfortably with other efforts to embellish the Brucian dynasty with the trappings of kingship and majesty. Known surviving remnants of the Canmore regalia potentially existed in Scotland: a mantle, royal banner and possibly the elusive papal sword. In addition, a small sceptre was fashioned by the goldsmith, Copyn, in 1331; although it is not clear from the records whether this small sceptre was made for the young king or his queen.[168] The fact that no other regalia items were purchased in either 1328 or 1331 indicates previous investment, in years without surviving financial accounts, to replace the regalia that Edward I

[161] *RPS*, 1334/1.
[162] Beam, *The Balliol Dynasty*, 202–9, 272–3.
[163] *RPS*, 1334/1.
[164] Ibid., A1334/5.
[165] Ibid., 1334/1.
[166] David II: *Chron. Melsa*, II, 361; *Chron. Fordun*, 346; *Chron. Bower*, 71–3; *Chron. Lanercost*, 268. Edward: *Chron. Melsa*, II, 366; 'Gesta Edwardi Tertii auctore canonico Bridlingtoniensi', in *Chronicles of the Reign of Edward I and Edward II*, ed. William Stubbs, 2 vols (London, 1882–83), II, 108–9; *Chron. Wyntoun*, V, 420–3; *Pluscarden*, 199. Some omit crowning for Edward, but these were known to have a tendency to minimalise the impact of either Balliol king: *Chron. Lanercost*, 271–2; *Chron. Fordun*, 347; *Chron. Bower*, VII, 81.
[167] Alexander J.S. Brook, 'Technical Description of the Regalia of Scotland', *PSAS* 24 (1889–90), 71–9. See Plate 20, 221.
[168] *ER*, I, 382. For further discussion on this, see Dean, 'Crowns, Rings and Processions', 125–7.

Plate 9   David II Great Seal [mounted and enthroned], c.1359. Crown Copyright, National Records of Scotland, Laing Seal Impressions, RH17/1/27–RH17/1/28.

had removed. While such objects would undoubtedly have been for an adult, there are few references to the fashioning of suitably sized regalia for minor kings' coronations elsewhere.[169] On David II's seal, the sceptre he holds in his right hand is elaborately floriated and bears a strong resemblance to that depicted on his father's seal. This could be the reuse of seal matrix designs, but there are other notable differences between David's and his father's seal. These include the introduction of a depiction of plate armour and a crown on the mounted image of the king, so the similarity in the sceptre may be indicative of a physical sceptre passed from father to son (see Plate 9).[170]

That Edward had a crown is confirmed in the manner that he ceded power in 1356: by delivering 'his golden crown and soil of the kingdom' to Edward III.[171] However, despite being raised to the throne at Scone in the presence of the abbot of that house, which claimed the right to hold the regalia, it is quite likely that the fleeing Bruce Scots carried the regalia with them.[172] Considering Edward III's known involvement in the promotion of Edward Balliol as king of Scots, and obvious efforts to bridge the gap between John and Edward's kingship, it seems quite possible that the Canmore crown, removed

---

[169] Contemporary commentary focuses on the strains on young kings enduring the weight of adult royal regalia; for example, the ten-year-old Richard II had to be carried from his coronation for a rest in 1377: Burden, 'Rituals of Royalty', 189.
[170] Henry Laing notes the plate armour: *Descriptive Catalogue of Impressions of Ancient Seals of Scotland* (Edinburgh, 1850), 7.
[171] CDS, III, nos 1591–2; *Scalacronica*, 140–1.
[172] A similar scene occurred in civil wars in Norway, when Magnus V was killed carrying his regalia: Brégiant, *Vox Regis*, 42–3.

Plate 10   Edward Balliol Great Seal [mounted and enthroned], 1350. Crown Copyright, National Records of Scotland, Laing Seal Impressions, RH17/1/30–1.

by Edward I in 1296, may have been returned.[173] Edward Balliol's seal design abandoned the French influence in later Brucian seals and returned to a style with an ornate high-backed throne, similar to both Alexander III and John Balliol (see Plate 10).[174] This was a typical design feature of Plantagenet kings' seals, but the rejection of the Bruce design for that of Alexander and John fits efforts to erase a period of Bruce kingship. Edward also holds both a simple single-flower sceptre and an orb, not seen on a Scottish seal for over a century, which may be indicative of the actual regalia returning to the use of the orb (apple) and papal rose sceptre retrieved from Westminster.[175] The use of this traditional regalia would have offered strong connections to both John Balliol and the Canmore dynasty for Edward, while also pointedly rejecting the interim Bruce kingship and any new regalia associated with it.

What is notably absent from the descriptions of Edward's inaugural ritual, and conspicuous in David's, is the act of anointing.[176] Unfortunately, surviving sources are sparse on details for this momentous event. The papal bull has instructions that the oath should promise to defend the Catholic Church and identified the bishop of St Andrews as the ecclesiastical officiant to anoint the king (followed by the bishop of Glasgow or other unnamed bishops in his absence), but there were no additional details about the prayers, appli-

---

[173] See 40–1, 80, 84.
[174] For comparison, see Plates 4, 8 and 9, 57, 82, 100.
[175] *Documents Illustrative of the History of Scotland*, II, 144.
[176] David II: *Chron. Melsa*, II, 361; *Chron. Fordun*, 346; *Chron. Bower*, 71–3; *Chron. Lanercost*, 268. Edward: *Chron. Melsa*, II, 366; 'Gesta Edwardi Tertii', 108–9; *Chron. Wyntoun*, V, 420–3; *Pluscarden*, 199; *Chron. Lanercost*, 271–2; *Chron. Fordun*, 347; *Chron. Bower*, VII, 81.

cation of the oil or the liturgical requirements.[177] The *Exchequer Rolls* record that a roll 'concerning the duty or service of the coronation' or an order of ceremony was composed, but there is no evidence to suggest this survived.[178] The chronicle of the northern English Cistercian house of Meaux or Melsa, composed in the later fourteenth century but possibly using an eye-witness account, records the coronation with most detail.[179] The chronicler does not favour David II; rather he accuses the young king of defiling the altar by soiling himself and dwells at some length on the absence of the famed stone of Scone, both of which appear to be additions designed to undermine the legitimacy of the Bruce coronation ceremonies.[180] He positions David's coronation – at least the crowning, anointing, Mass and oath-taking – within the church, and there is no mention of an outdoor enthronement. As with John, David's ceremony was taking place in November, so there may have been practical reasons for it largely taking place indoors. However, the absence in this narrative – or any other – of a ritual enthronement by the nobility who figured so prominently in previous inaugural ceremonies, including that of his father, is notable. It is also unclear whether the earl of Fife was present in 1331, as the only named secular attendants were Thomas Randolph, earl of Moray, John Stewart, earl of Angus, and Thomas Randolph, the son of earl of Moray (Appendix II, 'David II'). James Ben, bishop of St Andrews and the named officiator for anointing in the papal bull, was prominent in the brief narrative entries as the one who anointed David, and most sources explicitly note that the anointing was bestowed on a Scottish king for the first time with permission from the pope.[181] The prominence of the bishop and the potential shift to a wholly interior church space at this juncture may indicate changes in the ceremony to accommodate the act of anointing, but a lack of focus on the secular enthronement could also arise from the unique nature of this intrusion into the ceremony.

Another distinct factor observable for David II's coronation, which may speak to efforts by the leading secular lords to rebalance power, particularly

---

[177] 'Bull of John XXII Concerning the Coronation', 24–5. The papacy laid down specific distinctions between anointing of bishops and kings in the eleventh or twelfth century: Dale, *Inauguration and Liturgical Kingship*, 73–7.

[178] '*scriptura cuiusdam rotuli de officio coronacionis*': ER, I, 381. Duncan comments on 'the composition of a written *ordo* for the 1331 coronation' but provides no reference: Duncan, 'Before Coronation: Making a King at Scone', 153.

[179] *Chron. Melsa*, II, 361; King, 'Edward, by the Grace of God, King of Scotland'. The chronicle of Melsa, that is Meaux near Hull, is the most detailed. All entries that list the attendees in full seem to list exactly the same attendees, implying one eye-witness account that could have the basis for all.

[180] *Chron. Melsa*, II, 361. The description of the stone: '*Sed pro coronation ponebatur super unum lapidem jacentem juxta magnum altare in ecclesis monachorum apud Scone, concavum quidem et ad modum cathedrae confectum in parte.*' Note that this description of the stone is similar to that of Guisborough for 1292: *Chron. Guisborough*, 238–9; see 81–2.

[181] *Chron. Melsa*, II, 361; *Chron. Fordun*, 346; *Chron. Bower*, VII, 71–3; *Chron. Lanercost*, 268; Penman, *David II*, 45.

if there was no outdoor secular enthronement and the church appeared to be grasping power in the process of king-making, was the fact that the coronation on 24 November took place amidst a meeting of parliament that began on 22 November.[182] The gathering of the three estates for a parliament, with summoning notices sent over forty days previously, aided the chances of higher attendance at the ceremony even if surviving accounts name a relatively low numbers of specific attendees.[183] Additionally, placing David's coronation within a meeting of the estates, as Penman argues, would have forged a direct link between the king's investiture, oaths taken and the 'political role of his subjects'.[184] The prominence and authority of Scotland's parliament did not emerge through the king's need for taxes and support for war as in England, rather it lay in its role in royal succession and acclamation, minorities and the provision of lieutenants.[185] The political anxiety surrounding the accession of a child, combined with a potential reaction to the changes in ritual, further enmeshed the role of the estates and parliament into the investiture of royal power. Parliament was not directly connected to Edward Balliol's ritual elevation to kingship in the same way. The only surviving records of a meeting of parliament in Edward's reign are those from 1334 and are replete with evidence of Edward's loyalty to Edward III as a central facet of the Balliol succession.[186] This may not be an accident of source survival, but rather a means of illustrating the outside support required for Edward's accession and parliament's role in confirming the selection of a king of Scots.

The *Chronicle of Lanercost* states that Edward Balliol was raised to the throne 'according to the custom of the country'.[187] While this is an oft used generic description, in comparison to David II's coronation, this may well have appeared to be the case, and this may have been by design. Duncan, earl of Fife, enthroned the king amidst nobles and clerics of the realm including four earls, at least one bishop and a good number of abbots (Appendix II: 'Edward Balliol').[188] The attendees represented a relatively small geographic area of central-eastern Scotland, and included a number of disinherited

---

[182] *ER*, I, 376–92; *RPS*, A1331/1.
[183] Unfortunately, there is no list of attendees for the parliament of 1331, but the summons to the sheriffs and baillies of Berwick indicates that something similar was sent to all members of the three estates and those from beyond the realm who owed homage to the king, such as the bishop of Durham: *RPS*, A1331/1.
[184] Penman, *David II*, 46; Michael Penman, 'Parliament Lost, Parliament Regained? The Three Estates in the Reign of David II, 1329–1371', in Brown and Tanner (eds), *Parliament and Politics in Scotland, 1235–1560*, 77.
[185] Roland Tanner, *The Late Medieval Scottish Parliament: Politics and the Three Estates, 1424–1488* (East Linton, 2001), 12–13; Penman, 'The King Wishes and Commands', 125–41; Reid and Penman, 'Guardian – Lieutenant – Governor', 191–218, particularly 217–18.
[186] *RPS*, A1334/1–5.
[187] *Chron. Lanercost*, 271–2.
[188] *Chron. Melsa*, II, 366; 'Gesta Edwardi Tertii', 108–9; *Chron. Lanercost*, 271–2; *Chron. Fordun*, 347; *Chron. Bower*, VII, 81; *Chron. Wyntoun*, V, 420–3; *Pluscarden*, 199; *RPS*, 1334/4.

Plate 11 Edward Balliol, Privy Seal, c.1350, and David II, Privy Seal, c.1359. Crown Copyright, National Records of Scotland, Laing Seal Impressions, RH17/1/29, RH17/1/32.

lords, so Thomas Gray's suggestion that 'invading lords' raised Edward to the throne was perhaps warranted.[189] Nonetheless, the involvement of the earl of Fife was a crucial element in upholding traditions of king-making at Scone. All accounts are void of references to an anointing ritual for Edward Balliol, but it is most notable in the account of the Meaux chronicler who, only a few entries earlier, repeated the term anointed (*inuctus*) on three separate occasions for David.[190] While there are no explicit references made to the anointing of Robert I in 1306 either, a possibility proposed earlier in this chapter, the sharp distinction made between David and Edward within this one chronicle seems to reveal a purposeful, or even enforced, rejection of the inclusion of anointing as part of the Scottish coronation. The bishop of Dunkeld was recorded as the officiating cleric, and the Meaux chronicler states he 'invested [Edward]… with the crown of the kingdom', but both bishops named in the papal bull with the right to anoint were conspicuous in their absence.[191] While King argues for hindsight colouring Bower's statement regarding Edward being crowned 'in his own manner', there was a hybrid nature to Edward's ceremony that appears to have included a crowning and traditional outdoor enthronement, but not anointing, so this combination may have attracted such a statement.[192] The exclusion of anointing may have been a condition of Edward III of England's endorsement of Edward Balliol's kingship, particularly as omitting this act reinforced the inferiority

[189] *Scalacronica*, 110–11.
[190] *Chron. Melsa*, II, 361.
[191] *Chron. Melsa*, II, 366: '*Postea praefatus episcopus Dunkeldensis insignivit dictum Edwardum de Balliolo corona regni apud Scone…*'; 'Bull of John XXII Concerning the Coronation', 24–5.
[192] *Chron. Bower*, VII, 81; King, 'Edward, by the Grace of God, King of Scotland'.

of the Scottish king in this relationship. However, it also served to further whitewash the usurping Bruce dynasty's intervention, and the achievements associated with it, as found in the parliament documents of 1334.[193]

There is a marked difference in the Privy Seals of the two kings: David's features a royal heraldic shield lowered from clouds by heavenly arms, presumably those of God, and appears to be directly illustrative of the act of unction (see Plate 11, p. 104).[194] This intriguing material statement of divine kingship, example c.1359, is absent from Edward's seals – and indeed any other previous Scottish king's seal. It suggests a proactive effort to emphasise his anointed status was a necessity for David as an adult following his release from English captivity (1357) and in the wake of the campaign to attack the Bruce legacy that ended with the official removal of Balliol (1356). Liturgical and divine associations are largely absent from accounts of Edward's accession rituals. Yet, the *Chronicle of Lanercost* associated the ceremony with the feast day of St Francis on 4 October, even though he was raised to the throne in late September, to explain the miraculous multiplying of provisions to allow a small quantity to feed the 'immense multitude of men'.[195] Such miracles could be associated with the promises of future bounty, while also adding the gloss of saintly approval to Edward's kingship and implying that his right to the throne was sanctioned by God even without the anointing received by David.

Any actual feasting in 1332 is hard to assess. Financial accounts for Edward's reign are lacking; surviving *Exchequer Rolls* from the 1330s and 1340s indicate a continuation of Bruce bureaucracy. Comparably, David II's coronation and the accompanying parliament are well recorded, evidencing richly provisioned events with plentiful supplies of fine food, wine and music from minstrels. Wardrobe expenditures included imported silks and cloth of gold, red and white velvet for robes for the king and queen, a chair for the king, furs and expenses for merchants.[196] As with the coronation of fourteen-year-old Edward III in 1327, calculated effort was made to provide the 'impression of political stability and royal majesty'.[197] Antioch silk and cloth of gold were purchased for use 'in the making of the knights' and the chronicles record that John Stewart, earl of Angus, and Thomas Randolph (junior) were two of those belted with knighthood.[198] Such actions drew members of the royal household and wider political community into the performance to emphasise the position of prominent supporters and speaks to Hepburn's analogy as ritual as immersive theatre.[199] Knighting ceremonies frequently coincided

---

[193] See for example: *RPS*, 1334/1; *RPS*, A1334/5.
[194] Henry Laing, *Descriptive Catalogue of Ancient Seals of Scotland* (Edinburgh, 1850), 8.
[195] *Chron. Lanercost*, 271–2.
[196] *ER*, I, 375–404. For clothing, see 380–9. For minstrels, see 398.
[197] Ormrod, *Edward III*, 57.
[198] *ER*, I, 385; *Chron. Bower*, 71–3. Note: Antioch is located in modern-day Turkey.
[199] Hepburn, *The Household and Court of James IV*, particularly 102–6.

with Scottish coronations after 1331 to rally support around a leader and were witnessed at the coronation of young Edward III three years earlier.[200] The knighting ceremony, combined with the calling of the parliament, were concerted attempts to create a united support for the young king. Despite all such efforts, subsequent events cannot but help support Penman's proposal that this was still not enough to quell doubts across the realm.[201] Yet, the chronicle of Meaux's description of Edward Balliol's coronation feast makes explicit the challenges faced by Edward that were not apparent in the sumptuous celebrations for the young Bruce king:

> *Ubi omnes qui refectioni ipsius coronationis interfuerunt sufficienter armati, exceptis galeis, existebant.*[202]

> All the men at the feast of the coronation were in full armour, except for helmets.

Challenges lurked off-stage for David II's kingship. However, the coronation of Scotland's first anointed king and his young queen was undertaken in true Bruce style, with feasting and cloth of gold in abundance, even if both were only children. For Edward, the entry from Meaux does not suggest the triumphal use of an armed retinue as found in victorious royal entries, such as that made by Charles VII into Paris during the Hundred Years' War.[203] Rather, the image of the coronation guests in full armour unambiguously indicates that all were poised for the inevitable continuation of fighting reflecting the underlying contested nature of kingship in the early 1330s.

The Compromised Bruce Succession: Perpetuating Contested Rituals?

The Privy Seal impressions surviving from the late 1350s speak to decisive and demonstrable efforts by David II to re-establish and stabilise his kingship following his return to Scotland and the official removal of Edward Balliol (Plate 11, see p. 104). Such efforts have also been convincingly evidenced by Penman in explorations of the king's investments into pious devotion, such as the royal chapel at the 'pseudo-personal cult' centre for St Monan in Fife, and his chivalric court with semi-regular jousts that were commented on by continental observers.[204] Consequently, there is little doubt over whether David was capable of utilising rituals and display in his projections of royal

---

[200] Ormrod, *Edward III*, 55–7.
[201] Penman, *David II*, 46.
[202] *Chron. Melsa*, II, 366.
[203] Bryant, 'The Medieval Entry Ceremony at Paris', 104–5.
[204] Penman, 'Christian Days and Knights', particularly 258–61, 263–5. See also Penman, *David II, passim* (on St Monan, 261–7).

authority in a manner that emulated contemporaries and his father. It is also abundantly clear that the succession, and a desire to control the direction of this succession, underpinned many of his actions. This was particularly the case when it came to diverting the succession away from his nephew, Robert the Steward, whose position had been made law by Robert I's parliaments in 1318 and 1326.[205] Due to David's animosity towards the Steward and the entail of the succession upon him, the ceremonial occasions that might otherwise have marked key junctures in the ritual cycle tended to be dominated by the contested nature of the succession.

The most prominent example was David's second marriage to Margaret Logie (nee Drummond) in 1363. This marriage, and the coronation of his new queen, offered an opportunity to celebrate the promise of an heir through a union with a woman known to be capable of providing David with the long-sought-after heir.[206] Amy Hayes has demonstrated that Margaret was endowed with a sizeable dowry worthy of a queen when compared to her predecessor, an English princess, while a near contemporary chronicle comments that she was 'raised in honour' and provided with a royal crown.[207] Celebration of the marriage appears to have been combined with a ritualised submission and oath-giving performed by Robert the Steward – heir to the throne – following a failed, but nevertheless dangerous, threat of rebellion from the Steward and other magnates, notably the earls of Douglas and March.[208] Penman argues that this combination of public oath-giving of the Steward with the king's marriage sought to publicly 'legitimise his [David's] domestic and dynastic plans'.[209] Bower's account offers a text of the oath, indicating that the Steward swore allegiance under pain of disinheritance from the throne, with a list of witnesses that indicates possible attendees for the nuptials and the queen's coronation, such as prominent churchmen like William Landellis, bishop of St Andrews, and the bishop of Brechin.[210] Margaret Logie's marriage and crowning appear to have been exploited in a highly politicised way in front of a select but sizeable representation of the estates.

There are, however, many unknowns in the analysis of these two rituals and how they functioned alongside one another. The *Exchequers Rolls* are fragmentary for this period, and there is only an incomplete return from the clerk of the royal wardrobe, whose account likely held rich evidence for the provisioning of clothing and adornments for the wedding and associated cel-

---

[205] *RPS*, 1318/30; *RPS*, 1326/2. On the relationship between David II and his heir presumptive, see Penman, *David II*, *passim*; Boardman, *The Early Stewart Kings*, 1–38.
[206] Examples of David's favour towards his stepson, John Logie, Margaret's son from her first marriage: Penman, *David II*, 289, 302, 328, 354–5.
[207] Hayes, 'The Late Medieval Scottish Queen', 201–2; *Chron. Fordun*, 370.
[208] *Chron. Fordun*, 370; *Chron. Bower*, VII, 330–3; Rosalind K. Marshall, *Scottish Queens, 1034–1714* (Edinburgh, 2007), 38.
[209] Penman, *David II*, 281–95, quote 293.
[210] *Chron. Bower*, VII, 330–3. Landellis also recorded as 'de Landels', see 121.

ebrations.[211] Similarly, the physical site(s) of the ceremonies are unknown. The location for the submission is identified as Inchmurdoch in Fife, a parish held by the bishop of St Andrews.[212] St Andrews would have offered a prominent cathedral space in easy travelling distance from Inchmurdoch that was suitable – in both size and status – for the marriage and coronation, but the actual physical space used was not explicitly recorded. Using St Andrews Cathedral, or another location in Fife such as David's cult chapel to St Monan, would have complemented David's broader efforts to demonstrate his royal control over this region in the face of Stewart expansion.[213] It did not, however, have the rich associations with succession found at Scone, where David and his first wife, Joan, were crowned. With the limited evidence available, the submission of the Steward outweighs the nuptials in terms of what can be surmised about David's use of ritual actions.

For David, perpetuating the ritual cycle of succession was a challenge due to the lack of legitimate, or indeed illegitimate, heirs and an ingrained animosity towards his nephew, Robert the Steward, who his father had identified as the next legitimate heir. In addition to remarriage, David negotiated with Edward III – both via ambassadors and in person – to secure English support and a potential heir among Edward's sons, and he promoted his younger nephew, John of Sutherland, son of his full sister, during his short lifetime (c.1345x6–1361).[214] Yet, despite David's investment in proactive diplomacy, these efforts rarely got to the stage where ceremonies were arranged: John of Sutherland died in his mid-teens and the promotion of an English heir was routinely rejected in Scotland.[215] Subsequently, David shifted his focus onto the next generation of the Stewart line, favouring John of Kyle, Robert the Steward's eldest son: he granted John titles and arranged his marriage to Annabella Drummond.[216] However, there is little evidence of the actual matrimonial rituals and associated ceremony as this was part of David's wider efforts to strengthen his network of supporters, rather than being promoted as the marriage of an heir. Unfortunately, David II's inability to produce an heir compromised the way that ritual was employed in the promotion

---

[211] *ER*, II, 180–2. The incomplete account illustrates that the clerk of the wardrobe took in an income of over £766 for the period from 1361 to 1364, and amongst the expenses are fine spices and cloths, but it records only partial expenditure, and nothing specifically associated with the marriage preparations has been identified in the records. See also Penman, *David II*, 282, fn. 120; *ER*, II, liv.

[212] *Chron. Bower*, VII, 330–1.

[213] Penman, 'Christian Days and Knights', 258–60.

[214] Penman, *David II*, on negotiations with England, see particularly: 153–74, 221–8, 301–25. On the promotion of John, see Penman, *David II*, 114–16, 145, 210–11, 214, 269; Susan Marshall, *Illegitimacy in Medieval Scotland* (Woodbridge, 2021), 103–4.

[215] Diplomatic visits occurred in 1359, 1362–63 and 1369–70, see *ER*, II, xliv–xlv, l–li, lxxvi, 48, 130, 172, 183–4, 356; Penman, 'Christian Days and Knights', 246–72; Penman, *David II*, 220–1, 300–8.

[216] Ibid., 353–4, 357–8, 368–71; Hayes, 'The Late Medieval Scottish Queen', 112–13.

of the succession, while his decision to favour Robert the Steward's eldest son, John of Kyle and then Carrick, perpetuated the contested nature of the succession and arguably laid seeds for future internal discord in the decades that followed.

Despite the spin of partisan chroniclers, John Balliol was legitimised by the inauguration of 1292 making this, ironically perhaps, one of the least contested rituals of this period. After over two decades of Brucian efforts, there was little doubt over the legitimacy of David II between 1329 and 1331, even if the situation from 1332 onwards became rapidly more complicated. Descriptions of Edward Balliol's inauguration implied the presence of battle-ready guests poised for action and echoed the situation in 1306, when Robert I's inauguration was followed by attacks on the king and his supporters. This makes these two kings ripe for further comparison: both experienced criticism for 'making himself king' as both were seen to be usurping the throne from a legitimate claimant. Many accounts recorded kings being raised to the throne in the usual manner during the late thirteenth and fourteenth centuries but some traditions, such as the outdoor enthronement recorded for Alexander III, appear absent in 1292 and 1331. It would be tempting to suggest that English intervention and the introduction of unction provided the means for increasing church control over the rituals of king-making, but the vacillation occurring and the lack of details about the incorporation of the rite of unction in Scotland in the 1330s leads to the impression that the arrival of unction had a rather anticlimactic impact on the Scottish inaugural ceremony. Traditional people and places tend to dominate the brief chronicle accounts of the inaugural events. The centrality of Scone, whether the abbey housed the stone or not, was crucial to acquiring the Scottish throne and, indeed, to those wishing to dismantle the legitimacy of its kingship.

From the incorporation of Alexander III's heart burial within the journey to an inaugural parliament in 1286, through David Bruce's coronation being wholly integrated with a meeting of parliament, to Edward's kingship being ratified by parliament in 1334, this political institution and its members were increasingly enmeshed with the ceremonial cycle. The ritual importance of the members of the Scottish political elite, a group that demonstrably increased in size during this period, is pronounced in legitimising the kings of both dynasties. A clear mismatch appears between the presumed gravitas of unction and the role it played in 1331 to 1332, which raises questions about the importance of this rite in the eyes of the Scottish political community. The granting of the rite, which presumably arose from petitions perhaps after its unofficial use in 1306, coupled with Robert I's recurrent use of liturgical feast days for such occasions, indicate efforts to imbue his kingship with religiosity. As a king excommunicated for significant parts of his reign, this was a conventional response for retrieving papal favour. Yet, the necessity of keeping the national church and its representatives on side was more immediate and members of the Scottish church – such as Bishop Wishart in 1306 and Bishop Ben in 1332 – were instrumental in continuing efforts to secure unction. Even so, there were numerous abbots and at least one bishop present in 1332, so for some blood and dynasty were clearly thicker than holy oil. Any liturgical credence instilled by the act of anointing in 1331 must have partially evaporated in the subsequent raising of Edward Balliol to the throne by the earl of Fife in 1332, recognised by a substantial part of the political community. Indeed, David II's Privy Seal gives insight into his personal determination, after 1357 at least, to underscore the divine status anointing should have imparted upon him. The introduction of new ritual elements, however, involved the integration of the unfamiliar with the traditional – something that took time to navigate – so for this rite to be seamlessly incorporated would have been unusual. The negotiation between the secular and the divine in the making of Scottish kings was an ongoing process that continued long beyond the reign of David II, as will be explored in Chapter 3.

The closely intertwined cycle of death and royal succession, at first glance, appears noticeably fractured during this period. Memorialising the dead, however, still played a significant role in the transfer of power where it was feasible. The guardians sought legitimacy and connections between the funeral of Alexander III and the opening parliament that nominated the temporary guardians. The links between death and succession were also palpable in 1328 to 1329, with the preparations for Robert I's funeral and tomb intertwined with those for the triumphal wedding of David Bruce at Berwick. The heart burial of Robert I, as the conclusion to these elaborate funerary displays, also offers a plausible reason for the delay of David II's coronation that accentuates rather than confounds the ritual cycle. Where connections with the death of a predecessor were not possible, there was – for the Balliol kings at least – a shift of focus to the judicial process that provided legal basis for their accession. Thus, death was temporarily replaced in the cycle for the sake of necessity. This is most convincing for John Balliol, but the same judicial process provided the underpinning for his son's accession to kingship. There was no need to retrospectively manufacture an abdication for David because the basis in the parliamentary record ratifying Edward's kingship declared that the heirs of Bruce the Competitor had never been legitimate. Where there was neither funerary ritual nor judicial process, there was murder and Robert Bruce. Quite consciously sold to history over the centuries as a pre-eminent hero of the realm, his accession to the kingship caused the most dramatic ruptures in the cycle of succession and thus necessitated the most ritual creativity to provide legitimacy not only for himself, but also for his son. For each of these four rulers, ritual was still central to the transfer of power despite, or perhaps because of, how contested or compromised the succession appeared. These rituals had to be flexible and malleable, particularly in a period that witnessed disruption to the established cycle, the introduction of new elements, the absence of prominent individuals and the removal of ceremonial objects, but they remained unambiguously essential to being made and sustained as the king of Scots.

Genealogical Table 3 The Stewart Dynasty.

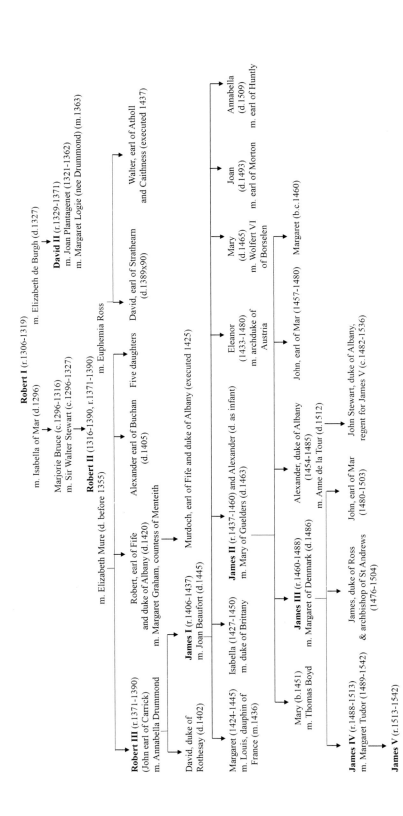

3

Stating Their Place: Ceremonial Legitimisation of the Stewart Dynasty, c.1371–c.1424

The Stewart dynasty was one of the longest reigning dynasties of late medieval and early modern Europe, but the stability and success of the dynasty were not certainties in the early decades. Traditional historiography has often dismissed Robert II and Robert III as weak and ineffectual.[1] However, in more recent years, scholarship has marked Robert II out as the significantly underestimated founder who was crucial to the dynasty's 'propaganda' offensive, while Robert III's failures have been tempered by a more nuanced understanding of the political context.[2] The reign of James I has fairly consistently been considered to herald increasing royal confidence and strong kingship, but his success, the nature of his rule and the impact of James's time in England are still areas of active debate.[3] The transition from Bruce to Stewart dynasties was far smoother than the prolonged succession crisis that ensued after 1286, but threats to the new dynasty came from within the wider Stewart kinship as much as from outside. Younger kin members challenged the authority of both Robert II and Robert III during their lifetimes, and – by 1406 – the surviving heir to the throne had been kidnapped by the English leading to the extended period of absentee kingship that marked the first twelve years of the reign of James I. Consequently, this period witnessed around thirty years of absentee kingship or proxy power on behalf of a monarch deemed incapable of ruling. The extent that such issues had an impact upon the language, practice and institutions of power in the fourteenth century and, more particularly, the legacy of this in the fifteenth century have become central features of more recent historiography.[4] This chapter will

---

[1] For example, see P. Hume Brown, *History of Scotland* (Cambridge, 1911), 149–50; Robert L. Mackie, *A Short History of Scotland* (Oxford, 1930), 149; Gordon Donaldson, *Scottish Kings* (London, 1967), 32–40; Nicholson, *Scotland: The Later Middle Ages*, 184–228.

[2] Alexander Grant, *Independence and Nationhood: Scotland 1306–1469*, reprint (Edinburgh, 2007), 171–87; Boardman, *Early Stewart Kings*, passim; Stevenson, *Power and Propaganda*, 182–214.

[3] Evan V.M. Balfour-Melville, *James I, King of Scots, 1406–1437* (London, 1936); Brown, *James I*; Nicola Scott, 'The Court and Household of James I of Scotland, 1424–1437' (PhD thesis, University of Stirling, 2007); Katy Jack, 'Political and Local Consequences of the Decline and Fall of the Earls of Mar, 1281–1513' (PhD thesis, University of Stirling, 2017), 213–24.

[4] Michael Brown, '"Lele counsale for the comoun profite": Kings, Guardians and

contribute to these ongoing debates about early Stewart kingship through an analysis of the ways in which these three monarchs were able, and at times unable, to harness the rituals and ceremonies associated with death and succession in their efforts establish the dynasty.

Financial materials do survive from the later fourteenth and early fifteenth centuries, along with some useful references to coronation and oath-taking practices in the *Records of the Parliament of Scotland*, but the fragmentary nature of official records means that there is a continued reliance on narrative sources. Some of the Scottish chronicle writers – particularly Wyntoun and Bower, working in the early fifteenth-century – were writing about an era through which they lived, or at least about which they could call on the living memory of others, but this does not lessen the need for caution in analysing their records of ritual action. Each wrote for a different sponsor and purpose, they sought to appeal to different audiences – with Wyntoun's work in rhyming Scots and Bower's in Latin – and they were influential on later chroniclers and history writers.[5] Equally, the level of detail they offer about ceremonies and rituals is very varied. For example, despite living during James I's reign and acting as royal official, Bower records the inauguration of Alexander III in 1249 with more detail than the return and coronation of James I in 1424, which is both frustrating and intriguing.[6] Bower does relay a fascinating example of a public response to a ceremony, or the impact of the gathering of crowds for a ceremony, at the time of the coronation of Robert III which will be discussed here.[7] Yet, otherwise, the records of ritual for the early Stewarts continue to demonstrate the 'ambivalence', lack of interest or, at the very least, inconsistency around relaying specific details of the roles of participants and/or the interaction or response of audiences making analysis of these aspects quite uneven.[8] Nonetheless, by examining this period through key transitional ritual moments, and the surviving records that captured them, this analysis confronts some of the core challenges faced by the first three Stewart monarchs, particularly concerning succession and royal authority, and thus contributes new insights into the means through which power was expressed and understood in this period.

Councils in the Scottish Kingdom c.1250–c.1450', in Jacqueline Rose (ed.), *The Politics of Counsel in England and Scotland, 1286–1707* (Oxford, 2016), 45–62, at 60; Penman and Reid, 'Guardian – Lieutenant – Governor', 217–18; Kilgallon, 'Communal Authority, Counsel and Resistance', 1–24, particularly 21–4.

[5] Edington, 'Wyntoun, Andrew (c.1350–c.1422)'; *Chron. Bower*, IX, particularly 204–9, 315–64.

[6] Bower can be found listed as an auditor for the collection of taxes in the records of the 1424 parliament (*RPS*, 1424/31), 1431 (*RPS*, 1431/10/2) and 1434 (*RPS*, 1434/2).

[7] *Chron. Bower*, VIII, 3–5; John J. McGavin, '"Robert III's Rough Music": Charivari and Diplomacy in a Medieval Scottish Court', *SHR* 74 (October, 1995), 144–58; John J. McGavin, *Theatricality and Narrative in Medieval and Early Modern Scotland* (Aldershot, 2007), 70–84.

[8] Andrews, 'Ritual and Space', 5.

The period 1371 to 1424 witnessed three revolutions of the cycle of death and succession that form the core of this chapter: the death of David II and the coronation of Robert II; the funeral of Robert II and coronation of Robert III; and the understated funeral of Robert III in 1406 to the return of James I in 1424. The chapter will argue that all the early Stewart adult monarchs (and associated lieutenants and governors) – not just James I – demonstrated a heightened awareness of the importance of display, even where they struggled to master the messages incorporated within such performances. This included the further integration of the acts of anointing and crowning with Scottish traditions, responsiveness to ceremonial developments occurring elsewhere and the focus of royal attention on Scone and Perth as a royal centre for the Stewart dynasty. Sacralisation and centralisation were tempered by the re-emergence and resilience of the tradition of secular outdoor enthronement. There was a recognition, particularly from Robert II, of the unique role developing for the political estates and parliament, which created a very Scottish scheme of events celebrating the process of succession. Public and open-access rituals were especially vital for a king whose ability to wield effective authority within the kingdom was challenged – an issue that all three of the early Stewarts faced, if for different reasons and with different results.

Robert II: from Steward to King

Named heir to Robert I in 1318 but superseded by David Bruce just six years later, Robert II's road to the throne was not an easy one.[9] As the Steward of Scotland, he ruled during his uncle's sustained absences (particularly post-1346), amassing land and power with a view to securing his position within the realm while producing a brood of sons and daughters.[10] Following the return of the childless David in 1357, the king repeatedly challenged the Steward's rights as heir and their relationship was fraught with tension as each sought to assert their own position at the expense of the other.[11] Yet, suggestions that the incoming Stewart monarch swept aside the legacy of David II in 1371 with a hurried burial, offering no 'symbolic continuity' to Robert II's coronation, or that a rapid funeral at Holyrood replaced plans for a second 'Bruce state funeral' at Dunfermline, seem highly unlikely.[12] Despite any personal animosity towards David, Robert stood to gain legitimacy

---

[9] RPS, 1318/30.
[10] Boardman argues that the legitimising of Robert's eldest children after David II's capture in 1346 was an attempt to bolster the position of his male heirs in terms of their right to succession: *Early Stewart Kings*, 8.
[11] On relations between Robert the Steward and David II, see ibid., 1–38; Penman, *David II*, 242–406.
[12] Penman, 'Christian Days and Knights', 269; Boardman, *Early Stewart Kings*, 39–40.

from building on the glorious dynastic foundations of his Bruce and Canmore predecessors. Equally, by the fourteenth century, across many European kingdoms including Scotland, death and burial held a prominent position in the accession of kings, and this was as much the case with an enemy or even a deposed king as it was with an elderly father who died in his bed.[13]

Extant evidence suggests that David had intended to be buried at Holyrood Abbey, in the Canongate near Edinburgh, rather than Dunfermline Abbey for many years before his death.[14] The surviving acts and charters of the reign are only remnants of a larger corpus of documents, but high proportions of those surviving relate to grants of land and other gifts, as these had value over generations as proof of ownership.[15] As such, the surviving material relating to Holyrood and Dunfermline offers evidence of David's favour towards them. Confirmation of Holyrood's existing rights was one of the earliest grants made after David's return from France (after Arbroath and Scone), including granting the 'office of the chaplain of the royal chapel' in 1342, and a number of confirmations and grants were also made in the final years of his life.[16] The majority of dated grants and confirmations for Dunfermline date from 1363, shortly after David's second marriage to Margaret Logie.[17] Assistance for conception and childbirth was frequently sought from St Margaret, whose shrine sat in Dunfermline Abbey, so this may have inspired generosity toward this house following their nuptials.[18] Furthermore, the only surviving petitions to the papacy on behalf of a monastery by David and his first wife Joan relate to Holyrood in 1348 and 1350; their joint interest in the site perhaps indicated plans to be interred there together.[19] There may have been no love lost between Robert II and David during the latter's lifetime, but evidence suggests Robert was continuing a plan of David's own making for his burial at Holyrood.

David's tomb demands our attention for similar reasons. Unfortunately, as with many Scottish royal tombs, the actual object was a victim of English attacks and Protestant zeal during the sixteenth and seventeenth centuries.

---

[13] For example, consider the funeral of Edward II, deposed by his wife, in 1327 but buried in state by Edward III, or the enemies of King Sverre in twelfth-century Norway, whose funerals were utilised in demonstrations of Sverre's right to the kingship: Joel F. Burden, 'Re-writing a Rite of Passage: The Peculiar Funeral of Edward II', in Nicola F. MacDonald and W. Mark Ormrod (eds), *Rites of Passage: Cultures of Transition in the Fourteenth Century* (York, 2004), 13–29; Brégiant, *Vox Regis*, 115–18.

[14] A suggestion also posited by Penman, see 'A Programme for Royal Tombs', 247–8.

[15] *RRS*, VI, iii–iv.

[16] Ibid., nos 59, 60, 71, 298, 446; *RMS*, I, nos 343, 347 and App. ii, nos 818, 1609, 1613. Unfortunately, there is no specific statement about burial at Holyrood.

[17] *RRS*, VI, nos 310–11; *RMS*, I, nos 144–5. Other dated grants are either made when David was a child (such as *RRS*, VI, no. 1) or linked to the royal confirmation of grants made by others (such as *RRS*, VI, no. 257; *RMS*, I, nos 944, 948).

[18] For the most recent discussions of St Margaret's role in childbirth, see Hayes, 'Late Medieval Scottish Queen', 132–4.

[19] *RRS*, VI, App. nos 15, 19.

Nonetheless, the surviving evidence of its construction confirms that David began the tomb in his lifetime and that Robert II continued with this task. Stone – particularly alabaster – for the monument made its way to Scotland from London and Flanders between 1367 and 1373, and English workmen were provided with a licence to work on the tomb of David II by Edward III of England in 1372.[20] Alabaster was a favoured material for effigies in fourteenth-century England, and the workmen who travelled north would have been immersed in the memorial culture of kinship tombs that was pervasive across England, the Low Countries and France.[21] Tombs displaying affinity and kin were definitely found in Scotland by the early fifteenth century, and the surviving tomb of Alexander Stewart, earl of Buchan, Robert II's fourth son, at Dunkeld Cathedral, c.1410x1430 (Plate 12), demonstrates that these were utilised by members of the royal family.[22] If statuettes of kin and affinity were included on David's tomb chest, Robert would likely have featured in a place of honour near his uncle's head as the deceased king's nephew and heir, offering a tangible and visual link between the two dynasties in stone. Some of the same English workmen who worked on David's tomb, along with similar materials, reappear in the costs for the programme of tombs and memorials that Robert embarked upon for his Stewart family in the ancestral mausoleum at Paisley and for his own tomb started in 1377.[23] Boardman has proposed that this tomb-building programme, combined with the remodelling of Dundonald castle (near Ayr in the heart of Stewart lands) and the patronage of literature, such as John Barbour's epic poem *The Bruce*, were 'a co-ordinated celebration of the monarch's paternal as well as maternal ancestry'.[24] Robert's actions reveal a heightened awareness of the need to

---

[20] *ER*, II, 300–48; *Rot. Scot.*, I, 949–50, 959. One of the workmen also worked on St Stephen's chapel, Westminster: Penman, 'A Programme of Royal Tombs', 248–9.

[21] Alabaster was used for the tombs of Edward II (d.1327), John of Eltham (d.1336), William Hatfield (d.1348), Isabelle de Valois (d.1356) and the joint tomb for the infant children of Edward III and Philippa, Blanche of the Tower (d.1342) and William of Windsor (d.1348): Duffy, *Royal Tombs*, 109–37. On kinship tombs: Morganstern, *Gothic Tombs of Kinship*, 82–102, 117–26.

[22] Initially, the figures on Buchan's tomb were thought to be weepers rather than kin members but, although they are now badly worn, the figures are dressed in armour, some hold shields and they are individually posed unlike archetypal pleurants or mourners found on fifteenth-century Burgundian tombs: A.V. Norman, 'The Effigy of Alexander Stewart Earl of Buchan and Lord of Badenoch (?1343–?1405)', *PSAS* 92 (1958–59), 104–13, at 105; Sophie Jugie, *The Mourners: Tomb Sculptures from the Court of Burgundy* (New Haven and London, 2010), 37–116; Morganstern, *Gothic Tombs of Kinship, passim*. Another prominent non-royal example from first half of fifteenth century survives in St Bride's church, Douglas, for Archibald, fifth earl of Douglas: David MacGibbon and Thomas Ross, *The Ecclesiastical Architecture of Scotland, from the Earliest Christian Times to the Seventeenth Century*, 3 vols (Edinburgh, 1896–98), I, 526, fig. 918. Thanks to Dr Lizzie Swarbrick for discussions and comparative examples on this subject.

[23] Paisley tombs: *ER*, II, 503, 622; III, 32, 222. Robert II's tomb: *ER*, II, 503, 585, 592, 608, 622; III, 348. See also Penman, 'A Programme of Royal Tombs', 248–9.

[24] Steve Boardman, 'Robert II (1371–1390)', in Brown and Tanner (eds), *Scottish Kingship*, 72–108, at 85.

Plate 12   Tomb of Alexander Stewart, 'the Wolf of Badenoch', c.1410x1420, Dunkeld Cathedral, photographed by the author, 2016.

secure permanent recognition of his personal dynastic lineage in stone and ink, as well as building on the memories of his royal predecessors.

While the tomb programme and other patronage demonstrate tangible connections being forged between the Bruce and Stewart dynasties, direct links between David II's funeral at Holyrood and Robert II's coronation at Scone are harder to extract from the extant sources. The chronicle accounts of 1371 indicate association between Robert II's coronation and that of David's father, Robert I, through the choice of date: 'Our Lady Day in Lentern' or 'the Annunciation of Our Lady' (25 March).[25] Wyntoun pointedly puts the choice of this date in Robert II's own hands, stating that the king 'gertset a certane day' for the event, but the parliament records state that the two-day coronation occurred on 26 and 27 March.[26] As the dates of the parliament records fall within the octave of the feast of the annunciation, the coronation would still have taken place in a period imbued with Marian liturgy and with the potential for guests to receive indulgences.[27] Nonetheless, this implies that it could have been the chronicler, rather than Robert II, who sought to make this direct connection with the anniversary of the inauguration of Robert I sixty-five years earlier as a means of cementing associations after the fact.

The fragmentary nature of financial materials, with missing accounts from the *Exchequer Rolls* for 1371–72, certainly hinders explorations of the

---

[25] *Chron. Wyntoun*, VI, 266–7; *Chron. Bower*, VII, 367; Boece, *Historia*, f. CCCLr; Bellenden's Boece, *Chronicle*, 336; *Chron. Fordun*, 370–1; Maior, *History*, 309.
[26] *Chron. Wyntoun*, VI, 266–7; *RPS*, A1371/1–2.
[27] On Marian feasts, see Harper, *The Forms and Orders of Western Liturgy*, 48–54; Fitch, *Search for Salvation*, 113–50, particularly at 120. For more on indulgences, see Duffy, *The Stripping of the Altars*, 193, 288–91.

ceremonies of 1371.[28] Indeed, the only expense specifically associated with Robert II's coronation was for the provision of wine.[29] A safe conduct for Andrew Peyntour [sic] and Henry Tankard, dated 14 July 1371, granted the men permission to pass from England to Scotland carrying items necessary for the funeral of David II.[30] This raises the possibility that, rather than rushing the funeral, months may have passed before the burial took place. Having the funeral later would have provided further time to work on David's tomb, but it was not unusual for kings to be buried prior to the completion of their tomb even when the work on that tomb was already underway.[31] The chronicle narratives state that David was honourably buried at Holyrood, after passing away in Edinburgh Castle; the ordering of events implicitly positioned the burial before the coronation but there are no details of the rituals that accompanied this. David's death is more clearly associated with the ritual 'election' of Robert as the rightful successor at Linlithgow.[32] Linlithgow was on a main land route north from Edinburgh to Scone so, had Robert attended David's burial at Holyrood prior to the coronation, this was a likely route north. With no mention from any narrative account as to who witnessed David's burial, however, it can only be speculated that Robert was present. Some of the most remarkable funerary rituals, particularly the treatment of medieval bodies, leave little – if any – mark in narrative chronicles and their analysis is often only possible where financial materials survive, as in the case of Robert I in 1329.[33] The fragmentary surviving evidence for 1371 means it must remain uncertain how much Robert was able to use David's funeral, associated processions and rituals to his advantage. Nonetheless, Robert's investment in the memory of his predecessor via the continuation of David's tomb monument does present the possibility that the funeral was employed in a similar manner.

Despite succession legislation that named Robert II as heir apparent, contemporary and later chronicle accounts record an assembly to choose, or acclaim, him as king following a stand made by the earl of Douglas at Linlithgow.[34] Boardman concludes that the most likely intent of the supposed confrontation was to remind Robert of the fragility of his claim and

---

[28] The custumar and baillies account, 1370–71, do not survive and there are only bulk summary totals from the clerks of liverance and the wardrobe accounts: Dean, 'Crowns, Wedding Rings, and Processions', 135.
[29] ER, II, 365.
[30] Rot. Scot., I, 945–6. Unlike other safe conducts discussed on 117, this one specifically states 'pro funere' rather than 'pro monumento sepulchral'.
[31] For example, see discussions of Henry III or Edward II: Duffy, Royal Tombs, 74–6, 146–8.
[32] 552 Chron. Fordon, 370–1; Wyntoun, VI, 264–7; Chron. Bower, VII, 364–7; Pluscarden, 234–6.
[33] See also Burden, 'Re-writing a Rite of Passage', 16.
[34] RPS, 1318/30; RPS, 1326/2; Chron. Wyntoun, VI, 264–7; Chron. Bower, VII, 364–7; Pluscarden, 234–6; Bellenden, Chronicle, 336–7; Maior, History, 309; Penman, 'Diffinicione successionis', 51–3.

the ease with which the English – promised the Scottish throne by David II on a number of occasions – might be drawn back into the fray.[35] While the rewards offered to Douglas, including a royal bride for his son, support the idea of Robert placating a potential rival, such generous behaviour was hardly unusual at the start of a new reign, especially one heralding dynastic shift. Concerning rituals of succession, the rhetoric of election and acclamation chosen by some of the chronicles offers insight into aspects deemed important to these Scottish writers in terms of ceremonial recognition of royal authority. Bower writes that:

> After the death of the splendid prince King David, the three estates of the realm met in the royal town of Linlithgow, and began to negotiate over the choice of their future king. They amicably voted in favour of the illustrious prince Sir Robert Stewart...[36]

The nature of the assembly and process of election described by Bower and later continuators emphasises the continued expectation of the three estates to be involved in the 'choice' of the monarch. This echoed the central role of acclamation in 1249 and their practical involvement in the judicial process of John Balliol's selection, as well as the rhetoric of the Appeal of the Seven Earls, the Declaration of the Clergy (1309) and the Declaration of Arbroath (1320).[37] These documents encompassed ideas about the right of the political community to choose the monarch or challenge one who did not protect the community of the realm. Such ideas, drawing on a range of classical and patristic sources, were found in treatises and royal handbooks in circulation in fourteenth-century Europe, combined with a general rise in representative political bodies around the ruler in the same era.[38] Moreover, in northern realms with elective kingship, such as Norway, the election – *Konungstekja* – was still integral to the king's accession even when coronation and unction were embraced; the election made the king and the coronation made him sacred.[39] With such Europe-wide developments and long-engrained traditions of election alongside hereditary succession in Scotland, it is unsurprising that the dynastic and political instability of the late thirteenth and fourteenth centuries shaped the ceremonies that followed in Scotland and created a heightened awareness for both the king and political community of their mutual inter-dependence.

The stylised pre-coronation acclamation recorded in the fourteenth-century English *Liber Regalis* holds some similarities, but the emphasis on choice, discussion and even voting recorded in the accounts of 1371 suggest a

---

[35] Boardman, *Early Stewart Kings*, 40–5.
[36] *Chron. Bower*, VII, 364–5. See also *Chron. Wyntoun*, VI, 264–7; *Pluscarden*, 235–6.
[37] 'Appeal of the Seven Earls'; *RPS*, 1309/2; *RPS*, 1320/4/1.
[38] Watts, *Making of Polities*, 233–86, particularly 254–63.
[39] Brégiant, *Vox Regis*, at 41–2, 262–4; for more on the *konungstejka* and its heritage and role, 33–159.

Scottish ritual borne of the political environment of late fourteenth-century Scotland.[40] As Lynn Kilgallon argues of a seemingly unique act of resistance to James I in the fifteenth century, the assembly and election-style event at Linlithgow did not emerge from a vacuum but was a product of the wider political context.[41] Boardman interprets this episode as indicative of a perceived weakness in Robert II's claim.[42] Conversely, by embracing the situation, arguably Robert strengthened his position by supporting the right of the political elite to invoke and confirm the authority of the 1326 act of succession and publicly acclaim his right to throne.[43] The Douglas 'outburst' or challenge also gave Robert the opportunity to settle the dispute through marriage alliance and negotiation rather than bloodshed as an initial demonstration of just kingship.[44] The role of the nobility and other estates remained central to the legitimising of the royal claim and, given his experience as a lieutenant of the realm and navigating power struggles with his predecessor, Robert II would have been keenly aware of the power of the political community.[45] Whether scripted to this effect or unexpected, this opening act of Robert's kingship was one that could be easily manipulated to emphasise public acceptance of Stewart kingship in Bower's narrative of the mid-fifteenth century.

The outdoor enthronement was reinstated as a central feature of the ceremony in 1371 for very similar reasons. The records of the coronation parliament provide a brief description of the main events – an unusual but happy survival – which clearly reveals the separation of events across two days. On the first day, in the abbey church, the king 'was crowned and anointed' by William de Landels, bishop of St Andrews before leading figures from around the realm.[46] Unfortunately, there is little further detail of the rituals, liturgy or objects used in the bestowal of Robert's kingship; in part, such absence is unsurprisingly muted by the brevity and secular nature of the parliamentary memoranda text that records the event. The second day relays a little more detail and was reminiscent – although certainly not a mirror image – of the outdoor inaugural enthronement ritual of the previous century:

> [...] the next day, with the king sitting on the royal throne upon the hill of Scone, as is the custom, the prelates, earls and barons and nobles written below assembled and compeared in his presence [...] All of whom individually made homage and oaths of fealty to our said lord the king [...][47]

[40] *Liber Regalis*, 83, 114; Burden, 'Rituals of Royalty', 35.
[41] Kilgallon, 'Communal Authority, Counsel and Resistance', 1–24, particularly at 2–3.
[42] Boardman, *Early Stewart Kings*, 44–5.
[43] *RPS*, 1326/2.
[44] *Wyntoun*, VI, 264–7; Boardman, *Early Stewart Kings*, 44–5.
[45] Robert's appointment and position of lieutenant during David II's minority and absences from the kingdom: *RPS*, 1339/1; *RPS*, 1357/1/1; *RPS*, 1357/9/1; *RPS*, 1357/9/2; Boardman, *Early Stewart Kings*, xvi, 1–38; Penman, *David II*, 55–60, 66–75, 140–53, 175–93; Brown, *Wars of Scotland*, 232–54, 316–41.
[46] *RPS*, 1371/1. William de Landels is also recorded as Landellis, see 107.
[47] *RPS*, 1371/2.

This reveals a physical and spatial division of the first day's religious and divine elements, held inside the church, from the second day's ceremony that centred upon the king enthroned outdoors to receive the homage and fealty of his people in an open air and raised accessible space.[48] This was also the first recorded use of the 'hill' at Scone for the enthronement, potentially marked out as a separate and distinctly royal political space within the abbey ground by a palisade fence, which suggests an innovation of situating the king's enthronement in a more visible and, arguably, a demonstrably secular position.[49] The manner in which the outdoor enthronement and the indoor coronation were divorced from one another in 1371 supports the argument that rituals were not static and their power resided in the ability to present both continuity and change.[50] The ritual enthronement for Robert II reflected descriptions of pre-1286 inaugurations at a first glance, but apparently sought to reject any blurring of boundaries between the ecclesiastical and secular ritual aspects of the king-making ceremony. This shift could represent a very conscious response by the secular lords – including the king perhaps – to the granting of unction, which had the potential to enhance ecclesiastical power in king-making ceremonies. Equally, positioning the outdoor enthronement and the accompanying homage-giving ceremony in a visibly prominent space also offered a second widely witnessed acceptance of Robert II's kingship: his coronation within Scone Abbey – viewed by the privileged few – was thus framed by the election at Linlithgow and this homage on the hill.

The parliament record provides a list of the individuals who paid homage and gave oaths to the king – including six bishops, five abbots and a prior, five earls and a host of barons, nobles, knights and lords, the hereditary High Constable of Scotland, Thomas de Hay, and Mariscal, William Keith, who held increasingly important ceremonial roles by the fifteenth century and beyond.[51] One key absentee from 1371 was an adult earl of Fife to enthrone Robert II on the Moot Hill. Isabella countess of Fife's husband, John Dunbar, was lord of Fife but the crown was contesting the title and lands, and these were granted to Robert Stewart, earl of Menteith and one of Robert's sons, on 30 March 1371.[52] The indenture recording the grant indicates that Isabella was at Perth, close to the coronation, and Boardman argues she took the

---

[48] Dean, 'Where to Make the King (or Queen)', 60–4.
[49] Oliver J.T. O'Grady, 'Accumulating Kingship: The Archaeology of Elite Assembly in Medieval Scotland', *World Archaeology*, 50:1 (2018), 137–49 at 139–44.
[50] For example, see Burden, 'Re-writing a Rite of Passage', 13–29, particularly 13–14, 28–9.
[51] *RPS*, 1371/2. See Appendix II. On role of the constable and mariscal, see Chapter 4, 155–6, 171.
[52] NLS, Charter no. 698; *The Red Book of Menteith*, ed. William Fraser, 2 vols (Edinburgh, 1880), II, 251–6.

hereditary role of the earl of Fife in enthroning Robert II.[53] There was a precedent for a female acting in this role: Isabella, countess of Buchan (of Fife by birth), performed it for Robert I. Thus, if the countess of Fife had enthroned Robert II, this 'complication' offered further visual ties to the Bruce's inauguration in 1306. Neither the oaths of the subjects nor that of the king survive, but the importance of making oaths upon a religious object is illuminated in contemporary descriptions of the bestowal of the royal lieutenancy in 1384.[54] In the record of attendees for 1371, the abbot of Dunfermline is listed above all other abbots in parliament, which could imply favoured status due to housing relics of St Margaret on which the king may have made his oath; although, this is speculative as there is no evidence of these relics being used in the Scottish ceremonies at Scone.[55]

In the wake of the Great Cause and the Wars of Independence, lineage was of heightened importance in Scotland.[56] Robert's sponsoring of history and genealogical texts, such as Barbour's *Bruce* and the now lost history of the house of Stewart, *The Stewartis Oryginalle* and/or *The Stewartis Genealogy*, and his tomb-building programme offer clear examples of his awareness of this.[57] However, there is no record of a poet reciting the genealogy in 1371, as featured so centrally in the inauguration of 1249. The early Stewarts had strong ties to the Gaelic world. Robert's acquisitions, pre-1371, were primarily Gaelic speaking and he acted as an intermediary for David II with communities in the west and north. Culturally, Robert venerated local saints like St Brendan of Bute and his father had a 'harpour' of high status, such as the figure found on the Scone seal from the thirteenth century (Plate 2, see p. 47).[58] An interest in promoting Stewart roots in the preceding Bruce and Canmore dynasties, and firm evidence that the practice of reciting genealogy continued into later centuries, albeit undertaken by a herald as discussed in

---

[53] Boardman, *Early Stewart Kings*, 50–2.
[54] When Robert's eldest son was made lieutenant records state that the three estates 'personally performed their oaths, touching the Holy Gospels': *RPS*, 1384/11/16.
[55] *RPS*, 1371/2.
[56] On elite interest in lineage demonstrated through literary patronage, see Michael Brown, '"Rejoice to Hear of Douglas": The House of Douglas and the Presentation of Magnate Power in Late Medieval Scotland', *SHR* 76 (Oct 1997), 161–84.
[57] *ER*, II, 566 (1377, £10 gratuity thought to be for the poem the *Brus*); *ER*, III, 136, 675, 681 (respectively 1386, £5; 1384, £10; 1386, £6, 8s. 4d.); *ER*, III, 208 (1388–89, charter granted for £10 annuity for life). In addition, there are also annual references to earlier annuities. *The Stewartis Oryginalle* and/or *The Stewartis Genealogy* was used by other chroniclers, such as Wyntoun: *Chron. Wyntoun*, V, 356–7. See also Roderick D. Lyall, 'The Lost Literature of Medieval Scotland', in J. Derrick McClure and Michael R.G. Spiller (eds), *Bryght Lanternis: Essays on the Literature of Medieval and Renaissance Scotland* (Aberdeen 1989), 33–47, at 39; Barbour, *Bruce*, 3; Boardman, *Early Stewart Kings*, 59–61.
[58] Steve Boardman, 'The Gaelic World and Early Stewart Court', in Dauvit Broun and Martin MacGregor (eds), Miorun Mor nan Gall, The Great Ill-Will of the Lowlander? (Glasgow, 2007), 83–109, particularly 84. The harpist was a recognisable figure on the Scone seal depicting Alexander III's inauguration: Bannerman, 'The King's Poet', 123–7, 134; Duncan, *Kingship of the Scots*, 134–9.

subsequent chapters, would strongly suggest that the traditional recitation of the genealogy occurred at Robert II's coronation and the Gaelic connections mean it was possibly undertaken by a poet.[59]

For M.G.J. Kinloch it was 'indisputable' that Robert II's coronation in 1371 was undertaken with 'the majestic ritual of Western Christendom', but he does not give the source of his information and surviving Scottish evidence makes this claim hard to quantify.[60] From the details Kinloch describes, it is likely that the *Ordo of Charles V* (c.1365), an illuminated copy of which was once thought to have been owned by the bishop of Glasgow, was a basis for his conclusions.[61] Orders of ceremony from France and England record ceremonies that embodied Jacques Le Goff's suggestion that royal consecration had evolved into extravagant representations of sacral monarchical power involving numerous additional elements, such as pre-coronation rituals and elaborate processions.[62] Of the attending bishops, Walter de Wardlaw, bishop of Glasgow and three others all attended French universities (predominantly Paris), while William de Landel, bishop of St Andrews, Walter de Coventry, bishop of Dunblane, and Bishop Wardlaw were all active ambassadorial figures in England and on the continent.[63] Wardlaw was in Paris in the

---

[59] This task was later undertaken by the Lyon herald who received fees in the reign of Robert II (see *ER*, III, 117; *RRS*, II, no. 63) but his name was not known: Francis J. Grant (ed.), *Court of the Lord Lyon: A List of His Majesty's Officers at Arms and Other Officials with Geographical Notes, 1318–1945* (Edinburgh, 1945), 1; Charles Burnett, 'Early Officers of Arms in Scotland', *Review of Scottish Culture* 9 (1996), 3–13, particularly 3–4; Katie Stevenson, 'Jurisdiction, Authority and Professionalisation: The Officers of Late Medieval Scotland', in Katie Stevenson (ed.), *The Herald in late Medieval Europe* (Woodbridge, 2009), 41–66.

[60] M.G.J. Kinloch, 'Scottish Coronations, AD 574–1651 (Part Two)', *Dublin Review* 131 (London, 1902), 34–52, at 47–8.

[61] BL, The Coronation Book of Charles V of France, MS Cotton Tiberius B VIII, fols 35–80; *The Coronation Book of Charles V. of France: Cotton MS Tiberius B VIII*, ed. Edward S. Dewick (London, 1899). For most detailed analysis of manuscript and text: Cara Ferguson O'Meara, *Monarchy and Consent: The Coronation Book of Charles V of France, British Library MS Cotton Tiberius B. VIII* (London and Turnhout, 2001). For debates about when the coronation book was added to the twelfth-century pontifical once owned by a bishop of Glasgow, see David McRoberts, *Catalogue of Scottish Liturgical Books and Fragments* (Glasgow, 1953), 4; Lyall, 'The Medieval Coronation Service', 17–20; Stephen M. Holmes, 'Catalogue of Liturgical Books and Fragments in Scotland before 1560', *IR* 62 (2011), 127–212, at 138; Ferguson O'Meara, *Monarchy and Consent*, 278–88.

[62] Le Goff, 'A Coronation Program for the Age of St Louis', 51–2. The *Ordo of Charles V*, dated c.1364, is one of the medieval French ordines used in the fourteenth and fifteenth centuries, see *Coronation Book of Charles V*; Jackson, *Vive le roi*, 24–40. The *Liber Regalis* dates from the fourteenth century: Andrew Hughes, 'The Origins and Descent of the Fourth Recension of the English Coronation', in Bak (ed.), *Coronations*, 197–216; *Liber Regalis*, 113–14; Strong, *Coronation*, 134–5.

[63] *RPS*, A1371/2; Robert Keith, *An Historical Catalogue of the Scottish Bishops Down to the Year 1688* (Edinburgh, 1824), 2–6, 246; Donald E.R. Watt, *A Biographical Dictionary of Scottish Graduates to A.D. 1410* (Oxford, 1977), 67–70, 114–15, 301–3, 328, 569–75; 'Landel, William de (d.1385), bishop of St Andrews and diplomat', *ODNB* (2004), https://doi.org/10.1093/ref:odnb/15970. Date accessed: 5 January 2021.

year prior to Robert's coronation, where Charles V's coronation manuscript and at least eight other *livres du sacre* were displayed at the Louvre, so it is possible that the bishop may have taken inspiration from viewing these on his visit.[64] The Scottish ceremony in 1371 was expanding and developing; not least by extending the proceedings over two days, or longer if the election is incorporated as a key aspect of the ceremonial in its entirety. Yet, even if the elusive coronation roll of David II's reign still existed or a copy of a French coronation manuscript influenced an attending bishop, the chance of replicating a ritual from a prescriptive texts was highly unlikely, if not impossible.[65] As stated previously, rituals were not static entities, rather they are actively reshaped in shifting contexts. As the first adult king officially anointed in Scotland, and first of his dynasty, Robert likely sought to stamp his own mark on the rite while maintaining continuity with what was recognisable to confirm his legitimacy.[66] Scottish literary and chronicle culture flourished in the late fourteenth and early fifteenth centuries, building on a corpus of earlier texts primarily originating from religious houses and cathedral chapters, including St Andrews and Dunfermline.[67] While no Scottish order of ceremony remains extant, texts such as the late thirteenth-century *Gesta Annalia I* containing descriptions of the inauguration of Alexander III in 1249 – featuring the rhetoric of election and acclamation, outdoor enthronement and the homage ceremony with recitation of the genealogy – were being circulated and incorporated into chronicle composites such as that of Fordun.[68] Records reveal that Robert's coronation offered an amalgamation of new and old, the divine and the secular and, arguably, the secular and traditional remained dominant.

Robert II's coronation in 1371 appears to have lacked tangible direct links to the funeral of his predecessor David II. However, the analysis is hampered by fragmentary evidence and the first Stewart king certainly took other opportunities to create symbolic connections to the Bruce dynasty and their shared Canmore predecessors through material remembrance, textual patronage and ceremonial display. It is notable that, despite apparent favour shown to the abbot of Dunfermline, there is no evidence to suggest there were efforts to link St Margaret to the act of unction through the holy oil, at this time or later, despite precedence for miracle stories linked to saints, dynastic lineage and the vessels (*ampullae*) for this substance in England or France and the incorporation of the relics of St Olaf into Norwegian king-making rituals.[69] Religiosity and the 'majestic rituals of Western Christendom' do

---

[64] Watt, *Dictionary of Scottish Graduates*, 573; Ferguson O'Meara, *Monarchy and Consent*, 278.
[65] The potential production of an order of coronation recorded in 1330s: *ER*, I, 381.
[66] Thiry, 'Rites of Reversion', 1391–1429; Burden, 'Re-writing A Rite of Passage', 14.
[67] Boardman, 'Chronicle Propaganda', 23–43; Watt commentary in *Chron. Bower*, passim; Broun, 'A New Look at Gesta Annalia', 9–30; Taylor, 'Historical Writing', 228–52; Broun, *Scottish Independence and the Idea of Britain*, 215–34.
[68] Ibid., 217.
[69] Amongst others see 'X. Letter of John XXII to Edward II about the Oil of Coronation',

Plate 13 Robert II Privy Seal, n.d. Crown Copyright, National Records of Scotland, Laing Seal Impressions, RH17/1/35.

not radiate from the surviving records of 1371. This may, in part, be due to the type of sources that survive but as a magnatial king – that is, one not born into kingship – and a longstanding member of the estates over which he now ruled, Robert II sought to recognise those elements of the coronation that would strengthen his position within the realm. Concentrating on the secular aspects of his inaugural rite, which emphasised his relationship with the political community, speaks to this aim. This could also account for the removal of the arms lowering the royal coat-of-arms from heaven on the Privy Seal, introduced by David II, and its replacement with a crown over the royal device that stepped away from such overt divine claims (Plate 13). Despite the incorporation of unction, those aspects of the ceremony that offered Robert II the ability to cast himself as a 'first among equals' were far more valuable.

Too Many Heirs and Spares?

Unlike his childless predecessor, Robert II had numerous male offspring but, far from securing his authority, Robert's male heirs proved a threat to dynastic stability.[70] Even in the opening years of his reign, issues of succession appear

in Legge, *English Coronation Records*, 69–76; Francis Oppenheimer, *The Legend of Ste. Ampoule* (London, 1953); T.A. Sandquist, 'The Holy Oil of St. Thomas of Canterbury', in T.A. Sandquist and Michael R. Powicke (eds), *Essays in Medieval History Presented to Bertie Wilkinson* (Toronto, 1969), 330–44; Jackson, *Vive le roi*, 31–4; Jacques Le Goff, 'La Structure et le contenu idéologique de cérémonie du sacre', in Jacques Le Goff et al., *Le Sacre royal a l'époque de Saint-Louis: d'après le manuscrit latin 1246 de la BNF* (Paris, 2001), 19–35; Brégiant, *Vox Regis*, 49–59.

[70] Robert II was certainly not alone in this challenge as adult sons caused strife for rulers elsewhere, including pertinently comparable examples of monarchs who were also the first of their dynasty in England: William Aird, 'Frustrated Masculinity: The Relationship

Plate 14   Seal of Euphemia queen of Scotland, 10 October 1375. Crown Copyright, National Records of Scotland, Laing Seal Impressions, RH17/1/36.

to have affected the ceremonies undertaken, as in the case of the coronation of Robert's queen, Euphemia. The exact date of Euphemia's coronation is unknown but, in contrast with other Scottish consorts married prior to coronation, it was separated by at least a year from that of Robert II's ceremony in March 1371.[71] There was an ongoing inheritance dispute over the order of succession that sought to honour the sons of Robert's first marriage to Elizabeth Mure, which was legitimised by papal dispensation after the birth of some of their children, before those of his second marriage to Euphemia.[72] Robert II favoured Euphemia's eldest son David, though he was still a child – created earl of Strathearn by 1371, swiftly followed by his receipt of the barony and castle of Urquhart (at the expense of one of Elizabeth's sons) – likely due to the influence of the queen and her powerful brother, William, earl of Ross (d.1372).[73] Nonetheless, the act of succession favouring Elizabeth's children was still agreed in a parliament held at Scone on 4 April 1373.[74] Euphemia's coronation receives minimal attention, but her surviving seal indicates

---

between William the Conqueror and his Eldest Son', in Dawn M. Hadley (ed.), *Masculinity in Medieval Europe* (Abingdon, 2014), 39–55; Katherine J. Lewis, *Kingship and Masculinity in Late Medieval England* (Abingdon, 2013), 67–83.

[71] *Chron. Bower*, VII, 375, 508. Fiona Downie suggests that the coronation took place between December 1372 and March 1373: *She is But a Woman: Queenship in Scotland 1424–1463* (Edinburgh, 2006), 89–90.

[72] By 1371 Robert II had three surviving adult sons by his first wife Elizabeth Mure – but these sons were only legitimised in the 1340s – and two sons, both children, with his second wife, Euphemia. There is some debate about whether contemporaries would have viewed the king's eldest sons as illegitimate, but Susan Marshall has convincingly argued it was unlikely due to the precedence it would have set more broadly for the rights of younger sons of second marriages for Scotland's elites: Marshall, *Illegitimacy in Medieval Scotland*, 100–16.

[73] Boardman, *Early Stewart Kings*, 74–6.

[74] *RPS*, 1373/3.

that she was perhaps both crowned and invested with a sceptre (Plate 14). The fifteenth-century chronicle accounts concur that the event took place at Scone in the same year as the death of Bridget of Sweden (1373).[75] As the year began on 25 March in Scotland, the queen's coronation must have taken place on or after this date. If concern existed that Euphemia's ceremonial elevation could give her sons precedence over their adult half-brothers – as occurred in the designation of Mael Coluim III's sons with St Margaret over the sons of his first wife in the eleventh century – it would make sense that the order of succession was settled in parliament beforehand.[76] This suggests that Euphemia's coronation was more significant than the brief comments in the chronicles imply. In purely practical terms, placing the coronation at the time of the parliament – which took place in March and April 1373 – meant that large numbers of the three estates could attend both events. Furthermore, proximity to the parliament in which the succession was formally decided, would have made a clear statement of Robert's royal authority and the subordinate authority of his queen despite her ritual elevation. A time lapse from 1371 to 1373 was unusual, but issues of succession provide a convincing explanation for a disruption to these proceedings.

In 1390, when Robert II died, the political situation surrounding the dynastic transfer of power was even more complex. Robert's ambitious eldest son, John earl of Carrick (who succeeded his father as Robert III), was installed as lieutenant of the realm between 1384 and 1388, only to be displaced by his younger brother, Robert earl of Fife, who became lieutenant in 1388 until his father's death.[77] A power struggle between the brothers – including Alexander, earl of Buchan (the Wolf of Badenoch), raising additional pressures in the north – have been identified as the reason for the delay between Robert II's death in April and his burial in August.[78] Months passing between death and burial were not unusual by the fourteenth century where power was contested: during the political confusion of late 1327, Edward II's regal burial at Gloucester took place three months after his murder.[79] Yet, there were also examples where monarchs dictated a significant date for burial: Henry IV died in late March 1413, but was buried on 18 July due to his request to be buried on Trinity Sunday in the Trinity Chapel at Canterbury.[80] Political instability extended the gap between Robert II's death and burial, but ceremonial reasons for the delay are also discernible. The

---

[75] *Chron. Bower*, VII, 375; *Pluscarden*, 238. St Bridget of Sweden died in July 1373 (canonised 1391) and was incredibly popular in England during the fifteenth century: Laura Saetvelt Miles, 'Bridget of Sweden', in Liz Herbert McAvoy and Diane Watt (eds), *The History of British Women's Writing, 700–1500, Volume 1* (Basingstoke, 2012), 207–15.
[76] For eleventh-century succession, see Chapter 1, 21–2, 24.
[77] RPS, 1384/11/4–5; RPS, 1388/12/1.
[78] Boardman, *Early Stewart Kings*; 173–5.
[79] Burden, 'Re-writing A Rite of Passage', 14–17.
[80] Griffiths, 'Succession and the Royal Dead', 102.

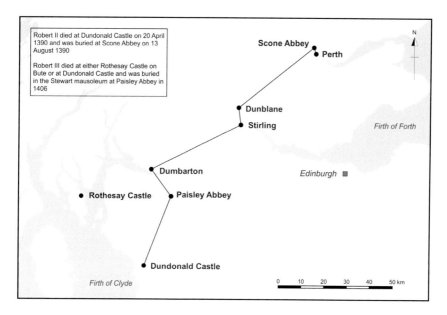

Map 6   Potential route of funeral processions of Robert II and Robert III, 1371 and 1390.

four-day event in August 1390 was centred on the feast of the Assumption of Our Lady on 15 August. This date may have been specifically chosen to link Robert III's succession to a feast of the Blessed Virgin and, thus, to his father and Robert I, both of whom were crowned during the octave of the feast of the Annunciation of the Virgin.[81] Burden and Griffiths have demonstrated that, in the case of England, challenges to a seamless cycle of succession facilitated some of the most notable ceremonial developments and can witness rituals performing 'overt political functions'.[82] By drawing together Robert II's funeral with the three-day coronation event for Robert III and his queen, Annabella Drummond, the ceremonial display in its entirety united the rituals of death and succession in the same temporal and physical space in a way that had not been witnessed in Scotland previously.[83]

In this final ceremony, Robert II, and his eldest son Robert III (John of Carrick), made determined moves to emphasise the direct dynastic transfer of power from father to eldest son. No will survives recording Robert II's wishes, but his hand in the design of these events speaks through surviving evidence. His death at Dundonald, a favourite seat in his ancestral lands of Ayrshire in the southwest, and his burial at Scone, a site he had selected for

[81]   See 118, and Chapter 2, 76, 85.
[82]   Burden, 'Rewriting A Rite of Passage', 14; Griffiths, 'Succession and the Royal Dead', 99–101.
[83]   *Chron. Bower*, VI, 3–4; *Pluscarden*, 252–3; *Chron. Wyntoun*, VI, 366–8.

burial in the late 1370s, made an extended procession between the two sites a necessity.[84]

> At Dundownald in his cuntre/ Off ane schort seiknes deyt he;/
> Fra þine to Scone his men him bair,/ And richely was he bereyt þair./
> Off all his kinryk þe prelatis,/ And uthir lords of hie estaitis/
> At his entyrment war their [...][85]

The exact route of this ninety- to one-hundred-mile journey is not known but possible stopping points can be identified between Dundonald and Scone: the family mausoleum at Paisley, the church at Dumbarton where offerings for Masses for the king's soul were made, Dunblane or Stirling and, finally, Perth (Map 6).[86] Importantly, whatever route was taken, Robert II's final journey travelled through his familial heartlands and, like Robert I, across the central belt of power in the realm. Perth would have provided a fitting place for the penultimate vigil, as well as enough accommodation and supplies for the members of the estates gathering for a funeral, coronation and parliament. The rhyming verse of Andrew of Wyntoun implies that the king was carried on the shoulders of his men: possibly knights, officers of arms or cadet family members. This last two-and-half-mile stretch, or a section of it as had been the case in 1214, would have provided the opportune time for such ceremonial display. The prominence and visual impact of such a procession, and demonstrations of loyalty to the king, were even more important due to the underlying tension between his sons. The efforts to project an image of unity may also have been mirrored in the design of Robert II's tomb if this included familial statuettes depicting progeny, rather than dynastic lineage, due to concerns around succession caused by having a plethora of legitimate children.[87]

By selecting the abbey at Scone for his final resting place, Robert II also united his interment with the crowning of Robert III at a significant site central to the governance of the kingdom. Scone's prominence as a meeting place for parliament, along with nearby Perth, was promoted by David II and the Stewart monarchs who followed him during the late fourteenth and early fifteenth century.[88] Five of the seven parliaments and councils of Robert II's reign, prior to Carrick's guardianship, were held at Scone or neighbouring

---

[84] Robert II's tomb was under construction at Scone long before his death: *ER*, II, 503, 585, 592, 608, 622; *ER*, III, 348. Stone for Robert's tomb was moved from Holyrood Abbey via Leith to Perth in 1377–78 (592), so the initial payments (1376–77) could suggest preparations for burial alongside his uncle and predecessor, David II (585). However, if there was a brief flirtation with creating a mausoleum at Holyrood, the idea was quickly replaced with Scone.
[85] 'Wemyss MS' in *Chron. Wyntoun*, VI, 354.
[86] *ER*, III, 231.
[87] See Morganstern on Edward III: *Gothic Tombs of Kinship*, 117–26.
[88] For more discussion, see Dean, 'Where to Make the King (or Queen)', 61–2.

Perth and all declarations regarding succession took place at Scone.[89] This mirrored Robert I's choice of Scone for the original 1318 entail of the throne of Scotland to the Stewart line (through the son of his daughter Marjory, Robert II).[90] The favour shown to Perth and Scone continued under Robert III, with ten out of sixteen known gatherings of the estates occurring there, while the royal exchequer most commonly conducted its business in Perth throughout both reigns.[91] In their selection of this ritual space, the first two Stewart kings – and those who advised them – actively centralised the mechanics of governance and the ceremonies of death and succession at one place, in a manner reminiscent of Westminster for England, signifying a proto-capital status for Perth and Scone.

Combining the funeral and coronation in a single event does present some challenges in deciphering expenses in the *Exchequer Rolls*, as the largest payment of £402, 15s. 4d. is a combined amount relating to both occasions.[92] Moreover, most expenses survive as bulk payments to officials, such as the king's clerk of the wardrobe, Walter Forester, who received over £250 to cover expenses associated with the funeral and almost £130 for wardrobe items for the coronation.[93] Without itemised lists, a better understanding of the objects and clothing purchased for these ceremonies is difficult to achieve. The expenses do offer hints at Perth's role as a royal base. For example, the clerk of the liverance, Ricardo Bard, received £27, 6s. 8d. for expenses for the king's household in Perth after the coronation, and two shillings were paid to the baillies of Perth for the delivery of letters at the time of the coronation.[94] This indicates that the local community was drawn into the preparations and may have financially benefited. However, Bower's account of the crushing of crops by 'the crowd from every part of the kingdom that gathered for the king's coronation' also speaks to the potential negative impact that such ceremonial events, and the resultant confluence of large numbers of people in one place, would have on everyday life.[95]

The damage caused to crops at Scone resulted in one of the earliest accounts of *charivari* or rough music – a custom in which people sought to shame an individual or group seen to have done wrong by parading and making of raucous noise on implements, such as pots and pans – in the northern British Isles.[96] The courtiers' reaction to this ritual behaviour from the

---

[89] *RPS* shows that parliaments or councils occurred at Scone in 1371, 1372, 1373 and 1382 with a fifth in Perth in 1382 also. Acts of succession: *RPS*, 1371/4; *RPS*, 1373/3.
[90] Ibid., 1318/30.
[91] *RPS* shows that parliaments or councils occurred at Scone in 1390, 1391, 1394, 1401, 1401–02, 1404, and in Perth in 1392, 1393, 1398 and 1399. For exchequer locations, see *ER*, II, vii–xxxi; *ER*, III, vii–xxxix.
[92] Ibid., 279.
[93] '*pro exquiis et sepultra regis nuper defuncti*' and '*pro diversis receptis in gardrobam ad expensas regis facta eciam* [sic] *apud Sconam eodem tempore [coronacione regis]*': *ER*, III, 279–80.
[94] Ibid., 227, 229, 235.
[95] *Chron. Bower*, VIII, 3–5.
[96] On *charivari* generally, see Jacques Le Goff and Jean-Claude Schmitt (eds), *Le*

common people was to demand punishment, but the king – 'wise man that he was' – had the damage assessed and reparations paid.[97] Whether such an event occurred is unclear. Bower could have introduced such an episode to emphasise Robert III's humility – a quality Bower repeatedly assigned to him. However, the coronation coincided with the nearing harvest and the granger canon, Robert Logy of Scone, who led the protest subsequently received royal favour. Due to this evidence John McGavin argues that this popular protest was likely and that, through his response, Robert III demonstrated his understanding of the ritualised language of his people.[98] The episode allowed popular access to the king's person at a crucial point in his reign, even though his courtiers may have deemed the intervention inappropriate. Moreover, it provides rare insight into the reception of a ceremonial gathering within a specific locality and the potential disruptions to daily activities that such proceedings could cause.

Wyntoun provides more information about both ritual objects and their bestowal on the king during the coronation ceremony within the abbey church in 1390 than previously found:

[Th]e Bischope of Sancte Androwis se,/ Walter, with gret solempnyte/
Gaf our kynge [th]ar [th]e crowne,/ His suerde, his sceptere, and vnccione./[99]

The regalia items – a crown, sword and sceptre – were tightly associated with the act of anointing as all these objects and the unction were 'given' to the king by Walter Trail, bishop of St Andrews.[100] The second pre-eminent Scottish bishop Matthew de Glendonwyn, the bishop of Glasgow, performed a 'collacion' within the coronation liturgy.[101] The splitting of roles reflected the fact that the papal bull of 1329 named both bishops as potential officiants.[102] The same two bishops also officiated at the funeral: here the impor-

---

Charivari: actes de la table ronde organisée à Paris (25–27 avril 1977) par l'École des Hautes Études en Sciences Sociales et le Centre National de la Recherche Scientifique (Paris, 1981); Tom Pettit, 'Protesting Inversions: Charivari as Folk Pageantry and Folk-Law', *Medieval English Theatre* 21 (1999), 21–51; Emma Dillon, *The Sense of Sound: Musical Meaning in France, 1260–1330* (Oxford and New York, 2012), specifically Chapter 3 on 'Charivari', 93–128. On Scottish *charivari* specifically: McGavin, 'Robert III's Rough Music', 144–58; McGavin, *Theatricality and Narrative*, 70–84.

97 *Chron. Bower*, VIII, 3–5.
98 McGavin, 'Robert III's Rough Music', 155.
99 'Cottonian MS' in *Chron. Wyntoun*, VI, 366–8.
100 When discussing the regalia in 1406 Wyntoun also mentions a ring within the regalia, but this is not referred to here: *Chron. Wyntoun*, VI, 416.
101 Collacion or collacioun likely translates as conference or talk in this context; this perhaps refers to the sermon, but Wyntoun uses this specific term in the same entry, so it may be a Scots term for the 'Collect' within the liturgy of the Mass: 'Collatioun, Collacioun', *Dictionary of the Old Scots Language (DSL)*, ed. Susan Rennie (February 2004): https://dsl.ac.uk/entry/dost/collatioun. Date accessed: 27 September 2022; Harper, *The Forms and Orders of Western Liturgy*, 85, 114–16, 122, 127–30, 294.
102 'Bull of John XXII Concerning the Coronation', 24–5.

tance of the roles was reversed as Glendonwyn undertook the requiem Mass and Trail performed the 'collacion'.[103] Having the same two bishops preside over the liturgical rites during these ceremonies provided a further tangible reinforcement of the succession from father to son within the performance of the rituals of death and succession.

Two other named bishops also took active roles in the three-day coronation event. John de Peebles, bishop of Dunkeld, crowned Annabella, Robert III's wife, and gave a sermon that 'accordande weil' with the feast of the Assumption of the Virgin, the day on which her coronation took place, while Thomas de Rossy, bishop of Galloway, 'gave a rycht pleyssande' sermon during the outdoor homage ritual.[104] Following the divorcing of secular and ecclesiastical elements in the coronation of Robert II in 1371, this was a notable addition that re-blurred the distinctive nature of the two parts to the king-making. The 1390 homage ceremony also potentially lacked a representative of the earl of Fife to perform the enthronement. The king's brother – Robert – was the earl of Fife and there is little evidence to suggest that he undertook the traditional role of enthroning the king. If effectively handled by Robert III, having the earl enthrone him could have acted as a visual confirmation that his brother accepted his authority as king, even after the reconfirmation of Fife's position as lieutenant in 1390.[105] Yet, Fife's apparent absence would have exposed the real tensions underpinning the ritual transferral of power, meaning that this ecclesiastical intervention in the homage ceremony may have been an effort to distract attention with a liturgical gloss to the proceedings. Ultimately, if Fife's absence from the chronicle accounts reflected reality, it had the potential to create visible fissures in the carefully crafted façade of stability that the combination of innovation and tradition within this ceremonial cycle had sought so hard to maintain.

Robert III's primary means of promoting the succession of his direct line in the subsequent decade revolved around his eldest son and heir David, earl of Carrick, who was a living symbol of the promise of stability offered by dynastic continuity. David's maturing on the political scene in the 1390s witnessed a temporary eclipse of the earl of Fife, a process that gathered momentum following Fife's removal from the role of lieutenant in 1393.[106] This period saw the creation of a separate household for the heir to the throne, thus providing another court and a new source of patronage.[107] Ceremonial occasions were utilised by both Robert III and Queen Annabella in these years to raise their eldest son into a position of political supremacy. Such events – including the pitched battle on the North Inch of Perth, for which stands were built for the

[103] 'Cottonian MS' in *Chron. Wyntoun*, VI, 336–8.
[104] Ibid.
[105] Fife was made lieutenant in 1388 and this was reconfirmed in 1390: Boardman, *Early Stewart Kings*; 148–53, 173–8.
[106] Boardman, *Early Stewart Kings*, 195–7.
[107] For most detailed analysis of David, earl of Carrick, see ibid., 194–254.

observing crowds, and a tournament orchestrated by Annabella to celebrate David's knighthood in 1398 – sought to place the heir at the centre of a Scottish chivalric culture made famous in the words of Barbour's *Bruce*.[108] Two rituals were key to David's promotion as the legitimate heir: his creation as duke of Rothesay in 1398 – along with Fife, who was made duke of Albany – and his subsequent elevation to the position of lieutenant of the realm in 1399.[109] The first took place at Scone: the site promoted as the symbolic centre of Scottish royal power and governance, intricately connected to the legitimacy of the Stewart dynasty and now also the site of the tomb of its founder, Robert II.[110] The second, centring on the taking of an oath in a general council, occurred in neighbouring Perth – the extension of the royal powerbase.[111] Bower's account of the ducal creation ceremony records Walter Trail, bishop of St Andrews, 'celebrating mass and preaching before the king and queen', which suggests that a direct liturgical intervention took place at this secular royal appointment.[112] The newly created duke of Rothesay was obliged by a general council that met in 1399 to take an oath – modelled on that taken by the king 'at his crowning' – prior to taking the role of king's lieutenant.[113] This demand reflects the concurrent need for acceptance of crown appointments by the estates, while the documenting of the process in the council's records indicates a collective interest in the rituals that confirmed such appointments. Consequently, these ceremonies for the heir reflected the necessity for spiritual and temporal affirmations of royal power as found in the coronations of Scottish kings. To firmly cement David's position and secure the succession, marriage was crucial. Unfortunately, David's romantic liaisons became a source of turmoil and tension within the realm rather than providing opportunities for ceremonial projections of stability.[114]

---

[108] *Chron. Bower*, VIII, 7–13; *ER*, III, 418, 436, 526, 596.

[109] Boardman suggests that these ducal creations, with titles of Gaelic origin, were linked to a wider crown-driven political and military campaign against the Lords of the Isles: *Early Stewart Kings*, 207–8.

[110] *Registrum Episcopatus Moraviensis*, ed. Cosmo Innes (Edinburgh, 1837), 382; *Chron. Bower*, VIII, 12–13; *Chron. Wyntoun*, VI, 383–4; *Pluscarden*, 254; *ER*, III, 460.

[111] *RPS*, 1399/1/3. The exact location in Perth is not identified in the surviving records.

[112] *Chron. Bower*, VIII, 12–13.

[113] Ibid. The oath performed by David in 1399 focused upon the protection of the kirk and people, the upholding of freedoms and privileges, keeping of laws and customs: *RPS*, 1399/1/3.

[114] Boardman, *Early Stewart Kings*, 200–1, 203–4, 226–7. Annabella sought out an English bride for her younger son, James (b. 1394), in communication with Richard II, but David's matches were with daughters of noblemen within the realm: 'Letter from Annabella Queen of Robert III, to Richard II of England … 1394', in *Facsimile of the National Manuscripts of Scotland*, 42; Hayes, 'Late Medieval Scottish Queens', 137–8.

Lost and Found: The Return of the King

The cycle of succession faced a far greater challenge in 1406 when Robert III died; as in 1286, the heir to the throne was a minor and physically absent from the realm. In 1402 David, duke of Rothesay, was murdered in his early twenties at the hand of his uncle, and shortly before Robert III's death his only surviving son and heir, twelve-year-old James, was captured by English pirates and imprisoned by Henry IV of England.[115] For a seamless transfer of power from father to son, the absence of the young heir to the throne was a serious practical problem, but it was not insurmountable nor without precedent in Scotland or beyond. Robert III had invested in the completion of his father's tomb at Scone, completed in 1394, along with funding Masses for the dead.[116] Nonetheless, rather than requesting burial at this centre of royal power, Robert was buried at the Stewart mausoleum at Paisley. This final resting place echoes a conversation, penned by Bower, that records Queen Annabella's concerns that her husband was not preparing a suitable royal tomb; to which, Robert responds with the often-quoted statement about wanting to be buried unnamed in a midden.[117] Yet, the actual owner of the decision for Robert III's burial at Paisley is unknown. Chronicle accounts indicate that his death occurred on Palm Sunday, a week before Easter Sunday, and it was directly associated with Christ's death by Bower.[118] Vigils for the king, and even the burial, could have been incorporated in the rich symbolism of Holy Week but there are no details surviving for this. The records are also quiet about who attended or how – if at all – the funeral was associated with the acceptance of Robert, duke of Albany and earl of Fife, as governor of the realm at Perth. The estates raised Albany to this position, likely following past precedent of 1384, 1388 and 1399, and records from the burgh of Aberdeen indicate that the general business of the council was paused.[119] Even without a burial at Scone, Albany could have still utilised the required rituals associated with death to bolster his own position. For example, Robert III's final vigils could have been observed conspicuously, while a procession from Paisley to Perth to attend the council meeting that made him governor would have encompassed wide swathes of the central belt. Yet, there is no evidence that Albany took advantage of making such ceremonial connec-

---

[115] David, duke of Rothesay, died in suspicious circumstances while in the care of his uncle, Robert, earl of Fife and duke of Albany: Boardman, *Early Stewart Kings*, 235–45, 291–5.
[116] *ER*, III, 297, 307, 348, 545, 579, 626, 631, 641.
[117] *Chron. Bower*, VIII, 64–5.
[118] Ibid., 63; *Wyntoun*, VI, 415.
[119] *RPS*, 1384/11/4–5; *RPS*, 1388/12/1; *RPS*, 1399/1/3; *RPS*, A1406/1; *Early Records of the Burgh Accounts of Aberdeen, 1317, 1398–1407*, ed. William Croft Dickinson (Edinburgh, 1957), 220.

tions between his brother's passing and his accession as governor of Scotland in 1406.

The use of the title 'governor', which seems to have emerged for Albany in this situation and vanished again for the fifteenth-century minority leaders, suggests that there was a recognition by Albany or the estates, or both, that the authority required in James's absence was different from that of Albany's former role as lieutenant for his father or brother.[120] Albany's quasi-royal pretensions are easily illustrated. He confirmed legislation and granted charters with no reference to the absent king, he recorded time passing by the number of years of his governorship rather than regnal years, made efforts to secure an advantageous marriage for his daughter to the second son of Henry IV and quartered the royal arms with his personal arms on his governor's seal.[121] These actions, combined with half-hearted attempts to secure James's release, underpin accusations that he sought the crown for himself.[122] However, Karen Hunt argues that the seal, in particular, was a 'necessary and practical prerequisite to good government' and could be likened to the seal used by the guardians in the succession crisis following the death of Alexander III in 1286.[123] In both cases, the long-term absence of a monarch encouraged the political community to adopt symbols of royal power in order to support the stability of the realm but, unlike the guardians in 1286, who used St Andrew on their guardian's seal (Plate 7, see p. 74), Albany inserted himself personally. Mimicking personal royal authority may have been a necessity. Nonetheless, it could equally have been perceived as a challenge to a long-absent monarch, particularly one who had not received a full coronation, when power was so clearly vested in one individual and passed down his dynastic line at his death.[124]

The documents that confirmed the transfer of power back to James I from the governor, then Robert's son, Murdoch, in April 1424 stated that this was '*Anno Regni nostri Decima Nono*' or the 'nineteenth year of our reign'.[125] This suggests that in Scotland – as in England by the fifteenth century – the point of 'actual' power transfer from one king to the next was deemed to be the death of the previous monarch.[126] However, the intervening period of absence for James – during which the governor dominated politically, making use of quasi-royal symbols, and other prominent Scottish nobles

[120] Ibid.; *RPS*, A1406/1; *Chron. Bower*, VIII, 65; *Chron. Wyntoun*, VI, 416–7.
[121] For example, see *RPS*, 1410/1–2; NRS, Letter from Henry IV to Robert Duke of Albany, SP6/10. On the governor's seal: *ER*, IV, 69, 86–7; Burnett, 'Preface', *ER*, IV, xlviii–xlix; Birch, *History of Scottish Seals*, 58; Karen Hunt, 'The Governorship of the First Duke of Albany, 1406–1420' (PhD thesis, University of Edinburgh, 1998), 26–8.
[122] Nicholson, *Scotland: The Later Middle Ages*, 256; Grant, *Independence and Nationhood*, 184–6; Brown, *James I*, 26.
[123] Hunt, 'The Governorship of the First Duke of Albany', 26–8.
[124] Robert, duke of Albany, died in 1420 and was succeeded by his son, Murdoch, both as duke and governor.
[125] *Foedera*, IV, part iv, 115; also see *RPS*, 1424/1.
[126] Griffiths, 'Succession and the Royal Dead', 104–5.

gained recognition in the service of foreign monarchs – left the returning king with many of the challenges faced by David II upon his return.[127] Unlike David though, while James I had been named king in 1406, contemporary commentators – such as Wyntoun – were careful to emphasise that James had not received the ritual objects that were, by then, recognisable symbols of kingship to contemporary Scots:

> Our king fra [th]ine callit be,
> Set he was in Ingland styll
> Haldyn all agane his will,
> [Th]at he mycht on nakyn wys,
> Take ony of his insignyis,
> As crowne, ceptoure, suerd or ring,
> Syk as afferis till a king
> Off kynd be rycht; [y]it neuir[th]eles
> Oure lege lorde and king he was […][128]

This situation offered James an opportunity – one not open to David II, who was crowned as a child – to utilise these physical symbols of rule in the reconstruction and reshaping of his relationship with the political community and the kingdom more broadly.[129] Brown states that 'the formal transition of power occurred in two stages': the sealing of the treaty that confirmed James I's release at Durham on 28 March 1424 and the surrender of the seals of office by Murdoch at Melrose on 5 April.[130] These two events certainly marked the start of the process of power transfer. Yet, after such a lengthy absence, this transition of power required wider public and symbolic legitimisation. This section explores the ritualised displays – including a royal entry, a double coronation with his wife and a separate enthronement, an inaugural parliament and a ceremonial dubbing of knights – that were harnessed to consolidate the legitimacy of James's kingship upon his return to Scotland.

If the early sixteenth-century humanist Hector Boece is correct in his description of the return of James I in 1424, this king made the first known Scottish *'ingressus'* or royal entry into the burgh of Edinburgh.[131] Boece was writing a century later, when Edinburgh had risen in importance as a centre

---

[127] Archibald Douglas, fourth earl of Douglas, was a prime example as his service to the French monarch, Charles VII, led to his creation as duke of Touraine on 29 April 1424, between James's arrival in Scotland and his coronation, and made a grand ducal entry into the town of Tours on 7 May: *Le Écossais en France, les Français en Écosse*, ed. F. Michel, 2 vols (London, 1862), I, 139–40; W. Forbes-Leith, *The Scots Men-At-Arms and Life-Guards in France. From their Formation until their Final Dissolution A.D. MCCCCXVIII–MDCCCXXX* (Edinburgh, 1882), 24–7.
[128] *Chron. Wyntoun*, VI, 416.
[129] Mörke, 'The Symbolism of Rulership', 34–6.
[130] *Foedera*, IV, part iv, 108–12, 115; Brown, *James I*, 40.
[131] Boece, *Historia*, fol. CCCLIXr. Translated, although with disparities on word choice and some minor details, in Bellenden's Boece, *Chronicle*, 382.

of government. Yet, urban environments offered a larger audience that the returning king could harness.[132] The more contemporary account of Regnault Girard – a member of the French embassy tasked with finalising negotiations and escorting James's eldest daughter, Margaret, to marry the dauphin of France – recorded his welcome to Edinburgh in 1435: on approaching the burgh, a delegation headed by the chamberlain, the keeper of the Privy Seal, the master of the king's household and numerous prelates emerged to greet the French party.[133] Girard was met by royal officials and clerics, which was perhaps unsurprising for a guest of the king, but the evidence is less certain about who took the lead in greeting James I in 1424. In Bellenden's translation of Boece's account the group who came to meet the king were the 'nobillis of Scotland', but in Boece's original Latin text it was the '*magistratibus ac clero*', or civil officials along with the clerics, of Edinburgh.[134] Representatives of a town or city coming out to meet the approaching ruler or visitor was a relatively common motif of European entry ceremonies and *joyeuse entrée* by the fifteenth century symbolising the beginning, or renewal, of a dialogue between the ruler and the ruled.[135] During his captivity, James had an active, if intermittent, role at the Lancastrian court and likely witnessed entries into both London and Paris, such as Henry V's victorious return from Agincourt in 1415, when ten thousand citizens and nobles dressed in red met the king on horseback outside the city of London at Blackheath.[136] It is not a stretch of the imagination to suggest that James was influenced by the elaborate ceremonial processions of Henry V's victorious years. Certainly, later in his reign, James was the first Scottish

[132] Brégiant, *Vox Regis*, 262.
[133] BNF, Manuscrits Français 17330, fols 128r, 132v (Girard also visited Dundee and St Andrews, including the recently founded university); L. Barbé, *Margaret of Scotland and the Dauphin Louis* (London, Glasgow and Bombay, 1917), 55, 62.
[134] Bellenden's Boece, *Chronicle*, 382; Boece, *Historia*, fol. CCCLIXr.
[135] Lawrence M. Bryant, *The King and the City in the Parisian Royal Entry Ceremony: Politics, Ritual, and Art in the Renaissance* (Geneva, 1986), 73–83; Andrew Brown and Graeme Small, *Court and Civic Society in the Burgundian Low Countries, c.1420–1530* (Manchester, 2007), 23–8, 165–7, 176–7; Wim Hüsken, 'Royal Entries in Flanders (1336–1515)', in Dagmar Eichberger, Anne-Marie Legaré and Wim Hüsken (eds), *Women at the Burgundian Court: Presence and Influence* (Turnhout, 2010), 37–42.
[136] For James's activities and expenditure on him, see *CDS*, IV, nos 723, 727, 739, 740, 777, 784, 837, 846–7, 850, 852, 857, 874, 877, 883, 886, 892, 895, 897–9, 908, 911–12, 918, 923, 931, 937; Brown, *James I*, 20–4; Michael Penman, 'The Lion Captive: Scottish Royals as Prisoners in England, c.1070–c.1424', *Quaestiones Medii Aevi Novae* 20 (2015), 413–34, at 429–33. For the 1415 entry: *Chronicle of Adam Usk, 1377–1421*, trans. and ed. Chris Given-Wilson (Oxford, 1997), 259–63. The best evidence for James' active involvement in Lancastrian ceremonies is for the wedding and coronation of Henry V's bride, Katherine of Valois: *The Chronica Maiora of Thomas Walsingham, 1376–1422*, trans. David Preest, ed. James G. Clark (Woodbridge, 2005), 437; TNA, Letter from Humphrey Duke of Gloucester [brother of Henry V] to the king [c. 1420], SC1/43/191; *CDS*, IV, nos 897–9; 'Chronicle of William Gregory, Skinner', in *The Historical Collections of a Citizen of London [viz. William Gregory] in the Fifteenth Century*, Vol. XVII of the Camden Society Series, ed. James Gairdner (London, 1876), 139; Burden, 'Rituals of Royalty', 197–220.

monarch known to have ensured oratory praise and celebration of his royal status during his lifetime, along with that of his queen and his children, through legislation passed in parliament that instructed the clergy to 'make processions and special prayers' for the royal family.[137]

These ritual meetings on the edges of towns were not, however, one-way conversations driven by the king; indeed, in many cases, they were orchestrated in part or wholly by the town hosting the entry. There is no evidence that James I's entry included the staged performances witnessed at royal and ducal entries into other European cities by the fifteenth century, as there are no burgh records or descriptive accounts recording this level of detail.[138] Nonetheless, the entry of 1424 coincided with – or was purposefully positioned on Palm Sunday, which featured liturgical processions symbolising Christ's entry into Jerusalem.[139] Biblical themes and narratives were prominent in royal entries during the fourteenth and fifteenth centuries, and Kipling notes that those drawing parallels between rulers and Christ were common, if widely varied, as they offered opportunities to 'explain and idealize political relationships' at a pertinent juncture in stabilising relations.[140] The choice of Palm Sunday – the day on which James's father was recorded to have died – also offered opportunities to make connections between the physical cycle of death and succession within the Stewart dynasty that had not been possible in 1406.[141] While there is a lack of clarity about which powerful group took the lead in greeting the king in 1424, both accounts agree about the presence of a large volume of people who gathered to see the king following his long absence.[142] In comparison to other ceremonies, such as James's coronation that would follow in May, a royal entry allowed the wider realm or community an opportunity to engage with the monarch and even actively participate in the ritual performance. Indeed, it is for this reason that Kipling likened inaugural entries to a public coronation.[143] In their shared confirmation of the high volume of spectators, the versions of Boece suggest

---

[137] *RPS*, 1425/3/19; *RPS*, 1426/15.

[138] For example, see Brown and Small, *Court and Civic Society*, 176–86; Jesse Hurlbutt, 'Symbols of Authority: Inaugural Ceremonies for Charles the Bold', in Wim Blockmans et al. (eds), *Staging the Court of Burgundy: Proceedings of the Conference 'The Splendour of Burgundy'* (Turnhout, 2013), 105–12.

[139] Craig Wright, 'The Palm Sunday Procession in Medieval Chartres', in Rebecca A. Baltzer and Margot E. Fassler (eds), *The Divine Office in the Latin Middle Ages: Methodology and Source Studies, Regional Development, Hagiography* (New York, 2000), 344–71; M. Birkedal Bruun, 'Procession and Contemplation in Bernard of Clairvaux's First Sermon for Palm Sunday', in Nils H. Petersen, Mette B. Bruun, Jeremy Llewellyn and Eyolf Østrem (eds), *The Appearance of Medieval Rituals: The Play of Construction and Modification* (Turnhout, 2004), 67–82; Monti, *A Sense of the Sacred*, 315–56; Penman, 'Who is this King of Glory?', 87–91; Harper, *The Forms and Orders of Western Liturgy*, 139–40.

[140] Kipling, *Enter the King*, 22–47, quote at 45.

[141] See Chapter 3, 135. Bruce also fused his coronation to this major liturgical feast, see Chapter 2, 76, 85, 87–8, and Penman, 'Who is this King of Glory?', 87–91.

[142] Bellenden's Boece, *Chronicle*, 382; Boece, *Historia*, fol. CCCLIXr.

[143] Kipling, *Enter the King*, 38.

that people took the opportunity to witness the return of the king, and the Christ-centric focus of the Palm Sunday liturgy in 1424 – whether orchestrated by town or crown – would have provided divine associations that all would have understood. Consequently, this was a powerful opportunity for James to legitimise his power in a public arena.

The coronation occurred at Scone on Sunday 21 May some thirty-five days after the royal entry to Edinburgh on Palm Sunday, where announcements regarding the coronation and parliament were likely made to allow the required forty days before the subsequent coronation parliament in Perth starting on 26 May.[144] The parliament was the first since the death of Robert III in 1406. This marked a distinct departure from the period of Albany's governorship, when there had only been General Councils, as only a king could call a full parliament during fifteenth century.[145] Holding an inaugural parliament after the coronation offered a means of further consolidating his singular right to the position at the top of the hierarchy. Such demonstrations were particularly necessary for a king who was undertaking his coronation with limited access to funds. The *Exchequer Rolls* are patchy at the start of the reign, and there is only one explicit reference to the coronation that relates to accommodation between his coronation and the parliament at Perth.[146] Later in James's reign examples of material demonstrations of power and wealth are plentiful. For example, a surviving account of John Turyne for 1429–30 contains everything from decorative ostrich feathers to Flemish purple velvet, from costumes for stage-players to collars encrusted with jewels and tapestries of the king's arms illustrating the development of symbols of power decorating royal spaces.[147] Moreover, extant general expenses of the king and queen's household from 1434–35 also refer to an abundance of meat and seafood, including the fact that the royal household consumed 45,100 oysters.[148] Yet, the situation in 1424 was arguably quite different. Legislation setting out the manner of repayment for the purveyance of goods indicates that the king had to raise money through the three estates retrospectively

---

[144] For the date of the coronation and entry: *Chron. Bower*, VIII, 221; *Pluscarden*, 278–9; Boece, *Historia*, fol. CCCLIXr; Bellenden's Boece, *Chronicle*, 382. Bellenden states 20 May rather than 21 May. Easter in 1424 was 23 April, so Palm Sunday would have been 16 April. Parliament preamble states parliament ran from 26 May: *RPS*, 1424/1; Bower states that the parliament began the day after the coronation: *Chron. Bower*, VIII, 221.

[145] From 1406 to 1424 there were only General Councils, see *RPS*, A1406/1 to *RPS*, 1423/8/1. Michael Brown argues that the difference between a General Council and a parliament are not clearcut, as councils could direct or even transfer authority, with examples of 1384 and 1388: 'Lele counsale', 58. However, parliament's role as the highest court and the fact that only the king could call a parliament separated it from General Councils at this time: Tanner, *Late Medieval Scottish Parliament*, 30–1.

[146] *ER*, IV, lxxxvii–lxxxviii, 383. *Exchequer Rolls* for James I's reign are fragmentary, with only two surviving chamberlain's account (1427 and 1435). Office of treasurer and *Treasurer's Accounts* begin in this reign, but the records do not survive.

[147] *ER*, IV, cxlvi–cxli, 676–85.

[148] Ibid., 617–18.

for his coronation costs.[149] Without fuller financial records it is impossible to assess how much money was collected, or what it was spent on, but James's coronation relied on the generosity of others for some supplies, thus creating further need for ritual statements of his authority and rewards for those who empowered it.

While the coronation feast may have been bankrolled by others, James had a powerful weapon in his arsenal for the promotion of a stable dynastic future under his kingship; his wife, Joan Beaufort, was a granddaughter of John of Gaunt, daughter of John Beaufort, earl of Somerset and the niece of Henry Beaufort, bishop of Winchester.[150] The chronicles agree that James and Joan were crowned side-by-side.[151] As a joint crowning had not occurred since the coronation of David II and Joan of the Tower in 1331, it could indicate that the now lost 'coronation roll' was consulted as a model by James.[152] More importantly, it reflected the close relationship between the royal couple, as exemplified in recent analysis of the *Kingis Quair*, and emphasised the manner in which James sought to promote his wife – who may have been showing early signs of pregnancy, as their first daughter was born later in 1424 – as second person of the realm.[153] Henry Wardlaw, bishop of St Andrews, presided over their joint coronation, but accounts describe James's enthronement to receive oaths of fealty separately, and with no mention of Joan, suggesting this did not involve the queen.[154] The joint coronation seems to have been indicative of their ruling partnership, and the potential that this offered for the security of the succession, while also demonstrating respect for the traditional enthronement ritual. By 1428, however, James had insisted that the political estates swore oaths of fealty to Joan in meetings of the General Council, and again in 1435, suggesting that as their ruling partnership matured – and once they had produced a brood of children – James desired further formal recognition of the queen's position.[155]

---

[149] 'Item, it is ordained that the yield taken to the purveyance of the king's crowning shall be allowed to those in the yield now being raised': *RPS*, 1424/32.

[150] Balfour-Melville suggests February, before 10 February, for the wedding: *James I, King of Scots*, 99–100.

[151] *Chron. Bower*, VIII, 221; *Pluscarden*, 279; Boece, *Historian*, fol. CCCLIXr; Bellenden's Boece, *Chronicle*, II, 382.

[152] See Chapter 2, 102.

[153] Brown, *James I*, 2–3, 24–6; Downie, *She is But a Woman*, 32–5. For recent analysis of the *Kingis Quair*, see Kylie Murray, '"Out of My Contree" Visions of Royal Authority in the Courts of James I and James II, 1424–1460', in Buchanan and Dean with Penman (eds), *Medieval and Early Modern Representations of Authority*, 214–34, at 215–22. On birth of Margaret, see Hayes, 'The Late Medieval Scottish Queen', 260.

[154] *Chron. Bower*, VIII, 221; *Pluscarden*, 279. Boece, and Bellenden's translation, merge the events with the duke of Albany and earl of Fife as sole officiator: Boece, *Historia*, fol. CCCLIXr; Bellenden's Boece, *Chronicle*, 382. The oath may have been similar to the aforementioned one recorded when David, duke of Rothesay, was made lieutenant of the realm in 1399: *RPS*, 1399/1/3.

[155] *RPS*, 1428/7/2; *RPS*, 1435/4. See also, 134.

Plate 15 James I Great Seal [enthroned], c.1436. Crown Copyright, National Records of Scotland, Laing Seal Impressions, RH17/1/42.

Of the coronation within Scone Abbey, and the regalia objects that James I and Joan received to provide the material confirmation of their accession, there is unfortunately limited evidence. James's Great Seal, like that of his father and grandfather, depicts him crowned and enthroned holding a sceptre in his left hand and mantle in his right, so the mantle retained a notable importance amongst the other regalia (Plate 15). Bower offers few details of the coronation in 1424, despite potentially being present or well informed as both a prominent abbot and a royal official.[156] However, he is notably the only commentator to suggest that Alexander III 'was clothed in royal purple' in 1249, which could point to the colour of the royal robe in his own time rather than the thirteenth century.[157] The regalia that Wyntoun associated with James's accession indicate that the chronicler expected James to receive a crown, sceptre and sword, along with a ring. This was the first mention of a ring as an item in the Scottish royal honours; however, as this was recorded in relation to James's inability to accept the regalia in 1406, it indicates this was not an English-inspired addition made by James and may have a much older heritage.[158] Wyntoun's discussion of the regalia, however, underscores how important the act of bestowing these objects was in the recognition of kingship and finalising the transition of power, even if their actual transformative qualities were minimal as James' reign had begun at the death of his father.

In a manner that his father had not managed, James was also able to manipulate the traditional privilege of the earl of Fife to enthrone the king, or 'set the said king upon the royal seat', as a further tangible demonstration

---

[156] Bower can be found listed as an auditor for the collection of taxes in the records of the 1424 parliament: *RPS*, 1424/31.
[157] *Chron. Bower*, V, 294–5.
[158] *Chron. Wyntoun*, VI, 416.

of the transfer of power from Murdoch, earl of Fife and duke of Albany, to the king.[159] Not only was the enthroning of the king by Albany a visual confirmation of the final stage in the transfer of power, it was also the final official ceremonial duty undertaken by the duke before his arrest and execution the following year.[160] Moreover, taking place in Scone and Perth, these events were positioned at the heart of Albany-Stewart power in lands subsequently forfeited to the crown.[161] Situating these events designed to project royal authority – coronation, parliament, oaths of fealty, and eventually burial – in this region served as a continual underlying reminder of James's initial victory in asserting his power upon his return.[162] Although undertaken on a shoestring, as far as the financial accounts can attest, James I made clear and absolute ceremonial statements about his royal authority.

The records of parliament for 1424 contain no sederunt list and give few clues to attendance at the coronation, beyond the key actors mentioned already, but the records of those knighted at the time of the coronation can offer some insight.[163] The inclusion of a knighting ceremony in the coronation was a visible demonstration of James I's potential as the source of royal favour and mirrors similar actions undertaken at the coronation of David II in 1331. Many of the men listed as receiving a knighthood were involved in James's release. George Dunbar, earl of March, was frequently found in commissions treating for the king's freedom, and at least eighteen of the twenty-five men knighted after the coronation had visited James at Brancepeth near Durham.[164] Such a favour is indicative that these men offered fealty to James on a previous occasion in anticipation of his return. Moreover, it illustrates the broad spectrum of attendees including earls, the constable of Scotland, other officials and lords. Brown suggests that the knighting ceremony aimed to ensure 'political harmony' and measures the success of this against James's ability to raise the taxes for his English ransom in his early reign on a scale that neither he nor later Stewarts managed to repeat.[165] While this knighting ceremony was certainly a clear demonstration and means of ensuring harmony, the ceremonial writ large – rather than one element – should be weighed into this equation. The combination of ritual elements harnessed in 1424, which sought to engage a range of audiences – including the inhabitants of Scotland's largest urban centre who were increasingly important

---

[159] *Chron. Bower*, VIII, 221; *Pluscarden*, 279.
[160] Brown, *James I*, 60–74.
[161] For most recent arguments on James I's forfeitures of major families after 1424, see Jack, 'Political and Local Consequences of the Decline and Fall of the Earls of Mar', 213–24.
[162] James I also attempted to have the recently established St Andrews University moved to Perth in 1426: Nicholson, *Scotland: The Later Middle Ages*, 300–1.
[163] See Appendix II, 'James I', for list of those knighted.
[164] Dunbar/March or family member as commissioners: CDS, IV, nos 805, 813, 872, 932. List of attendees at Brancepeth, including the earl of Dunbar/March: CDS, IV, no. 942.
[165] Brown, *James I*, 48–9.

contributors to raising taxes – worked as a ceremonial package to enhance and consolidate James's kingship in dialogue with representatives of each of the estates and the people more broadly.

Ceremony and rituals were employed with varying success to affirm, emphasise and visually acclaim the royal authority and stability of the dynasty during the first half century of Stewart rule. Elements of these displays for the early Stewart kings, particularly Robert II, speak to Reid's conclusions about Scottish kingship in the thirteenth century – that the monarch was 'first among equals' – due to ritual choices made to emphasise these origins within the ranks of the governing elite.[166] For Robert II, of course, this was an accurate reflection of his accession, unlike Alexander III who was the direct heir of an established dynasty. Yet, Robert also succeeded to the throne at a time of increasing liturgical encroachment upon rituals of succession and governance as the incorporation of unction and investment of regalia for an adult monarch was negotiated. The divine status of the Scottish monarch was notable in James I's displays, such as his entry to Edinburgh on Palm Sunday, but even this was arguably part of a natural progression and can be linked back to the choices of earlier kings, such as Robert I, and sits comfortably in a wider European context of royal entries in the fifteenth century. Moreover, with the entry occurring in Scotland's largest urban centre, the date may have appealed to those greeting their king as much as to James himself. Ultimately, the use of ceremony in 1424 indicated a developing role for urban environs and their inhabitants, the influence of Lancastrian kingly displays of majesty and an understanding of the traditional role of the estates in the affirmation of royal power. The fact that a secular enthronement at Scone retained its central place was a clear indicator of the latter, as were other choices: giving the role of enthroning the king to the earl of Fife, Murdoch, duke of Albany, and the direct connections between coronation and parliament. Whether these were James's personal choices, or undertaken on the advice of counsellors, is almost immaterial as either presents a case for the returning king engaging with and observing those traditions and rituals that were necessary and recognisable.

Real challenges to royal power existed throughout the first sixty-five years that Stewart kings reigned in Scotland, despite the relatively peaceful transition of power from the Bruce dynasty. Kingship was vulnerable at the point of power transfer, when political tensions were often at their most potent, and this was as much the case when power was contested between brothers as between distantly related claimants. There were ceremonial opportunities that do not seem to have been embraced, such as forging connections between the death of Robert III and the temporary succession of the guardian, Robert, duke of Albany, but such an explicit demonstration of power on the part of

[166] Reid, *Alexander III*, passim.

Albany shortly after James's capture could have been deemed a direct threat to a rightful king. Some challenges facilitated the drive to make ceremonial statements to present a necessary façade of stability, such as the fissures between Robert II's eldest sons that led to the centralising of ceremonies of succession, burial and the seat of governance in a Westminster-style royal centre. The forced years of absentee kingship from 1406, which denied James I and his father the opportunity to forge links between funeral and coronation, led to a distinctive break in styles of ruling that was reflected in ceremonial choices. Even so, there were demonstrable strands of continuity in rituals of death and succession that had far more secure roots than the dynasty itself. Despite the ceremonial displays in the reigns of the early Stewarts, featuring increasingly pronounced liturgical elements, material extravagance and the creeping incursions of divine kingship, the prominence of lay participation in king-making and the centrality of confirming political bonds remained central to the formation and enhancement of dynastic legitimacy for kings of Scots.

4

Foreign Queens, the Home-Grown Elite and Minor Kings, 1430s to 1470s

James I and Joan Beaufort had six daughters who survived into adulthood. Margaret – the eldest – was married in James's lifetime, offering an opportunity to entertain French ambassadors in Scotland and to present a Scottish entourage in France ahead of Margaret's nuptials to the dauphin.[1] More important to the cycle of succession, however, was the birth of twin boys, Alexander and James, in October 1430.[2] Riding high on the successful reestablishment of the alliance with France, including Margaret's initial betrothal in 1428, and the ritual submission of the Lord of the Isles in 1429, the birth and baptism of male heirs provided a fitting occasion to project royal authority by publicly celebrating the dynastic security they offered.[3] The birth took place at Holyrood Abbey in the Canongate, beside Edinburgh, presumably in the royal lodgings at the abbey as this was before the construction of the later palace.[4] The anonymous contemporary chronicler and continuator of Bower, the *Book of Pluscarden*, recorded outbursts of joy across the kingdom, with specific comment on Edinburgh's response:

> […] bonfires were lighted, flagons of wine were free to all and victuals publicly to all comers, with the sweetest harmony of all kinds of musical

---

[1] For further details: BNF, Manuscrits Français 17330, fols 119–48; Barbé, *Margaret of Scotland*; Lucinda H.S. Dean, 'Keeping Your Friends Close, But Your Enemies Closer? The Anglo-Franco-Scottish Marital Triangle, c.1200 to c.1625', in Marie-Claude Canova-Green and Sara Wolfson (eds), *Celebrations for the Wedding of Charles and Henrietta Maria* (Turnhout, 2020), 41–62. Of James and Joan's other daughters Isabella or Elizabeth married the Duke of Brittany (m.1442), Mary married the son of the lord of Veere (m.1444), and Eleanor married the duke of Austria-Tyrol (m.1448); and Annabella was betrothed to the heir of duchy of Savoy: Priscilla Bawcutt and Bridget Henisch, 'Scots Abroad in the Fifteenth Century: The Princesses Margaret, Isabella and Eleanor', in Elizabeth Ewan and Maureen M. Meikle (eds), *Women in Scotland, c.1100–c.1750* (East Linton, 1999), 45–55; Fiona Downie, '"La Voie quelle menace tenir": Annabella Stewart, Scotland, and the European Marriage Market, 1444–56', SHR 78 (1999), 170–91; Downie, *She is But a Woman*, 50–65.

[2] *Chron. Bower*, VIII, 263–5; *Pluscarden*, 284; Boece, *Historia*, fol. CCCLXIv; Bellenden's Boece, *Chronicle*, 386–8; Maior, *History*, 360; Buchanan, *History*, II, 95–6.

[3] *Chron. Bower*, VIII, 259–63; Balfour-Melville, *James I*, 159–73, Appendix B, 284; Brown, *James I*, 93–108.

[4] John G. Dunbar, *Scottish Royal Palaces: The Architecture of the Royal Residences during the Late Medieval and Early Renaissance Periods* (East Linton, 1999), 55–61.

instruments all night long proclaiming the praise and glory of God for all his gifts [...][5]

It is not clear from surviving evidence whether this was a spontaneous response by the burgh community or a crown-sponsored celebration, but this statement indicates there were public festivities in which all were encouraged to participate. Crown financial records indicate high levels of expenditure, including payments for foreign merchants, and confirm the king's residence in Edinburgh between September and January.[6] Large quantities of wax were also acquired by a burgess of Edinburgh: this would have been essential for the candles and torches required for the liturgy of the baptism and potentially in a procession from the birthing chamber to the church.[7] Bower also records James I honouring a number of young heirs with knighthoods, including the sons of Archibald, fifth earl of Douglas, Sir James Douglas of Balvenie, William Crichton, the chancellor, Sir William of Borthwick and the son of a visiting 'Roman Prince' Stephano de Porcari.[8] Knighting rituals were commonly used to cement bonds of loyalty to the king and his heirs through demonstrations of fealty, but they largely targeted a specific elite audience unlike the public celebrations that occurred in Edinburgh's streets. Evidence for the ceremonies generated by the birth and baptism of James and Joan's sons is not overly full. However, it indicates investment in the ritualised celebration of this important event in the cycle of death and succession for and by varied audiences, marked by further interactions with the urban spaces and communities of key towns, as witnessed in James's return to Scotland in 1424, which was a developing pattern as the fifteenth century progressed.

Underpinned by a relatively secure succession, the image of stability and shared public joy witnessed during the baptism celebrations, and the subsequent grandeur of Princess Margaret's betrothal and marriage, offered a counterbalance to the increasing disquiet with James's methods of rule during the 1430s. This came to the fore in 1436, when a public attempt was made to arrest the king in parliament for not upholding his duties as promised

---

[5] *Pluscarden*, 284. For the authorship of Pluscarden, see McGladdery, *James II*, 222–3.

[6] The surviving financial evidence for March 1430 to May 1431 is primarily recorded in bulk payments, such as the treasurer (received £640) and Genoese and German merchants (received £80), for which itemised accounts do not survive: *ER*, IV, 541–3.

[7] Stephen Lyon, burgess of Edinburgh, received nearly £40 for over 98 stone of white wax bought for the use of the king at this time: ibid., 543. For more on the use of candles and processions in later Scottish baptisms: Lucinda H.S. Dean, 'Raising Royal Scottish Babes: Baptisms, Gossibs and Godparents in Late Medieval and Early Modern Scotland', seminar paper, *History Live Talk*, University of the Highlands and Islands, 18 June 2020, https://www.youtube.com/watch? v=dFkcIy0m14c. Date accessed: 4 March 2021 (being prepared for publication under same title).

[8] *Chron. Bower*, VIII, 263; Leslie, *Historie*, II, 39; *ER*, IV, 543 (expenses of Porcari in Edinburgh). For more on Porcari: Stephen Miller, 'Political Oratory and the Public Sphere in Early Quattrocento Florence', *New Readings* 1 (1995), 41–64.

in his coronation.[9] Robert Graham's outburst was arguably misjudged and rapidly put down, but subsequent events indicate that James's response to this sanctioned form of resistance in parliament led to a far more violent outcome.[10] The murder of the king, at Blackfriars in Perth on 21 February 1437, shocked the political community and left a six-year-old heir to the throne. It was not a succession crisis on the scale of 1286, nor did it raise the problems of 1406, as there was an heir physically present in the realm. The youth of the king and the violent unexpected nature of his predecessor's death were the predominant challenges for representing the authority of this young heir when he succeeded the throne, as would also be the case for his son, James III. In some respects, these were quite different circumstances from those underpinning the ritual transfer of power between the first Stewart kings. However, as Lynn Kilgallon has most recently argued in relation to the use of counsel as a political tool, the absence or limitations of adult monarchical authority and extensive periods under lieutenants, guardians and governors since 1286 had already significantly influenced and shaped the ways that power was transferred, communicated and performed in Scotland.[11]

Murder, violent battlefield death, minor accessions and factional discord punctuated efforts to consolidate the Stewart dynasty. Nonetheless, the dynasty survived with observable growth of the crown demesne, despite more than twenty years of minority government between 1437 and 1488, and – according to Tanner – also witnessed the 'zenith of parliament'.[12] Consequently, it is not surprising that historical debates circle around the nature of power relations, particularly the impact of minorities and the extent to which the crown and nobility and/or parliament collaborated or had conflicted relations.[13] This debate continues. Claire Hawes has recently

---

[9] John Shirley, 'The Dethe of the Kynge of Scotis: A New Edition', ed. Margaret Connolly, *SHR* 71 (1992), 46–69, at 52–3; Michael Brown, '"I have thus slain a tyrant": The Dethe of the Kynge of Scotis and the Right to Resist in Early Fifteenth-Century Scotland', *IR* 47 (1996), 24–44; Brown, *James I*, 121–71; Tanner, *Late Medieval Scottish Parliament*, 7–75, particularly 66–75.

[10] Kilgallon, 'Communal Authority, Counsel and Resistance', 9–12.

[11] Ibid., 19–24.

[12] On the growth of crown demesne: Hawes, 'Community and Public Authority', 106–21. On the zenith of parliament: Tanner, *Late Medieval Scottish Parliament*, 264–78.

[13] Some key works on crown-magnate relations and minorities: Nicholson, *Scotland: The Later Middle Ages*, 325–52, 397–421; Jenny Wormald, 'Taming the Magnates', in Keith Stringer (ed.), *Essays on the Nobility of Medieval Scotland* (Edinburgh, 1985), 270–9; Grant, *Independence and Nationhood*, 171–99; Michael Brown, 'Scotland Tamed? Kings and Magnates in Late Medieval Scotland: A Review of Recent Work', *IR* 45 (1994), 120–46; Michael Brown, 'Public Authority and Factional Conflict: Crown, Parliament and Polity, 1424–1455', in Brown and Tanner (eds), *Parliament and Politics in Scotland, 1235–1560*, 133–44; McGladdery, *James II*, 12–85; Tanner, *Late Medieval Scottish Parliament*, 66–121, 169–90; Macdougall, *James III*, 40–67; Keith M. Brown, 'The Stewart Realm: Changing the Landscape', in Boardman and Goodare (eds), *Kings, Lords and Men in Scotland and Britain*, 19–36. For a useful recent summary of scholarship, see also Kilgallon, 'Communal Authority, Counsel and Resistance', 14–16.

advocated recognising the shared aims and responsibilities for the 'common good' and reimagines the political relationships as a negotiation of authority in the public domain.[14] This recasting of the political sphere in the fifteenth century speaks volumes to a researcher of ceremony. Althoff argues that 'medieval public communication was ritual and demonstrative', thus offering the physical manifestations of the rhetoric and discourse for kings, leading lords and ecclesiastics, burgh officials and the common people alike, and were essential for the legitimation of authority.[15] Yet, as Kilgallon notes, there is still an important place for the consideration of resistance and, by association, friction within these negotiations.[16]

By considering the period from the murder of James I (1437) to the marriage and progress of James III (1469–70), this chapter takes in two revolutions of the cycle of death and succession. In so doing, it includes the introduction and involvement of foreign-born queens – James I's consort, Joan (1424–45), introduced in Chapter 3, and Mary of Guelders (1449–63), wife of James II – as new forces in the landscape of minority alongside the political community and parliament. It also witnesses some dramatic breaks from ceremonial traditions, not least the deviations from the traditional inaugural site at Scone (Holyrood, 1437, and Kelso, 1460), and sees further notable interaction with urban spaces. Financial records do survive for this period, but the introduction of the treasurer in the reign of James I means that the *Exchequer Rolls* hold less detailed information about crown expenditure than in the later fourteenth and early fifteenth centuries. This is particularly the case with the personal and extraordinary expenditure of the king and royal household that was increasingly recorded in the *Treasurer's Accounts*, which do not survive consistently until the last decades of the fifteenth century.[17] The fifteenth century is also comparatively lacking in contemporary Scottish narrative accounts, so there is a greater reliance on sixteenth-century commentators.[18] Specific ceremonies, however, are better served by the accounts from foreign visitors – such as D'Escouchy's account of the marriage of James II and Mary of Guelders – and the first orders of ceremony for a Scottish coronation can also be tentatively dated to the mid-fifteenth century.[19] The analysis that follows utilises these records to address how and why different forces within the political community employed and shaped rituals, particularly considering what this illustrates about their involvement in the consolidation of the Stewart dynasty. Consequently, it will speak to debates about power distribution, using the ritual cycle as a barometer for the wider society and culture in which it sits, and lay down further challenge

[14] Hawes, 'Community and Public Authority', *passim*, particularly 1–7, 17–46.
[15] Althoff, 'The Variability of Rituals', 73–4.
[16] Kilgallon, 'Communal Authority, Counsel and Resistance', 14, *passim*.
[17] *TA*, I, xiii–xxv; Murray, 'The Exchequer and Crown Revenue', 272–319.
[18] On fifteenth-century sources, see McGladdery, *James II*, 203–34; Macdougall, *James III*, xiii–xvii.
[19] *Chron. D'Escouchy*, 175–83; Lyall, 'The Medieval Coronation Service', 3–21.

to Dougal Shaw's suggestion that long periods without adult kings impeded ritual development.[20]

A Queen Unleashed: Ceremonial Responses to Murder Most Foul

Despite James I's unexpected death at forty-two, plans for a royal burial site had been put into motion not long after his return from England in 1424.[21] Reflecting their partnership in life, James and Joan planned a shared mausoleum in their joint foundation of the Charterhouse at Perth to cement their bond in death. Joan was listed as *fundatrix* in the necrology of the Carthusian General Chapter, which confirms her shared role in the founding of the house, and her equal rights to intercessory prayers were secured and recorded in the order's *kalendar*.[22] The Charterhouse was the first and last Carthusian foundation established in Scotland and one of only a handful in the British Isles, such as Mount Grace Priory in North Yorkshire – transformed into a Beaufort mausoleum by a relative of Queen Joan during the 1420s – and Sheen Priory – founded by Henry V in 1414.[23] Neither the Charterhouse buildings nor any tombs remain intact following attacks on Perth's religious foundations in 1559 to 1560. John Knox recorded the Charterhouse's grandeur, if only to criticise excess, but unfortunately there are no detailed descriptions.[24] Monks of the Carthusian order lived largely isolated lives of prayer in individual cells with gardens and only came together in the main communal space of the church intermittently. Due to this often-solitary existence, Julian Luxford has argued that the decoration of the church would

---

[20] Shaw, 'Scotland's Place in Britain's Coronation Tradition', 47.
[21] The licence for founding a Carthusian house for thirteen monks at Perth was granted to James I on 19 August 1426 by the prior of the Grand Chartreuse in Grenoble: NRS, James VI Hospital Records, GD79/2/1. Bower's chronicle states that the founding was in 1429, which correlates with the first surviving land grants in the James VI Hospital records, even if the largest grant from the king (via the suppression of St Leonard's nunnery) was not confirmed until 1438: *Chron. Bower*, VIII, 269; NRS, James VI Hospital Records, GD79/2/2–4, 6.
[22] W.N.M. Beckett, 'The Perth Charterhouse before 1500', *Analecta Carthusiana* 128 (1988), 1–11, at 4–5; James Hogg, 'The Carthusians of Perth and the Carthusian General Chapter', *Analecta Carthusiana* 175 (2001), 151–241, at 188.
[23] For more details on the Charterhouse in Perth and comparators, see Henry Chester Mann, *A Cloistered Company: Essays on Monastic Life* (London, 1935), 113–18; W.N.M. Beckett, 'The Perth Charterhouse before 1500', *Analecta Carthusiana* 128 (1988), 1–11; John Cloake, *Richmond's Great Monastery, The Charterhouse of Jesus of Bethlehem of Shene* (London, 1990); Brown, *James I*, 116–17; Hogg, 'The Carthusians of Perth', 151–241; Scott, 'The Court and Household of James I of Scotland', 180–1.
[24] John Knox, *History of the Reformation in Scotland*, ed. William Croft Dickinson, 2 vols (London and Edinburgh, 1949), I, 163; Beckett, 'The Perth Charterhouse before 1500', 8–11. Beckett suggested a flat slab of blue marble at St John's church, outlining two figures, was part of James I and Joan's tomb, but Penman argues this is more likely a tomb of a noble couple, see 'A Programme for Royal Tombs', 250.

have been designed to inspire awe, in comparison to the simplicity of the monk's solitary living spaces, and that the art and sculpture, while sparingly used in comparison to other monastic orders, would have been sophisticated in design.[25]

Charterhouses such as Sheen and Mount Grace were situated in relatively rural areas, mirroring the idea of wilderness sought by the Grand Chartreuse near Grenoble. However, there were other urban Carthusian foundations, such as the London Charterhouse. Founded in 1371 by the English knight Sir Walter Manny, this foundation would have been a feature of the London landscape during James I's English captivity; although, there is no direct evidence that he visited the house. Luxford offers a thorough analysis of Manny's tomb, including sketches based on surviving pieces of the tomb: this relatively contemporary exemplar of a founder's tomb in a Carthusian foundation was made of painted alabaster, positioned near the altar, and included an effigy and kneeling niches (similar to a shrine).[26] While evidence for James's tomb is limited, white alabaster was not without precedent in Scotland: it was a favoured material in Scottish royal tombs at various locations through the previous century or more as evidenced above. Moreover, the extant expenses for metalwork and painted decoration after James's murder indicate that the tomb was both highly decorative and receiving finishing touches in 1437, so it was potentially built into the fabric of the church.[27] Unlike Sir Walter Manny's tomb, however, as co-founders, it was likely that James and Joan had a joint tomb to mark their unified royal authority even in death. Comparative examples that James and Joan would have seen, such as the double tomb of Richard II and Anne of Bohemia at Westminster, featured either weepers or familial figures and these also had precedent in Scotland. Considering the number of children that the couple had together, such figures may have combined progeny and dynastic ancestry.[28] Placed in a closed Carthusian community, this statement of unity was a less public one. However, positioned outside the south gates of one Scotland's notable urban centres, which frequently hosted parliament and sat around three miles south of the coronation site, the foundation in its entirety was a potent statement of the couple's conspicuous piety and their status as providers of patronage. It should also be considered alongside other overt ways James promoted Joan as second person of the realm, such as the joint coronation and oaths in parliament, as a project of ritualised promotion. The favouring of Joan caused some tensions within the political community.[29] Yet, tension suggests a palpable degree of strength in Joan's political position, even if temporarily, and made

---

[25] Julian M. Luxford, 'The Space of the Tomb in the Carthusian Consciousness', in Andrews (ed.), *Ritual and Space in the Middle Ages*, 259–81, at 269–70.
[26] Luxford, 'The Space of the Tomb', 259–74, especially plates 66–73.
[27] ER, V, 34, 73–4. The tomb was enclosed with Spanish iron (£30) in 1438 and decorated with further metalwork and painted decoration (£50) in 1440.
[28] Morganstern, *Gothic Tombs of Kinship*, 117–49. See also discussions in Chapters 2 and 3.
[29] Brown, *James I*, 153, 180–5; Downie, *She is But A Woman*, 99–103.

her involvement, if not control, of the subsequent transferral of power from father to son at James's death ever more probable.

The tomb and its mausoleum appear part of long-term planning, but the fraught political situation caused by the circumstances of James's demise had a marked impact on the ceremonies of death and succession that took place in 1437, including generating apparent one-off rituals. As repetition is often associated with the definition of a ritual, this could be considered problematic. However, as Andrews has argued, while a ritual may appear unique, this is very rarely the case as even a seemingly one-off ritual will use 'elements recognisable in other ritual contexts' to ground the actions in something familiar.[30] An apparent one-off appears in the *Book of Pluscarden*, which records the display of the king's wounded body as proof of death and an open accusation against the perpetrators.[31] There is no extant evidence that a Scottish royal body had been displayed in such a way before, but holding a vigil around a royal body (probably coffined or covered) was a recognisable tradition from at least 1214, when the queen, clerics and household officers had stayed in Stirling to 'abode with the king'.[32] Moreover, in other European countries – including England, where Joan had grown up – the display of the body as proof of death was a prominent feature in royal funerary practice into the fifteenth century and was particularly important where there were any unusual circumstances involved in the death of the king.[33] The display of a wounded body also had biblical connotations, such as Christ revealing his wounds to Thomas, which could be fruitfully employed to make statements about James's divine status. There is little evidence of where and how the body would have been put on display. However, a visiting papal legate, the Bishop of Urbino, fortuitously witnessed the body's display, according to a contemporary source, which recorded that he: 'uttered a great cry with tearful sighs and kissed his [James's] piteous wounds, and said before all bystanders that he would stake his soul on his having died in a state of grace, like a martyr'.[34] The inclusion of 'bystanders' suggest that Urbino saw the body in a public space open for observance of the corpse. Even if the bishop's acclamation was a fiction, in conjunction with the display of the body, it would have emphasised the divine and saintly nature of the king for the audience of the *Book of Pluscarden*, which may have been the intention of the text.[35] By

---

[30] Andrews, 'Ritual and Space', 1–29, particularly 6, 12.
[31] *Pluscarden*, 290.
[32] *Chron. Fordun*, 275–6. See Chapter 1, 32.
[33] Hallam, 'Royal Burial', 366–7; Joel F. Burden, 'How Do You Bury a Deposed King? The Funeral of Richard II and the Establishment of Royal Authority in 1400', in Gwilym Dodd and Donald Biggs (eds), *Henry IV: The Establishment of the Regime, 1399–1406* (York, 2003), 35–53, at 39–42, 51–2; Griffiths, 'Succession and the Royal Dead', 103.
[34] *Pluscarden*, 290; Brown, *James I*, 194–6; MacGladdery, *James II*, 7.
[35] Roberto Weiss states that Urbino's visit was to rectify poor relations between James and the pope, and the account he reproduces by Piero del Monto suggests no such proclamation over the body: 'The Earliest Account of the Murder of James I', *English Historical*

displaying the body, whether accompanied by the speech or not, the queen and her advisors may have manipulated ritual elements to make an important statement that could generate interest in the crimes against James I locally and beyond Scotland.[36]

One of the most challenging issues with the dramatic events of 1437 is that evidence for the funeral is sparse; although there are multiple accounts recording James's death, they focus almost exclusively on the murder.[37] Displaying James's wounded body may have served a certain political purpose but was not a dignified way to transport a king to his burial site at the Charterhouse. The procession from the Blackfriars or Dominican Priory, on the north side of the burgh, to the Charterhouse, at the southeast corner outside the burgh gates, likely included an enclosed and covered coffin, such as that illustrated in the fifteenth-century *Scotichronicon* manuscript illumination for Alexander III (Plate 6, see p. 73), or perhaps a temporary funeral effigy of the king.[38] James and Joan would have witnessed the use of an effigy at the funeral of Henry V, which travelled from Paris to Westminster in 1422 in one of the most elaborate funerary ceremonies of the fifteenth century.[39] The proximity of James's place of death to his burial site did not call for a long journey with multiple vigils. Yet, the urban setting of Perth provided controllable and largely walled spaces within which perform public funerary displays that would have been attractive in the circumstances.[40] Between Blackfriars and the Charterhouse, in the centre of the town between the High Street and South Street, sat the richly endowed parish church of St John's, which was 'of almost cathedral-like proportion, with its forty altars', via which a sombre procession could have made its way through the burgh to maximise intercessory prayers and public mourning.[41] The procession and funeral would also have taken place during Lent, which was a penitential period including fasting, processions and penitential prayers to saints.[42]

Review 52 (1937), 479–91, at 482–4, 490–1.
[36] Brown, *James I*, 194–5.
[37] Queen Joan sent a report of the murder to London: Weiss, 'The Earliest Account of the Murder', 481. For other examples: ibid., 479–80, 484–91; *Chron. Bower*, VIII, 300–3; *Pluscarden*, 288–90; Bellenden's Boece, *Chronicle*, 400; Shirley, 'Dethe of the Kynge of Scotis', 46–69.
[38] James reportedly had sixteen stab wounds and wounded hands from defending himself: Shirley, 'Dethe of the Kynge of Scotis', 62; Brown, *James I*, 187–8.
[39] Anthony Harvey and Richard Mortimer, *The Funeral Effigies of Westminster Abbey*, revised edition (Woodbridge, 2002), 41–2; Christopher Allmand, *Henry V* (London, 1992), 174–8.
[40] See R.M. Spearman, 'The Medieval Townscape of Perth', in Michael Lynch, Michael Spearman and Geoffrey Stell (eds), *The Scottish Medieval Town* (Edinburgh, 1988), 42–59, particularly town plan illustration on 53.
[41] Mann, *A Cloistered Company*, 112; 'Perth St John the Baptist Parish Church', *Corpus of Scottish Medieval Parish Churches* (St Andrews and Stirling, 2008), https://arts.st-andrews.ac.uk/corpusofscottishchurches/ site.php. Date accessed: 28 February 2021.
[42] Harper, *Forms and Orders of Western Liturgy*, 50–1, 136.

Lenten veils may also have been in use to cover religious iconography, as elsewhere in Europe, which would have distinctly altered the religious spaces used for any vigils or funeral liturgy.[43]

Mourning for James I's death took place over a relatively short time, perhaps less than a week, but there is evidence that Joan extended the ceremonial commemoration of James's death through other means.[44] The *Exchequer Rolls* record two payments in 1444–45 to a knight of St John of Jerusalem returning from Rhodes bearing the heart of James I, which was laid to rest in the Charterhouse.[45] The journey is reminiscent of the crusade journey of Robert I's heart around one hundred years earlier.[46] However, by the fifteenth century separate heart burials had declined in use from their peak between the 1100s and 1300s. More unusually, James's heart returned to the same site as his body. Considering over eighty separate heart burials in England and the Angevin territories from 1100 to 1327, Westerhof identifies no definite cases where the heart and body ended up at the same site.[47] In James's case, it could be that there were no clear instructions about where to house the heart upon its return following Joan's fall from power and then her death in 1445. The route of the journey undertaken by James's heart took, and the relative importance of the destinations on it, are unknown. Nonetheless, Rhodes was the central hub of the order of the Knights of St John situated on the route to Jerusalem. The heart was not returned until some six to seven years after 1437 but it must have been removed in the days immediately following James's death prior to burial. Consequently, this makes it credible to suggest that the remarkable but elusive journey was part of a larger programme embarked upon by the queen and her advisors at the time of James's death or that it may, as

---

[43] Easter would have been Sunday 31 March, so Lent would have started on forty days earlier on Ash Wednesday (Wednesday 20 February). For Lenten practices, see Monti, *Sense of the Sacred*, 297–300.

[44] A letter from Joan confirms that she was in Edinburgh by 7 March at the latest: David Marshall, 'Notes on the Record Room of the City of Perth', *PSAS* 33 (1899), 414–40, at 424–5; MacGladdery, *James II*, 6.

[45] *ER*, V, 156–79. Sir Alexander Seton of Gordon and Sir Herbert Herries of Caerlaverock could have carried the heart as both travelled to the Holy Land, c.1439, and Seton died on crusade, leaving his belongings to the Knights Hospitaller: Alan MacQuarrie, *Scotland and the Crusades, 1095–1560* (Edinburgh, 1997), 92–3. The Knights of St John, or Hospitallers, was a crusading order – a branch was established in twelfth-century Scotland with royal support. They faced decline between 1330s and 1380s but witnessed a revival in 1400s, including the rebuilding of Torphichen Priory by Sir Andrew Meldrum, preceptor. However, they were always heavily dependent on English support so their involvement may have been linked to Joan or James's own time in England. See Ian B. Cowan, P.H.R. Mackay and Alan MacQuarrie, *The Knights of St John of Jerusalem in Scotland*, Scottish History Society Series 19 (Edinburgh, 1983), particularly xxvi–lv; Historic Environment Scotland, *Statement of Significance: Torphichen Preceptory* (Edinburgh, 2019), 1–4, https://www.historicenvironment.scot/archives-and-research/publications/publication/?publicationid=84caa975-2c4c-4c5d-91e0-a6c9010ff06e. Date accessed, 7 January 2023.

[46] Hallam, 'Royal Burial', 364–6; Simpson, 'The Heart of King Robert I', 178.

[47] Westerhof, *Death and the Noble Body*, 75–96, App. 1, 141–9; Brown, *The Monarchy of Capetian France*, see 'Death and the Human Body in the Later Middle Ages', 263.

with their joint mausoleum, have been a decision taken prior to the murder, despite the sudden nature of the death.

Both Brown and McGladdery have identified that the queen's position was reliant on her personal control of the young king and to achieve this she needed to be in Edinburgh, where the young king resided.[48] This led to significant ceremonial change: the most notable was that Holyrood Abbey and Edinburgh, rather than Scone and Perth, became locations for the ritual transition of power to the young James II. This led to a dramatic shift in the use of space.[49] One of the extant secular orders of ceremony for Scotland locates the coronation it records at Holyrood Abbey, with a ritual wholly conducted inside the church. This document resides in the seventeenth-century heraldic collections of Sir James Balfour of Denmilne (c.1590–1657) and shares similarities with the Scottish coronation order compiled at the behest of Charles I in the late 1620s by Jerome Lindsay, who was the Lyon herald.[50] The medieval origins claimed for these two orders of ceremony are difficult to confirm as they only survive in these later copies.[51] Nonetheless, the documents do chart developments that would sensibly date to changes necessary in 1437, including the unusual instruction to position the crown on the floor before the king during the giving of oaths, which could have been introduced due to the crown being too heavy for a small boy to wear.[52] Moreover, the emergence of an order of ceremony at a point of change, or when a particular religious institution – in this case Holyrood – sought to stake its claim to the coronation, would certainly have precedents elsewhere.[53]

These orders retained and expanded the roles for secular individuals. Considering the heraldic credentials of the seventeenth-century copyists, the increased importance of heraldic and secular royal officials must be treated with caution. However, the absorption of the earldom of Fife by the crown in 1425 – following James I's destruction of the Albany Stewarts – removed a traditional secular figure permanently from the enthronement.[54] This left a ceremonial gap and an opportunity for the advancement of other nobles, heraldic or household officers within the coronation, such as the Marischal

---

[48] Brown, *James I*, 195–8; McGladdery, *James II*, 6, 12–36, particularly 12–15.
[49] Dean, 'Where to Make the King (or Queen)', 65–70.
[50] NLS, Adv. MS. 33.7.10, fols 6r–14r, and Adv. MS. 33.2.26, fols 30–31. The former includes note about the origin of the text (f. 14r) and an oath with the deleted date of 1445 (fols 12r–14r). For Lindsay's 1620s order, see NRS, Privy Council: Register of Royal Letters, 19 September 1623–17 May 1633, PC5/4, fols 138v–9r; Lindsay, 'Forme of the coronatioun', 393–5.
[51] Roderick Lyall suggests both copyists may have had access to similar fifteenth-century materials: 'The Medieval Coronation Service', 14–5.
[52] Dean, 'Crowns, Wedding Rings and Processions', 159–65; Dean, 'Crowning the Child', 271–6.
[53] Balfour states that the copy in his manuscript was taken from a manuscript at Holyrood: NLS, Adv. MS. 33.2.26, fol. 30r. Nelson discusses the influences of houses such as Reims and St Denis on early Frankish orders of ceremony: *Politics and Ritual*, 283–308, 329–40.
[54] On destruction of the Albany Stewarts, see Brown, *James I*, 73–92.

and Constable.[55] The order also emphasises the role of the three estates to offer legitimacy through consent, oath giving and acclamation:

> The Churchmen Nobles Barrons and Burgesses askit at ye king If he wer Lawfull successor or Not and wes villing to accept the dignity of ye Croune wich they did Now offer to his Ma[jes]tie: then wes hes Geneologie recitted.[56]

The recitation of genealogy occurred twice: once in the opening actions and again after the coronation, which marked a continued emphasis of the young king's dynastic rights due to lineage – a facet made ever more potent following the murder of James I, ostensibly directed by another branch of the dynasty.[57]

Despite the ecclesiastical setting, the extant orders downplay the divine elements of the ritual. Taking place on 25 March, the accession of James II in 1437 could have been associated with the feast of the Annunciation of the Blessed Virgin, thus the anniversary of the inaugural ceremonies of both Robert I (1306) and Robert II (1371).[58] Moreover, with Easter Sunday falling upon 31 March in 1437, the coronation occurred on the first day of Holy Week. It is unlikely that such a congruence of liturgical richness was not fully harnessed by the organisers to emphasise James II's dynastic and divine right to the succession in the wake of his father's murder. The desire to enhance the coronation ceremonial by combining it with such a potent date could also explain why there was not strict adherence to the forty days required for calling parliament. Balfour's order of ceremony offers details of the anointing with notable differences from the other seventeenth-century document created for the coronation of Charles I, which follows the English pattern for anointing, so Balfour potentially recorded a distinct Scottish practice.[59] The anointing was ascribed to a bishop, but the roles of ecclesiastics are otherwise muted. Balfour does admit, however, that he did not record all ceremonial

---

[55] William Hay, hereditary constable, and William Keith, hereditary marischal, were both belted as earls in James II's reign, respectively 1452 and 1458. Neither received much more than the title and had long been prominent in the king's household, including the organisation of tournaments and other royal events, so their increased responsibility in the coronation may have been a factor: *Scots Peerage*, III, 564, VI, 39–40; McGladdery, *James II*, 198–9.

[56] NLS, Adv. MS. 33.2.26, fol. 30r. The recitation of the genealogy was potentially based upon Barbour's now lost, *Stewartis Original*.

[57] Brown, 'That Old Serpent and Ancient of Evil Days', 23–45.

[58] *RPS*, 1437/3/1–2; Bower, IX, 139; Leslie, *Historie*, II, 56–8. See Chapter 2, 76, 85 and Chapter 3, 118, 129.

[59] Balfour records anointing on 'the Croune of the head, boughes of hes armes, shoulder blades and palmes of hes handes' by a bishop with oil only but Lindsay's order of anointing reflects English *ordines* from the twelfth century onwards, which included anointing the breast and the use of the chrism for anointing the king's head: NLS, Adv. MS. 33.2.26, fol. 30r.; NRS, PC5/4, fol. 138v; Lindsay, 'Forme of the coronatioun', 394; 'Twelfth Century Coronation Order' and '*Liber Regalis*', in *English Coronation Records*, 30–42, 81–130.

components.⁶⁰ Consequently, the balance of the secular and ecclesiastical involvement in the ceremony was likely skewed by a post-Reformation distancing from Catholic overtones.

The extent to which the shift to Holyrood altered the coronation of James II is hard to quantify with extant evidence, but the removal of the outdoor enthronement would have been a notable change. The ritual offering of fealty, though still central in the orders of ceremony, was undertaken within an ecclesiastic closed space and, as such, was reserved for a select elite audience. However, James II was paraded between Edinburgh Castle and Holyrood in a coronation procession.⁶¹ This was a truncated version of the entry route through the burgh that developed across the later fifteenth and sixteenth centuries: moving past secular and ecclesiastical features of the High Street that were central to daily life in the burgh, including the Mercat Cross, the Tron and St Giles.⁶² This echoes similar urban processions, such as that from the Tower of London to Westminster for the coronations of English monarchs with which Joan would have been familiar, and it may have mirrored the entry of James and Joan to the town in 1424.⁶³ This procession through a public urban space made the boy king very visible, if only briefly, and provided potentially wider popular access to the ruler before and after the important transitional ritual that occurred in the abbey.

The same processional route, exiting the castle and making its way around the streets of Edinburgh, had recently hosted a rather different form of spectacle for the cheering crowds to observe and even participate in, but one that also unquestionably resulted from the death of James I. In the days before James II's coronation, John Shirley's contemporary English translation – considered one of the fullest accounts of the events of 1437 – recorded the ritual torture and execution of the first two of the conspirators captured.⁶⁴ After public torture and confession, the near naked Robert Stewart and John Chambers, fastened to large crosses mounted on a cart, were processed from Edinburgh Castle around the streets of the burgh so, as Shirley states, '[th]at alle peple myght beholde and wonder uppoun hem'.⁶⁵ The crowds that

---

⁶⁰ NLS, Adv. MS. 33.2.26, fol. 31r.
⁶¹ RPS, 1437/3/2; Leslie, *Historie*, II, 56–8.
⁶² By the sixteenth century the route started at the West Port, went to the castle, down the High Street via various key stopping points, such as the Tron, and out of the Netherbow Gate to Holyrood: Douglas Gray, 'The Royal Entry in Sixteenth-Century Scotland', in Sally Mapstone and Juliette Hood (eds), *The Rose and the Thistle: Essays on the Culture of Late Medieval and Renaissance Scotland* (East Linton, 1998), 10–32, at 12.
⁶³ A coronation procession from the Tower of London to Westminster first occurred for Richard II in 1377 and continued under the Lancastrian kings: John Brückman, 'The Ordines of the Third Recension of the Medieval English Coronation Order', in Sandquist and Powick (eds), *Essays in Medieval History*, 99–115, at 100–1; Burden, 'Rituals of Royalty', 185–9.
⁶⁴ Shirley, 'Dethe of the Kynge of Scotis', 63–4. Brown comments that Shirley's translation 'must come from a source close to the events' due to its knowledge of Scottish politics: *James I*, 4–5.
⁶⁵ Shirley, 'Dethe of the Kynge of Scotis', 64.

welcomed their new king on 25 March 1437 cannot have helped but make connections between these two events. Subsequently, the trial of the earl of Atholl also took place in Edinburgh, where Shirley described the elderly earl being publicly pilloried in the town – most probably outside the tolbooth – wearing a paper crown indicating his pretensions to the throne prior to execution.[66] Following the legitimate coronation of the young king in Holyrood Abbey, such ritualised punishments took on ever more potency. By using the same physical spaces, celebratory acclamation was juxtaposed with visceral punishment and a show trial to create a demonstrable statement about James II's right to succeed, despite his father's violent removal. The malleability of ritual, through combining traditions and inventions, and the potency of associations with physical spaces, provided a means of creating a veneer of stability and control in response to a crisis.

Oaths, Jousting and Marriage: Succeeding to Adulthood

Urban spaces dominated the ceremonies confirming the transition of power in 1437 and this was a feature of the subsequent reign of James II; indeed, David Ditchburn suggests James was an 'urban king' in terms of the spaces favoured for ceremonial occasions.[67] On 3 July 1449, aged eighteen, James arrived at Holyrood Abbey on horseback amid an entourage of knights. Dressed in a long fur-lined grey and white robe, the king made his way through the Burgundian, Guelderian and Scottish elite to his bride.[68] This triumphant wedding celebration witnessing the union of James with Mary of Guelders marked a significant coming of age moment for the king: ostensibly one where his minority officially ended and his majority began.[69] During this minority, McGladdery states that James was 'a shadowy figure', but there were ritual moments where the young king was briefly visible, at least when it was beneficial for the leading faction.[70] For example, during attacks on William, lord Crichton and chancellor, and the queen dowager by William, eighth earl of Douglas, during 1443 and 1444, Douglas deployed the presence

---

[66] Ibid.: Shirley's account suggests that Atholl's trial occurred 'the nyghe [th]e fest of Pasque' (64), or the night before Easter (30 March 1437) but McGladdery states 26 March: *James II*, 8–9. The tolbooth was the common site for the pillory or stocks: Dennison, *The Evolution of Scotland's Towns*, 34.

[67] Ditchburn, 'Rituals, Space and the Marriage of James II', 192–3.

[68] *Chron. D'Escouchy*, 180–1.

[69] For example, see Nicholson, *Scotland: The Later Middle Ages*, 348; McGladdery, *James II*, 81, 86; Ditchburn, 'Rituals, Space and the Marriage of James II', 176–96. See also Dean, 'Crowns, Rings and Processions', Chapter 3.

[70] For more details on the minority, see Tanner, *Late Medieval Scottish Parliament*, 76–92; McGladdery, *James II*, 14–48, quote 86; Brown, *James I*, 194–211; Annie I. Dunlop, *The Life and Times of James Kennedy, Bishop of St Andrews* (Edinburgh, 1950), 20–99.

of the king and royal insignia at the sieges of Barnton and Methven.[71] Aged thirteen, in November 1443, James was also found 'personally presiding' over the general council that 'blew the horn' on Crichton – an action which proclaimed Crichton's downfall by making it 'common knowledge' through public announcement.[72] The prominence of the king increased further in 1445 when he took part in Scotland's first parliament since the coronation in 1437, which marked a significant departure from the rest of the minority.

This parliament, which started in Perth and continued at Edinburgh, saw the introduction of amended reciprocal oaths taken by the king and the estates.[73] The oaths and legislation protecting the royal demesne until the king reached the 'lawful age' have dominated historians' discussions of this parliament, particularly the importance of these oaths as a restriction on royal power and a renegotiation of the crown-estate relationship.[74] Claire Hawes has argued that, rather than signalling a renegotiation, these oaths confirmed the status quo, in which the king could not change a law without consent of parliament, and emphasised the continuation of a relationship between the king and the estates as one of mutual reciprocity.[75] The Scottish coronation ceremony, with oaths exchanged between king and estates as part of the enthronement at Scone from at least the fourteenth century, demonstrates that the rituals of kingship had sought to encapsulate such ideas of reciprocity for some time.[76] The orders of ceremony linked to the coronation at Holyrood, discussed above, also allude to the oaths being symbolic of the partnership between the crown and the estates.[77] The oaths of 1445 were not coronation oaths but evidence suggests that choices were made to offer echoes of a coronation within the parliament space.[78] In a rare glimpse of a ritual undertaken in parliament, the records of the creation of Lord Hamilton – which occurred later in the same parliament – described the young king 'sitting in royal garment and majesty on the platform, in the presence of the three estates'.[79] Physically positioned above the estates, the king was centre stage and notably elevated in a manner similar to the

---

[71] Ibid., 46–8.
[72] *RPS*, 1443/11/1–3, 11; *Chron. Auchinleck*, fol. 110v, 263; McGladdery, *James II*, 47–8; Hawes, 'Community and Public Authority', 33.
[73] *RPS*, 1445/2–7, *RPS*, A1445/10. See also NLS, Regiam Maiestatem, statutes, burgh and guild laws, etc., c.1488, Adv. MS. 25.5.6, fols 203–5.
[74] McGladdery, *James II*, 53–61; Tanner, *Late Medieval Scottish Parliament*, 112–18, 266.
[75] Hawes, 'Community and Public Authority', 122–6.
[76] See previous chapters.
[77] NLS, Adv. MS. 33.7.10, fols 6r–14r; NLS, Adv. MS. 33.2.26, fols 30–1; NRS, PC5/4, fols 138v–9r; Lindsay, 'Forme of the coronatioun', 393–5. The Scottish king's oath came after anointing and immediately preceding those of the estates, meaning the oath was not a pre-condition of receiving the crown, as in England and France, but reflected the symbolic partnership between king and estates, see Lyall, 'The Medieval Coronation Service', 17–20.
[78] Tanner, *Late Medieval Scottish Parliament*, 112–13; McGladdery, *James II*, 53, fn. 69.
[79] *RPS*, A1445/10.

coronation, either on the Moot Hill at Scone or on a stage as in Balfour's order of ceremony.[80] The event may also have taken place in Perth, close to the former traditional coronation site at Scone, which had only seen one general council through the rest of the reign to this point despite its previous prominence.[81] Following a coronation in Edinburgh, largely orchestrated by the queen and her advisors, this parliament and the amended oaths offered the estates of the realm a new ceremonial opportunity prior to James's succession to full royal power. The oaths of 1445 were not necessarily advocating anything new, nor was the event a coronation, but it did ritualise the status quo in a public forum and the oaths were subsequently embedded into Scottish ritual culture of succession.[82]

Despite the young king's physical presence centre stage in these ceremonies, the calling of the parliament and the ritual actions taken within have largely been discussed as demonstrations of Douglas's hold on power.[83] However, this conclusion assumes James was still a pawn in the power games of others and appears to overlook the fact that Douglas was only five years James's senior.[84] In 1445, James turned fifteen and Douglas turned twenty. Contemporary didactic literature commenting on coming of age, such as the *Ratis Raving*, stated that the prime age of reason for a man was thirty. As youths, between fifteen and thirty, both James and Douglas occupied a period in the life cycle in which they were to learn and demonstrate the type of men they would become – virtuous or otherwise – through engaging with 'the work of men'.[85] Didactic sources such as this need to be treated cautiously, but Douglas's rapid rise to power often overshadows the fact that he too was also a young man. Knighted as a child with other young heirs at the baptism of James and his deceased twin brother, Alexander, Douglas was one of James's generation and a peer rather than a seasoned political actor.[86] Nonetheless, at five years older with a prominent role in government from at least 1443

---

[80] Balfour's manuscripts refer to the coronation taking place on a scaffold: NLS, Adv. MS. 33.2.26, fol. 31r. The English *Liber Regalis* records that the platform in Westminster Abbey was designed to make the king visible to all: *Liber Regalis*, 112.

[81] The only other general council in Perth after 1437 was in 1442: *RPS*, A1442/3/1. Tanner and McGladdery both suggest the oaths were taken in Perth, but the oaths are listed as undated so this cannot be confirmed: *Late Medieval Scottish Parliament*, 112–14; *James II*, 53–4; *RPS*, 1445/3–6.

[82] The 1445 oaths appear in a manuscript copy of the *Regiam Maiestatem* and other legal texts composed in the year of James IV's coronation, and in one of Balfour's coronation collections with the fifteenth-century order of ceremony: NLS, Adv. MS. 25.5.6, fols 203–5; NLS, Adv. MS. 33.7.10, fols 6r–14v.

[83] McGladdery, *James II*, 52–61; Tanner, *Late Medieval Scottish Parliament*, 112–18.

[84] Michael Brown suggests Douglas was born late 1424 or early 1425: 'Douglas, William, eighth earl of Douglas and second earl of Avondale', *ODNB* (2004), https://doi.org/10.1093/ref:odnb/7928. Date accessed: 1 March 2021.

[85] *Ratis Raving and Other Moral and Religious Pieces in Prose and Verse from Cambridge University MS KK. I. 5*, ed. J. Rawson Lumby (London, 1890), 59, 63, at lines 1150–8, 1336–43.

[86] See Chapter 3, 146–7; *Chron. Bower*, VIII, 263; Leslie, *Historie*, II, 39.

and one of the largest landholdings in Scotland, Douglas was indeed a powerful young man.[87] While the concept of a political community and crown that worked toward the same goals is often convincing in a Scottish context, this is a case where a confrontation of individuals impacting this status quo was inevitable. James's position at the top of the hegemonic masculine order was under threat.[88] The king's marriage to Mary of Guelders, niece of the duke of Burgundy – particularly when Douglas's own marriage to his cousin Margaret Douglas of Galloway had not yet produced children – offered James an opportunity to secure a stable succession and confirm his superior position in the hierarchy in Scotland and beyond. James played an active role in these ongoing marriage negotiations from at least 1447, when the Guelderian knight, Otto de Puflich, visited Scotland.[89] Moreover, the objectives of this agreement included trade, military support and marriage; it also involved other parties, such as Francis, duke of Brittany, married to James's sister Isabella, whom – as a couple – the treaty named as James's heir should he die childless.[90] The treaty thus reflected efforts to protect the cycle of succession in more than one way, while strengthening relations that would see Douglas's pretensions on the continent snubbed in later years.[91] It is in the light of such ongoing machinations that the tournament held at Stirling on Shrove Tuesday 1449 (25 February) between Burgundian and Scottish knights – the latter led by Sir James Douglas, William's brother and heir apparent – should be assessed.

Often discussed as a Douglas-driven event, Ditchburn convincingly argues the tournament was a Burgundian initiative, capitalised upon by the king.[92]

---

[87] Michael Brown, *The Black Douglases: War and Lordship in Late Medieval Scotland, 1300–1455* (Edinburgh, 1998), 272–80.
[88] Hegemonic masculinity is the dominant or most culturally revered form of masculinity within a particular society, functioning alongside other stratified masculinities such as subordinate and complicit. In the case of a king, who should ideally be the epitome of manhood within society, he should be within this category with his nobles complicit to his prime position. See Lewis, *Kingship and Masculinity*, particularly, 7, 34–5; Raewyn W. Connell and James W. Messerschmidt, 'Hegemonic Masculinity: Rethinking the Concept', *Gender and Society* 19 (2005), 829–59; Lucinda H.S. Dean, 'Negotiating Youth, Old Age and Manhood: A Comparative Approach to Late Medieval Scottish Kingship', in Mairi Cowan, Janay Nugent and Cathryn Spence (eds), *Gender and Identity in Scotland, 1200–1800: Power, Politics, and Faith* (Edinburgh, forthcoming 2024).
[89] ER, V, 273. Letters indicate James II's direct communications with Charles VII and the dukes of Burgundy, Brittany and Guelders, regarding his marriage and those of his sisters: Downie, *She is But A Woman*, 50–80. For example, see NRS, State Papers: Treaties with the Low Countries, Letter of Elizabeth, Duchess of Burgundy, requesting King James II allow his sister, Eleanor to proceed to France […] (20 April 1445), SP9/2; *Letters and Papers Illustrative of the Wars of the English in France during the Reign of Henry VI, King of England*, ed. Joseph Stevenson, 2 vols (London, 1861–64), I, 194–8, 221–3.
[90] Michael Brown, 'War, Marriage, Tournament: Scottish Politics and the Anglo-French War, 1448–1450', *SHR* 98 (2019), 1–21.
[91] Ibid., 17–21.
[92] Carol Edington, 'The Tournament in Medieval Scotland', in Matthew Strickland (ed.), *Armies, Chivalry and Warfare in Medieval Britain and France: Proceedings of the 1995*

The contemporary Picardian chronicler, Mathieu D'Escouchy, states that the three challengers were people of 'the house of Burgundy', who had notable ambassadorial credentials and direct financial support from Philip, duke of Burgundy.[93] Both the Burgundians and James needed to tackle the potential threat of Douglas's power eclipsing the young king at a crucial point in the negotiations.[94] This was a very public opening gambit to the ritual demonstration of royal authority connected to James's marriage. The young king does not appear to have taken part in the jousting in February 1449, but he took advantage of the opportunities offered by presiding over the event. It was the king who 'had the lists made ready at Stirling'.[95] Stirling was a strategically important burgh positioned prominently above the landscape, with a sizeable royal castle and potent Arthurian connections.[96] Though the captain of the castle, Livingstone, was a Douglas adherent, his family would soon face its downfall at James's hand.[97] By orchestrating the martial display at Stirling, the king asserted his position by reclaiming this royal space. Both contemporary continental commentators, Jacques de Lalaing and D'Escouchy, also state that the king entertained these foreign guests before and after the joust.[98] Although not recording specific expenses accrued for this event, the *Exchequer Rolls* list purchases of rich cloths, jousting gear and harnesses, as well as large quantities of spices, wine and other supplies for the royal household in the relevant year, and these expenses are significantly higher than the previous year on the same goods.[99] Footing of the expense does not con-

---

Harlaxton Symposium (Stamford, 1998), 55–8; Katie Stevenson, 'Contesting Chivalry: James II and the Control of Chivalric Culture in the 1450s', *Journal of Medieval History* 33 (2007), 197–214, at 207–8; Ditchburn, 'Rituals, Space and the Marriage of James II', 179–96.

[93] Ibid., 179–83: Mériadac was counsellor to Philip the Good and bought a horse for the journey, Simon de Lalaing, knight of the Golden Fleece, had previous diplomatic experience and Jacques de Lalaing was son of a *chevalier d'honneur* of Isabella duchess of Burgundy. See also *Chron. D'Escouchy*, 148.

[94] For more on the negotiations, see Dunlop, *Life and Times of James Kennedy*, 65–7, 84–96, 99–101; David Ditchburn, 'The Place of Guelders in Scottish Foreign Policy, c.1449–c.1542', in Grant G. Simpson (ed.), *Scotland and the Low Countries, 1124–1994* (East Linton, 1996), 59–75, at 59–69; Downie, *She is But A Woman*, 66–80.

[95] 'Histoire du Bon Chevalier Messire Jacques de Lalain', in *Early Travellers in Scotland*, ed. P. Hume Brown (Edinburgh, 1891), 33.

[96] Ditchburn, 'Rituals, Space and the Marriage of James II', 192–4.

[97] On the fall of the Livingstones, see McGladdery, *James II*, 88–92.

[98] 'Histoire du ... Jacques de Lalain', 38; *Chron. D'Escouchy*, 150. Lalaing's account reports that the king footed the cost of feasting and gifts for the foreign guests, rather than Douglas.

[99] ER, V, 338–40, 344–9. Annual expenditure is difficult to calculate accurately without the comptroller's account, but comparative expenditure for similar items between September 1448 to mid-July 1449 and the previous twelve months indicates an increase in expenditure of over £700. For entries 1447–48, see ER, V, 299–300, 302, 306, 309–15, 317–18. The 1448–49 account covers the Shrove Tuesday tournament and the wedding in July, but costs for the wedding also appear in the next account as this began in July 1449. Absent *Treasurer's Accounts* mean much is missing as these accounts increasingly recorded the king's personal and 'extraordinary' expenses.

firm that king orchestrated the event independently, but it certainly returns agency to him. The only specific reference to William, earl of Douglas, was his entrance to the field amidst a large entourage of nobles and knights, following the three Scottish combatants, which also included the Lyon herald, chief herald and the king's steward, who would have been dressed in their royal livery.[100] Notably, the attention of the foreign commentators lingers on the combat and the enthroned king who presided as fair judge in concluding the fight rather than on Douglas. James also took advantage of the occasion to bestow knighthoods on the three competing Douglas adherents, publicly tying their loyalty to the crown as James I had done at his sons' baptism, and James II also extended the same honour to the visiting knights.[101] Douglas's dominance of the minority and even the early adult reign is not in question, but James's agency seems to be subsumed in the existing narrative. If it is an accepted fact that Douglas was leader of the minority government in 1443, aged around eighteen, it is unlikely that the king was quietly waiting in the wings as he too reached this age in late 1448. The young king was aware of his ceremonial and political role prior to July 1449, so the Shrove Tuesday joust should be assessed as part of a larger programme with this in mind.

In the wedding of July 1449, following the Treaty of Brussels on 1 April, Douglas and his adherents are notably absent in the contemporary records of these events.[102] Two of the Scottish ambassadors, William Crichton, chancellor, and John Ralston, bishop of Dunkeld, led the welcoming crowd at Leith and presented Mary of Guelders to James in their first meeting.[103] Ralston may also have officiated at the marriage and the queen's coronation to support William Turnbull, bishop of Glasgow.[104] All three were also king's men who actively supported subsequent moves against Douglas.[105] Another leading figure in the ceremonial was William Sinclair, earl of Orkney and admiral of the Scottish fleet, along with his wife, Elizabeth, who led the

---

[100] *Chron. D'Escouchy*, 150; RMS, II, no. 319; Stevenson, 'Contesting Chivalry', 207; 'Histoire du ... Jacques de Lalain', 33–4.
[101] Ibid.; *Chron. D'Escouchy*, 150.
[102] For details of the marriage treaty: J.H. Baxter, 'The Marriage of James II', SHR 25 (1927), 69–72; Ditchburn, 'The Place of Guelders in Scottish Foreign Policy', 59–69.
[103] *Chron. Auchinleck*, fols 121v, 274; *Chron. D'Escouchy*, 178–9; Dunlop, *Life and Times of John Kennedy*, 96; Lucinda H.S. Dean, 'Enter the Alien: Foreign Consorts and their Royal Entries into Scottish Cities, c.1449–1590', in Ronnie Mulryne and Anna Maria Testaverde with Ines Aliverti (eds), *The Iconography of Power: Ceremonial Entries in Early Modern Europe* (Farnham, 2015), 267–95, at 285–7.
[104] *Chron. D'Escouchy* does not offer names, but both signed the ratification of the marriage treaty and James Kennedy, bishop of St Andrews, did not: NRS, SP7/14; Dunlop, *Life and Times of Bishop Kennedy*, 101–2. For background on the bishops: Alan R. Borthwick, 'Ralston, John (d.1451/2)', ODNB (2004), https://doi.org/10.1093/ref:odnb/23061. Date accessed: 1 March 2021; John Durkan, 'Turnbull, William (c.1400–1454)', ODNB (2004), https://doi.org/10.1093/ref:odnb/27838. Date accessed: 1 March 2021.
[105] Tanner, *Late Medieval Scottish Parliament*, 128–47; McGladdery, *James II*, 93–6, 101, 110–11, 119, 130–1, 135–6.

female welcoming party and accompanied the queen to her marriage.[106] Orkney was a longstanding royal servant, who had accompanied Margaret Stewart to France in 1436, served on the minority council and was later made chancellor (1454), and, like Turnbull and Crichton, supported the king in bringing down Douglas.[107] Douglas's conspicuous absence from the accounts of foreign commentaries, despite the family's European renown, suggests that the king purposefully sought to keep Douglas involvement to a minimum to reassert royal authority.

Mary of Guelders' welcome was an elaborate one, focusing initially on her alone.[108] A crowd headed by Bishop Ralston and Chancellor Crichton with three hundred 'men in harness', who were likely liveried men-at-arms on horseback, along with the churchmen, burgesses and people of Leith, met Mary and her entourage on 18 June.[109] After lodging at the monastery of St Anthony of Vienne in Leith, the queen made her entry to Edinburgh without the king and was the primary focus of the urban audience who welcomed her.[110] A large company – stated as ten-thousand-strong – paraded 'in rather beautiful order according to the estates of the country', leading the young queen to Edinburgh where her entry was heralded by music from many diverse instruments.[111] The route of the entry is not recorded but, considering that Mary was housed at the royal lodgings at Holyrood Abbey, potential precedent existed in James's own coronation procession that passed down the High Street from the castle, or James I's entry in 1424 that would have started at one of the town's gates.[112] Crichton and Ralston continued their ambassadorial role by escorting the queen to her husband after his arrival.[113] There was a choreographed formality to this first meeting: Mary knelt before James II, who raised her up to standing

---

[106] *Chron. D'Escouchy*, 179–80, 182.
[107] Ibid., 176; Barbara Crawford, 'Sinclair Family', *ODNB* (2009), http://doi.org/10.1093/ref:odnb/54321. Date accessed: 1 March 2021.
[108] Dean, 'Enter the Alien', 285–7.
[109] *Chron. Auchinleck*, fol. 121v, 274; *Chron. D'Escouchy*, 178. Her entourage included: Henry van Borselen, lord of Veere (father of Wolfaert van Borselen married to Mary Stewart, James II's sister), Anthoine de Rochebaron and his wife, Philipotte of Bourgogne (illegitimate daughter of the duke of Burgundy) and Isabel, daughter of Jacques de Lalaing.
[110] The Latin records note the expenses for the '*adventus domine regine infra regnum*': ER, V, 381–2, 387–8. The monastery of Saint Anthony's had strong Burgundians ties and was last in a series of religious sites visited on Mary's journey to Edinburgh, including St Adrian's on the Isle of May: Ditchburn, 'Rituals, Space and the Marriage of James II', 183–5. James II ratified the marriage treaty in Stirling before meeting the queen in Edinburgh: NRS, Confirmation under the Great Seal of Scotland of marriage contract between King James II and Marie de Gueldres (Stirling, 25 June 1449), SP7/14.
[111] French text: '… en assez belle ordonnance, selon de estatz du pays, qui lui firrent comme paravant la reverence, chascun en droit soy': *Chron. D'Escouchy*, 178–9.
[112] See Chapter 3, 137–40, and Chapter 4, 157–8. Royal funds for work to the building fabric of Holyrood: ER, V, 346–7. This was unusual during the mid-fifteenth century as the upkeep of the abbey and lodgings was usually left to the Augustinian brethren prior to the construction of the palace: Dunbar, *Scottish Royal Palaces*, 55–6.
[113] *Chron. D'Escouchy*, 179.

and only once the king had welcomed his queen were the Burgundian and Scottish nobles permitted to greet each other.[114] Both the queen's entry and the first royal meeting were replete with efforts to impress upon foreign and Scottish onlookers the ordered state of the realm.

This desire to present ordered civility continued through other elements of subsequent ceremonies, but the extent to which this performance convinced the foreign guests is debatable. At the dinner, for example, thirty to forty individuals served the guests, who were seated by rank in the hall, and each server knelt before the guest they served until the guest began eating. This is indicative of rigid formal etiquette. However, D'Escouchy's subsequent description of prelates and knights drinking liberally from an enormous wooden goblet, presumably shared between them, offers a contrasting image of the raucous celebrations of some attendees, indicating that the rougher edges of the Scottish court could not be entirely smoothed off.[115] Similar comparisons are apparent in other aspects of the celebrations described by D'Escouchy. The two main decorative dishes – embracing heraldic and symbolic devices that were prominent across Europe – arrived with great ceremony.[116] The first was a painted stuffed boar's head, the stuffing of which was set alight 'to the joy of all observers', surrounded by banners of the arms of the king and key nobles, including the newly created earl of Huntly, Alexander Seton, who was son-in-law to Chancellor Crichton. The second was an exquisitely crafted ship with silver cords carried by Orkney, admiral of the Scottish fleet, accompanied by four knights, which perhaps sought to offer symbolic references to both the trade alliances and military support that the marriage treaty confirmed. D'Escouchy's account suggests he was suitably impressed by these displays, but he also labelled the ensuing entertainments as rough and strange in French eyes.[117]

Specifics of these later festivities are lacking, but financial records illustrate that instruments such as the 'gittar' or 'gythorn' were played at James's court and that regular expenses were made for plays, jesters and entertainers in the late 1440s and early 1450s.[118] Payments for gear necessary for jousting, including an armoured tabard for the Albany pursuivant, and pieces of armour purchased for the king's own use between September 1448 and late July 1449 indicate that martial activities were prominent, and that the king participated in these – beyond his role as host for the Shrove Tuesday

---

[114] Ibid.
[115] Ibid., 181–2. Richard Vaughan has translated part of the account of the feast by D'Escouchy: *Philip the Good: The Apogee of Burgundy* (Woodbridge, 2011), 112.
[116] On *soltetes* of Queen Katherine of England in 1421: Burden, 'Rituals of Royalty', 197–220. This kind of symbolism is rife in the Feast of the Pheasant, organised at Lille by Duke Philip of Burgundy in 1454; see, the account of Olivier de la Marche translated and discussed in Brown and Small, *Court and Civic Society*, 36–53.
[117] *Chron. D'Escouchy*, 181–2. French text on the entertainments: '*rude et estranges aux regards des parties de France*', 182.
[118] *ER*, V, 263, 302, 311, 339, 377–8. A gittar or gythorn was similar to a guitar.

DEATH AND THE ROYAL SUCCESSION IN SCOTLAND

tournament – during this accounting period.[119] Stevenson argues that James's personal involvement in such chivalric pursuits should be considered central to his projections of authority and status.[120] Consequently, it is curious that there does not appear to have been any jousting to celebrate the wedding, according to D'Escouchy. It is not clear whether an absence of jousting was one of the things that he found strange about the entertainments or whether he just was not present for subsequent martial entertainments, if they took place. Here a firm conclusion is not possible as the *Exchequer Rolls* cover both Shrove Tuesday and the wedding without clarity of what was used when, and the corresponding *Treasurer's Accounts* have not survived.

The marriage ceremony and Mary's coronation offered James II further opportunities in terms of ritual display.[121] The liturgy of the Mass was that of the feast of the Visitation of the Blessed Virgin, which was both suitable for marriage and provided a liturgical hook between James's own coronation – on the anniversary of Annunciation of the Blessed Virgin – and that of his wife.[122] Between the wedding Mass and the consort crowning, Mary was led into a side chapel where she was dressed in a robe of royal purple. James had entered the abbey in a long grey and white fur-lined robe but exited wearing purple also, suggesting a simultaneous re-robing to signify the unity of the royal couple through marriage made visibly manifest in these sartorial choices.[123] The use of purple robes by James II has been cautiously connected to imperial ambitions and Ditchburn also associates the colour choice to a statement of adulthood and independent power on the part of James at this juncture.[124] It is not entirely clear when this particular colour of coronation robe was first used in Scotland; however, the use of a purple robe may have been a feature from previous centuries, possibly stretching back to the inauguration of Alexander III.[125] The extant *Exchequer Rolls* also record only a small payment for cloth purchased for the royal robe at the time of the marriage, which was indicative of a repair to an existing robe rather than a new item.[126] If James used a purple robe passed down through generations as part of the regalia, thus of an older style or cut, and gave his new queen matching attire, this might explain D'Escouchy's comments about the robes

---

[119] *ER*, V, 339, 344–46, 385–6.
[120] Stevenson, 'Contesting Chivalry', 210.
[121] *Chron. D'Escouchy*, 180.
[122] The marriage was on 3 July 1449 and the annual Visitation feast was 2 July, but this was a major Marian feast and was performed for eight days: Harper, *Forms and Orders of Western Liturgy*, 49–57. See 156.
[123] *Chron. D'Escouchy*, 180–1. See also Downie, *She is But A Woman*, 79.
[124] Ditchburn, 'Rituals, Space and the Marriage of James II', 185–6, 190; McGladdery, *James II*, 79.
[125] *Chron. Bower*, V, 294–5. Bower states Alexander III 'was clothed in royal purple' in 1249, but he is the only commentator to do so. See Chapter 2, 80 and Chapter 3, 142.
[126] *ER*, V, 387.

being of a strange fashion.[127] However, for local audiences, this reuse of the robe could have spoken to connections to forebears and the dynastic lineage that this union promised to continue. This speaks to the importance of recognising that all records of ritual are filtered through the senses, memories and experiences of those viewing and recording them.

The marriage ceremony in 1449 included a possible innovation: a reading of the 'letters' regarding Mary's surety and dower lands in the church prior to the marriage sacrament taking place.[128] This action made a very public and celebratory statement about the king's ability to provide for his queen, and symbolically emphasised her position in the realm as a political figure with landed power and gravitas that echoed James I's efforts to have Joan's status within the realm recognised.[129] The subsequent parliament in January 1450, held at the tolbooth in Edinburgh, saw the grants confirmed by the estates and a public act of stage-managed intercession by the queen on behalf of the Scottish bishops.[130] This was a prime opportunity for James II to project his importance as the sole giver of pardons and justice, building on the image he presented at the tournament of February 1448. However, it also drew his foreign queen into an active relationship with the estates at the opening parliament of their reign together as a couple. A parliament held in Edinburgh, presumably at the tolbooth but this is not confirmed, also witnessed a public celebratory declaration about the first fruit of this union in June 1452, following the birth of Prince James (later James III) at St Andrews.[131] This was an important event for James II, but particularly so in the wake of the murder of William, earl of Douglas, at the king's hand.[132] During the confirmation of privileges to St Andrews, also known as Bishop Kennedy's 'golden charter', in parliament the king announced:

> [...] the birth of our eldest son within the place and chief messuage of our same patron [St Andrews] [a] fortunate [event], by the favour of divine

---

[127] *Chron. D'Escouchy*, 180–1.
[128] Ibid., 180.
[129] Amy Hayes demonstrates that Mary of Guelders did not hold all of her landholdings prior to James II's death, as such this was a symbolic act rather than one practically putting the land in her charge: 'Late Medieval Scottish Queens', 231–8.
[130] *RPS*, 1450/1/32; *RPS*, 1450/1/34; Downie, *She is But A Woman*, 94–5.
[131] *RPS*, 1479/10/12. Expenses of the queen at St Andrews between May and August 1452: *ER*, V, 685. Land grants were also made to a royal servant, Robert Norry, in June 1452, rewarded '*pro jocundus novis per ipsum regi primitus de nativite Jacobi principis, heredis et filiis regis legitimi relatis*' [for delivering the good news to the king of the birth of his son]: *RMS*, II, no. 566. Reference to the birthing shirt of St Margaret brought to the queen in 1451 (*ER*, V, 497, 512) caused some confusion regarding James III's year of birth (*ER*, V, lxxxviii–lxxxix); however, the delivery of the shirt has been linked to the birth of James III's elder sister, Mary, see Dunlop, *Life and Times of Bishop Kennedy*, 135–6; Macdougall, *James III*, 1.
[132] McGladdery, *James II*, 126–9; Brown, *The Black Douglases*, 292–9; Macdougall, *James III*, 1–6. The *Chron. Auchinleck* records the brutal murder of Douglas and subsequent events, fols 114v–15v, 265–6.

clemency, pleasing and joyful to us and our realm's inhabitants [...] which, with God's favour, has also achieved the assured future and lineal succession of our royal majesty and brought us most pleasing advancement in the world [...][133]

The birth of a male heir, considering the potential political crisis that loomed, was utilised to full advantage within the parliament as deflection of criticism and to offer an element of stability in uncertain times. Celebrations like those that erupted in Edinburgh for James II's birth were not recorded in narrative accounts, but this period is poorly served by such. Considering the significance of urban spaces to ritual celebrations, and indeed punishments, through the course of James' life, it would have been surprising if the promise of dynastic succession and stability that their union and offspring offered was not celebrated in some public way.

Crowning the Boy and Burying the Unfortunate Warrior

Mary of Guelders gave birth to three more sons and two daughters during the 1450s, thus fulfilling one of her pre-eminent roles as queen consort in terms of succession.[134] She was also prominent in the ceremonies marking the transferral of power from her husband, James II, to their son, James III, following the king's tragic death, aged twenty-nine, during the siege of Roxburgh in August 1460. Unlike Joan Beaufort, however, Mary's control over the young king and her role in government was not limited to the first few months of her son's reign and continued until her own early death in 1463. This indicates that the dialogue between James II, Mary and the estates, initiated in the rituals undertaken at the time of the couple's marriage, had developed sufficiently during the reign to make this possible. Mary had also been brought up in the culturally refined Burgundian court with Isabella of Portugal, duchess of Burgundy – a powerful and intelligent female role model, who negotiated and even ruled in lieu of Philip, duke of Burgundy, at times.[135] Consequently, Mary's education imbued her with a sense of status, a knowledge of factional politics and an appreciation of the importance of ritual, ceremony and court culture. The events surrounding James II's funeral and his son's coronation suffer from a scarcity of documentary evidence, but

---

[133] *RPS*, 1479/10/12. See also *RMS*, II, no. 1444.

[134] One daughter was born before James III and one of these sons, David, lived only a year or so, and there was an additional stillborn infant recorded in 1450, see Hayes, 'Late Medieval Scottish Queens', Appendix 1, 271.

[135] From the mid-1430s, Isabella was centrally important to the Burgundian administration; she negotiated with Burgundian cities and foreign powers (England and France), acted as regent during absences of the duke, oversaw the rebuilding of the ducal palace in Bruges (1448–52) and helped raise funds and men for wars: *Philip the Good*, 83, 89, 101, 114–15, 116–20, 124, 167–8, 171–2, 219–20; Downie, *She is But a Woman*, 68–9.

the following draws what has survived into discussion with past precedent and wider contextual detail to consider how the role of the deceased king, widowed queen consort and the Scottish political elite manifested during this unexpected ceremonial transfer of power.[136]

James II died on 3 August 1460, during the final days of the siege of Roxburgh, and men were sent to Edinburgh to inform the prince and the queen:

> And the said lordis Incontinent sent till Edinburgh for the Prince and the said Prince with his modere the quene and bischopis and uther nobillis come to Kelso on the fryday efter the deid of the king and remanit ther quhill he was crownit [...][137]

The coronation of eight-year-old James III took place at Kelso Abbey on Sunday 10 August 1460.[138] The haste of the arrangements for the coronation – without forty days for gathering the estates or sufficient time to inter the king's body some fifty miles away at Holyrood – was reminiscent of thirteenth-century Scotland, when hereditary succession from father to son was a relatively new and fragile concept.[139] By 1460 the actual point of power transfer was the death of the previous monarch, rather than at the coronation or funeral, and had been for some time. Yet, this had not lessened the value of these ceremonies in providing visible and tangible expressions of the transfer of power that marked the cycle of succession. Potential logistical challenges arose with the king's unexpected death so far from the centres of power and ritual, particularly as surviving evidence points to his desire to be buried at Holyrood Abbey, as considered below. However, there was precedent for waiting to make a powerful ceremonial statement with a funeral and coronation in one location, such as occurred in 1390, and Holyrood Abbey was the primary ritual space with which Mary of Guelders would have been most familiar. Kelso and nearby Roxburgh, on the other hand, had not hosted a royal ceremony since the weddings of the thirteenth century and there were no obvious links between the Augustinian houses of Holyrood or Scone, and the Tironensian monastery of Kelso.[140] Moreover, the date of the coronation was not one of note in the religious calendar, despite the proximity to the feast

---

[136] For chronicle and later histories, see 11–12, 149. The *Exchequer Rolls* record purchase of fustian and cotton for James's groom (*veletis*) for the ride to his coronation: *ER*, VII, 34. Otherwise financial record of James III's coronation are limited as there are no surviving *Treasurer's Accounts* and the *ER* is fragmentary; see Introduction, 12–13.

[137] *Chron. Auchinleck*, fol. 119v, 272.

[138] Ibid.; Maior, 387; Leslie, *Historie*, II, 82; Buchanan, *History*, II, 168. See also McGladdery, *James II*, 111–12; Macdougall, *James III*, 34.

[139] See Chapter 1.

[140] There are records settling a dispute (in Kelso's favour) c.1159 regarding rights to lands around Duddingston Crag, now part of Holyrood Park: *RRS*, I, no. 131. See also *People of Medieval Scotland*, 1/5/24 (RRS, I, no. 131), https://www.poms.ac.uk/record/source/92/. Date accessed: 1 March 2021; Henderson, *Kelso Abbey*, 10–12.

of the Assumption of the Virgin Mary on 15 August. Against the backdrop of James II's relatively recent overthrow of the Douglases, the acceleration of civil war in England and increased intergenerational tensions around the succession in Mary's native Guelders, the choices made would suggest an urgency to ritually confirm the succession through a coronation that overrode other concerns, traditions and expectations.[141]

Following the victorious siege of Roxburgh, the Scots continued to press their advantage by attacking northern England and took the settlement of Wark prior to the coronation.[142] Taking the child king to the region offered the opportunity to cement military victory with the passage of dynastic power between father and son. Moreover, despite being removed from the usual centres of Scottish power, Macdougall suggests the audience that witnessed James III's coronation was the largest to gather in Scotland for some time.[143] Such a statement is challenging to quantify with the paucity of evidence around coronation attendance in 1460, but combining the siege army with key court figures summoned to accompany the queen and the heir, and the urban communities at Kelso and Roxburgh, certainly offered the potential for large numbers (see Appendix II, 'James III'). The first parliament of James III's reign took place in February 1461 in Edinburgh, rather than immediately after the coronation, so parliament records must be used cautiously to comment on attendees at Kelso; nonetheless, they prove valuable when combined with other sources (see Appendix II, 'James III').

The *Auchinleck Chronicle* states that both bishops and nobles travelled with the queen and prince from Edinburgh in August 1460, but their identities are not confirmed.[144] James Kennedy, bishop of St Andrews, was not in Scotland to take his role as officiant, nor did he attend the first parliament, as he did not return from foreign travels until around May 1461.[145] Five bishops attended the first parliament of 1461: Andrew Durisdeer, bishop of Glasgow, and Thomas Lauder, bishop of Dunkeld, were first of the clerical estate in witness lists for that parliament, as well as being selected as lord auditors, and precedent existed for both of these bishops officiating in Scottish coronations.[146] The first parliament officially placed significant power in the hands of the king's mother, Mary of Guelders, William Sinclair, earl of Orkney and a council consisting largely of people who had served in the former king's council.[147] As the guardianship of the eight-year-old king was a likely sub-

---

[141] Brown, *The Black Douglases*, 282–334; McGladdery, *James II*, 125–208; David Grummit, *The Wars of the Roses* (London, 2013), 43–82; Gerard Nijsten, *In the Shadow of Burgundy: The Court of Guelders in the Late Middle Ages* (Cambridge, 2004), xviii–xix.
[142] Macdougall, *James III*, 31–5.
[143] Ibid., 40.
[144] *Chron. Auchinleck*, fol. 119v, 272.
[145] Dunlop, *Life and Times of Bishop Kennedy*, 211–15; Macdougall, *James III*, 46.
[146] *RPS*, A1461/2–3, 1461/5. For the list of witnesses and lord auditors, see Appendix II 'James III'.
[147] Ibid.; *Chron. Auchinleck*, fols 120r–v, 273. Sinclair's guardianship of the king is not

ject of discussion at Kelso, these important players had a vested interest in accompanying the queen to the coronation, if they were not at the siege site already, to secure their place in power. Men reliant on the queen's patronage, such as James Lindsay, provost of Lincluden and, later, keeper of the Privy Seal, were equally likely to have accompanied her for the ceremonial installation of the king.[148]

The choice of Kelso also meant that many of those who fought alongside James II would have been able to attend. The *Auchinleck Chronicle* records the knighting of one hundred men at the coronation: now a common ritual within the Scottish coronation for creating and consolidating loyalty to the new king, the knighting was harnessed here also to honour those loyal to the fallen king.[149] Stevenson has identified ten men who may have received knighthoods on this occasion, including Alexander Napier of Merchiston – a 'typical merchant-turned-laird', upon whom the Scottish crown was becoming increasingly reliant.[150] Napier served as comptroller several times from 1449 to 1460–61 and was recorded in a witness list as the '*scutifer regis*' or 'shield-bearer' of the king in 1459, which indicates a position in the royal household with physical closeness to the former king.[151] Other figures, with increasingly important ceremonial roles, who were likely to have accompanied the king to the battlefield included household officers, such as the Marischal and the Constable, who were both belted as earls by James II.[152] Heraldic officials, particularly the Lyon herald, also gained importance in the ceremonies of kingship and the royal household through the fifteenth century and, clad in striking royal Stewart livery, they visually emphasised dynastic continuity.

Many of these people – clerics, nobles, knights, heraldic officials, household officers and presumably the young king – also became the funeral entourage for James II's body on the journey from Kelso to Edinburgh. The journey would have been at least fifty miles, dependent on the route, and may have required four or more stopping points that could create interim vigils.[153]

---

recorded in extant parliament sources or the chronicles; however, it is recorded in a letter to the king of Norway in July 1461: *Records of the Earldom of Orkney, 1299–1614*, ed. Joseph Storer Clouston (Edinburgh, 1914), 54; Macdougall, 40–1.

[148] RPS, A1461/2; *Chron. Auchinleck*, fol. 120v, 273; Macdougall, *James III*, 40–4.

[149] *Chron. Auchinleck*, fol. 119v, 272.

[150] Katie Stevenson, *Chivalry and Knighthood in Scotland, 1424–1513* (Woodbridge, 2006), 183.

[151] Atholl Murray, 'The Comptroller, 1425–1488', SHR 52 (1973), 1–29, at 5–6; RMS, II, no. 700 (17 May 1459). He also starts being called '*domino*' in the *Exchequer Rolls* from the account rendered in March 1461; see ER, VII, 7.

[152] See Chapter 4, 156 n.55. The constable was responsible for the king's guards, so he would have been with either James II or his heir: 'The Scottish King's Household and Other Fragments from a Fourteenth-Century Manuscript in the Library of Corpus Christi College, Cambridge', ed. Mary Bateson, in *Miscellany of the Scottish History Society Second Volume* (Edinburgh, 1904), 1–43, at 39–40.

[153] Distance covered by an army carrying siege weapons was unlikely to be more than 10 to 12 miles per day, see Barrow, *Scotland and Its Neighbours*, 204.

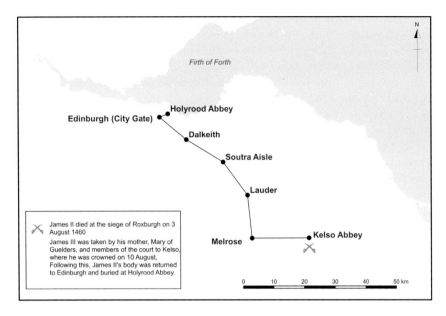

Map 7 Potential route of funeral procession of James II, 1460. Contains Ordnance Survey data © Crown Copyright and database right (2023).

There is no record of any of the exact stops, so any suggestions are necessarily speculative. The road between the border abbeys and Edinburgh was one of the numerous major land routes in Scotland known as the king's road, and it passed near or through places of note including the royal burgh of Lauder, the Augustinian hospital of the Holy Trinity at Soutra, the castle of Dalkeith and Newbattle Abbey, situated two miles south of Dalkeith (see Map 7).[154] The latter two were both positioned a comfortable distance from Edinburgh (approximately six to eight miles) to allow for a final procession to Holyrood Abbey. The distance from Kelso or Roxburgh to Lauder, if this was a stop on the route, would have been too long to cover in one day; the imposing abbey at Melrose, where Alexander II and the heart of Robert I were buried, offered a potential first stop even though it was off the direct route. If the

---

[154] Barrow, *Scotland and Its Neighbours*, 202–3, 206, 212. Soutra was a rich royal foundation in the fifteenth century, although Mary of Guelders later transferred the rich revenues of Soutra to her Holy Trinity foundation in Edinburgh: *Registrum Domus de Soltre necnon Ecclesie Collegiate S. Trinitatis prope Edinburgh etc.*, ed. David Laing (Edinburgh, 1861), x, 3–70, particularly 57–70; James Hunter, *Fala and Soutra including a History of the Ancient 'Domus de Soltre' with its Masters and Great Revenues, and of other Historical Associations and Buildings* (Edinburgh, 1892), 5, 30–49. Dalkeith was neither a royal burgh nor an abbey or royal religious foundation, but the castle was held by James Douglas, the newly created earl of Morton (1458) and husband of James II's sister Joanna (m.1459), rewarded for Red Douglas loyalty to the crown during the king's power struggle with the Black Douglases: Roland Tanner, 'Douglas, James, first earl of Morton', *ODNB* (2004), https://doi.org/10.1093/ref: odnb/54167. Date accessed: 1 March 2021.

route incorporated a royal resting place of former famous warrior kings of Scots, there was a further opportunity to emphasise the martial prowess of the dynastic line from which the young king inherited the throne that would appear to tie in with the decision to take the heir to Kelso for his coronation.

On arrival in Edinburgh, it is likely that crowds gathered in the streets to mourn James II on his route to Holyrood – just as they had cheered him in 1437 and marched in 'beautiful order' from Leith with Mary of Guelders in 1449. With so many royal officials and knights in the entourage, this would have been a heraldic display of some scale within this urban space. The prominence of processions and public vigils had long existed in Scottish royal funerary practices, but the burial sites used before 1460 were situated in or near much smaller burghs, including Dunfermline, Arbroath, Melrose and Scone. Other than David II, there had been no other royal burials in Holyrood Abbey. Edinburgh and Holyrood Abbey were, however, central to the ceremonies of James II's reign including his marriage to Mary of Guelders, so the choice of Holyrood Abbey as a burial place fits a wider pattern in the couple's ritual undertakings and built on the increasing focus on the ritual opportunities that Edinburgh's urban environment offered from 1424 onwards. It also speaks to the influence of the urban-centred courts in which Mary of Guelders grew up, both in Guelders and Burgundy. Nijsten comments that the commemoration ceremonies held for James II in Arnhem and Venslo, at the behest of Mary's father, demonstrated the central role of civic administration in ritual performances in Guelders, with bailiffs gathering mourners and organising the ringing of bells.[155] Considering the development of interactions between royalty and the burghs in orchestrating royal occasions, including James I's return in 1424, Mary's own entry in 1449 and the subsequent better-recorded events of the sixteenth century, it is entirely plausible that the urban population of Edinburgh and Canongate was mobilised to respond in a similar way in 1460 to mourn James II and welcome the return of their new king.[156] Consequently, an argument emerges for a joint organisational effort between the living and the dead: the widowed queen, the deceased monarch, the political elite and the urban community through which they traversed.

James II's involvement in preparations reveals itself in the extant references for the tomb at Holyrood Abbey. The fees for a painter and carpenter, along with wax and black cloth, in the *Exchequer Rolls* indicate an ongoing project – perhaps in collaboration with Mary – to build a tomb that was already underway by 1460 despite the king's young age.[157] Notably, records describe James's monument as a *sepulcrum* or *sepulcri*, which translates to tomb-shrine, rather than the more commonly used *tumba*. *Sepulcrum* often refers to the structure placed in the north chancel used as the tomb of Christ

---

[155] Nijsten, *In the Shadow of Burgundy*, 372–5.
[156] For example, see Gray, 'The Royal Entry', 10–31, and Chapter 5.
[157] ER, VII, 34–5.

during Easter and Holy Week, and wealthy patrons in England and elsewhere had begun to request burial in this area so that their tombs would take on a temporary liturgical role at one of the most holy times of year.[158] Burial in this location may have been following broader fashions, but there were arguably echoes of ritual demonstrations of links between the king and Christ that occurred during James I's life – such as the amalgamation of Palm Sunday and the royal entry – which points to an increasing Stewart engagement with notions of sacral kingship.

The way the late king was conveyed in the extended processions, and whether a body was visible, is unclear. Extant purchases of new garments and pieces of armour for the 'late' king do imply the dressing of the body – or perhaps an effigy – for public consumption during the ceremony.[159] The substantial hiatus between James II's death and burial, as well as his mortal wound from a cannon backfire, provide very practical reasons for an effigy if there was an expectation for the body to be on display. Ideas circulating in Scotland, as in the work of Gilbert Hay, the Scot who was former chamberlain of Charles VII of France, imply a broad understanding of the theories of the king's two bodies – that is the body politic, which continued eternally, and the body natural that perished – rooted in the earlier ideology of *dignitas non moritur* (dignity does not die).[160] However, the order of the rituals in 1460, with James III being anointed at Kelso before the burial and accompanying the king's body back to Edinburgh and Holyrood, meant that the 'royal dignity' had already been ritually passed from father to son, arguably undermining any tangible representations of the king's two bodies in an effigy of James II. Thus, if such an object existed, it was likely for the practical purpose of proving death and presenting the warrior king in final glory.

The armour prepared for the dead king – such as the two pieces ordered from Ligerio Gallico by the queen and the council – could also have been used as funerary offerings rather than for the display of the king's body or his effigy.[161] The fifteenth-century work of Adam Loutfout, who was in the service of the Marchmond herald, Sir William of Cummyn of Inverlochy, and later works based on this, bear testament to an established understanding of contemporary European developments in heraldic culture and rituals, including the offerings of knightly accoutrements during a funeral.[162] Heraldic dis-

---

[158] Duffy, *The Stripping of the Altars*, 29–35. James was neither founder nor first king buried in Holyrood, as David II was buried there in 1371, so was unlikely to be positioned at the high altar and this would have been a viable high-status alternative.

[159] ER, VII, 34–6.

[160] Sally L. Mapstone, 'The Advice to Princes Tradition in Scottish Literature, 1450–1500' (DPhil thesis, University of Oxford, 1986), 70. The prose works of Hay were commissioned for William Sinclair, earl of Orkney (chancellor for part of James II's reign) and the poetic *Buik of King Alexander* for Lord Erskine. See also Kantorowicz, *The King's Two Bodies*, particularly 383–437.

[161] ER, VII, 34.

[162] BL, Fifteenth-Century Heraldic Treatise (*The Deidis of Armorie*), Harley MS 6149; *The Deidis of Armorie: A Heraldic Treatise and Bestiary*, ed. Luuk A.J.R. Houwen, 2 vols

plays were also realised in the commemoration for the queen, whose funeral costs in 1463 reached £212, 16s. 2d. without any costs for a tomb, in the form of a number of painted escutcheons.[163] The final expenses for James II's tomb, made under the command of James III, also included the addition of more heraldic decoration.[164] The use of knightly accoutrements in the funeral would have been fitting following James's death in a siege, while also reflecting the wider 'chivalric ethos' of his kingship that demonstrated the influence of both Burgundian and Scottish traditions and fashions.[165]

The unusual order of the events in 1460, reverting to that of an earlier age, with a notably curious setting for the coronation, make the treatment of these events as a ceremonial whole rather than as disparate parts a logical approach. The rapidity with which the crowning was undertaken appears rooted in the anxieties of the queen and her advisors, perhaps based on personal experience or just forced by circumstance. Yet, by combining the young king's coronation, a large-scale knighting ceremony at the siege site, and his father's heraldic funeral procession from the borders, the minority government – led by the queen and Sinclair – offered a coherent statement about the continuity and stability of the dynasty through death and succession. This was further extended in the funeral and tomb, which carried hallmarks of James II's own influence.

Becoming an Emperor within His Kingdom and Securing Succession

Following James III's coronation near the front line of the siege of Roxburgh in 1460, he continued to be used as tangible proof of power for subsequent minority councils and the leading individuals within them through his youthful years. This included being a military figurehead at Norham in 1463 – a failed campaign to support the Lancastrian king, Henry VI – and making formal royal entries and entertaining guests in northern burghs on a progress around the realm

---

(Edinburgh, 1994). See Appendix I for transcript of the later sixteenth-century work of John Scrymheour based on Loutfout: NLS, Adv. MS. 31.5.2, fols 15r–16v. There is an extensive literature, but for some European examples, see *Liber Regie Capelle*, 112–14; Malcolm Vale, 'A Burgundian Funeral: Olivier de la Marche and the Obsequies of Adolf of Cleves, lord of Ravenstein', *English Historical Review* 111 (1996), 920–38, at 934–8; Lisa Monnas, 'Textiles from the Funerary Achievements of Henry V', in Jenny Stratford (ed.), *The Lancastrian Court: Proceedings of the 2001 Harlaxton Symposium* (Donington, 2003), 125–46; Chris Given-Wilson, 'The Exequies of Edward III and the Royal Funeral Ceremony in Late Medieval England', *English Historical Review* 134 (2009), 257–82, at 271–5.

[163] ER, VII, 241, 243, 284, 286. Considering that the funeral expenses for Henry IV (d.1413) were around £333 (sterling), this would suggest a ceremony of some scale for Mary: Duffy, *Royal Tombs*, 200. In the 1460s there were approx. £2 to £3 Scots to £1 sterling, see the Note on Money, xviii.

[164] ER, VII, 422.

[165] Stevenson, 'Contesting Chivalry', 197–214.

in 1464 under the new guardianship of Bishop Kennedy.[166] As his father had been enthroned in the parliament of 1445, so too was the fourteen-year-old James III recorded as 'sitting on his royal throne' in the parliament of October 1466 at a critical juncture.[167] Robert, lord Boyd – whose faction seized power in July 1466 – used the words of the monarch in an accepted and recognised theatre of power to legitimise his actions: the young king declared from his throne that he bore Boyd no ill will 'authoritatively and in a clear voice' after receiving 'mature and well-considered advice'.[168] However, even at fourteen, Macdougall stresses that James was fast becoming a risk to the Boyd faction through his increased independent activities around the realm.[169] Between 1466 and 1469 this included travelling north to Inverness and Aberdeenshire, taking hunting trips to Perthshire and visiting Falkland to take part in justice ayres with his younger brother, Alexander, duke of Albany.[170] During 1465–66, as noted above, James ordered further heraldic decoration on his father's tomb: he added painted arms of the king and four smaller escutcheons, as well as candles and cloths of satin and buckram for the tomb.[171] The date and type of ceremony that occurred are unknown, but selecting the anniversary of James II's death or burial, or the Easter festival, would be logical suggestions. The timing of James III's direct interaction with his father's tomb monument, while another faction manhandled the young king into their grasp, indicate that he sought ritualised means to assert his own royal authority through making visible connections to his father and the succession.

Key to the continuation of the succession, and for James's independence, was securing a marriage and an heir. The parliament of January 1468 agreed to levy a tax of £3,000 from the three estates to send a high-powered embassy to Denmark to treat for a union, which was concluded later that year.[172]

---

[166] On Norham: Macdougall, *James III*, 53–4. On the Kennedy progresses: *RMS*, II, nos 796 (Dundee, 7 July), 797–9 (Aberdeen, 17 July), 800–5 (Inverness, 16–17 August), 806 (Elgin, 21 August), 807–10 (Dundee, 31 August–1 September), 811 (Edinburgh, first charter after trip dated 11 October). At Aberdeen, repairs were done '*ergo adventum regis*', and tables and chairs were repaired at the castle and *palacii* in Inverness, suggestive of the king entertaining guests: *ER*, VII, 304, 357–9. Further details are lacking without *Treasurer's Accounts* or burgh records from the mid-fifteenth century: the Aberdeen burgh accounts survive but offer little on this period of James III's reign. See also Macdougall, *James III*, 54, 59–60.

[167] *RPS*, A1466/2.

[168] Ibid. Robert, lord Boyd, was an Ayrshire lord of parliament who used the position of royal chamberlain held by his younger brother, Sir Alexander of Boyd of Drumcoll, to kidnap the king and overthrow the Kennedy government. For details of the rise and fall of the Boyds, see Macdougall, *James III*, 63, 68–83. James also affirmed Boyd's position as 'governor' in the same parliament: *RPS*, A1466/1.

[169] Macdougall, *James III*, 76.

[170] For examples, see *ER*, VII, 383, 488, 502, 512, 533, 555, 560, 569.

[171] Ibid., VII, 422.

[172] *APS*, II, 90; *RPS*, 1468/1/2–3; NRS, Treaty between Christian, King of Denmark, Sweden and Norway, and King James III, SP8/2 (badly damaged photograph only

The terms of this union were particularly important for the statements that James could make about his adult kingship: the union with Princess Margaret brought the potential to lay rightful and complete claim to the Danish-controlled islands of Orkney and Shetland.[173] Margaret arrived in Scotland with a large and splendid entourage in July 1469, she stayed at the royal lodgings at Holyrood Abbey and they were married in the abbey church. Details, however, are sparse and contradictory. Even the date of the union is uncertain, with various suggestions ranging between 10 and 20 July in the chronicle accounts.[174] If the marriage ceremony in 1469 included a ritual confirmation of the dower lands in the abbey church, as occurred in the marriage of James II and Mary of Guelders, the date on the formal diplomatic of 24 July 1469 may be closer to the actual date.[175]

While details of the specifics of 1469 are lacking, a surviving inventory list from 1488 offers insight into the materiality of the Scottish court during this period. For example, a section recording items in a chest belonging to Margaret identifies a 'surples of the rob royall'.[176] A surples or surplice is an item of clerical attire – a white cotton or linen garment worn over a cassock by a priest or monk with long sleeves, which can be associated with repentance or baptism – so could be linked to the act of anointing.[177] However, the word comes from the Latin *superpelliceo*, which means 'over skins or furs', so this could be indicative of an item made of fur worn over the royal robe.[178] The same inventory refers to a covering of purple cloth, embroidered with unicorn and thistle decorations, with a roof and pendicles (or valance) that indicates a canopy for either a throne or bed of state: either of these could have been central in the wedding celebrations, placing these Scottish heraldic devices at the core of proceedings, as was the case some thirty-five years later for the marriage of James IV and Margaret Tudor.[179] The use of the unicorn and thistle as heraldic symbols of Scottish royal power increased

---

available); Statens Archiver Copenhagen, Kongehuset Christian 1., Princesse Margarethe: Pergamentsbreve 1468–1469, a–1, 1468 9 8; b–1, 1468 7 28; b–3, 1469 7 24; *ER*, VIII, xl. Note: a–1 is a Danish copy of the final treaty with seals and lists the bishops of Glasgow and Orkney, earl of Arran [Boyd's son Thomas] and Lord Avandale, Martin Wan [the king's confessor or secretary], Gilbertus de Rerik, archdeacon of Glasgow, David Creichton of Cranstoun and John Schaw.

[173] Macdougall, *James III*, 79–80, 90–3.
[174] BL, A Short Prose Chronicle to 1482, appended to Andrew of Wyntoun, Original Chronicle of Scotland, in verse, with other tracts, Royal MS 17 D XX, fol. 307r (dates the wedding to 13 July, MS dated to late fifteenth century); Leslie, *Historie*, II, 89 (10 July); Pitscottie, *Historie*, I, 161 (20 July 1473?).
[175] Statens Archiver Copenhagen, b–3, 1469 7 24.
[176] NRS, Exchequer Records: Accounts of the Treasurer, June 1488 to July 1492, E21/2, fol. 3v; *TA*, I, 85.
[177] Harper, *Forms and Orders of Western Liturgy*, 316.
[178] 'Surples', 'Surplice' and 'Superpellice', *Dictionary of the Scots Language*, www.dsl.ac.uk. Date accessed: 22 January 2023.
[179] NRS, E21/2, fol. 3v; *TA*, I, 85. See Chapter 5 regarding use of bed of state in the wedding of James IV and Margaret Tudor, 1503, 194–5.

Plate 16 Coin (obverse), unicorn, from reign of James III (1484–1488 issue). The Hunterian, Lord Stewartby Collection, S/4779.

during the fifteenth century, with both introduced onto Scottish coinage during James III's reign (Plates 16 and 17).[180] The Danish envoy present at James's court at Yule in 1474 received a collar of gold thistles from the king: a gift in return for the Order of the Elephant jewel – the symbol of the chivalric order of the Danish king – given to James as part of the ceremonies marking his union with Margaret.[181] Gifts of heraldic badges and the use of livery were increasingly common and politically fuelled as the fifteenth century progressed.[182] For example, when the Lyon herald travelled to England as an ambassador to secure the betrothal contract between Margaret and James's first-born son, James (later James IV), and Cecilia, daughter of Edward IV, he was sent with a gown of cloth of gold, lined with satin, to offer as a gift to the English herald.[183] James appears to have understood and exploited symbolic emblems of royal power during his reign, so it seems plausible to suggest that the displays at his wedding similarly made use of them.

---

[180] The thistle appeared on coinage from c.1470, whereas the collared and chained unicorn was later in the reign, c.1484/5: Stewart, *Scottish Coinage*, 60–2, 141; McAndrew, *Scotland's Historical Heraldry*, 275.

[181] NRS, E21/1, fol. 49v; NRS, E21/2, fol. 1v; TA, I, liv–lv, 68, 81; *A Collection of Inventories and Other Records of the Royal Wardrobe and Jewelhouse; and of Artillery and Munitions in some of the Royal Castles MCCCCLXXXVIII–MDCVI*, ed. Thomas Thomson (Edinburgh, 1815), 6; Macdougall, *James III*, 82.

[182] Bryony Coombs, 'Material Diplomacy: A Continental Manuscript Produced for James III, Edinburgh University Library, MS 195', *SHR* 98 (2019), 183–213; Ailes, 'Heraldry in Medieval England', 85–104.

[183] *CDS*, IV, nos 1414, 1417–25; NRS, Indenture (26 Oct. 1474) and Obligation (26 Nov. 1474), SP6/23–4; *ER*, VIII, 287, 292, 294, 387; NRS, E21/1, fols 20v, 37r, 38r, 39r; *TA*, I, 27, 50, 52, 54. The Scottish ambassadors included Thomas Spens, bishop of Aberdeen, John Colquhon of Luss, the Chamberlain, James Shaw of Sauchie, and the Lyon herald. For more on James III's foreign policy, see Macdougall, *James III*, particularly 110–25.

Plate 17 Coin (obverse), groat, from reign of James III (c.1471–1483 issue). The Hunterian, Lord Stewartby Collection, S/2372.

Writing much later, in the sixteenth century, John Lesley recorded a curiosity in relation to Margaret's coronation when he states that she was crowned some four months after the marriage at a meeting of the parliament.[184] If this is correct, it would have marked a significant change from 1449, when Mary of Guelders's coronation was incorporated into the wedding. This meeting of the parliament took place in the tolbooth in Edinburgh in November.[185] The parliament records for 1469 do not confirm the presence of the queen in parliament, despite having a sederunt list, but they are not complete records and the queen may have just been in attendance for one day.[186] There was a pattern developing around ritual interactions between the consort and the political community across the fifteenth century: oaths were sworn by the estates to Joan Beaufort and Mary of Guelders undertook choreographed intercessory action within the parliament. In the wake of the minorities of the fifteenth century, facilitating such interactions via ritualised dialogue with the political community seems a logical step for securing a role for the queen consort should her husband predecease her. Yet, to take the coronation of the queen out of an ecclesiastical setting entirely does seem unusual. For the sixteenth-century consorts – Madeleine of France, Marie de Guise and Anne of Denmark – with whom Leslie would have been more familiar, there was more temporal and geographical space between royal marriages and consort coronations. However, this was due to the specific circumstances, such as marriages occurring abroad, and the coronations were still in church spaces. If there was a crowning or crown wearing in parliament, as Leslie's statement suggests, it was perhaps a subsequent swearing of oaths in parliament – akin to those sworn to Joan Beaufort – where Margaret wore a crown received in an earlier church-bound coronation.

[184] Leslie, *Historie*, II, 89.
[185] *RPS*, 1469/2.
[186] *RPS*, 1469/1–36, A1469/1–3.

Following the marriage and subsequent parliament, the royal couple went on a progress of the realm as far north as Inverness in 1470.[187] The dearth of direct evidence for this journey, indicating an apparent lack of official business, has led Macdougall to suggest that it was 'less elaborate' than that led by Kennedy in 1464.[188] Nonetheless, the progress of 1470 followed a statement made in parliament about the king having 'full jurisdiction and free empire within his realm' and accusations of degrading royal majesty were implicit in the forfeiture of the Boyds.[189] The rhetoric in both instances offers insight into James's kingship and the people who guided him. James was educated by proto-humanist scholars, such as Archibald Whitelaw, and the mid-fifteenth century witnessed a vastly increased size and reach of the royal demesne, leading to shifts in administrative practice that would only be fully incorporated by the reign of James IV.[190] With greater landed power came increased responsibility but also inflated attitudes about royal status, particularly when fanned by ideas of imperial majesty. It is no great leap of the imagination to suppose that these same attitudes and ideals were displayed during this post-wedding progress, especially when it heralded the emergence of an adult king, celebrated the promise of the union with Margaret and portrayed the reach of the Scottish crown into newly acquired territories secured through the marriage. Prior to their departure in June 1470, James granted Margaret lands for her lifetime that were specifically recorded in the charter as to provide for the maintenance of her robes of state and the ornaments of her head.[191] This indicates that Margaret's appearance as a visible symbol of royalty and promise for the dynastic succession was crucial. Moreover, evidence from the extant fragmentary *Treasurer's Accounts*, although not for this specific period of the reign, reveal evidence of a couple investing in a wealth of richly decorative clothing, accessories, riding gear and harnesses throughout their reigns.[192] Source survival for 1469–1470 hinders fuller conclusions about the progress, but it provided potential ceremonial opportunities for projections

---

[187] *ER*, VIII, 80–6, 131; Leslie, *Historie*, II, 89. See also Dean, 'Enter the Alien', 282–4.
[188] Macdougall, *James III*, 89.
[189] *RPS*, 1469/20; *RPS*, A1469/2; Macdougall, *James III*, 89.
[190] On cultural and ideological influences: Roger Mason, 'The Realm of Scotland is an Empire? Imperial Ideas and Iconography in Early Renaissance Scotland', in Crawford (ed.), *Church, Chronicle and Learning*, 73–91, at 76–7; Roger Mason, 'Laicisation and the Law: The Reception of Humanism in Early Renaissance Scotland', in Luuk A.J.R. Houwen, Alistair A. MacDonald and Sally Mapstone (eds), *A Palace in the Wild: Essays on Vernacular Culture and Humanism in Late-Medieval and Renaissance Scotland* (Leuven, 2000), 1–25, at 14–17; Macdougall, *James III*, 86; Coombs, 'Material Diplomacy', 184–97. On the royal demesne and changing structures: Hawes, 'Community and Public Authority', 108–21.
[191] *RMS*, II, no. 992.
[192] NRS, E21/1, fols 10v–54v; NRS, E21/2, fols 1r–4v; *TA*, I, 13–75, 79–87; *A Collection of Inventories*, 1–18. From the treasures, there is a wealth of objects but a stomok (ornamental chest covering) with a heart made of 'precious stanis and perle' and the collar of swans made of gold, diamonds, rubies and pearls particularly stand out: *TA*, I, 80, 85.

of royal authority and the promise of dynastic succession at a crucial point in James's reign that seem unlikely to have been overlooked.

The rituals of the fifteenth century illustrate that, while power theoretically and legally transferred to an heir at the death of the previous king, the importance of the rituals that cemented this transferal of power remained high on the agenda. This was just as much the case when the monarch was not old enough to organise these ceremonies himself. As in previous centuries, those invested in the power of the crown – including parliament, the three estates and widowed queens – recognised the value of ceremonial occasions that made palpable public statements. Thus, these individuals and groups helped to oversee further ritual development rather than stagnation. The deceased kings of the fifteenth century also contributed to rituals that occurred to commemorate them and – in choices they made in life – made marks on the ceremonies of power transfer. Despite unexpected early deaths, both James I and James II prepared for death through investment in burial monuments and each etched their own mark into the subsequent funeral ceremonies, with assistance from their respective wives and the consistency in royal office holders and day-to-day government officials at the initial transfer of power. These conclusions speak directly to Hawes's suggestions that the political community (from the king down) held shared aims and responsibilities for the 'common good' in the form of the maintenance and continuation of the dynasty.[193] Due to young ages at accession in the fifteenth century, however, the coronation became a stage in a longer ritual process of power transfer and distribution including other ritual moments, such as coming of age and marriage. The monarchs that emerged through this process were – for better or worse – increasingly assured of their own royal prerogative and displays of majesty grew in elaboration and embellishment. This could generate potential frictions in negotiations of authority and ritual displays could be harnessed by emerging kings to make overt statements about personal power, such as those made by James II during the rituals associated with his marriage in 1449.

The early and violent deaths of James I and James II did lead to some dramatic breaks with tradition, particularly with the rejection of Scone Abbey and the associated outdoor fealty ritual within the coronation, and introduced some apparent ceremonial one-offs, including a potential display of a royal body marked with wounds and a coronation beside a siege site. However, as Kilgallon argues of Graham's outburst in parliament in 1436, casting such episodes as one-offs is problematic: rhetoric and performance do not emerge from a vacuum but reflect the political milieu from which they

---

[193] Hawes, 'Community and Public Authority', *passim*, particularly 1–7, 17–46.

emerge.[194] Rituals similarly gain their cultural and social meaning through recognisable elements and their ability to mirror reality or model expectations or aspirations of a particular society. For example, while the monarchs of the early Stewart dynasty recognised value in the distinctive indoor and outdoor spaces utilised in the coronations of 1371, 1390 and 1424, the most potent need for the outdoor recognition of the first Stewart monarchs was one generated by Robert II's accession from the role of earl – an equal to his peers – to that of monarch. Even by 1390 there were new religious encroachments into this outdoor ritual and James I's reign was marked by a renewed vigour for invoking divine connections for the monarch through rituals, art and rhetoric. Consequently, moving the coronation into a wholly church-bound space may have been a future possibility that was merely accelerated through crisis.

The rejection of Scone for the coronation in 1437 was, ultimately, an action taken in response to the crisis of James I's murder. While crowning James II at Scone following the funeral of the king in Perth could have offered a powerful visible message about continuity, the situation in 1437 and the queen's desire to maintain control of her son, then resident in Edinburgh for protection, motivated a significant change. This arguably also set a precedent for location being less important than the audience and content of the coronation ritual, making the choice of Kelso in 1460 less unusual than it might have been otherwise. It is impossible to prove the extent to which Joan Beaufort and Mary of Guelders influenced the change of location in these cases, but it is notable that they occurred when foreign-born queens were central to the performance of power.

Together with the introduction of anointing from the previous century, relocating most of the rites that made up the Scottish coronation within a church had the potential to create a ritual dominated by ecclesiastics, especially with the removal of the earl of Fife as a prominent secular actor after 1425. However, this does not appear to have been the case as far as the evidence can demonstrate. In fact, the surviving orders of ceremony suggest that traditional secular elements – like the fealty ceremony, which emphasised the relationship between king and political community, and the recitation of the genealogy highlighting the longevity of the royal line – remained dominant in the written record of ritual into the seventeenth century. Moreover, the minorities of the fifteenth century meant that the secular space of parliament gained, or at least maintained, importance as the site of ritual negotiation between the king and the estates established throughout the fourteenth century. Indeed, increasingly, it became a space in which royal wives also undertook ritual actions designed to open a dialogue with the political community. Urban spaces – particularly the streets marking the route from Edinburgh Castle to Holyrood Abbey and out to Leith – and the communities that inhabited these also appeared to hold an increasingly important role in the

---

[194] Kilgallon, 'Communal Authority, Counsel and Resistance', 3.

dialogues generated by rituals of death and succession as the fifteenth century progressed. Despite changes in location and physical space, the emphasis on the permanence of dynasty and the manner that royal power was confirmed via the political community remained a constant. The maintenance and prominence of these ritual aspects offered examples of continuity and were modelled on the desires and expectations of the political elite.

5

The Pinnacle of Stewart Power? James IV and James V

The late fifteenth and sixteenth centuries witnessed European monarchs, such as Henry VIII, François I and Emperor Charles V, harnessing cultural patronage, ritual and spectacle in increasingly elaborate expressions of royal power.[1] Scotland was no different, and more recent historiography of this period – encompassing the reigns of James IV and James V – actively examines how these kings, and their kingdom, fit into this European renaissance mould.[2] These enquiries have been enhanced by explorations of material culture, such as Morvern French's research into Flemish material culture in Scotland, which illustrated James IV's keen ability to engage in modes of conspicuous consumption that spoke volumes on a wider European stage.[3] Extensive work around the recreation of James V's renaissance palace at Stirling Castle turned eyes afresh to the built fabric and material culture of the reign, while portraiture as a form of display in sixteenth-century Scotland has also received renewed attention.[4] Blessed with a relative abundance

---

[1] For example, see Glenn Richardson, *Renaissance Monarchy: The Reigns of Henry VIII, Francis I and Charles V* (London, 2002), 32–4, 145–92; Glenn Richardson, *Field of the Cloth of Gold* (New Haven, 2013); Sharpe, *Selling the Tudor Dynasty*, 79–185; Anglo, *Spectacles, Pageantry and Early Tudor Policy*, 124–237; Robert J. Knecht, *Renaissance Warrior and Patron: The Reign of Francis I* (Cambridge, 1994), 105–41, 425–77; Robert J. Knecht, *Francis I and Sixteenth-Century France* (Farnham, 2016), Chapters III, IV and XV; Giesey, *The Royal Funeral Ceremony in Renaissance France*, particularly 1–18; Peter Burke, 'Presenting and Representing Charles V', in Hugo Soly and Willem P. Blockmans (eds), *Charles V (1500–1558) and His Times* (Antwerp, 1999), 393–476; Bryant, *Ritual, Ceremony and the Changing Monarchy in France*, 155–86; Roy Strong, *Art and Power, Renaissance Festivals 1450–1650* (Woodbridge, 1982), *passim*.

[2] For example, see Macdougall, *James IV*, *passim*; Norman Macdougall, '"The geattest schip that ewer saillit in England or France": James IV's Great Michael', in Norman Macdougall (ed.), *Scotland and War AD 79–1918* (Edinburgh, 1991), 36–60; Alastair A. MacDonald, 'Princely Culture in Scotland Under James III and James IV', in Gosman, MacDonald and Vanderjagt (eds), *Princes and Princely Culture*, I, 147–72; Thomas, *Princelie Majestie*; Andrea Thomas, *Glory and Honour: The Renaissance in Scotland* (Edinburgh, 2013); Dunbar, *Scottish Royal Palaces*; Edington, *Court and Culture in Renaissance Scotland*; Janet Hadley Williams (ed.), *Stewart Style 1513–1542: Essays on the Court of James V* (East Linton, 1996), various essays; Roger Mason, 'The Realm of Scotland is an Empire?', 73–91; Roger Mason, 'Renaissance Monarchy? Stewart Kingship (1469–1542)', in Brown and Tanner, *Scottish Kingship 1306–1542*, 255–78.

[3] French, 'Magnificence and Materiality', particularly 90–134.

[4] Sally Rush, *Stirling Castle: The Stirling Heads Gallery*, Exhibition (2011–present); Sally

of sources, coupled with James IV's historical popularity and the diplomatic importance of his marriage to Margaret Tudor in 1503, the Stewart-Tudor wedding has a substantial historiography that explores various aspects of performance and display, while rituals also form part of a wider discussion of court culture in the reign of James V.[5] For the very good reason of providing a robust challenge to the lingering belief that Scotland was culturally backward, research into the cultural display, patronage and court ceremony during these reigns has largely focused on their successes.

Scholarship on the reigns of James IV and James V more broadly classically identified a stark contrast between the two kings in which James V was lambasted where his father was praised. This was particularly the case in terms of their characters and their relationships with magnates, leading Jenny Wormald to the conclusion that James V was the 'most unpleasant of all the Stewarts'.[6] However, more recent work by Jamie Cameron, Ken Emond, Andrea Thomas and Amy Blakeway has presented a far more nuanced pic-

---

Rush, 'French Fashions in Sixteenth-Century Scotland: The 1539 Inventory of James V's Wardrobe', *Furniture History* 42 (2007), 1–26; John Harrison, *Rebirth of a Palace: The Royal Court at Stirling Castle* (Edinburgh, 2011); Sally Rush, 'The Stirling Heads: An Essay in Nobility', in Birgitte Bøggild Johannsen and Koen A. Ottenhym (eds), *Beyond Scylla and Charybdis: European Courts and Court Residences outside Habsburg and Valois Territories, 1500–1700* (Odense, 2015), 225–36; Kate Anderson, 'Portraits of James V from Renaissance Prince to Ruling Monarch', conference paper, *The Presence of Majestie: James V and Sir David Lyndsay*, Heraldry Society Conference, Edinburgh, September 2015; Hannah Woodward-Reed, 'The Context and Material Techniques of Royal Portraiture Production within Jacobean Scotland: The Courts of James V and James VI' (PhD thesis, University of Glasgow, 2018).

[5] Two key source collections are fuller surviving *Treasurer's Accounts* and the detailed account of John Young, Somerset herald, who accompanied Margaret Tudor: NRS, Exchequer Records: Accounts of the Treasurer, September 1502–February 1504, E21/6; TA, II, 197–395: *Fyancells MS*, fols 75–115v; *Fyancells Coll.*, 258–300. On Stewart-Tudor marriage: Louise O. Fradenburg, *City, Marriage, Tournament: Arts of Rule in Later Medieval Scotland* (Madison, 1991), particularly 67–152; Louise O. Fradenburg, 'Sovereign Love: The Wedding of Margaret Tudor and James IV of Scotland', in Fradenburg (ed.), *Women and Sovereignty*, 78–97; Ian Campbell, 'James IV and Edinburgh's First Triumphal Arches', in Deborah Mays (ed.), *The Architecture of Scottish Cities, Essays in Honour of David Walker* (East Linton, 1997), 26–33; Gray, 'The Royal Entry', 16–22; Lorna G. Barrow, '"The Kynge sent to the Qwene, by a Gentylman, a grett tame Hart": Marriage, Gift Exchange and Politics: Margaret Tudor and James IV, 1502–13', *Parergon* 21 (2004), 65–84; Carpenter, 'Thexaltacyon of Noblesse', 104–20; Dean, 'Enter the Alien', 279–82; Michelle L. Beer, 'Translating a Queen: Material Culture and the Creation as Queen of Scots', *Medieval Clothing and Textiles* 10 (2014), 151–64. On ritual and court culture in reign of James V: Thomas, *Princelie Majestie*, 182–217; Thomas, 'Crown Imperial', 43–67; Edington, *Court and Culture in Renaissance Scotland*, 107–14; Perin Westerhof Nyman, 'Mourning Madeleine and Margaret: Dress and Meaning in the Memorials for Two Scottish Queens, 1537 and 1541', *SHR* 100 (2021), 359–77. In addition, the work of Giovanna Guidicini offers insights across royal entries in Scotland of the early modern period: *Triumphal Entries and Festivals*.

[6] Jenny Wormald, *Court, Kirk and Community: Scotland 1470–1625*, reprint (Edinburgh, 2007), 12.

ture of the reign of James V, his relationships with magnates and institutions, and his role in presiding over a glittering royal court.[7] This chapter seeks to further complicate the existing narrative around royal ceremony and display in the reigns of both kings. As adults, both kings mastered the use of ritual display as a means of dynastic and personal aggrandisement through their marriages, the births of their heirs and the burials of royal relatives and spouses. However, as Anglo picked holes in the thesis of a well-oiled 'Tudor propaganda machine' by questioning the long-term coherence of royal ceremonial schemes, this chapter will play devil's advocate in the manner it addresses ritual and commonly-held views of the later Stewarts' command of such forms of display by focusing on the chronological cycle of death and succession.[8] Ceremonies in this era – roughly 1488 to 1540 – were often as reactive and hard to prepare for as any other period. Both kings succeeded to the throne as minors – indeed, James V was the youngest heir considered in this study – and the situation at each accession was exacerbated by issues associated with their predecessor's deaths: the murder of James III by an army that used his son as a figurehead in 1488 and the loss of James IV's body (taken by the English as a trophy of war) after the battle of Flodden in 1513. The period also saw increasing challenges in securing the legitimate succession due to a string of infant deaths for both royal couples and the death of James V's first French bride, Madeleine of Valois, before she was even able to make her royal entry in Scotland. This chapter confronts how the complexities of the period affected the ability of the crown and those who were invested in its continued stability and success to use these ceremonies in challenging times. Consequently, it asks new questions of the stability projected through ritual statements during the adult reigns of these kings and of the use of the ceremonial tools by those acting on the minor monarch's behalf. In so doing, it provides a more comprehensive and nuanced understanding of how the Scottish crown both struggled and succeeded in projecting royal authority at crucial points in the cycle of death and succession.

Deposing the Father to Crown the Son

James III was the second Scottish king to be murdered in the fifteenth century, but the circumstances were quite different from that of James I in 1437. James III was killed at Sauchieburn on 11 June 1488 when the king and his supporters faced rebels using his eldest son and heir as the figurehead of their campaign. James IV's active involvement in this violent rebellion meant that

---

[7] Jamie Cameron, *James V: The Personal Rule, 1528–1542*, ed. Norman Macdougall (East Linton, 1998); Emond, William K., *The Minority of James V: Scotland in Europe, 1513–1528* (Edinburgh, 2019); Thomas, *Princelie Majestie*; Amy Blakeway, *Parliament and Convention in the Personal Rule of James V of Scotland, 1528–1542* (Cham, 2022).
[8] Anglo, *Images of Tudor Kingship, passim* (argument outlined at 3–4).

clear-cut retribution and revenge for the murder of the king, as meted out following the murder of James I in 1437 and incorporated into the rituals of death and succession, was not an option.[9] The challenges of representing royal authority in such situations had arisen elsewhere. While most of the kings deposed in fourteenth- and fifteenth-century England were removed by competing dynasties – such as Richard II, Henry VI and Richard III – the deposition of Edward II in 1327 offers a comparison where the king was removed in favour of his son. Edward II's son, Edward III, was crowned before Edward II was even dead let alone buried. Joel Burden argues that these abnormal circumstances led to some innovations in the delayed funeral for Edward II, but the unusual events also required that the ceremony retained recognisable elements to retrospectively present 'the normal passage of royal succession' and bolster wavering royal authority.[10] James III was dead before James IV's coronation, so this progression was more straightforward than Burden's case study. Nonetheless, James IV's involvement in the deposition and regicide of his father had the same potential to undermine the new king's authority. The incoming government had to restore confidence, so ceremonial displays around death and succession in 1488 should have been paramount in legitimising the incoming government. Macdougall identified that significant effort was put into the hastily organised coronation of James IV to provide this highly sought-after legitimacy.[11] However, as explored throughout this study, the transferral of power did not occur at a single point but was tied into a cycle of rituals that followed the death of the king. Consequently, the burial of James III appears conspicuous in its absence from existing discussions.

In 1488 the coronation of fifteen-year-old James IV returned to Scone after a sixty-four-year break with tradition. As Queen Margaret had predeceased James III, there was no widowed queen involved in orchestrating the events so this was a choice dictated by the Scottish nobles who had rebelled against James III, and likely spoke to concerns about legitimising the transfer of power in a period of divided loyalties. Relocation to Scone may also have witnessed the return of other traditional elements, such as performing the religious ceremony in the church and the secular enthronement and offering of fealty outside. There is no evidence for this, however, and the nature of the surviving sources means that what occurred at Scone in 1488 is largely lost. The date of the coronation – 24 June – was both the feast day of St John the Baptist and the anniversary of Robert I's victory at Bannockburn.[12] The

---

[9] Leslie J. Macfarlane, *William Elphinstone and the Kingdom of Scotland, 1431–1514: The Struggle for Order* (Aberdeen, 1985), 403–5; Macdougall, *James IV*, 49.
[10] Burden, 'Re-writing a Rite of Passage', 26–9.
[11] Macdougall, *James IV*, 53–4.
[12] Adam Abell notes that the king was crowned on St John the Baptist day (24 June): NLS, The Roit or Qhuiell of Tyme, MS 1746, fol. 111r; Stephanie M. Thorson, 'Adam Abell's *The Roit and Qhueill of Tyme*: An Edition' (PhD thesis, University of St Andrews, 1998), 224.

young king appears to have observed and possibly celebrated St Fillan's (or Fáelán's) feast day (20 June) as the surviving *Treasurer's Accounts* included a payment for a man bearing 'Sanct Fyllanis bell, at the kingis commande'.[13] The relic and saint were significant to the Perthshire area and had been revered by Robert I, who revived interest in the ninth-century saint following his escape from Perthshire in 1306.[14] Other Brucian items were found in James III's treasure, including a shirt and the Bruce maces, and the relics of saints and kings could have been employed to connect the young king to a glorious chivalric past.[15] While connections to Robert I potentially carried a degree of tragic irony, as James III is thought to have carried Robert's sword into the battle in which he died, casting back to former and more glorious occasions at Bannockburn offered opportunities to whitewash the immediate past.[16] Ultimately, due to the nature of available sources, all such suggestions must remain speculation.

The records do indicate that processional entrances were a prominent feature in these early ceremonies. Prior to arriving at Scone, the royal party returned to Edinburgh and purchases of clothing for the king 'sen the tyme of his entra' around 15 June suggest that the young king may have made a royal entry to the burgh.[17] Velvet to cover the saddles and harnesses was provided for three horses for the king 'aganis the Coronatioune' and eight finely attired henchmen were purchased black velvet gowns and satin doublets to accompany the king.[18] The additional horses were perhaps decked out for the king's two brothers, as appears to have been the case in the first parliament of October 1488 when clothing for all the king's siblings was purchased for the event.[19] The processional element of the October parliament is further evidenced in the silver, gold and azure coats of arms made for heralds and pursuivants, as well as in velvet coverings provided for the king's horse ahead of the continuation of parliament in January 1489.[20] The first official record of a 'riding of parliament' – the public procession to open meetings of the estates – occurred in 1578, when an act was passed to penalise members of the estates for not taking part in the procession, but the very existence of this

---

[13] *TA*, I, 88, 164; Macdougall, *James IV*, 51.
[14] Dickson (ed.), 'Preface', in *TA*, I, lxxii–lxxiv. On Fillan, see Simon Taylor, 'The Cult of St Fillan in Scotland', in Thomas R. Liszka and Lorna E.M. Walker (eds), *The North Sea World in the Middle Ages: Studies in the Cultural History of North-Western Europe* (Dublin, 2001), 175–209, particularly 181–90.
[15] *ER*, X, 82; NRS, E21/2, fol. 2v; *TA*, I, 83; *A Collection of Inventories*, 8.
[16] Macdougall, *James IV*, 51; ibid., *James III*, 346.
[17] *TA*, I, 139–40. Extant Edinburgh burgh records are patchy for the 1480s with nothing surviving for June 1488: *Extracts Edinburgh*, 54–6. On reasons to return to Edinburgh, see Macdougall, *James IV*, 50.
[18] *TA*, I, 147, 164.
[19] James, duke of Ross, received two fine gowns, John, earl of Mar, received a velvet coat and gown, and Lady Margaret received a gown and kirtill ahead of the parliament; additionally, John also received a coat and gown in June: *TA*, I, 140, 152, 159, 162.
[20] Ibid., 147, 163.

act indicates that this ritual had much earlier origins.[21] The preparations occurring in 1488 and 1489 indicate that, at the very least, there was a processional arrival for the king and his entourage to these parliament events. Parading the royal siblings in public spaces demonstrated the vitality of the dynasty and the stability of the succession, despite the king's young age and corresponding lack of a wife or children of his own.

The king was conspicuously recorded in full regalia at the parliament of October 1488 in the tolbooth in Edinburgh.[22] A private act passed on 14 October, regarding the forfeiture of lands and privileges of John Ramsay, late lord Bothwell, and their re-granting to Patrick Hepburn, lord Hailes, records that the king was 'enthroned on his seat of justice or royal throne, bearing the crown of the realm and the sceptre in his hand [...]'.[23] This parliament had a notably higher level of attendance than the coronation – which, with only two bishops and two earls present, had poorer attendance than the much criticised inauguration of Robert I – so the parliament would have been the first occasion that many had seen the king in majesty (see Appendix II, Robert I and James IV). Thus, despite attempts to project legitimacy by holding the coronation at Scone, the performance in June 1488 potentially had limited impact. In this light, Pitscottie's suggestion that the estates were called together to 'sie the king crownit' in Edinburgh at the parliament is less outlandish than it might initially appear.[24] While not arguing for a second coronation, the high attendance, and need for a public acclamation by a full complement of the three estates with the king present in full majesty, hints at a potential reciprocal offering of oaths similar to that of 1445 occurring in October 1488. The extant parliamentary records for 1488 hold no record of oaths exchanged, but interest in them at this juncture is evidenced in a copy of the *Regiam Maiestatem* compiled by James Monynet, including a copy of the 1445 oaths (those of king and estates), dated to c.1488.[25] While there was no record of a knighting ceremony at the coronation of James IV, the parliament in October also incorporated the bestowal of new titles as the king belted Patrick Hepburn as the earl of Bothwell. Hepburn was touched by the sword of the king 'as is customary' in a display of royal power usually connected with the coronation.[26] The ceremonial in and around the parliament that confirmed and rewarded the Hepburns demonstrated a growing confidence in the incoming regime by October 1488 that was not present at the coronation in June.

This parliament also 'ascertained the truth of the king's death', however vaguely and unsatisfactorily.[27] Consequently, it offered a prime opportunity

---

[21] Mann, 'The Scottish Parliaments: The Role of Ritual and Procession', 140–4.
[22] Location of parliament at tolbooth: *RPS*, 1488/10/7. On parliament of 1488, see Macdougall, *James IV*, 58–60.
[23] *RPS*, 1488/10/29.
[24] Pitscottie, *Historie*, I, 216–17.
[25] NLS, Adv. MS. 25.5.6.
[26] *RPS*, 1488/10/36.
[27] *RPS*, A1488/10/1.

to hold an elaborate funeral or memorial for James III to provide the retrospective normality of the progression of the succession sought in the funerary arrangements of Edward II in 1327.[28] Yet, the *Treasurer's Accounts* for this month do not record any evidence of this. Nineteenth-century excavations of tombs at Cambuskenneth – where James III and Margaret of Denmark were buried – confirmed that a double or triple tomb with a bluish marble top slab and monumental brasses was that of the royal couple.[29] As Margaret died two years previously, in 1486, and James III sought her canonisation to 'enhance his own position' through association, this tomb may well have been near completion in 1488.[30] Despite this, records are confusingly silent on the manner, or even date, of James's burial. The only chronicle or history to comment on James III's funeral was George Buchanan, writing in the late sixteenth century, who stated:

> The council then breaking up, proceeded to Edinburgh, where, having ascertained the truth of the king's death, they caused a magnificent funeral to be given to him, at the abbey of Cambuskenneth, in the vicinity of Stirling, on the 25th June [1488].[31]

As the formal declaration regarding the death of James III was not produced until the parliament in October 1488, Buchanan's retrospective ordering and dating of events is problematic.[32] Moreover, royal grants were made at Perth on 26 June and it was not until 28 June that James IV returned to Stirling, which was the nearest royal residence to Cambuskenneth Abbey.[33]

Although Buchanan's dating appears questionable, it is quite possible that – as with his father before him – James IV was crowned before the burial of his father, especially as he remained at Stirling for nearly a month after the coronation. A solitary payment of £100 to the abbot of Cambuskenneth was made in mid-August, but the reason for the payment was not stated.[34] This was a substantial fee, and was similar to one of £92 made to the dean and canons at St Andrews after the death of James IV's brother in 1504, although this was one amongst a number of payments so this fee alone was hardly extravagant.[35] The extant expenses for Mary of Guelders' funeral ceremony,

---

[28] Burden, 'Re-writing a Rite of Passage', 13–29.
[29] James E. Alexander, 'An Account of the Excavations of Cambuskenneth Abbey in May 1864', *PSAS* 6 (1864–66), 14–25, at 20–1. See also David Laing, 'Notes Relating to the Interment of King James III of Scotland and of His Queen, Margaret of Denmark, in the Abbey Church of Cambuskenneth', *PSAS* 6 (1864–66), 26–33.
[30] Macdougall explores efforts of James III to canonise his wife, including raising a papal commission, following her death in the turmoil of the years before his own death: *James III*, 305–7; *James IV*, 39–41.
[31] Buchanan, *History*, II, 223.
[32] *RPS*, A1488/10/1.
[33] Macdougall, *James IV*, 52, see also fn. 13; *RMS*, II, nos 1740–43, 1746.
[34] *TA*, I, 93.
[35] Ibid., II, 418.

for example, were over £212 excluding any costs for a tomb.[36] The book of hours created for Margaret Tudor as a wedding gift from James IV includes an image that has been posited as a representation of James III's funeral (Plate 18).[37] The scene is set in a church decorated with Scottish heraldic flags and escutcheons, featuring a wooden hearse or *chapelle ardente* covered by black cloth and candles, and surrounded by nine mourners clad in black, as well as canons in the stalls of the choir. While the Flemish piece indicates familiarity with Scottish heraldic designs, it is also similar to other contemporary illustrations of this type indicative of a standardised image that was suitably adorned with relevant heraldry.[38] The image provides potential evidence of a heraldic funeral, but there are no references to dule wear, funeral furniture, heraldry or other material evidence to support this kind of display in the *Treasurer's Accounts*, even though these remain extant from mid-June 1488.[39]

The depiction in the book of hours and Buchanan's retrospective claim of a magnificent funeral on or after 25 June lack substantive evidence. This is compounded by the fact that the first known payment to priests to sing for the late king's soul does not appear until January 1489, and it was not until 1491 that the anniversary of the king's death witnessed more elaborate memorial dirges, with candles and heraldry, in his memory.[40] Notably, it was in February 1492 that James IV offered a further reward for information on the murder of his father, and the dirges and masses continue with some regularity in surviving records after this point, which suggests James IV's own increasing role in the manner his father was memorialised.[41] This, combined with the lack of evidence of the material objects needed for a funeral, raises questions about the level of memorialisation for the late king in 1488. Unlike 1437 and 1460, there was no widowed queen to push forward with any pre-arranged funeral proceedings and a split existed within the political elite following the rebellion.[42] It had become common that the previous king should be buried before the coronation, particularly in France where pre-coronation rituals around displaying the body provided symbolic continuity between the passing of one king and the succession of the next.[43] Nonetheless, the haste and apparent lack of ceremony in 1488 appears indicative of a quick and panicked burial caused by the manner of the king's death rather than a careful ritual response.

---

[36] ER, VII, 241, 243, 284, 286.
[37] ON, 'Dirge of the King of Scots', in Das Gebetbuch Jakobs IV. von Schottland (Book of Hours of James IV of Scotland), Cod.1897, fol. 141v.
[38] Leslie J. Macfarlane, 'The Book of Hours of James IV and Margaret Tudor', IR 9 (1960), 3–20, at 8, 12, 21; French, 'Magnificence and Materiality', 33–6, 91–100.
[39] Expenses for sixteenth-century funerals arrangements appear across household books and the *Treasurer's Accounts*; while the absence of a household book for 1488 may obscure some details, references should also appear in the *Treasurer's Accounts*.
[40] TA, I, 102, 178.
[41] Ibid., 92, 200, 229; II, 73, 252; III, 60, 75, 290; IV, 42, 188.
[42] Macdougall, *James IV*, 49–79.
[43] Giesey, *The Royal Funeral Ceremony*, 41–9.

Plate 18   'Dirge of the King of Scots' from Das Gebetbuch Jakobs IV. von Schottland (Book of Hours of James IV of Scotland). Österreichische Nationalbibliothek, Cod.1897, fol. 141v.

There were ceremonial statements made in 1488 to legitimise the new king, such as the return to Scone augmented by processional entries and the enthroned king in parliament. Yet, some of the crucial cyclical elements of the rituals of death and succession appear to have been lost, or largely understated, during the initial months following James III's death. That the active memorialisation of James III only appeared as James IV matured and took personal control of such displays suggests that, unlike previous moments when power was transferred in the fifteenth century, the minority leaders in 1488 did not appreciate the crucial role a funeral could play in legitimising the succession in times of crisis.

The Thistle and the Rose: A Long-Awaited Union?

By 1503, when James IV married Margaret Tudor, and even more so in 1507, when the couple celebrated the birth of their first son, any lack of confidence apparent in the earlier reign appeared to have been fully compensated for by an energetic and proactive adult king. There is no doubt that James mastered and exploited the full arsenal of modes of display, and there is an increasingly wide range of scholarship addressing this.[44] Stevenson has emphasised, for example, that James used chivalric symbols and performance in promoting Scottish designs on British sovereignty in competition with Henry VII, particularly in the celebrations of 1507.[45] Yet, here and elsewhere, there is a tendency to analyse these ceremonies as a coherent and confident programme of ritual posturing and royal performance; this needs problematising.

Something not addressed, for example, is the fact that in 1502 the *Treasurer's Accounts* record the first work done on the tomb of James IV at Cambuskenneth: the digging of the *lair* for his *sepultur*.[46] In February, March and May 1503 payments were made to David Pret [Pratt], the *payntour*, for costs of making the *sepultur* itself.[47] The tomb's creation in parallel with the negotiations and preparations for James's marriage, agreed in the Treaty of Perpetual Peace of 1502, offer a poignant reminder of the fragility of hereditary succession. As previous chapters have illustrated, death was never far away from the minds of medieval rulers even when young: indeed, tombs were often in preparation, or even complete, at the death of kings across Europe. At thirty years old in 1503, James IV was a man in his prime according to near-contemporary literature, such as the *Ratis Raving*, but his energetic warlike grandfather had died before he had reached this age and James's father had been murdered at thirty-six.[48] Moreover, both his pre-

---

[44] See 185 n.5.
[45] Stevenson, 'Chivalry, British Sovereignty and Dynastic Politics', 601–18.
[46] TA, II, 140, 150, 153–4, 351.
[47] Ibid., 289, 360, 390.
[48] *Ratis Raving*, 59, 63, particularly at lines 1150–8, 1336–43.

decessors had married relatively young and sired three legitimate male heirs by the time they were thirty. James's relations with at least three mistresses during the 1490s and early 1500s provide adequate evidence of the king's ability to produce an heir, but this meant little if they could not be promoted in the official dynastic succession.[49] James's predecessors also married wives of a similar age whereas his bride was a thirteen-year-old princess, which could cause further delay to the succession as Margaret was considered too young to consummate the marriage.[50] Margaret was also English, witnessing a return of the revamped unpopular policy of James III. As such, while James IV's marriage did not mark the end of his minority, the importance of the union and the surrounding ceremonies in 1503 was no less than in 1449 or 1469. The situation in 1503 demanded ritual statements promoting dynastic security and the continuation of the cycle of succession to mask a whole host of anxieties, including underscoring the strength of the Stewarts in the face of rising Tudor power in England. The Stewart dynasty had reigned for one hundred and thirty years. In comparison, it was less than twenty years since Henry VII had seized power on the battlefield and the English king lost his eldest son and heir in 1502, which Stevenson argues gave James the upper hand in their relations.[51] However, Henry still had surviving legitimate children. James's insecurities, on the other hand, quietly but physically manifested themselves in the marble *sepultur* being built at Cambuskenneth.

To say that James IV took every opportunity to mask any dynastic anxiety with the effort and expense that he threw into the wedding ceremonial would be an understatement. Macdougall stated that James had the 'one-off expense of a lavish wedding' costing him £6,125, 4s. 6d., but this significantly underestimated James's financial input.[52] These costs in the *Exchequer Rolls* were for provisions – such as food, wine, candles, spices, coals and charcoal – only. The current running total, which underestimates rather than overestimates due to issues with extracting information specifically for the wedding, stands at £18,677, 6s. 8d. (see Appendix III).[53] This was over half of the dowry of £35,000 agreed in the marriage treaty.[54] The

---

[49] The three mistresses were Marion Boyd, Margaret Drummond and Janet Kennedy; the last had her own section in the *Treasurer's Accounts* of 1502–1504 totalling over £788: TA, II, 294–8. For brief information on mistresses: Macdougall, *James IV*, 98–9, 113–14, 162–3, 180, 197, 286.
[50] Hayes, 'Late Medieval Scottish Queens', 117–22.
[51] Stevenson, 'Chivalry, British Sovereignty and Dynastic Politics', 604–6.
[52] Macdougall, *James IV*, 155. The figure appears to be based on information in the *Exchequer Rolls* only: NRS, Exchequer Records: Exchequer Rolls, Comptroller's Account [Sept 1503], E38/326; *ER*, XII, liv, 181–2.
[53] This calculation includes a wide range of material goods and provisions, but it does not include building work at Holyrood or all service charges, carriage costs, wages and fees as these are difficult to extract from general expenditure. The *Treasurer's Accounts* edition is an abridgement, so the original manuscript has been consulted for this section and the appendix. The manuscript has a digital surrogate at the NRS (Virtual Volume) that is now produced, but the folio numbers are those from the original manuscript.
[54] NRS, Indenture on treaty of perpetual peace (24 January 1501–02), SP6/29; NRS,

queen's chambers were lavishly decorated with a cloth of state that matched one made for the king, a state bed largely made of cloth of gold, a large number of cushions and carpets, hangings of velvet and Arras tapestries.[55] In addition to Arras tapestries, as French has discussed, James sought other goods through his Burgundian factors including an extensive range of silver plate to exhibit in an open cupboard.[56] The king's own lavish clothing – so attentively commented upon by John Young that it is possible to extract the components of the outfits from the *Treasurer's Accounts* – was one of the largest costs across the whole event.[57]

Sartorial display was not only a concern for the king personally. As Young states on the day of the wedding 'every Man apoynted hymselfe rychly, for the Honor of the noble Maryage' and the same went for the women, particularly those Scottish noblewomen who accompanied the queen.[58] The burgh records from Aberdeen identify that only 'the best and worthiest of the town ordered to attend the marriage of his majesty'.[59] This implies that only those who could afford to dress were invited to attend, thus suggesting a degree of audience management. The financial records reveal that the king also spent large sums on rich fabrics – silks, velvets, cloth of gold – for clothing attending nobles, courtiers, household officials and servants, including musicians, henchmen and heralds. The latter received red taffeta and gold coats of arms for the ceremonies further amplifying the symbols and colours of royal authority that permeated the wedding celebrations.[60] These demonstrations of 'noblesse' were necessary to honour the bride, the king and the visitors, and it was paramount to James's own demonstrations of princely control.[61] Moreover, James' investment in clothing for his court and household speaks directly to Hepburn's suggestion that the Scottish court could be likened to 'immersive theatre' in which member of the household were not just functioning behind the scenes but were important participants in the performance.[62]

Ratification by Henry VII of indenture of treaty of Perpetual Peace (31 October 1502), SP6/31; TNA, Treaty of perpetual peace (24 January 1502), E39/92/12; TNA, Treaty of marriage between the King of Scots and the Princess Margaret. (24 January 1501–02), E39/92/18; TNA, Confirmation by James, King of Scots, of the dowry of Queen Margaret (6 June 1503), E39/79; CDS, IV, nos 1690–7.

[55] E21/6, fols 22r–4r; TA, II, 213–17. For more on the Flemish tapestries, see French, 'Magnificence and Materiality', 70–9 (on Arras tapestries generally), 115–18 (on 1503 tapestries).

[56] E21/6, fol. 37r; TA, II, 241. For exploration of the use of plate, see French, 'Magnificence and Materiality', 110–14.

[57] E21/6, fols 18v–22r; TA, II, 206–13; *Fyancells MS*, fols 95r–115v; *Fyancells Coll.*, 283–300. See Carpenter on the manner that Young's details can be identified in the *Treasurer's Accounts*: 'To Thexactacyon of Nobless', 108–9.

[58] *Fyancells MS*, fol. 104v; *Fyancells Coll.*, 291.

[59] ACA, Council, Baillie and Guild Court Book, VIII, CA/1/1/8, fol. 239.

[60] E21/6, fols 78r–83r, 132v; TA, II, 306–13, 395.

[61] For more on the use of textiles in the wedding: Dean, 'richesse in fassone and in fairenesse', 378–96.

[62] Hepburn, *The Household and Court of James IV*, 102–7.

Plate 19   'King James IV at Prayer' from Das Gebetbuch Jakobs IV. von Schottland (Book of Hours of James IV of Scotland). Österreichische Nationalbibliothek, Cod.1897, fol. 24v.

The marriage and coronation of the consort, which took place on 8 August, began with the king in a separate chamber seated under a great cloth of state with his brother, archbishop of St Andrews, on his right-hand side and the earl of Surrey on the left, while they heard an opening oration with members of the three estates.[63] Following this the king received 'reverence' from the three estates, before he offered the same in return.[64] This ceremonial offering of reverence echoes an exchange of reciprocal oaths in a way not observed previously in the context of marriage. Though subtle and overlooked in other studies, this opening display offered an opportunity for the king to restate his position in the realm via the fealty owed to him, but also emphasised the reciprocal promises made by him to the political community. Unlike other examples of enthroned Scottish kings accepting oaths or presiding over parliament, it seems unlikely that James was wearing a crown during this ritual. Young comments that the king greeted the lords on entering the hall holding his 'bonnet' in this hand and 'maid Reverence to every man' before sitting in the throne.[65] Moreover, Young's frequent references to the king's 'barre head' throughout the processions and rituals imply that, like James II in 1449, the king was rather conspicuously not wearing his crown at various points during the proceedings.[66] While there are many examples of James IV demonstrating his superior majesty during the events of 1503, subtle examples of humble reverence by the king to others are notable in the English herald's account, suggesting this was of interest to the author. This offers an important insight into the way that James used symbolic gestures to balance extravagant shows of majesty with the 'first among equals' qualities of kingship expected from the native political community.

The sword of honour was prominent in descriptions of events. It was paraded before the king on numerous occasions in a purple velvet scabbard decorated with pearls arranged to read 'God my defende', the mending of which is recorded in the *Treasurer's Accounts*.[67] It is not as clear whether the crown and sceptre were similarly displayed, but an ounce and half of additional gold was added to the crown and the sceptre was re-gilded at this time.[68] Extant images of James IV's regalia leave some uncertainty about the crown's design. Despite the introduction of the closed imperial crown on the coinage of James III in the 1480s, his son's coinage returned to the use of an open circlet and his seal continued with an almost identical design to the three previous kings, which depicted the same open style. However, in the book of hours commissioned

---

[63] The opening oration is called a 'preposition' by Young.
[64] *Fyancells* MS, fols 205r–6r; *Fyancells Coll.*, 292.
[65] Ibid.; *Fyancells* MS, fols 205r–v.
[66] Ibid., fols 97v, 101v–2r, 107r; *Fyancells Coll.*, 285, 289, 293.
[67] Ibid., 287, 293; *Fyancells* MS, fols, 100v, 107r; E21/6, fols 18v–19v; *TA*, II, 206–7.
[68] E21/6, fols 19v, 22v, 127v; *TA*, II, 207, 385. An ounce and a half was a small amount of gold, but the total weight of gold used for the queen's crown was only eleven and half ounces. Brooks has noted that even in the remodelled crown (which survives to the present day) the arches are of a significantly lighter and daintier design than the rest of the crown: Brooks, 'Technical Description of the Regalia of Scotland', 83–5.

for Margaret Tudor on her marriage to James (c.1502x1503), the king was illustrated wearing a closed crown (see Plate 19).[69] Thomas has stated that either one or both of these conflicting images must be inaccurate.[70] However, in 1504 ahead of the first parliament after the wedding, the bonnet of the crown received decorative embellishments – or 'powderings' – and a bordering of ermine.[71] That there was a bonnet indicates that, by this point at least, the crown was enclosed with imperial arches as a bonnet was rarely found on a simple circlet.[72] Consequently, it could be that the various images of James's crown are correct but reflect different periods of the reign, and the respective levels of confidence found therein.

The fact that regalia items and royal robes underwent repair prior to the parliament in March 1504 suggests that this occasion was also used to demonstrate and renegotiate royal power. This parliament saw the production of charters and other documents regarding the fulfilment of Margaret Tudor's marriage dower and confirmation of her morning gift.[73] Parliamentary records do not confirm Margaret's attendance explicitly, but she was made a 'gret goun' of white and gold damask at this time.[74] As with Margaret of Denmark, John Leslie records that Margaret Tudor was crowned in this first parliament.[75] The consort's presence in parliament wearing a crown early in her reign appears as a recurring theme for the fifteenth-century queens consort. The frequency of parliaments notably declined in James's adult reign from 1496.[76] However, this ritual use of parliament following the royal wedding, in conjunction with the reverent exchange of oaths in the chamber before the marriage, implies a recognition of the continuing role of the three estates in the ratification of royal power. The exchange of a material object during the joint wedding and coronation ceremony in Holyrood in 1503, however, sent a different message. After the consort's anointing, Young observes that the king, rather than a prelate, invested the queen with her sceptre.[77] This was

---

[69] 'King James IV at Prayer' from ON, Cod.1897, fol. 24v; Macfarlane, 'The Book of Hours of James IV and Margaret Tudor', 4–5.

[70] Thomas, 'Crown Imperial', 59–61.

[71] E21/6, fol. 27v; TA, II, 225.

[72] A bonnet was only usually found on an arched crown, supporting Brook's thesis of a slowly developing crown with arches added and remodelled at various points, rather than Thomas's conclusion that arches were only added in 1532: Brooks, 'Technical Description of the Regalia of Scotland', 83–5; Thomas, 'Crown Imperial', 59–60.

[73] RPS, 1504/3/7, A1504/3/147–8.

[74] E21/6, fol. 27v; TA, II, 224–5.

[75] Leslie, *History*, II, 73. This statement only appears in the one-volume edition of Leslie, based on the earliest known manuscripts of Leslie's *History*. It is not found in the 1888 two-volume edition, nor in the Latin version *De Origine Moribus, et Rebus Gestis Scotorum Libri Decem* (Rome, 1578) from which it was translated. See E.G. Cody's introduction to Leslie, *Historie*, I, xviii–xxii. This has been taken as fact in some cases: Everett Green, *Lives of the Princesses*, IV, 19; Barrow, 'the Kynge sent to the Qwene', 72, fn. 25.

[76] On the demise of parliament, see Macdougall, *James IV*, 170–95.

[77] *Fyancells MS*, fol. 108r; *Fyancells Coll.*, 294. English queens received a sceptre from the ecclesiastic celebrant from at least the fourteenth century: Carmi Parsons, 'Ritual

symbolic confirmation of her role in assisting the king in matters of justice and ruling the realm, while also clearly emphasising her powers were gifted by the king. This was potentially loaded with meaning about James's divine right as God's anointed who was able to pass aspects of royal power to his partner, but it could also be analysed as the secularising of an object usually invested by a cleric so its meaning in this sense is a little opaque. The actions and objects utilised and exchanged within the marriage, consort coronation and the subsequent parliament reveal the delicate balance in the negotiation of power undertaken at this juncture.

James did not solely orchestrate the events of 1503, which occurred in four distinct parts. First, Henry VII arranged Margaret's journey northward to Scotland. This walking statement of Tudor authority wound its way through the English countryside, in particular the northern areas where the Tudor king had faced rebellions earlier in his rule.[78] Second, the unusually drawn out – in a Scottish context at least – period of ritualised courtship between James and Margaret included interactions of Scottish and English design.[79] Third, the burgh of Edinburgh took the lead role in organising the royal entry. Even though James chose to accompany Margaret, whereas previous and later queens made this entry alone, this was an opportunity for the town and people to welcome the queen rather than a strictly royal display.[80] Lastly, came the wedding and coronation followed by days of entertainments directly orchestrated and funded by the king and his advisors. This range of phases with their different organisers had the potential to produce rather mixed messages. Douglas Gray concludes that the burgh created a coherent blend of 'celebration, welcome and advice' through a royal entry designed to promote harmony and unity, but the use of Tudor and Stewart iconography in the border regions to promote the dynastic glory of the rival monarchs sits rather uncomfortably alongside this.[81] The king's appropriation of British or English icons, as discussed by Stevenson, also challenges this idea of peace and harmony. Although Stevenson's argument centres more on the baptism of 1507, she comments on the use of a brooch of St George and the dragon,

---

and Symbol in the English Medieval Queenship', 64–5; Joanna L. Laynesmith, *The Last Medieval Queens: English Queenship 1445–1503* (Oxford, 2004), 104–7.

[78] The entourage entered all the following towns between Richmond and Berwick: Colleweston [sic], Grantham, Newark, Sirowsby [sic], Doncaster, Pontefract, Tadcaster, York, Newbrough, Allerton [Northallerton?], Hexham, Darnton, Durham, Newcastle, Morpeth and Alnwick. See *Fyancells MS*, fols 76v–91r; *Fyancells Coll.*, 266–78; TNA, King's Remembrancer: Wardrobe and Household: Documents subsidiary to accounts of the great wardrobe (22 August 1501–21 August 1503), E101/415/7, fols 91–2, 95–9, 104–5, 107–22, 138, 141; *CDS*, IV, nos 1715–7, 1720–7; Carpenter, 'Thexaltacyon of Noblesse', 107–8; Dean, 'Keeping Your Friends Close', 49–51; Beer, 'Translating a Queen', 151–64.

[79] *Fyancells MS*, fols 93v–101v; *Fyancells Coll.*, 281–9. A number of scholars discuss this, including:: Barrow, '"the Kynge sent to the Qwene, by a Gentylman, a grett tame Hart", 74–6; Guidicini, *Triumphal Entries and Festivals*, 64–7.

[80] Dean, 'Enter the Alien', 269–95; Gray, 'The Royal Entry', 10–31.

[81] Ibid., 16–22, quote at 22; *Fyancells MS*, fols 92r–5v; *Fyancells Coll.*, 281–3.

worn by the king to Mass on the day after the wedding, and suggests that Young records the jewelled brooch because 'it was so striking'.[82] Yet, the herald's observations of clothing, jewels and human decorations are consistently detailed:

> ...a riche Robbe of Cloth of Gold fourred of fyne blak Bougye, his Doublett of cramfyn Satyn, blak Hofys couved abouff, of Cloth of Gold, a blak Bonnet, a Saunt George of Gold, apon the Dragon a Ruby, a crafyn Hat, a Payre of gold Beads haungyng to his Gyrdle, to the Nombre of xiij more or leffe, and a Dagar beforre hym.[83]

This brooch is described amidst a full list of the king's outfit and is given no special attention. Moreover, St George was not an exclusively English saint and had a presence in Scotland.[84] James's understanding of ritual and display supports Stevenson's argument that such small gestures were potentially significant and calculatingly provocative, but caution should be taken in making too much of this as it could be that James adopted the symbol to emphasise the union.

Subtle provocation there may have been in 1503, but the entry, wedding and subsequent festivities were typically reflective of peace and friendship. In the church ceremony, and at other times, Young observes how English and Scottish ladies walked in groups of four, made up of two women from each realm, and comments that James demanded equal numbers of the royal couple's coats of arms to be displayed.[85] Demonstrations of the harmonious union also extended to the decorations of food, the last course of which – according to the *London Chronicle* – included jellies with the arms of the respective countries both separately and combined.[86] English and Scottish minstrels and trumpeters provided the music for subsequent dancing, demonstrating an aural manifestation of unity.[87] Such ideals were also evident in

---

[82] Stevenson, 'Chivalry, British Sovereignty and Dynastic Politics', 615–16.
[83] *Fyancells MS*, fols 110v–11r; *Fyancells Coll.*, 297.
[84] The Trinity Altar depicts James IV's mother, Margaret of Denmark, alongside a saint identified as St George, which could be connected to Margaret's Danish heritage or due to the altarpiece being destined for the Trinity College, which was dedicated to St George: Colin Thompson and Lorne Campbell, *Hugo Van der Goes and the Trinity Altar Panels in Edinburgh* (Edinburgh, 1974), 11–13. On popular devotion to St George in Scotland, see Steve Boardman, 'The Cult of St George in Scotland', in Steve Boardman, John R. Davies and Eila Williamson (eds), *Saints' Cults in the Celtic World* (Woodbridge, 2009), 146–59.
[85] *Fyancells MS*, fol. 106v, fol. 109r; *Fyancells Coll.*, 293, 295.
[86] *Great Chronicle of London*, ed. Arthur H. Thomas and Isobel D. Thornley (London and Aylesbury, 1938), 323–5.
[87] *Treasurer's Accounts* indicates payments to Scottish and English minstrels and musicians, while Aberdeen burgh minutes recorded payments for local minstrels to travel 'to the fest of our soverane lords marriage, at commaunde of his hienes and to the plesour of his maieste': E21/6, fols 127v–8v; *TA*, II, 386–7; ACA, CA/1/1/8, fol. 241. Italian minstrels were also present at the court c.1502–c. 48: Helena M. Shire, 'Music for the "Goddis Glore and the Kingis"', in Hadley Williams (ed.), *Stewart Style*, 119–21.

the king's overt reverence towards his young queen throughout the extended celebrations. For example, when offered relics to kiss by the mendicant friars of Edinburgh, members of the College of St Giles and the Archbishop of St Andrews during the entry, 'he wold not before the Quene; and he had hys Hed barre during the ceremonies'.[88] Young's comments on the king's reverential behaviour may have been innocent observation, but the frequent and pointed comments suggest that it was unusually conspicuous. The same could be said of the time that James spent with the queen leading up to her coronation; this included accompanying her in the entry, which Mary of Guelders had certainly made alone in 1449 as others would after her.[89] The king's efforts in welcoming his royal bride were perhaps a simple reflection of hopes pinned on their marriage and the offspring it promised. Yet, the exaggeration of reverential behaviour could also have been to divert attention from James's choice to move his mistress, Janet Kennedy, and the children he had borne by her, to Stirling Castle during August of 1503 from their usual home at Darnaway Castle near Forres.[90] The motivations behind this are not immediately clear but, considering the young age of his bride, it raises questions about James's conviction in the union as a cure for his anxieties about producing a legitimate heir.

Underlying unease about death and the royal succession in 1503 may have factored into the king's choice to observe rather than participate in the jousting and martial entertainments held before the royal palace at Holyrood.[91] The birth of James and Margaret's first son and heir, James, in February 1507 saw such anxieties alleviated, and the king actively participated in the elaborate tournament that occurred in the summer of that year.[92] This event took James's earlier displays of martial prowess through standard tournament activities – such as jousting held in January 1496 for the wedding of Perkin Warbeck, pretender to the English throne, and Lady Catherine Gordon – and transformed them into a truly Renaissance allegorical performance centred on the Wild Knight and the Black Lady.[93] The intended audience

---

[88] *Fyancells MS*, fols 96v, 101v–3v; *Fyancells Coll.*, 284, 289–90. See also Carpenter, 'To Thexaltacyon of Noblesse', 110.
[89] Dean, 'Enter the Alien', 269–95.
[90] James visited Janet on route to St Duthac's, Tain, in October 1503. However, there were expenses accrued by 'the lady at Darnaway' and her children while at Stirling paid on 24 August to cover the previous twenty-two days: *TA*, II, xxxvi–xxxvii, 294–8 (at 297), 401–3.
[91] *Fyancells MS*, fols 112v–14v; *Fyancells Coll.*, 298–9. See also Dunbar, *Scottish Royal Palaces*, 59; Dean, 'Making the Best of What They Had', 110–14.
[92] For James's role in the tournament, see Leslie, *Historie*, II, 128; Stevenson, *Chivalry and Knighthood*, 94–7; Frandenburg, *City, Marriage, Tournament*, 231–4. The birth and baptism took place in February 1507, the latter on 23 February, see NRS, E21/8, fols 31r–3r, 89v–90v; *TA*, III, 272–7, 369–71; Dean, 'Raising Royal Scottish Babes'.
[93] The Wild Knight and Black Lady tournament was orchestrated twice by James IV, once in 1507 and again in 1508 for Bernard Stewart, lord of Aubigny, and his accompanying French envoy. On the 1496 marriage tournament: *TA*, I, 257, 261–4; Macdougall, *James IV*, 122–3; Stevenson, *Chivalry and Knighthood*, 84; Stevenson, 'Chivalry, British

for this event included continental observers, as evidenced by the articles illuminated with gold leaf sent to France advertising the tournament.[94] The *Treasurer's Accounts* record the scale and design of the tournament with details of winged beasts, apparel for knights and wild men, and the clothing and triumphal chair of the Black Lady.[95] The ceremony's sophistication has been much discussed, and even Anglo admits – if a little reluctantly – that James IV's spectacle to celebrate his first born had a marked influence on Henry VIII's subsequent tournament for the birth of his short-lived son in 1511.[96] This elaborate display also saw James appropriate the typically British (English) visual symbol of King Arthur's round table.[97] Here, there was no subtle use of a jewel of St George and the dragon as found at the wedding, but a far more public declaration of James's right to claim British sovereignty through the person of his son. James was not the first Scottish king to claim Arthur and the round table for Scotland, but he was the first to be able to use it to declare realistic designs on the English throne, through the young child that the great tournament celebrated.[98] Where the wedding celebrations may have masked genuine ongoing apprehensions, the 1507 ceremonial celebration of the royal heir – arguably the pinnacle of display in the reign of James IV – was one of confidence in the promise of the succession.

Tragedy of Flodden Field: How to Bury a King Without His Body

Such confidence was short lived. The *Treasurer's Accounts* record the tragedy of the young prince's death in February 1508 merely by ceasing to record purchases for him.[99] There are no obvious costs for a funeral for the infant in surviving records, although this was perhaps not unusual for infant deaths in this era.[100]

Sovereignty and Dynastic Politics', 603–4. For more on Perkin Warbeck in Scotland, see David Dunlop, 'The "Masked Comedian": Perkin Warbeck's Adventures in Scotland and England from 1495 to 1497', *SHR* 70 (1991), 97–128; Macdougall, *James IV*, 117–45.

[94] NRS, E21/8, fols 88r, 91r; *TA*, III, 365, 372. For the content of these articles, see M. de Wulson [Vulson], Sieur de la Colombière, *Le vray theatre d'honneur et de chevalerie ou le miroir héroïque de la noblesse* (Paris, 1648), 271–2.

[95] *TA*, III, xlv–lii, 255–61, 393–8.

[96] Fradenburg, *City, Marriage, Tournament*, 172–264; Stevenson, *Chivalry and Knighthood*, 94–7; Sydney Anglo, 'Introductory Text', in *The Great Tournament Roll of Westminster: A Collotype Reproduction of the Manuscript*, ed. Sydney Anglo (Oxford, 1968), 9–15.

[97] Leslie, *Historie*, II, 128.

[98] Stevenson, 'Chivalry, British Sovereignty and Dynastic Politics', 605–14.

[99] Final purchases for Prince James included a scarlet cloth for a 'litill cote' and cloth and ribbons for a 'hurle-stule' (child's chair on wheels) rather than medical supplies, suggesting his death was sudden: *TA*, IV, 33. An infant's skeleton found in James III and Margaret's tomb has been posited as that of one of James IV's children: Alexander, 'An Account of the Excavations of Cambuskenneth', 20–1.

[100] English examples show that Edward IV's two-year old son, Prince George, received a familial funeral with dule attire purchased for thirty people, but the record of this only survives in Great Wardrobe accounts (which rarely survive for Scotland) and there is little evidence for any funerary arrangements for Henry VIII's two-month-old son: Anne

A priest at Stirling, where the infant and queen were resident, was paid a one-off fee on 22 February of £3, 10s. and cloth for a black gown was purchased for Margaret on 23 February, but neither was explicitly linked to the prince's death.[101] By 1510 James and Margaret had lost two more infants. Wider public concern about the Stewart succession may have been made visible when Margaret made a royal entry to Aberdeen in 1511. According to Dunbar's poetic record of the event, which was orchestrated by the burgh, there was a *tableau vivant* featuring a family tree 'with branches new and greine'.[102] Margaret was only twenty-one and imagery focused on productivity of dynastic marital unions was not uncommon in entries of young queens but, following a string of infant deaths, such a display was potentially tinged with criticism or concern about the future of the succession. By 1512 an additional dark cloud hung over Scotland; war with England was becoming increasingly likely.[103] The birth of a third son, also named James, on 11 April 1512 must have been a glimmer of light, particularly as the prince's birth fell at the heart of the Easter festival.

Easter had a close affinity with baptism. In earlier centuries, before the move toward infant baptisms held close to birth, baptisms of Christians occurred annually at Easter to directly link the liturgy and ritual of baptism with the resurrection of Christ, which was representative of rebirth and the washing away of sins.[104] Reassociating an infant baptism with the liturgical richness of Easter offered the royal couple opportunities to make conspicuous connections between the royal heir and Christ's sacrifice by inserting baptismal liturgy and ritual – such as the placing of a candle 'in the Princis hand at the Font' – into the Holy Day's Mass undertaken at St Michael's in Linlithgow.[105] Moreover, this significant feasting period celebrating the end of fasting during lent was one for which the court at Linlithgow would have naturally swelled in size as visiting courtiers and even foreign guests arrived for feasting, rejoicing and annual gift giving.[106] The first surviving *Libri Emptorum* (household accounts) attests to a sizeable increase in food stuffs purchased, and the *Treasurer's Accounts* contain fees for performers, mending of Arras cloths – hangings and possibly tapestries – and transporting the 'king's cupboard' used for the dis-

---

F. Sutton and Livia Visser-Fuchs, with Ralph A. Griffiths, *The Royal Funerals of the House of York at Windsor* (London, 2005), 47–57; Anglo, 'The Tournaments of King Henry VIII', in *The Great Tournament Roll of Westminster*, 58.
[101] *TA*, IV, 30, 101.
[102] William Dunbar, '*To Aberdeen: Be Blyth and blissfull, burgh of Aberdeen*', in *William Dunbar: The Complete Works*, ed. John Conlee (Kalamazoo, 2004), 81–3, at line 38. Stevenson suggests that this was a statement by the king, but the town would have been the main orchestrators of this event: 'Chivalry, British Sovereignty and Dynastic Politics', 605–6; Gray, 'The Royal Entry', 22–3.
[103] Macdougall, *James IV*, 248–64.
[104] Bryan D. Spinks, *Early and Medieval Rituals and Theologies of Baptism: From the New Testament to the Council of Trent* (Farnham, 2006), 64–6, 109–33.
[105] *TA*, IV, 185–6; E21/10, f. 22r–v; Monti, *A Sense of the Sacred*, 104–25, particularly at 122.
[106] Payment made to an Italian man in Scotland on behalf of the pope in April: *TA*, IV, 340.

play of gold and silver plate.[107] As Hepburn explores in his analysis of courtly dancing, gambling and gift giving in the court of James IV, performances such as these – designed for 'internal courtly audiences' – were ones in which important opportunities arose to confirm and create relationships within the household and court.[108] With the arrival of a new heir, this was a critical moment for bonds with the new arrival to be created and for members of the court to situate or advance themselves. James V's baptism was then far more lavish and poignant than previously assumed: a fitting celebration to welcome a new heir to the throne and establish a network to support him.

The death of James IV at Flodden on 9 September the following year, however, left the youngest heir to the Scottish throne yet witnessed. James V was seventeen months old. The removal of James IV's body from the battlefield as an English trophy of war also left the Scots with no king to bury.[109] Expenses for James's tomb at Cambuskenneth Abbey indicate that work had been ongoing on a marble construction for over ten years with the king actively engaged with overseeing the work; for example, in 1511 he visited and rewarded workmen with drink silver.[110] While any mourning for James and Margaret's infant children seems to have been muted, the accounts allude to James's adherence to contemporary ideals of public mourning for others and funerary rituals formed part of a wider symbolic dialogue with foreign powers.[111] Payments for dirge Masses were made for his own parents and Margaret's parents, Henry VII and Elizabeth of York, dule attire worth over £66 was purchased for the king and others at the time of the death of his uncle, the king of Denmark, and an embroidered velvet cloth decorated with the royal arms in gold, red and yellow silks and taffeta, costing over £40, was provided for his grandfather's tomb at Holyrood in November 1511.[112] The funeral of his younger brother and heir apparent, James Stewart, duke of Ross and archbishop-designate of St Andrews, who died in Edinburgh in January 1504, incurred significant expense despite the young duke purchas-

---

[107] The daily expenditure increases from £5, 1s. 1d. when the king and queen arrived on the day of the *Cena Domini* was £10, 12s. 2d. but rose to £102, 8s. 6d. for Easter: E32/1, fols 100v–3v; *TA*, IV, 339–40. See also Dean, 'Raising Royal Scottish Babes'; Everett-Green, *Lives of the Princesses of England*, IV, 148 (her figures cannot be located in the extant rolls).

[108] Hepburn, *The Household and Court of James IV*, 108–20.

[109] Polydore Vergil records that Henry VIII sought to have James's excommunication lifted to bury him with royal honour, but there is no evidence to suggest this occurred and it has been argued that James IV's body rotted away at Sheen: *The Anglica Historia of Polydore Vergil, A.D. 1485–1537*, ed. and trans. D. Hay (London, 1950), 221; Macdougall, *James IV*, 300; Tony Pollard, 'The Sad Tale of James IV's Body', *BBC News Scotland* (9 Sept 2013), http://www.bbc.co.uk/news/uk-scotland-23993363. Date accessed: 1 March 2021.

[110] *TA*, II, 130, 140, 150, 289–90, 360; IV, 132, 269, 311–12, 315. Missing years of financial records between 1508 and 1511 mean that the full amount spent on the tomb is unknown.

[111] See discussions published recently by Westerhof Nyman, 'Mourning Madeleine and Margaret', 361–2.

[112] *TA*, II, 249; III, 56, 287; IV, 38, 187, 195, 422. See also, soul Mass paid for Bernard Stewart, lord of Aubigny, *TA*, IV, 42.

ing his own tomb of Tournai limestone prior to his death.[113] Letters were sent out instructing attendance at the archbishop's 'tyrment', the grey friars and priests of St Andrews received over £90 for preparations for the funeral, near £70 was spent on torches and candles and a further £28, 2s. on 303 'dosane armes' (3,636 arms).[114] This was the highest number of arms prepared for a Scottish royal funeral located across the four centuries covered here and likely included royal, ducal and archbishop-designate heraldic designs, plus those of other religious houses of which he was commendator, including Holyrood, Dunfermline and Arbroath, and secular lordships, such as Brechin.[115] Such a display provided a visual demonstration of power by James IV at a time when the stability of the succession was weakened with the loss of a valuable heir for this childless king.

James IV's responses to the deaths of others and the building of his own marble tomb in the dynastic burial site adopted by his mother and father offer indications about the scale of the funeral he may have desired, but no instructions have survived and the *Treasurer's Accounts* from summer 1513 to 1515 are no longer extant. The fragmentary *Exchequer Rolls* record that the queen 'at her time of bereavement and widowhood' set up a fee to sustain the collegiate church of Restalrig to ensure the chaplains offered prayers for the souls of both James IV and his father.[116] Beyond this, the records are silent. No chronicles or histories comment on ceremonies performed to honour the dead king. Numerous funerals previously discussed prove that a lack of descriptive records does not mean nothing happened, but there is little evidence to indicate what occurred to mark James IV's death or how this was linked to the succession of his infant son. The provision of an effigy around which to focus prayers, or perhaps even to bury, could have been used to provide an embodiment of the perpetuation of the body politic or 'royal dignity' to be passed from father to son, as seen elsewhere, despite the forcible removal of the body natural by the enemy.[117] Powerful as this would have been, the lack of evidence means it is impossible to know whether such

---

[113] TA, II, 257, 415–17. The tomb was imported from Bruges c.1498, when he was only twenty-two years old, and the slab (3.175m × 2.32m) was cut to hold a monumental brass that could be one of the largest in Europe from this era: Trevor Chalmers, 'James Stewart, duke of Ross (1476–1504), archbishop-designate of St Andrews', *ODNB* (September 2012), https://doi.org/10.1093/ref:odnb/26477. Date accessed: 1 March 2021; Richard Oram, 'Bishops' Tombs in Medieval Scotland', in Penman (ed.), *Monuments and Monumentality*, 171–98, at 183. It is notable that the death of his other brother, John earl of Mar, occurred in April 1503, but little attention was lavished on him with only one soul Mass occurred and some debts settled: TA, II, 249, 365, 367, 408; III, 174.

[114] TA, II, 257, 416–17; for the arms specifically: NRS, E21/6, fol. 285.

[115] Chalmers, 'James Stewart, duke of Ross (1476–1504)'.

[116] ER, XIV, 76. These payments continue through to 1528–29 with some variation on size of payment: XIV, 219, 286, 354, 464; XV, 92–3, 196, 286, 379, 459, 532. Payments were made later in James V's reign for perpetual prayers for James IV at Orkney and Brechin: XVII, 84, 203, 354, 428.

[117] Giesey, *Royal Funeral Ceremony*, *passim*; Kantorowicz, *The King's Two Bodies*, particularly 383–437.

a ceremony was organised for James IV *in absentia* or whether the shock of loss prevented the minority regime's ability to make such a cogent statement.

One tangible link between death and succession may potentially have been found in the music of the coronation Mass, which occurred on 21 September 1513. Robert Carver's *Dum sacrum mysterium* Mass, although originally conceived in 1506, was re-dated in the manuscript *Choirbook* to 1513. D. James Ross posits it was revived to welcome James IV's glorious return from battle with 'an ocean of sound … a sumptuous representation of his monarch's dream of Christendom triumphant and at peace'.[118] With the outcome of Flodden being the accession of a new heir, rather than the triumphant homecoming of the king, this was rather problematic. Nonetheless, if rehearsals of the piece were underway for James IV's return from battle, it meant that 'the most impressive work in the whole *Carver Choirbook*' was ready and waiting for the coronation despite the rapidity of its organisation.[119] James V's coronation has earned the title of 'mourning coronation' due to the high numbers of casualties at Flodden, but the use of a Mass revived to celebrate James IV's designs of victory and peace potentially offered aural promise for the future in complicated times.[120]

Beyond this insight into the choral performance of Carver's Mass, many of the finer details of James V's coronation in 1513 are lost in the same evidentiary black hole as any memorial or funeral for James IV.[121] In the surviving evidence, however, there was one notable change in location; the chapel royal within Stirling Castle hosted the coronation. While three different coronation sites had been used during the fifteenth century, the space was always an abbey church and public processions were used to replace potential restrictions of access through the loss of the outdoor ceremonial space at Scone.[122] Stirling Castle was an architectural jewel in the Scottish crown on which James IV lavished attention, including building a new Great Hall and completing the chapel royal, which received papal approval as a collegiate church in 1501.[123] The castle was increasingly a royal favourite as both a nursery and household for the heir, particularly following the establishment of a separate household there for Margaret of Denmark and her sons.[124] Yet, the chapel at Stirling was small in comparison to an abbey and positioned within a closed royal – highly fortified – space that limited access to the ritual

---

[118] D. James Ross, *Musick Fyne: Robert Carver and the Art of Music in Sixteenth-Century Scotland* (Edinburgh, 1993), 30–3; *Robert Carver: O Bone Jesu; Missa Dum Sacrum Mysterium; Magnificat,* The Sixteen Harry Christophers, Coro (2007) [CD].
[119] Ross, *Musick Fyne,* xxiii–xxiv, 29–33.
[120] Kinloch, 'Scottish Coronations, AD 574–1651', Part II, 52; Thomas, 'Crown Imperial', 43; Emond, 'The Minority of King James V, 1513–1528', 1–36, 633–6 (Appendix A).
[121] Andrea Thomas utilises Jerome Lindsey's *Forme* from the seventeenth century to undertake a speculative reconstruction of the ceremony, but there are issues with this as noted on 8–10, 155: 'Crown Imperial', 49–55.
[122] See Chapter 4.
[123] Dunbar, *Scottish Royal Palaces,* 40–8; Thomas, 'Crown Imperial', 49–51.
[124] Hayes, 'Late Medieval Scottish Queens', 144–6, 176–9.

more than any previous site. The limited surviving records omit reference to a public procession, but the castle was situated in close proximity to the former king's desired burial place at the new Stewart mausoleum at Cambuskenneth Abbey, with the abbey tower visible from the large oriel windows of the Great Hall.[125] The easy distance between the two meant that a requiem Mass at Cambuskenneth could have been followed by a processional entry to Stirling prior to the coronation, but this is speculation based on basic logistical possibilities only. Despite the physical and spatial connection, the retreat into a closed royal space – potentially without a procession to and from a coronation church and no immediate parliament – had the potential to undermine the central facet of public acclamation that was so crucial in previous ceremonies of accession.

One thing the records confirm is that haste was paramount in orchestrating the coronation of James V.[126] The council that met on 19 September 1513 was neither a parliament nor a general council, similar to the non-parliamentary pre-coronation gatherings of 1460 and 1488 in the wake of previous tragedies.[127] Surviving records indicate that the council's main purpose was to install a daily council and arrange the coronation, which occurred two days later on Wednesday 21 September, as it 'pleis the quenis grace' and the lords.[128] This was less than two weeks after the death of James IV but it was hardly unusual in comparison to 1460 or 1488, where gaps between death and coronation were between about a week and two weeks. A fundamental difference in 1513 was the age of the king: James III had been nine and James IV had been fifteen, but James V was under two years old. The nine-month-old Henry VI, who succeeded the thrones of both England and France in 1422, offers a comparable example but Henry VI's coronations, respectively held in 1428 (London) and 1431 (Paris), were postponed until he could both walk and talk.[129] In fourteenth-century Scotland the same considerations may have factored into the postponing of David II's coronation from 1329 until 1331, when David was seven rather than five, but a potential pre-coronation crowning occurred for David during his father's lifetime.[130] The immediacy of James V's coronation, despite the incapacity of an infant to undertake the rituals required, suggests that – for the esteemed members of this council and the queen, at least – the coronation and what it bestowed, particularly in times of crisis, were still essential to legitimise the transferral of royal power in Scotland.

---

[125] Investment in the castle suggest the development of a royal showpiece around Stirling, thus explaining the siting of a new mausoleum at Cambuskenneth: Dunbar, *Scottish Royal Palaces*, 40–9; Harrison, *Rebirth of a Palace*, 15. Thanks to Katherine Buchanan for inspiring me to look out of windows to find that perfect view.
[126] Emond, *The Minority of James V*, 8–9.
[127] See Chapter 4, 170–1, 187–9.
[128] ADCP, 1.
[129] Lewis, *Kingship and Masculinity*, 144.
[130] See Chapter 2, 92–3, 95–7.

Lists of attendees at both the council in September 1513 and the first general council in November offer some indication of potential participation in the ceremony.[131] There were thirty-three members of the September council, including seven bishops, nine earls and various key officials from the previous reign, and the numbers rose to around fifty in the November meeting (see Appendix II, 'James V'). Even if the coronation was only witnessed by the members of the September council, there were numerous coronations with poorer attendance including that of James's father at Scone in 1488. However, representation from across the three estates was potentially limited, as the September council had no burgh representatives and only a small number of barons and lairds. Combined with a possible absence of public processions and outdoor enthronement, this speaks to a far more select audience witnessing the coronation even if the numbers of leading nobles and clerics were relatively robust. The roles for individuals within the coronation are even less clear. Blakeway suggests Margaret Tudor may have taken the oath on behalf of James V.[132] Sixteenth-century histories all confirm that Margaret was made governor and *tutrix* to the king, as long as she did not remarry, and the council records indicate that the organisation of the coronation involved her, but her role beyond this is obscure.[133] Thomas's speculative reconstruction of the coronation – using Jerome Lindsay's seventeenth-century order of ceremony as a starting point – includes hereditary household officers, like the Marischal and Constable.[134] However, neither William Keith, second earl Marischal, nor William Hay, fifth earl of Errol, attended the September council meeting, so they may not have been present two days later to carry out the roles assigned to them in Lindsay's order of ceremony (see Appendix II, 'James V'). The scant information about the attendees, and more particularly the roles that they undertook, means that only the role of James Beaton, archbishop of Glasgow, as officiant – in absence of an archbishop of St Andrews – can be comfortably confirmed, and he may not have acted in this role alone.

The heir apparent, John Stewart, duke of Albany, was inaugurated as regent and governor in the parliament following his celebrated arrival in 1515.[135] Had he been in Scotland in 1513, he would likely have played a sig-

---

[131] ADCP, 1; RPS, A1513/1.

[132] Blakeway, *Regency in Sixteenth-Century Scotland*, 61. For more on Margaret and her claim to the regency, see ibid., 24–30.

[133] Buchanan names her 'regent' but others use governor: *History*, II, 262–3; Pitscottie, I, 279; *Diurnal of Occurrents*, 4; Leslie, *Historie*, II, 148; ADCP, 1.

[134] Thomas, 'Crown Imperial', 49–55.

[135] John Stewart was the son of Alexander Stewart, duke of Albany and forfeited brother of James III, who was raised in France: Blakeway, *Regency in Sixteenth-Century Scotland*, *passim*, particularly 25–30; Bryony Coombs, 'John Stuart, Duke of Albany and his contribution to military science in Scotland and Italy, 1514–36', *PSAS*, 148 (2019), 231–66. For his arrival, processions and expenses, see *Diurnal of Occurrents*, 5; TA, V, 13–14, 16. There is no evidence of the infant king's involvement in the ceremonies as he was still in Margaret's care, and she reportedly dropped the portcullis of [Edinburgh] castle when

nificant role in the coronation itself. The records of the lords of the council identify that in 1515:

> [...] the lordis forsaid being thar with ripelie avisit thinkis expedient that my said lord governour weir ane mantill of ane duk, the crounale of ane duke, the sceptour in signe of regiment and governyng the realme, and the suerd in signe of justice within the samin.[136]

Blakeway emphasises that the inauguration of the duke as regent was significantly removed from the coronation of the monarch, taking place in a secular space and with no ecclesiastical involvement.[137] Nonetheless, the description of this ritual – with Albany 'wearing' the sceptre and the sword of honour – marks a departure from previous minorities with the suggestion that he was to carry the royal dignity attached to these objects until the king was of age.[138] These instructions in 1515 imply a quasi-royal role for Albany not found since the early Stewarts, when the seal of Robert Stewart, duke of Albany and governor from 1402 to 1420, depicted him enthroned with the sword and ducal coronet during the physical absence of James I.[139] There is evidence of Albany using progresses around the realm with the four-year-old James V to bolster his authority in 1516 and 1517, and the rush to crown and anoint the young king indicate an immediate transferral of the royal dignity was important.[140] Yet, the incapacity of James's tiny 'body natural' to carry the full weight of this royal dignity saw it more markedly and visually lodged with someone else, who also had a claim to the succession, once they were available in the realm to do so.

To Have Loved and Lost and Loved Again? The Marriages of James V

The youth of James V at his accession meant an inevitably long period without an adult monarch. The ritual investment of Albany as temporary holder of the royal dignity alleviated some challenges, but his tenure did not last the duration of the minority. From 1524 to 1527, between the ages of twelve and fifteen, James V was declared to be ruling Scotland in his own name at least three times by different individuals vying for power during his minority, who

---

representatives arrived to collect her children: *LPHVIII*, 'Letter from Dacre, English ambassador, to London', II, part i, no. 779.
[136] *ADCP*, 50; Emond, *The Minority of James V*, 40.
[137] Blakeway, *Regency in Sixteenth-Century Scotland*, 30–1, 55–9.
[138] The regalia was carried in the ridings of parliament and other processions, but it was not usually worn by others: Mann, 'The Scottish Parliaments: The Role of Ritual and Procession', 140–4.
[139] Birch, *Scottish Seals*, I, 58–9. See Chapter 3, 136.
[140] *ER*, XIV, 144; Blakeway, *Regency in Sixteenth-Century Scotland*, 176 (Table 9), 258 (Appendix 4).

then ceremonially paraded him before his people and parliament.[141] As seen in the previous century, particularly with James II, this created a young king determined to make active statements about his own personal authority from the moment that he took power into his own hands, aged sixteen, in 1528. A wedding did not mark the end of his minority – as was the case for James II and James III – but, unlike James IV, there was no shortage of potential brides for James V, and he married long before his thirtieth birthday. Due to the vagaries of European politics, eight different realms offered seventeen different brides in the two decades after James's accession.[142] The wedding of James to Madeleine of France in Paris on 1 January 1537 was thus a ritual climax to ceremonial statements centred on the king's coming of age and increasing adult authority at home while these negotiations for a bride had been undertaken.[143]

In travelling to France for his wedding, James V was the first Scottish king to venture outside his realm, for purposes other than war or involuntary detention, since the fourteenth century when David II made pilgrimage journeys to England.[144] A desire to influence the choice of bride may have been a motivating factor for James's journey: the first French bride he was promised was Marie de Bourbon, daughter of the duke of Vendôme, rather than the daughter of the king of France, but on 31 December he made a royal entry to Paris as the future son-in-law of the king of France, François I.[145] It may also have been deemed necessary to underscore James V's dedication to a foreign match after he actively pursued efforts to marry one of his mistresses, Margaret Erskine, in the previous year.[146] Jamie Cameron has also argued that

---

[141] *RPS*, 1524/8/2; *RPS*, 1525/2/9; *RPS*, 1525/2/16; *RPS*, 1525/2/11; *RPS*, 1526/6/5; ADCP, 1 August 1524, 204–5; *Diurnal of Occurrents*, 9; *Extracts Edinburgh*, I, 219; Leslie, *Historie*, II, 202; Emond, *The Minority of James V*, 189–90, 235–6.

[142] Cameron, *James V*, 60–1, 132–3 (list of all proposed matches, 153, fn. 15). See also NRS, Caprington MS, Royal Letter Book, 1524/5–1548/9, GD149/264; NRS, Tyningham MS, Royal Letter Book, 1529–1627, GD249/2/2/1; Edmond Bapst, *Les Mariages de Jacques V* (Paris, 1889), 7–281; *The Letters of James V*, ed. Robert K. Hannay and Denys Hay (Edinburgh, 1954), *passim*; Thomas, *Princelie Majestie*, 183–4.

[143] On earlier ceremonies and James's coming of age: Lucinda H.S. Dean, 'Reaching the "Estate of Manhood": A Case Study of James V of Scotland', seminar paper, *Centre for Gender History Seminar Series*, University of Glasgow, January 2018 (being prepared for publication under same title). Earlier version of the seminar paper accessible online, 2017: https://www.youtube.com/watch?v=RUakt04ftZk&t=102s. Date accessed: 4 March 2020.

[144] Penman, 'Christian Days and Knights', 249–72.

[145] Pitscottie, *Historie*, I, 357–68; Leslie, *Historie*, II, 234–8; *Cronique du roy Francoys, premier de ce nom. Publiée pour la première fois d'après un manuscrit de la Bibliothèque Impériale*, ed. Georges Guiffrey (Paris, 1860), 200–5; *LPHVIII*, XI, nos 848, 916, 1012, 1183, 1352; *Papiers d'état, pièces et documents inédits ou peu connus relatifs a l'histoire de l'Écosse au XVIème siècle*, ed. Alexandre Teulet, 3 vols (Edinburgh, 1852–60), I, 109–24; Bapst, *Les Mariages de Jacques V*, 230–308; Thomas, *Princelie Majestie*, 183–8.

[146] James sought the pope's permission for Erskine's divorce (as she was married) and rumours were still circulating about this affair when James was in France: *Letters of James V*, 320; *LPHVIII*, XI, no. 916. See also Cameron, *James V*, 151, 160 (n. 253), 177, 188 (n. 176).

undertaking this journey, which lasted nine months, demonstrated the stability created in Scotland since the end of his minority.[147] In the thirteenth century and earlier, the action of travelling into another monarch's realm during negotiations was considered to emphasise the inferior status of the monarch, and indeed his realm.[148] Yet, by the sixteenth century, there were exemplars that suggest that the journeys of kings were less associated with such notions. In 1520 François I and Henry VIII arranged a ceremonial bonanza, known as the Field of the Cloth of Gold, near Calais. This was a highly contested place for both kings, but the event epitomised the way that Renaissance monarchs postured outside the field of war through chivalric spectacles in richly elaborate ephemeral settings.[149] Indeed, later in the sixteenth and seventeenth centuries, royal entries by visiting monarchs to foreign capital cities were made without the visitor being presumed inferior.[150] By virtue of his youth, James may have been considered subordinate to François in the masculine hierarchy and evidence suggests that James complicity accepted this position as a 'son' rather than an equal.[151] Yet, neither this nor James's presence in France appear to have been directly linked to Scotland's inferior status.

The level of sartorial and material display undertaken by James V in France has previously been understated due to a presumption that his wedding was 'paid for by the French king'.[152] This grossly underestimates James's own financial input and efforts to perform alongside his royal peers on the European stage. The costs identified in Appendix IV, which are select costs rather than a full total, amount to significantly more than half of the dowry James received for his marriage to Madeleine. Although descriptions in narrative records of James's trip are limited in detail, the financial records composed by Kirkcaldy of the Grange and David Beaton offer fascinating insights

---

[147] Cameron, *James V*, 131–60.
[148] Benham, *Peacemaking in the Middle Ages*, 19–68. See also discussions in Chapter 1.
[149] Richardson, *Field of the Cloth of Gold*.
[150] Examples include the visit of Charles V, Holy Roman Emperor, to Paris in 1540 and Christian IV of Denmark's visit and entry to London: Robert J. Knecht, 'Charles V's Journey Through France, 1539–1540', in J.R. Mulryne and Elizabeth Goldring (eds), *Court Festivals in the European Renaissance: Art, Politics and Performance* (Aldershot, 2002), 153–70; Geoffrey Parker, *Emperor: A New life of Charles V* (New Haven, 2020), 265; Henry Robarts, *The King of Denmarkes welcome: Containing his ariuall, abode, and entertainement, both in the Citie and other places* (London, 1606). See also Philippa Woodcock, 'Early Modern Monarchy and Foreign Travel', in Woodacre, Dean, Jones et al. (eds), *The Routledge History of Monarchy*, 282–99.
[151] Dean, 'richesse in fassone and in fairenesse', 394–5.
[152] Thomas, *Princelie Majestie*, 183–8, quote at 183. A total of 14,615 livres 10d. is recorded as being accrued by the French king for the expenses of James V, Madeleine and her sister Marguerite between October 1536 and April 1537: *Inventaire chronologique des documents relatifs àl'histoire d'Écosse*, 84; *Papiers d'état*, I, 125. The Scottish accounts show an exchange rate of between 9s. and 10s. 6d. to one franc; thus, the known amount spent by the French king was approximately £7,500. The exchange rate from the *Treasurer's Accounts* is used by Gilbert: 'The Usual Money of Scotland', 144; see Note on Money, xviii.

into material display and the ways in which the royal household functioned in supporting James' performances abroad.[153] For example, they illustrate that the king's tailors, Thomas Arthur and Richard Hill, a furrier (possibly called Sande) and their servants accompanied the king from Scotland to procure and produce textiles and clothing for him at Blois, Paris and Rouen.[154] James also employed embroiderers, including Robinet, known the 'brodstar de roy': their fees were at least 1,125 francs and they received 1,320 francs worth of gold and silver silk threads from Florence 'for the fassoun of all the kingies abilȝements and claithis the time his grace was in France'.[155] The combination of fees and expenses on fine fabrics, furs, cloths of gold and an exquisite range of accessories, including buttons, gold thistles, jewels and points, reveal an active process of providing new clothing for the king's wardrobe *in situ* (see Appendix IV). Similar processes can be observed for the provision of the elaborate horse gear and tourneying equipment: Scottish royal household servants and French craftsmen were employed to procure and fashion an array of goods, including harnesses overgilt with gold, caparisons of velvet with gold fringes, jousting saddles and green damask purchased for a tourney pavilion.[156] Such evidence emphasises the importance of James's servants and local craftsmen, such as armourers, wrights and goldsmiths, in the projection of this royal image of magnificence and martial prowess.

The active procurement of material display was feverish enough to warrant criticism from an English ambassador who reported that James was 'running up and down the streets of Paris buying every trifle himself'.[157] However, with numerous unknown variables – including the identity of the bride – and a journey of unspecified length, James's need for an army of servants purchasing and making what he needed to respond to situations as they changed is hardly surprising. There is also little evidence to suggest that the royal regalia was taken to France: there are no packing or carriage fees for them nor do extant descriptions refer to them. Consequently, James's attire and wider material displays had to convey his status and identity without such

---

[153] NRS, James Kirkcaldy of Grange, now Treasurer, accounting for receipts and expenses outwith his office of Treasury, 11 Sept. 1536–22 Sept. 1538, E21/35, fols 1r–15v (Income: fols 1r–v); *TA*, VI, 449–68 (Income: 449–50); NRS, Accounts by Cardinal Beaton of James V's Expenses in France and of the receipt and expenditure of the dowries of Queens Magdalene and Marie of Guise-Lorraine, E30/5; *TA*, VII, 1–64 (Income: 1–2, 47–8). The income was primarily generated by the dowries of Madeleine, and in Beaton's account also Mary of Guise. For expenses accrued, see 'Appendix IV: Select Expenses from James V's French Journey, 1536–37'.

[154] NRS, E21/35, fols 8r–9v; *TA*, VI, 458–60; NRS, E30/5, fols 17r–19r, 20r–v, 25r–6v; *TA*, VII, 17–21, 26–7.

[155] NRS, E21/35, fol. 7v; E30/5, fol. 10v; *TA*, VI, 457; VII, 7–8.

[156] NRS, E21/35, fols 7r–10v; NRS, E30/5, fols 7v, 11r–13r, 14v–15v, 17r, 18r, 20v, 21v, 22r, 26r, 27r–8v, 35r, 43v–4v; *TA*, VI, 457–61; VII, 5, 8–10, 12–14, 16–17, 21–2, 27–30, 37, 48–51.

[157] *LPHVIII*, XI, no. 916.

overt royal objects to rely upon.[158] Indeed, he also invested in an array of items that any respectable royal should have on show in his residence, even if the residence was a semi-permanent one owned by another monarch. This included sets of tapestries, such as the story of the triumph of the dames, a set of gold and silver plate, worth over ten thousand francs or around a tenth of the dowry he received, and a fine bed of green velvet and other furnishings.[159] While many of these items were purchased as investments to take back to Scotland, costs for the repacking of tapestries, purchased from Flanders and Paris, at Rouen and boxing up the silverware to move it with the royal party, imply that such items were conspicuously displayed in James and Madeleine's rooms as they travelled and entertained.[160] As noted in regards to James IV, such items were commonly used for demonstrating wealth, status and engagement with the material world that flourished in Renaissance Europe.[161]

The French visit also allowed opportunities for James V to demonstrate a range of other kingly qualities for the foreign audiences that observed him both directly and indirectly through ambassadorial correspondence. The trip was punctuated with extensive gift giving to illustrate the kingly qualities of beneficence and generosity on the part of both monarchs. On James's part this included the distribution of fine fabrics, such as cloth of gold for gowns gifted to Madeleine, Madame le Dauphiné, Madame Marguerite – Madeleine's younger sister – and Madame de Vendôme.[162] James also spent over one thousand crowns on a diamond 'spousing ring' for his young queen.[163] The exchanging of rings is largely absent in earlier Scottish ceremonies, but the ring-giving ritual in sixteenth-century French royal weddings was centrally important to the affirmation of the queen's shared power with her husband.[164] Consequently, particularly if uncommon in Scotland, James's gift indicates a ritual literacy that spoke to French norms. Other gifts ranged from the expensive and opulent New Year and parting gifts for the extended royal family and officials to smaller signs of munificence, such as almsgiving, a habit gifted to a friar, candles provided at Easter and a lining for an altar

---

[158] Dean, 'richesse in fassone and in fairenesse', 392–3.
[159] NRS, E30/5, fols 17v, 18v, 26v, 32r–3v, 36v; TA, VII, 17–18, 28, 34–6, 39, 43. In addition, there are costs for further tapestries in the 1538–39 account, but it is unclear at what point these were purchased: NRS, E30/5, fol. 45v; TA, VII, 51. See also Rush, 'French Fashion in Sixteenth-Century Scotland', 1–26.
[160] NRS, E30/5, fols 17r, 19v, 39r–40r; TA, VII, 16, 19, 43–4.
[161] See 194–5; French, 'Magnificence and Materiality', 110–18.
[162] NRS, E30/5, fols 47r–v; TA, VII, 52–3.
[163] NRS, E30/5, fols 16r, 34r; TA, VII, 14, 37. The accounts give some of the figures in crowns worked out into francs/ livre: 100 crowns noted as 225 francs (TA, VII, 51), therefore, possible to calculate a rough exchange rate for the crowns as the exchange rate for Scots pound to francs was 1:2, making 100 crowns around £112, 6s. This would make this approx. £1,123 Scots for the ring: Note on Money, xviii.
[164] Elizabeth McCartney, 'Ceremonies and Privileges of Office: Queenship in Late Medieval France', in Jennifer Carpenter and Sally-Beth MacLean (eds), *Power of the Weak: Studies on Medieval Women* (Urbana and Chicago, 1995), 178–220, at 187.

cloth donated at Rouen.[165] Prior to the couple's departure, both kings made one final elaborate show of gift giving. James and Madeleine received horses, jewels, cloths of gold and other rich fabrics.[166] In return James had great gold cups made by 'Hoitman' or 'Hottmannis', a goldsmith, to gift to the French king and queen and the 'master of France' which were valued at over 7,500 francs, and on their arrival in Scotland a silver cup overgilt with gold was gifted to the French ambassador.[167] James engaged actively in gift exchange and with more extravagance than found with gifts exchanged in earlier Scottish wedding diplomacy, perhaps due to his personal presence in France.

James also found plenty of opportunities to portray his kingly virility through participating in tournaments and hunting expeditions, which took place throughout his visit.[168] Both English and Italian commentators also observed the young king practising and assessing his horses and equipment, and he also had his own coursing and hunting horses, dogs and falcons brought over from Scotland in December by Sir James Lindsay.[169] James's investment in material display for such activities was complimented in French sources, such as the *Cronique du Roy Francoys*, which stated that James and the Dauphin were the most wonderfully mounted and equipped throughout all the days of jousting.[170] Martial sport and 'manly' exhibitions of prowess and vigour were central to James's image at home in Scotland, and prominent in the posturing between Henry VIII and François I at the Field of the Cloth of Gold, so it is unsurprising to see such commitment to these displays in France also.[171] James V's demonstrations of his royal majesty and kingly attributes in France were both elaborate and expensive, as found for James IV in 1503, and the modes of display reflected wider European trends in terms of exhibiting majesty through material wealth and conspicuous consumption. However, by physically placing himself on the European stage, the active promotion of his kingship and his quest for a bride were primarily performed for a foreign audience. Thus, his return with Madeleine was a critical opportunity to relay the promise for the succession that the union offered and open a more direct dialogue between the wider Scottish community and his new bride.

---

[165] Gifts for the royal family and monetary gifts were also given to members of the French household: NRS, E30/5, fols 10r, 16r–17r, 31r; *TA*, VII, 7, 14–15. Smaller charitable gifts: NRS, E30/5, fols 18r, 20r–v, 35v; *TA*, VII, 17, 21, 38.
[166] Pitscottie, *Historie*, I, 367–8.
[167] NRS, E30/5, fols 23v, 30r, 34v; *TA*, VII, 25, 31–2, 37. These gifts would have been worth around £3,750 Scots. No references have been located to suggest the survival of any of the gifts.
[168] This included a theatrical tourney display for the wedding, not dissimilar to James IV's 'Wild Knight and Black Lady' tournament, but also more impromptu displays: Pitscottie, *Historie*, I, 364–7; *Cronique du Roy Francoys*, 204–5.
[169] *LPHVIII*, IX, nos 1305, 1315; NRS, GD149/264, fols 92v–3r; *Letters of James V*, 326.
[170] *Cronique du Roy Francoys*, 205.
[171] Dean, 'Reaching the Estate of Manhood'; Richardson, *Field of the Cloth of Gold*, 107–40.

Seven short weeks after the young couple returned to Scotland and before such a dialogue could begin, tragedy stole away the promise for the succession and dynastic stability arising from the union as, before her royal entry or coronation could be performed in Scotland, Madeleine had passed away.[172] Sir David Lindsay's poem immortalised how the plans for her celebratory royal entry turned quickly to preparations for public mourning.[173] The death of his queen had the potential to undermine the confident and nuanced Scottish royal statement made in France. James V had to provide ceremonial mourning that would honour his young queen in a manner befitting her status, while also looking beyond the tragedy to secure the succession through seeking a new marital alliance. Not only did a sizeable French entourage remain in Scotland, awaiting the entry that would never happen, but Madeleine's death also resulted in an outpouring of public grief in print that points to the technological advances of the sixteenth century. Alongside the Scottish offerings from David Lindsay, the death of Madeleine inspired literary laments in French and Latin from the continent by the likes of Jehan Desmontiers and Giles Corozet.[174] Literary responses to death existed for earlier Scottish royals: Bower recalls an eighty-eight line epitaph composed in memory of Robert Bruce and the *Book of Pluscarden* notes that James II had an epitaph in memory of his sister, Margaret dauphine of France, translated into Scots.[175] Nevertheless, the outpouring of printed memorials for the young French queen illuminates the fact that a wider sixteenth-century European audience was focused on Scotland, which made the subsequent funerary display all the more significant.

The heraldic and chivalric nature of the wedding bled through into the funeral arrangements. The king appears to have ridden in the funeral procession in knightly attire with the sword carried before him. Accounts refer to 'ane grete suerd' carried to and from the abbey at the time of Madeleine's funeral, while the king also received a 'mailze and ane hudskull' at the abbey and his saddle was newly covered with black fabric.[176] James had also purchased a great wealth of armour and horse gear in France, including a set of

---

[172] Pitscottie, *Historie*, I, 369; Leslie, *Historie*, II, 238; Lindsay, 'The Deploratioun of the Deith of Quene Magdalene', in *Sir David Lyndsay: Selected Poems*, 101–8; *TA*, VI, 298–300, 303, 305, 310–13; Thomas, 'Crown Imperial', 56. Madeleine's health delayed departure from France and was an ongoing concern: Cameron, *James V*, 133; Thomas, *Princelie Majestie*, 188–9; Bapst, *Les Mariages de Jacques V*, passim, particularly 301–3.

[173] Lindsay, 'The Deploratioun of the Deith of Quene Magdalene', 105.

[174] Giles Corozet, *Deploration fur le trefpas de tref noble Princeffe dame Magdeleine de France Royne Defcoce* (Paris, 1537); *Cronique du Roy Françoys*, 216–20. For both the Latin and translations of epitaphs by Desmontiers, see A.H. Miller, 'Scotland Described for Queen Magdalene: A Curious Volume', *SHR* 1 (1904), 37–8.

[175] *Chron. Bower*, VII, 44–5; *Pluscarden*, 288.

[176] NRS, E21/32, fol. 13v; *TA*, VI, 337. The sword could have been the papal sword gifted to James V in 1537: *TA*, VII, 18; Burns, 'Papal Gifts', 150–95, particularly 180–3; Thomas, *Princelie Majestie*, 207–8.

gold-gilt horse armour, which could also have been utilised.[177] Black liveries were purchased for nineteen pages – nine for the queen and ten for the king – presumably identified by representative coats-of-arms.[178] In addition to the liveried members of the processional party, both courtiers and the wider public were provisioned with dule wear, including four French ladies and two ladies of honour, with the latter receiving fur-lined hoods for their gowns.[179] This indicates the importance of female mourners for the young queen, echoing the pronounced part played by women in the royal entries and coronations of queens consort, and emphasises the 'immersive' nature of such ritual performances for prominent members of the court, wider society and visitors alike.[180] The volume of black cloth and dule attire purchased in July 1537 led near-contemporary Buchanan to comment that the very public nature of the mourning, with the wearing of dule clothes on such a scale, had rarely been seen in Scotland.[181] Public mourning and the wearing of dule garments were not new to Scotland, as evidenced from Robert I and his black-clad knights in 1329 and more recently in James IV's purchases of dule wear for himself and others. However, the scale of the mourning ceremony for Madeleine – particularly staged for an international audience – was unlikely to have been witnessed in the living memory for any king or a queen.

Within Holyrood Abbey a *castrum deloris* was constructed for Madeleine. Employed in Scotland since at least 1329, when it was called a hearse or later a *chapelle ardent*, the newly adopted term for the decorative structure gives an impression of its size and grandeur.[182] The structure would have been glittering with candlelight and colour in the black-clad surroundings, with two hundred large candles on spikes and four hundred coats of arms.[183] A black and purple cloth embroidered with 'sex grete armys and sex small' along with one large cross and one small cross was made, indicating an elaborate pall cloth draped over the coffin rather than any evidence for an effigy as later used for James V.[184] The flickering heraldic focal point at the heart of this display was a sombre statement of James's royal authority, which also signalled ongoing desires for continuing the union between the

---

[177] A 'bard' (breast and flank armour for a horse) overgilt with gold was purchased for the king for 270 francs: NRS, E30/5, fol. 45r; TA, VII, 51. For further information about armour and horse gear purchased, see Appendix IV.

[178] NRS, E21/32, fols 20–1v; TA, VI, 342–4.

[179] NRS, E21/32, fols 9–20, 24–8r; TA, VI, 330–44, 349–52, 354. For further analysis of the dule clothing provided, particularly for the French entourage, see Westerhof Nyman, 'Mourning Madeleine and Margaret', 365–9.

[180] For 'immersive theatre' analogy, see Hepburn, *The Household and Court of James IV*, 102–22.

[181] Buchanan, *History*, II, 315.

[182] See Chapter 2, 90–1.

[183] NRS, Exchequer Records: Household Books, E31/7, fols 98v, 102v; NRS, E21/32, fol. 11v; TA, VI, 334. An image of the *chapelle ardent* survives for the elaborate funeral of Anne of Brittany in 1514: McCartney, 'Ceremonies and Privileges of Office', fig. 6; Giesey, *Royal Funeral Ceremonies*, fig. 11.

[184] NRS, E21/32, fol. 26; TA, VI, 352.

two countries beyond the tragedy. Such statements continued through the king's lifetime, with memorials each year which witnessed the rehanging of the abbey in black, up to seventy-two escutcheons prepared and Masses sung by up to two hundred chaplains.[185] It is possible that these later ceremonies centred on a tomb, perhaps a double tomb with James: it was not unusual, after all, for a monarch to have started or even completed their own tomb during their reign, nor was it unusual to be buried with a first spouse after remarriage, even where the marriage was childless.[186] Giesey states that the burial of Anne of Brittany in 1514 – wife of Louis XII – was 'modelled in every way possible on the traditional rites for the king'.[187] While there were differences between Madeleine's funeral and James's own, such as the inclusion of an effigy of James in 1543, the similarities underscore the necessity to emphasise her status as queen, despite never receiving her crown nor continuing the succession.

No amount of elaborate mourning, widely provided dule wear, candles or Masses for the dead could resolve the challenge to the succession that Madeleine's death caused. James V needed an heir, and the honour shown to Madeleine in death enabled continued strong relations with François I, who helped secure a second bride for his widowed son-in-law. The recently widowed duchess de Longueville, Marie de Guise, was still in her early twenties and had produced two healthy sons by her first marriage, proving her capacity to bear healthy male heirs to term.[188] The dynastic continuation of the Stewart line was a central feature in the ceremonies orchestrated for Marie. Although she arrived in Scotland in June 1538, Marie was not crowned until she was heavily pregnant in February 1540, over eighteen months after her arrival.[189] Indeed, whereas barons were invited to attend Madeleine's coronation in 1537, despite her ill health, there was no sign of a coronation being planned for Marie until October 1539 – by which point she was pregnant – when John Mosman, goldsmith, was paid for making the queen's crown.[190] In France postponing the queen's coronation until politically or dynastically pertinent was not uncommon but this was rare in Scotland.[191] The date selected for Marie's coronation was Sunday 8 February. Consequently, this would have permitted conspicuous liturgical connections to be made by the presiding cleric, David Beaton, archbishop of St Andrews and instrumental ambassador in both of James's French marriages, as the date marked the

---

[185] Ibid., 422–3; VII, 181, 321, 466; VIII, 90–1; NRS, E31/8, fols 126r, 131r.
[186] The most prominent example of this being Richard II and Anne of Bohemia at Westminster: Duffy, *Royal Tombs*, 163–7, 169 (including figs 69–72).
[187] Giesey, *Royal Funeral Ceremonies*, 75.
[188] *LPHVIII*, II, part ii, nos. 1201, 1285, 1292–3; Bapst, *Les Mariages de Jacques V*, 318–25; Thomas, *Princelie Majestie*, 194; Pamela E. Ritchie, *Mary of Guise, 1548–1560: A Political Career* (East Linton, 2002), 10–13.
[189] Thomas, *Princelie Majestie*, 94; Thomas, 'Crown Imperial', 63.
[190] *TA*, VI, 298–300, 303, 305, 310–13; *TA*, VII, 254.
[191] McCartney, 'Ceremonies and Privileges of Office', 178–219; Laynesmith, *Last Medieval Queens*, 75. For Scotland, see example of Euphemia Ross, Chapter 3, 126–8.

close of the octave of the Marian feast of the Purification of the Virgin, also known as Candlemas, on 2 February.[192] Association with Virgin feasts was common in Scottish royal ceremonies of previous centuries, but this specific Marian feast marked the presentation of Christ's mother at her post-birth purification (after forty days) and was firmly associated with childbirth.[193] The potency of James and Marie's marital union may also have been visually emphasised as the queen was fashioned a gold belt, decorated with a sapphire, for the occasion that would undoubtedly have drawn attention to her pregnant belly.[194] Madeleine's early death and the threat it caused to the succession appear to have directly impacted choices associated with the coronation of James's second queen. In particular, postponing the ritual until there was evidence that Marie would survive to produce children inferred that her position – more so than any of her predecessors – rested on her ability to produce children.

This was not the only way in which Madeleine's death affected the ceremonies surrounding Marie's arrival and coronation. Purchases of fine clothing – including a hood of the 'French sort' and a gold 'chafferoun' in 'Paris werk' – for James's eldest illegitimate child, Lady Jane, suggest she was presented to the new queen on her arrival at St Andrews in 1538.[195] It seems that James V's own fertility – illustrated through his illegitimate offspring – was a factor to showcase in the wake of a potential dynastic crisis following his first wife's death. The choice of St Andrews for Marie's arrival was also unusual.[196] St Andrews was a prominent town – the seat of the premier archbishop and the site of the oldest university in the country, which was central to the guided-tour Marie received following their marriage rite. Yet, most queens arriving via the North Sea docked at Leith for ease of access to Edinburgh. Consequently, St Andrews was perhaps chosen, in part, to draw attention away from Leith where Madeleine's ill-fated arrival had occurred a little over a year previously.[197] Arriving at St Andrews in Fife also provided the means to introduce the queen consort to the realm in a very public manner through a longer journey of welcome. Following a number of weeks of feasting, dancing, plays and jousting at St Andrews, the royal party was welcomed at a number of palaces and burghs, including Cupar, Falkland,

---

[192] *Diurnal of Occurrents*, 23: uses title of abbot of Arbroath, but Beaton was both archbishop and cardinal by this point.
[193] For coronations of Robert I, Robert II, Robert III and James II, and Annabella and possibly Euphemia, see 76, 85, 118, 129, 133, 156, 166. On the prominence of Marian worship in Scotland: Fitch, *Search for Salvation*, 113–50.
[194] *TA*, VII, 278.
[195] *TA*, VI, 406. James's illegitimate sons were also all schooled in St Andrews by 1539 but is not clear if they were present in 1538: *TA*, VII, 103, 130, 163–4, 312–14, 396–7, 442. See also Cameron, *James V*, 261–2.
[196] Pitscottie, *Historie*, I, 380; *Diurnal of Occurrents*, 22; NRS, E31/7, fol. 70r; *TA*, VI, 394–419; *Accounts of the Masters of Works*, I, 21–2; Thomas, *Princelie Majestie*, 191–2; Dean, 'Enter the Alien', 275–7; ibid., 'Making the Best of What They Had', 110.
[197] Guidicini, *Triumphal Entries and Festivals*, 50.

Stirling, Linlithgow and Corstorphine.[198] In addition to this, following her formal entry to Edinburgh on 20 July, Marie made subsequent entries at Perth and Dundee, where the king and archbishop of Glasgow presided over the wedding of the earl of Errol to the sister of the earl of Lennox in August 1538.[199] Madeleine's illness meant that she did not leave Holyrood for seven weeks until her funerary procession, whereas the extended processional journey with multiple royal entries and celebrations in 1538 offered the king opportunities to promote Marie quickly and coherently within the Scottish court and the kingdom more broadly, particularly facilitating dialogues with the wider population in urban centres. Nonetheless, Marie's rapid departure from Edinburgh after her royal entry on 20 July without a coronation left the rituals of queenship unfinished, particularly in relation to her official role as consort and her position within the political community.

The evidence for Marie's coronation is primarily extracted from the financial records due to a lack of detailed descriptions. Ladies (unnamed) from across the realm were summonsed, emphasising the prominence of female presence found for both Madeleine's funeral and earlier consort coronations.[200] Timber was delivered to Holyrood Abbey for the coronation preparations, presumably to create a raised stage for the proceedings.[201] Two chairs were recovered with purple velvet, silk ribbons and fringes specifically for the queen in February 1540, likely for the couple to sit on during the proceedings as with those provided for James IV and Margaret in 1503.[202] The royal chapel gear was transported to the abbey for use in the ceremony.[203] Much of this had been purchased on James's visit to France and included two 'crowatis' or small vials for oil or water for liturgical use which were potentially used in anointing Marie.[204] There were also payments made for eleven additional chaplains from the king's chapel royal at Stirling, with new clothing purchased on 6 February for one of the chaplains.[205] The chaplains of the chapel royal were 'highly-trained' choristers at the forefront of Scottish

---

[198] Pitscottie, *Historie*, I, 380–1; NRS, E31/7, fols 70r–80r; *TA*, VI, 431–2. The location of the royal household in the margins of the household account verify Pitscottie's descriptions of the queen's journey.

[199] NLS, Volume of Extracts from the Records of the City preserved in the Advocates Library, Adv. MS 31.4.9, fols 189r–90v; *Extracts Edinburgh*, II, 89–91; *Accounts of the Masters of Works*, I, 224; Pitscottie, *Historie*, I, 380–1; *Diurnal*, 22; Lindsay, 'Deploratioun of the Deith of Queen Madeleine', 105; Dean, 'Enter the Alien', 276–9; *Princelie Majestie*, 190–1.

[200] *TA*, VII, 302.

[201] Ibid., 487. Thomas suggests 'tiered stands' were erected for the congregation. Tiered seating was used in Westminster from the seventeenth-century post-Reformation coronations of Charles II and James II and VII onwards, but there was no earlier precedence for this in Scotland: Thomas, *Princelie Majestie*, 197; Strong, *Coronations*, 311–27, particularly images at 312, 316–17, 319–21.

[202] *TA*, VII, 284–5.

[203] Ibid., 280.

[204] Ibid., 36–7; NRS, E30/5, fols 34r–v.

[205] *TA*, VII, li, 288, 290.

religious musical performance and, during the 1540s, they would almost certainly have counted Robert Carver amongst their number, as his choir book has datable pieces in 1513 and 1546.[206] Thomas's proposal that these men were just there to boost the number of clerics and assist with the ceremonies misses a key facet of the inclusion of these particular men.[207] Their presence in Holyrood Abbey in February 1540 illustrates the aural extravagance that would have accompanied the visual splendour of the occasion.

Preparations undertaken for James, including the making of a vast hooded royal robe of purple velvet lined with ermine to replace the former 'rob ryall', illuminate his prominence alongside Marie in the ceremony.[208] Marie was made a matching robe of velvet continuing the emphasis on marital unity through sartorial choices as found in both 1449 and 1503, but the volume of cloth used in their respective robes – twenty-two ells of cloth for Marie to thirty-eight ells used for James – suggests that the king had a significantly more impressive train on his robe.[209] Consequently, while the material display marked their unity and the royal pedigree of their offspring, James left little doubt as to his own prominence in this relationship: he was the ultimate source of royal authority and this event provided a perfect opportunity to underscore this. The remodelling of the king's regalia from 1532 onwards offers further evidence for this (Plate 20): more gold was used to increase the weight of the crown, additional pearls and precious stones were added and the arches were completed with the exquisite French globe and cross.[210] This material display focused on the king and his regalia arguably speaks to a different character of coronation ritual (and king perhaps) than 1503 when James IV so conspicuously chose to be seen with a 'barre head' at his marriage and the coronation of his queen.

Marie was also provided with a lighter-weight crown, made of thirty-five ounces of gold and precious stones by John Mosman; although, notably, this was over three times the weight of gold as used in Margaret's crown in 1503.[211] Marie's sceptre, also made for the occasion, was topped with a white hand, similar to the *main de justice* found in the French regalia.[212] By ordering the queen's sceptre fashioned in this manner, James did more than show admiration for French design. In the speech composed for her arrival at St Andrews, Marie was reportedly advised about her duties to her new hus-

---

[206] Isobel Woods Preece, *'Our awin Scottis Use'*: *Music in the Scottish Church up to 1603*, ed. Sally Harper (Glasgow, 2000), 106–25, 163–4. One of Carver's masses may have been used in 1513, see 206.
[207] Thomas, *Princelie Majestie*, 197–8.
[208] Ibid., 277.
[209] Ibid.
[210] TA, VI, 25–6, 73, 179; VII, 204, 278, 285; Thomas, *Princelie Majestie*, 194–8; Thomas, 'Crown Imperial', 55–67. Other works on the remodelling of the regalia: Brook, 'Technical Description of the Regalia', 94–104; Charles J. Burnett and Chris J. Tabraham, *The Honours of Scotland: The History of the Scottish Crown Jewels* (Edinburgh, 1993).
[211] TA, VII, 254.
[212] *A Collection of Inventories*, 76; Thomas, 'Crown Imperial', 64.

Plate 20   The Royal Honours of Scotland (crown, bonnet, scabbard, sceptre and sword). Historic Environment Scotland, SCRAN 008-001-008-645-C.

band including her support in upholding justice and preserving the peace.[213] There are no explicit references to Marie taking an oath at her coronation or appearing in a parliament to do so; a convention of the estates was planned to coincide with the coronation, but it is not clear if this occurred or not.[214] However, her investiture with the sceptre demonstrated the proxy power bestowed upon her and emphasised the role of the king in providing her with such power, particularly if it was presented to her by the king as James IV had done for Margaret Tudor in 1503. For a king who could not perform in his own coronation, this was also an opportunity to manipulate royal ritual and material culture to reemphasise his royal authority, but the marital union and its promise for the succession physically manifested in Marie's pregnancy appears to have been the primary message.

In May 1540, James V and Marie de Guise welcomed a new infant son and heir into the world, bringing widespread public celebration, according to Leslie's later sixteenth-century history, that included the lighting of fires, offerings of prayers and public triumph reminiscent of fifteenth-century celebrations.[215] The financial records inform of the making of a 'paill' or canopy for a crib of state, white cloth purchased to carry torches, messages requesting attendance sent to Scottish nobles and the courts of France and England, and these celebrations may have included some of the first fireworks used in a Scottish ceremony.[216] Moreover, the parliament of December 1540 introduced an act calling for prayers for the royal family, in the mould of James I, including the couple's first-born son – titled James 'the sext' – and possibly witnessed proclamations about Marie de Guise's second pregnancy to the political community.[217] Yet, by the spring of 1541, the couple had lost two sons – James and a second son who lived only a few weeks.[218] Herein lies the juxtaposition at the heart of this chapter: very real difficulties with the physical ability to continue the legitimate Stewart succession underpinned some of the most elaborate adult demonstrations of kingly majesty in the sixteenth century, which perhaps hints at a level of anxious overcompensation fuelling these displays. With fuller surviving records than for earlier periods, particularly so when placed in direct comparison with the mid-fifteenth century, it is not difficult to demonstrate that James IV and James V sought and maintained a position amongst their Renaissance European counterparts, but asking more questions of these performances and putting them more consciously into a

---

[213] Pitscottie, *Historie*, I, 380.
[214] See *RPS* from December 1540. On the convention, see Blakeway, *Parliament and Convention in the Personal Rule of James V*, 3, 67.
[215] Leslie, *Historie*, II, 243; Pitscottie, *Historie*, 382.
[216] NRS, E21/37, fols 55v–6r, 58v, 59v–60r; TA, VII, 304, 307, 309, 357.
[217] RPS, 1540/12/56; Blakeway, *Parliament and Convention in the Personal Rule of James V*, 251–2.
[218] NRS, E21/37, fol. 55v; TA, VII, 304, 442; *Diurnal of Occurents*, 23.

cycle of death and succession offers a more nuanced understanding. These Scottish kings embraced contemporary forms of display as adults. This led to notable innovations in ritual performance, enhanced engagement with material culture and sartorial splendour, increased expenditure and growing performative confidence. However, this period still suffers from incomplete official records and silences from narrative sources at pertinent moments for gauging the role of ritual at critical transitional moments. Notably, this was particularly the case when the king was a minor and the ceremonies were under the control of others.

The rapid organisation of coronations in both 1488 and 1513 implies that this ritual confirmation of royal power – even for a small infant – remained central to monarchical power and legitimacy in the eyes of those who sought to restabilise power after unexpected deaths. However, the physical spaces chosen for the ceremony in each case indicates that different concerns were a priority: the choice of Scone appeared to reflect desires for tradition and the legitimacy by elite Scottish men amidst a period of internal strife, whereas the use of the chapel royal at Stirling Castle speaks to the response of a political community – perhaps adhering to the desires of a widowed queen – fearing external threats after Flodden. These choices and the wider context affected the number and roles of attendees, and the extent to which subsequent rituals – often using the political environment of parliament – were utilised to continue to confirm and re-establish power. The funeral had historically functioned in conjunction with the coronation as the legitimate transitional opening of the reign, even where minor kings were involved and despite subtle shifts in the order of events. Unfortunately, the evidence for such a combined use of funeral and coronation is elusive in the case of James IV's death so only speculative suggestions can be made. Moreover, where a delayed royal funeral offered ceremonial stability during political turmoil, or a smoothing over of questionable political actions elsewhere, no such retrospective use of funerary ritual appears to have been employed to paste over the cracks between James III's death and his son's accession. Death still had a marked impact on the rituals of succession, particularly so in the ceremonial of queenship in the 1530s. Yet, despite the impressive ceremonies orchestrated by the adult monarchs in this period offering exquisite demonstrations of Scottish engagement with European ceremonial culture, this period also raises questions about the changing nature of the integration of the rituals of death with those of succession.

Conclusion

'The king is dead. Long live the queen.'

Death and funerary display reclaimed an elaborately prominent position in the ritual cycle of succession with the funeral of James V in January 1543, described in the opening of this book. The coronation for his daughter, Mary, did not take place immediately, so the funeral was not directly connected to the ceremony that confirmed and celebrated her accession. Yet, James Hamilton, earl of Arran, the heir presumptive after Mary, took a prominent role in the funerary proceedings: he used this ritual mourning to state his claim clearly.[1] Subsequently, in the parliament of March 1543, the power of the crown to maintain the 'common good' was temporarily vested in Arran by representatives of the three estates.[2] The governor produced coinage marked with 'IG' for '*Iohannes Gubernator*' and paid for the production of a new seal for the infant queen, but Mary remained with her mother, the widowed Queen Marie.[3] Mother and daughter moved to Stirling Castle in August 1543 and Marie was involved in personally bankrolling some of the provisions for the feasting that occurred to celebrate the coronation on 9 September, within the octave of the Feast of the Nativity of the Virgin (on 8 September). Tensions appear to have arisen around the temporary guardianship of the royal dignity due to the presence of an adult male, who stood next in the hereditary succession in Scotland, and a widowed queen, who sought to protect her daughter. This coronation took place in the Chapel Royal at the castle, with the Mass possibly accompanied by one of Robert Carver's famed compositions, in a manner that echoed her father's coronation.[4] Lead-

---

[1] NRS, E21/40, fols 13r–14v; TA, VIII, 163–5.
[2] RPS, 1543/9–10; RPS, A1543/3/1.
[3] Marcus Merriman, *The Rough Wooings, Mary Queen of Scots, 1542–1551* (East Linton, 2000), 92; NRS, E21/40, fol. 27r; TA, VIII, 184.
[4] TA, VIII, 224; NRS, E33/3/4, Déspences De La Maison Royale, Mary of Guise-Lorrain: Accounts (extraordinary), Feb 1542/3 to Jan 1543/4, fols 26–30; Lucinda H.S. Dean, 'In the Absence of an Adult Monarch: The Ceremonial Representations of Authority by Marie de Guise, c.1543–1558', in Buchanan and Dean with Penman (eds), *Medieval and Early Modern Representations of Authority*, 143–62, at 146–9. Ross proposes that the *Pater Creator omnium* Mass, dated 1543, was the kind of composition 'reserved for solemnities of the highest order': *Musick Fyne*, 40–4.

ing earls, including the governor Arran, carried the regalia in the coronation procession, while senior churchmen were also prominent and led by the Cardinal David Beaton, archbishop of St Andrews, who performed the role of officiant.[5] Despite, or perhaps because of, the tensions about where power lay with the accession of another infant, rituals were still actively utilised to navigate the transfer and negotiation of royal power following the death of James V just as they had been with his predecessors.

Many of the features found in the displays of 1543, outlined here and in the introduction, had long roots into the past. Yet, equally, the context of this period of power transition was unique so there were both subtle and marked developments and innovations caused by these specific circumstances. The very nature of ceremonies that marked the cycle of death and succession meant that they often occurred in times of heightened tension and – in many cases in the Scottish context particularly – with little warning or time to prepare. Burden, and other ritual scholars, have argued that the 'apparent conservatism of ritual practices will often veil a reality in which ritual traditions are not static, but continually reproduced'.[6] This is critical to understanding the development of rituals within the Scottish ceremonial cycle of succession. There was, of course, a necessity for elements that were rooted in continuity and repetition that spoke to shared understanding of precedent and expectation. However, even where known scripts or models to follow existed, a carbon copy of an earlier ritual was almost impossible in such irregularly held ceremonies situated in complex varying contexts.[7] These variables and their impact upon the rituals performed was the reason for approaching this study chronologically. Taking the events of 1543 as a starting point, the remainder of this conclusion will reflect on elements of continuity and change across key areas – the temporal connections between ceremonies of death and succession; the use of locations, spaces and associations of place; the use of objects and material display; and the roles of participants, organisers and audiences – before drawing final conclusions.

The coronation of Mary, queen of Scots, was separated from the funeral of her father by nine months and from his death by ten months. This was unusual in the Scottish context: the haste with which inaugurations or coronations were orchestrated was quite a consistent feature across the centuries addressed in this book. The gap between the death of the predecessor and the subsequent inauguration or coronation was usually one month or less, with only two other exceptions when the direct heir was present in the realm,

---

[5] 'Parr to Suffolk, 13 Sept 1543', *The Hamilton Papers: Letters and Papers Illustrating the Political Relations of England and Scotland in the XVIth Century*, ed. Joseph Bain, 2 vols (Edinburgh, 1890–92), II, no. 30; Ralph Sadler, *Letters and Negotiations of Sir Ralph Sadler, ambassador of King Henry VIII to Scotland* (Edinburgh, 1720), 359–67.
[6] Burden, 'Re-writing A Rite of Passage', 14. Other examples include: Burke, 'Performing History', 35–52; Fantoni, 'Symbols and Rituals', 25–6.
[7] Steven Thiry, 'Rites of Reversion: Ceremonial Memory and Community in the Funeral of Philip II in the Netherlands (1598), *Renaissance Quarterly*, 71/4 (2018), 1391–429.

and rarely allowed for what became the standard of forty days for calling the estates to parliament.[8] This was the case both before and after the Wars of Independence, and includes the accessions of both adults and minors alike. Moreover, despite being named king in absentia in 1406 at the death of his father, James I also sought to employ ceremonial to proclaim his kingship quickly upon his return in 1424, with his coronation occurring thirty-six days after his official entry to Edinburgh. Thus, while the dating of reigns indicates that a theoretical transfer of power occurred at the death of the predecessor, in practice there was a clear desire to confirm and acclaim a new king promptly using an inaugural ritual in a public arena. Therefore, Scottish inaugurations and coronations fall under Muir's definition of an enacting ritual: one that elicited change or, at the very least, indicated change had occurred in a formal setting.[9] While the monarch's right to the throne was rooted in his or her hereditary claim in Scotland, this analysis of ritual demonstrates that the late medieval and early modern political sphere was an inherently performative one that required visible manifestations of such ideas to consolidate and stabilise the succession.

James V's funeral witnessed the first confirmable use of an effigy within a Scottish monarch's funeral ceremony. Effigy usage elsewhere has been associated with either a simple replacement for the body, once used as proof of death, around which to centre mourning, or as an embodiment of the idea of the king's two bodies – the body natural and the body politic that continues beyond death. The latter resulted in particularly elaborate funerary developments elsewhere, particularly in sixteenth-century France.[10] While an effigy was prepared for James V, there does not appear to have been one made for his first queen, Madeleine, five and half years earlier; this could suggest that the effigy was more than an object around which to centre mourning. The accession of two infants under two-years old since 1500 also led to adults of royal blood – Albany (1515) and Arran (1543) – being invested with the royal dignity temporarily. As early as 1286, evidence indicates that the estates sought to invest royal dignity in the chosen guardians through recognisable ceremonial and material means. Moreover, works of fifteenth-century Scots, such as Gilbert Hay and John Ireland, indicate that a developed understanding of the ideology of the king's two bodies existed in Scotland.[11] Yet, beyond this, the surviving evidence of its incorporation into the ritual activities associated with death and succession are limited, particularly as the temporal relationships between death, funeral and ceremonies of accession are inconsistent, particularly in terms of which ceremony occurred first.[12]

[8] Periods between death and inauguration or coronation where this was one month or less: 1214, one day; 1249, nearly one week; 1371, approximately one month; 1437, one month; 1460, near one week; 1488, near two weeks; 1513, under two weeks.
[9] Muir, *Ritual in Early Modern*, 247.
[10] Giesey, *Royal Funeral Ceremony*, 1–18, 106–24.
[11] Mapstone, 'The Advice to Princes Tradition', 45–142, 355–452.
[12] Where the order of death/funeral and inauguration/coronation can be confirmed, the

Instances where significant gaps existed between death, funeral and accession rituals do offer further interesting insights. If the delaying of David II's coronation to 1331 was linked, as argued here, to awaiting the return of Robert's heart for burial, this speaks more directly to a choice imbued with the ideologies associated with the royal bodies politic and mortal in which the royal dignity could not be fully invested until the mortal remains were buried. The other significant hiatus, occurring in 1390, witnessed the delayed funeral and coronation combined into one extended ceremonial occasion at Scone four months after Robert II's death. The descriptions in Wyntoun's and Bower's chronicle, with the ceremonies occurring seamlessly one after the other, should potentially raise alarm bells: as Buc argues, where rituals are recorded as perfectly ordered 'we are free to suspect that it masks a struggle for authority'.[13] In 1390 there was a palpable struggle for authority between Robert II's eldest sons, so the choices made – whether by Robert II, Robert III or the chronicler in his decision to record the ceremonial proceedings in this way – indicate the desire for this ceremonial programme to present an idealised model of societal order for an uncertain future, rather than a mirror of reality.[14] However, through this model they presented a physical and tangible transfer of the royal dignity through this series of temporarily and spatially interconnected rituals. The choices made regarding the ordering of funerals and accession ceremonies appear to have been more pragmatic than ideological in the Scottish context across the period in its entirety. However, the political community used ritualised performance to make tangible the transfer of royal dignity as an important means of upholding stability, or the façade of such at least, if not fully incorporating the same elaborate ritual use of effigies found in France.

In 1543 the coronation of Mary, queen of Scots, was performed on 9 September, in the octave of the Feast of the Nativity of the Blessed Virgin, which linked to similar usage of another Marian feast for her mother's coronation in February 1540. This could, tentatively, be linked to frequent associations between major feast days of the Blessed Virgin and accession rituals of early Stewart kings following the inauguration of Robert I on, or near, the Annunciation of the Virgin in 1306. It was not only feasts of the Blessed Virgin that were appropriated in this way. Indeed, there are numerous examples where royal ceremonies were combined with a religious festival from Alexander III's wedding on Christmas Day in 1251 to James V's baptism at Easter in 1512. The symbolic value of such date choices, particularly those that linked the monarch to Christ, or a queen with the Blessed Virgin, would not have been lost on a population whose lives rotated around the religious calendar and whose chroniclers often record events by mentioning

---

inauguration or coronation occurs first in 1214, 1249 and again in 1460, while the funeral occurred first in 1390, 1437 and 1543.
[13] Buc, 'Ritual and Interpretation', 201. *Chron. Wyntoun*, VI, 366–8; *Chron. Bower*, VIII, 3–5.
[14] Muir, *Ritual in Early Modern*, 4–6.

major feasts rather than dates. There are also occasions where secular dates of importance may have been used for similar reasons, such as the anniversary of the victory at Bannockburn for the funeral of Robert I in 1329 and the coronation of James IV in 1488, but it is also important not to impose modern enthusiasm for anniversary celebrations onto the past. Religious feast days would certainly have brought accompanying benefits – enhanced levels of worship, specific prayer cycles, processional activities, opportunities for indulgences, associated feasting and gift giving – that could be effectively harnessed by shrewd organisers to enhance and embellish royal ceremonies. There was no consistent dating pattern for ceremonies associated with death and succession for the very simple reason that death was not predictable, and even well-laid plans of monarchs, their spouses and advisors could easily be impacted by early or unexpected death. Yet, where possible, significant religious feasts, or personal victories, were used to elevate royal ceremonial by association with existing celebrations without adding greatly to cost.

Just as dates could be harnessed, the importance of physical settings in enhancing and communicating specific messages and encouraging certain dialogues was very apparent in Scottish ceremonies. Such sites were material spaces that carried relational connections to wider expressions of kingship and the exercise of power across the generations and were imbued with meaning and significance for the individual, couple or group who selected it, the participants of the ceremony and the audiences who observed the ritual actions.[15] Consequently, even if selected for practical reasons or due to the pressures of a particular situation, the locations utilised were far more than backdrops. From 1214 to 1543, one of the most notable factors about the locations of Scottish ceremonies in the cycle of death and succession was their variety: eight different sites were chosen for burial by the twelve reigning monarchs who died in Scotland during this period;[16] four different sites hosted the inaugurations and coronations for the fourteen monarchs who were raised to the throne;[17] where evidence survives for them, consort coronations were slightly more settled, occurring at Scone Abbey until 1424 and at Holyrood Abbey thereafter; and the weddings of reigning monarchs used at least eight sites, including locations outside the realm.[18] For coronations and funerals particularly, a comparison to kingdoms such as England and France, where ceremonial was often bound to traditional fixed locations,

---

[15] For work on spatial theories underpinning this discussion, see Leif Jerram, 'Space: A Useless Category for Historical Analysis?', *History and Theory*, 52 (2013), 400–19 at 403–7; Mike Rapport, 'The Bricks and Mortar of Revolution: Space and Place in Revolutionary Paris', *University of Glasgow School of Humanities Lecture Series 2018–29*, 6 December 2018. https://www.youtube.com/watch?v=jxL8P_N2xs8. Date accessed: 29 September 2020. Thanks to Dr Mike Rapport and participants/organisers of SGSAH workshop on spatial history, St Andrews, 2019, for helpful discussions on this topic.

[16] The abbeys at Arbroath, Melrose, Dunfermline, Holyrood, Scone, Paisley, Cambuskenneth and the Carthusian Charterhouse at Perth.

[17] The abbeys of Scone, Holyrood, Kelso and the Chapel Royal at Stirling Castle.

[18] York, Roxburgh, Jedburgh, Berwick, London, Holyrood Abbey, Paris and St Andrews.

makes such variability seem unusual.[19] Yet, in late medieval Scandinavian kingdoms at least two, but often more, sites were used for 'making' kings during the same period: in Sweden an assembly site with a stone gave way to a capital city over time; Norwegian coronations occurred at the burial site of St Olaf in Trondheim initially, but the royal centres at Bergen and Oslo dominated in later centuries; and in Denmark the coronation site shifted frequently between dominant episcopal sites dependent on the monarch's location.[20] These similarities require more exploration and offer compelling evidence for pursuing further comparative work between Scotland and other peripheral kingdoms in the future to better understand connections and differences between the rituals, kingship and governance across these regions.

The reasons for the variant choices of site in Scotland were multi-layered and understanding them will always be speculative to a degree, but the role of specific individuals or groups (such as widowed queens or leading political figures in minorities), familial, marital or dynastic connections, personal or conspicuous piety and the need to stabilise royal authority all played important roles across the centuries in question. For weddings where the bride was from another realm, Scotland's place (desired or realised) on a wider European political stage was also a factor in the choice or use of space. In some cases, these choices were dictated by others, which could require careful management in the earlier centuries covered here to avoid space being used to reinforce perceived superiority. Yet, over the period, as the ease of travel increased and celebratory entries of foreign monarchs to cities increased, the connotations of royals travelling beyond their realms changed quite significantly. The sites used in 1543 – Holyrood Abbey with a procession from Falkland for the funeral and the Chapel Royal at Stirling Castle for the coronation – were situated in two locations that gained importance as royal centres during the fifteenth and sixteenth centuries. The abbey, and the palace constructed by James IV and James V, at Holyrood had witnessed a notable number of royal ceremonies from the fourteenth century onwards hosting one coronation, two funerals of monarchs and one consort's funeral, all consort coronations since 1449, three out of five royal weddings in the same period and it was the concluding point for several royal entries and processions. For James V, while not emerging as a sole ceremonial centre, the abbey hosted two important ceremonies that were inextricably linked with the cycle of death and succession: the funeral of his first wife, Madeleine, with whom

---

[19] In England coronations and, by the late thirteenth century, funerals primarily – although, not exclusively – occurred at Westminster Abbey, as did many royal weddings and consort coronations; whereas, France favoured one site for coronation – the cathedral at Reims – and another for funerals – the abbey at Saint-Denis.

[20] Erich Hoffman, 'Coronation Ordines in Medieval Scandinavia', in Bak (ed.), *Coronations*, 125–43 at 130–2, 137–9. See also John Ljungkvist and Joakim Kjellberg, 'Monuments and History-making – the Creation and Destruction of Gamla Uppsala Monuments in the Medieval Period' and Dean, 'Where to Make the King (or Queen)', in O'Grady and Oram (eds), *Royal and Lordly Inauguration and Assembly Places*, 48–73, 202–25.

he may have shared a double tomb, and the coronation of his second wife, Marie, for which he conspicuously remodelled the regalia. Unlike William I's deviation from the dynastic Canmore burial site at Dunfermline or James I and Joan's burial at the Charterhouse at Perth, James V did not select a personal foundation. However, the decision – that led to a procession from Falkland Palace in Fife – did offer the possibility of being temporarily housed with his ancestors and St Margaret at Dunfermline for a vigil on the journey. More importantly, it facilitated a public procession in the urban space of Edinburgh – centred on what is now the Royal Mile – that had been used in processions marking all the key moments since the end of his minority and had rapidly claimed prominence as the major processional space in Scotland.

From 1214 to 1543, processions – whether connecting ritual locations or entering specific spaces at critical junctures – were frequently embraced as integral aspects of the use of space in Scottish rituals, particularly due to the opportunities for being seen. In many cases, particularly at the death or marriage of a monarch, these processional elements covered significant distances via prominent locations within (and beyond) the kingdom. This was especially the case in earlier centuries – such as the funeral processions of William I, Robert I and Robert II, or the journeys of Alexander II and Alexander III to York for their marriages. In comparison, James V's funeral procession travelled a shorter distance from Falkland to Holyrood. It would be tempting to associate this apparent change with a centralising of governance and associated reduction in the peripatetic nature of Scottish kingship, but this would be too simplistic. James V also travelled with an entourage to France to marry his first wife, Madeleine, and chose to welcome his second wife, Marie, at St Andrews – rather than the more commonly used Leith – to provide an extended progress through several other burghs before reaching Edinburgh. Even James III, a king accused of being too sedentary, recognised the potential of processional movement at key transitional moments when he travelled as far north as Inverness with his new wife, Margaret of Denmark, following their marriage in 1469. Yet, during the fifteenth century, there was an undeniable increase in the use of urban spaces for royal ceremonial, particularly processions. While the funeral processions of William I and Robert I travelled large distances, evidence suggests that their journeys were predominantly marked by stops at pertinent ecclesiastic sites or monastic houses. Indeed, when William's funeral procession and Alexander II's inauguration entourage converged at Perth, this ritual meeting occurred quite specifically in the liminal space outside the burgh. James II has been identified as an urban king, particularly in his location choices for ceremonies, but arguably this begins with the entry of James I and Joan Beaufort to Edinburgh in 1424 and their subsequent use of urban environments.[21] Such urban locations offered captive audiences, confined spaces that could be lavishly decorated and in which attendance could be controlled, while also generating place associa-

---

[21] Ditchburn, 'Rituals, Space and the Marriage of James II', 192–3.

tions that could be harnessed and the potential to tap into merchant wealth in supporting crown demonstrations of authority. With the increased role of burgh representatives in parliament from the reign of Robert I onwards, it is important to recognise that the royal use of urban spaces was not driven by the crown alone but also by a growing need to engage in a dialogue with the urban elite.

Stirling had grown in significance ceremonially from the fifteenth century also, but most particularly following the division of the royal household between Queen Margaret and James III, with the former taking up residence at Stirling Castle with her heirs and the latter in Edinburgh, and their decision to request burial at Cambuskenneth Abbey. Yet, the choice of the Chapel Royal at Stirling Castle for the coronations of 1513 and 1543 marked one of two major spatial shifts that had the potential to significantly alter the coronation ceremony. The choice of location and use of space in royal ceremonies were interwoven with issues of access to the monarch at critical junctures. The Chapel Royal was a notably smaller space than an abbey church, and Stirling Castle was an identifiably royal and defensive space that restricted access to the ceremony in significant ways when compared to inaugurations and coronations at Scone. From at least the thirteenth century onwards, Scone had offered a unique combination of secular and ecclesiastical spaces for the making of Scottish monarchs that featured an outdoor and accessible enthronement with a widely viewed homage exchange ritual and the recitation of the genealogy at its heart. Robert II's use of secular and ecclesiastic spaces at Scone in 1371 – with the re-emphasis on the outdoor enthronement situated on the Moot Hill – sought to capitalise on the value of the open-air homage exchange to dampen any doubts of his right to rise from the ranks of the nobility to rule. In comparison, the ability to abandon this setting during the fifteenth and sixteenth centuries suggests that the increased stability of the Stewart dynasty and its succession likely had a part to play in the acceptance of variable locations with more restricted access. The response of Robert III's nobles, according to Bower, to the *charivari* incident – where some commoners sought reparations from the king – indicates that there were some members of the elite who might have encouraged restricted access to the king. However, the initial departure from Scone in the fifteenth century – when coronations occurred entirely within ecclesiastical spaces in 1437 and 1460 – resulted in the increased prominence of publicly accessible processional elements. There is circumstantial evidence of a procession between Cambuskenneth Abbey and Stirling Castle in 1513, but Mary was moved to Stirling Castle accompanied by an armed force from Linlithgow Palace in August 1543, a month before the coronation, so the sixteenth-century evidence for this use of celebratory coronation processions is less convincing.[22] The young age of both James V and Mary, combined with internal power struggles and ongoing tensions with England, seem likely

[22] *TA*, VIII, 224.

to have influenced the choice of this royal space within a castle, but it also speaks to longer term developments in the kingdom.

The dominance of Scone, and its outdoor enthronement site, for both accession ceremonies and meetings of parliament had waned significantly, except where the legitimacy of this traditional space was sought in 1488. However, the distinctly Scottish aspects of the coronation that developed there – such as the recitation of the genealogy and the reciprocal oaths or homage between the enthroned king and the political community – were retained as features that the seventeenth-century herald promoted in his order of ceremony to Charles I in 1633. Consequently, there was still significant potency to ritual aspects that developed and were associated with this place during the fifteenth, sixteenth and even seventeenth centuries. In the same period that Scone's dominance waned, the parliament – wherever it might be physically located – emerged as an important space in which to enthrone and acclaim the young king, as well as becoming increasingly associated with the coronations, or at the very least oath-taking associated with her dower lands, of Scotland's queens consort. This was not directly associated with the departure from Scone, as it had often hosted parliaments and gathering of the three estates. From 1331 – when David II's coronation took place amidst a session of the parliament, and both the king and queen were provided with robes suited for attending parliament – the accession of the Scottish monarch, and his union with his wife, had increasingly been directly or indirectly associated with a meeting of the three estates. However, both the departure from Scone and the frequent accessions of minors from the fifteenth century onwards certainly further entrenched the use of parliament meetings, in various locations, as a place for enthronement and acclamation. This shift also suggests that the physical location of the coronation was less important as the centuries passed, but that the consensual acceptance of the king – so prominently developed at Scone – was transferred into the places that parliament inhabited as time passed.

One of the challenges to fully appreciating the use of space in Scottish ceremonies is linked to the loss or significant alteration of much of the built environment. While there is fascinating work ongoing to reimagine these physical locations, where possible, the fragmented documentary evidence is essential to researching the possible use and decorations of these spaces.[23] This is often also the case with ritual objects and material display. While there are key surviving regalia items, it is important to remember that these were a product of the last decades of the period explored here. An inventory of the jewels and clothing of James V was recorded in November 1542, which provides a list of the regalia that was available for Mary's coronation: a crown

---

[23] Oliver J. T. O'Grady, 'Tracing the Medieval Royal Centre at Scone', *Medieval Archaeology*, 52 (2008), 376–8; O'Grady, 'Accumulating Kingship', 139–44; Open Virtual Worlds, 'Scone Abbey – 1390', *Open Virtual Worlds 3D Reconstructions*, https://blogs.cs.st-andrews.ac.uk/openvirtualworlds/reconstructions/ scone-abbey/. Date accessed: 29 September 2020; Penman and Utsi, *In Search of the Scottish Royal Mausoleum*.

with precious stones and oriental pearls, a sceptre with 'ane greit barrell', two swords of honour with belts that required some work, an ermine lined 'rob royall' of purple velvet and a matching kirtill, a grey velvet papal hat set with oriental pearls, various items associated with royal heraldic orders of other realms, as well as a bejewelled crown and sceptre, made with a white hand, for the queen consort.[24] While this regalia was extensively redesigned by James V, it would appear that the crown was remodelled from its earlier counterpart rather than made anew. Evidence for a new royal robe being made for the king was only found in James's case; previously, where information survives, the costs were for mending this garment indicating its reuse. The consort regalia appears to have been made for each queen, at least in the sixteenth century, as financial records indicate that both Margaret Tudor and Marie de Guise had their own regalia made so these jewels were perhaps more directly associated with an individual queen than the monarch's regalia. Understanding the design of the Scottish regalia prior to this point has, as discussed earlier, various challenges associated with it, but there are points where its apparent absence from ceremonies is particularly intriguing: neither James II nor James IV appear to have worn the crown during the coronation of their queens. In Young's account, the bare head of the king is associated with a reverence for the queen and his lords in the pre-marital exchange of reverence or oaths between king and subject. This suggests that the absence of objects could be used to make as powerful or notable statements as their presence in royal ceremonies.

Another ceremony where the regalia is noticeably absent in the available source material is the funeral, until that of James V in 1543 where mock regalia was painted for an effigy. The demonstrations of royal grandeur and pomp undertaken for the funeral of Robert I, and subsequent funerals, would imply that these status symbols were deployed in some way. However, the absence of any costs for regalia or descriptions of their usage where records remain would suggest that the coronation regalia was displayed nearby, perhaps atop a coffin or other prominent place, but that regalia was not buried with the king. The value of the regalia in representations of royal authority was understood by kings and minority guardians alike: the prominence of these items in rituals involving minor monarchs, whether in parliament or processions through major burghs, reflected a commonly held belief in their value as items representative of royal power. Yet it is telling that the most intensive work on the production and elaboration of the regalia occurred in conjunction with international marriages.

Many of the highest expenditures on material display occurred in the ceremonies where foreign audiences were likely to attend, particularly for royal marriages to foreign queens including David and Joan Plantagenet, James

---

[24] 'Ane Inventur of the kingis graces abilyementis beand in his graces wardrop in Edinburgh givinup be Johne Tennand the xxviii day of November in the yeir of god J^{m}v^c fourty twa yeiris': *A collection of inventories*, 76.

IV and Margaret Tudor, and James V and Madeleine. This speaks to the employment of an economy of scale to counteract the relative poverty of the Scottish monarchy, but to take this on too readily would be to court oversimplification. In 1329, with no known invited foreign audience, the scale and expense recorded in the preparation and execution of Robert I's funeral appears remarkable, and comparable with some of his far wealthier contemporaries. However, the dearth of financial materials for other funerals with extended processions, such as that for William I in 1214 and Robert II in 1390, make it impossible to state that expenses in 1329 were 'remarkable' in the context of comparative funerals of the thirteenth and fourteenth centuries. Such elaborations around death and burial may have been more of the norm when emphasis was laid more heavily on securing dynastic succession. One thing that these relatively 'native' ceremonies and the 'foreign audience events' had in common was the control or prior investment of an adult monarch. With the complexities of minorities and contested accessions providing the context for many Scottish funerals, inaugurations and coronations in this period, marriage and its interrelated ceremonial often provided one of the first occasions for Scottish monarchs, particularly of the fifteenth and sixteenth centuries, to have control and thus to demonstrate their independent royal authority. Ceremonial development certainly occurred in periods with no adult monarch directing the ceremonies of death and succession, but there were obstacles for those who undertook the ceremonial displays on behalf of the monarch, or for a monarch whose financial situation was unstable. This economy of scale was often enforced by contingent circumstances.

There is no surviving information about the wider response to enclosing Mary's coronation, or that of her father before her, within the walls of Stirling Castle. One of the most fulsome reports of a public response was that at the time of Robert III's coronation, but such direct interaction with everyday people's experiences of or responses to the ceremonies of death and succession are rare. There are often generic statements about the shared great joy of cheering crowds and occasional references to general celebration, such as the lighting of fires and distribution of food or drink at the birth of a royal child. Even positing who made up the audience of ceremonies is difficult as Scottish and foreign commentators alike tend to present the crowds in attendance as rather amorphous group, with occasional comments about the ordering of audiences by social strata. Indeed, it is often tricky to ascertain the roles of the participants of ritual, let alone the audiences. Those offering the most insight into the participants in Scottish ceremonies are commonly foreign visitors for weddings, consort coronations and associated celebrations in the fifteenth and early sixteenth centuries. In Mary's case, it is letters to and between diplomatic figures in 1543 that offer the most information about the participants and their roles in the coronation.[25] Throughout the period,

---

[25] 'Parr to Suffolk, 13 Sept 1543', no. 30; Sadler, *Letters and Negotiations*, 359–67.

however, two groups of people retain central importance: leading secular figures and prominent members of the ecclesiastical estate.

Even prior to the introduction of unction for Scottish kings, there had been an ecclesiastical presence in all the main ceremony types considered in this study: the sacramental nature of funerary rights and marriage ceremonies guaranteed their involvement in these increasingly church-bound rites, while their education combined with their status likely put them at the forefront of techniques associated with body preservation and embalming. The Bishop, or Archbishop from 1472, of St Andrews was a prominent feature in Scottish ceremonies of death and succession – he officiated at coronations in both 1214 and 1543, but not at each one between.[26] As the Bull of 1329 indicated, other bishops could stand in for him as officiant in anointing the king, and there were several examples where this was the case, usually when the bishop of St Andrews was not resident in the realm or where various ecclesiastics were involved. The specific roles and ritual activities of the bishops – beyond anointing, leading the Mass and providing sermons – in royal ceremonies of death and succession are often obscured by the lack of liturgical orders of ceremony. Yet, individual churchmen had both the ability and desire to affect the course of ceremonial and ideological development. This was witnessed through figures including the abbot of Dunfermline in the thirteenth century, Robert Wishart, bishop of Glasgow, in the fourteenth century, the canons of Holyrood in the fifteenth century, and influential churchmen in the minorities of the fifteenth and sixteenth centuries. The increasing 'liturgification' of Scottish ceremonies, particularly inauguration and coronation, advanced by churchmen and kings was tempered by the secular roots of many aspects of these ceremonies, such as acts of homage and fealty, and the prominent secular actors involved, including nobility, heralds, the poet and household officers.

In 1543, the leading nobles taking prominent roles, carrying items of the regalia in the coronation procession within the Chapel Royal, were the earls of Arran (also the governor), Lennox and Argyll. This presents a significant departure from the named earls who dominated ceremonial roles in the rituals of the thirteenth and fourteenth centuries, but also mirrors the rise and fall, erasure and emergence, of baronial families across the centuries.[27] Of the seven earls often associated with early inaugurations and the 'selection' of the king, the earls of Fife and Strathearn were most prominent. Indeed, the earl of Fife, or a representative, was deemed so essential that, on at least one occasion, a female representative of the house was sought to perform the ritual enthronement. However, the destruction of the Albany Stewarts with the crown's assumption of that forfeited earldom after 1425 left a significant ceremonial void. By the sixteenth century, as Arran, Argyll and Lennox's

[26] Seven out of twelve inaugurations/coronations saw the bishop or archbishop of St Andrews as the officiant (solely or with others), see Appendix II.
[27] See Appendix II.

central participation in Mary's coronation indicate, this had – in part – been filled by the new ranks of leading earls, particularly those who were closely related to the monarch, but their roles in the ceremony were different. These figures were located at the centre of processions carrying items from the regalia, but the role of enthroning the monarch and bestowing the royal mantle had shifted. The surviving evidence – in the seventeenth-century heraldic texts that claim fifteenth-century origins – suggests that the heraldic and household officers had prominent roles in supporting bishops and in proclaiming the king's lineage; a task previously undertaken by the poet in Gaelic. However, the period where such changes must have taken place, are those about which there is the least certainty. Some of these changes could sensibly date to the ceremonial gap left by the earl of Fife, but the nature of the surviving materials makes this hard to confirm so looking wider to other ceremonies within the cycle is essential.

The introduction of the heraldic funeral – such as those witnessed for James V and the people that he buried in the sixteenth century – cannot be pinpointed exactly for Scotland. Yet, there were elements witnessed as early as 1329 and, by the funerals of James II and Mary of Guelders in the 1460s, heraldic culture was permeating many aspects of funerary practices. Moreover, the increasing use of heraldic messengers emblazoned with the Scottish royal arms followed a similar trajectory, undergoing a veritable explosion in the fifteenth century and accompanied by a corresponding rise in the use of livery and distinctive official clothing, embellished and elaborated with the extensive use of rich fabrics, colours and cloths of gold across the later fifteenth and sixteenth centuries. Underlying the ceremonial developments of this later era were cultural movements amongst the elites and lower laity, particularly lairds and wealthier merchant classes, radiating from the acculturation of humanist and renaissance ideals.[28] This generated a body of non-religious men with the skills for government or household offices, which had usually been the reserve of clerics, who were far more reliant upon the crown for their position as they rose through the ranks as *noblesse de robe*. In royal ceremony, and particularly so in processional components, this was mirrored by an increasing focus upon rank and order notably emerging in the records of foreign observers of Scottish weddings and consort coronations, as an awareness of office, civic duty and honour grew. During the precarious accessions of ever younger minors, there was a notable re-emphasis on the roles of higher-ranking nobles – often involving the regalia – in the high-profile ceremonies. If the seventeenth-century heraldic document reflects a reality when the royal household and heraldic officials had been accelerated into the forefront of ceremony, there was arguably a reactionary reclaiming of deeply traditional rights of the Scottish earls by the higher nobility, which focused on proximity to the monarch and the symbols of gravitas and royal power, within royal ceremony.

---

[28] For example, see Mason, 'Regnum et Imperium', 104–38; ibid., 'Laicisation and Law', 1–25.

CONCLUSION

The fifteenth and sixteenth centuries also witnessed the increasing prominence of queens consort in ritual activity associated with the cycle of succession as participants in the ritual actions and/or as an orchestrator of ceremonial occasions. Across the fourteenth and fifteenth centuries the lack of hard evidence confirming that the queens of Scotland were anointed as consort seems unusual, as it would perhaps be presumed that anointing the future mother of royal heirs might be a top priority. However, in fifteenth-century France, there are examples illustrating that a queen could still function as a consort without undergoing a coronation.[29] The ceremonial of queenship in Scotland appears to have been under negotiation; much like, one might argue, the position of the queen herself in the political and royal sphere of influence. It was only during the sixteenth century, from Margaret Tudor onwards, that anointing was clearly described for a queen. This was accompanied by the investiture of the sceptre by the king: this reflected fairly common understanding that a queen's power emanated from the king via her marriage, but the investiture does appear to be a uniquely Scottish ritual action. Considering the concurrent references to the queen undergoing a ritual in parliament – potentially emerging from James I's insistence on oaths being given to Joan after their marriage – confirming her dower portion and relationship with the realm, this ritual investiture may have been a means of reasserting the monarch's role in her position. It is not clear what direct role these queens played in the coronation rituals of their children. From the thirteenth and fourteenth centuries, queens, such as Marie de Coucy and Queen Annabella, took an active role in organising ceremonies for their heirs, and by the later period – particularly in the cases of Joan, Mary of Guelders and Marie de Guise – the queen consort was notably influential in marking the final farewell to her husband and in orchestrating the inaugural rites of her children, either in collaboration or contest with her male counterparts at the forefront of the minority government.

One significant conclusion to draw through these themes relates to the presumed negative impact of minorities and absentee kingship over this long period. The extent to which widowed queens and leading members of the political community have been shown to exploit ceremonial practices firmly rebuts the suggestion that Scottish rituals of kingship stagnated during periods of minority rule. It is true that some ceremonial opportunities were missed during minorities, but adult kings might equally struggle to make the ritual statements expected of them, particularly those without heirs or who seized the throne with questionable legitimacy. While challenges existed in performing power, adult monarchs and minority leaders alike employed ritual as visible manifestations of legitimate authority performed in public and semi-public spaces, even if those efforts were not always successful. That the ceremonial cycle of death and succession was not only used but developed in the absence of adult rulers underscores the integral role of the Scottish political community to its perpetuation. This analysis confirms and extends

---

[29] McCartney, 'Queenship in Late Medieval France', 182–3.

recent conclusions that suggestions of a political elite in opposition to or competition with the monarch can be misleading and unhelpful, for evidence largely points to a shared set of goals, if not methods, in terms of keeping the crown functioning and maintaining the royal dignity. It is important to stress that this ritual dialogue did not lack confrontational posturing. However, as Brégiant suggests, the monarch did not have 'the monopoly over royal ideas, myths and messages', and such examples demonstrate how the renegotiation of power through ritual was part of an ongoing dialogue.[30]

Just as Scotland's parliament has now been proven different rather than inferior to that in England, another important conclusion to draw is that Scottish ceremony was unique not inferior or immature in relation to comparable kingdoms.[31] Rituals reflect polities and the influences that come to bear upon them. There were discernible incidents of Scottish kings drawing on English examples or acting in direct competition with English monarchs. Yet, Scotland was a melting pot in which external ideas and internal traditions intermingled. Acquisitive borrowing was folded into the existing ceremonial cycle as it was critical not to create something that was entirely alien to that which had come before. Comparisons with other countries are certainly valid. Indeed, exploring more direct comparisons with other countries deemed 'periphery' is a direction that should be pursued. Yet, the rituals of Scottish kingship were different from those of their European counterparts because they reflected the inner workings and political context that produced them. Shaw's suggestion that Scottish ceremony was 'immature' in a comparison with England's elaborate coronation misses this vital point.[32] Scotland's coronation did not look like those performed elsewhere, but this was not a limitation, nor an indication of its immaturity, but rather evidence that Scottish kingship developed along a different trajectory.

Unction was just one element of the Christianisation in Scotland's kingship rituals. The increased inclusion of prayers, sermons and clerics in ceremonies previously deemed secular, the prominence of saints and Christo-centric feast day associations, the use of relics and papal gifts, the importance of candles and vigils in commemorating the dead, and the exploitation of separate heart burial, all speak to the adoption of 'Christianised norms of the West'. Whether Scottish kings fully embraced the idea of their own divine right, or the sacral nature of their kingship, is a debate that this book navigates with much caution. The reason for this is twofold: this subject is one that arguably requires a study of its own, but also because there are too many gaps in the evidence of ritual to come to a definitive conclusion. There are certainly prominent examples where Scottish kings pressed their personal connection to the divine in ceremonies that go beyond the conventional piety of the age. Yet, despite accepting the honour of unction with holy oil, no elaborate

---

[30] Brégiant, *Vox Regis*, 5.
[31] For example: Brown and Tanner (eds), *Parliament and Politics in Scotland, 1235–1560*; Tanner, *Medieval Scottish Parliament*.
[32] Shaw, 'Scotland's Place in Britain's Coronation Tradition', 47.

myth survives about the Scottish holy oil of coronation as in other European countries, despite there being a dynastic saint in Scotland from whose legend or miracles this could have been drawn. The lack of extant liturgical texts means that the only orders of ceremony for inaugural events and funerals emerge from secular pens, and details of unction and prayers that underpin sacral kingship as explored by Dale for England, France and the Empire do not survive.[33] The records that do survive contain oaths underlining the reciprocal nature of the monarch's relationship with the estates. Funerals were increasingly dominated by heraldic secular features and the continuity of acclamation underscores the role of the people as much as God. Although it is important to note that the chronicle descriptions of inaugurations and coronations offer some balance to this, the prominence of the secular is also found in the words of clerical authors. Ultimately, the hybrid blending of secular and liturgical ritual elements in the Scottish ceremonial cycle of death and succession reveals the complexities of navigating around the idea of divine kingship in a country where the political community retained the right to grant power to, or at least acclaim, the monarch.

The use of an effigy invested with the royal dignity that lives on while the mortal body died in 1543 suggests engagement with the concept of the king's two bodies in a very tangible representational sense in the sixteenth century. However, effigy use and the physical representation of two bodies was not the only way that ritual can inform us about the separation of the person of the king from the perpetuation of the royal dignity. The continuation and development of the ritual cycle itself, with or without adult monarchs, provides unique evidence for the investment by king and community alike in the concept of the crown or royal dignity that transcended the individuals who became king. In exploring this cycle, this study of ceremony offers a new platform for exploring not only Scottish kingship but also the political, social and cultural milieu in which it evolved.

---

[33] Dale, *Inaugurations and Liturgical Kingship*.

Timeline of Key Events

1165	(9 December) Funeral of Mael Coluim IV
	(24 December) Inauguration of William I
1174	(July) William I captured by Henry II of England at Alnwick
	(December) William I signed the Treaty of Falaise, recognising English overlordship
1176	(30 July) Papal bull *Super anxietatibus*
1186	(5 September) William married Ermengarde de Beaumont at Woodstock Palace
1189	Death of Henry II. Accession of Richard I of England
	(5 December) Quitclaim of Canterbury signed and nullified the Treaty of Falaise
1189x1192	Papal Bull *Cum universi* (also known as 'special daughter' status)
1194	William I carried one of three swords in an English ceremony of thanksgiving at Winchester, akin to a coronation, to celebrate the return of Richard I
1195	William I attempted to have his eldest daughter, Margaret, and husband, Otto of Brunswick, recognised as heirs to the throne (unsuccessfully)
1198	(August) Birth of William's son, Alexander
1199	Death of Richard I. Accession of John of England
1201	(October) Scottish nobles swore allegiance to William's son, Alexander, at Musselburgh
1209	William I capitulated to John at Norham following suspicions of Scottish overtures for alliance with Philip II of France (r.1180–1223). William's daughters taken as hostages to be married off by John as a term of the Treaty of Norham
1211–12	Re-emergence of MacWilliam threat with arrival of Guthred, son of Donald MacWilliam, from Ireland
1212	Negotiations for marriage between Alexander, son of William, and daughter of John, Joanna. Alexander travelled to London to be knighted by John
1214	(4 December) Death of William I at Stirling
	(5 December) Inauguration of Alexander II at Scone
	(10 December) Funeral of William I at Arbroath Abbey
1215	Opening of the Fourth Lateran Council

TIMELINE OF KEY EVENTS

1215–17	Alexander II involved in northern rising against John. Received homage from northern elites and travelled to Dover to meet the French
1216	Death of John. Accession of Henry III of England
1217	Papal interdict against rebels, including Alexander II
1218	Papal interdict against Alexander raised and 'special daughter' status reconfirmed
1220	Marriage negotiations at York to secure Anglo-Scottish royal marriage. Alexander requests a crowning ceremony from the papal legate in Scotland
1221	(June) Marriage of Alexander II to Joanna, daughter of John, at York
1229–30	Alexander II ended MacWilliam threat by killing remaining family members
1238	Joanna, wife of Alexander II, died in England
1239	(May) Alexander II married Marie de Coucy, daughter of Enquerraud or Ingram de Coucy, at Roxburgh
1241	(September) Birth of Alexander II and Marie's son, Alexander
1244	Alexander suspected of seeking alliance with Louis IX of France (r.1226–1270). Betrothal secured between Alexander II's son and daughter of Henry III, Margaret, to resolve rising tensions between England and Scotland
1245	Alexander II and Robert de Kenleith, abbot of Dunfermline, pursued canonisation of Margaret, wife of Mael Coluim III
1247	Håkon IV, king of Norway, received papal permission for unction
1249	(June–July) Alexander II led an expedition to Lorn (8 July) Death of Alexander II on the island of Kerrara (13 July) Inauguration of Alexander III at Scone (date unknown, but probably late July) Alexander II buried at Melrose Abbey
1250	Canonisation of St Margaret and translation of her remains within Dunfermline Abbey
1251	Request for unction and coronation of the kings of Scots refused by the pope (25 December) Alexander III married to Margaret Plantagenet at York
1256	Alexander III and Margaret, queen of Scots, travel to Woodstock and London on a progress to the court of Henry III
1261	Birth of Alexander III and Margaret's first child, Margaret, in England. Scottish envoy at the Norwegian court of Håkon IV, negotiating control of Hebridean islands, witnessed the wedding and coronation of Håkon's son, Magnus
1263	Battle of Largs between king of Scots and king of Norway. Håkon IV died in Orkney when returning from the campaign

TIMELINE OF KEY EVENTS

1264	(January) Birth of Alexander III and Margaret's son, Alexander, in Scotland
	(summer) King Magnus of Man, former liege of Håkon IV, submitted to Alexander III. The Isle of Man is annexed following Magnus's death
1266	(July) Treaty of Perth ended confrontations between Scottish king and Magnus VI, king of Norway, and Scots received control of the western isles
1272	(March) Birth of Alexander III and Margaret's second son, David
	(November) Death of Henry III and accession of Edward I of England
1274	(August) Alexander III attended the coronation of Edward I at Westminster
1275	(February) Death of Queen Margaret. Alexander III's son, Alexander, granted the lordship of Man as part of a royal appanage
1282	(November) Young Alexander married Marguerite or Margaret of Flanders, daughter of the count of Flanders, at Roxburgh
1281	(summer) Marriage of Alexander III's daughter, Margaret, to Eric II, king of Norway. Death of Alexander III's younger son, David
1283	(March–April) Death of Alexander III's daughter, queen of Norway, possibly in childbirth with her first daughter, Margaret (later known as Maid of Norway)
1284	Death of Alexander III's eldest son, Alexander. Alexander III sought recognition of his granddaughter, Margaret Maid of Norway, as heir to the Scottish throne, and many nobles and clerics swore oaths of allegiance to her
1285	Alexander III married Yolande of Dreux at Jedburgh Abbey
1286	(19 March) Death of Alexander III near Kinghorn
	(29 March) Funeral at Dunfermline. Envoys are sent to Edward I
	(April) Parliament or assembly at Scone elected six guardians of the kingdom
1289	Edward I sought papal dispensation for a marriage between his infant son, Edward, and Margaret Maid of Norway
1290	(18 July) Treaty of Birgham agreed the Anglo-Scot marriage
	(September) Death of Margaret Maid of Norway near Orkney. She was returned to Norway and buried at Christ Church in Bergen
1290x1291	The Appeal of the Seven Earls presented to Edward I as one of several appeals by Robert Bruce the competitor
1291	(April–May) Edward I received submissions various claimants to Scottish throne. Robert Bruce the competitor, grandfather of Robert I, and John Balliol identified as main claimants

TIMELINE OF KEY EVENTS

1291–92	Great Cause: process of selecting a Scottish heir, managed by Edward I at Berwick
1292	(19 November) Symbolic breaking of the seal of the guardians
	(20 November) John Balliol undertook oath-giving ceremonies at Norham
	(30 November) Inauguration of John Balliol at Scone
	(December) John Balliol gave oaths of homage to Edward I at Newcastle
1294	Edward I demanded service of Scots against Philip IV of France (r.1285–1314), but Scots sought papal permission to remove this obligation to Edward I
1295	John Balliol and the guardians sought an alliance with France
1296	(30 March) Edward I sacked Berwick
	(27 April) English victory over the Scots at the Battle of Dunbar
	(June) John Balliol removed from the throne of Scotland. The regalia, stone of Scone and Holy Rood of St Margaret are confiscated by the English
	(August) Leading Scots submitted to Edward at Berwick
1297	Uprising against English rule in the north and southwest, culminating in the Battle of Stirling Bridge (September)
1297–1328	First War of Independence in Scotland (civil war and war with England)
1301	Baldred Bisset's pleading presented to the pope in response to Edward I's claims of sovereignty over Scotland
1302	Robert Bruce married to Elizabeth de Burgh, daughter of lord of Ulster
1306	(10 February) Robert Bruce murdered John Comyn at Greyfriars in Dumfries
	(25–27 March) Inauguration of Robert Bruce as Robert I at Scone
	(June) English victory over Robert I and his supporters at the Battle of Methven. Robert fled west. Elizabeth, his wife, and other supporters captured on their flight north; many remain in captivity for several years
1307	Edward I died on a journey to Scotland. Edward II acceded as king of England
1309	Declaration of the Clergy of Scotland in support of Robert I
1314	(June) Battle of Bannockburn: victory for Robert I over the forces of Edward II, which led to the release of prisoners including Robert's wife, Elizabeth
	(November) Nobles who had not come into Robert's peace were forfeited at a parliament at Cambuskenneth
	(Late in the year) John Balliol died in France
1315	(April) Robert I entailed throne to his brother, Edward Bruce, who subsequently led Bruce attacks in Ireland. Edward was crowned high king of Ireland

TIMELINE OF KEY EVENTS

1316	Birth of Robert Stewart, son of Walter Stewart and Robert I's daughter, Marjory
1318	(April) Siege of Berwick: significant victory for Robert I
	(June) Robert I excommunicated; Scotland placed under interdict
	(5 July) Consecration of St Andrews Cathedral
	(October) Edward Bruce died at the Battle of Faughart or Fochart
	(December) Crown entailed to Robert Stewart, Robert I's grandson, in parliament
1318–20	Soules conspiracy against Robert I
1320	(6 April) Declaration of Arbroath
1324	(March) Birth of Robert I and Elizabeth de Burgh's sons, David and John (although, it is not clear how long John lived)
1326	(July) Parliamentary legislation secured succession for Robert's son, David II, identified guardians for a minority and reconfirmed Robert Stewart's position as heir apparent after sons of Robert I
1327	Deposition of Edward II by his queen, Isabella of France, in the name of their son, Edward III. Edward II was subsequently murdered
1328	(March) Treaty of Edinburgh-Northampton ended the First War of Independence; secured English recognition of Robert's kingship and an Anglo-Scottish marriage union
	(July) Marriage of David Bruce and Joan, sister of Edward III, at Berwick
1329	(7 June) Robert I died at Cardross
	(13 June) Papal bull permitted unction and coronation for kings of Scots
	(Later in June) Robert I buried at Dunfermline Abbey
1330	Sir James Douglas took Robert I's heart on crusade but died in Spain in August
1331	(August) Retrospective permission for separate heart burial of Robert I received
	(September) Summons sent out for a coronation of David II and parliament
	(24 November) David II was crowned and anointed at Scone
1332	(July) Death of Thomas Randolph, earl of Moray and guardian
	(6 August) Edward Balliol, son of John Balliol, arrived in Scotland
	(11 August) Battle of Dupplin Moor: Balliol victory over Bruce forces
	(24 September) Edward Balliol enthroned and crowned at Scone
1332–57	Second Scottish War of Independence
1333	Siege of Berwick and Scottish defeat at the Battle of Halidon Hill

TIMELINE OF KEY EVENTS

1334	(May) David II and Joan sent to France for safety
	(June) Edward Balliol performed homage to Edward III at York
1335–36	Campaigns of Edward III in Scotland to support Edward Balliol, including capture of Perth and attacks on the northeast
1338	Robert Stewart named sole guardian
1339	Robert Stewart recaptured Perth for Bruce cause
1341	(April) William Douglas recaptured Edinburgh for David II
	(June) David II and Joan returned from France
1346	(17 October) Battle of Neville's Cross: English victory and capture of David II
1347	Robert Stewart renamed guardian in David's absence
1351–52	Parliament attempted to negotiate release of David II, but David's proposals around succession were rejected
1355	French forces arrived in Scotland. Franco-Scottish army recaptured Berwick
1356	Edward Balliol ceded his right to the Scottish throne to Edward III
1357	Treaty of Berwick confirmed the release of David II
1362	Death of David II's queen, Joan; no issue from the marriage
1363	(Spring) David II married his mistress, Margaret Logie (née Drummond)
	(May) David II forced submission of Robert Stewart and others after a rebellion
1366–67	David II supported marriage between John Stewart of Kyle, Robert Stewart's eldest son, and Annabella Drummond, Margaret Logie's niece
1368	David II granted John Stewart the earldom of Carrick, part of the Bruce's dynastic patrimony, indicating favour for John as his heir
1371	(February) Death of David II at Edinburgh (buried at Holyrood Abbey, date unknown)
	(March) Coronation of Robert II at Scone following confrontation at Linlithgow
1372	Robert II secured a licence for English workmen to complete David II's tomb
1373	(April) Parliamentary confirmation of succession of Robert II's sons from his first marriage, and coronation of Robert II's second wife, Euphemia, at Scone
1377	Work started on tomb of Robert II at Scone
1378	(October) Birth of John, earl of Carrick, and Annabella's first son, David
1384	John, earl of Carrick, made lieutenant of the realm in parliament
1385	Renewed hostility with England; French forces brought to Scotland
1388	(August) Scottish incursions into England ended in victory for Scots at the Battle of Otterburn, but also the death of James, earl of Douglas

TIMELINE OF KEY EVENTS

	(December) Carrick forced to resign lieutenancy to his younger brother, Robert, earl of Fife
1390	(April) Death of Robert II
	Confirmation of Fife's lieutenancy
	(August) Funeral of Robert II and coronation of Robert III (formerly John, earl of Carrick) and his wife, Annabella
1393	Removal of Fife from the role of lieutenant
1394	Birth of James Stewart, second son of Robert III and Annabella
1396	Battle of the North Inch (a performance clan fight orchestrated by the king)
1398	David, son of Robert III, knighted. David and Robert, earl of Fife, raised to dukedoms, respectively of Rothesay and Albany, at Scone
1399	David, duke of Rothesay, made lieutenant at parliament in Perth
1401	Death of Annabella, queen of Scots
1402	Imprisonment and death (murder) of David, duke of Rothesay
1406	(March) Robert III sent his younger son, James, to France for protection but James was captured and taken to England as a prisoner
	(April) Robert III died and was buried at Paisley Abbey. Robert, duke of Albany, was proclaimed governor of the realm in a General Council meeting at Perth
1420	Robert, duke of Albany, died and his son, Murdoch, inherited the titles of earl of Fife and duke of Albany, and the role of governor
	James I campaigned in France with Henry V against Franco-Scottish forces
1421	James I took part in the coronation of Katherine of Valois, queen of Henry V
1422	James I witnessed the funeral of Henry V in England
1424	(February) James I married Joan Beaufort in London; arranged as part of the treaty around his release
	(March) Treaty sealed at Durham finalised James I's release
	(April) Murdoch surrendered seals of office to James I at Melrose Abbey. James I's royal entry to Edinburgh on Palm Sunday
	(21 May) Coronation of James I and Joan at Scone, followed by parliament in Perth from 26 May
	(Late 1424) Birth of Margaret, first daughter of James I and Joan
1425	Forfeiture and execution of Murdoch Stewart and other Albany Stewarts
1426	Founding licence for the Carthusian Priory at Perth
1427	Birth of Isabella, second daughter of James I and Joan
1428	First negotiations for betrothal between Princess Margaret and Louis, dauphin of France
1429	Submission of Alexander, Lord of the Isles

TIMELINE OF KEY EVENTS

1430	(October) Birth of Alexander and James, twin sons of James I and Joan, at Holyrood Abbey in the Canongate beside Edinburgh
1431	Death of Alexander, son of James I and Joan
1433	Birth of Eleanor, daughter of James I and Joan[1]
1435–6	French embassy in Scotland secured marriage of Princess Margaret and Dauphin Louis
	(June 1436) Margaret travelled to France and married the dauphin
1436	Robert Graham attempted to arrest James I as a tyrant in parliament
1437	(21 February) James I murdered at Blackfriars in Perth
	(March) Robert Stewart and John Chambers, two of the men accused of murdering James I, were tortured and executed in Edinburgh
	(25 March) Coronation of James II at Holyrood Abbey
	(Late March) Trial and execution of Walter Stewart, earl of Atholl, considered to be the leading actor in the murder of James I, in Edinburgh
1440	The Black Dinner: James II witnessed the execution of William, sixth earl of Douglas, instigated by James Douglas of Balvenie, William Crichton and Alexander Livingstone
1442	Isabella, daughter of James I and Joan, married to the Duke of Brittany
1443	(August) James II accompanied William, eighth earl of Douglas, at the siege of Barnton
	(November) James II presided over the general council at Stirling, which 'blew the horn' on William Crichton and signalled his downfall
1443–44	William, eighth earl of Douglas, made lieutenant-general of the kingdom
	Mary, daughter of James I and Joan, married to the son of Lord of Veere
	(November) James II accompanied William, eighth earl of Douglas, at the siege of Methven
1444–45	Knight of St John of Jerusalem returned to Scotland with the embalmed heart of James I, which was taken on crusade
1445	(June) James II and three estates took reciprocal oaths at a parliament in Edinburgh and Perth
	(July) Death of Joan Beaufort, widow of James I
1447	James II active in his marriage negotiations
1448	Eleanor, daughter of James I and Joan, married to the Duke of Austria-Tyrol

---

[1] James I and Joan Beaufort had three other daughters whose birth dates are not known: Mary, Joan and Annabella: Hayes, 'The Late Medieval Scottish Queen', 260–1.

TIMELINE OF KEY EVENTS

1449	(February) Burgundian knights travelled to Scotland for jousting tournament hosted by James II with Douglas men as the Scottish combatants
	(April) Treaty of Brussels secured marriage between James II and Mary of Guelders, niece of the Duke of Burgandy
	(July) Marriage of James II and Mary of Guelders at Holyrood Abbey following her arrival at Leith and royal entry to Edinburgh
1450–51	William, eighth earl of Douglas, and James Kennedy, bishop of St Andrews, travelled to Rome for the papal jubilee amidst increased tensions between James II and Douglas
1451	(July) Birth of Mary, daughter of Mary of Guelders and James II
1452	(February) James II killed William, eighth earl of Douglas, at Stirling Castle
	(March) James, ninth earl of Douglas and brother to William, 'blew the horn' on James II and dragged a letter of safe conduct through the streets of Stirling
	(May) Birth of James, first son of James II and Mary, at the episcopal castle of James Kennedy, bishop of St Andrews, where Mary was moved for safety
	(June) James II submitted himself to the judgment of parliament and handed out rewards to supporters, such as Kennedy
	(August) Efforts to bring settlement between earl of Douglas and James II
1454	Birth of Alexander, second son of James II and Mary
1455	James II attacked James, ninth earl of Douglas, who fled to England and his land and titles were forfeited
1455–57	James II raided northern England and attacked Berwick and Roxburgh
1456	Birth of David, third son of James II and Mary
1457	Birth of John, fourth son of James II and Mary. Death of David
1460	Birth of Margaret, daughter of James II and Mary
	(August) Siege of Roxburgh
	(3 August) Death of James II
	(10 August) Coronation of James III at Kelso Abbey, where he was brought by Mary and leading members of the court who were not at the siege
	(Later in August) Funeral of James II at Holyrood Abbey
1461	(February) First parliament of the reign of James III
1463	(July) James III present at the siege of Norham
	(December) Death of Mary of Guelders, queen of Scots; buried at Trinity College Kirk, Edinburgh
1464	James Kennedy, bishop of St Andrews and guardian of the king, took James III on a progress around the realm
1466	(July) Robert, lord Boyd, seized power
	(October) James III appeared enthroned in parliament that

248

TIMELINE OF KEY EVENTS

	secured Boyd power
1468	(January) Parliament agreed to support embassy to Denmark to secure a royal marriage (concluded later in the year)
	(Spring) Failed coup by uncles of James III to overturn Boyd leadership
1469	(July) Overthrow of Boyd rule. Marriage of James III and Margaret of Denmark
1470	(Summer) Progress of the royal couple as far north as Inverness
1473	(17 March) Birth of James, first son of James III and Margaret
1474	James III and ambassadors secured a betrothal agreement for Anglo-Scottish marriage between Prince James and Cecilia, daughter of Edward IV of England
1475–79	Increased tensions between James III and his brother, Alexander duke of Albany
1476	Birth of James, second son of James III and Margaret
1479	(September) Alexander, duke of Albany, fled Scotland for France
	(October) James III failed to gain parliamentary support for the full forfeiture of his brother, Alexander, for accusations of treason
1480	(12 July) Birth of John, third son of James III and Margaret
	(by July) James III's younger brother, John earl of Mar, was arrested and forfeited titles and lands; he was later executed
1480–82	Increased Anglo-Scottish tensions after failure of James III's policies
1482	(June) Treaty of Fotheringhay, between Albany and Edward IV, to supplant James III with support of English force, led by Richard, duke of Gloucester
	(July) Scottish muster at Lauder ends with the arrest of the king by Scottish opponents and the execution of several of his favourites
	(August–September) Siege of Edinburgh Castle ended with the 'freeing' of James III by Albany who ruled briefly as lieutenant-general
1483	(March) Indenture signed between James III and Albany to restore peace and avoid civil war
	(April–June) Death of Edward IV and accession of Edward V, leading to the accession of Richard III of England
1484	(February) Parliament agreed to more forfeitures of Albany supporters
	(March) James III renewed treaty of mutual support with the French king, Charles VIII (r.1483–1498), in response to continued threat of English invasion
	(July) Battle of Lochmaben ended with Albany finally fleeing from Scotland

TIMELINE OF KEY EVENTS

	(September–October) Truce agreed between James III and Richard III, including prospective marriage between James III's eldest son and Richard III's niece
1485	Albany imprisoned; escaped to France but died there later in the year
1486	Death of Margaret of Denmark, queen of Scots; buried at Cambuskenneth Abbey
1488	(11 June) James III killed after the Battle of Sauchieburn, in which his eldest son, James, was presented as a figurehead of opposing force and was crowned later the same month (October) First parliament of the reign with James IV in full regalia at the Tolbooth in Edinburgh
1495–97	James IV's support for pretender to English throne, Perkin Warbeck, led to raids of northern England and confrontations with Henry VII of England (r.1485–1509)
1501	Chapel Royal at Stirling Castle received papal approval as a collegiate church
1502	(February–May) First payments made by James IV for his tomb at Cambuskenneth Abbey (Winter) Treaty of Perpetual Peace between England and Scotland
1503	(August) Marriage of James IV and Margaret Tudor of England
1504	(January) Death and funeral of James IV's brother, James Stewart, archbishop of St Andrews (March) Parliament confirmed Margaret Tudor's dower
1507	(Feb) Birth of James IV and Margaret's first son, James, celebrated with an elaborate baptism and the tournament of the Wild Knight and the Black Lady
1508	Death of Prince James[2]
1509	(April) Death of Henry VII and accession of Henry VIII of England, which led to worsening relations between Scotland and England (Oct) Birth of James IV and Margaret's second son, Arthur
1510	Death of Prince Arthur
1511	Birth and baptism of Henry VIII's short-lived son, Arthur. Margaret Tudor, queen of Scots, made a royal entry to Aberdeen. James IV visited Cambuskenneth to oversee work on his tomb at Cambuskenneth
1512	Birth of James IV and Margaret's third son, James, which was celebrated at Easter at Linlithgow Palace[3]
1513	(9 September) Death of James IV at the Battle of Flodden

[2] James IV and Margaret also had a daughter born in 1508, but she died within a day of her birth: Hayes, 'The Late Medieval Scottish Queen', 261.

[3] James IV and Margaret had another daughter either before or after James' birth, but she did not live long.

TIMELINE OF KEY EVENTS

	(21 September) Coronation of James V at the Chapel Royal, Stirling Castle
1514	(April) Birth of James IV and Margaret's fourth son, Alexander (August) Margaret Tudor married her second husband, Archibald Douglas, sixth earl of Angus
1515	John Stewart, duke of Albany, son of James III's brother, arrived in Scotland from France as regent and governor
1516–17	Albany took the young king, James V, on a progress around the realm
1517	Treaty of Rouen included the first mention of a marriage between James V and a daughter of François I of France[4]
1517–28	Remainder of James V's minority witnessed power changing hands between Albany, the earls of Arran and Angus, and Margaret regained control briefly
1520	Field of the Cloth of Gold: ceremonial meeting of Henry VIII and François I near Calais
1528	(May–June) James V escaped from control of Angus and treason was proclaimed against the former governor (December) Treaty of Berwick secured peace with England
1536	(September) James V travelled to France to marry Marie de Bourbon, daughter of the duke of Vendôme (October–November) James V travelled to meet François I and spent this period travelling with the French king and his court (26 November) Marriage treaty between James V and Madeleine, daughter of François I, agreed at Blois (31 December) James V made a royal entry to Paris
1537	(1 January) James V married Madeleine de Valois in Paris (January–May) James V and Madeleine travelled around France (May) James V and Madeleine returned to Scotland delayed by Madeleine's ill health (July) Madeleine died prior to receiving royal entry or coronation. Funeral held at Holyrood Abbey
1538	(May) Embassy led by Robert Lord Maxwell, Lord High Admiral, travelled to France to complete arrangements for marriage of Marie de Guise to James V (June) Marie de Guise arrived at St Andrews (July) Marie made her entry to Edinburgh after an extensive progress (August) Marie made royal entries to Dundee and Perth
1539	(October) Commission to John Mossman for a crown for the queen
1540	(9 February) Marie de Guise's coronation

[4] Seventeen brides from eight different countries were potentially discussed for James V: Cameron, *James V*, 132.

TIMELINE OF KEY EVENTS

	(22 May) Birth of Marie and James V's first son, James
1541	(12 April) Birth of Marie and James V's second son, Arthur or Robert
	(20–21 April) Deaths of both of Marie and James V's sons
1542	(December) Birth of Mary Queen of Scots. Death of James V at Falkland Palace
1543	(January) Funeral of James V at Holyrood Abbey
	(9 September) Coronation of Mary Queen of Scots at the Chapel Royal, Stirling

Appendix I:
Transcription from John Scrymgeour of Myres, NLS, Adv. MS 31.5.2, fols 15r–16r[1]

Part (i) A treatise on tournaments [fols 1–18].
Transcription from fols 15r–16r

[fol. 15r] 'The Maner hou herrauldis and purſevantis ſould knau of obſequis'[2] Herrauldis and Puirſevantis ſould knaw how obſequis ſould be done bot mony kepis na weele ffor ſum makis [th]ame for deuotion of meβ [and] littil ly[ch] t [and] litill apprareling[3] And v[ther]is makis [th]ame w[i]t[h] grit appareling [and] grit pompes [and] few meſſ [and] w[i]t[h] gritar magnificens nor appertenis to [th]ame Bot pri[n] – cipall[is] [th]e hono[ur] of s[yr]uice of wardly esat[is] it is to takken how [th]ai mak [and] gangis till offerand[is] Off [th]e quhilk[is] [th]air wes in auld tymes about [th]e beir throw [th]e luminar[4] ſome cierg[is][5] at [th]e four rowk[is][6] at ilk a cierge ane eſcuſſ[i]on[7] The first [th]e armes of [th]e mother The ſecond [th]e armes of [loſle][8] The third [th]e armes

---

[1] Signature on the document is 'Ex libris petri thomsoune ylay heraldi' on fol. 2v. The transcription has retained long 's' and original spellings; contractions have been elongated in square brackets where possible. Some obscure words and queries marked in footnote form. Thanks to Alasdair Ross and Ulrike Hogg (NLS) for assistance with palaeography queries, and to Ralph Moffat and David Sellar (Lord Lyon King of Arms, 2008–2014) for help with heraldic vocabulary queries. Transcription of 'The Maner hou herrauldis and purſevantis ſould knau of obſequis' from the heraldic collection by John Scrymgeour of Myres, NLS, Adv. MS 31.5.21136 (Reproduced with kind permission of the National Library of Scotland).
[2] From Part (i) A treatise on tournaments, fols 1–18. Transcription from fols 15r–16r. Title in red. Obsequis or obsequies: funeral rite or ceremony.
[3] Apparelling: making ready/fitting up.
[4] Luminar: source of light, lamp, celestial light.
[5] Ciergis: Large or monumental candle (also spelt 'serge' or sierge).
[6] Rowk in old Scots, is the verb 'to stack' so it could be that this term was used to indicate the stacks of timber used to construct the bier. In Middle English 'Rok' or 'Rowk' means 'oak'. In the context of the source, it could be that 'four rowkis' means 'four branches' (as in branches of a family).
[7] Escutcheons.
[8] This section describes four escutcheons that are placed with a candle around the bier.

of be[z]ele[9] The fert [th]e armes of [th]e fu[z]elle[10] Ilk fhield partit as [th]e armes of a Womane fould be quhame [th]air husband[is] War levand.[11] And at [th]e feit of [th]e beir ane efcufl[i]on with [th]e armes of [th]e deid And all [th]e luminar [and] [th]e fanctuar of [th]e kirk fould be armoyit W[i]t[h] [th]e famin efcufl[i]onis bot far les. And [th]at efcufl[i]on fould be armoyit on tua fyd[is]e and fa thik [th]at it may ftand vp ry[ch]t quhen it is laid vpoun [th]e feit of [th]e beir And [th]ai fould offer And [th]e eldeft sone fould bere [th]e offrand w[i]t[h] c[om]pany of fowr of [th]e narrest efcuffonis of armes of [th]e vary[is] cierg[is] armoyit as saidis And [the]r by he is kend [tha]t beir[is] [th]e fcheild he is gentill man of fowr branchis And be [th]e armes and [th]ai [th] at beir[is] [th]e vary[is] in [th]air c[om]pany ar [kend] quhat fo[ur] branchis [th]ai ar Defceindit fra And quhat anciennete he be of Eftir [th]e linnage of fo[ur] branchis he fould be honorit And quhen a man hes tane ligne of fo[ur] branchis in [th]e maner foirsaid he may call him gentilman.

[fol. 15v] And for [th]is caus all gentillmen fould defyre to be maryit in no – bill ligne And bot gif it be throw [th]at falt his ligne fall evir be callit noble quhat evir he do and [y]it [th]e noble man of his natur fould evir do nobilneff quhat evir he do of werk[is] or ellis he fchannis his nature

Item [th]e secund offerand fould be [th]e heallme[12] quhilk [th]e gritest Lord [th]at bene in [thai]r obfequis sould offer Item [th]e thrid offerand f[hou]ld be [th]e fwerd[13] [th]e q[uhi]lk fould be offrit be [th]e hand[is] of [th]e tua maist vailliant men of all [th]e obfequis Item [th]e ferd offerand of a horβ coverit w[i]t[h] [th]e armes of [th]e deid And a gentillman salbe vpon him or a freind of [th]e deid quhilk fall beir his baner or be [th]e bachileir his pe[n]non[14] And he salbe [cum]panit w[i]t[h] tua noble men [th]e maist vailliant and [th]e maist of renown to be capitanes [and] [go -----][15] of men of armes [th]at salbe in all [th]e obfequis.

The first certainly shows the arms of the mother of the deceased, but the following three arms are less clear. The meaning of this word 'losle' is not clear, the closest heraldic term is 'lozenge'. However, considering the previous content and that Scrymgeour may have copied his information from Loutfut, who is known to use French sources for his manuscript collections, it may come from the Middle French 'l'aiel' meaning grandfather.

[9] Bezele, also spelt bezel or bevill, could be from Middle English 'bisaile' or Middle French 'bessaile' meaning great grandfather; or otherwise from French *biseau*, 'sloping edge', or *bijou*, 'jewel'.
[10] Fuzelle or fuselle or fusil is a heraldic word meaning either a heraldic elongated lozenge, or 'firesteel'. The latter was a symbol used on the arms of the Burgundian dukes.
[11] Levand: living or alive or existing.
[12] Heallme: helmet.
[13] Swerd: sword.
[14] Pennon: small flag or streamer.
[15] Unknown word.

APPENDIX I

Item [th]e fyft offrand falbe ficlyck of ane horß coverit w[i]t[h] his loveray and a man aboue quhilk salbe led [and] offerit be [th]e tua maift gratious [and] maift wardly amang[st] ladyis [and] damoy - fellis w[i]t[h]out reproche of all the obfequis

Item in sum places [th]e offerand[is] ar double [th]e half for [th]e were half for [th]e tournay of thing[is] befeir faid And in mony en[n]treis no[ch]t

Item in fum places quhair [th]e offerand[is] ar [th]us maid [th]e blak cled offer[is] no[ch]t bot he [th]at hes [th]e scheild bot in places quhair [th]ai gang to [th]e offerand [th]ai fould be led and convoyit be [th]e gritest of [th]e obfequis [th]er hes no[ch]t offerit [th]e thingis befoir said.

Item [th]e said[is] offerand[is] fould be offerit [and] borne to [th]e lord[is] be [th]e king[is] of armes or herauld[is] fayand to [th]ame gif it pleis [th]ame till excuß [th]ame to do [th]is for it is fua ordanit.

And [th]ai quhom to [th]ai ar presentit fould ans[yr] thai have lakit evill about [th]ame to present in fic honour for it is no[ch]t aucht to me befour v[the]r[is] in [thi]s cumpany bot of [th]er charge of [th]ame [tha]t hes maid [th]e ordinance I will do it [and] no[ch]t of my will. Th[e] quhilk[is] ordinances or s[er]vices ar left in [th]is prefent tyme for thre thing[is] Ane is for mony [th]at fchawis [th]ame felf[is] folk[is] of grit efstait can no[cht] armoyer [th]e cierg[is] of fo[ur] lignes.

[fol. 16r] becaus [th]ai ar no[ch]t cu[m]in of fic nobilnes. The fecund is for [th]e [I]nvyes[16] [th]at war of offerand[is]. The thrid for [th]e gritcost maid [th]air vpon bot [th]ai war thing[is] quhair throw [the] eftat of [per]fone my[ch]t be knawin and quhair be men fould knaw quhat hono[ur] fould be done to [th]ame And it wes [th]r prin – cipall caus quharfoir [th]e herauld[is] tuk mair tent to [th]e offerand[is] [th]an ony v[th]ir thing[is] [per]tein[in]g to [th]e s[yr]uice [th]e quhilk[is] may be knawin be demanding or be veriteis or be v[th]er[is] buk[is] of [th]is mater.

[The account has another copy in Adv. MS. 31.3.20 – Sir David Lindsay Heraldic Collection]

---

[16] The first letter of this word is not clear.

Appendix II: Attendees and Officiators at Scottish Inaugurations and Coronations

Few lists of attendance exist for Scottish inaugurations and coronations. Note these are not total attendees, rather the lists offer information about known or possible attendees from a range of sources, as well as details on known or possible ecclesiastic and secular officiators. Where attendance is drawn from Records of the Parliament of Scotland (www.rps.ac.uk), titles are given rather than full names as these are easily searchable online.

Alexander II

Inauguration: 1214

Officiating Bishop: William Malveisin bishop of St Andrews
Secular Officiator: Unknown – possibly earl of Fife or 'seven' earls?
Other Known Attendees:
Earls of Fife, Strathearn, Atholl, Angus, Menteith, Buchan and Lothian or Dunbar
Other members of the three estates
Not in Attendance (as Stayed to 'Abode' with the late King William):
Queen Ermengarde
Earl of Huntingdon (David, William's brother) – joins the party at Perth
Bishops of Glasgow (Walter), Ross (Robert)
Others: William del Blois (chancellor), other household officials

[References: Chron. Bower, V, 3; Chron. Fordun, 279]

APPENDIX II

Alexander III

Inauguration: 1249

Officiating Bishop: David de Berham, bishop of St Andrews
Secular Officiator: Mael Coluim , earl of Fife, Malise, earl of Strathearn, and Walter Comyn, earl of Menteith[1]
Other Known Attendees:
Earls of as above
Bishop of Dunkeld (Geoffrey or Galfrid)
Abbot of Scone [Robert]
Others: Alan Durward (justiciar of Scotia), the 'poet' or *filid* [2]
Probably Not in Attendance (Travelled with Body of Alexander II):
Bishops of Dunblane (Clement)
Officials: David of Lindsay (justiciar of Lothian), Alexander (Steward)
Others: Walter of Moray (or Murray), William of Brechin, Walter Bissett, Robert of Meynors

[Ref: *Chron. Fordun*, 289–90; *Chron. Bower*, V, 291–3; *Chron. Melrose*, 87; *RMS*, II, no. 3136; Oram, *Alexander II*, 190]

John Balliol

Inauguration: 1292

Officiating Bishop: Not clear, bishops present listed below
Secular Officiator: John de St John (English knight, in place of earl of Fife, minor)[3]
Other Attendees: There is no definitive list of attendees to Balliol's inauguration, rather the records of those present at the various homage giving ceremonies, first in Norham and then Newcastle
Present at Norham on 20 November When John offered Homage to Edward:
Archbishop of Dublin (John [Sanford])
Bishops of Durham (Anthony [Bek]), St Andrews (William [Fraser]), Glasgow (Robert [Wishart]), Ely (William [de Luda]), Carlisle (John [de Halton])
Earls of Lincoln (Henry de Lacy), Buchan (John), Ross (William), March

---

[1] Singled out by *Gesta Annalia* but not by Bower or Melrose – not clear that there was one key noble, but the earls of Fife and Strathearn are likely to be those depicted in the Bower image of Alexander III's inauguration and in the Scone seal (Plates 2 and 3, see 47, 48).
[2] Bannerman offers suggestions of the family descent of the harper and the poet in 1249: 'The King's Poet', 120–49.
[3] *Foedera*, I, pt. iii, 115.

APPENDIX II

(Patrick), Menteith (Walter)
Lords of Lorne (Alexander Macdougall), Cavers (Alexander Balliol)
Others: James (the Steward), Patrick de Graham, William de Saint Clare [Sinclair]

Present at Newcastle at Christmas Witnesses to John Swearing Homage to Edward:
Attendance as above, plus the following:
Abbot of Jedworth (John)
Earls of Surrey (John de Warenne), Angus (Gilbert de Unfraville), Atholl (John)
English Knights: John de St John, Robert of Typetot [sic], Nicholas de Segrave, William de Leyburn, Brian son of Alan, Gilbert of Thornton, Roger Brebanzon [sic], Robert Malet
Others: John de Lanetone (chancellor of England), Master John Lovell, Master Walter de Langetone, John Comyn, Thomas Randolph, Galfridi de Montbray, Richard Seward, Andrew Murray, Thomas Randolph (son of David of Torthorald), Michael de Wymss, Richard Fraser,
Andrew Fraser, Alexander de Bonkil, John de Stirling
Not at Newcastle but attended Norham: bishops of Ely and Carlisle, earls of Ross and Menteith, Alexander lord of Lorne.

[Ref: *Foedera*, I, part iii, 112–3.]

Robert I

Inauguration (Coronation) 1306

Officiating Bishop: Robert Wishart, bishop of Glasgow [possibly anointed Robert?] and William Lamberton, bishop of St Andrews [conducted Palm Sunday Mass]
Secular Officiator: Isabella Countess of Buchan, adult representative of the earldom of Fife
Other Attendees:
Bishops of Glasgow (Wishart), St Andrews (Lamberton), Moray [David], Dunkeld, Brechin[4]
Abbots of Scone (Henry Mann), Coupar [?]
Earls of Atholl (John of Strathbogie), Lennox (Mael Coluim), Menteith, Malise, Strathearne, Mar[5]
Lord of Atholl (John, son of earl of Atholl)

---

[4] Penman, *Robert the Bruce*, 98.
[5] Ibid. Attended as a minor.

Knights or knighted at ceremony: Christopher de Seton, Alexander of Scrymgeour (royal standard bearer), James Douglas, Thomas Randolph of Morton, Robert Boyd, Alexander Lyndsay (and son David), Patrick Graham, Mael Coluim of Innerpeffray, Ranald de Crawford

Others: Simon Fraser, Alexander, Neil, Edward and Thomas Bruce (brothers of Robert Bruce), James (Steward), John de Seton, Michael of Wymss, Gilbert de la Hay, Hugh Lovell, William de Moray of Sandford, Walter de Moray, Gilbert Mauduyt [sic], Hugh Oliphant[6]

Female Attendees: Isabella Comyn, countess of Buchan (nee Fife), Marjory Bruce (Bruce's daughter), Elizabeth de Burgh (Bruce's second wife), Christine and Mary Bruce (Bruce's sisters)

Executed as prisoners of war after Methven and Perth: David de Inchemartyn, John de Cambhon (knight), John Somerville, Ralph Herries, Alexander Scrymegeour (standard bearer), Robert Wycher (possibly Wishart), Bernard de Mohaut [sic], Cuthbert de Carrick, William de Bae, William de Botharm, Roger le Taillur, Ughtred le Marechal, Duncan Boyd, William Rusky, Adam Turry (messenger of Simon Fraser), and John de Seton

[Ref: *CDS*, II, nos 1771, 1775, 1777, 1780, 1782, 1785–7, 1790, 1807, 1811–18, 1820, 1823–29, 1836–37, 1841–43, 1849–52, 1854, 1856–58, 1860–62, 1885, 1894, 1907, 1910; *Passio Scotorum Perjutatorum*, 167–84; Penman, *Robert the Bruce*, 98–100.]

David II

Coronation 1331

Officiating Bishop: James Ben, bishop of St Andrews
Secular Officiator: possibly Thomas Randolph, earl of Moray (?)
Other Attendees:
Earls of Moray (Thomas Randolph), Angus (John Stewart)
Knights or knighted: Thomas Randolph (son of Moray)
Female Attendees: Queen Joan (also crowned), Christian Bruce (king's aunt), Margaret, Matilda and Elizabeth (David II's sisters)
Others: Sheriffs asked to give homage along with others; for example, Robert [Lauder] sheriff of Berwick

[Ref: *Chron. Bower*, VII, 70–3; *Chron. Fordun*, 346; *ER*, I, 389–90; *RPS*, A1331/1]

---

[6] Penman lists additional – Walter Logan, Alexander Menzies, Gilbert Herries, Gilbert of Carrick and Walter Bickerton: *Robert the Bruce*, 98–100.

APPENDIX II

Edward Balliol

Inauguration (Coronation): 1332

Officiating Bishop: William of St Clair, bishop of Dunkeld
Secular Officiator: Duncan, earl of Fife
Other Attendees:
Earls of Atholl, Fife, Angus, Buchan (Henry de Beaumont)
Abbots of Dunfermline, Cupar-Angus, Inchaffray, Arbroath, Scone
Other: *communitas* of Fife and Fothreve, Stratherne, Gowry
List of Parliament Named Attendees, 9 February 1334:
Bishops of Glasgow, Aberdeen, Dunkeld, Dunblane, Brechin
Earls of Buchan, Atholl, March
Other: Richard Talbot (lord of Mar), Henry of Galloway, John of Ross, Alexander de Seton, Alexander de Mowbray, William de Keith (steward of royal household)
English knights: Ranulph of Dacre, R. de Stafford, John Kingston, Thomas West, Peter Middleton, Master William Brisbane

[Ref: *Chron. Fordun*, 379; *Chron. Brindlington*, 366; *Chron. Lanercost*, II, 271–2; *RPS*, 1334/1–4, A1334/5–11]

Robert II

Coronation: 1371

Officiating Bishop: William de Landels, bishop of St Andrews
Secular Officiator: *Possibly Isabella MacDuff, countess of Fife, enthroned the king (?)*
Other Attendees:
Bishops of St Andrews, Glasgow, Aberdeen, Moray, Brechin, Dunblane
Priors of St Andrews
Abbots of Dunfermline, Arbroath, Holyrood, Lindores, Scone
Earls of Carrick, Strathearne, Mar, Douglas, Menteith, March, Moray
Lords of Lennox, Livingstone, Seton
Knights: Alexander Stewart, William de Keith (marischal), Archibald de Douglas, Robert de Erskine, Alexander de Lindsay,[7] David de Graham, Walter de Haliburton, John de Carrick (chancellor), Walter de Biggar (chamberlain), Alexander Stewart, Andrew Campbell, Robert Erskine

---

[7] Bellenden states that James Lindsay of Glennesk was created earl of Crawford in a knighting ceremony at Robert II's coronation, but the earldom was first created in 1398 by Robert III (David Lindsay, son of the Alexander): Boece, *Chronicle*, 336–7; *The Complete Peerage of England, Scotland, Ireland, Great Britain and the United Kingdom, Extant, Extinct or Dormant*, ed. George E. Cokayne et al., 6 vols, new edition (Gloucester, 2000), III, 508.

260

Others: Thomas de Hay (constable), William de Cunningham, James de Douglas, James Fraser, Alexander Fraser, William de Dishington, David Watson, David de Annan, Roger de Mortimer, Robert de Ramsay, Alan Stewart, Duncan Wallace, Robert Stewart, George de Abernethy, David Fleming, Nicholas de Erskine, John de Lyle, Simon de Preston, John de Maxwell, John de Strachan, Robert de Dalziel and Walter de Ogilvy, John de Tours, John Kennedy, Gillespic Campbell, William de Fenton, John de Sinclair, John de Crawford, Alexander de Straton, Alexander Scrimgeour, John de Crichton, Patrick Gray, John de Menzies, Robert de Normanville, John de Cragie, Hugh Fraser, Alexander de Strachan, and Donald MacNair

[Ref: *RPS*, 1371/2; *Chron. Wyntoun*, VI, 264–6; *Chron. Bower*, VII, 364–7; *Bellenden's Boece Chronicle*, 336–7.]

Robert III

Coronation: 1390

Officiating Bishops: Walter Trail, bishop of St Andrews
Secular Officiator: Unknown, Robert earl of Fife (Robert III's brother, lieutenant of realm) is not recorded as attending
Other Attendees:
Bishops of Glasgow (Matthew de Glendonwyn), Dunkeld (John de Peebles), Galloway (Thomas de Rossy)
Abbot of Cambuskenneth (William de Blackburn)

[Refs: *Chron. Wyntoun*, VI, 366–8; *RPS*, 1390/1]

James I

Coronation: 1424

Officiating Bishop: Henry Wardlaw, bishop of St Andrews
Secular Officiator: Murdoch Stewart, earl of Fife and duke of Albany
Other Attendees:
Men knighted at the coronation:
Earls of: Douglas or Wigtown (Archibald),[8] Angus (William), March (George Dunbar)

---

[8] Archibald still heir to the earldom of Douglas, his father, Archibald II (the fourth earl and Duke of Touraine) was in France and died at the battle of Verneuil, August 1424. Younger Archibald was styling himself earl of Wigtown earlier in 1424: *CDS*, IV, no. 942; Brown, *The Black Douglases*, 220–3.

APPENDIX II

Others: Alexander Stewart (son of duke of Albany), Adam Hepburn of Hailes; Thomas Hay of Yester, Walter de Haliburton, Walter de Ogilvy, David Stewart of Rossyth, Alexander de Seton of Gordon, [Alexander Lindsay earl of Crawford], Patrick Ogilvy of Auchterhouse, John Red Stewart of Dundonald, David Murray of Gask, John Stewart of Cardney, [William Erskine of Kinnoull], William Hay of Errol (constable); John Scrimegeour, Alexander Irvine of Drum, Herbert Maxwell of Caerlaverock, Herbert Herries of Terregles, Andrew Gray of Fowlis, Robert Cunningham of Kilmaurs, Alexander Ramsay of Dalhousie, William Crichton of Crichton

[Ref: *Chron. Bower*, VIII, 242–3; *Pluscarden*, 279; Maior, *History*, 354–5][9]

James II

Coronation: 1437

Officiating Bishops: Michael Ociltree, bishop of Dunblane[10]
Secular Officials: Unknown, possible increase in role for Lyon, Constable [William Hay] and Marischal [William Keith][11]
Other Attendees:[12]
Queen Joan
Earls of Angus (William), Douglas (Archibald)
Lords and officials: Alexander Livingstone of Callander, William Crichton, Walter Ogilvy, William Foulis. John Forrester of Corstorphine, James Livingstone [?]
Known not to be in attendance: Cameron, bishop of Glasgow (at Council of Basle), Wardlaw, bishop of St Andrews, reason unknown, possible feud with James I

[Ref: *Extra e Varriis Cronicis Scocie* (Edinburgh, 1842), 237; McGladdery, *James II*, 8–9, 12–17]

---

[9] Pluscarden indicates that Hepburn, Hay, Seton, Erskine, Cunnigham, Ramsay and Crichton were all lords.
[10] McGladdery and Tanner suggest Wardlaw, bishop of St Andrews, absented himself due to the long-term conflict with James I: *James II*, 8–9; *Medieval Scottish Parliament*, 78.
[11] See Chapter 4, 155–6.
[12] There is little direct evidence in narrative or parliament records for who attended this coronation, but the suggestion is that it was well attended, despite key absences: McGladdery, *James II*, 8–9.

APPENDIX II

James III

Coronation: 1460

Officiating Bishops: In the absence of James Kennedy, bishop of St Andrews, Andrew Durisdeer, bishop of Glasgow, and Thomas Lauder, bishop of Dunkeld, seem likely candidates
Secular Officials: *Lyon herald, Mairschal and Constable likely in attendance*
Other Attendees:
George Douglas, earl of Angus[13]
Men knighted at the coronation (as identified by Katie Stevenson):
Patrick Maitland, James Crichton of Carnis, John Colquhoun of that Ilk, William Wallace of Craigie, Alexander Napier of Merchiston, John Herries, lord of Terregles, Alexander Forrester of Corstorphine, William Hay of Nactane, Alexander Lauder of Hatton, and William, thane of Cawdor

Named witnesses to acts at the first parliament in 1461:
Bishops of <u>Glasgow, Dunkeld,</u> Aberdeen, Argyll, Galloway
Abbots of Holyrood, Arbroath, Paisley, Dunfermline, Newbattle
Earl of Argyll
Lords of <u>Avondale (chancellor), Gray, Borthwick,</u> Montgomery, Lindsay, Hailes, Kennedy
Others: Thomas Brown (notary), James Lindsay (provost of Lincluden, keeper of the Privy Seal), Alexander Home, Thomas Cranstoun, Robert Semple of Elliston, Archibald Stewart, Stephen of Angus, Archibald Whitelaw (clerk of the rolls), Thomas Brown, Robert Laing (vicar of Maryton)

Auditors: those underlined above also named auditors
Earls of Angus, Orkney and Caithness
Lords of Graham, Glamis
Others: Walter Lindsay of 'Kinblac hinour', Master George Liddale (king's secretary), Sir Walter Graham, William Cranstoun and Thomas Lamont

[Ref: *RPS*, A1461/2–3, 1461/5; Stevenson, *Chivalry and Knighthood*, 183, fn. 64.]

---

[13] David Hume of Godscroft (seventeenth-century Douglas biographer) claims that George Douglas, earl of Angus, demanded the right to crown James III, but Macdougall demonstrates that Douglas was likely wounded and Godcroft overplaying his involvement: Macdougall, *James III*, 41.

APPENDIX II

James IV

Coronation: 1488

Officiating Bishops: Robert Blacader, bishop of Glasgow
Secular Officials: William Hay, third earl of Errol and hereditary Constable, and William Keith, second earl Marischal and hereditary Marischal, were definitely absent

Witnesses on a charter produced the day after the coronation:
Bishops of Glasgow (Robert Blackadder), Dunkeld (George Brown)
Prior of St Andrew (John Hepburn, keeper of the Privy Seal)
Earls of Argyll (Colin Campbell, chancellor), Angus (Archibald Douglas)
Lords: Hailes (Patrick), Lyle (Robert), Oliphant (Laurence), Gray (Andrew), Drummond (John) *Others:* Alexander Inglis (archdeacon of St Andrews, keeper of the Rolls), Archibald Whitelaw (subdeacon of Glasgow, king's secretary), William Hepburn (vicar of Linlithgow, clerk register William Knollis (preceptor of Torphichin, treasurer)

Attendance at Parliament, 7 October 1488
Archbishop of St Andrews [Scheves]
Bishops of Glasgow, Aberdeen [Elphinstone], Dunkeld, Galloway [Vaus], Dunblane [Chisolm], Isles [Campbell]
Abbots of Paisley, Kelso, Holyrood, Cambuskenneth, Melrose, Newbattle, Lindores, Inchaffray, Inchcolm, Soulseat, Coupar Angus, Balmerino, Kilwinning, Dryburgh
Priors of St Andrews, Whithorn, Pluscarden, Restenneth
Other clerics: archdeacons of St Andrews and Lothian [Whitelaw, royal secretary], rector of St Andrews, officials of St Andrews and Balmerino, provost of St Salvator's college, dean of St Andrews, Hugh Spens, Martin Wan
Earls of Argyll, Angus, Huntly, Morton, Erroll, Marischal, Lennox, Rothes, Atholl, Buchan.
Lords: Hailes [Hepburn], Hamilton, Lyle, Lyon, Gray, Oliphant, Montgomery, Drummond, Maxwell, Graham, Carlyle, Dirleton, Craigie, Drum
Others: Alexander Home (chamberlain), Archibald Cambell (master of Argyll), Matthew Stewart (master of Lennox), Alexander Stewart of Avondale, Constable of Dundee, James Ogilvy of Finlater, Walter Kerr, Patrick Home, Archibald Edmonstone, Sheriff of Ayr, Willaim Seton of Meldrum
Burgh Commissioner of: Edinburgh, Dundee, Stirling, Perth, Linlithgow, Haddington, St Andrews, Renfrew, Rutherglen, Aberdeen, Dumfries, Elgin and Forres, Rothesay, Irvine, Ayr

[Refs: *RMS*, II, no. 1739; *RPS*, 1488/10/3]

APPENDIX II

James V

Coronation: 1513

Officiating Bishops: James Beaton, archbishop of Glasgow
Secular Officials: Unknown
Other Attendees: Margaret Tudor, widowed queen dowager

Members of the Council of 19 September 1513
Archbishop of Glasgow [James Beaton]
Bishops of Aberdeen [William Elphinstone], Galloway [David Arnot], Dunblane [James Chisholm], Caithness [Andrew Stewart], Argyll [David Hamilton], Orkney [Edward Stewart] *Prior of* St Andrews [John Hepburn]
Abbots of Holyrood [George Crichton], Paisley [Robert Shaw], Cambuskenneth [Patrick Paniter
Other clerics: [Gavin Dunbar, archdeacon of St Andrews], Clerk of the Register, provost of St Giles Kirk, dean of Dunkeld, dean of Glesgow, provost of Crichtoun, Master David Seton, the official of Lothian
Earls of Angus [Archibald Douglas], Huntly [Alexander Gordon], Morton [James Douglas], Argyll [Colin Campbell], Crawford [Alexander Lindsey], Lennox [John Stewart], Eglinton [Hugh Montgomery], Glencairn [William Cunningham], Atholl [John Stewart]
Lords and lairds: Home [Alexander, chamberlain], Ruthven [William], Drummon [John], Forbes [John], laird of Inverugie, laird of Bass

[Ref: *ADCP*, 1: to identify names of individuals, utilised: *RPS*, A1513/1 and A1517/10/1; Emond, 'The Minority of King James V, 1513–1528', 7]

Attendees First General Council, 26 November 1513
Archbishop of Glasgow (Beaton, chancellor)
Bishops of Aberdeen, Dunblane, Caithness, Argyll, Orkney
Prior of St Andrews
Abbots of Holyroodhouse, Paisley, Coupar Angus, Lindores, Jedburgh
Postulate of Dunfermline, Cambuskenneth, Caithness
Other clerics: archdean of St Andrews, dean of Glasgow, dean of Dunblane
Earls of Argyll, Arran, Morton, Lennox, Erroll, Crawford, Marischal, Atholl, Cassilis, Eglinton
Lords: Home, Drummond, Fleming, Oliphant, Erskine, Ruthven, Maxwell, Forbes, Ross [of Hawkhead], Sanquhar
Master of Marischal, Montgomery
Knights: William Murray of Tullibardine, William Menteith of Kerse, Patrick Crichton of Cranston, Patrick Hamilton of Glencavill, James Shaw of Sauchie

265

Others: David Bruce of Clackmannan, Andrew Kerr of Ferniehirst, Philip Nisbet, Alexander Home of Spott, Gilbert Menzies [of Findon], Master James Wishart of Pittarrow, justice clerk
Provosts of Aberdeen and Perth

[Ref: *RPS*, A1513/1]

Appendix III: James IV and Margaret's Wedding Costs, 1503

This calculation includes main material goods and provisions to elucidate the scale and expense of the event, but it does not include building work at Holyrood or all service charges, carriage costs, wages and fees as these are difficult to extract from general expenditure.[1]

King's clothes	£3,159, 14s. ½d.[2]
King and queen wedding gowns	£210, 17s. 5d.[3]
Work on king's crown, sceptre, sword of honour	£15, 12s. 11½d.[4]
Queen's crown	£96, 5d.[5]
Other jewels	£17, 13s. 8d.[6]
Cloths of state/state bed (king and queen)	£841, 5s.[7]
Trevis (not specifically for beds)	£130, 6s.[8]
Liars [rug/ coverlet] of velvet	£169, 14s.[9]

[1] As noted in the main text, the manuscript NRS, E21/6 has a digital surrogate (Virtual Volume); the folio numbers listed here are for the original folios (visible on digital version) not the Virtual Volume pages.

[2] NRS, E21/6, fols 18v–22r; TA, II, 206–13. Notably most of the key outfits made in this section can be identified in Young's account of the wedding

[3] NRS, E21/6, fol. 20v; TA, II, 209.

[4] NRS, E21/6, fols 18v–19r, 127v; TA, II, 205–7, 385. This includes amendments to the crown with additional gold (this could be arches to the crown and seems more likely considering that a bonnet was added in January 1504 as this was an addition for an imperial closed crown rather than an open one), gilting on the sceptre and a pair of spurs, adding a new hilt and pommel to the sword, mending or a making purple velvet sheath embroidered with pearls (costs suggest mending rather than making).

[5] NRS, E21/6, fol. 19r; TA, II, 206. Made by John Currour, goldsmith, weighing 11 ounces and one angel – no jewels listed.

[6] NRS, E21/6, fol. 24r; TA, II, 217–18. This includes a unicorn of gold adorned with a pearl, a gold ring, three little rings of gold, a hart/heart of gold, image of Our Lady, a cross of gold, a ring with a ruby.

[7] NRS, E21/6, fol. 22r; TA, II, 213. The king and queen's cloths of state are made of 18 elne and a quarter of cloth of gold each; 71 elne and one quarter of cloth of gold used for second cloth of state and state bed for the queen.

[8] NRS, E21/6, fol. 22r; TA, II, 213.

[9] NRS, E21/6 fol. 22v; TA, II, 213–14.

APPENDIX III

Hangings, cushions, tapestries royal chambers	£1,392, 14s. 4d.[10]
Five chairs of state from Flanders	£175, 15s. 3d.[11]
Cupboard of plate	£704, 3s.[12]
Offerings	£9, 17s.[13]
Undisclosed wedding items from Flanders	£659, 19s. 8d.[14]
Provisions (comptroller)	£8,362, ½d.[15]
Clothing for guests and officers	£1,736, 9s. 10½d.[16]
Gifts to English/fees to English minstrels/musicians	£758, 8s. 7d.[17]
Jousting gear (specifically identified for wedding)	£45, 9s.[18]
King's riding sword/caparison of cloth of gold	£48, 4s. 8d.[19]
Heralds coats of arms	£16, 1s.[20]
Saddle for the queen	£127, 10d.[21]
Total	**£18,677, 6s. 8d.**

1504 Parliament

Work on 'rob riall' and bonnet for crown	£23, 5s. 3d.[22]
Queen's great gown of white damask gold	£99, 10s. 6d.[23]

---

[10] NRS, E21/6, fols 22r–4r; *TA*, II, 213–17.

[11] NRS, E21/6, fol. 29r; *TA*, II, 227–8. These are paid for in May 1504, but for a discussion of these chairs and connection to marriage, see French, 'Magnificence and Materiality', 114–15, 221 (App. 8).

[12] NRS, E21/6, fol. 37r; *TA*, II, 241. For exploration of use of plate, see: French, 'Magnificence and Materiality', 110–14.

[13] NRS, E21/6, fols 44v, 127v; *TA*, II, 254, 385. This includes offering on the Mass book during marriage and candles for the same.

[14] NRS, E21/6, fol. 37r; *TA*, II, 241–2.

[15] NRS, E21/6, fol. 37v; *TA*, II, 242; *ER*, XII, 164–5, 181–2, 186, 205, 228, 234. These are only the expenses specifically identified as specifically for the wedding in the *Exchequer Rolls*, there are others recorded at a similar date that could arguably be included.

[16] NRS, E21/6, fols 78r–83r; *TA*, II, 306–14. The entries in the published *Treasurer's Accounts* for the clothing purchased for guests, servants and officials are substantially abridged when compared to the original manuscripts.

[17] NRS, E21/6, fols 83v, 127v–8v; *TA*, II, 314, 386–7. There are other fees regarding the English, such as carriage of goods, fees for passage home – these are not included, only obvious gifts and fees for musicians who seem to be very prominent.

[18] NRS, E21/6, fols 129r–30r; *TA*, II, 388–90.

[19] NRS, E21/6, fols 19v, 22v; *TA*, II, 207, 214. These are only traceable in Young, particularly the gold caparison. However, there are many other expenses for horses and horse gear that could be relevant, 204–7, which include gilting of stirrups, daggers and fashioning of gold and silver bridle pieces.

[20] NRS, E21/6, fol. 132v; *TA*, II, 395.

[21] NRS, E21/6, fol. 23r; *TA*, II, 214–5.

[22] NRS, E21/6, fol. 27v; *TA*, II, 224–5.

[23] NRS, E21/6, fol. 27v; *TA*, II, 225.

Appendix IV: Select Expenses from James V's French Journey, 1536–37

This appendix highlights select costs demonstrating the king's workforce and purchases for means of display in France. This does not include all fees, services or purchases, and does not attempt to provide a total cost for the wedding as it looks specifically at expenses made in France so does not take into account previous preparatory spend.

Cloths and fabrics (incl. cloth of gold, furs, silk, satin etc.)	3,110 crowns, 5,945 fr. 18s. 7d.[1]
Specific items of clothing for the king	637 crowns, 557 fr. 12s.[2]
Fees for embroiders, tailors and furriers	799 crowns, 1,277 fr. 8s.[3]
Accessories and jewels (incl. pearls, gold thistles, buttons, gold silk threads etc.)	2,734 crowns, 6,217 fr. 5s. 5d.[4]
Horses, horse gear and jousting equipment	435 crowns, 2,400 fr. 12s. 9d.[5]
Additional armour and weapons	9,722 fr. 14s.[6]
For the Queen of Scotland's saddle	226 fr. 12s. 3d.[7]

---

[1] NRS, E21/35, fols 5v, 7v–8r; NRS, E30/5, fols 7r–8r, 22v, 35r–6r; TA, VI, 454, 457–8, VII, 3–5, 23, 37–9.

[2] NRS, E21/35, fols 5v, 7r–8r, 9v; NRS, E30/5, fols 9v, 14v, 21r, 38r; TA, VI, 454, 456–8, 460–2, VII, 6–7, 21, 41.

[3] NRS, E21/35, fols 7r–8r, 9v; NRS, E30/5, fols 10r, 16r, 17v–20v, 25r–26r; TA, VI, 457–60, VII, 8, 14, 17–21.

[4] NRS, E21/35, fol. 8r; NRS, E30/5, fols 10r–10v, 16r, 19r–20r, 21r, 31r–v, 36r; TA, VI, 458, VII, 7–8, 14, 18–20, 22, 32–34, 39.

[5] NRS, E21/35, fols 8r–11v; NRS E30/5, fols 7v, 11r–13r, 14v–15v, 18r, 20v, 21v–2r, 26r, 27r–8r, 35r; TA, VI, 457–63, VII, 5, 8–10, 12–14, 16–17, 21–2, 27–30, 37.

[6] This is recorded in the 1538–39 account but appears to have been purchased in France. Some of it is horse gear and armour for display, including horse armour overgilt with gold for the king, but the bulk of it – around 7,733 fr. – is for artillery 'bullets' or cannon shot: NRS, E30/5, fols 43v–5v; TA, VII, 48–51.

[7] NRS, E30/5, fols 29r–v; TA, VII, 30–1.

APPENDIX IV

Fees and wages for yeoman of the stables, grooms, master of dogs, gamekeepers	556 crowns, 112 fr. 9s.[8]
Furnishings, furniture and napery	100 crowns, 1,458 fr. 12s. 2d.[9]
Tapestries and tapister fees	103 crowns, 2,333 fr. 5s.[10]
Gifts (New Year gifts at court and gifts at departure)	6,328 crowns, 27 fr. 6d.[11]
Queen's spousing ring	1,100 crowns, 22 fr. 10s.[12]
Silver and gold plate, including new chapel plate	11,852 fr. 19 s. 15 d.[13]

These expenses come in at over 15,000 crowns (approximately 33,750 francs)[14] and over 32,000 francs, totalling around 65,750 francs. James received c.100,000 francs for dowry from Madeleine and this was prior to James knowing he would receive a second dowry. Even reducing this by 7,773 francs on artillery (see fn. 6), leaves a total of 57,977 francs.

---

[8] NRS, E21/5, fols 7v, 9v, 11r; NRS, E30/5, fols 17r–21r, 22r–2v, 23v; TA, VI, 457–8, 460, 462, VII, 16–24.
[9] NRS, E21/35, fols 7r–8r; NRS, E30/5, fols 8v, 13–14v, 17v, 18v, 21v–2r, 39r–40r; TA, VI, 457–8, VII, 5–6, 11–12, 17–18, 22, 39r–40r.
[10] NRS, E30/5, fols 17v, 18v, 24r, 26v, 36v, 39r–40r; TA, VII, 17–18 25, 28, 39, 43–4.
[11] NRS, E30/5, fols 10r, 16r–18r, 23r, 23v, 30r, 31v, 34v; TA, VII, 7, 14–16, 17, 25, 31–3, 37.
[12] NRS, E30/5, fols 16r, 34r; TA, VII, 14, 37.
[13] NRS, E30/5, fols 32r–2v, 33v–4v; TA, VII, 34–7.
[14] See example of exchange rate: NRS, E30/5, fol. 45v; TA, VII, 51.

Bibliography

Primary Sources

National Records of Scotland [NRS]

E21/1–2, E21/6–8, E21/31–7, Exchequer Records: Accounts of the Treasurer
E30/5, Accounts by Cardinal Beaton of James V's Expenses in France
E31/7–8, Exchequer Records: Libri Domicilli, James V
E32/1, E32/8, Exchequer Records: Libri Emptorum
E33/4/4, Déspences de la maison royale, Mary of Guise-Lorraine
E38/7–10, E38/326, Exchequer Records: Exchequer Rolls
GD79/2, James VI Hospital Records (relating to the Charterhouse at Perth)
GD149/264, Caprington MS, Royal Letter Book, 1524/5–1548/9
GD249/2/2/1, Tyningham MS, Royal Letter Book, 1529–1627
PC5/4, Privy Council: Register of Royal Letters, 19 September 1623–17 May 1633
SP6–SP9, State Papers, Treaties with England, France, Scandinavia and the Low Countries

National Library of Scotland [NLS]

Adv. MS. 25.5.6, Regiam Maiestatem, statutes, burgh and guild laws, etc. c.1488
Adv. MS 31.4.9, Volume of Extracts from the Records of the City preserved in the Advocates Library
Adv. MS. 31.5.2, John Scrymgeour's Heraldic Collection
Adv. MS. 33.2.26, Sir James Balfour of Denmilne's Manuscript Collection
Adv. MS. 33.7.10, Sir James Balfour of Denmilne's Manuscript Collection
Charter No. 698
MS 1746, Adam Abell, The Roit or Quiell of Tyme

Aberdeen Burgh Archive [ACA]

CA/1/1/5, CA/1/1/8, Council, Baillie and Guild Court Registers

British Library [BL]

Add. MS 4575, Thomas Rymer Collections Hen. I–Edw. I
Add. MS 5444, Annales Angliæ ab anno 1195 ad anno 1316
Cotton MS Nero A IV, Chronicle of English History to 1274, fols 75v–111v
Cotton MS Tiberius B VIII, The Coronation Book of Charles V of France

Cotton MS Vespasian A II, Miscellaneous Treatises, Gloucester Chronicle AM 1–AD 1303, fols 41–74
Harley MS 688, Monachus de Bridlington
Harley MS 4690, Old Chronicle
Harley MS 6149, Fifteenth Century Heraldic Treatise (*The Deidis of Armorie*)
Royal MS 17 D XX, A Short Prose Chronicle to 1482, appended to Andrew of Wyntoun, Original Chronicle of Scotland, in verse, with other tracts

National Archives, Kew [TNA]

C54/24, C54/64–5, Close Rolls
C62/28, Liberate Rolls
C66/24, C66/63, Patent Rolls
E39/79, E39/92, Exchequer: Treasury Receipts: Scottish Documents
E101/415/7, King's Remembrancer: Wardrobe and Household
E372/95, Pipe Rolls
SC1/1/134–9, SC1/5/9, SC1/43/191, Special Collections: Ancient Correspondence
SC7/20/11, Special Collections: Papal Bulls

Other Archival Sources

Bibliothèque nationale de France [BNF]
Manuscrits Français 17330

College of Arms [CA]
MS 1st M.13 bis., [John Young] The Marr. of Margarete da: to Hen: VII to the King of Scots, fols 75–115v

Österreichische Nationalbibliothek [ON]
Cod.1897, Das Gebetbuch Jakobs IV. von Schottland (Book of Hours of James IV of Scotland)

Statens Archiver Copenhagen [SAC]
Kongehuset Christian 1., Princesse Margarethe: Pergamentsbreve 1468–1469

Printed Primary Sources

Accounts of the Lord High Treasurer of Scotland, ed. Thomas Dickson and James Balfour Paul, 12 vols (Edinburgh, 1877–1916)
Accounts of the Masters of Works for Building and Repairing Royal Palaces and Castles, ed. Henry M. Paton et al., 2 vols (Edinburgh, 1957–82)
Acts of the Lords of Council in Public Affairs 1501–1554: Selections from the Acta Dominorum Concilii, ed. Robert K. Hannay (Edinburgh, 1932)
The Acts of Parliament of Scotland, ed. Thomas Thomson and Cosmo Innes, 12 vols (Edinburgh, 1814–75)
The Anglica Historia of Polydore Vergil, A.D. 1485–1537, trans. and ed. Denys Hay (London, 1950)
Anglo-Scottish Relations, 1174–1328: Some Selected Documents, trans. and ed. Edward L.G. Stones (London, 1965)

BIBLIOGRAPHY

Annales Monastici, ed. Henry Richard Luard, 5 vols (London, 1864–69)

Annals of the Reigns of Malcolm and William, 1153–1214, ed. Archibald C. Lawrie (Glasgow, 1910)

'The Auchinleck Chronicle', from the Asloan MS. (NLS MS. Acc. 4233), 'Appendix 2' in Christine McGladdery, *James II* (Edinburgh, 2015), 261–76

Barbour, John, *The Bruce*, ed. Archibald A.M. Duncan (Edinburgh, 1997)

Boece, Hector, *Scotorum historiae a prima gentis origine cum aliarum & rerum & gentium illustration non vulgari: præmissa epistola nu[n]cupatoria, tabellisq[ue] amplissimis, & non pœnitenda Isagoge quæ ab huius tergo explicanbuntur diffusius* (Paris, 1526)

Boece, Hector, *The Chronicles of Scotland Compiled by Hector Boece. Translated into Scots by John Bellenden, 1531*, ed. Edith Batho and H. Winifred Husbands, 2 vols (Edinburgh and London, 1941)

The Book of Pluscarden, Vol. II, ed. Felix J.H. Skene, The Historians of Scotland Series 10 (Edinburgh, 1880)

Bower, Walter, *Scotichronicon*, ed. D.E.R. Watt et al., 9 vols (Aberdeen and Edinburgh, 1987–98)

Buchanan, George, *The History of Scotland Translated from the Latin of George Buchanan: with Notes and Continuation to the Reign of Queen Anne*, ed. James Aikman, 4 vols (Glasgow, 1827)

Calendar of Documents relating to Scotland preserved in her Majesty's Public Record Office, London, ed. Joseph Bain et al., 5 vols (Edinburgh, 1881–1986)

Calendar of Entries in the Papal Registers relating to Great Britain and Ireland: Papal Letters, ed. W.H. Bliss et al., 16 vols (London, 1893)

Chronica Buriensis: The Chronicle of Bury St Edmunds, 1212–1301, ed. Antonia Edmunds (Edinburgh and London, 1964)

Chronica Monasterii de Melsa. A fundatione usque ad annum 1396, auctore Thoma de Burton, Abbate, accredit continuation ad annum 1406 – A monacho quadam ipsium domus, ed. Edward A. Bond, 3 vols (London, 1867)

The Chronica Maiora of Thomas Walsingham, 1376–1422, trans. David Preest and ed. James G. Clark (Woodbridge, 2005)

Chronicle of Adam Usk, 1377–1421, trans. and ed. Chris Given-Wilson (Oxford, 1997)

The Chronicle of Jhon Hardyng, from the firste begynnynge of Englande, vnto the reigne of kyng Edward the fourth And from that tyme is added a continuacion [by Richard Grafton], facsimile edition (Amsterdam, 1976)

The Chronicle of Lanercost, 1272–1346, trans. and ed. Herbert Maxwell (Cribyn, reprint 2001)

The Chronicle of Walter of Guisborough: Previously edited as the Chronicle of Walter of Hemingford or Hemingburgh, ed. Harry Rothwell (London, 1957)

'Chronicle of William Gregory, Skinner', in *The Historical Collections of a Citizen of London [viz. William Gregory] in the Fifteenth Century*, Camden Society Series 17, ed. James Gairdner (London, 1876), Part III

Chronicles of the Reign of Edward I and Edward II, ed. William Stubbs, 2 vols (London, 1882–83)

Chronicles of the Reigns of Stephen, Henry II and Richard I, Rolls Series 82, ed. Richard Howlett, 4 vols (London, 1881–89)

Chronicles of the Revolution, 1397–1400, trans. and ed. Chris Given-Wilson (Manchester, 1993)

Chronique de Mathieu D'Escouchy, ed. Gaston du Fresne de Beaucourt (Paris, 1863)
A Collection of Inventories and Other Records of the Royal Wardrobe and Jewelhouse; and of Artillery and Munitions in some of the Royal Castles MCCCCLXXXVIII–MDCVI, ed. Thomas Thomson (Edinburgh, 1815)
The Coronation Book of Charles V. of France: Cottonian MS. Tiberius B. VIII, ed. Edward S. Dewick (London, 1899)
Corozet, Giles, *Deploration ſur le treſpas de treſ noble Priceſſe dame Magdeleine de France Royne Deſcoce* (Paris, 1537)
Cronique du roy françoys, premier de ce nom. Publiée pour la première fois d'après un manuscrit de la Bibliothèque Impériale, ed. Georges Guiffrey (Paris, 1860)
The Deidis of Armorie: A Heraldic Treatise and Bestiary, Scottish Text Society Fourth Series 22–23, ed. Luuk A.J.R. Houwen (Edinburgh, 1994)
Disciplinary Decrees of the General Councils: Text, Translation and Commentary, ed. Henry J. Schroeder (St. Louis, 1937)
An Diurnal of Remarkable Occurrents that have passed within the country of Scotland since the Death of King James the Fourth til the Year MDLXXV [1575] (Edinburgh, 1833)
Documents Illustrative of the History of Scotland from the Death of King Alexander the Third to the Accession of Robert Bruce MCCLXXXVI–MCCCVI, ed. Joseph Stevenson, 2 vols (Edinburgh, 1870)
Early Records of the Burgh Accounts of Aberdeen, 1317, 1398–1407, ed. William Croft Dickinson (Edinburgh, 1957)
Early Sources of Scottish History A.D. 500 to 1286, ed. Alan Orr Anderson, 2 vols (Edinburgh, 1922)
Early Travellers in Scotland, ed. P. Hume Brown (Edinburgh, 1891)
Les Écossais en France les Français en Écosse, ed. Francisque-Michel, 2 vols (London, 1862)
Edward I and the Throne of Scotland, 1290–1296: An Edition of the Record Sources for the Great Cause, ed. Grant Simpson and E.L.G. Stone, 2 vols (Oxford, 1977–78)
English Coronation Records, ed. Leopold G. Wickham Legge (Westminster, 1901)
The Exchequer Rolls of Scotland: Rotuli Scaccarii Regum Scotorum, ed. John Stuart, George Burnett et al., 23 vols (Edinburgh, 1878–1908)
Extracta E Variis Cronicis Scocie from Ancient Manuscripts in the Advocates Library, ed. William B.D.D. Turnbull (Edinburgh, 1842)
Extracts from the Council Register of the Burgh of Aberdeen, 1398–1625, ed. John Stuart, 2 vols (Aberdeen, 1844–48)
Extracts of the Records of the Burgh of Edinburgh, 1403–1589, ed. James D. Marwick, 5 vols (Edinburgh, 1869–92)
Facsimile of the National Manuscripts of Scotland, 3 vols (Edinburgh, 1867–72)
Foedera, Conventiones, Literæ, et cujuscunque generis Acta Publica inter Reges Angliæ. Et alios quosvis Imperatores, Reges, Pontifices, Principes, vel Communitates etc., ed. Thomas Rhymer et al., third edition, 10 vols (Hague, 1739–45)
Fordun, John, *Chronicle of the Scottish Nation*, trans. and ed. William F. Skene (Edinburgh, 1872)
John Froissart, *Chronicles of England, France, Spain and the Adjoining Countries from the Latter Part of the Reign of Edward II to the Coronation of Henry IV*, trans. Thomas Johnes, 12 vols, third edition (London, 1803–10)

Great Chronicle of London, ed. Arthur H. Thomas and Isobel D. Thornley (London and Aylesbury, 1938)

Gilbert Haye's Prose Manuscript (d. 1456) Vol. II: The Buke of the Knychtehede and the Buke of the Gouvernance of Princis, ed. J.H. Stevenson (Edinburgh and London, 1914)

Gray, Thomas, *Scalacronica, 1272–1363*, trans. and ed. Andy King (Woodbridge, 2005)

The Great Tournament Roll of Westminster: A Collotype Reproduction of the Manuscript, ed. Sydney Anglo (Oxford, 1968)

The Hamilton Papers: Letters and Papers Illustrating the Political Relations of England and Scotland in the XVIth Century, ed. J. Bain, 2 vols (Edinburgh, 1890–92)

The Historical Works of Gervase of Canterbury, Rolls Series, 73, ed. William Stubbs, 2 vols (London, 1879–80)

Howden, Roger de, *The Annals of Roger de Hoveden comprising the History of England and other countries of Europe from AD 732 to AD 1201*, trans. and ed. Henry T. Riley, 2 vols (London, 1853)

Inventaire chronologique des documents relatifs à l'histoire d'Écosse conservés aux archives du royaume à Paris. Suivi d'une indication sommaire des manuscrits de la bibliothèque royale, ed. Jean B.A.T. Teulet (Edinburgh, 1839)

Knox, John, *History of the Reformation in Scotland*, ed. William Croft Dickinson, 2 vols (London and Edinburgh, 1949)

Leslie, John, *The History of Scotland from the Death of King James I in the year MCCCXXXVI to the year MDLXI* (Edinburgh, 1830)

——, *The Historie of Scotland wrytten first in latin by the most reuerrend and worthy Jhone Leslie, Bishop of Ross*, trans. James Dalyrmple (1596), ed. E. G. Cody and William Murison, 2 vols (Edinburgh and London, 1888–95)

Letters and Negotiations of Sir Ralph Sadler, Ambassador of King Henry VIII to Scotland (Edinburgh, 1720)

Letters and Papers, Foreign and Domestic, of the Reign of Henry VIII, ed. John S. Brewer, James Gardiner and R.H. Brodie, 21 vols (London, 1862–1932)

Letters and Papers Illustrative of the Wars of the English in France during the Reign of Henry VI, King of England, ed. Joseph Stevenson, 2 vols (London, 1861–64)

The Letters of James V, ed. Robert K. Hannay and Denys Hay (Edinburgh, 1954)

Liber Regalis seu Ordo Consecrandi Regem Solum, Ordo Reginam cum Rege, Ordo Consecrandi Reginam Solam, Rubrica de Regis Exequiis [E Codice Westmonasteriensi Editus] (London, 1870)

Liber Regie Capelle: A Manuscript in the Biblioteca Pública, Évora, ed. Walter Ullmann (London and Cambridge, 1961)

Life of Saint Columba (Colum-kille) AD 521–597 founder of the Monastery of Iona and first Christian missionary to the Pagan Tribes of North Britain, trans. and ed. Wentworth Huyshe (London, 1900)

Lindesay of Pitscottie, Robert, *The Historie and Cronicles of Scotland: From the Slauchter of King James the First To the Ane thousande five hundrieth thrie scoir fyftein seir*, ed. Æneas J.G. Mackay, 2 vols (Edinburgh and London, 1899)

Lindsay, Jerome, 'Forme of the coronatioun of the Kings of Scotland', *Register of the Privy Council of Scotland*, ed. John H. Burton et al., 36 vols (Edinburgh, 1877–1933), Second Series, II, 393–5

Magna Carta, with A New Commentary, trans. and ed. David A. Carpenter (London, 2015)

Maior, John, *A History of Greater Britain as well England as Scotland, Compiled from the Ancient Authorities by John Major, by name indeed a Scot, but by profession a Theologian 1521*, trans. and ed. Archibald Constable and Æneas J.G. Mackay (Edinburgh, 1892)

Matthew of Paris's English History from the Year 1235 to 1273, trans. and ed. John A. Giles, 3 vols (London, 1852–54)

Medieval Chronicles of Scotland: The Chronicle of Melrose (from 1136 to 1264) and The Chronicle of Holyrood (to 1163), trans. and ed. Joseph Stephenson, reprint (Dyfed, 1988)

The Miracles of Saint Æbbe of Coldingham and Saint Margaret of Scotland, trans. and ed. Robert Bartlett (Oxford, 2003)

'Notice of a Manuscript of the Latter part of the Fourteenth Century, entitled *Passio Scotorum Perjutatorum*', trans. and ed. John Stuart, *PSAS* 19 (1884–85), 166–92

Papiers d'état, pièces et documents inédits ou peu connus relatifs a l'histoire de l'Écosse au XVIème siècle, ed. Alexandre Teulet, 3 vols (Edinburgh, 1852–60)

Ratis Raving and Other Moral and Religious Pieces in Prose and Verse, from Cambridge University MS KK. I. 5, ed. Joseph Rawson Lumby (London, 1890)

Records of the Earldom of Orkney, 1299–1614, ed. Joseph Storer Clouston (Edinburgh, 1914)

Records of the Parliament of Scotland, ed. Gillian H. MacIntosh, Alastair J. Mann, Roland J. Tanner et al. (St Andrews, 2007–13), accessed online at www.rps.ac.uk

The Red Book of Menteith, ed. William Fraser, 2 vols (Edinburgh, 1880)

Regesta Regum Scottorum. Handlist of the Acts of Alexander II, 1214–1249, ed. James Maclean Scouler (Edinburgh, 1960)

Regesta Regum Scottorum. Handlist of the Acts of Alexander III, the Guardians and John, 1249–1296, ed. Grant G. Simpson (Edinburgh, 1960)

Regesta Regum Scottorum Vol. I: The Acts of Malcolm IV, 1153–1165, ed. Geoffrey W.S. Barrow (Edinburgh, 1960)

Regesta Regum Scottorum Vol. II: The Acts of William I, 1165–1214, ed. Geoffrey W.S. Barrow and W.W. Scott (Edinburgh, 1971)

Regesta Regum Scottorum Vol. IV, Part I: The Acts of Alexander III, ed. Cynthia Neville and Grant G. Simpson (Edinburgh, 2013)

Regesta Regum Scottorum Vol. V: The Acts of Robert I, 1306–1329, ed. Archibald A.M. Duncan (Edinburgh, 1988)

Regesta Regum Scottorum Vol. VI: The Acts of David II, 1329–1371, ed. Bruce Webster (Edinburgh, 1982)

Register of the Privy Council of Scotland, ed. John H. Burton et al., 36 vols (Edinburgh, 1877–1933)

Registrum de Dunfermlyn, ed. Cosmo Innes (Edinburgh, 1842)

Registrum Domus de Soltre necnon Ecclesie Collegiate S. Trinitatis prope Edinburgh etc., ed. David Laing (Edinburgh, 1861)

Registrum Episcopatus Moraviensis, ed. Cosmo Innes (Edinburgh, 1837)

Registrum Magni Sigilli Regum Scotorum, ed. John M. Thomson et al., 11 vols (Edinburgh, 1882–1914)

Registrum Secreti Sigilli Regum Scotorum, ed. Matthew Livingstone et al., 8 vols (Edinburgh, 1908–)

Robarts, Henry, *The King of Denmarkes welcome: Containing his ariuall, abode, and entertainement, both in the Citie and other places* (London, 1606)

Rotuli Scotiae in Turri Londonensi et in Domo Capitulari Westmonasteriensi Asservati [Scottish Rolls Preserved in the Tower of London and the Chapter House of Westminster Abbey], ed. David Macpherson et al., 2 vols (London, 1814–19)

Scotland: Documents and Records Illustrating the History of Scotland, and the Transactions between the Crowns of Scotland and England, preserved in her Majesty's Exchequer, ed. Frances Palgrave, 2 vols (London and Edinburgh, 1837)

'The Scottish King's Household and Other Fragments from a Fourteenth-century Manuscript in the Library of Corpus Christi College, Cambridge', ed. Mary Bateson, in *Miscellany of the Scottish History Society Second Volume* (Edinburgh, 1904), 1–43

Shirley, John, 'The Dethe of the Kynge of Scotis: A New Edition', ed. Margaret Connolly, *SHR* 71 (1992), 46–69

Sir David Lyndsay: Selected Poems, ed. Janet Hadley Williams (Glasgow, 2000)

The True Chronicles of Jean le Bel, 1290–1360, trans. Nigel Bryant (Woodbridge, 2015)

William Dunbar: The Complete Works, ed. John Conlee (Kalamazoo, 2004)

Wulson [Vulson], M. de, Sieur de la Colombière, *Le vray théâtre d'honneuret de chevalerie ou le miroir heroique de la noblesse* (Paris, 1648)

Wyntoun, Andrew of, *The Original Chronicles of Andrew of Wyntoun*, ed. F.J. Amours, 6 vols (Edinburgh and London, 1903–14)

Young, John, 'The Fyancells of Margaret, eldeft Daughter of King of the King Henry VIIth to James King of Scotland', in *Johannis Lelandi antiquarii De rebus Brittannicis Collectanea*, ed. Thomas Hearne, 6 vols (London, 1774), IV, 258–300

Secondary Sources

Books, Articles and Chapters

Abrams, Lynn, and Elizabeth L. Ewan (eds), *Nine Centuries of Man: Manhood and Masculinity in Scottish History* (Edinburgh, 2017)

Ailes, Adrian, 'Governmental Seals of Richard I', in Phillipp Schofield (ed.), *Seals and Their Context in the Middle Ages* (Oxford, 2015), 101–10

——, 'Heraldry in Medieval England: Symbols of Politics and Propaganda', in Peter Coss and Maurice Keen (eds), *Heraldry, Pageantry and Social Display in Medieval England* (Woodbridge, 2008), 83–104

Aird, William, 'Frustrated Masculinity: The Relationship between William the Conqueror and his Eldest Son', in Dawn M. Hadley (ed.), *Masculinity in Medieval Europe* (Abingdon, 2014), 39–55.

Aitchison, Nick, *Scotland's Stone of Destiny: Myth, History and Nationhood* (Stroud, 2000)

Alexander, James E., 'An Account of the Excavations of Cambuskenneth Abbey in May 1864', *PSAS* 6 (1864–66), 14–25

Allmand, Christopher, *Henry V* (London, 1992)

Althoff, Gerd, Johannes Fried and Patrick J. Geary (eds), *Medieval Concepts of the Past: Ritual, Memory and Historiography* (Cambridge, 2002)

——, 'The Variability of Rituals in the Middle Ages', in Gerd Althoff, Johannes Fried and Patrick J. Geary (eds), *Medieval Concepts of the Past: Ritual, Memory and Historiography* (Cambridge, 2002), 71–89

Ambler, Sophie, and Nicholas Vincent (eds), *Magna Carta: New Interpretations* (forthcoming)

Andrews, Frances, 'Ritual and Space: Definitions and Ways Forward', in Frances Andrews (ed.), *Ritual and Space in the Middle Ages: Proceedings of the 2009 Harlaxton Symposium* (Donington, 2011), 1–29

——, (ed.), *Ritual and Space in the Middle Ages: Proceedings of the 2009 Harlaxton Symposium* (Donington, 2011)

Anglo, Sydney, *Spectacle, Pageantry and Early Tudor Policy* (Oxford, 1969)

Arnade, Peter, *Realms of Ritual: Burgundian Ceremony and Civic Life in Late Medieval Ghent* (Ithaca and London, 1996)

Ashley, Kathleen, and Wim Hüsken (eds), *Moving Subjects: Processional Performance in the Middle Ages and the Renaissance* (Amsterdam, 2001)

Auslander, Leora, 'Beyond Words', *American Historical Review* 110 (2005), 1015–44

Bagge, Sverre, *From Viking Stronghold to Christian Kingdom: State Formation in Norway, c.900–1350* (Copenhagen, 2010)

Bak, Janos M. (ed.), *Coronations: Medieval and Early Modern Monarchic Ritual* (Berkeley, 1990)

Balfour-Melville, Evan V.M., *James I, King of Scots, 1406–1437* (London, 1936)

Baltzer, Rebecca A., and Margot E. Fassler (eds), *The Divine Office in the Latin Middle Ages: Methodology and Source Studies, Regional Development, Hagiography* (New York, 2000)

Bannerman, John, 'The King's Poet and the Inauguration of Alexander III', *SHR* 68 (1989), 120–49

Bapst, Edmond, *Les Mariages de Jacques V* (Paris, 1889)

Barbé, Louis, *Margaret of Scotland and the Dauphin Louis* (London, Glasgow and Bombay, 1917)

Barrell, A.D.M., *Medieval Scotland* (Cambridge, 2000)

Barrow, Geoffrey W.S., (ed.), *The Declaration of Arbroath: History, Significance, Setting* (Edinburgh, 2003)

——, 'A Kingdom in Crisis: Scotland and the Maid of Norway', *SHR* 69 (1990), 120–41

——, *The Kingdom of the Scots: Government, Church and Society from the Eleventh to the Fourteenth Century*, second edition (Edinburgh, 2003)

——, *Kingship and Unity: Scotland 1000–1306*, revised edition (Edinburgh, 2003)

——, *Robert Bruce and the Community of the Realm*, third edition (Edinburgh, 2001)

——, *Scotland and its Neighbours in the Middle Ages* (London, 1992)

Barrow, Lorna G., '"the Kynge sent to the Qwene, by a Gentylman, a grett tame Hart": Marriage, Gift Exchange, and Politics: Margaret Tudor and James IV, 1502-13', *Parergon* 21 (2004), 65–84

Bawcutt, Priscilla, and Bridget Henisch, 'Scots Abroad in the Fifteenth Century: The Princesses Margaret, Isabella and Eleanor', in Elizabeth Ewan and Maureen M. Meikle (eds), *Women in Scotland, c.1100–c.1750* (East Linton, 1999), 45–55

Baxter, J.H., 'The Marriage of James II', *SHR* 25 (1927), 69–72
Beam, Amanda G., *The Balliol Dynasty 1210–1364* (Edinburgh, 2008)
Beckett, W.N.M., 'The Perth Charterhouse before 1500', *Analecta Carthusiana* 128 (1988), i–xii, 1–75
Beem, Charles, '"Have Not Wee a Noble Kynge?" The Minority of Edward VI', in Charles Beem (ed.), *The Royal Minorities of Medieval and Early Modern England* (New York, 2008), 211–48
——, (ed.), *The Royal Minorities of Medieval and Early Modern England* (New York, 2008)
Beer, Michelle M., '"Translating" a Queen: Material Culture and the Creation of Margaret Tudor as Queen of Scots', *Medieval Clothing and Textiles* 10 (2014), 151–64
Benham, Jenny, *Peacemaking in the Middle Ages: Principles and Practice* (Manchester, 2011)
Bennett, Matthew, and Katherine Weikert (eds), *Medieval Hostageship, c.700–c.1500: Hostage, Captive, Prisoner of War, Guarantee, Peacemaker* (Abingdon, 2017)
Bernhardt, John W., 'King Henry II of Germany: Royal Self-Representation and Historical Memory', in Gerd Althoff, Johannes Fried and Patrick J. Geary (eds), *Medieval Concepts of the Past: Ritual, Memory and Historiography* (Cambridge, 2002), 39–69
Bertelli, Sergio, *The King's Body: Sacred Rituals of Power in Medieval and Early Modern Europe*, trans. R. Burr Litchfield (University Park, PA, 2001)
Binski, Paul, *Westminster Abbey and the Plantagenets: Kingship and the Representation of Power, 1200–1400* (New Haven and London, 1995)
Birch, Walter de Gray, *History of Scottish Seals from the Eleventh to the Seventeenth Century*, 2 vols (Stirling, 1905)
Blakeway, Amy, *Parliament and Convention in the Personal Rule of James V of Scotland, 1528–1542* (Cham, 2022)
——, *Regency in Sixteenth-Century Scotland* (Woodbridge, 2015)
Blockmans, Wim, Till-Holger Borchert, Nele Gabriëls, Johan Oosterman and Anne Van Oosterwijk (eds), *Staging the Court of Burgundy: Proceedings of the Conference 'The Splendour of Burgundy'* (Turnhout, 2013)
Boardman, Stephen I., 'Chronicle Propaganda in Fourteenth-Century Scotland: Robert the Steward, John Fordun, and the "Anonymous Chronicle"', *SHR* 76 (1997), 23–43
——, 'The Cult of St George in Scotland', in Steve Boardman, John R. Davies and Eila Williamson (eds), *Saints' Cults in the Celtic World* (Woodbridge, 2009), 146–59
——, 'Dunfermline as a Royal Mausoleum', in Richard Fawcett (ed.), *Royal Dunfermline* (Edinburgh, 2005), 139–54
——, *The Early Stewart Kings: Robert II and Robert III, 1371–1406* (East Linton, 1996)
——, 'The Gaelic World and Early Stewart Court', in Dauvit Broun and Martin MacGregor (eds), *Miorun Mor nan Gall, The Great Ill-Will of the Lowlander?* (Glasgow, 2007), 83–109
——, 'Robert II (1371–1390)', in Michael Brown and Roland Tanner (eds), *Scottish Kingship 1306–1542: Essays in Honour of Norman MacDougall* (Edinburgh, 2008), 72–108

——, John R. Davies and Eila Williamson (eds), *Saints' Cults in the Celtic World* (Woodbridge, 2009)

——, and S. Foran (eds), *Barbour's Bruce and its Cultural Contexts: Politics, Chivalry and Literature in Late Medieval Scotland* (Cambridge, 2015)

——, and Julian Goodare (eds), *Kings, Lords and Men in Scotland and Britain, 1300–1625: Essays in Honour of Jenny Wormald* (Edinburgh, 2014)

Boogaart II, T.A., 'Our Saviour's Blood: Procession and Community in Late Medieval Bruges', in Kathleen Ashley and Wim Hüsken (eds), *Moving Subjects: Processional Performance in the Middle Ages and the Renaissance* (Amsterdam, 2001), 69–116

Bothwell, James S., 'The More Things Change: Isabella and Mortimer, Edward III and the Painful Delay of a Royal Majority', in Charles Beem (ed.), *The Royal Minorities of Medieval and Early Modern England* (New York, 2008), 67–102

Brégiant, David, *Vox Regis: Royal Communication in High Medieval Norway* (Leiden, 2016)

Brook, Alexander J.S., 'Technical Description of the Regalia of Scotland', *PSAS* 24 (1889–90), 49–146

Brotherstone, Terry, and David Ditchburn (eds), *Freedom and Authority, Scotland c.1050–c.1650: Historical and Historiographical Essays Presented to Grant G. Simpson* (East Linton, 2000)

Broun, Dauvit, 'The Church and the Origins of Scottish Independence in the Twelfth Century', *Records of the Scottish Church History Society* 31 (2002), 22–33

——, 'Contemporary Perspectives on Alexander II's Succession: The Evidence of King-Lists', in Richard D. Oram (ed.), *The Reign of Alexander II* (Leiden, 2005), 79–97

——, *The Irish Identity of the Kingdom of the Scots in the Twelfth and Thirteenth Centuries* (Woodbridge, 1999)

——, 'A New Look at *Gesta Annalia* Attributed to John of Fordun', in Barbara E. Crawford (ed.), *Church, Chronicle and Learning in Medieval and Early Renaissance Scotland: Essays presented to Donald Watt on the Occasion of the Completion of Bower's Scotichronicon* (Edinburgh, 1999), 9–30

——, 'The Origin of the Stone of Scone as a National Icon', in Richard Welander, David Breeze and Thomas O. Clancy (eds), *The Stone of Destiny: Artefact and Icon* (Edinburgh, 2003), 183–97

——, *Scottish Independence and the Idea of Britain From the Picts to Alexander III* (Edinburgh, 2007)

——, 'The Seven Kingdoms in *De Situ Albanie*: A Record of Pictish Political Geography or Imaginary Map of Alba?' in Edward J. Cowan and R. Andrew MacDonald (eds), *Alba: Celtic Scotland in the Medieval Era* (Edinburgh, 2012), 24–42

——, and Martin MacGregor (eds), *Miorun Mor nan Gall, The Great Ill-Will of the Lowlander?* (Glasgow, 2007)

Brown, Andrew, *Civic Ceremony and Religion in Medieval Bruges, c.1300–1520* (Cambridge, 2011)

——, and Graeme Small, *Court and Civic Society in the Burgundian Low Countries, c.1420–1530* (Manchester, 2007)

Brown, Elizabeth A.R., *The Monarchy of Capetian France and Royal Ceremonial* (Aldershot, 1991)

Brown, Keith M., 'The Stewart Realm: Changing the Landscape', in Steve Boardman and Julian Goodare (eds), *Kings, Lords and Men in Scotland and Britain, 1300–1625: Essays in Honour of Jenny Wormald* (Edinburgh, 2014), 19–36

——, and Roland Tanner, Alastair J. Mann and Alan R. MacDonald (eds), *The History of the Scottish Parliament Series*, 3 vols (Edinburgh, 2004–2010)

——, and Roland Tanner, 'Introduction', in Keith Brown and Roland Tanner (eds), *The History of the Scottish Parliament 1: Parliament and Politics, 1235–1560* (Edinburgh, 2004), 1–28

Brown, Michael, *The Black Douglases: War and Lordship in Late Medieval Scotland, 1300–1455* (Edinburgh, 1998)

——, *James I* (Edinburgh, 1994)

——, '"I have thus slain a tyrant": The Dethe of the Kynge of Scotis and the Right to Resist in Early Fifteenth-Century Scotland', *IR* 47 (1996), 24–44.

——, '"Lele counsale for the comoun profite": Kings, Guardians and Councils in the Scottish Kingdom c. 1250–c. 1450', in Jacqueline Rose (ed.), *The Politics of Counsel in England and Scotland, 1286–1707* (Oxford, 2016), 45–62

——, 'Public Authority and Factional Conflict: Crown, Parliament and Polity, 1424–1455', in in Keith Brown and Roland Tanner (eds), *The History of the Scottish Parliament 1: Parliament and Politics, 1235–1560* (Edinburgh, 2004), 133–44

——, '"Rejoice to hear of Douglas": The House of Douglas and the Presentation of Magnate Power in Late Medieval Scotland', *SHR* 76 (1997), 161–84

——, 'Scotland Tamed? Kings and Magnates in Late Medieval Scotland: A Review of Recent Work', *IR* 45 (1994), 120–46

——, '"That Old Serpent and Ancient of Evil Days": Walter, Earl of Atholl and the Death of James I', *SHR* 71 (1992), 23–45

——, 'War, Marriage, Tournament: Scottish Politics and the Anglo-French War, 1448–1450', *SHR* 98 (2019), 1–21

——, *Wars of Scotland 1214–1371*, reprint (Edinburgh, 2010)

——, and Roland Tanner (eds), *Scottish Kingship 1306–1542: Essays in Honour of Norman MacDougall* (Edinburgh, 2008)

Brückman, John, 'The Ordines of the Third Recension of the Medieval English Coronation Order', in T.A. Sandquist and Michael R. Powick (eds), *Essays in Medieval History Presented to Bertie Wilkinson* (Toronto, 1969), 99–115

Bruun, M. Birkedal, 'Procession and Contemplation in Bernard of Clairvaux's First Sermon for Palm Sunday', in Nils H. Peterson, Mette B. Bruun, Jeremy Llewellyn and Eyolf Østrem (eds), *The Appearance of Medieval Rituals: The Play of Construction and Modification* (Turnhout, 2004), 67–82

Bryant, Lawrence M., *The King and the City in the Parisian Royal Entry Ceremony: Politics, Ritual, and Art in the Renaissance* (Geneva, 1986)

——, 'The Medieval Entry Ceremony at Paris', in Janos M. Bak (ed.), *Coronations: Medieval and Early Modern Monarchic Ritual* (Berkeley, 1990), 88–118

——, *Ritual, Ceremony and the Changing Monarchy in France, 1350–1789* (Farnham, 2010)

Buc, Philippe, *The Dangers of Ritual: Between Early Medieval Texts and Social Scientific Theory* (Princeton, 2001)

——, 'Ritual and Interpretation: The Early Medieval Case', *Early Medieval Europe* 9 (July 2000), 183–210

Buchanan, Katherine, and Lucinda H.S. Dean with Michael Penman (eds), *Medieval and Early Modern Representations of Authority in Scotland and the British Isles* (Abingdon, 2016)

Burden, Joel F., 'How Do You Bury a Deposed King? The Funeral of Richard II and the Establishment of Royal Authority in 1400', in Gwilym Dodd and Donald Biggs (eds), *Henry IV: The Establishment of the Regime, 1399–1406* (York, 2003), 35–53

——, 'Re-writing a Rite of Passage: The Peculiar Funeral of Edward II', in Nicola F. MacDonald and W. Mark Ormrod (eds), *Rites of Passage: Cultures of Transition in the Fourteenth Century* (York, 2004), 13–29

Burke, Peter, 'Performing History: The Importance of Occasions', *Rethinking History* 9 (2005), 35–52

——, 'Presenting and Representing Charles V', in Hugo Soly and Willem P. Blockmans (eds), *Charles V (1500–1558) and His Times* (Antwerp, 1999), 393–476

Burnett, Charles J., 'Early Officers of Arms in Scotland', *Review of Scottish Culture* 9 (1996), 3–13

——, and Chris J. Tabraham, *The Honours of Scotland: The History of the Scottish Crown Jewels* (Edinburgh, 1993)

Burns, Charles, 'Papal Gifts to Scottish Monarchs: The Golden Rose and the Blessed Sword', *IR* 20 (1969), 150–95

Burton, Janet, Phillipp Schofield and Björn Weiler (eds), *Thirteenth Century England XII: Proceedings of the Gregynog Conference, 2007* (Woodbridge, 2009)

——, Phillipp Schofield and Björn Weiler (eds), *Thirteenth Century England XIV: Proceedings of the Aberystwyth and Lampeter Conference, 2011* (Woodbridge, 2013)

Caldwell, David, 'Finlaggan, Islay – Stones and Inauguration Ceremonies', in Richard Welander, David Breeze and Thomas O. Clancy (eds), *The Stone of Destiny: Artefact and Icon* (Edinburgh, 2003), 61–75

Cameron, Jamie, *James V: The Personal Rule, 1528–1542*, ed. Norman Macdougall (East Linton, 1998)

Cameron, Sonja, 'Sir James Douglas, Spain and the Holy Land', in Terry Brotherstone and David Ditchburn (eds), *Freedom and Authority, Scotland c.1050–c.1650: Historical and Historiographical Essays presented to Grant G. Simpson* (East Linton, 2000), 108–17

——, Sonja, and Alasdair Ross, 'The Treaty of Edinburgh and the Disinherited (1328–1332)', *History* 84 (1999), 237–56

Campbell, Ian, 'James IV and Edinburgh's First Triumphal Arches', in Deborah Mays (ed.), *The Architecture of Scottish Cities, Essays in Honour of David Walker* (East Linton, 1997), 26–33

Canova-Green, Marie-Claude, and Sara Wolfson (eds), *Celebrations for the Wedding of Charles and Henrietta Maria* (Turnhout, 2020)

Carpenter, David A., *The Minority of Henry III* (London, 1990)

——, *The Reign of Henry III* (London, 1996)

Carpenter, Jennifer, and Sally–Beth MacLean (eds), *Power of the Weak: Studies on Medieval Women* (Urbana and Chicago, 1995)

Carpenter, Sarah, '"To Thexaltacyon of Noblesse": A Herald's Account of the Marriage of Margaret Tudor and James IV', *Medieval English Theatre* 29 (2007), 104–120

Cherry, John, 'Medieval and Post-Medieval Seals', in Dominique Collon (ed.), *7000 Years of Seals* (London, 1997), 124–42
Church, Stephen D. (ed.), *King John: New Interpretations* (Woodbridge, 1999)
Cloake, John, *Richmond's Great Monastery, The Charterhouse of Jesus of Bethlehem of Shene* (London, 1990)
Cohn Jr, Samual, and Marcello Fantoni, Franco Franceschi and Fabrizio Ricciardelli (eds), *Late Medieval and Early Modern Rituals: Studies in Italian Urban Culture* (Turnhout, 2013)
Collon, Dominique (ed.), *7000 Years of Seals* (London, 1997)
The Complete Peerage of England, Scotland, Ireland, Great Britain and the United Kingdom, Extant, Extinct or Dormant, ed. George E. Cokayne et al., 6 vols, new edition (Gloucester, 2000)
Connell, Raewyn W., and James W. Messerschmidt, 'Hegemonic Masculinity: Rethinking the Concept', *Gender and Society* 19 (2005), 829–59
Coombs, Bryony, 'John Stuart, Duke of Albany and his contribution to military science in Scotland and Italy, 1514–36', *PSAS*, 148 (2019), 231–66
——, 'Material Diplomacy: A Continental Manuscript Produced for James III, Edinburgh University Library, MS 195', *SHR* 98 (2019), 183–213
Cooper, J., 'Four Scottish Coronations Since the Reformation', *Transactions of the Aberdeen Ecclesiological Society and Transactions of the Glasgow Ecclesiological Society*, Special Issue (Aberdeen, 1902)
Coss, Peter, 'Knighthood, Heraldry and Social Exclusion in Edwardian England', in Peter Coss and Maurice Keen (eds), *Heraldry, Pageantry and Social Display in Medieval England* (Woodbridge, 2008), 39–68
——, and Maurice Keen (eds), *Heraldry, Pageantry and Social Display in Medieval England* (Woodbridge, 2008)
Cowan, Edward J., and R. Andrew MacDonald (eds), *Alba: Celtic Scotland in the Medieval Era* (Edinburgh, 2012)
Cowan, Ian. B., P.H.R. Mackay, and Alan MacQuarrie, *The Knights of St John of Jerusalem in Scotland*, Scottish History Society Series 19 (Edinburgh, 1983)
Cowan, Mairi, Janay Nugent and Cathryn Spence (eds), *Gender and Identity in Scotland, 1200–1800: Power, Politics, and Faith* (Edinburgh, forthcoming 2024)
Crawford, Barbara E. (ed.), *Church, Chronicle and Learning in Medieval and Early Renaissance Scotland: Essays Presented to Donald Watt on the Occasion of the Completion of Bower's Scotichronicon* (Edinburgh, 1999)
Crewe, Emma, and Marion G. Müller (eds), *Rituals in Parliaments, Political, Anthropological and Historical Perspectives on Europe and the United States* (Frankfurt, 2006)
Dale, Johanna, *Inauguration and Liturgical Kingship in the Long Twelfth Century* (York, 2019)
Damen, Mario, Jelle Haemers and Alastair J. Mann (eds), *Political Representation: Communities, Ideas and Institutions in Europe, c.1200–c.1690* (Leiden, 2018)
Davies, Rees R., *The First English Empire* (Oxford, 2000)
Davis, Rachel M., 'Material Evidence? Re-approaching Elite Women's Seals and Charters in Late Medieval Scotland', *PSAS* 150 (2021), 301–26
Dean, Lucinda H.S., 'Crowning the Child: Representing Authority in the Inaugurations and Coronations of Minors in Scotland, c.1214 to c.1567', in Elena Woodacre and Sean McGlyn (eds), *The Image and Perception of Monarchy in Medieval and Early Modern Europe* (Newcastle, 2014), 254–280

——, 'Enter the Alien: Foreign Consorts and their Royal Entries into Scottish Cities, c.1449–1590', in J. Ronnie Mulryne and Anna Maria Testaverde with Ines Aliverti (eds), *The Iconography of Power: Ceremonial Entries in Early Modern Europe* (Farnham, 2015), 267–95

——, 'In the Absence of an Adult Monarch: The Ceremonial Representations of Authority by Marie de Guise, c.1543–1558', in Katherine Buchanan and Lucinda H.S. Dean with Michael Penman (eds), *Medieval and Early Modern Representations of Authority in Scotland and the British Isles* (Abingdon, 2016), 143–62

——, 'Keeping Your Friends Close, But Your Enemies Closer? The Anglo-Franco-Scottish Marital Triangle, c.1200 to c.1625', in Marie-Claude Canova-Green and Sara Wolfson (eds), *Celebrations for the Wedding of Charles and Henrietta Maria* (Turnhout, 2020), 41–62

——, 'Making the Most of What They Had: Adapting Indoor and Outdoor Spaces for Royal Ceremony in Scotland, c. 1214 to c. 1603', in Krista De Jonge and J. Ronnie Mulryne with Richard Morris (eds), *Architectures of Festival in Early Modern Europe* (Abingdon, 2017), 99–117

——, 'Negotiating Youth, Old Age and Manhood: A Comparative Approach to Late Medieval Scottish Kingship', in Mairi Cowan, Janay Nugent and Cathryn Spence (eds), *Gender and Identity in Scotland, 1200–1800: Power, Politics, and Faith* (Edinburgh, forthcoming 2024)

——, 'Projecting Dynastic Majesty: State Ceremony in the Reign of Robert the Bruce', *International Review of Scottish Studies* 40 (2015), 34–60

——, '"Richesse in Fassone and in Fairenesse": Material Display and Sartorial Splendour in Sixteenth-Century Scottish Royal Weddings', *SHR* 100 (2021), 378–96

——, 'Where to Make the King (or Queen): The Importance of Place in Scottish Inaugurations and Coronations from 1214 to 1651', in Oliver O'Grady and Richard Oram (eds), *Royal and Lordly Inauguration and Assembly Places in North-West Europe* (Donington, 2023), 48–73

Dennison, E. Patricia, *The Evolution of Scotland's Towns: Creation, Growth and Fragmentation* (Edinburgh, 2018)

Dillon, Emma, *The Sense of Sound: Musical Meaning in France, 1260–1330* (Oxford and New York, 2012)

Ditchburn, David, 'The Place of Guelders in Scottish Foreign Policy, c.1449–c.1542', in Grant G. Simpson (ed.), *Scotland and the Low Countries, 1124–1994* (East Linton, 1996), 59–75

——, 'Rituals, Space and the Marriage of James II', in Frances Andrews (ed.), *Ritual and Space in the Middle Ages: Proceedings of the 2009 Harlaxton Symposium* (Donington, 2011), 176–96

——, 'Scotland and Europe', in Bob Harrison and Alan R. MacDonald (eds), *Scotland: The Making and Unmaking of the Nation, 1100–1707, Vol. I* (Dundee, 2006), 103–120

——, and Alastair J. Macdonald, 'Medieval Scotland, 1100–1560', in Robert A. Houston and William W.J. Knox (eds), *The New Penguin History of Scotland: From the Earliest Times to the Present Day* (London, 2001), 96–181

Dodd, Gwilym, 'Richard II and the Fiction of Majority Rule', in Charles Beem (ed.), *The Royal Minorities of Medieval and Early Modern England* (New York, 2008), 103–159

——, and Douglas Biggs (eds), *Henry IV: The Establishment of the Regime, 1399–1406* (York, 2003)
Donaldson, Gordon, 'Reflections on the Royal Succession', in James Kirk (ed.), *Scotland's History: Approaches and Reflections* (Edinburgh, 1995), 103–17
——, *Scottish Kings* (London, 1967)
Dowden, John, *The Bishops of Scotland* (Glasgow, 1912)
Downie, Fiona, '"La Voie quelle menace tenir": Annabella Stewart, Scotland, and the European Marriage Market, 1444–56', SHR 78 (1999), 170–91
——, *She is But a Woman: Queenship in Scotland 1424–1463* (Edinburgh, 2006)
Driscoll, Stephen T., 'Govan: An Early Medieval Royal Centre on the Clyde', in Richard Welander, David Breeze and Thomas O. Clancy (eds), *The Stone of Destiny: Artefact and Icon* (Edinburgh, 2003), 77–83
Duffy, Eamon, *The Stripping of the Altars: Traditional Religion in England 1400–1580* (New Haven, 1993)
Duffy, Mark, *Royal Tombs in England* (Stroud, 2003)
Dunbar, John G. *Scottish Royal Palaces: The Architecture of the Royal Residences during the Late Medieval and Early Renaissance Periods* (East Linton, 1999)
Duncan, Archibald A.M., 'Before Coronation: Making a King at Scone in the Thirteenth Century', in Richard Welander, David Breeze and Thomas O. Clancy (eds), *The Stone of Destiny: Artefact and Icon* (Edinburgh, 2003), 139–67
——, 'The Early Parliaments of Scotland', SHR 45 (1966), 36–58
——, 'John King of England and the King of Scots', in Stephen D. Church (ed.), *King John: New Interpretations* (Woodbridge, 1999), 247–71
——, *The Kingship of the Scots 842–1242: Succession and Independence* (Edinburgh, 2002)
——, *Scotland: The Making of the Kingdom*, reprint (Edinburgh, 1996)
——, 'The Wars of the Scots, 1306–23', *Transactions of the Royal Historical Society* 2 (1992), 125–51
Dunlop, Annie I., *The Life and Times of James Kennedy, Bishop of St Andrews* (Edinburgh, 1950)
Dunlop, David, 'The "Masked Comedian": Perkin Warbeck's Adventures in Scotland and England from 1495 to 1497', SHR 70 (1991), 97–128
Edington, Carol, *Court and Culture in Renaissance Scotland, David Lindsay of the Mount* (Amherst, 1994)
——, 'The Tournament in Medieval Scotland', in Matthew Strickland (ed.), *Armies, Chivalry and Warfare in Medieval Britain and France: Proceedings of the 1995 Harlaxton Symposium* (Stamford, 1998), 46–62
Eichberger, Dagmar, Anne-Marie Legaré and Wim Hüsken (eds), *Women at the Burgundian Court: Presence and Influence* (Turnhout, 2010)
Emond, Ken, *The Minority of James V: Scotland in Europe, 1513–1528* (Edinburgh, 2019)
Erlande-Brandenburg, Alain, *Le Roi est mort: étude sur les funérailles les sépultures et les tombeaux des rois de France jusqu'à la fin du XIIIe siècle* (Paris and Geneva, 1975)
Everett Green, Mary Anne, *Lives of the Princesses of England from the Norman Conquest*, 6 vols (London, 1849)
Ewan, Elizabeth, and Maureen M. Meikle (eds), *Women in Scotland, c.1100–c.1750* (East Linton, 1999)

——, and Janay Nugent (eds), *Childhood and Youth in Pre-Modern Scotland* (Woodbridge, 2015)

Fantoni, Marcello, 'Symbols and Rituals: Definition of a Field of Study', in Samual Cohn Jr, Marcello Fantoni, Franco Franceschi and Fabrizio Ricciardelli (eds), *Late Medieval and Early Modern Rituals: Studies in Italian Urban Culture* (Turnhout, 2013), 15–40

Farmer, David H., *The Oxford Dictionary of Saints* (Oxford, 1978)

Fawcett, Richard (ed.), *Royal Dunfermline* (Edinburgh, 2005)

Ferguson, Paul C., *Medieval Papal Representatives in Scotland: Legates, Nuncios, and Judge-Delegate, 1125–1286* (Edinburgh, 1997)

Ferguson O'Meara, Cara, *Monarchy and Consent: The Coronation Book of Charles V of France, British Library MS Cotton Tiberius B. VIII* (London and Turnhout, 2001)

Fitch, Audrey-Beth, *The Search for Salvation: Lay Faith in Scotland 1480–1560*, ed. Elizabeth Ewan (Edinburgh, 2009)

Fitzpatrick, Elizabeth, *Royal Inauguration in Gaelic Ireland, c. 1100–1600: A Cultural Landscape Study* (Woodbridge, 2004)

Foran, Susan, 'A Nation of Knights? Chivalry and the Community of the Realm in Barbour's *Bruce*', in Steve Boardman and Susan Foran (eds), *Barbour's Bruce and its Cultural Contexts: Politics, Chivalry and Literature in Late Medieval Scotland* (Cambridge, 2015), 137–48

Forbes-Leith, William, *The Scots Men-at-Arms and Life-Guards in France. From their Formation until their Final Dissolution A.D. MCCCCXVIII–MDCCCXXX* (Edinburgh, 1882)

Fradenburg, Louise O., *City, Marriage, Tournament: Arts of Rule in Later Medieval Scotland* (Madison, 1991)

——, 'Sovereign Love: The Wedding of Margaret Tudor and James IV of Scotland', in Louise O. Fradenburg (ed.), *Women and Sovereignty* (Edinburgh, 1992), 78–97

——, (ed.), *Women and Sovereignty* (Edinburgh, 1992)

Fraser, Iain, 'The Tomb of the Hero King: The Death and Burial of Robert I and Discoveries of 1818–19', in Richard Fawcett (ed.), *Royal Dunfermline* (Edinburgh, 2005), 155–76

Gemmill, Elizabeth, and Nicholas Mayhew, *Changing Values in Medieval Scotland: A Study of Prices, Money, and Weights and Measures* (Cambridge, 1995)

Gerristen, Anne, and Giorgio Riello, 'Introduction: Writing Material Culture History', in Anne Gerristen and Giorgio Riello (eds), *Writing Material Culture History* (London, 2015), 1–14

——, and Giorgio Riello (eds), *Writing Material Culture History* (London, 2015)

Giesey, Ralph, 'Inaugural Aspects of French Royal Ceremonials', in Janos M. Bak (ed.), *Coronations: Medieval and Early Modern Monarchic Ritual* (Berkeley, 1990), 35–45

——, *The Royal Funeral Ceremony in Renaissance France* (Geneva, 1960)

Gilbert, John M. 'The Usual Money of Scotland and Exchange Rates Against Foreign Coin', in David M. Metcalf (ed.), *Coinage in Medieval Scotland (1100–1600): The Second Oxford Symposium on Coinage and Monetary History*, British Archaeological Report 45 (Oxford, 1977), 131–53

Gimson, G.S., 'Lion Hunt: A Royal Tomb-Effigy at Arbroath Abbey', *PSAS* 125 (1995), 901–16

Gittos, Brian, and Moira Gittos, 'Motivation and Choice: The Selection of Medieval Secular Effigies', in Peter Coss and Maurice Keen (eds), *Heraldry, Pageantry and Social Display in Medieval England* (Woodbridge, 2008), 143–67

Given-Wilson, Chris, *Chronicles: The Writings of History in Medieval England* (London and New York, 2004)

Goff, Jacques Le, 'A Coronation Program for the Age of St Louis: The Ordo of 1250', in Janos M. Bak (ed.), *Coronations: Medieval and Early Modern Monarchic Ritual* (Berkeley, 1990), 46–57

——, 'The Exequies of Edward III and the Royal Funeral Ceremony in Late Medieval England', *English Historical Review* 134 (2009), 257–82

——, 'La Structure et le contenu idéologique de cérémonie du sacre', in Jacques Le Goff et al., *Le Sacre royal a l'époque de Saint-Louis: d'après le manuscrit latin 1246 de la BNF* (Paris, 2001), 19–35

——, and Jean-Claude Schmitt (eds), *Le Charivari: actes de la table ronde organisée à Paris (25–27 avril 1977) par l'École des Hautes Études en Sciences Sociales et le Centre National de la Recherche Scientifique* (Paris, 1981)

——, et al. (eds), *Le Sacre royal a l'époque de Saint-Louis: d'après le manuscrit latin 1246 de la BNF* (Paris, 2001)

Goodare, Julian, and Alastair A. MacDonald (eds), *Sixteenth-Century Scotland: Essays in Honour of Michael Lynch* (Leiden, 2008)

Gosman, Martin, Alastair A. MacDonald and Arie Johan Vanderjagt (eds), *Princes and Princely Culture, 1450–1650*, 2 vols (Leiden, 2003–5)

Grant, Alexander, 'The Death of John Comyn: What Was Going On?' *SHR* 86 (2007), 176–224

——, *Independence and Nationhood: Scotland 1306–1469*, reprint (Edinburgh, 2007)

——, and Keith Stringer (eds), *Medieval Scotland: Crown, Lordship and Community: Essays Presented to G.W.S Barrow* (Edinburgh, 1993)

Grant, Francis J. (ed.), *Court of the Lord Lyon: A List of his Majesty's Officers at Arms and Other Officials with Geographical Notes, 1318–1945* (Edinburgh, 1945)

Gray, Douglas, 'The Royal Entry in Sixteenth-Century Scotland', in Sally Mapstone and Juliette Hood (eds), *The Rose and the Thistle, Essays on the Culture of Late Medieval and Renaissance Scotland* (East Linton, 1998), 10–32

Griffiths, Ralph A., 'The Minority of Henry VI, King of England and France', in Charles Beem (ed.), *The Royal Minorities of Medieval and Early Modern England* (New York, 2008), 161–93

——, 'Succession and the Royal Dead in Later Medieval England', in Frédérique Lachaud and Michael Penman (eds), *Making and Breaking the Rules: Succession in Medieval Europe, c.1000–1600* (Turnhout, 2008), 97–109

Grummit, David, *The Wars of the Roses* (London, 2013)

Guidicini, Giovanna, *Triumphal Entries and Festivals in Early Modern Scotland: Performing Spaces* (Turnhout, 2020)

Hadley, Dawn M., (ed.), *Masculinity in Medieval Europe* (Abingdon, 2014)

Hadley Williams, Janet, (ed.), *Stewart Style 1513–1542: Essays on the Court of James V* (East Linton, 1996)

Hallam, Elizabeth M., 'Royal Burial and the Cult of Kingship in France and England, 1060–1330', *Journal of Medieval History* 8 (1982), 359–80

Harper, John, *The Forms and Orders of Western Liturgy from the Tenth to the Eighteenth Century: A Historical Introduction for Students and Musicians*, reprint (Oxford, 2001)

Harrison, Bob, and Alan R. MacDonald (eds), *Scotland: The Making and Unmaking of the Nation, 1100–1707, Vol. I* (Dundee, 2006)

Harrison, John, *Rebirth of a Palace: The Royal Court at Stirling Castle* (Edinburgh, 2011)

Harvey, Anthony, and Richard Mortimer, *The Funeral Effigies of Westminster Abbey*, revised edition (Woodbridge, 2003)

The Heads of Religious Houses in Scotland from the Twelfth to the Sixteenth Centuries, ed. Donald E.R. Watt and N.F. Shead (Edinburgh, 2001)

Helle, Knut, 'Norwegian Foreign Policy and the Maid of Norway', *SHR* 69 (1990), 142–56

Henderson, Christine, *Kelso Abbey: A Brief History* (Kelso, 2012)

Henderson, George D.S., 'Royal Effigy at Arbroath', in W. Mark Ormrod (ed.), *England in the Fourteenth Century: Proceedings from the 1985 Harlaxton Symposium* (Woodbridge, 1986), 88–98

Hepburn, William, *The Household and Court of James IV of Scotland, 1488–1513* (Woodbridge, 2023)

Hillen, Christian, and Frank Wiswall, 'The Minority of Henry III in the Context of Europe', in Charles Beem (ed.), *The Royal Minorities of Medieval and Early Modern England* (New York, 2008), 17–66

Hoffman, Erich, 'Coronation Ordines in Medieval Scandinavia', in Bak (ed.), *Coronations: Medieval and Early Modern Monarchic Rituals* (Berkeley, 1990), 125–43

Hogg, James, 'The Carthusians of Perth and the Carthusian General Chapter', *Analecta Carthusiana* 175 (2001), 151–241

Holmes, Stephen M., 'Catalogue of Liturgical Books and Fragments in Scotland before 1560', *IR* 62 (2011), 127–212

Houston, Robert A., and William W.J. Knox (eds), *The New Penguin History of Scotland: From the Earliest Times to the Present Day* (London, 2001)

Houwen, Luuk A.J.R., (ed.), *Literature and Religion in Late Medieval and Early Modern Scotland* (Leuven, 2012)

——, Alistair A. MacDonald and Sally Mapstone (eds), *A Palace in the Wild: Essays on Vernacular Culture and Humanism in Late-Medieval and Renaissance Scotland* (Leuven, 2000)

Hughes, Andrew, 'The Origins and Descent of the Fourth Recension of the English Coronation', in Janos M. Bak (ed.), *Coronations: Medieval and Early Modern Monarchic Ritual* (Berkeley, 1990), 197–216

Hunt, Karen, 'The Governorship of Robert Duke of Albany (1406–1420)', in Michael Brown and Roland Tanner (eds), *Scottish Kingship 1306–1542: Essays in Honour of Norman MacDougall* (Edinburgh, 2008), 126–54

Hunter, James, *Fala and Soutra Including A History of the Ancient 'Domus de Soltre' with its Masters and Great Revenues, and of other Historical Associations and Buildings* (Edinburgh, 1892)

Hume Brown, P., *History of Scotland* (Cambridge, 1911)

Hurlbutt, Jesse, 'Symbols of Authority: Inaugural Ceremonies for Charles the Bold', in Wim Blockmans, Till-Holger Borchert, Nele Gabriëls, Johan Oosterman and Anne Van Oosterwijk (eds), *Staging the Court of Burgundy: Proceedings of the Conference 'The Splendour of Burgundy'* (Turnhout, 2013), 105–112

Hüsken, Wim, 'Royal Entries in Flanders (1336–1515)', in Dagmar Eichberger, Anne-Marie Legaré and Wim Hüsken (eds), *Women at the Burgundian Court: Presence and Influence* (Turnhout: Brepols, 2010), 37–42

Jackson, Richard A., *Vive le roi! A History of the French Coronation From Charles V to Charles X* (Chapel Hill and London, 1984)

Jardine, Henry, 'Extracts from the Report made by Henry Jardine […] relative to the Tomb of King Robert Bruce and the Church of Dunfermline', *Archaeologia Scotica: The Transactions of the Society of Antiquaries of Scotland* 2 (1822), 435–54

Jaski, Bart, *Early Irish Kingship and Succession* (Dublin, 2000)

Jerram, Leif, 'Space: A Useless Category for Historical Analysis?', *History and Theory* 52 (2013), 400–19

Johannsen, Birgitte Bøggild, and Koen A. Ottenhym (eds), *Beyond Scylla and Charybdis: European Courts and Court Residences Outside Habsburg and Valois Territories, 1500–1700* (Odense, 2015)

Jugie, Sophie, *The Mourners: Tomb Sculptures from the Court of Burgundy* (New Haven and London, 2010)

Jonge, Krista De, and Ronnie Mulryne with Richard Morris (eds), *Architectures of Festival in Early Modern Europe* (Abingdon, 2017)

Kantorowicz, Ernst H., *The King's Two Bodies: A Study in Medieval Political Theology*, reprint (Princeton, 1997)

Kaufman, Matthew H., and William J. MacLennan, 'King Robert the Bruce and Leprosy', *Proceedings of the College of Physicians* 30 (2000), 75–80

Keen, Maurice, *Chivalry*, reprint (New Haven and London, 2005)

Keith, Robert, *An Historical Catalogue of the Scottish Bishops down to the Year 1688* (Edinburgh, 1824)

Kempshall, Matthew, *Rhetoric and the Writing of History* (Manchester, 2011)

Kilgallon, Lynn, 'Communal Authority, Counsel and Resistance in the Reign of James I: A Conceptual Approach', *SHR* 100 (2021), 1–24

Kinloch, M.G.J., 'Scottish Coronations, AD 574–1651', Part One and Two, *Dublin Review* 130 (1902), 263–77 and 131 (1902), 34–52

Kipling, Gordon, *Enter the King: Theatre, Liturgy, and Ritual in the Medieval Civic Triumph* (Oxford, 1998)

Kirk, James (ed.), *Scotland's History: Approaches and Reflections* (Edinburgh, 1995)

Kjær, Lars, 'Food, Drink and Ritualised Communication in the Household of Eleanor de Montfort, February to August 1265', *Journal of Medieval History* 37 (2011), 75–89

——, 'Matthew Paris and the Royal Christmas: Ritualised Communication in Text and Practice', in Janet Burton, Phillip Scholfield and Björn Weiler (eds), *Thirteenth Century England XIV: Proceedings of the Aberystwyth and Lampeter Conference 2011* (Woodbridge, 2013), 141–52

Knecht, Robert J., 'Charles V's Journey Through France, 1539–1540', in J. Ronnie Mulryne and Elizabeth Goldring (eds), *Court Festivals in the European Renaissance: Art, Politics and Performance* (Aldershot, 2002), 153–70

——, *Francis I and Sixteenth-Century France* (Farnham, 2016)

——, *Renaissance Warrior and Patron: The Reign of Francis I* (Cambridge, 1994)

Laing, Henry, *Descriptive Catalogue of Impressions of Ancient Seals of Scotland* (Edinburgh, 1850)

——, 'Notes Relating to the Interment of King James III of Scotland and of His Queen, Margaret of Denmark, in the Abbey Church of Cambuskenneth', *PSAS* 6 (1864–66), 26–33

Lachaud, Frédérique, and Michael Penman (eds), *Absentee Authority Across Medieval Europe* (Woodbridge, 2017)

——, and Michael Penman (eds), *Making and Breaking the Rules: Succession in Medieval Europe, c.1000–1600* (Turnhout, 2008)

Laynesmith, Joanna L., *The Last Medieval Queens: English Queenship 1445–1503* (Oxford, 2004)

Legge, M.D., 'Inauguration of Alexander III', *PSAS* 80 (1945–46), 73–82

Lewis, Katherine J., *Kingship and Masculinity in Late Medieval England* (Abingdon, 2013)

Liszka, Thomas R., and Lorna E.M. Walker (eds), *The North Sea World in the Middle Ages: Studies in the Cultural History of North-Western Europe* (Dublin, 2001)

Little, A.G., 'Authorship of the Lanercost Chronicle', *English Historical Review*, 31/2 (1916), 269–79

Ljungkvist, John, and Joakim Kjellberg, 'Monuments and History-making – the Creation and Destruction of Gamla Uppsala Monuments in the Medieval Period', in Oliver O'Grady and Richard Oram (eds), *Royal and Lordly Inauguration and Assembly Places in North-West Europe* (Donnington, 2023), 202–225

Luxford, Julian M., 'The Space of the Tomb in the Carthusian Consciousness', in Frances Andrews (ed.), *Ritual and Space in the Middle Ages: Proceedings of the 2009 Harlaxton Symposium* (Donington, 2011), 259–81

Lyall, Roderick, 'The Lost Literature of Medieval Scotland', in J. Derrick McClure and Michael R.G. Spiller (eds), *Bryght Lanternis: Essays on the Language and Literature of Medieval and Renaissance Scotland* (Aberdeen, 1989), 33–47

——, 'The Medieval Coronation Service: Some Seventeenth Century Evidence', *IR*, 28/1 (1977), 3–21

Lynch, Michael, 'Queen Mary's Triumph: The Baptismal Celebrations at Stirling in December 1566', *SHR* 69 (1990), 1–21

——, 'Scotland's First Protestant Coronation: Revolutionaries, Sovereignty and the Culture of Nostalgia', in Luuk A.J.R. Houwen (ed.), *Literature and Religion in Late Medieval and Early Modern Scotland* (Leuven, 2012), 177–207

——, Michael Spearman and Geoffrey Stell (eds), *The Scottish Medieval Town* (Edinburgh, 1988)

MacDonald, Alastair A., 'Princely Culture in Scotland Under James III and James IV', in Martin Gosman, Alastair A. MacDonald and Arie Johan Vanderjagt (eds), *Princes and Princely Culture, 1450–1650*, 2 vols (Leiden, 2003–2005), I, 147–72

MacDonald, Nicola F., and W. Mark Ormrod (eds), *Rites of Passage: Cultures of Transition in the Fourteenth Century* (York, 2004)

MacDonald, R. Andrew, *Outlaws of Medieval Scotland: Challenges to the Canmore Kings, 1058–1266* (East Linton, 2003)

Macdougall, Norman, '"The greattest schip that ewer saillit in England or France": James IV's Great Michael', in Norman Macdougall (ed.), *Scotland and War AD 79–1918* (Edinburgh, 1991), 36–60

——, *James III*, revised edition (Edinburgh, 2009)

——, *James IV*, reprint (Edinburgh, 2006)

——, (ed.), *Scotland and War AD 79–1918* (Edinburgh, 1991)

Macfarlane, Leslie J., 'The Book of Hours of James IV and Margaret Tudor', *IR* 9 (1960), 3–20

——, *William Elphinstone and the Kingdom of Scotland, 1431–1514: The Struggle for Order* (Aberdeen, 1985)

MacGibbon, David, and Thomas Ross, *The Ecclesiastical Architecture of Scotland, from the Earliest Christian Times to the Seventeenth Century*, 3 vols (Edinburgh, 1896–98)

MacGregor, Martin and Caroline Wilkinson 'In Search of Robert Bruce, Part III: Medieval Royal Burial at Dunfermline and the Tomb Investigations of 1818–19', *IR* 70/2 (2019), 171–201

Mackie, Robert L., *A Short History of Scotland* (Oxford, 1930)

MacQuarrie, Alan, *Scotland and the Crusades, 1095–1560* (Edinburgh, 1997)

Malden, John, 'Alexander and the Double Tressure', in Richard D. Oram (ed.), *The Reign of Alexander II* (Leiden, 2005), 211–20

Mann, Alastair J., 'The Scottish Parliaments: The Role of Ritual and Procession in Pre–1707 Parliament and the New Parliament of 1999', in Emma Crewe and Marion G. Müller (eds), *Rituals in Parliaments, Political, Anthropological and Historical Perspectives on Europe and the United States* (Frankfurt, 2006), 135–58

Mann, Henry Chester, *A Cloistered Company: Essays on Monastic Life* (London, 1935)

Mapstone, Sally, and Juliette Hood (eds), *The Rose and the Thistle, Essays on the Culture of Late Medieval and Renaissance Scotland* (East Linton, 1998)

Marshall, David, 'Notes on the Record Room of the City of Perth', *PSAS* 33 (1899), 414–40

Marshall, Rosalind K., *Scottish Queens, 1034–1714* (Edinburgh, 2007)

Marshall, Susan, *Illegitimacy in Medieval Scotland* (Woodbridge, 2021)

Mason, Roger, 'Beyond the Declaration of Arbroath: Kingship, Counsel and Consent in Late Medieval and Early Modern Scotland', in Steve Boardman and Julian Goodare (eds), *Kings, Lords and Men in Scotland and Britain, 1300–1625: Essays in Honour of Jenny Wormald* (Edinburgh, 2014), 265–82

——, *Kingship and the Commonweal: Political Thought in Renaissance and Reformation Scotland* (East Linton, 1998)

——, 'Laicisation and the Law: The Reception of Humanism in Early Renaissance Scotland', in Luuk A.J.R. Houwen, Alistair A. MacDonald, and Sally Mapstone (eds), *A Palace in the Wild: Essays on Vernacular Culture and Humanism in Late-Medieval and Renaissance Scotland* (Leuven, 2000), 1–25

——, 'The Realm of Scotland is an Empire? Imperial Ideas and Iconography in Early Renaissance Scotland', in Barbara E. Crawford (ed.), *Church, Chronicle and Learning in Medieval and Early Renaissance Scotland: Essays Presented to Donald Watt on the Occasion of the Completion of Bower's Scotichronicon* (Edinburgh, 1999), 73–91

——, 'Renaissance Monarchy? Stewart Kingship (1469–1542)', in Michael Brown and Roland Tanner (eds), *Scottish Kingship 1306–1542: Essays in Honour of Norman MacDougall* (Edinburgh, 2008), 255–78

Mays, Deborah (ed.), *The Architecture of Scottish Cities, Essays in Honour of David Walker* (East Linton, 1997)

McAndrew, Bruce A., *Scotland's Historic Heraldry* (Woodbridge, 2006)

McAvoy, Liz Herbert, and Diane Watt (eds), *The History of British Women's Writing, 700–1500, Volume 1* (Basingstoke, 2012)

McCartney, Elizabeth, 'Ceremonies and Privileges of Office: Queenship in Late Medieval France', in Jennifer Carpenter and Sally-Beth MacLean (eds), *Power of the Weak: Studies on Medieval Women* (Urbana and Chicago, 1995), 178–220

McClure, J. Derrick, and Michael R.G. Spiller (eds), *Bryght Lanternis: Essays on the Language and Literature of Medieval and Renaissance Scotland* (Aberdeen, 1989)

McGavin, John J., '"Robert III's Rough Music": Charivari and Diplomacy in a Medieval Scottish Court', *SHR* 74 (1995), 144–58

——, *Theatricality and Narrative in Medieval and Early Modern Scotland* (Aldershot, 2007)

McGladdery, Christine, *James II*, revised edition (Edinburgh, 2015)

McNamee, Colm, *The Wars of the Bruces: Scotland, England, Ireland, 1306–1328* (East Linton, 1997)

McQueen, Alison A.B., 'Parliament, the Guardians and John Balliol, 1284–1296', in Keith Brown and Roland Tanner (eds), *The History of the Scottish Parliament 1: Parliament and Politics, 1235–1560* (Edinburgh, 2004), 29–49

McRoberts, David, *Catalogue of Scottish Liturgical Books and Fragments* (Glasgow, 1953)

Metcalf, David M. (ed.), *Coinage in Medieval Scotland (1100–1600): The Second Oxford Symposium on Coinage and Monetary History*, British Archaeological Report 45 (Oxford, 1977)

Mill, Anna J., *Medieval Plays in Scotland* (Edinburgh, 1927)

Miller, A.H., 'Scotland Described for Queen Magdalene: A Curious Volume', *SHR* 1 (1904), 27–35

Miller, Stephen, 'Political Oratory and the Public Sphere in Early Quattrocento Florence', *New Readings* 1 (1995), 41–64

Monnas, Lisa, 'Textiles from the Funerary Achievements of Henry V', in Jenny Stratford (ed.), *The Lancastrian Court: Proceedings of the 2001 Harlaxton Symposium* (Donington, 2003), 125–46

Monti, James, *A Sense of the Sacred: Roman Catholic Worship in the Middle Ages* (San Francisco, 2012)

Morganstern, Anne M., *Gothic Tombs of Kinship in France, the Low Countries and England* (Pennsylvania, 2000)

Mörke, Olaf, 'The Symbolism of Rulership', in Martin Gosman, Alasdair MacDonald and Arjo Vanderjagt (eds), *Princes and Princely Culture 1450–1650, Vol I* (Leiden: Brill, 2003), 31–49

Moroni, Gaetano, *Dizionario di erudizione storico-ecclesiastica*, 103 vols (Venice, 1840–61)

Morris, Marc, *A Great and Terrible King: Edward I and the Forging of Britain* (London, 2008)

Muir, Edward, *Ritual in Early Modern Europe* (Cambridge, 1999)

Mulryne, J. Ronnie, and Elizabeth Goldring (eds), *Court Festivals in the European Renaissance: Art, Politics and Performance* (Aldershot, 2002)

——, and Anna Maria Testaverde with Ines Aliverti (eds), *The Iconography of Power: Ceremonial Entries in Early Modern Europe* (Farnham: Ashgate, 2015)

Murray, Atholl, 'The Comptroller, 1425–1488', *SHR* 52 (1973), 1–29

Murray, Kylie, '"Out of My Contree" Visions of Royal Authority in the Courts of James I and James II, 1424–1460', in Katherine Buchanan and Lucinda Dean with Michael Penman (eds), *Medieval and Early Modern Representations of Authority in Scotland and the British Isles* (Abingdon, 2016), 214–34

Nelson, Janet L., *Politics and Ritual in Early Medieval Europe* (London, 1999)

Neville, Cynthia J., 'Making a Manly Impression: The Image of Kingship on Scottish Royal Seals of the High Middle Ages', in Lynn Abrams and Elizabeth L. Ewan (eds), *Nine Centuries of Man: Manhood and Masculinity in Scottish History* (Edinburgh, 2017), 101–21

——, 'Preparing for Kingship: Prince Alexander of Scotland, 1264–1284', in Elizabeth Ewan and Janay Nugent (eds), *Childhood and Youth in Pre-Modern Scotland* (Woodbridge, 2015), 155–72

Nicholson, Ranald, *Scotland: The Later Middle Ages* (Edinburgh, 1978)

Nijsten, Gerard, *In the Shadow of Burgundy: The Court of Guelders in the Late Middle Ages* (Cambridge, 2004)

Norman, A.V., 'The Effigy of Alexander Stewart Earl of Buchan and Lord of Badenoch (?1343 –?1405)', *PSAS* 92 (1958–59), 104–13

Old Roxburgh, Floors Castle Estates, Kelso: An Archaeological Evaluation and an Assessment of their Results, Document Reference: 52568.06 (Salisbury, 2004)

O'Grady, Oliver J.T., 'Accumulating Kingship: The Archaeology of Elite Assembly in Medieval Scotland', *World Archaeology* 50 (2018), 137–49

——, 'Tracing the Medieval Royal Centre at Scone', *Medieval Archaeology*, 52 (2008), 376–8

——, and Richard Oram (eds), *Royal and Lordly Inauguration and Assembly Places in North-West Europe* (Donington, 2023)

Oppenheimer, Francis, *The Legend of Ste. Ampoule* (London, 1953)

Oram, Richard D., *Alexander II: King of Scots, 1214–1249* (Edinburgh, 2012)

——, 'Bishops' Tombs in Medieval Scotland', in Michael Penman (ed.), *Monuments and Monumentality in Later Medieval and Early Modern Europe* (Donington, 2013), 171–98

——, *Domination and Lordship: Scotland 1070–1230* (Edinburgh, 2011)

——, 'An Overview of the Reign of Alexander II', in Richard D. Oram (ed.), *The Reign of Alexander II* (Leiden, 2005), 1–49

——, (ed.), *The Reign of Alexander II* (Leiden, 2005)

Ormrod, W. Mark, *Edward III* (New Haven, 2013)

——, (ed.), *England in the Fourteenth Century: Proceedings from the 1985 Harlaxton Symposium* (Woodbridge, 1986)

——, (ed.), *Fourteenth Century England III* (Woodbridge, 2004)

Palliser, D.M., 'Royal Mausolea in the Long Fourteenth Century (1272–1422)', in W. Mark Ormrod (ed.), *Fourteenth Century England III* (Woodbridge, 2004), 1–16

Parker, Geoffrey, *Emperor: A New life of Charles V* (New Haven, 2020)

Parsons, John Carmi, 'Ritual and Symbol in the English Medieval Queenship to 1500', in Louise O. Fradenburg (ed.), *Women and Sovereignty* (Edinburgh, 1992), 60–77

Penman, Michael, 'The Bruces, Becket and Scottish Pilgrimage to Canterbury, c.1174–c.1406', *Journal of Medieval History* 32 (2006), 346–70

——, 'Christian Days and Knights: The Religious Devotions and Court of David II of Scotland, 1329–71', *HR* 75 (Aug. 2002), 249–72

——, *David II* (Edinburgh, 2005)

——, '*Diffinicione successionis ad regnum Scottorum*: Royal Succession in Scotland in the Later Middle Ages', in Frédérique Lachaud and Michael Penman (eds), *Making and Breaking the Rules: Succession in Medieval Europe, c.1000–1600* (Turnhout, 2008), 43–59

——, '"A fell coniuracioun agayn Robert the douchty king": The Soules Conspiracy of 1318–1320', *IR* 50 (1999), 25–57

——, '"The King Wishes and Commands"? Reassessing Political Assembly in Scotland, c.1286–1329', in Mario Damen, Jelle Haemers and Alastair J. Mann (eds), *Political Representation: Communities, Ideas and Institutions in Europe, c.1200–c.1690* (Leiden, 2018), 125–41

——, 'The Lion Captive: Scottish Royals as Prisoners in England, c.1070–c.1424', *Quaestiones Medii Aevi Novae* 20 (2015), 413–34

—— (ed.), *Monuments and Monumentality in Later Medieval and Early Modern Europe* (Donington, 2013)

——, 'Parliament Lost, Parliament Regained? The Three Estates in the Reign of David II, 1329–1371', in Keith Brown and Roland Tanner (eds), *The History of the Scottish Parliament 1: Parliament and Politics, 1235–1560* (Edinburgh, 2004), 74–101

——, 'A Programme for Royal Tombs in Scotland? A Review of the Evidence, c.1093–c.1542', in Michael Penman (ed.), *Monuments and Monumentality in Later Medieval and Early Modern Europe* (Donington, 2013), 239–53

——, *Robert the Bruce, King of Scots* (New Haven and London, 2014)

——, 'Royal Piety in Thirteenth-Century Scotland: The Religion and Religiosity of Alexander II (1214–49) and Alexander II (1249–86)', in Janet Burton, Phillipp Schofield and Björn Weiler (eds), *Thirteenth Century England XII, Proceedings of the Gregynog Conference, 2007* (Woodbridge, 2009), 13–30

——, 'Sacred Food for the Soul: In Search of the Personal Piety and Devotions to Saints of Robert Bruce, King of Scotland, 1306–1329', *Speculum* 88 (2013), 1035–62

——, 'Who is this King of Glory? Robert I of Scotland (1306–1329), Holy Week and the Consecration of St Andrews', in Katherine Buchanan and Lucinda Dean with Michael Penman (eds), *Medieval and Early Modern Representations of Authority in Scotland and the British Isles* (Abingdon, 2016), 85–104

——, and Erica Carrick Utsi, *In Search of the Scottish Royal Mausoleum at the Benedictine Abbey of Dunfermline, Fife: Medieval Liturgy, Antiquarianism, and a Ground-Penetrating Radar Pilot Survey, 2016–19* (Stirling and Ely, 2020)

Peterson, Nils H., Mette B. Bruun, Jeremy Llewellyn and Eyolf Østrem (eds), *The Appearance of Medieval Rituals: The Play of Construction and Modification* (Turnhout, 2004)

Pettit, Tom, 'Protesting Inversions: Charivari as Folk Pageantry and Folk-Law', *Medieval English Theatre* 21 (1999), 21–51

Phillips, Seymour, *Edward II* (New Haven, 2011)

Prestwich, Michael, 'Edward I and the Maid of Norway', *SHR* 69 (1990), 157–74

Raffensperger, Christian, 'The Kingdom of Rus: Towards A New Theoretical Model of Rulership in Medieval Europe', Grischa Vercamer and Dušan Zupka (eds), *Rulership in Medieval East Central Europe: Power, Ritual and Legitimacy in Bohemia, Hungary and Poland* (Leiden, 2021), 325–39

Reid, Norman H., *Alexander III, 1249–1286: First Among Equals* (Edinburgh, 2019)

——, 'Alexander III: The Historiography of a Myth', in Norman H. Reid (ed.), *Scotland in the Reign of Alexander III, 1249–1286* (Edinburgh, 1990), 181–213

——, 'The Kingless Kingdom: The Scottish Guardianship of 1286–1306', *SHR* 61 (1982), 105–29

——, (ed.), *Scotland in the Reign of Alexander III, 1249–1286* (Edinburgh, 1990)

——, and Michael Penman, 'Guardian – Lieutenant – Governor: Absentee Monarchy and Proxy Power in Scotland's Long Fourteenth Century', in Frédérique Lachaud and Michael Penman (eds), *Absentee Authority Across Medieval Europe* (Woodbridge, 2017), 191–218

Richardson, Catherine, 'Written Texts and the Performance of Materiality', in Anne Gerristen and Giorgio Riello (eds), *Writing Material Culture History* (London, 2015), 43–58

Richardson, Glenn, *Field of the Cloth of Gold* (New Haven, 2013)

——, *Renaissance Monarchy: The Reigns of Henry VIII, Francis I and Charles V* (London, 2002)

Ristvet, Lauren, *Ritual, Performance, and Politics in the Ancient Near East* (Cambridge, 2015)

Ritchie, Pamela E., *Mary of Guise in Scotland, 1548–1560: A Political Career* (East Linton, 2002)

Rose, Jacqueline (ed.), *The Politics of Counsel in England and Scotland, 1286–1707* (Oxford, 2016)

Ross, Alasdair, *Kings of Alba* (Edinburgh, 2011)

Ross, D. James, *Musick Fyne: Robert Carver and the Art of Music in Sixteenth-Century Scotland* (Edinburgh, 1993)

Ruiz, Teófilo F., 'Unsacred Monarchy: The Kings of Castile in the Late Middle Ages', in Sean Wilentz (ed.), *Rites of Power: Symbolism, Ritual and Politics Since the Middle Ages* (Philadelphia, 1999), 109–44

Rush, Sally, 'French Fashions in Sixteenth-Century Scotland: The 1539 Inventory of James V's Wardrobe', *Furniture History* 42 (2007), 1–26

——, 'The Stirling Heads: An Essay in Nobility', in Birgitte Bøggild Johannsen and Koen A. Ottenhym (eds), *Beyond Scylla and Charybdis: European Courts and Court Residences Outside Habsburg and Valois Territories, 1500–1700* (Odense, 2015), 225–36

Saetvelt Miles, Laura, 'Bridget of Sweden', in Liz Herbert McAvoy and Diane Watt (eds), *The History of British Women's Writing, 700–1500, Volume 1* (Basingstoke, 2012), 207–15

Sandquist, T.A., 'The Holy Oil of St Thomas of Canterbury', in T.A. Sandquist and Michael R. Powick (eds), *Essays in Medieval History Presented to Bertie Wilkinson* (Toronto, 1969), 330–44

——, and Michael R. Powick (eds), *Essays in Medieval History Presented to Bertie Wilkinson* (Toronto, 1969)

Saul, Nigel, *The Three Richards: Richard I, Richard II and Richard III* (London, 2006)

Schnettger, Matthias, 'Dynastic Succession in an Elective Monarchy: The Habsburgs and the Holy Roman Empire', in Elena Woodacre, Lucinda H.S. Dean, Chris Jones et al. (eds), *The Routledge History of Monarchy* (London, 2019), 112–29

Schofield, Philipp (ed.), *Seals and Their Context in the Middle Ages* (Oxford, 2015)

Schuessler Bond, Melanie, *Dressing the Scottish Court, 1543–1553: Clothing in the Accounts of the Lord High Treasurer of Scotland* (Woodbridge, 2019)

The Scots Peerage founded on Woods edition of Sir Robert Douglas's Peerage of Scotland Containing an Historical and Genealogical Account of the Nobility of the Kingdom, ed. James P. Balfour Paul, 9 vols (Edinburgh, 1904–14)

Scott, W.W., 'Fordun's Description of the Inauguration of Alexander II', *SHR* 50

(1971), 198–200
Sharpe, Kevin, *Selling the Tudor Dynasty: Authority and Image in Sixteenth-Century England* (New Haven, 2009)
Shaw, Dougal, 'Scotland's Place in Britain's Coronation Tradition', *Court Historian* 9 (2004), 41–60
Shenton, Caroline, 'Edward III and the Symbol of the Leopard', in Peter Coss and Maurice Keen (eds), *Heraldry, Pageantry and Social Display in Medieval England* (Woodbridge, 2008), 69–81
Shire, Helena M., 'Music for the "Goddis Glore and the Kingis"', in Janet Hadley Williams (ed.), *Stewart Style 1513–1542: Essays on the Court of James V* (East Linton, 1996), 118–41
Simpson, Grant G., 'Declaration of Arbroath Revitalised', *SHR* 56 (1977), 11–33
——, 'The Heart of King Robert I: Pious Crusade or Marketing Gambit?' in Barbara E. Crawford (ed.), *Church, Chronicle and Learning in Medieval and Early Renaissance Scotland: Essays Presented to Donald Watt on the Occasion of the Completion of Bower's Scotichronicon* (Edinburgh, 1999), 173–86
——, 'Kingship in Miniature: A Seal of Minority of Alexander III, 1249–1257', in Alexander Grant and Keith Stringer (eds), *Medieval Scotland: Crown, Lordship and Community: Essays Presented to G.W.S Barrow* (Edinburgh, 1993), 131–9
——, (ed.), *Scotland and the Low Countries, 1124–1994* (East Linton, 1996)
——, 'Why Was John Balliol Called Toom Tabard?', *SHR* 47 (1968), 196–9
Spearman, R.M., 'The Medieval Townscape of Perth', in Michael Lynch, Michael Spearman and Geoffrey Stell (eds), *The Scottish Medieval Town* (Edinburgh, 1988), 42–59
Soly, Hugo, and Willem P. Blockmans (eds), *Charles V (1500–1558) and His Times* (Antwerp, 1999)
Spiegel, Gabrielle M., *The Past as Text: The Theory and Practice of Medieval Historiography* (Baltimore and London, 1999)
Spinks, Bryan D., *Early and Medieval Rituals and Theologies of Baptism: From the New Testament to the Council of Trent* (Farnham, 2006)
Staniland, Kay, 'The Nuptials of Alexander III of Scotland and Margaret Plantagenet', *Nottingham Medieval Studies* 30 (1986), 20–45
Steane, John, *Archaeology of the Medieval English Monarchy* (London, 1999)
Stephenson, J.H., 'The Law of the Throne: Tanistry and the Introduction of the Law of Primogeniture: A Note on Succession from Kenneth MacAlpin to Robert the Bruce', *SHR* 25 (1927), 1–12
Stevenson, Katie, 'Chivalry, British Sovereignty and Dynastic Politics: Undercurrents of Antagonism in Tudor-Stewart Relations, c.1490–c.1513', *HR* 86 (2013), 601–18
——, *Chivalry and Knighthood in Scotland, 1424–1513* (Woodbridge, 2006)
——, 'Contesting Chivalry: James II and the Control of Chivalric Culture in the 1450s', *Journal of Medieval History* 33 (2007), 197–214
——, (ed.), *The Herald in Late Medieval Europe* (Woodbridge, 2009)
——, 'Jurisdiction, Authority and Professionalisation: The Officers of Late Medieval Scotland', in Katie Stevenson (ed.), *The Herald in Late Medieval Europe* (Woodbridge, 2009), 41–66
——, *Power and Propaganda, Scotland 1306–1488* (Edinburgh, 2014)
Stewart, Ian H., *The Scottish Coinage* (London, 1955)

Stratford, Jenny (ed.), *The Lancastrian Court: Proceedings of the 2001 Harlaxton Symposium* (Donington, 2003)

Strickland, Matthew, (ed.), *Armies, Chivalry and Warfare in Medieval Britain and France: Proceedings of the 1995 Harlaxton Symposium* (Stamford, 1998)

——, *Henry the Young King, 1155–1183* (New Haven, 2016)

Stringer, Keith, 'Arbroath Abbey in Context, 1178–1320', in Geoffrey W.S. Barrow (ed.), *The Declaration of Arbroath: History, Significance, Setting* (Edinburgh, 2003), 117–41

——, (ed.), *Essays on the Nobility of Medieval Scotland* (Edinburgh, 1985)

——, 'Kingship, Conflict and State-Making in the Reign of Alexander II: The War of 1215–17 and Its Context', in Richard D. Oram (ed.), *The Reign of Alexander II* (Leiden, 2005), 99–156

Strong, Roy, *Art and Power, Renaissance Festivals 1450–1650* (Woodbridge, 1982)

——, *Coronations: A History of Kingship and the British Monarchy* (London, 2005)

Stuart, John P.C., *Scottish Coronations* (Paisley, 1902)

Sutton, Anne F. and Livia Visser-Fuchs, with Ralph A. Griffiths, *The Royal Funerals of the House of York at Windsor* (London, 2005)

Tanner, Roland, 'Cowing the Community? Coercion and Falsification in Robert Bruce's Parliaments', in Keith Brown and Roland Tanner (eds), *The History of the Scottish Parliament 1: Parliament and Politics, 1235–1560* (Edinburgh, 2004), 50–73

——, *The Late Medieval Scottish Parliament: Politics and the Three Estates, 1424–1488* (East Linton, 2001)

Taylor, Alice, 'Historical Writing in Twelfth- and Thirteenth-Century Scotland: The Dunfermline Compilation', *HR* 83 (2010), 228–52

——, 'The Scottish Clause in the Magna Carta in Context: Homage, Overlordship and the Consequence of Peace in the Early Thirteenth Century', in Sophie Ambler and Nicholas Vincent (eds), *Magna Carta: New Interpretations* (forthcoming)

——, *The Shape of the State in Medieval Scotland, 1124–1290* (Oxford, 2016)

Taylor, Simon, 'The Cult of St Fillan in Scotland', in Thomas R. Liszka and Lorna E.M. Walker (eds), *The North Sea World in the Middle Ages: Studies in the Cultural History of North-Western Europe* (Dublin, 2001), 175–209

Thiry, Steven, 'Rites of Reversion: Ceremonial Memory and Community in the Funeral of Philip II in the Netherlands (1598)', *Renaissance Quarterly*, 71/4 (2018), 1391–429

Thomas, Andrea, 'Crown Imperial: Coronation Ritual and Regalia in the Reign of James V', in Julian Goodare and Alastair A. MacDonald (eds), *Sixteenth-Century Scotland: Essays in Honour of Michael Lynch* (Leiden, 2008), 42–67

——, *Glory and Honour: The Renaissance in Scotland* (Edinburgh, 2013)

——, *Princelie Majestie, The Court of James V of Scotland, 1528–1542* (Edinburgh, 2005)

Thompson, Colin, and Lorne Campbell, *Hugo Van der Goes and the Trinity Altar Panels in Edinburgh* (Edinburgh, 1974)

Turner, Ralph V., and Richard R. Heiser, *The Reign of Richard the Lionheart: Ruler of the Angevin Empire, 1189–1199* (Harlow, 2000)

Turpie, Tom, 'A Monk from Melrose? St Cuthbert and the Scots in the Later Middle Ages, c.1371–1560', *IR* 62 (2011), 47–69

——, 'Scottish or British? The Scottish Authorities, Richard III and the Cult of St Ninian in Late Medieval Scotland and Northern England', in Katherine Buchanan and Lucinda H.S. Dean with Michael Penman (eds), *Medieval and Early Modern Representations of Authority in Scotland and the British Isles* (Abingdon, 2016), 124–40

Vale, Malcolm, 'A Burgundian Funeral: Olivier de la Marche and the Obsequies of Adolf of Cleves, lord of Ravenstein', *English Historical Review* 111 (1996), 920–38

——, *The Princely Court: Medieval Courts and Culture in North-West Europe, 1270–1380* (Oxford, 2001)

Vaughan, Richard, *Philip the Good: The Apogee of Burgundy* (Woodbridge, 2011)

Vercamer, Grischa, and Dušan Zupka (eds), *Rulership in Medieval East Central Europe: Power, Ritual and Legitimacy in Bohemia, Hungary and Poland* (Leiden, 2021)

Vincent, Nicholas, *The Holy Blood: King Henry III and the Westminster Blood Relic* (Cambridge, 2001)

——, 'The Seals of King Henry II and his Court', in Phillipp Schofield (ed.), *Seals and Their Context in the Middle Ages* (Oxford, 2015), 7–34

Waley, Daniel, and Peter Denley, *Later Medieval Europe, 1250–1520*, third edition (Abingdon, 2013)

Ward, Jennifer, *Women in Medieval Europe, 1200–1500* (Harlow and London, 2002)

Watt, Donald E.R., *A Biographical Dictionary of Scottish Graduates to A.D. 1410* (Oxford, 1977)

——, *Medieval Church Councils* (Edinburgh, 2000)

——, 'The Minority of Alexander III in Scotland', *Transactions of the Royal Historical Society*, Fifth Series 21 (1971), 1–23

Watts, John, *The Making of Polities: Europe, 1300–1500* (Cambridge, 2009)

Weikert, Katherine, 'The Princesses Who Might Have Been Hostages: The Custody and Marriages of Margaret and Isabella of Scotland, 1209–1220s', in Matthew Bennett and Katherine Weikert (eds), *Medieval Hostageship, c.700–c.1500: Hostage, Captive, Prisoner of War, Guarantee, Peacemaker* (Abingdon, 2017), 122–39

Weiss, Robert, 'The Earliest Account of the Murder of James I', *English Historical Review* 52 (1937), 479–91

Welander, Richard, David Breeze and Thomas O. Clancy (eds), *The Stone of Destiny: Artefact and Icon* (Edinburgh, 2003)

Westerhof, Danielle, *Death and the Noble Body in Medieval England* (Woodbridge, 2008)

Westerhof Nyman, Perin, 'Mourning Madeleine and Margaret: Dress and Meaning in the Memorials for Two Scottish Queens, 1537 and 1541', *SHR* 100 (2021), 359–77

Wild, Benjamin, 'Secrecy, Splendour and Statecraft: The Jewel Accounts of Henry III', *HR* 83 (2010), 409–30

Wilentz, Sean (ed.), *Rites of Power: Symbolism, Ritual and Politics Since the Middle Ages* (Philadelphia, 1999)

Woodacre, Elena, Lucinda H.S. Dean, Chris Jones et al. (eds), *The Routledge History of Monarchy* (London, 2019)

——, and Sean McGlyn (eds), *The Image and Perception of Monarchy in Medieval and Early Modern Europe* (Newcastle, 2014)

Woodcock, Philippa, 'Early Modern Monarchy and Foreign Travel', in Elena

Woodacre, Lucinda H.S. Dean, Chris Jones et al. (eds), *The Routledge History of Monarchy* (London, 2019), 282–99.
Woods Preece, Isobel, *'Our Awin Scottis Use': Music in the Scottish Church up to 1603*, ed. Sally Harper (Glasgow, 2000)
Woolf, Alex, 'The Song of the Death of Somerled and the Destruction of Glasgow in 1153', *Journal of the Sydney Society for Scottish History* 14 (2013), 1–11
Wormald, Jenny, *Court, Kirk and Community: Scotland 1470–1625*, reprint (Edinburgh, 2007)
——, 'Taming the Magnates?', in Keith Stringer (ed.), *Essays on the Nobility of Medieval Scotland* (Edinburgh, 1985), 270–80
Wright, Craig, 'The Palm Sunday Procession in Medieval Chartres', in Rebecca A. Baltzer and Margot E. Fassler (eds), *The Divine Office in the Latin Middle Ages: Methodology and Source Studies, Regional Development, Hagiography* (New York, 2000), 344–71
Young, Alan, *Robert the Bruce's Rivals: The Comyns, 1212–1314* (East Linton, 2001)
——, and George Cumming, *The Real Patriots of Early Scottish Independence* (Edinburgh, 2014)

Audio Source

Robert Carver: O bone Jesu: Missa Dum sacrum mysterium: Magnificat, The Sixteen, Harry Christophers, Coro (2007) [CD]

Exhibition

Rush, Sally, *Stirling Castle: The Stirling Heads Gallery*, Exhibition (2011–present)

Report

Dean, Lucinda H.S., *The Scottish Royal Honours: Objects, Ceremony, Use* (Edinburgh, forthcoming)

Online Sources

Corpus of Scottish Medieval Parish Churches (St Andrews and Stirling, 2008), https://arts.st-andrews.ac.uk/corpusofscottishchurches/sites.php. Date accessed: 28 February 2021
Dictionary of the Old Scots Language (DSL), ed. Susan Rennie (Feb. 2004): www.dsl.ac.uk. Date accessed: 27 September 2022.
Historic Environment Scotland, *Statement of Significance: Torphichen Preceptory* (Edinburgh, 2019), https://www.historicenvironment.scot/archives-and-research/publications/publication/?publicationid=84caa975-2c4c-4c5d-91e0-a6c9010ff06e. Date accessed, 7 January 2023.
'Lost Tomb of Robert the Bruce Finds Its Final Resting Place', *Historic Environment Scotland: About Us – News* (HES, 26 April 2019), https://www.historicenvironment.scot/about-us/news/lost-tomb-of-robert-the-bruce-finds-its-final-resting-place/. Date accessed: 28 February 2021
Open Virtual Worlds, *'Scone Abbey – 1390'*, *Open Virtual Worlds 3D Reconstructions*, https://blogs.cs.st-andrews.ac.uk/openvirtualworlds/reconstructions/scone-abbey/. Date accessed: 29 September 2020

Oxford Dictionary of National Biography (ODNB), Oxford University Press (2004–2013) https://www.oxforddnb.com/. Date accessed: 1 March 2021

People of Medieval Scotland, 1093–1286 Database, https://www.poms.ac.uk/. Date accessed: 1 March 2021

Pollard, Tony, 'The Sad Tale of James IV's Body', *BBC News Scotland* (9 Sept 2013), http://www.bbc.co.uk/news/uk-scotland-23993363. Date accessed: 1 March 2021

Taylor, Alice et al., 'The Declaration of Arbroath: A New Dynamic Digital Edition', *The Community of the Realm. 1249–1424: History, Law and Charters in a Recreated Kingdom* (COTR project, 2019), https://cotr.ac.uk/guidelines/dynamic-declaration-arbroath/. Date accessed: 28 February 2021

Unpublished Works

Conference Papers and Working Papers

Anderson, Kate, 'Portraits of James V from Renaissance Prince to Ruling Monarch', conference paper, *The Presence of Majestie: James V and Sir David Lyndsay* (Heraldry Society Conference, Edinburgh, September 2015)

Cameron, Sonja, and Alasdair Ross, 'The Bad Bishop: Robert Wishart and the Scottish Wars of Independence' (working paper)

Dean, Lucinda H.S., 'Raising Royal Scottish Babes: Baptisms, "Gossibs" and Godparents in Late Medieval and Early Modern Scotland', seminar paper, *History Live Talk*, University of the Highlands and Islands, 18 June 2020, https://www.youtube.com/watch?v=dFkcIy0m14c. Date accessed: 4 March 2021 (being prepared for publication under same title)

——, 'Reaching the "Estate of Manhood": A Case Study of James V of Scotland', seminar paper, *Centre for Gender History Seminar Series*, University of Glasgow, January 2018 (being prepared for publication under same title). Earlier version of the paper accessible online, 2017: https://www.youtube.com/watch?v=RU-akt04ftZk&t=102s. Date accessed: 4 March 2020

King, Andy, 'Edward, by the Grace of God, King of Scotland: Perceptions of the Kingship of Edward Balliol, 1332–1356' (working paper)

Rapport, Mike, 'The Bricks and Mortar of Revolution: Space and Place in Revolutionary Paris', *University of Glasgow School of Humanities Lecture Series 2018–29*, 6 December 2018. https://www.youtube.com/watch?v=jxL8P_N2xs8. Date accessed 29 Sept 2020

Theses

Burden, Joel F. 'Rituals of Royalty: Prescription, Politics and Practice in English Coronation and Royal Funeral Rituals c.1327 to c.1485' (PhD thesis, University of York, Dec 1999)

Dean, Lucinda H.S., 'Crowns, Wedding Rings, and Processions: Continuity and Change in the Representations of Scottish Royal Authority in State Ceremony, c.1214–c.1603' (PhD thesis, University of Stirling, 2013)

Duch, Anna, 'My Crown Is in My Heart, Not on My Head: Heart Burial in England, France, and the Holy Roman Empire from Medieval Times to the

Present' (Masters thesis, University of North Texas, 2013)

——, 'The Royal Funerary and Burial Ceremonies of Medieval English Kings, 1216–1509' (PhD thesis, University of York, 2016)

Emond, William K., 'The Minority of King James V, 1513–1528' (PhD thesis, University of St Andrews, 1988)

French, Morvern, 'Magnificence and Materiality: The Commerce and Culture of Flemish Luxuries in Late Medieval Scotland' (PhD thesis, St Andrews, 2016)

Hawes, Claire, 'Community and Public Authority in Later Fifteenth-Century Scotland' (PhD thesis, University of St Andrews, 2015)

Hayes, Amy V., 'The Late Medieval Scottish Queen, c.1371–c.1513' (PhD thesis, Aberdeen, 2015)

Holmes, Stephen M., 'Liturgical Interpretation and Church Reform in Renaissance Scotland c.1488–c.1590' (PhD thesis, Edinburgh, 2013)

Hunt, Karen, 'The Governorship of the First Duke of Albany, 1406–1420' (PhD thesis, University of Edinburgh, 1998)

Jack, Katy, 'Political and Local Consequences of the Decline and Fall of the Earls of Mar, 1281–1513' (PhD thesis, Stirling, 2017)

Lee, SangDong, 'The Development of Dunfermline Abbey as a Royal Cult Centre, c.1070–c.1420' (PhD thesis, University of Stirling, 2014)

Mapstone, Sally L., 'The Advice to Princes Tradition in Scottish Literature, 1450–1500' (DPhil thesis, Oxford, 1986)

Murray, Atholl L., 'The Exchequer and Crown Revenue, 1437–1542' (PhD thesis, Edinburgh, 1961)

O'Grady, Oliver J.T., 'The Setting and Practice of Open-air Judicial Assemblies in Medieval Scotland: A Multidisciplinary Study' (PhD thesis, University of Glasgow, 2008)

Scott, Nicola, 'The Court and Household of James I of Scotland, 1424–1437' (PhD thesis, University of Stirling)

Thorson, S.M., 'Adam Abell's *The Roit and Qhueill of Tyme*: An Edition' (PhD thesis, University of St Andrews, 1998)

Woodward-Reed, Hannah, 'The Context and Material Techniques of Royal Portraiture Production within Jacobean Scotland: The Courts of James V and James VI' (PhD thesis, University of Glasgow, 2018)

Index

Notes about index: Page numbers marked in **bold** indicate plates or maps and their captions. Names, places and titles (secular and clerical) in the timeline and appendices are only included in the index if they have appeared in the main body of the text. Listings of chronicles and other primary sources in the index are only included where the author or source is discussed in the main body of the text, or where a footnote provides useful information about the source or author not included in the main text.

Aberdeen   176 n.166, 203, 250
   bishop of   260, 263, 264, 265
      Thomas Spens   178 n.183
   burgh commissioners or provosts of   264
   burgh records of   135, 176 n.166, 195, 200 n.87
   See also royal entry to Aberdeen *under* Margaret Tudor, queen of Scots
Aberdeenshire   176
Aberdour, parish church of   71–2
absentee kingship   15 (n.71), 17–19, 113, 135–7, 145, 148, 226, 237–8
   See also minority *under* succession
acclamation   24, 103, 189, 232, 239
   See also under coronation; inauguration
Adomnán, *Life of St Columba*   29
Adrian, St, shrine of, on Isle of May   164 n.110
Áedán   29, 52
Agincourt, battle of   138
Albany pursuivant   165
Alexander, son of Alexander III, king of Scots, and heir to throne   242
   burial of, with his brother, David   68, 242
   creation of appanage, including lordship of Man, and household for   58, 242
   education of   58
   understanding of royal status, use of seals and letter diplomatic   60
   wedding of *see* wedding and marriage orchestrated by *under* Alexander III
Alexander I, king of Scots   29
   illegitimate children of   22
Alexander II, king of Scots   24, 34–5, 240–1
   canonisation of St Margaret   42–3, 49, 51–2, 241
   death on military campaign of   42–3, 45–6, 241
   efforts to secure unction and crowning   38, 40, 49, 52–3, 61, 241
   funeral and burial of   43–4, 51, 172, 241, 257
      preparation of body for   45
      heart burial   53, 72
   homage to England or requests for   26
   ill health of   42
   inauguration of   21, 24, 26–30, 40, 230, 240, 256
   pre-mortuary recognition as heir   24–6, 58, 62, 96, 240

INDEX

seal of 40, **41**
sister of, Margaret 39 n.93
wedding of
    first marriage, to Joanna
        Plantagenet 35–41, 53,
        230, 240–1
    second marriage, to Marie de
        Coucy 41–2, 59, 241
Alexander III, king of Scots 39, 93,
    96, 144, 153, 241–2
    birth of 42, 241
    death of 65, 67–8, 71, 136, 242
    designation of succession and
        heirs 57–8, 60, 62
    funeral and burial of 68, 71–5,
        78, 90, 110, 242
        heart burial 72, 74, 109
    Great Seal of **57**, 82
    inauguration of 3, 43–5, 46–50,
        61, 81, 109, 114, 120, 123,
        125, 142, 166, 241, 257
        debate over ceremonial pro-
            cedure at 46
    influences on during minori-
        ty 56–7
    journeys to England 56–7
    lack of effort to secure unc-
        tion 60–1, 69
    refusal of homage to England for
        Scotland 54
    seals of 52, 54, **57**, 82, 101
    tomb of 68–71
    translation/ reinterment of St
        Maragaret, attended 51–2, 68
    wedding of
        first marriage, to Margaret
            Plantagenet 53–6, 227,
            230, 241
            pardons granted by Henry
                III on behalf of 55–6
            Alexander knighted by
                English king during 46
                n.128, 55
        second marriage, to Yolande
            of Dreux 67, 242
    wedding and marriage orchestrat-
        ed by
        Margaret and Eric of Nor-
            way 57–8
        Alexander and Marguerite
            or Margaret of Flanders,
            daughter of Guy, Count of
            Flanders 58–60, 242
Alfred, king of England 52
almsgiving *see under* gifts and gift
    giving
Alnwick 199 n.78, 240
Alpin, Cinead mac 43
Andrew, St 74, 136 *see also under*
    feast days
Angus, earl of 29–30, 251, 256, 258,
    260, 261, 262, 263, 264, 265
    John Stewart *see* Stewart, John,
        earl of Angus
Anne of Bohemia, queen of England
    and wife of Richard II, tomb of *see*
    tomb of *under* Richard II
Anne of Brittany, queen of France and
    wife of Louis XII 217
Anne of Denmark, queen of Scots and
    wife of James VI 179
Annabella Drummond, queen of Scots
    and wife of Robert III 108, 129,
    133–4, 134 n.114, 135, 237, 245–6
    coronation of 129, 133–4 *see
        also* coronation of *under* Robert
        III
anointing 15–17, 24, 26, 30 n.51,
    38–9, 49, 52, 60–1, 83, 84–5, 95–6,
    101–2, 104, 105, 109–10, 115,
    121–2, 125–6, 132, 144, 156–7
    (156 n.59), 174, 182, 209, 235,
    238–9, 244, 258
    holy oil for 96, 125, 238–9
        vials for (crowats) 219
    See also anointing of consorts
        under wedding and consort
        coronation
Anthony of Vienne, St, church at
    Leith 164
Appeal of the Seven Earls 29, 83–4,
    120
Arbroath
    abbey of (Tironensian) 21,
        31–3, 35, 116, 173, 205, 228
        n.16, 240

INDEX

abbot of 260, 263
 David Beaton, later Cardinal Beaton 211 *see also* St Andrews *under* archbishop of
Declaration of 120, 244
Argyll
 bishop or diocese of 45, 263, 265
 earl of 235–6, 263, 264, 265
 Somerled 22
armour 106, 165, 174–5, 215–16, 269
 depictions of **41, 57, 82, 100–1**, 117 n.22, **118**
Arnhem 173
Arran, earl of 251, 265
 See also Hamilton, James, earl of Arran
Arras, tapestries and hangings from 195, 203
Arthur, Thomas, tailor to the king 212
Atholl, earl of 29–30, 256, 258, 260, 264, 265
 Alan, son of the earl of Atholl (1250), pardoned by Henry III at request of Margaret Plantagenet 55–6
 Walter Stewart *see* Stewart, Walter, earl of Atholl
Auchinleck Chronicle 170–1
Austria-Tyrol, duke of, Sigismund, husband of Eleanor Stewart 149 n.1

Badenoch, lord of
 John Comyn, murder of 76, 78, 80, 84, 243
 Walter Comyn *see* Walter Comyn, lord of Badenoch *under* Menteith, earl of
Balliol, Edward *see* Edward Balliol, king of Scots
Balliol, John *see* John Balliol, king of Scots
Bannockburn, near Stirling 94–5
 battle of 87, 187–8, 228, 243

baptism 3, 85, 146–7, 177, 202–4, 234, 250
 bonfires to celebrate 146, 222, 234
 candles and/or torches, use at 147, 203
 Charles James Stewart (b.1566, later James VI), son of Mary 4 n.11
 feasting and provisions for 203–4 (n.107), 234
 fireworks associated with 222
 knighting at 147, 160
 liturgy of 147, 203
 prayers for heirs 222
 procession at 147
 public celebration of birth 146–7
 See also birth and baptism of *under* James II, king of Scots; birth and baptism of heirs *under* James IV, king of Scots; birth and baptism of heirs *under* James V, king of Scots
 tournaments associated with 201–2
Barbour, John
 The Bruce 78, 89, 91–2, 117, 123, 134
 The Stewartis Oryginalle or Genealogy 123
Barnton, siege of 159
Bauzan, Stephen 54 n.172
Beaufort, Joan *see* Joan Beaufort, queen of Scots and wife of James I
Beaufort, John, earl of Somerset, father of Joan Beaufort 140
Beaumont, Ermengarde de *see* Ermengarde Beaumont, queen of Scots
bed 213
 of state or state bed 177, 195, 267
 crib of state for baptism 222
Bellenden, John, translation of Boece 138
Berwick 42, 59, 89, 92–3, 110, 199 n.78, 228 n.18, 243, 244, 245, 248, 251

INDEX

Bruce entry into   87
  sheriff of   259
  siege of   87, 244
  Trinity Church at   89
Birgham, treaty of   74 n.33, 75, 242
bishops, as a collective group (unnamed) *see* prelates, as a collective group (unnamed)
Bissett, Baldred, pleading of   80, 243
Bissett, Walter   45, 257
Blois
  Stephen of *see* Stephen, king of England (contested)
  textiles from   212
  William del *see under* Lothian, archdeacon of
Boece, Hector, *Historia* of   137–8
Boniface VIII, pope   98
book of hours   191, **192**, 196–8
Borselen, Henry van, lord of Veere, father-in-law of Mary Stewart   149 n.1, 164 n.109
Borselen, Wolfaert van, son of lord of Veere, husband of Mary Stewart   149 n.1, 164 n.109, 247
Borthwick, Sir William of   147
Bothwell, earl of *see* Hepburn, Patrick, earl of Bothwell
Bothwell, late lord of *see* Ramsay, John, lord Bothwell
Bourbon, Marie de, daughter of duke of Vendôme and proposed wife for James V   210, 251
Bourgogne, Philipotte of, illegitimate daughter of Philip, duke of Burgundy   164 n.109
Bower, Walter   114 (n. 6), 142 n.156
  Scotichronicon of   10, 29–30, 30, 46–9, 67–8, 71–2, **73**, 77, 80, 98, 104, 107, 114, 120–1, 131–2, 134, 135, 142, 147, 215, 227, 231
Boyd, Marion, mistress of James IV   194 n.49
Boyd, Robert, lord Boyd   176
  rise of   176 n.168, 248–9
  forfeiture of   180, 249
Brancepeth (near Durham)   143
Brechin   205 (n.116)

bishop of   107, 258, 260
  See also William of Brechin
Brendan of Bute, St   123
Bridget of Sweden, St, death of   128
Briggelak, Ridellus de   54 n.172
Brittany, duke of, Francis, husband of Isabella Stewart   149 n.1, 161 (n.89), 247
Bruce, David *see* David II, king of Scots
Bruce, dynasty of   66, 113, 115–16, 118, 123, 125 *see also* David II, king of Scots; Robert I, king of Scots
Bruce, Marjory, daughter of Robert I   131, 244, 259
Bruce, Robert, of Annandale, the Competitor   76 n.40, 83, 98–9, 110, 242
Bruce, Robert, earl of Carrick *see* Robert I, king of Scots
Bruges, limestone imported from   205 n.113
Brunswick, Otto of, husband of daughter of William I   22, 240
Brussels, treaty of   163
Buchan, countess of, Isabella, aunt of the earl of Fife   76–7, 79, 86, 123, 259
  death of in captivity   86 n.97
Buchan, earl of   29–30, 256, 257, 260, 264
  Alexander Stewart *see* Stewart, Alexander, earl of Buchan
Buchanan, George, *History* of   190–1, 216
burgh elites, burgesses or urban community   1, 8, 144, 147, 156, 164, 170, 173, 208, 219, 231
  See also burgh commissioner *under* Edinburgh; Linlithgow; Perth; St Andrews; Stirling
Burgh, Elizabeth de *see* Elizabeth de Burgh, queen of Scots
Burgh, Hubert de   39 n.93
Burgundy
  court of   168, 173
  duchess of, Isabella of Portugal   162 n.93, 168 (n. 135)
  duke of, Philip the Good   161

305

(n.89), 162, 165 n.116, 168
factors from   195
influence of   175
involvement in tournament and marriage of James II   161–3
Burntisland *see* Kinghorn-Wester

Cambuskenneth
    abbey of (Augustinian)   94, 190, 193–4, 204, 207, 228 n.16, 231, 250
        excavations at   190
    abbot of   190, 261, 264, 265
    parliament at   92, 243
candles and torches   1, 89–90, 147 (n.7), 176, 191, 194, 203, 205, 213, 216–17, 222, 238 *see also* wax
Canmore dynasty   43, 101, 115–16, 123, 125
Canongate   146, 173
Cantelupe, Matilda   54 n.172
Canterbury
    archbishop of   25, 28
        Lanfranc   47
    Quitclaim of   26, 240
    Trinity Chapel at   128
Cardross   89, 94–5, 244
    rector of   94 n.140
Carlisle   36
    bishop of, John de Halton   83, 257, 258
Carnato, Thomas de   89, 95
Carrick, earl of
    David Bruce   92 *see also* David II, king of Scots
    David Stewart *see* Stewart, David, earl of Carrick and duke of Rothesay
    John Stewart *see* Stewart, John, of Kyle and earl of Carrick
Carver, Robert, musical composer   206, 220, 224
    choir book of   206, 220
Castile, coronation traditions of   30
castrum deloris *see* hearse
ceremony
    attendees and participants in   1, 28–31, 36–8, 41, 43–7, 53, 77–9, 83, 85–6, 91–2, 96, 102–4, 107, 122–3, 124, 128, 132–3, 138, 143–4, 152, 162–4, 165, 167, 170–1, 173, 189, 195, 203, 205, 208–9, 216, 217, 218, 222, 223, 235–6, App II
    audience at or for   1, 6, 7–8, 26, 31, 34, 38, 62, 65, 78, 83–5, 92, 103, 114, 130–2, 137–8, 143–4, 147, 152–3, 157–8, 164–5, 166–7, 170, 182, 189, 201–2, 203–4, 208, 213–14, 215, 216, 218–19, 225, 228, 230–1, 233–5
    audience management   147, 157, 195, 203–4, 208, 230
    definitions and scholarly debate upon   4–5, 6–8, 66 *see also under* ritual
    impact of crowds or damage done by   89, 131–2
    role of urban environments and people in   38, 39, 41–2, 59, 88–9, 93, 137–40, 143–4, 146–7, 149, 151, 153, 157, 158, 164, 168, 170, 173, 182, 218–19, 230–32
    sources for   8–15, 39, 53, 76, 114 *see also under* ritual
    See also baptism; coronation; funeral; inauguration; ritual; wedding and consort coronation
chair   105, 176 n.166, 202 n.99, 219, 268
    triumphal   202
Chambers, John, murderer of James I   157, 247
chapel gear   219
chapelle ardent *see* hearse
chaplain/s   116, 205, 217, 219–20
Charles I   155
    coronation of   156
Charles II, coronation of   219 n.201
Charles IV, emperor   30 n.52
Charles V, emperor   184, 211 n.150
Charles VII, king of France   137 n.127, 174
charivari or rough music   131–2, 231

306

INDEX

chivalric culture 91–2, 106, 134, 166, 174–5, 188, 193, 211, 214, 215–16
   Arthurian connections 161, 202
   Orders of chivalry 233
   Order of the Elephant 178
Christ, Jesus 152, 173–4, 203, 227
   see also Christo-centric *under* feast days
Christian I, king of Denmark, father of Margaret, wife of James III 178
Christian IV, king of Denmark, entry and visit to London 211 n.150
clergy, as a collective group (unnamed) 28, 71, 74, 85, 99, 139
   see also Declaration of; cleric *and* ecclesiastics
cleric or clerical estate, as a collective group (unnamed) 35, 46, 52, 61, 62, 103, 138, 152, 171, 199, 208, 217, 220, 236, 238, 242 *see also* ecclesiastics, as a collective group (unnamed) and clergy (above)
   clerical authors, as a collective group (unnamed) 29–30, 239
clothing, fabric and soft furnishings 55, 89, 91, 105–6, 162, 180, 188, 195, 202, 202 n.99, 213, 218, 236, 267–70
   accessories 12, 180 (n.192), 212, 218, 269 *see also* jewels and jewellery
   black fabric 1, 90–1, 173, 188, 191, 203, 215–17
   buckram 176
   canopy 27, 177, 222
   chafferoun 218
   cloth of gold 55 n.177, 91, 105–6, 178, 195, 198, 200, 212, 213–4, 236, 267 n.7, 268, 269
      threads of 212, 269 *see also under* Florence
   cloth of state 195, 197, 267
   damask 198, 212, 268
   embroidery 177, 204, 216, 267 n.4
   furs 59, 105 158, 166, 177, 212, 216, 269
   hood 91, 216, 220
      of French sort 218
   livery *see under* heraldic decoration
   ostrich feathers 140
   sartorial display or splendour 12, 55, 59, 166, 195, 211, 220, 223
   satin 176, 178, 188, 200
   silk 13, 28, 53, 55, 89, 91, 105, 195, 204, 212, 219
   taffeta 195, 204
   velvet 105, 140, 188, 195, 197, 212, 213, 219, 220, 233, 269
   white cloth 105, 158, 166, 198, 222, 268
   See also dule wear
Cluny, loch (Perthshire) 59
coats-of-arms *see* heraldic decoration
coffin 71–2, 135, 153, 216, 233
   coffin bearer 35
Coigners, Geoffrey de 84
coins 40, 46, 90 177, **178**, **179**, 197, 224
Colleweston [sic] 199 n.78
Colquhon of Luss, John, chamberlain 178 n.183, 263
Columba, St 29, 52
community of the realm 17, 65–6, 77–8, 120, 161 *see also* political community; three estates
conspicuous consumption 54, 59, 184, 213, 214
Copyn, goldsmith 99
coronation 2, 9, 14, 15–19, 114, 159, 181–3, 187, 209, 223, 225–6, 231, 234, 239, 241, 259–66
   acclamation or election at 17, 119–21, 156, 158, 207
   anointing or unction *see* anointing
   collacion or collect in 131 (n.101)
   enthronement or enthroning at 17, 102–3, 115, 121–3, 133, 137, 141–3 (**142**), 144, 155, 157, 159, 181, 187, 208
   feasting and provisions for 96, 105–6, 119, 131, 140–1, 224

307

homage (offering fealty) 121–2, 125, 133, 157, 181, 182, 187, 235 *see also* oath-giving/ taking at
knighting at 105–6, 137, 143, 171, 175, 189
liturgification of, influence of the church over 122, 133, 144, 156–7, 181–3, 235, 238 *see also under* inauguration
Mass and liturgy at 101–2, 118, 121, 132, 206, 219–20, 224, 235
oath-giving/ taking at 102, 103, 121–3, 141, 155–6, 208, 211, 222, 232
procession associated with 28, 124, 157–8, 164, 188–9, 206–207, 208, 225, 231, 235–6
recitation of genealogy at 17, 123–4, 124 n.59, 156, 182, 231–2
sermon at 132–3, 235
See also at coronation *and* at queen's coronation under crowning or crown wearing; at time of coronation *under* parliament; attending second coronation of Richard I of England *under* William I, king of Scots; coronations at *under* Scone; coronations in *under* Edinburgh
See also coronation of *under* Annabella Drummond, queen of Scots and wife of Robert III; Charles I; Charles II; David II, king of Scots; Edward I; Edward III; Edward Balliol; Euphemia Ross, queen of Scots and wife of Robert II; James I, king of Scots; James II, king of Scots; James III, king of Scots; James IV, king of Scots; James V, king of Scots; Joan Beaufort, queen of Scots; Margaret of Denmark, queen of Scots and wife of James III; Margaret Logie (nee Drummond), queen of Scots and second wife of David II; Margaret Tudor, queen of Scots and wife of James IV; Marie de Guise, queen of Scots and second wife of James V; Mary of Guelders, queen of Scots and wife of James II; Mary, queen of Scots; Robert II, king of Scots; Robert III, king of Scots

See also coronation traditions of *under* Castile; Empire; England; France; Norway

See also Eleanor of Provence, queen of England; coronation of Henry VI in *under* London and *under* Paris; Richard I, second coronation of

See also sites for coronation in *under* Denmark; Norway; Sweden

Corozet, Giles, poet 215
Corstorphine 219
Coucy, Enquerrand (or Ingram) de, father of Marie de Coucy, wife of Alexander II 41, 241
Coucy, Marie de *see* Marie de Coucy, queen of Scots
Coupar Angus (also spelt Cupar-Angus)
  abbey of (Cistercian) 33
  abbot of 260, 264, 265
Crichton, William, lord Crichton 147, 158–9, 163–4, 247, 261, 262
  son of, William 147
Cronique du Roy Francoys 214
crowat *see* vials for oil
crown (term for royal government power) 5, 8, 16, 23, 37, 39, 46, 60, 88, 90, 122, 134, 140, 143, 147, 148–9, 155, 159, 161, 163, 171, 172 n.154, 180–1, 186, 224, 231, 235, 236, 238, 239
crown, or coronet (object) 28, 40, 76, 84–5, 99–101, 132, 137, 142, 155, 189, 197–8, 209, 217, 220, **221**, 232–3, 268,

INDEX

bonnet of 198 (n.72)
depictions of 40, **41**, 54, **57**, **82**, **100**, **101**, **126**, **127**–8, **142**, **196**, 197–8
of queen consorts 107, 180 (ornaments of her head), 217, 220, 251, 269
paper crown 156
crowning or crown wearing 2, 17, 23, 24 n.18, 28, 30 n.51, 34, 38, 40 (n.103), 49–50 n.144, 52 n.159, 60, 88 n.105, 92–3, 166, 189, 197, 198, 207, 233, 241, 243
  at coronation 38–9, 96, 99–100, 102, 115, 121, 128, 129, 130, 132, 134, 141, 155, 159 n.77, 169, 175, 182, 187 (n.12), 190, 209, 244
  at inauguration 28, 77, 83, 84–5, 99–101, 104, 244
  at weddings 40, 54, 92–3, 166, 179, 197, 217
  at queen's coronations/ of consorts 18, 38, 40, 55–6, 92–3, 107–8, 127–8, 133, 141, 166, 179, 198, 217, 233
  See also inauguration, coronation, unction, wedding and consort coronation
Cummyn of Inverlochy, Sir William, Marchmond herald 174
Cupar 218
Culross 94–5

Dalkeith, burgh and castle of 172 (n.154)
Darnaway Castle (near Forres) 201
Darnton 199 n.78
Dauphiné, Madame de 213
David, earl of Huntingdon, brother of William I 22, 34–5, 255
David I, king of Scots 22, 27, 37 n.82, 70
  Henry, son of 22
  depiction of 27, 40
David II, king of Scots 65, 106, 109, 123, 130 n.84, 135, 244–5
  absence from realm 115
  animosity towards Robert the Steward (later Robert II) 67, 107–9, 115–16
  role at funeral of Robert I 91, 95
  capture in 1346 115 n.10,
  coronation of (as minor) 65, 66, 95–7, 99–100, 101–4, 105–6, 109, 141, 143, 207, 232, 244, 259
    anointing at 101–2, 104
    crowning at 99–100
    coronation roll 102, 125, 141
    defiling altar at 102
    delay to 65, 96–8, 110, 227
    sceptre made for 99
  death of 115, 245
  funeral and burial of 115–16, 118–19, 125, 173, 174 n.158, 245
  lack of heir 65, 108–9, 115
  pilgrimage journeys to England 210
  seals of **100**, 126, **104**, 105, 106, 110
  pre-accession crowning of 92–3, 96, 207
  succession policy of 108–9, 119–20
  tomb of 116–19
    English workmen granted licence to work on 117, 245
  wedding of
    first marriage, to Joan Plantagenet 67, 88–9, 90–3, 95, 110, 233–4, 244
    second marriage, to Margaret Logie (nee Drummond) 67, 107–8, 116, 245
De Situ Albanie 29
Declaration of the Clergy (1309) 120, 243
Denmark
  marriage negotiations for James III with 176–8, 249
  kings of *see* Christian I; Christian IV; John
  sites for coronation in 229

deposition 76 n.41, 88, 96, 186–7, 244
Desmontiers, Jehan, poet 215
Domnall Bán, son of Donnchad II 24
Domnall mac Donnchad III 22
Doncaster 199 n.78
Donnchad II 24
Douglas, family, overthrow of by James II 170
Douglas, earl of 107, 119–21, 260
  Archibald Douglas, fourth earl, and duke of Touraine 137 n.127, 261 n.8
  Archibald Douglas, fifth earl, son of knighted 147, 261, 262
  William Douglas, eighth earl 158–64
    marriage to Margaret Douglas of Galloway 161
    murder of 167
Douglas of Galloway, Margaret 161
Douglas, Sir James 89, 92, 97–8, 259
Douglas, Sir James, brother of eighth earl 161, 163
Douglas, Sir James of Balvenie, son of knighted 147
Dover 36
Drummond, Annabella *see* Annabella Drummond, queen of Scots and wife of Robert III
Drummond, Maragret, mistress of James IV 194 n.49
Dublin, archbishop of, John Sandford 83, 257
dule wear 1, 91, 191, 202 n.100, 204, 216
Dumbarton 130
Dumfries, priory of the Grey Friars at 76, 78, 243
Dunbar, earl of, also known as earl of Lothian in 1214 29, 256
Dunbar, John, lord of Fife 122
Dunbar, William, poet 203
Dunblane
  bishop of 260, 262, 264, 265
    Clement 45, 257
    Walter de Coventry 124
  cathedral of 33, 130

Dundee 176 n.166, 219, 251
  representatives of 264
Dundonald, castle (near Ayr) 117, 129–30
Dunfermline
  abbey of (Benedictine) 1, 31–2, 33, 43, 51–3, 68–72, 89–90, 93–5, 96, 115–16, 125, 173, 205, 228 n.16, 230, 241
    excavations at 51
    Robert I installs perpetual light at 96–7 n.148
  abbot of 46, 96–7 n.148, 123, 125, 260, 263, 265
    See also Kenleith, Robert of (or de Leldeleth)
  compilation of 52
  See also funeral of *under* Alexander III, king of Scots; Robert I, king of Scots
Dunipace 94
Dunkeld
  bishop of 104, 258, 260, 264, 265
    Geoffrey or Galfrid 46, 257
    John de Peebles 133, 261
    John Ralston 163–4
    Thomas Lauder 170, 263
  cathedral of 117
Dupplin Moor, battle of 98
Durham 137, 199 n.78
  bishop of 38, 103 n.183
    Anthony Bek 83
  Frosterly marble from 69–70, 93
Durward, Alan, justiciar 45–6, 52, 257

Earl Marshal of England 54
Easingwold 38
ecclesiastics, a collective group (unnamed) 28–31, 46, 49, 61–2, 65, 83, 84–5, 133, 149, 156, 157, 182, 209, 235 *see* clergy, a collective group (unnamed) *and* cleric, a collective group (unnamed)
Edinburgh 119, 146–7, 154 n.44, 155, 157–8, 168, 169, 170, 171–2, 174, 176 n.166, 182, 190, 204, 218, 230, 231, 245, 247, 249

INDEX

burgess of *see* Lyons, Stephen
burgh commissioner of 264
burgh records of 188 n.17
coronation in 155–8, 160
civic officials and clerics of 138
Edinburgh Castle 119, 157, 164, 182, 208 n.135
funeral processions in 1, 173, 230
High Street 157, 164
Holy Trinity College in 172 n.154, 200 n.84, 248
mendicant friars of 201
Mercat Cross in 157
parliament at 159–60, 167, 170, 247
    in the Tolbooth 167, 179, 189, 250
royal entries at 38, 137–8, 140, 144, 164, 188, 219, 226, 230, 246, 248, 251
    entry route 157 (n.62), 164
    role in organising 199
treaty of Edinburgh-Northampton 95, 244
St Giles 157
    college of 201
Tolbooth in 167 *see also* in the Tolbooth *under* parliament at
Tron 157
West Port of 157 n.62
Edith (also known as Matilda), queen of England, daughter of Mael Coluim III and Margaret 36 n.77
Edward I, king of England 29, 32 n.64, 58 n.193, 68–9, 75, 76–80, 82–4, 85–6, 242–3
    coronation of 57, 242
    as Prince Edward 55, 56
    removal of royal honours and stone of Scone (or Destiny) 27, 40, 80, 99–100
    wife of *see* Eleanor of Castile, queen of England
Edward II, king of England 243
    burial and funeral of 90, 116 n. 13, 128, 187, 190
    deposition or removal of 88, 98, 187, 244
    as Prince of Wales 75
    tomb of 117 n.21
    wife of *see* Isabella of France, queen of England
Edward III, king of England
    accession of 97, 244
    burial and funeral of father 116 n. 13, 187
    coronation of 105–6, 187
    grants licence to workmen for David II's tomb 117
    mother of *see* Isabella of France, queen of England 97
    negotiations with David II 108
    seizure of power 98
    sister of *see* Joan of the Tower, queen of Scots and first wife of David II
    support for Edward Balliol 99–100, 103–4, 245
    tomb for children of, Blanch and William 117 n.21
Edward IV, king of England 249
    daughter of, Celia 178, 249
    son of, George, funeral for 202 n.100
Edward Balliol, king of Scots 65, 66, 96, 244–5
    contractual nature of kingship 99
    claim to the throne 98
    crown of/ crowning of 99–100, 244
    inauguration or coronation of 96, 98–101, 103–6, 109–10, 244, 260
    removal of 106
    seal of **101, 104**, 105
Edward the Confessor, king of England 32 n.64, 68
effigy (funeral) *see* effigy use in *under* funeral
Eleanor of Austria, queen of France and second queen of François I 214
Eleanor of Castile, queen of England and wife of Edward I, funeral of and monuments for 32 n.64, 45 n.127, 90

311

Eleanor of Provence, queen of
  England and wife of Henry III,
  coronation and staged intercession
  of 55–6
Elgin 176 n.166
Elizabeth de Burgh, queen of Scots
  and wife of Robert I 86, 243, 244,
  259
Elizabeth of York, queen of England,
  wife of Henry VII, mother of Margaret Tudor 204
Eltham, John of, tomb 117 n.21
Ely, bishop of, William de Luda 83,
  257
embalming *see under* preparation of
  the body *under* funeral
Empire, later Holy Roman Empire
  coronation traditions of 30, 239
    Golden Bull (1356) of 30
      n.52
  funeral traditions in 35 n.76
England 15–16, 58, 103, 203, 222,
  228–9, 238, 241
  claims of supremacy or presumed
    superiority of 23, 25–26, 35,
    36–7, 55–6, 65, 80
  commentators from (unnamed) 214
  civil war or turmoil in 36, 92
    n.132, 97, 170
  coronation traditions of 15–16,
    24, 30, 46, 84, 120–1, 124–5,
    157 (n.63), 159 n.77, 219
    n.201, 238–9
  Edwardian era of war 91–2
  expenses for Anglo-Scot weddings 39
  funeral traditions and death practices in 30, 31 (n. 56–7, 61),
    34, 91, 152, 153, 154, 174
  heralds of 178
    See also Young, John, Somerset herald
  homage from Scottish kings or
    elites (requested or granted) 26, 54, 76–7, 243, 245,
    257–8
  intervention in Scottish affairs/
    tensions with 22, 69, 77–8,
    79–80, 83, 99, 100–1, 103–5,
    109, 203, 231, 242–4, 245,
    248, 250
  kings of *see* Alfred; Edward the
    Confessor; Edward I; Edward
    II; Edward III; Edward IV; Henry I; Henry II; Henry III; Henry
    IV; Henry V; Henry VI; Henry
    VII; John; Richard I; Richard
    II; Richard III; Stephen
  peace with 36, 88, 92, 95, 97,
    199–200, 250, 251
    treaty of Perpetual Peace
      with 193, 250 *see also*
      wedding or marriage of *under* James IV, king of Scots
  queens of *see* Anne of Bohemia;
    Edith (also known as Matilda);
    Eleanor of Castile; Elizabeth of
    York; Isabella of France; Katherine of Valois; Matilda, queen
    of England
  refusal to recognise Bruce kingship 88
  removal of James IV's body as
    trophy of war 204
  rise of Tudor power in 194
  Scottish kings in England *see*
    Alexander II, king of Scots;
    Alexander III, king of Scots;
    David II, king of Scots; James
    I, king of Scots
  tomb design in 117, 151
    See also Eltham, John of,
      tomb; Hatfield, William,
      tomb; Manny, Sir Walter,
      tomb; tomb for children of
      under Edward III; tomb of
      under Edward II; Richard
      II; Isabella of France or de
      Valois
  workmen from 117 (n.20)
enthronement or enthroning 17,
  159, 163, 176, 181, 189, 193, 197,
  209, 231–2, 235–6, 248
  See also under coronation, inauguration
  See also ritual in, including enthroning *under* parliament

entrail burial *see under* funeral
Eric II, king of Norway   57, 242
Ermengarde de Beaumont, queen of Scots and wife of William I   28, 30
Errol, earl of   219, 264, 265
   See also Constable of Scotland *under* household officers
Erskine, Margaret, mistress of James V   210
D'Escouchy, Mathieu
   Chronique of   149, 162, 165–6
Euphemia Ross, queen of Scots and wife of Robert II
   children of   127
   coronation of   127–8, 245
   seal of   126–**127**
evisceration *see under* preparation of the body *under* funeral

Falaise, treaty of   26, 32, 240
Falkland Palace (Fife)   1, 176, 218, 229–30, 252
feast days   109, 227–8
   All Saints   67
   Andrew, St   76, 77–8
   Annunciation of the Virgin   76, 85, 118, 129, 156, 166, 227
   Assumption of the Virgin   56, 129, 133, 170
   Candlemas *see* Purification of the Virgin
   Christmas Day   33 n.70, 53, 227
   Christo-centric feast days   238
     see also Christmas Day; Easter; Lent; Palm Sunday; Shrove Tuesday *under* feast days
   Easter or Holy Day   74, 135, 156, 158 n.66, 174, 176, 203, 213, 227
     feasting and provisions for   203–4
     Mass on   203
   Fillan, St, feast day   188
   Francis, St, feast day   105
   Holy Week   135, 156, 174
   indulgences on   51, 118, 228
   John the Baptist, St, feast day   187
   Lent   118, 153–4, 203
     Lenten veil   154
   Marian feasts and liturgy   51 n.155, 85 n.89, 118, 166, 217–18, 227–8, *see also* Annunciation of; Assumption of; Purification of; Nativity of *under* feast days
   Martinmas   58
   Margaret, St, feast day   58–9
   Nativity of the Virgin   224
   New Year   213
   Nicholas, St, feast day of   28 n.41
   Palm Sunday   76, 85, 87–8, 135, 139–40, 144, 174, 246
   Purification of the Virgin   218
   Shrove Tuesday   161, 162 n.99, 163, 165–6
   Trinity Sunday   128
   Visitation of the Blessed Virgin   166
   Whitsunday   41
Feast of the Pheasant *see under* Lille
feasting *see under* baptism; coronation; inauguration; wedding and consort coronation
Field of the Cloth of Gold (near Calais)   211, 214, 243, 251
Fife   71, 94, 218–19
   chapel for St Monan in   106, 108
   countess of, Isabella   122–3
     husband, John Dunbar, lord of Fife, 122
   earl of   29, 44–5, 46, 76–7, 79, 81, 102, 110, 122–3, 133, 142, 155, 235, 256, 257
     absorption of earldom by crown   155 n.54, 182
     Duncan, ninth earl of   79, 102, 103–4, 110, 260
     Isabella, countess of Buchan, acting for *see* Buchan, countess of, Isabella, aunt of the earl of Fife
     Robert Stewart *see* Stewart, Robert, earl of Fife
     Murdoch Stewart *see* Stewart,

Murdoch, earl of Fife
  lord of *see* Dunbar, John, lord of Fife
  See also Falkland Palace
Fillan, St   188
  bell of   188
  See also under feast days
Fitz Alan, Sir Walter, justiciar   41
Flanders   117
  count of, Guy, father of Marguerite or Margaret of Flanders   41, 58
  Flemish material culture   184, 191, 268
  Marguerite or Margaret of *see* Marguerite or Margaret of Flanders, queen of Scots
  tapestries from   213
Flodden   204, 206
  battle of   186, 250 *see also* death of *under* James IV
Florence, gold and silver threads from   212
Fordun, John of   10, 81, 125 *see also Gesta Annalia*
Forfar, royal residence at   33, 59
Fourth Lateran Council, 1215   49, 240
France   15, 58, 202, 210, 211 n.150, 212, 222, 228–9 (n.19), 243, 245, 246, 247, 250, 251, 269–70
  coronation tradition of   15, 24, 30, 46, 61, 124–5, 159 n.77, 191, 237, 239
  Ordo of Charles V   124–5
  funeral traditions and death practices of   31 (n. 57 and 61), 34, 35 n.76, 89–90, 153, 191, 226–7
  kings of *see* Charles VII; François I; Henri II; Henry VI (of England); Louis VIII; Louis IX; Louis X; Louis XI; Philip August; Philip IV; Philip V
  queens consort of *see* Anne of Brittany; Eleanor of Austria; Margaret of Provence
  tomb design in   70, 117
  wedding traditions in   213
  See also wedding of, journey to France for *under* James V
Francis, St, feast day of *see under* feast days
François I, king of France   184, 210, 211, 214, 251
  expenses for James V and Madeleine's wedding   211 n. 152
  Robinet, 'borstar de roy', 212
  second wife of *see* Eleanor of Austria, queen of France
  See also Field of the Cloth of Gold, near Calais
funeral   62, 204, 223, 234, 235
  display of body   31 (n.56), 34, 45, 152–3, 174–5, 181, 191
  effigy use in   1, 153, 174, 205–6, 226, 233, 239
  entrail burial   31, 45 (n.127), 62, 94 n.140
  heart burial or heart removal   31, 51, 53, 62, 72, 74, 88 n.105, 89, 97–8, 109, 110, 154–5, 172, 227, 238, 244, 247
  heraldic nature of   236, 238 *see also* heraldic decoration
  liturgy at   31, 89, 89–90 n.115, 95, 133, 153–4
  Masses and prayers for the soul related to   1, 31, 102, 130, 133, 135, 150, 153, 191, 204–5, 207, 217
  mourners and mourning at   31, 34, 68, 74, 117 n.22, 153–4, 173, 191, 204, 215–16, 217, 225, 226
  offerings at   91, 95, 130, 174–5
  preparation of body for   1, 30–1 (31 n.56), 45, 62, 235
    embalming   1, 31, 72, 89, 94 n.140, 235
    evisceration (removal of entrails or viscera)   31, 45, 72, 89, 94 n.140
  provisions for   131
  procession for   1, 21, 32–5 (**33**), **44**, 62, 71–4 (**72**, **73**), 74, 89–90, 93–5 (**94**), 119, **129**–30, 135, 153–4, 171–3 (**172**), 174, 175, 215–16, 219, 229–30, 234

INDEX

cross raised to mark   34
viscera burial *see* entrail burial
vigil/s   1, 21, 31, 32–4, 71, 72 n.30, 89, 94–5, 130, 135–6, 152, 153–4, 171–2, 173, 230, 238
See also burials and funerals of others organised by *and* funeral or lack thereof for *under* James IV, king of Scots
See also death of *under* Joan Beaufort, queen of Scots; Joanna Plantagenet, queen of Scots; death and burial *under* Margaret of Denmark, queen of Scots; Mary of Guelders, queen of Scots; death and funeral of *under* Henry IV, king of England; Madeleine de Valoise or of France, queen of Scots; Stewart, James, duke of Ross and brother of James IV
See also funeral and burial of *under* Alexander II, king of Scots; Alexander III, king of Scots; David II, king of Scots; James I, king of Scots; James II, king of Scots; James III, king of Scots; Robert I, king of Scots; Robert II, king of Scots; Robert III, king of Scots; William I, king of Scots;
See also funeral and/or death of *under* James V, king of Scots
See also funeral traditions and death practices of *under* England; France; Norway
See also Louis X, king of France, funeral of; Philip V, king of France, funeral of

Gaelic poet   46, 50, 123–4, 235–6
Gallico, Ligerio, armourer   174
Galloway, bishop of   263, 264, 265
  Thomas de Rossy   133, 261
guardian/s or guardianship   15, 18, 65, 74–5, 77–8, 92, 97–8, 110, 115, 136, 144–5, 148, 170–1 n.147, 175–6, 224–5, 226, 233, 242, 243, 244, 245, 248
  seal of   **74**, 77–8, 136, 243
  See also Randolph, Thomas, earl of Moray and guardian; Stewart, Robert, earl of Menteith, Fife and duke of Albany; Sinclair, William, earl of Orkney and admiral of Scottish fleet; James Kennedy *under* St Andrews, bishop of
Gaunt, John of, grandfather of Joan Beaufort   141
General Council   140, 141, 159, 160, 207–8, 246, 247, 265
  difference between parliament and general council *see under* parliament
  oaths exchanged at   134
George, St   199–200, 202
Gesta Annalia   10, 21 n.1, 29–30, 31, 34–5, 46–7, 49, 52, 62, 67–8, 71, 77, 80, 81–2, 125
gifts and gift giving   13, 39, 55 (n.177), 56–7, 162 n.98, 178, 191, 199, 203–4, 213–14, 228, 268, 270
  almsgiving and offerings   56, 91, 95, 130, 174–5, 213–14, 222, 268
  papal gifts   25, 27, 40, 49, 215 n.176, 238
Girard, Regnault, ambassador for Charles VII   138
Glasgow
  archbishop of   219
    James Beaton   208, 265
  bishop of   79, 101, 104, 260, 262, 264
    Andrew Durisdeer   170, 263
    Matthew de Glendowyn   132–3, 261
    Robert Wishart   79, 80, 83, 84–6, 110, 235, 257, 258
    Walter   28, 30–1, 256
    Walter de Wardlaw   124–5, 260
    William de Bondington   41
    William Turnbull   163–4
Gloucester   128

INDEX

Gordon, Lady Catherine 201
governor or governorship 135–6, 140, 148, 176 n.168, 208–9, 224–5, 235, 246, 251
   bestowal of governorship 135, 208
   See also Stewart, Robert, earl of Menteith, Fife and duke of Albany; Boyd, Robert, lord Boyd; Stewart, John, duke of Albany; Hamilton, James, earl of Arran
Graham, Robert 148, 247
Grand Chartreuse (near Grenoble) 151
   prior of 159 n.21
Grantham 199 n.78
Gray, Thomas, *Scalachronica* 104
Great Cause 3, 29, 65, 75, 83, 123, 243
Guelders
   court of 173
   duke of, Arnold, father of Mary of Guelders 161 n.89, 173
   intergenerational tensions in 170
   ritual tradition in 173
   See also Mary of Guelders, queen of Scots and wife of James II
Guisborough, Walter of, chronicle of 78, 79, 81–2, 84

Håkon IV, king of Norway 24, 31 n.56, 35, 60, 92, 241
Hamilton, James, second earl of Arran, also duke of Châtellerault and governor 1, 224–5, 226, 235–6
Hamilton, lord of 159, 264
Harpour or harpist 123–4 *see also* Scone seal *under* Scone
Hatfield, William, tomb 117 n.21
Hay family *see* constable of Scotland *under* household officers or officials
Hay, Gilbert 174, 226
   Buke of the Gouvernance of Princis by 12
hearse 1, 90, 191, **192**, 216–17
heart burial *see under* funeral
Hebridean Islands 60, 241
hegemonic masculinity or masculine

hierarchy 161 (n.88), 211
Hélicourt 98
Henri II, king of France, as dauphin 214
Henry II, emperor 35 n.76
Henry VI, emperor 28
Henry I, king of England 36 n.77, 45 n.127
Henry II, king of England 24–5 n.18, 26, 92 n.132, 240
Henry III, king of England 37–8, 40, 41 n.106, 51–2, 53–7, 68, 71, 83, 241–2
   criticism of in Matthew of Paris 53, 55
   daughter of *see* Margaret Plantagenet, queen of Scotland and wife of Alexander III
   gift of seal matrix to 55
   influence exerted in minority of Alexander III 56
   knighted Alexander III and bestows gifts 46 n.128, 55
   pardons granted on behalf of Margaret, daughter, and Alexander III following marriage 55
   sister of *see* Joanna, queen of Scots and wife of Alexander II
   translation of Edward the Confessor 32 n.64, 51–2
   wife of *see* Eleanor of Provence, queen of England and wife of Henry III
Henry IV, king of England 135, 135
   death and funeral of 128, 175 n.163
Henry V, king of England 45 n.127, 138, 150, 153, 246
Henry VI, king of England 175, 187, 207
   accedes to French throne 207
Henry VII, king of England 193–4, 199, 204, 250
Henry VIII, king of England 184, 202, 211, 214, 250
   Arthur, son of 202 (n.100), 250
   attempt to bury James IV 204 n.109
   See also Field of the Cloth of

316

INDEX

Gold, near Calais
Hepburn, Patrick, earl of Bothwell   189
Hepburn, Patrick, lord Hailes   189, 264
heraldic decoration and coats of arms   1, 40, 42, 57, 90–1, 136, 140, 165, 173, 174–5, 176, 177–8, 188–9, 191, 193, 195, 200, 205, 216–17, 236, 253–5, 268
   badges   178
   depicted in seal   **57, 104**–5, **126**
     see also seals
   livery   163, 171, 178, 216, 236
   See also chivalric culture; symbols and symbolism
heralds and heraldic officials   1, 9, 123, 155, 171, 188, 195, 235–6
   Marchmond herald *see* Cummyn of Inverlochy, Sir William
   pursuivants   188
     see also Albany Persuivant
   receiving red taffeta and gold coats of arms   195
   See also Lord Lyon King of Arms
Herries of Caerlaverock, Sir Herbert   154 n.45
Hexham   199 n.78
Hill, Richard, tailor to the king   212
Hoitman or Hottmannis, goldsmith   214
Holy Land *see* Jerusalem
Holyrood
   abbey of (Augustinian)   1, 115–116, 118, 119, 130 n.84, 146, 149, 155, 157–8, 159, 164 (n.112), 169, 171, 173–4, 177, 182, 204, 205, 215, 216–17, 219–20, 228 (n.16), 228 n.17, 228 n.18, 229–30, 245, 247, 248, 251, 252
     abbot of   260, 263, 264, 265
     canons of   235
   building costs at   194 n.53, 267
   palace of   201
homage *see under* homage from Scottish kings or elites *under* England; homage given at *under* inauguration; homage (offering fealty) *under* coronation; homage to England *under* Alexander II; refusal of homage to England for Scotland *under* Alexander III
Honorius III, pope   36, 38
   Cum universi (1192), renewal of in 1218   36
honours of Scotland *see* regalia
horse/s   1, 34, 39–40, 71, 138, 158, 162 n.93, 164, 188, 214
   carriage or chariot or litter drawn by   1, 34, 91, 194 n.53, 212, 267–8
   depictions of   **57** *see also* seals
   gear and harnesses for   57, 162, 180, 188–9, 212, 214, 215–16, 268, 269
   see also under hunting; tournament
household officers or officials   30–1, 45, 138, 152, 155, 171, 195, 212, 235–6
   clerk of the liverance
     Ricardo Bard   131
   clerk of the wardrobe
     Walter Forester   131
   constable of Scotland   143, 155–6, 264
     Thomas de Hay   122
     William Hay, belted as earl   156 n.55, 171 (n.152), 262, 263
     William Hay, fifth earl of Errol   208
   henchmen   188, 195
   marischal   155–6
     William Keith (d.1410)   122, 260
     William Keith, belted earl   156 n.55, 171, 262
     William Keith, second earl Marischal   208, 264
   master of the king's household   138
   pages   216
   shield-bearer of the king or *scutifer regis*
     See Napier of Merchiston, Alexander, comptroller

and shield-bearer
Howden, Roger of, Annals of   22
hunting   176, 214
  dogs for   214
  falcons for   214
  horses for   214
Huntingdon, earl of, David, brother of William I   22, 34–5, 256
Huntly, earl of   264
  Alexander Seton, son-in-law to Chancellor Crichton   165

inauguration   17, 62, 74–5, 225–6, 231, 234, 239, 256–60
  acclamation at   46, 61–2, 74, 125 *see also* election *under* succession
  enthronement or enthroning at   21, 27, 29, 34, 46, **48**–**50**, **57**, 61–2, 76–7, 79–83 (**82**), 103–4, 109, 125, 244
  feasting and provisions for   21, 28 n.41, 29, 31, 105–6
  homage given at   46 *see also* oath-giving *under* inauguration
  knighting associated with   46–7
  liturgification of, influence of the church over   16–17, 49–50, 60–2, 82–6, 109–10
  Mass or blessings at   28–9, 49, 62, 83, 85
  of governor   208–9
  oath-giving/ taking at   49, 76, 77, 81, 83
  procession at   62
  pre-mortuary inauguration or crowning   24–25, 60, 92–3, 96, 207 *see also* Rex designatus or heir designate *under* succession
  recitation of genealogy   17, 46, 47, 50, 61–2, 125, 231–2
  See under crowning or crown wearing
  See also inauguration of *under* Alexander II, king of Scots; Alexander III, king of Scots; Edward Balliol, king of Scots; John Balliol, king of Scots; Robert I, king of Scots; William I, king of Scots
  See also inauguration tradition of *under* Ireland

Inchmurdoch (Fife)   108
Ingibörg, first wife of Mael Colium III *see* heirs of with *under* Mael Colium III
Inverkeithing, parish church of   71–2
Inverness   176, 180, 230
  castle or palace at   176 n.166
Iona, abbey of (Benedictine)   27, 29
Ireland
  inauguration traditions of   29
  succession in   21 (n.5)
Ireland, John   226
Isabella of France or de Valois, queen of England and mother of Edward III   97
  tomb of   117 n.21
Italy, commentators from   214

James I, king of Scots   113, 121, 134 n.114, 135–6, 144–5, 246–7
  coronation of   114, 137, 139, 140–4, 147–8, 151, 226, 246, 261–2
  daughters of   138, 146, 146 n.1
  death or murder of   148, 149, 150–6 (153 n.38), 158, 181, 182, 186–7, 247
  destruction of Albany Stewarts by   155, 235
  display of body in death   152–4
  disquiet caused by style of ruling   147–8
  English captivity of   113, 135–6, 138 n.136, 145, 151, 209, 246
  ensuring oratory praise for royal family   138–9, 222
  founding of Carthusian house   150–2
  funeral or burial of   150, 153–5, 181, 182, 230
  heart removal, crusade journey and burial of   154–5, 247
  heirs of   146–7
    conferring knighthoods at

INDEX

baptisms of 147
influence of English captivity and Lancastrian court on 113, 138–9, 144, 154 n.45,
Kingis Quair 141
relationship with the pope 152 n.35
return to Scotland 114–15, 136–7, 150, 226
royal entry of 137–40, 157, 164, 173, 174, 230, 246
seal of **142**
tomb of, with Joan Beaufort 150 n.24, 151–2
wife of *see* Joan, queen of Scots and wife of James I
James II, king of Scots 158, 169, 171, 173, 182, 215, 247–8
  accession of 148
  birth and baptism of, along with twin brother Alexander 146–7, 160, 163, 247
  birth of male heir, James III 167–8, 248
  coronation of 155–8, 159, 166, 173, 182, 247, 262
  death of 168–9, 175, 176, 181, 193, 248
  dynastic rights of 156, 158
  enthroned in parliament 159
  funeral or burial of 168, 169, 171–5, 236
    influence upon 173–5, 181
  minority and coming of age of 158–63, 210
  murder of Douglas and potential political crisis 167–8 *see also* Douglas, William, eighth earl of
  named sister, Isabella, duchess of Brittany, as heir 161
  overthrow of Douglases 170
  tomb or tomb-shrine of 173–5, 176, 204
  and tournament at Stirling (1449) 161–3 (162 n.99)
    bestows knighthoods at 163
    enthroned at 163
  urban king 158, 230

  wedding of, to Mary of Guelders 158, 161, 162 (n.99), 163–7, 173, 177, 181, 193–4, 197, 233, 247–8
    ratified treaty at Stirling 164 n.110
    role in marriage negotiations 161 (n.89)
James III, king of Scots 148, 168, 169, 170, 187, 207, 231, 248–50
  attending funeral of James II 171
  betrothal of heir of 178, 249
  birth of 167–8 (167 n.131)
  canonisation of Margaret of Denmark, wife 190 (n.30)
  carrying Bruce sword at Sauchieburn 188
  coinage with imperial crown 197
  coming of age of 176–81
  coronation of 168, 169–71, 173, 174, 175, 181, 207, 248, 263
    clothing and supplies at time of 169 n.136
  death and murder of 186–7, 193, 250
    declaration about 189–90
  English foreign policy 178, 194
  funeral and/or burial of 187, 190–2
    representation of 191, **192**
  minority of 170–1, 175–7, 210
    enthroned in parliament during 176
    independent activity during 176
    as military figurehead 175
  royal progress and entries during 175–6 (176 n.166)
  prayers for the soul of 191, 193, 204–5
  tomb 190, 202 n.99
  treasure of 188
  wedding (marriage) of, to Margaret of Denmark 149, 176–81, 193–4, 249
    grant of lands to Margaret 180

319

progress associated
  with   149, 180–1, 230
 tax for   176
 work on tomb of James II   175, 176
James IV, king of Scots   184–6, 190, 193–4, 206, 207, 210, 213, 214, 222–3, 249–50
 betrothal as prince   178 (n.183)
 birth and baptism of heirs   186, 250
  James (b.1507), first son   193, 199, 201–2
   James IV participating in tournament   201
  James (b. 1512), later James V   203–4, 227
 burials and funerals of others organised by   186, 204–5, 216
 claims to British sovereignty   199–200, 202
 clothing for   188
 coronation of   187–9, 190, 207, 208, 223, 228, 264
 court and household of   8, 204
 death and removal of body of   186, 204 (n.109), 205, 207, 250
 death/s of children of   186, 202–3, 204
 direction of commemoration for James III   191, 193
 funeral or lack thereof for   205–6
 historical popularity of   185
 horse gear for   188–9
 illegitimate children   194, 201
 minority of/ accession as minor   186–93
  as figurehead in rebellion against James III   186–7
 mistresses   194 (n. 49) see also Boyd, Marion; Drummond, Margaret; Kennedy, Janet
 prayers for the soul of   205 (n.116)
 tomb (or mausoleum) of   193–4, 204–5, 207, 250
  overseeing work on   204
 wedding of, to Margaret Tudor, daughter of Henry VII   177, 185, 186, 193–201, 202, 219, 222, 250
  bare-headed at   197, 220, 233
  clothing at   195
  costs of   194–5 (194 n.53), 233–4, 267–8
  gifts to Margaret   190
  reciprocal reverence exchanged at   197
 work at Holyrood   229
 work at Stirling Castle   206–7
James V, king of Scots   184–86, 207, 217, 219, 222–3, 231, 250–2
 birth and baptism of see birth and baptism of heirs under James IV, king of Scots
 birth and baptism of heirs   186, 222, 252
 brides proposed for   210
 coronation of   206–9, 223, 224, 231, 234, 251, 265–6
  known as mourning coronation   206
 court culture of   185–6
 criticism of   185
 death of children of   186, 222, 252
 ensuring oratory praise for royal family   222
 funeral and/or death of   1–2, 4, 6, 90, 216–17, 224–5, 226, 229–30, 233, 236, 252
  date of death   1 n.1
  role of women at   1
 funeral arrangements for Madeleine of France see under Madeleine of France, queen of Scots
 illegitimate children of see Stewart, Lady Jane
 inventory of jewels and clothing of   232
 minority of/ accession as minor   186, 204–9, 209–11
 mistress of see Erskine, Margaret, mistress of James V
 prayers for soul of father   205 n.116
 tomb of   230

see also tomb of *under* Madeleine, queen of Scotland
weddings of 186, 217
   first marriage, to Madeleine of France 210–14, 251
   clothing for 211–12
   costs and expenses for 211–12, 233–4, 269–70
   journey to France for 210–11, 230
   procurement of goods in France for 212–13
   royal entry to Paris 210
   second marriage, to Marie de Guise, duchess de Longueville *see Marie de Guise, queen of Scots*
   preparations and clothing for coronation of Marie 220
   See also royal robe; regalia; crown
work at Holyrood 229
James VII of Scotland, or II of England 219 n.201
Jedburgh, abbey of (Augustinian) 228 n.18
Jerusalem 154
   Holy Sepulchre in 97 n.154
   Knights of St John of, or Hospitallers 154 (n.45), 247
jewels and jewellery 99, 178, 199–200, 202, 212, 214, 232–3, 267, 269
   collars 140, 178, 180 n.192
   ring 28, 132 n.100, 137, 142, 267 n.6
     spousing ring 213, 270
Joan Beaufort, queen of Scots and wife of James I 137, 141, 149, 151–5, 158, 160, 168, 182, 230, 237, 246–7, 262
   daughters of 138, 146, 146 n.1, 246–7
   death of 154, 247
   royal entry, with James 157 *see also* royal entry *under* James I
   estates swear oaths to 141, 179, 237

   foundation of Charterhouse (fundatrix), with James 150, 230, 246
   coronation of, with James I 137, 141–2, 152, 246
   James's promotion of as second person of the realm 141, 151, 167
   Knights of St John or Hospitallers 154 n.45
   letter of 154 n.44
   sons of 146–7 *see also* James II, king of Scots
   See also tomb of, with Joan Beaufort *under* James I
Joan of the Tower, queen of Scots and first wife of David II 99, 105, 108, 244, 245, 259
   See also wedding of *under* David II
Joanna Plantagenet, queen of Scots and first wife of Alexander II 35–6, 39, 41, 116, 241
   burial of 41 n.106
   dower of 39
   See also wedding of, first marriage *under* Alexander II
John Balliol, king of Scots 76, 98, 242–3
   death of 99, 243
   inauguration of 65, 66, 76–9, 81–4, 86, 96, 109–10, 120, 243, 257–8
   removal of 65, 80, 85, 99, 243
   seal of **82**, 101
John the Baptist, St 70, 187
   See also under feast days
John, king of Denmark and brother of Margaret, wife of James III 204
John, king of England 25–6, 36, 240–1
jousting *see* tournaments
justice ayres 176

Katherine of Valois, queen of England and wife of Henry V 90 n.122, 165 n.116, 246
Keith family *see* marischal *under* household officers or officials
Kelso
   abbey of (Tironensian) 59, 149,

321

INDEX

169–70, 171–3, 174, 182, 228 n.17, 248
   abbot of   59 n.198, 264
Kenleith, Robert of (or de Leldeleth), abbot of Dunfermline   42–3, 49 n.144, 51–3, 61, 68, 235, 241
Kennedy, Janet, mistress of James IV   194 n.49, 200 (n.90)
Kerrara, island of   42, 43, 45
king's two bodies (bodies politic and mortal)   1, 75, 174, 205–6, 226–7, 239
   Le roi est mort, vive le roi (the king is dead, long live the king)   2, 224
   See also royal dignity; sacral or sacred kingship
Kinghorn   71–2, 242
   Kinghorn-Wester, parish church of   71–2
Kirkcaldy of the Grange, James, treasurer   211–12
knight/s or men-at-arms   39, 54 n.172, 59, 78, 79, 90, 91–3, 122, 130, 151, 164, 165, 171, 173, 201–2, 216, 247, 248, 250, 257, 258, 259, 260, 265
   Scottish and Burgundian   161–3
   See also Knights of St John of *under* Jerusalem
knighting   25–6, 134, 160, 163, 241, 246, 259, 260 n.7, 261, 263,
   See also knighting associated with *under* inauguration; knighting at *under* baptism, coronation, wedding; knighting or belting associated *with* under parliament
Knox, John   150

Lalaing, Isabel de, daughter of Jaques de Lalaing   164 n.109
Lalaing, Jacques de
   as combatant   162
   Histoire of   162
Lalaing, Simon de, knight of Golden Fleece   162 n. 93
Lanercost, chronicle of   67–8, 103, 105

authorship of   67 n.7
Langele, Geoffrey de, justiciar of the forest (English)   54 n.172
Lauder   172, 249
Leith   163, 173, 182, 218, 230, 248
   people of   164
   See also Anthony of Vienne, St, church at
Lennox, earl of   219, 235–6, 258, 260, 264, 265
Lesley, John, history of   179
Liber Extravagans   70
lieutenants   103, 115, 121 (n.45), 128, 133–4 (133 n.105), 136, 148, 245, 246, 247, 249, 261
   bestowal of lieutenancy, ceremony associated with   123, 133, 134, 141 n.154
   See also Stewart, Robert, the Steward; Stewart, John, of Kyle and earl of Carrick; Stewart, Robert, earl of Menteith, Fife and duke of Albany; Stewart, David, earl of Carrick and duke of Rothesay
Lille, feast of Pheasan at   165 n.116
Lincoln   45 n.127
Lindsay, James, provost of Lincluden   171
Lindsay, Sir David   215
   'The Deploratioun of the Deith of Quene Magdalene'   215
Linlithgow   119–21, 122, 219, 245
   burgh commissioner of   264
   palace at   219, 231, 250
   St Michael's church at   203
liturgy   66, 74, 139–40 *see also* Mass or liturgy *under* coronation; Mass or liturgy *under* coronation *under* wedding and queens; liturgy at *under* funeral; liturgification *under* coronation and inauguration
Livingstone of Callendar, Sir Alexander, keeper or captain of Stirling Castle   162, 247, 262
Logie (nee Drummond), Margaret *see* Margaret Logie, queen of Scots
   son of, from first marriage, Logie, John   107 n.206

INDEX

London 25, 37, 56, 117, 138, 211 n.150, 228 n.18, 240, 246
  Charterhouse at 151
  Chronicle of 200
  coronation of Henry VI in 207
  Tower of 157 (n.63)
Lord of the Isles 134 n.109, 146, 246
  See also Argyll, earl of
Lord Lyon King of Arms or Lyon herald 124 n.59, 163, 171, 178 (n.183), 262, 263
  Sir James Balfour of Denmilne 155–7, 160
  Jerome Lindsay 155
  See also Lindsay, Sir David
Lothian, archdeacon of 264
  William del Blois, chancellor 30–1, 256
Louis VIII, king of France, as dauphin 35 n.76, 36
Louis IX, king of France and later St Louis 41 n.107, 68–9, 241
Louis X, king of France, funeral of 90
Louis XI, king of France, as dauphin 138, 146, 246–7
Louis XII, king of France 217
Loutfout, Adam 174
Louvre 125
Lovel, Philip, receives pardon from Henry III at behest of Alexander III 56
Low Countries
  See also Bruges; Flanders; Sluys
  tomb design in 70, 117
  Tournai, limestone from 205
Lucius III, pope 27 n.31
Lyon, Stephen, burgess of Edinburgh 147 (n.7)

MacWilliam (also known as FitzDuncan) family 24, 35, 42, 240, 241
  See also Domnall Bán, son of Donnchad II
Mael Colium III 21–2, 31, 36 n.77, 43, 128
  heirs of, with Ingibörg, first wife 24, 128
Mael Colium IV 70
  accession of 22

  funeral of 21, 240
  depiction of 27, 40
  Cistercian foundation of Coupar Angus 33
Madeleine de Valois or of France, first wife of James V 179, 230, 251
  death and funeral of 90, 186, 215–17, 218, 219, 226, 229, 251
    in knightly attire at 215
    role of women at 216
    outpouring of printed grief/mourning following 215
  ill health of 219
  sister of *see* Valois, Marguerite
  tomb for 217, 230
  See also weddings of, first marriage *under* James V
  gifts given to Madeleine at 213
Magnus Erlingsson, or Magnus V, king of Norway 96, 100 n.172
Magnus VI, king of Norway, as heir 24, 35, 60, 92
Man, Isle or lordship of 58, 242
Manny, Sir Walter, tomb 151 *see also* charterhouse at *under* London
Mar, earl of 258, 260
  See also Stewart, John, earl of Mar
March, earl of 107, 257, 260
  George Dunbar 143, 251
Marche, Olivier de la 165 n.116
Margaret of Denmark, queen of Scots and wife of James III 249–50
  betrothal of first son 178
  canonisation attempt for 190 (n.30)
  coronation of 179, 198
  death and burial of 187, 190, 250
  depiction on Trinity Altar piece 200 n.84
  grants of land to 180
  progress with James III 180–1, 230
  robes and regalia of 177, 180
  separate household at Stirling of 206, 231
  tomb of 190, 202 n.99
  wedding and marriage of *see*

323

wedding (marriage) of *under* James III
Margaret Logie (nee Drummond), queen of Scots and second wife of David II 107–8, 116, 245
  coronation of 107–8
  See also wedding of, second marriage *under* David II
Margaret, maid of Norway 71–2, 74–5, 242
Margaret Plantagenet, queen of Scots and first wife of Alexander III 42, 53, 54–7, 68, 241–2
  See also wedding of, first marriage *under* Alexander III
Margaret of Provence, queen of France 41 n.107
Margaret, queen of Norway, daughter of Alexander III 57–8, 242
Margaret, St, queen of Scots and wife of Mael Coluim III 31, 36 n.77, 4358–9, 96, 116, 123, 125, 128, 230
  birthing shirt associated with 167 n.131
  canonisation of 42–3, 49, 51–2, 54, 241
  feast day of *see under* feast days
  relics of 123
  tomb shrine of **69**–71, 93, 116
  translation and reinterment of 51–2, 54, 68
Margaret Tudor, queen of Scots and wife of James IV 220, 223, 233, 250–1
  birth and baptism of son 193, 201–2, 250
  black gown bought for 203
  coronation of 195, 198–9, 237
  crowned or crown wearing in parliament 198
  death/s of children of 186, 202–3, 204
  dowry of 194
  governor and *tutrix* for James V 208
  gown made for parliament 198
  involvement in James V's coronation 207–8
  journey to Scotland 199
  marriage of 177, 185, 193, 194–201, 202, 219, 222, 250, 267–8
    chambers decorated for 194–5
    confirmation of dower in parliament 198
    gifts from James IV to 190, 197–8
    royal entry associated with 199 (n.78), 200–1
    reverence of king to Margaret in 200–1
    young age at time of 194
    See also wedding of *under* James IV
  prayers for the soul of James IV paid for by 205
  retaining control of her children 208–9 n.135
  royal entry to Aberdeen 203
Marguerite (or Margaret) of Flanders, wife of Alexander, son of Alexander III 58–60, 242
  See also wedding of *under* Alexander, son of Alexander III
Marguerite de Valois, sister of Madeleine 211 n.152, 213
Marie de Coucy, queen of Scots and second wife of Alexander II 41–2, 45, 51–2, 53, 57, 59, 237, 241
  See also wedding of, second marriage *under* Alexander II
Marie de Guise, queen of Scots and second wife of James V 1, 179, 217, 233, 251–2
  arrival and progress of 218–19
  birth of heir/ pregnancy 186, 222, 252
  coronation of 217–18, 219–20, 230
    investiture with sceptre at 222
    ladies (unnamed) attending coronation 219, 251
    postponing until pregnant 217–18
  death/s of children of 186, 222, 252

role in minority and coronation of
Mary 224, 237
wedding of 218, 230
Marischal, earl *see* marischal *under* household officers or officials
Mary, Blessed Mother of Jesus Christ 227
See also Marian feasts *under* feast days
Mary of Guelders, queen of Scots and wife of James II 149, 182, 248
birth of male heir, James III, and other children 167–8 (168 n.134), 248
at St Andrews for and use of birthing shirt of St Margaret at, 167 n.131
coronation of 163, 166, 179
purple robe at 166
death and burial of 168, 175, 190–1, 236
diverting funds from Soutra to Holy Trinity College, Edinburgh 172 n.154
education of 168
intercession by 167, 179
land holdings of 167 n.129
religious sites visited by 164 (n.110)
role in government and transferal of power 168–71, 173–5, 237, 248
comparison to Joan Beaufort 168
royal entry of 164–5, 173, 201, 248
wedding of, to James II 149, 158, 161, 165–7, 168, 173, 248
Marian liturgy at 166
reading of letters of surety 167, 177
See also wedding of *under* James II
Mary, queen of Scots 1–2, 224, 231
coronation of 224–5, 227, 229, 231, 232, 234, 235–6, 252
Mass or blessing 134, 199–200 *see also under* coronation; funeral; inauguration; wedding

Matilda, queen of England 24–5 n.18, 92 n.132
May, Isle of *see* Adrian, St, shrine of
Meaux, or Melsa, abbey of (Cistercian)
chronicle of 102, 104, 106
Melrose 37, 137
abbey of (Cistercian) 42, 43, 45, 51, 97–8, 172, 173, 228 n.16, 241, 246
abbot of 264
chronicle of 29, 43, 46, 49, 50
Menteith, earl or mormaer of 29–30, 44–5, 79, 256
See also Stewart, Robert, earl of Menteith, Fife and duke of Albany
Walter Comyn, lord of Badenoch 46, 257, 258
Mériadac, counsellor of Philip, duke of Burgundy 162 n.91
Methven
battle at 243
siege of 159, 247
minority *see under* succession
minority councils or government or leaders 46, 51, 52, 54, 136, 148, 163, 164, 170, 174–6, 193, 205, 237–8
Monan, St 106, 108
Monynet, James 189
Moray
bishop of 258, 260
earl of 257, 260
Thomas Randolph *see* Randolph, Thomas, earl of Moray and guardian
Thomas Randolph, son of 102, 105, 259
Morpeth 199 n.78
Morton, earl of 264, 265
James Douglas 172 n.154
wife of *see* Stewart, Joanna, countess of Morton
Mosman, John, goldsmith 217, 220
Mount Grace Priory (North Yorkshire) 150, 151
Mure, Elizabeth, first wife of Robert II 127 (n.72)

325

music and entertainment   1, 10, 105, 146–7, 164, 206, 219–20
  gythorn or gittar   165
  jesters   165
  minstrels   105, 200 (n.87), 268
  musicians   195, 200 n.87, 268
  plays and players   165, 218
  costumes for   140
  trumpets or trumpeters   1, 200
  See also charivari (rough music); liturgy
Musselburgh   25

Napier of Merchiston, Alexander, comptroller and shield-bearer   171, 263
Newark   199 n.78
Newbourgh   199 n.78
Newcastle   76, 77, 83, 199 n.78, 243, 257–8
Neville, Geoffrey de   37
Nicholas, St, feast day of *see under* feast days
Nidaros, archbishop of, Eystein Erlendsson   49–50 n.144, 60
Norham   83, 175, 240, 243, 248, 257–8
  treaty of   26, 32, 240
nobility or earls, as a collective group (unnamed)
  noblewomen (unnamed)   195, 200
  northern nobles of England   36, 38
  Scottish   21, 25, 29–30, 46, 50, 51, 59, 62–3, 71, 74, 76, 77, 78–9, 83, 99, 102–3, 121–2, 138, 165, 169, 170, 171, 187, 195, 208, 222, 223, 224–5, 231, 235–6
  noblesse de robe   236
North Queensferry   71
Northallerton   199 n.78
Northampton   37
  See also treaty of *under* Edinburgh
Northumberland   51
  sheriffs, nobles and barons of   38
Norway   35
  coronation traditions of   24, 30, 60
  influence of the church over   16–17, 49–50, 60–1, 84–5, 92, 96, 120, 125
  funeral traditions and death practices of   31 (n. 56 and 61), 35
  kings of   45 *see also* Eric II; Håkon IV; Magnus Erlingsson, or Magnus V; Magnus VI; Sverre
  succession in   21 (n.5)
  laws of succession in   49–50 n.144
  sites for coronation in   229
  Thing   24
Nory, Robert, royal servant of James II and Mary of Gueders   167 n.131

oath-giving or taking   25, 71, 92, 115, 123 n.54, 134 (n.113), 159–60 (159 n.77), 197, 198, 239 *see also under* coronation; inauguration; wedding and consort coronation; oaths given at *under* parliament
Olaf, St   49–50 n.144, 229
orders of ceremony or *ordines*   9, 102, 120, 121–2, 124–5, 141, 155 n.53, 156 n.59, 235, 239
  Liber regalis   120–1, 159–60 n.80
  Liber regie capelle   91
  Northumbrian pontifical (eleventh century)   27, 29
  orders in heraldic texts   9, 91, 149, 155–6, 157, 159–60, 182, 208, 232, 236
  See also Ordo of Charles V
Orkney   177, 205 n.116, 241, 242
  bishop of   265
  earl of *see* Sinclair, William, earl of Orkney and admiral of Scottish fleet
  wife of, Elizabeth, countess of   163–4
  Kirkwall   31 n.56
Otto III, emperor   35 n.76, 240

Paisley
  abbey of (Cluniac)   117, 130, 135, 228 n.16, 246
  abbot   263, 264, 265

papacy, petitions to 116, 241
papal bulls
   Cum universi 25, 36, 240
   Desterande feritatis 98
   permitting unction in Scotland 84, 95–6, 101–2, 104, 132, 235, 244
   Super anxietatibus 25, 240
papal gifts *see under* gifts and gift giving
papal hat 25, 233
papal legates
   Master James 38, 241
   Pandulf 36, 40–1
   Giovanni di (John of) Salerno 25
   unnamed Italian man 203 n.106
   bishop of Urbino 152 (n.35)
papal rose 27, 40, 54, 101
papal sword *see under* sword/s
Paris 93–4 n.139, 138, 153, 210, 228 n.18, 251
   coronation of Henry VI in 207
   textiles and tapestries from 212–13
Paris, Matthew of 53–6
   Chronica Majora (published in translation as *Matthew of Paris's English History*) 53–6
parliament 8, 15, 17, 75, 96, 99, 107, 109–10, 115, 127–8, 135, 137–8, 147–9, 151, 168, 176, 180, 181, 188, 190, 198, 207, 224, 231–2, 233, 238, 244, 245, 248–9, 256, 260, 263, 264, 268
   at time of coronation/ coronation parliament 98, 103, 105, 121, 127–8, 140–1, 143, 144, 179, 232
   difference between parliament and general council 140 n.145
   knighting or belting associated with 106, 189
   oaths given at 141, 151, 159–60 (160, n.82), 179, 189
   riding of parliament/ processions associated with 188–9, 209 n.138
   ritual in, including enthroning 159–60, 176, 179, 182, 189, 193, 198–9, 223, 232, 237
   Records of Parliament 9, 98–9, 103, 105, 110, 114, 118, 121, 122, 143, 170, 179, 198
   time for parliament to gather 78, 103, 140, 156, 169, 226
   See also parliament at *under* Cambuskenneth; Edinburgh; Perth; Scone
paupers, black-clad 1
Perth 21, 31, 33–4, 72, 74, 115, 122, 130 (n.84), 131, 134, 135, 140, 151, 153, 182, 190, 219, 242, 245, 251
   attempt of James I to move St Andrews University to 143 n.162
   baillies and community of 131
   battle at the North Inch of 133
   Blackfriars or Dominicans at 148, 153, 247
   bridge at 34, 230
   burgh commissioner or provost of 264, 265
   Carthusian charterhouse at 150 (fn.21), 151–2, 153, 154, 228 n.16, 230, 246
   Exchequer at 131
   parliament or General Council at 130–1, 140, 159–60, 246, 247
   royal centre with Scone 115, 130–1, 134, 143, 155, 160
   St John's parish church in 150 n.24, 153
Perthshire 176, 188
Petrus machinarum or Peter the machinist 89
Peyntour, Andrew 119
Philip Augustus, king of France 35 n.76, 36 n.77
Philip IV, king of France 84, 243
Philip V, king of France, funeral of 90
Picardy 76
plate, silver and/or gold 195, 204, 213, 214, 270

327

cupboard for display of 195, 203–4, 268
Pluscarden, chronicle, *liber* or book of 77, 84, 146–7, 152, 215
political community or elite 8, 18, 44, 53, 66, 74–5, 78, 83, 85, 86, 105, 109–10, 120–1, 126, 136, 137, 148–9, 161, 169, 173, 179, 181, 182–3, 191, 197, 219, 222–3, 227, 232, 237–9 *see also* community of the realm; three estates
Pontefract 199 n.78
Porcari, Stephano de, son of 147
prayers 138–9, 222, 228, 238, 239 *see also* liturgy; Masses and prayers for the soul *under* funeral; prayers for heirs *under* baptism
prelates as a collective group (unnamed) 21, 51, 59, 78–9, 101, 121, 138, 165, 167, 169, 170, 208
Pret [Pratt], David, painter 193
Puflich, Otto de, Guelderian knight 161
procession 228, 230, 233, 236 *see also under* baptism; coronation; funeral; inauguration; wedding and consort coronation; royal entry or progress

queens consort of Scotland 181, 191, 232, 236, 237
See also Annabella Drummond; Anne of Denmark; Elizabeth de Burgh; Ermengarde de Beaumont; Euphemia Ross; Ingibörg; Joan Beaufort; Joan of the Tower; Joanna Plantagenet; Madeleine of Valois; Margaret, St; Margaret Platagenet; Margaret Tudor; Marguerite or Margaret of Flanders; Marie de Coucy; Mary of Guelders; Marie de Guise; Yolande of Dreux

Ramsay, John, lord Bothwell 189
Randolph, Thomas, earl of Moray and guardian 92, 97, 98, 102, 244, 259
Ratis Raving 160, 193
recitation of genealogy *see under* coronation; inauguration

reformation (Scotland) 9, 11, 150, 157
regalia (or material symbols of majesty) 1, 14, 27, 28, 40, 49, 54, 57, 76, 79, 80, 83, 84, 96, 99–101, 132, 142, 144, 166, 189, 197–8, 209 n.138, 212, 220, 225, 232–3, 235–6, 243, 250,
depiction of **142, 221** *see also* depiction of *under* crown; royal robe; sceptre; sword
orb 27, **41, 101**
rod 27
remodelling of 220, 230, 233
See also crown; royal robe; sceptre; sword
regent 208 *see also* Stewart, John, duke of Albany
Regiam Maiestatem 160 n.82, 189
regicide 187 *see also* death and murder of *under* James I and James III
Reims 155 n.53, 229 n.19
relics 49–50 n.144, 86
use of in ritual 51–2, 82 n.74, 123, 125–6, 188, 201, 238
See also Stone of Destiny
renaissance 4, 5, 184, 201, 211, 213, 222, 236
associated humanist ideals and scholars 180, 236
Restalrig, collegiate church of 205
Rhodes 154
Richard I, king of England 240
second coronation of 27–8, 40, 240
Richard II, king of England 100 n.169, 134 n.114, 157 n.63,
deposition of 187
tomb of with Anne of Bohemia 151
Richard III, king of England, deposition of 87, 249–50
Richmond 199 n.78
ring exchange *see under* wedding and consort coronation
ritual
confirming ducal or lieutenant appointments 134 *see also* of governor *under* inauguration

definitions of and debate
  about 4–5, 6–8, 15–19, 44,
  105, 110–11, 125, 149, 152,
  158, 167, 181–2, 195, 225–39
ritual cycle of death and succession *see* cycle of death and *under* succession
sources for 8–15, 23–4, 39, 53,
  65–6, 76, 88, 114, 139, 140,
  149, 155, 166, 176 n.166, 179,
  184–5 (185 n.5), 187–8 *see also* ordines; Scottish financial records
torture and execution 157–8
use of space in, conclusions on 228–32
See also acclamation; anointing; ceremony; *charivari*; crowning or crown wearing; embalming *under* preparation of the body *under* funeral; enthronement or enthroning; entrail burial *under* funeral; evisceration *under* preparation of the body *under* funeral; feasting; gifts, gift-giving; heart burial *under* funeral; knighting; liturgy; Mass or blessing; oath-giving or taking; prayers; procession; relics, use of in; recitation of genealogy; ring exchange; royal entry or progress; sermons; tournaments
Robert I, king of Scots 31, 66, 76 (n.40), 87, 144, 188, 231, 243–4
  absence from David II and Joan's wedding 92
  birth of heir 65, 88
  daughter of *see* Bruce, Marjory
  death of 88–9, 94–5, 244
  deathbed speech 89
  epitaph for 215
  excommunication of 87, 109–10
  funeral and burial of 88–91, 93–5, 119, 130, 216, 228, 230, 233, 234, 236, 244
    evisceration and embalming 89
    heart burial and crusade 89, 97–8, 110, 154, 172, 227, 244
  illness of 88, 92, 95
  inauguration of 66, 76–7, 78–81, 84–6, 87, 95, 109–10, 118, 123, 129, 156, 189, 227, 243, 258–9
    crowned by Isabella, countess of Buchan 76–7, 79, 123
  investment in the regalia 99
  secured peace with England 88
  succession legislation of 107, 131
  reinterment of William I, king of Scots 93
  relics associated with 188
  reverence toward St Fillan 188
  seal of 100
  Soules Conspiracy 87
  tomb of 51, 70, 93–4,
  use of ceremony to validate kingship 84–7
  usurpation of 65, 87, 109
  victory at Bannockburn *see* battle of *under* Bannockburn
Robert II, king of Scots 5 n.18, 113, 115, 129, 131, 144, 227, 245–6 *see also* Stewart, Robert, the Steward
  animosity towards David II 115–116
  coronation of 115, 118–26, 127, 129, 133, 156, 182, 231, 245, 260–1
    Marian liturgy at 118
    acclamation or election at 119–21
  death of 128, 129, 227, 246
  election of 119–21, 122
  funeral and burial of 115, 128–9, 130–1 (130 n.84), 132–3, 230, 234, 246
  heirs and children of (unnamed) 115 n. 10, 126–8, 130, 145
  legitimacy of 127 n.72
  magnatial king 126
  perceived weakness of claim to throne 121
  programme of Stewart tombs 117–18, 123
  seals of **126**, 209

tomb of 117, 130 n. 84, 135, 245
veneration of local saints 123
wives of see Mure, Elizabeth, first wife of Robert II; Euphemia Ross, queen of Scots
work on David II's tomb 117–18
Robert III, king of Scots 113, 129, 132, 133–5, 227, 246
challenges to authority of 113
death of 135, 139, 140, 144, 246
coronation of 114–15, 129–33, 231, 234, 246, 261
funeral and burial of 115, 135
tomb of 135
wife of see Annabella Drummond, queen of Scots
Robert of Meynors 45, 257
Robert of Norwich 54 n.172
Rochebaron, Antoine de, husband of Philipotte of Bourgogne 164 n.109
Rome 96
Ross
bishop-elect of, Robert 28, 30–1, 255
duke of see Stewart, James, duke of Ross and brother of James IV
earl of 257, 258
William, brother of Euphemia Ross, queen of Scots 127
Ross, Euphemia see Euphemia Ross, queen of Scots
Rouen 45 n.127
James V at 213
provision of altar cloth at 213–14
textiles from 212
Roxburgh 41–2, 59, 169, 172, 175, 228 n.18, 241
siege of 168, 169, 170–1, 175, 181, 248
St John's church in 59
royal banner/s 40, 56, 80, 99, 165
royal dignity 1, 18–19, 74–6, 78, 87, 95, 156, 174, 205–6, 209, 224, 226–7, 238 see also sacral kingship; king's two bodies
royal entry or progress 54, 175–6

(176 n.166), 180–1, 189, 193, 197, 203, 209, 210, 211, 215, 218
of foreign monarchs visiting other realms 211 n.150
See also royal entries at under Edinburgh; royal entry associated with under marriage of under Margaret Tudor, queen of Scots; royal entry of under James I, king of Scots; weddings of under James V, king of Scots; Joan Beaufort, queen of Scots; Mary of Guelders, queen of Scots
tableau vivant in 203
royal mantle see royal robe
royal or government officers or officials 45, 61, 138, 142, 155, 173, 181
chamberlain 138, 260, 264, 265
see also Colquhon of Luss, John
chancellor 260, 263, 264
See also Crichton, William lord Crichton; Kenleith, Robert, abbot of Dunfermline; William del Blois under Lothian, archdeacon of; William de Bondington under bishop of under Glasgow
comptroller see Napier of Merchiston, Alexander, comptroller and shield-bearer
justiciar
of Lothian, David Lindsay 45, 257
of Scotia see Durward, Alan
See also Fitz Alan, Sir Walter, justiciar
keeper of Privy Seal 138
See also Lindsay, James, provost of Lincluden
secretary to the king 263
See Whitelaw, Archibald, secretary to James III
steward of Scotland
Alexander (1249) 45, 257
James (1296–1306) 79, 258, 259

INDEX

See also Stewart, Robert, the Steward
  treasurer of Scotland 264
  See also Kirkcaldy of the Grange, James
royal robe 28, 80, 99, 105, 158, 198, 209, 220, 232–3, 236
  depictions of **47**, **48**, **57**, **82**, **100**, **142**
  for queen 105, **127**, 166, 177, 180, 220, 232
  repair to and reuse of 166–7, 199
  re-robing 166
  use of a purple robe 142, 166–7, 220

sacral or sacred kingship (including reference to divine kingship or saintly nature) 17, 28, 54, 56, 60–1, 63, 83, 85, 105, 110, 120, 124, 140, 144, 145, 152, 156, 174, 182, 199, 238–9 *see also* royal dignity; king's two bodies
saints (unnamed) 32, 59, 123, 125, 153, 238
  canonisation 52, 190 *see also under* Margaret, St, queen of Scots and wife of Mael Coluim III
Saint-Denis 31–2, 68, 155 n.53, 229 n.19
  abbot of, abbot Suger 49–50 n.144
Saint Maur de Fosse 45 n.127
Sande, furrier 212
Savoy, Louis of, son of duke of Savoy, betrothed to Annabella Stewart 149 n.1
Scandinavia 229 *see also* Denmark; Norway; Sweden
sceptre 27, 28, 40, 54, 132, 137, 142, 189, 197, 209, 233, 267
  depictions of **57**, **82**, **100**, **101**, **127**, **142**, **221**
  small sceptre 99–100
  for queen (*main de justice*) **127**–8, 199–200, 220, 222, 233, 237
Scone 173
  abbey of (Augustinian) 28, 29, 82, 85–6, 96, 102, 104, 108, 109, 116, 119, 134, 149, 169, 227, 246
    abandonment for coronation 181–2, 231–2
    abbot of 28, 46, 100, 257, 260
      Thomas Balmerino 96–7 n.148
      Henry Mann 86, 258
    burial and tomb at 129–30, 130 n.84, 135, 173, 228 n.16, 245
    inauguration or enthronement at 21, 26, 43, 45, 76, 78, 100, 231–2, 240, 241, 243, 244
    coronation at 98, 118, 121–2, 123, 128, 130–1, 140, 142, 187–8, 189, 193, 208, 223, 228, 231–2, 244, 245, 246
    damage to crops at 131–2
    granger canon of, Robert Logy 132
    Hill or Moot Hill at 121–2, 160, 231
    outside enthronement at 29, 144, 159, 206, 231–2
    right to house the royal honours 96–7 n.148
    seal of 3 n.7, 46–**47**, 123, 257 n.1
  parliaments and councils at 72, 74, 96–7 n.148, 98, 127, 130–1, 231, 242
  royal centre with Perth 115, 130–1, 134, 143, 155, 160
  Stone of *see* Stone of Destiny
Scottish financial records 39, 114, 147 (n.6), 149, 219
  Exchequer Rolls 13, 88–91, 102, 105, 107, 118, 131, 140 (n.146), 149, 162 (n.99), 166, 173, 194, 205
  Household Books 13, 191 n.39, 203–4

331

INDEX

Treasurer's Accounts   13, 149, 162 n.99, 166, 180, 188, 190–1, 193, 195, 202, 203–4, 205
Scrope, Sir Galfrid, Edward III's justiciar in Scotland   99
Scrymgeour, John   91, 253–5
seal   14–15, 27, 60, 80, 90, 137, 197, 224, 246
   matrix   14, 100
      for Margaret Plantagenet gifted by Henry III   55
      for David II   95
   of guardians *see under* guardian/s
   of Robert Stewart, duke of Albany as governor *see under* Stewart, Robert, earl of Menteith, Fife and duke of Albany
   of Scone *see under* Scone
   See also under Alexander II, king of Scots; Alexander III, king of Scots; David II, king of Scots; Edward Balliol, king of Scots; Euphemia Ross, queen of Scots; James I, king of Scots; John Balliol, king of Scots; Robert I, king of Scots; Robert II, king of Scots
Serf, St   95
sermons   238 *see also under* coronation; wedding and consort coronations
Seton of Gordon, Sir Alexander   154 n.45, 262
Shaw of Sauchie, James   178 n.183, 265
Sheen Priory (now Richmond, London), 150, 151
Shetland   177
Shirley, John, account of James I's murder   157–8
Sinclair, William, earl of Orkney and admiral of Scottish fleet   163–4, 165, 170 (n.147), 175, 263
Sirowsby [sic]   199 n.78
Sluys   97
Soutra, Hospital of the Holy Trinity at (Augustinian)   172
Spain   98
St Albans   56

St Andrews   167–8, 218, 220, 228 n.18, 230, 251
   archbishop of   208, 235
      David Beaton, chancellor   217, 225, 265 *see also* abbot of Arbroath
      James Stewart   201 *see also* Stewart, James, duke of Ross, brother of James IV
   bishop of   29, 62, 79, 101, 104, 235, 261, 262, 264
      David de Bernham   46, 47, 49, 257
      James Ben   102, 110, 259
      James Kennedy   163 n.104, 167–8, 170, 175–6, 248
      Walter Trail   132–3, 134, 261
      William Fraser   79, 83, 257
      William de Lamberton   79, 85–6, 258
      William Landellis or de Landels   107–8, 121, 124, 260
      William Malveisin   21, 28, 256
   burgh commissioners   264
   cathedral at   108, 125
      consecration of   87–8, 244
      archdeacon, dean, prior and canons of   190, 264, 265
   Grey friars and priests of   205
   university at   218
St John, Johnde   79
Stephen, king of England (contested)   24–5 n.18, 92 n.132
Stewart, Alexander, earl of Buchan, also known as Wolf of Badenoch, son of Robert II   128
   tomb of   **117–18**
Stewart, Alexander, duke of Albany, younger brother of James III   176, 208 n.135, 248, 249
Stewart, Annabella, daughter of James I   146 n.1, 247 n.1
Stewart, Bernard, lord of Aubigny   201 n.93
Stewart, David, earl of Strathearn, eldest son of Robert II and Euphemia Ross   127

332

INDEX

Stewart, David, earl of Carrick and duke of Rothesay, son of Robert III   133–4, 135, 245–6
   created duke of Rothesay   134, 246
   marriage and romantic liaisons of   134
   murder of   135 (n.115), 246
   oath as lieutenant   134 (n.113)
Stewart, dynasty   66, 113, 194, 231 *see also* Charles I; Charles II; James I, king of Scots; James II, king of Scots; James III, king of Scots; James IV, king of Scots; James V, king of Scots; James VII and II; Mary, queen of Scots; Robert II, king of Scots; Robert III, king of Scots
Stewart, Eleanor, daughter of James I   146 n.1, 247
Stewart, Isabella, daughter of James I   146 n.1, 161, 246, 247
Stewart, James, duke of Ross and brother of James IV   188 (n.19), 197
   death and funeral   190, 204–5, 250
   See also Stewart, James *under* archbishop of St Andrews
   tomb of   205
Stewart, James (b. 1507), first son of James IV and Margret   201–2, 250
   death of   202–3, 250
   little coat and 'hurle-stule' for   202 n.99
Stewart, James (b.1512), later James V   203–4, 250 *see also* James V, king of Scots
Stewart, James (b.1540), son of James V and Marie de Guise   222, 252
Stewart, Lady Jane, illegitimate daughter of James V   218
Stewart, Joanna (or Joan), countess of Morton, wife of James Douglas, earl of Morton, and daughter of James I   172 n.154, 247 n.1
Stewart, John, duke of Albany, regent   208–9, 226
   arrival and processions of   208 n.135

Stewart, John, earl of Angus   102, 105, 259
Stewart, John, earl of Mar, brother of James IV   188 (n.19), 205 n.113, 249
Stewart, John, of Kyle and earl of Carrick   108–9, 128, 245, 260 *see also* Robert III, king of Scots
Stewart, Margaret, daughter of James I and dauphine of France   138, 146, 147, 164, 215
Stewart, Margaret, sister of James IV   188 n.19
Stewart, Mary, daughter of James I   146 n.1, 164 n. 109, 246–7
Stewart, Murdoch, earl of Fife and duke of Albany, son of Robert Stewart, earl of Menteith, Fife and duke of Albany   136–7, 142–3, 144, 246, 261
   forfeiture of   143 (n.161)
Stewart, Robert, earl of Menteith, Fife and duke of Albany, son of Robert II   5–6 n.18, 122, 128, 133–4, 135–6, 246, 260, 261
   created duke of Albany   134, 246
   governor of the realm   5–6 n.18, 135–6, 140, 144, 209, 246
   murder of David duke of Rothesay   5–6 n.18, 135 n.115
   seal of as governor   136, 209
Stewart, Robert, murderer of James I   157
Stewart, Robert, the Steward   67, 91–2, 95, 107–9, 115, 121 (n.45), 123, 244–5 *see also* Robert II, king of Scots
Stewart, Walter, earl of Atholl, second son of Robert II and Euphemia Ross   158, 247
   date of trial   158 n.66
Stirling   21, 30, 31, 130, 161–2, 164 n.110, 190, 202–3, 207, 219, 240, 247, 248
   Arthurian connections of   162
   burgh commissioner of   264
   Castle   201, 206–7, 224, 231, 234, 248
   Chapel Royal at   206–7, 219–20,

223, 224, 228 n.17, 229, 231, 235, 250, 251, 252
    favoured as nursery and household for heirs 206
    James IV's great hall at 206–207
    keeper or captain of see Livingstone of Callendar, Sir Alexander
    unnamed priest at 203
    palace at 184
Stone of Destiny 47, 62, 71, 79, 80, 81–2, 96, 102, 109, 243 see also removal of royal honours and stone of Scone
Strathearn, earl of 29–30, 44–5, 46, 235, 256, 257, 258, 260
    David Stewart see Stewart, David, earl of Strathearn, eldest son of Robert II and Euphemia Ross
succession
    concerns about/ issues with/ precarious nature of 30, 55, 58, 62, 68, 70, 86–7, 88, 102–3, 108–9, 126–9, 130, 133, 144–5, 170, 186, 193–4, 201, 202–3, 215, 217–18, 222–3, 227
    confidence in the 60, 97, 202
    confirmations, legislation or Acts of 92, 96–7 n.148, 107, 115, 119, 121, 127–8, 131
    contested nature of 79, 96, 107–9, 110–11, 113, 234
    contested nature of kingship associated with 65–6, 79, 87–8, 96, 106–7, 144, 197
    crisis of or at time of 5, 65–6, 67–8, 71, 135–6, 148, 193
    cycle of death and 2, 4–5, 15, 17–19, 23, 35, 41, 43, 62–3, 65, 67, 68, 69, 76, 95, 97–8, 108, 109–11, 114–15, 129, 131, 133, 135, 146–7, 149, 152, 161, 169, 182–3, 186–7, 193, 194, 206, 222–3, 224, 225–7, 228, 229, 234, 236, 237–9
    election/ selection of monarch 21–2, 24, 30 (n.52), 46, 50, 74, 76, 77, 96, 120
    'first among equals'/ *primus inter pares* 26, 60–1, 63, 126, 144, 197
    hereditary or dynastic succession 28, 43, 58, 120, 133, 156, 168–9, 180–1, 193, 234 see also primogeniture under succession
    minority/ succession of minor kings 15, 17–19, 36, 45, 46, 52, 103, 135, 148–50, 158–63, 170–1, 175–7, 179, 181, 186, 232, 234, 237–8
    primogeniture 21–2, 24, 35, 60, 62, 74, 169
    Rex designatus or heir designate (designating heir) 22, 24–6, 58, 67, 108–9, 128
        See also designation of succession under Alexander III
    temporal gap between death, accession and funeral 225–8
    securing through marriage or agreements of 42, 57–8, 60, 134, 141, 161, 176, 214–15
    stability of (real or projected) 18, 24, 26, 34–5, 42–3, 55, 57–8, 71, 92, 96, 105–6, 133–4, 144–5, 147, 158, 161, 167–8, 175, 186, 189–90, 191, 205, 222–3, 226–7, 231
    See also succession in under Ireland, Norway; succession legislation or policy of under Robert I, David II
    temporary nature of 74, 144–5
Surrey, earl of 258
    Thomas Howard 197
    William de Warenne 37
Sutherland, John of, nephew of David II 108
Sverre, king of Norway 96, 116 n.13
Sweden
    sites of coronation in 229
sword/s 1, 27–8, 40, 55, 80, 99, 132, 137, 189, 197, 209, 215, 233, 240, 254, 267, 268
    depictions of **41, 57, 82, 100, 101, 142, 221**
    papal sword 25, 40, 54, 80, 99

INDEX

scabbard for   55, 197, **221**
symbols and symbolism   22, 33–4, 34, 40–1, 43, 45, 51, 54, 74, 77–8, 80, 85, 95, 115, 125, 133–4, 135–40, 159, 165, 167, 178, 180, 191, 197, 199, 204, 227, 233, 236, 243
   Arthur's Roundtable   202
   of Christian kingship   17, 23, 61
   definitions and scholarly debate upon   6–7
   double tressure flory counter-flory   42
   fleur-de-lys   57
   imperial crown   197
   lion rampant   40, 42, 57, 74, 90–1
   leopards, English royal arms   55
   royal or Stewart insignia   159, 171, 176, 199, 236
      See also heraldic decoration
   St Andrew   74
   St George   199–200, 202
   thistle   7, 177–8, 212
   Tudor iconography   186, 199
   unicorn   7, 177–8 (**178**), 267 n.6

Tadcaster   199 n.78
Tankard, Henry   119
tapestries and hangings   55 n.177, 140, 195, 203, 213, 216–17, 268, 270
   packing and repacking of   213
Tees, sheriffs, nobles and barons of   38
Thomas, St and Apostle   152
Thomas of Becket, St   21, 32
three estates   30, 92, 99, 103, 115, 120–2, 123 n.54, 128, 130, 134, 135–6, 140–1, 156, 159–60, 176, 181, 188, 189, 197, 198, 208, 224, 232, 239, 247, 256 see also community of the realm; political community or elite
throne   49, 50, 62, 76, 80–2, 121, 142, 176, 177, 189, 197
   depiction of   **41, 57, 82, 100, 101, 142**
   See also Stone of Destiny

tomb   31, 32 n.64, 110, 123, 134, 173–4, 175, 176, 181, 245, 250
   effigies on   93–4 n.139, 117, 118, 151
   See also under Alexander III, king of Scots; David II, king of Scots; Edward II, king of England; Edward III, king of England; Isabella of France or de Valoise, queen of England; James I, king of Scots; James II, king of Scots; James III, king of Scots; James IV, king of Scots; James V, king of Scots; Madeleine de Valois or of France; Margaret of Denmark, queen of Scots; Richard II, king of England; Robert I, king of Scots; Robert II, king of Scots; Robert III, king of Scots; Stewart, Alexander, earl of Buchan; Stewart, James, duke of Ross and brother of James IV;
   See also Eltham, John of, tomb; Hatfield, William, tomb; Manny, Sir Walter, tomb
   See tomb design in *under* England; France; Low Countries
   See tomb shrine of *under* Margaret, St, queen of Scots
Torphichen
   preceptor of, Meldrum, Sir Andrew   154 n.45
   priory of   154 n.45
tournaments   3, 91 (n.124), 106, 133–4, 156 n.55, 161–3 (162 n.99), 165–6, 167, 201–2, 214, 218, 248, 250
   gear for   91 n.123, 162, 165–6, 212, 268, 269
   horses for   214
   illuminated articles for   202
Tours, ducal entry to   137 n.127
Trinity altar piece   200 n.87
Turgot, *Life of Saint Margaret*   59
Turyne, John   140

unction *see* anointing

Vendôme, Madame de   213

Venslo 173
Vieuxpont, Robert de 37
Virgil, Polydore 204 n.109

Wales 80
Walter of Moray (Murray) 45, 257
Waltheof, St 51
Wars of Independence 3, 123, 236, 243, 244
Warbeck, Perkin, pretender to English throne 201, 250
Wark 170
wedding and consort coronation 3, 49, 66–7, 234, 235, 236
   coronations of queens consort 179, 215
      anointing of queens consort 177, 198–9, 219, 237
      oath-taking at or associated with 92, 107, 141, 179, 232, 237
      See also coronation of *under* Annabella Drummond, queen of Scots; Euphemia Ross, queen of Scots; Joan Beaufort, queen of Scots; Margaret of Denmark, queen of Scots; Margaret Logie (nee Drummond), queen of Scots; Margaret Tudor, queen of Scots; Marie de Guise, queen of Scots; Mary of Guelders, queen of Scots
      See under crowning or crown wearing
   dancing at 200, 218
   feasting and provisions for 39, 54–5, 59–60, 67, 88–9, 90–91, 165, 194, 200, 218
   intercession (granting of pardons) in association with 55–6, 167
   investiture with regalia (sceptre) 198, 222, 237
   knighting at 46 n.128, 55
   Mass or liturgy at 58–9, 166, 167
   processions 37–8 (**37**), 53–4, 91, 197, 218–19, 229–30 *see also* royal entry and progress
   reading of letters of surety (confirmation of dower at) 167, 177, 198, 232, 237, 259
   ring exchange 213
   ritualised courtship at 199, 201
   roles of women in 59, 163–4, 195, 200, 216, 218, 219
   sermons at 58–9, 133
   See also marriage *under* Margaret Tudor, queen of Scots
   See also marriage negotiations for James III *under* Denmark
   See also wedding/s of *under* Alexander II, king of Scots; Alexander III, king of Scots; David II, king of Scots; James II, king of Scots; James III, king of Scots; James IV, king of Scots; James V, king of Scots; Marie de Guise, queen of Scots; Mary of Guelders, queen of Scots
   See also wedding and marriage orchestrated by *under* Alexander III
   See also wedding tradition in *under* France
wax 55, 89–90, 147, 173 *see also* candles and torches
Westminster, abbey of (Benedictine) 32 (n. 64), 47, 68, 82, 101, 117 n.20, 131, 145, 153, 157 (n.63), 160 n.80, 219 n.201, 229 n.19, 242
   St Stephen's chapel at 117 n.20
Whitelaw, Archibald, secretary to James III 180, 263, 264
wild men 202
William of Brechin 45, 257
William I, king of Scots (also known as the Lion) 21–2, 24, 30 n.51, 37 n.82, 42–3, 240
   accession and inauguration of 2, 26–7, 29, 240
   attending second coronation of Richard I of England 27–8, 40
   brother of *see* Huntingdon, earl of, David
   daughters, Margaret (*see also* sister

under Alexander II) and Isabella, held hostage   26
  funeral and burial of   4, 21, 24, 26, 30–5, 71–2, 130, 152, 230, 234
  designation of heir and pre-mortuary recognition   24–6, 58, 62
  old age and ill health of   21, 28
  papal gifts to   25, 27, 40, 49
  reinterment of   93
  See also Treaty of Falaise
Winchester   27, 37
  bishop of, Henry Beaufort   141
Woodstock   56, 240, 241
Wyntoun, Andrew of, *Original Chronicle*   10, 98, 114, 118, 130, 132–3, 137, 142, 227

Yolande of Dreux, queen of Scots and second wife of Alexander III   67, 70, 242
York   25 n.19, 36–9, 41, 53, 199 n.78, 228 n.18, 230, 241, 245
  archbishop of
    supposed supremacy of   25, 36
    Walter de Gray   37–9, 41
  cathedral/ minster of   36
  mayor of   39
  sheriffs, nobles and barons of   38
  St Peter's church in   37 n.82
Yorkshire, men of   36–7
Young, John, Somerset herald   12, 195, 198, 200–1, 233

St Andrews Studies in Scottish History
Previously published

I
Elite Women and Polite Society in Eighteenth-Century Scotland
Katharine Glover

II
Regency in Sixteenth-Century Scotland
Amy Blakeway

III
Scotland, England and France after the Loss of Normandy, 1204–1296
'Auld Amitie'
M. A. Pollock

IV
Children and Youth in Premodern Scotland
Edited by Janay Nugent and Elizabeth Ewan

V
Medieval St Andrews: Church, Cult, City
Edited by Michael Brown and Katie Stevenson

VI
The Life and Works of Robert Baillie (1602–1662)
Politics, Religion and Record-Keeping in the British Civil Wars
Alexander D. Campbell

VII
The Parish and the Chapel in Medieval Britain and Norway
Sarah E. Thomas

VIII
A Protestant Lord in James VI's Scotland
George Keith, Fifth Earl Marischal (1554–1623)
Miles Kerr-Peterson

IX
The Clergy in Early Modern Scotland
Edited by Chris R. Langley, Catherine E. McMillan and Russell Newton

X
Kingship, Lordship and Sanctity in Medieval Britain
Essays in Honour of Alexander Grant
Edited by Steve Boardman and David Ditchburn

XI
Rethinking the Renaissance and Reformation in Scotland
Essays in Honour of Roger A. Mason
Edited by Steven J. Reid

XII
Life at the Margins in Early Modern Scotland
Edited by Allan Kennedy and Susanne Weston